The Discovery of
a Norse Settlement in America

The Discovery of a Norse Settlement in America

Excavations at L'Anse aux Meadows, Newfoundland 1961–1968

By Anne Stine Ingstad

WITH CONTRIBUTIONS BY
Charles J. Bareis and
Jon H. Winston
Arne Emil Christensen jr.
Kari E. Henningsmoen
Kristján Eldjárn
Reidar Nydal
Leif M. Paulssen
Rolf Petré
Anna M. Rosenqvist

Universitetsforlaget

OSLO – BERGEN – TROMSØ

© The Norwegian Research Council for Science and the Humanities 1977
(Norges almenvitenskapelige forskningsråd)
Section: A.19.37-3T

Cover design: Per Syversen
Translated by: Elizabeth Seeberg
Printed in Norway by: Grøndahl & Søn Trykkeri A.s

ISBN: 82-00-01513-0

Distribution offices:

NORWAY
Universitetsforlaget
Box 6589, Rodeløkka
Oslo 5

UNITED KINGDOM
Global Book Resources Ltd.
37 Queen Street
Henley on Thames
Oxon RG9 1AJ

UNITED STATES and CANADA
Columbia University Press
136 South Broadway
Irvington-on-Hudson
New York 10533

*To the Memory
of my Mother and Father
Louise and Eilif Moe*

Contents

PART III

Foreword

BY HELGE INGSTAD

This book forms the first part of a larger, two-volume work. Written by Anne Stine Ingstad, it gives her archaeological assessment of an excavated settlement site at L'Anse aux Meadows, on the northern point of Newfoundland (51°36' N 55°32'W).

The writer of this preface, who led the archaeological expeditions, will shortly publish the second volume, which will take the form of a historical assessment of the Norse voyages to Vinland, partly viewed in the light of the settlement at L'Anse aux Meadows.

The site was excavated in the course of seven archaeological expeditions, which took place in the period 1961–68. Throughout this period, Anne Stine Ingstad was in charge of the archaeological work. The present volume deals with the excavations of eight, possibly nine house-sites, four boat-sheds, a charcoal kiln and several other features, situated on a marine terrace at Épaves Bay, which lies a short distance from a small fishing settlement – L'Anse aux Meadows. It also includes articles and reports by several other scholars, whose names appear below.

As regards the background for these expeditions, I would here merely mention some of the aspects which will be dealt with in detail in the historical discussion included in Volume II. In 1953, I conducted exhaustive examinations of the Norse settlements in south-western Greenland together with Anne Stine Ingstad. This colony, which was founded by Eirik the Red in A.D. 986, consisted of two settlements – the East settlement in the south, and the West Settlement, which lay further to the north. The ruins of about 300 farms, 19 churches and two monasteries have been found – the farm buildings are constructed of turf and stone. At its most prosperous, this society probably numbered about 4,000 people, who lived in these two settlements. They lived by stock-keeping, hunting and fishing. They must have had great difficulty in obtaining material for ship building, for the only timber available in Greenland was knurled birch and drift-wood. Ships went directly – although irregularly – from Bergen in Norway to Greenland and back again. The Greenland episcopal see was established in A.D. 1152, as part of the archiepiscopal see of Nidaros (Trondheim, Norway). In A.D. 1261, Greenland became part of the Norwegian realm. The Norse settlements on this distant arctic island continued to exist until about A.D. 1500 – after this date, they disappeared mysteriously.

A point of particular interest is the fact that the so-called Vinland voyages started from Eirik the Red's farm in the East Settlement, Brattahlið. According to the Grœnlendinga Saga and Eirik's Saga, the expeditions of Leif Eiriksson and Þorfinnr Karlsefni, as well as others, left from Brattahlið around the year A.D. 1000, and sailed to an unknown land which they called Vinland. The Grœnlendinga Saga states that Leif built "large houses" there. It appears clearly that this region must have been in North America, but where? The problem of the position of Vinland has been discussed for generations, but the many investigations carried out yielded no certain traces of the Norsemen.

It has generally been held that Vinland must have lain fairly far to the south, as the sagas mention wild grapes. However, after having investigated the Norse settlements of Greenland, my continued studies led me to the conclusion that Sven Söderberg (1898), the Swedish philologist, was right in asserting that the syllable *vin* referred not to wine, but to the Old Norse word *vin* (f), which means meadow or pasture; a misunderstanding of the name may be responsible for the mention of grapes in the sagas. Taking also a number of other factors into consideration, such as the sailing times and the old Icelandic map of Sigurður Stefansson, I arrived at the conclusion that it seemed likely that Vinland should have lain on Newfoundland. In *Land under the Pole Star** I accounted for this conclusion in detail; a discussion of this view and its background will also be included in volume II of the present work. A few other scholars had previously held the view that Vinland was most likely to have lain in Newfoundland, including A. W. Munn (1929), V. Tanner (1941), A. H. Mallery (1951) and Jørgen Meldgaard (1961).

I further maintained that it should be possible to find traces of Norse settlers if one undertook a systematic investigation of the coasts of Newfoundland by boat and from the air. Such an investigation was undertaken in 1960, and then I discovered a group of densely overgrown house-sites near Épaves Bay, at L'Anse aux Meadows on the northern point of Newfoundland. There was a small fishing village close by, almost completely isolated from the rest of the world: there was no road, and the coast boat did not call here. A large plain covered with grass and heather stretched facing the Labrador Sea – here there was better pasture than anywhere else along the coast on the same latitude. If the Norsemen sailed southwards along the coast of Labrador, they would come straight on to the northern point of Newfoundland, and they could hardly avoid this particular area.

* Helge Ingstad: *Landet under Leidarstjernen,* Oslo, 1959. *(Land under the Pole Star,* London & New York. 1966.)

I then led the seven archaeological expeditions (1961–68) during which the settlement site was excavated, and other scientific investigations were carried out. The scholars taking part in this work formed international teams. The participants from Norway were mag.art Anne Stine Ingstad, mag.art. Arne Emil Christensen jr., mag.art. Sigrid Hillern Hansen Kaland, Kari Henningsmoen, cand. real., and myself. From Iceland: Dr. Kristján Eldjárn, Gísli Gestsson, curator, and Professor Þórhallur Vilmundarson. From Sweden: Rolf Petré, fil. lic.; from Canada: Dr. William Taylor jr. and Dr. Jan Whitaker; from U.S.A.: Dr. Junius Bird, Dr. Henry Collins, Birgitta L. Wallace, fil. cand., Dr. Charles Bareis, Dr. Jon Winston, and Professor Elmer Harp jr. with his students.

These expeditions would not have been possible without considerable economic help from many quarters. We are deeply indebted to the institutions and persons who in this way gave proof of their confidence in our enterprise, which was of so extraordinary a character that the prospects of success may not have seemed very promising.

First I would mention the Norwegian Research Council for Science and the Humanities, who not only rendered financial support to our expeditions, but also took the financial responsibility for publication upon itself. Special mention must also be made of the National Geographic Society, Washington D.C., not only because of the considerable financial support granted to us, but also because of the attitude of the Society – at a very early stage of our work, they fully accepted the Norse character of the settlement, advocating this view with the full weight of their great prestige. Their support meant a great deal to us, especially during the first years, when we were experiencing many difficulties.

Our grateful thanks are due to the following, private persons, firms and institutions, all of whom have helped us with contributions:

A/S Ancas, Oslo; A.O. Andersen & Co's Eft., and A.O. Andersen's Shipping Company A/S, repr. by Mr. Ole Schrøder, ship-owner, Oslo; Askim Gummivarefabrik A/S, Oslo; Mr. Nils Astrup, ship-owner, Oslo; A/S Auto Supply Co., Oslo; Johan H. Bentzon A/S, Oslo; Bergans Meis og Ryggsekk A/S, Oslo; A/S Bergens Mekaniske Verksteder, Bergen; A/S Bergens Privatbank, Bergen; Mr. Sigval Bergesen d.y., ship-owner, Oslo; Shipping Company Harry Borthen & Co., Oslo; Mr. Ludv. G. Bråthen, ship-owner, Oslo; A/S Christiania Glasmagasin, Oslo; A/S Christiania Portland Cementfabrik, Oslo; Shipping Company Ditlev-Simonsen, Oslo; Early Sites Foundation, New Hampshire; Elektrokemisk A/S, Oslo; Elkem-Spigerverket A/S, Oslo; Fiskereidskap P/L, Ålesund; Framhuset A/S, Oslo; A/S Freia Oslo; G.R. Fuglesangs Sønner A/S, Oslo; W. Giertsen A/S, Bergen; A/S Gresvig, Oslo; A/S Gyldendal Norsk Forlag, Oslo; Sigurd Herlofsen & Co., Oslo; Yngvar

Husebye, Oslo; Shipping Company Kristian Jebsen A/S, Bergen; Mr. Joh. Johannesen, director, Oslo; Mr. Jørgen Jørgensen, director, Oslo; A/S Jøtul, Oslo; Kolbjørn Knutsen & Co., Oslo; The Kon-Tiki Fund, Oslo; Mr. Ludvig Lorentzen, ship-owner, Oslo; Mr. Øivind Lorentzen, ship-owner, Oslo; Mandals Reperbane A/S, Mandal; A/S Margarinsentralen, Oslo; Dr. Terris Moore, The Arctic Institute of North America, Montreal; Mr. F.H.Münster, director, Oslo; The Nansen Fund, Oslo; The National Historic Parks and Sites Branch, Ottawa; The National Geographic Society, Washington D.C.; A/S Nera, Oslo; A/S Nestlé, Oslo; Norsk Brændselolje A/S, Oslo; Norsk Philips A/S, Oslo; Norsk Polarinstitutt, Oslo; A/S Norske Esso, Oslo; Norske Meieriers Salgssentral, Oslo; The Norwegian America Line A/S, Oslo; The Norwegian Council for Science and the Humanities, Oslo; The Norwegian Association of Sports Dealers, Oslo; Shipping Company B.D. Oddfjell A/S, Bergen; Mr. Fred Olsen, ship-owner, Oslo; Mr. Thomas Olsen, ship-owner, Oslo; Shipping Company Olsen & Ugelstad A/S, Oslo; A/S Rieber & Co., Bergen; The Royal Norwegian Foreign Office; The Royal Norwegian Ministry for Church and Education; Shipping Company Erling H. Samuelsen A/S, Oslo; Mr. Gunnar Schjelderup, director, Oslo; Mr. Peder Smedvig, ship-owner, Stavanger; Smith-Corona Inc., Oslo; Stabburet A/S, Fredrikstad; Mr. Otto Staib, director, Oslo; Steen & Strøm A/S, Oslo; A/S Sydvaranger, Oslo; J.L.Tiedemanns Tobaksfabrik, Oslo; Tingstad A/S, Oslo; A/S Trondheims Wirefabrik, Trondheim; Mr. Brede Villestad, Oslo; Mr. Nordahl Wallem, ship-owner, Hong Kong; Wallem Steckmest & Co. A/S, Oslo; Mr. Niels Werring, ship-owner, Oslo; Weswitco A/S, Oslo; With & Wessel A/S, Oslo.

Here I would add that ship-owners Thomas Olsen and Niels Werring not only supported these expeditions; they had also financed my previous expedition to the Norse settlements of Greenland, which was of great importance for my North America expeditions.

For transport across the Atlantic, I should like to thank the Scandinavian Airlines System, A/S Loftleiðir, the shipping company Olsen & Ugelstad and the Norwegian America Line for their valuable help. For transport in Newfoundland and Labrador we are greatly indebted to the Royal Canadian Airforce and the Royal Canadian Navy and, not least, to the International Grenfell Association, St. Anthony. Dr. Gordon Thomas, the superintendent of this institution, I might almost describe as our sheet anchor while we were working in Newfoundland; he was always willing to give his help, whenever it was needed.

There are many others who rendered invaluable assistance during the many years covered by these expeditions. I would here single out the late Professor Bjørn Hougen, former director of the Oslo University Museum of National Antiquities. We were in close contact with him all the time, and the fact that

14

so great an authority in the field of Norse archaeology showed such a never-wavering faith in the Norse character of the settlement, from the moment the results of the first year's excavation were available, meant a great deal to us.

The late Professor Mårten Stenberger, Stockholm, regarded our work with a similar attitude. At the request of the Newfoundland Government, they both came to L'Anse aux Meadows in order to study and assess the excavation. We greatly appreciated this visit, which enabled us to discuss the many problems involved with these experts. Our special thanks are also due to the following Norwegians: Professor Hallvard Magerøy, the late Professor T. F. W. Barth, Geological Museum, University of Oslo and Professor Knut Bergsland, who have rendered us assistance of very great value in their particular fields, mag. art. Charlotte Blindheim, Haakon Christie, architect, Dr. Tore Gjelsvik, Dr. Thor Heyerdahl, Ambassador Kaare Ingstad, Professor Reichborn Kjennerud, Professor Sverre Marstrander, Dr. Erling Christoffersen and Professor Fridtjof Isaachsen, Odd Medbøe, press officer, Svein Molaug, Director of the Maritime Museum, Oslo, and the late mag.art. Søren Richter. The assistance of the National Museum of Iceland, Reykjavik, was of great importance. The former director of the museum, Kristján Eldjárn, Þór Magnússon, its present director, and Gísli Gestsson, curator, were at all times willing to supply any information we needed.

The cooperation of Swedish scholars was also of great value to us: apart from Professor Mårten Stenberger I would here mention the late Professor Hans W:son Ahlmann, Dr. Sverker Jansson, the late Professor Holger Arbmann and Dr. L. Engstrand.

During all the expeditions we worked in close cooperation with the authorities of Newfoundland, Prime Minister Joseph Smallwood, other members of the government, and government officials, particularly David Webber. We were always met with an attitude of understanding of the importance of our work. Our thanks go also to many other people in Newfoundland, to Henry Collingwood, the Norwegian Consul, and to a number of members of the International Grenfell Association. Apart from Dr. Gordon Thomas, they include, among others, Mrs. Gordon Thomas, Dr. W.A.Paddon, Miss Pamela Sweet and Miss Louise Greenfield.

In Ottawa and in other parts of Canada we were also met with great courtesy and goodwill. At our request the Engineering Service Division of the National and Historic Parks and Sites Branch prepared an excellent map of the L'Anse aux Meadows district, which we found extremely useful. We are greatly indebted also to Dr. William Taylor jr., Director of the Museum of Man, the National Museum of Canada, Ottawa, the Hon. J.W. Pickersill, Ottawa, Deputy Minister E.A. Coté, Professor Olav Løken, Ottawa, and Mr. Karl Karlsen, ship-owner, Halifax. I would make special mention of our good friends Dr. Graham Rowley and his wife Diana, Ottawa, Dr. Trevor Lloyd, Director for Northern Studies and Research, McGill University, Montreal, and Dr. R.A. MacKay, Ottawa.

Our thanks go also to the U.S.A., to Dr. Henry Collins, The Smithsonian Institution, Washington D.C., Professor Elmer Harp jr., Dartmouth College, Hanover, New Hampshire, Melvin M. Payne, President of The National Geographic Society, Washington D.C., and to Andrew H. Brown, Assistant Editor of this society. We are particularly indebted to our good friend Dr. Junius Bird of the Museum of Natural History, New York. He took part in two of our expeditions – on one he was accompanied by his wife Peggy and Jon Beardsley – and he also rendered us valuable assistance in many other ways over the years.

We would express our heartfelt gratitude to all those who took part in the expeditions and excavations or carried out other scientific investigation in the area. Their names appear above; some of them have contributed to this volume, and valuable scientific contributions from other scholars are also included. The contributors will be listed in Anne Stine Ingstad's Preface to this Volume.

We shall never forget the people of L'Anse aux Meadows, who became our good friends. Many of them took an active part in the work, quickly gaining so much skill that they were a real help to us. Here we must be permitted to single out the late George Decker and his late wife, Mae Decker, who did so much for us, sterling people who will always be remembered. It was he who first showed me the site in 1960, when I was searching for traces of the Norsemen along the coasts of Newfoundland.

My heartfelt thanks go to the crew of our ship, the *Halten:* our skipper Paul Sørnes, Erling Brunborg, Odd Martens and Benedicte Ingstad Sandberg.

But the one to whom I owe most is my wife, the author of this volume. For almost fourteen years she devoted all her time and energy to this work, and had to renounce so much else on the way. Our expeditions covered many years, and the varying conditions at sea and on land must have been hard for a woman. Not only did the excavation of the remains of ancient turf houses with vague and diffuse features present many difficulties, but the climate at its worst, when cold winds, fog or rain come in from the Labrador Sea, can be downright abominable. It is hard for anyone to spend any length of time excavating under such conditions. But for all these years she went on with unflagging determination and courage.

Oslo, September 1975

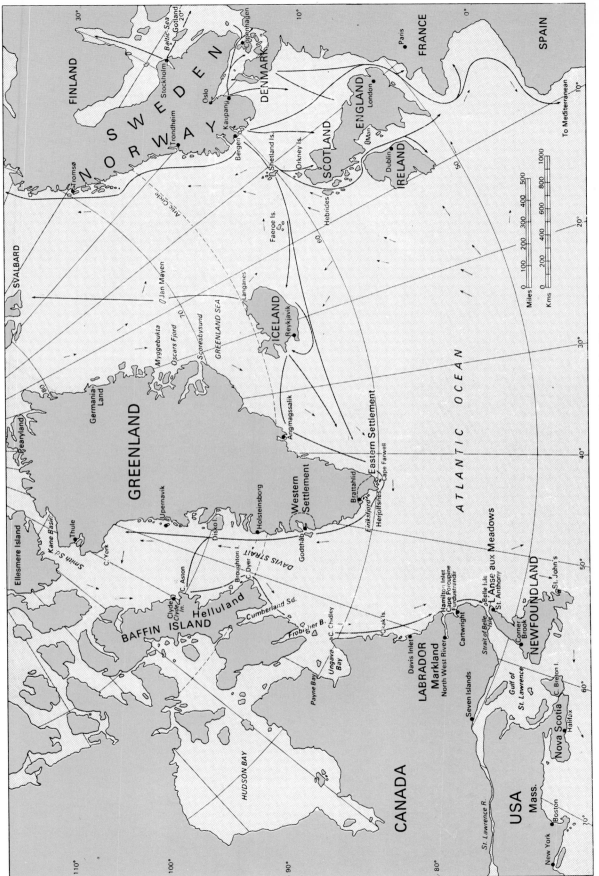

General map showing the Viking routes, including the «Way West», the route from Norway to Iceland, to the Norse settlements in Greenland and thence to North America. Drawn by G. Furuholmen. After Canada Department of Mines and technical Surveys.

Fig. 1. Épaves Bay, with the large plain covered in grass and heather. Part of the terrace with the house-sites appears on the right.

Preface

BY ANNE STINE INGSTAD

In this volume the results of the excavations of a settlement discovered by Helge Ingstad in 1960 on the northern point of Newfoundland are presented together with an archaeological assessment of the finds, which comprise house-sites and other archaeological material. The site is located at Épaves Bay, near the little fishing settlement of L'Anse aux Meadows.

During the period 1961–1968, Helge Ingstad organized seven archaeological expeditions, in the course of which these house-sites were excavated. The scholars participating in these expeditions formed international teams, and their names are listed in Helge Ingstad's foreword to this book; I would use this opportunity to thank each and every one of them not only for excellent work done, but also for the atmosphere of friendship which obtained during our life and work at these expeditions. Some of them have contributed to this volume, and valuable scientific contributions from other scholars are also included. The contributors are Dr. Charles J. Bareis, Assistant Professor at the University of Illinois, Arne Emil Christensen jr., Keeper at the University Museum of National Antiquities, Oslo; Dr. Kristján Eldjárn, President of Iceland, at the time Director of the National Museum of Iceland; Dr. Reidar Nydal, Laboratory for Radiological Dating, Institute of Physics, Trondheim, Norway; Kari E. Henningsmoen, Scientific Officer at the Geological Institute, University of Oslo; Leif M. Paulssen, Senior Scientific Officer at the Department of Pharmaceutical Chemistry, Institute of Pharmacy, University of Oslo; Rolf Petré, Keeper at the Museum in Lund, Sweden; Anna M. Rosenqvist, Keeper at the University Museum of National Antiquities, Oslo; Dr. William Taylor jr., Director of the Museum of Man, Ottawa (the assessment of the Stone Age material is based on his analyses) and Dr. Jon H. Winston.

My special thanks are due to Professor Bjørn Hougen, the former director of the University Museum of National Antiquities, Oslo. He supported and encouraged us in our work right from the beginning, and he has, moreover, read my entire manuscript – this was of great value to me in the preparation of this book. My heartfelt thanks also to Professor Hallvard Magerøy;

17

without his great kindness and valuable help there might well have been a number of mistakes in the spelling of old Norse terms and names.

We are also indebted to the late Professor T.F.W. Barth, The Geological Museum, University of Oslo, Charlotte Blindheim, Keeper at the University Museum of National Antiquities, Oslo, Dr. L. Engstrand, Radioactive Dating Laboratory, Stockholm, Rolf W. Lie, Keeper at the Zoological Museum, University of Bergen, I. Martens, Keeper at the University Museum of National Antiquities, Oslo, R. Monsen, Keeper at the Institute of Comparative Cultural Research, Oslo, B. Myhre, Keeper at the Historical Museum, University of Bergen, Håkon Olsen, Keeper at the Zoological Museum, University of Bergen, Perry Rolfsen, Keeper at the University Museum of National Antiquities, Oslo, Diana Stensdal, Librarian at the University Museum of National Antiquities, Oslo, Gunvor Ingstad Trætteberg, Oslo, and Bergljot Mauritz Messel.

Tone Strenger has made the final drawings from those prepared in the field, and she has also drawn some of the stone implements found. Her help has been invaluable and I should like to express my thanks to her in this connection.

Ragnhild Johannessen has typed my Norwegian manuscript, no easy task, and my thanks go to her.

Erling Brunborg, Hans Hvide Bang and Nicolay Eckhoff have covered the excavations photographically and I thank them all for their excellent work.

Elizabeth Seeberg has translated the book, and I am very grateful to her for the personal interest which she has taken in its progress, and for the time we spent preparing the English manuscript together. I should also like to thank her for having arranged the catalogue.

Oslo, November 1974

Part I
Excavations 1961–1968

Introduction

The northern part of Newfoundland is a long promontory, extending north into the Labrador Sea. At its northern point, at 51°35' N and 55°32' W, lies L'Anse aux Meadows, an almost isolated fishing village, the home of about seventy people (figs. 1 and 2). South of L'Anse aux Meadows the land opens up – there are low hillocks here, the land between them having been formed by late glacial deposits, at a time when the level of the sea lay 60–100 metres higher than today. Characteristic of these parts are the meadows by the shore, that at Épaves Bay being the largest. Nowhere else at this latitude are such expanses of meadow-land to be found. But the land is not only meadow and hillocks – there is forest, many of whose trees are stunted, there are extensive bogs and innumerable small lakes.

In summer, wild iris turns the plains near L'Anse aux Meadows into a blue carpet strewn with many other kinds of flowers. In warm summers, all sorts of wild berries ripen here: red currants and black, gooseberries, cranberries, crowberries, blueberries, bilberries, cloudberries, strawberries, raspberries and squashberries (Viburnum edule) (see Kari Henningsmoen, p. 295), to mention the most common only.

Today the fauna is not numerous, but there are still wild caribou, limited in number, at Long Range and elsewhere, and a few black bears and other wild animals. But in the past there was more life here: we have several accounts from the time immediately following Cabot's rediscovery of Newfoundland in 1497, and from Pasgualigo's contemporary account of Gaspar Cortreal's expedition in 1501 we know that the fauna of all Newfoundland was unusually rich and varied – the species mentioned include reindeer, lynx, wolf, fox, sable (marten), and falcons. In the sea there were large numbers of whale, seal, salmon and cod.[2]

Life in Newfoundland today is mostly confined to the coast, agriculture is of little importance. The people depend for their livelihood mostly on the sea, and live in scattered, small fishing villages, lying where bays and firths afford some protection from the ocean. These small communities live primarily by fishing cod along the coast, and seal catching forms an important supplement to their economy. The breeding grounds of the Greenland seal lie off the coast of Labrador and in the Gulf of St. Lawrence. These animals trek from Greenland and Baffin Land, arriving at their breeding grounds around the end of September. The young are thrown on the ice at the beginning of March, and in April-May, the seals move northwards again. Great numbers of these animals frequent the waters off the coast of Newfoundland in autumn.

These parts have a pronounced maritime climate, greatly influenced by the Labrador Current with its ice-floes, which meets the warm Gulf Stream off Newfoundland. High winds, and heavy fog and rain are commonplace. Abrupt changes in the weather are typical – a sunny summer's day may well be as warm as any in southern Norway, but when the wind changes to N or NE, as it is apt to do very suddenly, heavy fog may roll in over the plains in the van of the icy blast from the ocean. Then the temperature can fall considerably. This changeable climate can also lead to greatly differing summers: one year, the prevalent wind may be a warm, westerly breeze, and the sun may shine for weeks on end – but more often the cooler on shore winds dominate, making for raw, chilly summers (cf. Kari Henningsmoen's account of the climate).

Before this land was rediscovered in about A.D.1500, the inhabitants of northern Newfoundland were Beothuk Indians, the so-called Red Indians. These nomads, who migrated between the coast and the inland areas, lived by hunting and fishing. In autumn they moved inland along the great rivers, one of their most favoured regions being the parts by Red Indian Lake. There they lived mainly by hunting the wild caribou – there were large herds of these animals here in the past. In the spring, the Beothuk returned to the coast, some of them reaching the northernmost parts of Newfoundland.[3]

This Indian tribe was mercilessly persecuted by the white settlers, who allied themselves with the Micmac Indians in their war on the Beothuk. Early in the nineteenth century the Beothuk Indians had almost been exterminated, and the last surviving member of their tribe died in 1829.[4]

About ten minutes walk west from L'Anse aux Meadows lies Épaves Bay (fig. 3). This bay is so shallow for a long way out to sea that not even small fishing boats can put in to shore here. A small river, Black Duck Brook, which rises in Black Duck Pond about three miles inland from the coast, runs out into the bay.

The Labrador Current carries with it icebergs from the north, many of them foundering off L'Anse aux Meadows, where they break down in the course of the summer. Épaves Bay is a typical driftwood bay, and driftwood – most of it from Labrador, but also some from the Strait of Belle Isle – is forever being washed ashore here. In fact the very name, Épaves Bay, means a bay where flotsam and jetsam collect.

About 70–100 metres from the shore a curving marine terrace rises about 4 metres above the highest water level. It consists mostly of gravel and sand;

the layer of humus on top is, on the average, 5–10 cm thick, and covered by grass and heather. There is very little stone on the terrace and in its immediate vicinity. Kari Henningsmoen concludes that this marine terrace must have risen out of the sea about 5000 years ago, basing her view on pollen analyses and radiocarbon datings (see p. 329 below). D.R. Grant has arrived at a similar result.[5]

The land between the terrace and the shore is marshy, and lies at a lower level. Bush-willow grows here, and there are willows also along the banks of Black Duck Brook. This brook cuts through the terrace, and for a short part of its lowest reaches it turns to flow first east, then north, finally emptying into the bay. In its last stretch it runs very slowly, and deposits sandbanks which may change from year to year. Sometimes a rim of sand forms at the mouth of the brook, so that the water is dammed up into a small pond. If the water level 1000 years ago lay 0.5–0.75 metres higher than today – and this Kari Henningsmoen considers most probable (see p. 329) – the lower stretches near the mouth of Black Duck Brook must have been under water. In that case a boat which did not draw much water might well have entered the river; however Arne Emil Christensen does not consider this likely (cf. his article, pp. 109–127 below).

In the south, the gravel terrace merges into a bog, where low, windswept trees rising no more than three feet or so cover the ground with the spread umbrella of their crowns. In the west, a hilly ridge, some 20–40 metres high, runs towards the sea, blocking the view beyond.

The terrace which curves around the bay, sloping down to the sea, passes into a level plain covered by grass and heather, from which a headland projects northwards into the sea, from the eastern shore of Épaves Bay. Beyond lies Little Sacred Isle and some other, smaller islands and, further out, Great Sacred Isle. These shallow coastal waters abound with skerries; apart from these, the land lies naked and unprotected, open to the Labrador Sea. This is the marine terrace where Helge Ingstad in 1960 discovered the house-sites and other features with which we shall deal below.[6]

The problems involved

In the present paper the main interest has been concentrated on the determination of the cultural origin of the settlement by means of a critical analysis and assessment of the material and by adducing for comparison cultural material from all the ethnic groups which might have lived in these parts at any time.

It will be seen that a number of archaeological features are of a type which makes it clear to anyone familiar with Norse archaeology that this must have been a Norse settlement; however, I decided to discuss our findings in a larger context as well. This method should also make the character of the settlement clearer to those readers who are not familiar with Norse archaeology.

The walls of the houses were of turf, and the lower layers were preserved in many places. But few other structural details came to light as a result of the excavations, in spite of the fact that we constantly had the importance of finding features indicating how the houses were built in mind. For this reason, only a limited discussion of structural techniques is included, as there would seem to be little point in hypothetical reflections as long as so little new evidence is available.

After this work had gone to press, two articles by Elmer Harp jr. came to my notice (1974/75 and 1976). They contain very interesting information regarding the problem of the Norse culture viewed in the light of the Dorset culture. At this late stage, I cannot discuss these articles in any detail, unfortunately, but must confine myself to mentioning some important aspects: in the south-eastern part of Hudson Bay, several Dorset settlement sites have been excavated, and in one of their houses (Gulf Hazard house 1), a copper amulet was found *in situ*. Analysis revealed that this amulet was "almost certainly made of metal that derived from the old world". Harp assumes that it originally derives from the Norse people in Greenland. The house has been dated to A.D.1200. This date, as well as Harp's late dates of certain other Dorset houses in the Hudson Bay area, are of particular interest: they correspond with the fact that the houses at L'Anse aux Meadows yielded Dorset artifacts lying above the Norse strata.

The Stone Age material deriving from Eskimoes and Indians which was found during the excavations in and around the house-sites is significant, not least because it adds to our conception of the ethnic groups whom the Norsemen may have met. I have chosen to present this material in such a way that experts in these fields may study and assess it in greater detail. For my own part, I have merely attempted to relate it to the Norse houses and to the material found within them. My conclusions are based on William Taylor jr.'s analysis of the stone implements, and I would take this opportunity of thanking him for his help.

Elmer Harp jr. 1976: Dorset Settlement Patterns in Newfoundland and Southern Hudson Bay. Memoirs of the Society for American Archaeology, No. 31, 1976
Elmer Harp jr. 1974/1975: A late Dorset Copper Amulet from Southeastern Hudson Bay. Eastern Arctic Prehistory, 16–17

I Investigations

BY ANNE STINE INGSTAD

Test Excavations, 1961

At the beginning of June 1961, our boat, the *Halten*, cast anchor off Épaves Bay, Newfoundland. We had a long voyage behind us, having started from Montreal on one of the last days of April, and sailed down the St. Lawrence River, along the entire coast of the province of Quebec, to Pinnware Bay in Labrador. Then we crossed the Strait of Belle Isle, heading for the northern point of Newfoundland.

We had been ashore at many places on the way, examining the terrain with a view to ascertaining whether there might perhaps be ruins deriving from the Norsemen there. Some scholars have held that the Norsemen might quite feasibly have settled along this coast.[7] We discovered some house-sites, but test digs soon revealed that they must be fairly recent, deriving from white settlers. Moreover, nowhere along the coast did we see land with enough grass to have tempted the Norsemen to settle there. In our opinion, the most important requirement inducing them to settle in a particular place must have been pasture land, for their ancient culture was primarily based on stock-keeping. Nowhere along the coast of Quebec did we see so much grass that their animals might have found enough fodder.

At last we reached L'Anse aux Meadows. The *Halten* cast anchor fairly far out, for the bay is very shallow. We used our small boat on the way into Épaves Bay, but for the final stretch we had to wade, hauling in the boat.

In front of us, a wide, open plain curved around the bay (fig. 3). A small river had its outlet here. The land rose in terraces, gradually sloping up from the water. On the largest of these terraces lay the house-sites which Helge Ingstad had found the previous year, and which we were now going to investigate.

The house-sites could be dimly discerned along the curving marine terrace. Nearest the brook there were three house-sites, quite clearly visible, and marked by sods which had subsided. Two of these were rectangular, the third approximately round. At the middle of the terrace, apparently entirely on their own, there were indistinct traces of a rectangular house-site; a little way beyond, a roundish site, cut into the edge of the terrace, could be seen. The

25

Fig. 3. Aerial photograph of the marine terrace at Épaves Bay, showing the partially excavated house-sites. In the foreground, Black Duck Brook; in the background, Great and Little Sacred Isles.

other house-sites which we discovered later were practically without any visible traces: here and there stones were sticking up, that was all. But these stones were remarkable enough in themselves, for there is practically no natural occurrence of stone in the ground here. We also noted a couple of depressions in the edge of the terrace and some shallow pits in the ground: these, it later appeared, represented small houses and other features.

We hired some men from L'Anse aux Meadows, the fishing village close by, to help us.

The ground from the shore up to the terrace with the house-sites was levelled. It appeared that this terrace lay about 4 metres above the highest water-level, measured on 14th June 1961.

During the first year of excavation it was imperative that we should ascertain whether these house-sites represented Norse settlers or natives – Eskimoes or Indians – or more recent white fishermen or whalers. Unless we could establish this, we would hardly be in a position to decide whether we should continue to search for a Norse settlement elsewhere along the coast, abandoning the house-sites at Épaves Bay, or whether we should concentrate exclusively on this site, and continue to excavate here the following year.

Excavating all the house-sites completely in the course of one short summer and autumn was out of the question; therefore the 1961 excavation was organized as a test dig, a partial investigation of the actual floor-layer of each of the visible house-sites, within the walls. In some places we cut through the walls, in order to ascertain the materials and methods of construction employed. These test digs were based on a grid system consisting of squares of 1 square metre. All profiles were drawn and some photographed.

It soon became clear that we were here dealing with turf houses, highly eroded in part. At some places it was very difficult to distinguish between the cultural layer and the walls because the earth in both places was black, and thus there was a great risk that the walls might be removed without our having noticed them. In other places, the walls were so diffuse, almost resembling sterile sand, that it was practically impossible to see the difference between the walls and the sterile sand outside the houses when we were scraping from above. In these latter cases, the presence of a wall could be established only by means of the profiles. The most distinct of these showed the layers of turf as black, reddishbrown and grey stripes overlying one another. Where the erosion of the walls was most severe, the layers of the walls could only just be discerned as indistinct stripes in various shades of grey. Some of these could, in fact, be seen only in humid weather conditions.

Test excavation of several of the house-sites showed that these had many features in common, and the experience we gained during this first season was to prove very valuable during the later excavations.

We worked along these lines in the five house-sites which were visible above ground. One fact emerged with certainty from these first test digs: we found no evidence to show that these were Norse house-sites, but neither any evidence suggesting any of the other possible occupants of the houses. As far as we were able to tell after these test digs, the house-sites were primitive in character, with open hearths and cooking pits, but not a single fragment of any Stone Age tool or implement was found. This was certainly encouraging; but even so, two months' digging did not provide us with enough evidence to prove that we had actually found a Norse settlement. We therefore decided to leave Épaves Bay for a while, and go north to Labrador in order to investigate the coast-line there. Later I was to fly back alone, and resume the excavations at Épaves Bay, while the others were to continue their investigations in the north. We had now come to the beginning of August, and the remaining long days of daylight had to be utilized for the expedition along the coast of Labrador.

I returned to L'Anse aux Meadows at the end of August, and continued work on the excavations.

This time I decided to investigate an area where some stones were sticking up above the ground; one evening, when the sun was low in the sky, I had noticed some irregularities in the ground here, irregularities which might indicate the presence of a house. By that particular light I was just able to make out the faint outline of a corner as well as something which might possibly be the remains of a wall.

The system employed for this excavation was based on test trenches 2.5 m wide, running NW-SE, aligned with the presumed wall. Between these, a 30 cm wide section was reserved, and the profiles of these parts were drawn and photographed. This was slow work, as I constantly had to keep an eye on the men to make sure that they exercised great care in their work, for our only guiding lines were the changes in the colour and consistency of the soil. There was practically no stone which might have indicated the position of the walls.

It became clear as work progressed that we had here found a house of a very special type which, in our view, had many parallels in Norse material; moreover, it could hardly represent any of the other peoples who might reasonably be considered here. Further – we found iron rivets which were so corroded that they must be of considerable age, and we found hearths of types known from Iceland and Greenland, as well as other details which occur in the Norse material. Now we realized that we would have to return to this spot, and excavate all the house-sites completely, and also other parts of the area in as far as this proved necessary.

Then, one day, I sighted the *Halten* – the others had returned from Labrador. This was towards the end of September, and it was quite chilly. We had to sail south to Halifax before the autumn storms set in and on our way south we intended to investigate parts of the west coast of Newfoundland.

Six more seasons of excavation were to come: all in all we have uncovered eight or possibly nine house-sites and several smaller structures; four boat-sheds have also been partially investigated.

Excavation Procedure

In 1962, the entire area around Épaves Bay was surveyed by The Historic Parks Division Branch Engineering Services, Department of Indian and Northern Affairs and National Resources, Ottawa. All the house-sites and other features which came to light were plotted on to this map. All terraces and elevations were levelled, and all contour lines were mapped here. This was of great help to us in our work, for it turned out that the various features were scattered over quite a large area.

The experience gained during the test excavations of 1961 had made it clear that we could hope to carry out an entirely satisfactory excavation of these houses only if we planned the excavation of each individual house in a way which would give us a number of parallel profiles. We realized that we would have to base the excavation of every site on an individual grid system, so that the profiles would – as far as possible – run along the length of each site and at right angles to this. Only in this way could we be certain of following the line of the walls and the limits of the floor of each house. This proved to be a very practical method, and in the majority of cases it enabled us to establish with a fairly high degree of certainty where the walls began and ended. The closer to each other the profiles were, the more certain could we be of finding the walls. All the house-sites were excavated, drawn and photographed in three levels. As a rule, only the lowest level will be published in this paper, as the available space does not permit of a detailed publication of all levels.

The excavation of house A was planned according to a system of coordinates whose x axis ran east-west, with the positive values to the east, the negative values to the west. The y axis ran north-south, its positive values to the north and its negative values to the south. (Pl. 3).

Since house B lies close to house A, parallel with the latter, the same system of coordinates was employed for this house, and also for house C.

Similar systems of coordinates were employed for DI and DII. As concerns house F, which had in 1961 been investigated by means of test trenches from a base line (p. 65), we continued using this original system, since a great part of the site had been excavated during the first year. We extended the area southwards, assigning negative values to locations within this new, southern part.

Each of the other archaeologists responsible for parts of the excavation has accounted for the system employed, as appears from the reports below.

During the 1963 season we decided to dig a number of test trenches beyond the house-sites and between them. It then became necessary to establish a common grid system for the entire area on both sides of Black Duck Brook (see p. 97).

All the house-sites were plotted also on to this grid.

As soon as we realized that the settlement was Norse, we decided that as much of it as possible ought to be preserved. For one thing, we considered it important that the walls should remain, as they provide not only documentation of cultural history, but also material for future scientific studies. Moreover, we had cut a great number of profiles through them, without finding any structural details below, and thus it seemed very unlikely that such details would come to light even if we scraped away the entire remains of the walls. We felt that any possible scientific information concerning these walls which might thus be concealed would be insignificant as compared to the importance of preserving as much as possible of the Norse houses for posterity.

It was also our intention that the remaining, unexcavated part of the terrace and neighbouring area should remain untouched, for later generations with more advanced facilities to investigate.

After we had finished our excavations in 1968, the Historic Parks Division Branch, Department of Indian and Northern Affairs and National Resources has declared a large area around the site a National Park, and a museum is to be built here. Extensive excavations were undertaken in connection with this project. For these later excavations we are not responsible.

House-site A (fig. 4 and pls. 3–12)

House-site A lies on the east bank of Black Duck Brook, at the point where the brook cuts through the terrace. The longitudinal axis of this house (x-axis) runs almost true east-west. The north side wall is aligned with the edge of the terrace, and the west end wall lies right by the bank of the brook.

In 1961 a test excavation had been carried out in the eastern part of this house-site, between two clearly marked, parallel turf walls, about 4.5 m apart. The cultural layer was then found to be so poor that, pressed for time as we were, we decided against further excavation here for the time being.

Later we were to realize why the cultural layer of this part of the house-site was so indistinct: each spring, when the brook is full of drifting ice, the banks are flooded at this very spot. Every year the water must have washed away a great deal of the cultural layer, while depositing gravel and sand on the floor of the house-site instead. This applies particularly to the eastern part of the house; less such activity of the brook was apparent in the western part of this test excavation.

In 1962, the Icelandic members of our expedition, headed by Dr. Kristján Eldjárn, partially investigated the area between the excavated part and the brook. "A 17 m long and 50 cm wide trench, running west-east, and five trenches running south-north, right up to the edge of the terrace in the north, were dug. The three eastern trenches were 1 m wide, the other two 50 cm. Starting from the west, the trenches were 6.5 m, 13 m, 5.5 m, 6 m and 10 m long. All these test trenches were cut right down to the sterile sub-soil. At the top there was greensward and earth containing some sand, 5 – 15 cm thick, and below this we found the cultural layer, up to 30 cm thick in places, but thinner on the whole, with an average thickness of 15 – 20 cm. Below the cultural layer lay virgin soil, gravel mixed with clay, and with patches of grey sand.

"The cultural layer consisted mainly of earth, fine gravel and sand, irregularly mixed, and containing large and small lumps of decayed sods of grass and clean, grey sand. This mixture conveyed a general impression of somewhat grizzled soil, and scattered stones, most of them small, could be seen here and there at the edges of the trenches. They lay at greatly varying depths

30

within the cultural layer, and there were probably more of them at the edges than at the centre, but nowhere did they form any kind of row which might be reminiscent of a wall. The greatest dimension of most of these stones did not exceed 25 cm, but the largest of them, which was found immediately below the grass, measured 50 cm across. At the end closest to the area excavated in 1961, a very clearly defined boundary could be observed in the cultural layer, but it obviously extended some way into this previously excavated patch. The trenches showed the limits of the cultural layer sufficiently clearly. It was largely in the form of a continuation of the area excavated in 1961, about 14 m long and about 5 m wide. At most places it diminished rapidly towards the edge, as though it were lying in a shallow depression whose edges sloped upwards. The edges were uneven, and the entire bottom was extremely rough . . . At the eastern end of trench L–M, an iron rivet was found." (From Kristján Eldjárn's report; cf. the profiles of the test trenches, pls. 5 and 6.)

Then the trenches were filled up again, and the site lay undisturbed until 1967, when work was resumed. This last excavation was completed in the autumn of 1968; the entire house-site had then been excavated.

Excavation of House-site A, 1966-68

We started work at the western end of the house-site, where we investigated the reserved sections between the 1962 trenches. Our observations largely agreed with those made by Kristján Eldjárn: in all directions we found the same boundaries of the cultural layer. We cut through the northern edge of the terrace in several places and found a distinct wall consisting of layers of turf laid horizontally on top of one another (pls. 8–12). This was clearly a westerly continuation of the north wall of that part of the house which had been excavated during the test dig of 1961. In some places the stratification was so distinct that we were able to count as many as twenty layers of turf, in other places it was less clear. Our Icelandic colleagues had demonstrated that the cultural layer seemed to lie within a shallow depression with sloping sides; now the reason for this was apparent, for we had found the wall which formed the natural boundary of the cultural layer. The southern extent and boundary of the cultural layer were very indistinct, as the wall bounding the house here had been highly eroded by the water of the brook. Hardly more than a slightly raised part of sterile ground remained here, but the profiles revealed darker and lighter shades of grey, indicating layers of turf. The remains of this wall formed the southern limit of the cultural layer. In some places the cultural layer continued indistinctly beyond the wall – this was a midden outside the south wall of the house, which will be discussed below. With this one exception, the limits of the cultural layer were clear.

On the whole we found that the cultural layer corresponded to Kristján Eldjárn's description, but in several places a distinct floor layer of compact

31

earth, partly blackened by soot and containing charcoal appeared. The sub-soil below was scorched red in many places. Towards the western limit of the house, between x=1m and x=2.5m, the cultural layer showed a high content of large and small fragments of slate slabs broken as a result of fire; these lay above each other in layers, with burned clay in between. The clay had clearly been conveyed there, for all the layers were light in colour below, and black and burned red on top. Under this mound of brittle-burned stone, clay and ashes we found an oblong depression which was also burned red – undoubtedly the primary hearth.

In the west, at about x=11m, in the direction of the area test-excavated in 1961, the cultural layer continued under that part which we had in 1961 assumed to be sterile. Now we realized why – the brook had carried with it a great deal of gravel and sand, which had been deposited above the cultural layer here. The underlying cultural layer became greyer and more eroded the further east we proceeded. Strangely enough we found the most distinct remains of a wall in this part of the house, while the southern wall in the west of the house had been almost completely washed away. The cultural layer, however, was darker and more distinct here. The reason must be the following: the brook in flood burst through the southern turf wall, at its western end, but was stopped by the sturdy north turf wall. Then the water must have taken a right turn into the eastern part of the house, where it remained as a pool which washed out the cultural layer for a considerable period of time. Then the water flowed westwards, taking with it most of the western end wall, and found its way back to the brook. Thus here, in the part where the water found an outlet, its effect was limited to a shorter period, and thus the cultural layer was not eroded as badly as in the eastern part of the house. At the point where trench L-M, cut by the Icelandic archaeologists, stopped, the cultural layer was approaching a fairly uniform grey colour, but near the bottom there were parts where the sub-soil was burned red and where a fairly large number of pieces of charcoal was found. These were also greyish in colour, and resembled gravel. Both the large cooking pits in the eastern part of the house contained this light grey, monochrome material, which proved to consist of pieces of charcoal mixed with gravel and river sand. Farthest east, between x=17.50 m and x=25 m, where there was most erosion, any difference between the cultural layer and the sterile ground was difficult to detect. Fortunately the remains of the walls in this part of the house-site were very distinct, so we were never in any doubt about the limits of the site here.

Internally, house A measured c. 24 m in length and 4–5 m in width, measured at the widest point. The house consisted of four rooms, aligned along the length of the site, which runs in an east-west direction. A door opening connects the two eastern rooms, and there is another between the two

32

Fig. 4. House-site A, seen from east. The curving south wall continues into the excavated area
in the background; there are two door openings in that part of the wall.

Fig. 5. The ring-headed pin of bronze from house-site A in situ, Scale 1 : 1.

western rooms, but it is extremely doubtful whether there was a door between the two rooms in the middle of the house (I and III).

The external walls, as already stated, were built of turf, and the same material was used also for the partition walls. These were of approximately the same thickness as the external walls, 1–2 m. Before excavation, they could not be seen at all.

Two entrance doors led into the house, both of them on the south wall. The western door led into room I, the eastern into room III. The position of the western door has been established quite securely, but the eastern door we were not able to locate; however, a wide though not very deep midden outside the south wall of room III makes it appear probable that there must have been a door nearby. Only between $x = 11.5$ m and $x = 13.5$ m did we find a cultural layer running through the wall. We are thus fairly sure that there must have been a door here. Moreover, middens usually indicate the presence of an entrance door in the vicinity.

A sooty, hard-trodden patch of ground leading out through the wall marks the western door.

Room I

Room I is 5.5 m long and 4 m wide at its widest point, these being the internal dimensions. There is a hearth in the middle of the floor, at $x = 5.80$ m – $x = 8.20$ m, a longish lengthwise depression, 2.4 m long and 80 cm wide at its widest point. No stone setting marks this hearth, which was filled with ashes and coal, while the sand below was burned red. The floor around the hearth was firm and sooty, and fragments of charcoal had been trodden into it. Along the walls north and south of the hearth there was no such firm floor, and it is likely that there were earthen benches along the walls here, covered with some material or other – twigs or hides – which prevented this part becoming sooty and hard-trodden.

A few depressions at the edge of the hard-trodden floor around the hearth may be post holes. They were not lined with stone, but as they occur at regular intervals also in other parts of the house-site, this is a likely interpretation.

Two stones in the floor on either side of the entrance door on the south wall may have had some connection with this door. On the inside of the door there were large amounts of brittle-burned stones and charred fragments of bone on the floor, almost giving the appearance of a midden. This is probably refuse thrown out of room II.

Room II

Room II, which is wider than it is long, measures 3.3 m $\times$ 4 m. There is a hearth in the middle of the floor, at $x = 1.20$ m – $x = 2.50$ m, a longish depression

Fig. 6. Western end of house-site A, room II, showing impression of a post in the clay.

running along the length of the house (pl. 3). This hearth was 1.10 m long, 0.5 m wide and 10 cm deep. It was completely concealed under a heap of charcoal, ashes and brittle-burned stones, including some fairly large slabs of slate. We were brought into touch with this hearth at an early stage, as the top of the heap of charcoal and ashes came right up to the layer interpreted as the turf roof of the house. (This layer was much more distinct in the other houses than in house A.)

There were some depressions in the floor also of this room (fig. 6), probably post holes representing posts to support the roof. They are without any stone lining, and were filled with black earth. The deepest is 8 cm deep.

Room III

Room III lies east of room I, but our findings indicate that there probably was no door connecting these two rooms. At the place where there could have been a door, there is a small depression, possibly a post hole. If this interpretation is correct, the post housed in this hole cannot possibly have been a door post,

Fig. 7. The cooking pit in house-site A, room III. The ring-headed pin of bronze was found on the edge of this pit. At the right side of the pit, a post-hole may be seen.

for it would, as such, have stood in the middle of the door opening. As has already been pointed out, it seems likely that this room was entered by a door in the south wall.

The main hearth of room III seems to have been a large cooking pit in the north-east corner (fig. 7). The largest diameter of its opening is 1.8 m, the greatest depth is 15 cm. It was full of charcoal and brittle-burned stones, and partly covered by the collapsed north wall and the partition wall separating room III from room IV.

In the north-west corner, up against the north wall, at x = 12 m – x = 13 m, there is a second hearth, orientated north-south, across the room. It was covered by thick layers of charcoal and ashes. This hearth did not extend below floor level, but the floor below was burned very red and showed up clearly against the rest of the floor of the room, which was hard-trodden and sooty-black. About 1 m east of this hearth, the floor slopes gently down towards the cooking pit at the north-east corner.

West of the presumed entrance in the south wall of room III there is yet a third hearth, at x= 12 m – x= 13.3 m and y=–3.5 m – y=–4 m. This is quite small, and appears as an irregular depression in the floor. It was full of charcoal and ashes, and the sand at the bottom was hard and burned red.

There is a depression at the south-east corner, 50 cm in diameter and 10 cm deep, at x=17.3 m – x=17.8 m, y=–3m – y=–3.5 m. This was filled with large, clean pieces of charcoal. It is very unlikely to have served as a post hole, as immediately beside it there is a definite post hole, full of dark earth. It is possible, of course, that the end of the post which may have stood here might have been burned in order to make it more durable, but in that case the hole would hardly have been as chock-full of clean charcoal as it in fact is. The most reasonable explanation seems to be that this was a small ember pit, where the glowing charcoals were stored at night in order to facilitate the lighting of fires next morning. We shall later see that several of the other houses on the terrace also had ember pits of this kind.

As we have already stated, there was a depression close beside this presumed ember pit, probably a post hole. Immediately opposite, at the east edge of the cooking pit at the north corner, there is a corresponding post hole. Both these are 12–15 cm deep and 50 cm in diameter.

Strangely enough this post must have stood at the edge of the cooking pit, a position where it would easily burn, but there seems to be no other explanation for this depression but as a post hole (pl. 3).

A third hole, 30 cm in diameter and 6 cm deep, was found at the south-west corner, at x= 11.10 m – x= 11.40 m, y= –3.5 m – y= –3.75 m. This is probably also a post hole. On the opposite side of the room, a flat slab of stone corresponds to this hole, and this may have formed the foundation of a post. We found a small hole in the ground below this stone slab, 10 cm in diameter; it was completely empty. One more depression was found in this room, to the east of the presumed door in the south wall, at x= 13.60 m – x= 13.80 m, y= –4.60 m – y=–4.80 m. This may be a post hole which once housed a door post. It measured 20 cm in diameter, and was only 5 cm deep.

Room IV

Room IV, which lies east of room III, is connected to the latter by a door opening. The room is 5.65 m long and 3 m wide.*

In this room, too, the main hearth was a cooking pit in the north-east corner. The depression is 2.4 m long and its maximum width is 90 cm; it is 15 cm deep and was filled with charcoal, ashes and brittle-burned stones.

There was another hearth in this room, a shallow depression in the middle

---

* In my preliminary report on this subject in Acta Archaeologica 1970, I found this room to be 6.15 m long. It seems in fact to be a little shorter, and thus the cooking pit is placed in the corner.

Fig. 8. Dorset projectile point, found in
the west wall of house-site A, LaM 140.

of the western part of the floor. Its maximum width is 1.1 m, at x = 20 m – x =
21 m, and it is 6 cm deep. The floor underneath was burned red.

It seems quite evident that the flooding brook had destroyed many details
in this room. The cultural layer here was full of river sand and gravel, and it
was almost sterile – even the pieces of charcoal in the hearths were greyish in
colour. But even so, it seems that traces of an earthen bench running across
the eastern end of the room, along the end wall, could be detected. The walls
of this room were, as pointed out on p. 32 above, very distinct.
The turf of which the walls were built was subjected to two radio-carbon
analyses, which yielded the dates:

T-530: 950 ± 90, A.D.1000
T-818: 1320 ± 80, A.D. 630
Scattered charcoals from the cultural layer, very highly eroded by the brook,
were also tested by a radio-carbon analysis,
T-310: 1310 ± 130, A.D.640 (fig. 9).*

Finds

1 ring-headed pin of bronze, LaM 169, fig. 5.
4 fragmentary iron rivets, LaM 65.158.160.168.
13 fragments of iron, LaM 141.147.148.154.155.157(3).163.165.167.179(2).
6 lumps of slag, LaM 149.159.161.162.164.172.
1 arrow-head, Dorset Eskimo type, LaM 140, fig. 8.
2 pieces of red jasper, LaM 143.151.
1 flint chippings, LaM 142.
1 piece of iron pyrites, LaM 146.
1 fragment of bone(pig), LaM 182. App.I
Unidentifiable bone fragments.

* All radio-carbon analyses except one were carried out by the Radiological Dating Laboratory
in Trondheim, Norway. The remaining analysis was carried out by the Radioactive Laboratory
in Stockholm. cf. fig.9, and R. Nydal below. Cf. also Kari Henningsmoen's assessment of the
radio-carbon datings of the turf from the walls below.

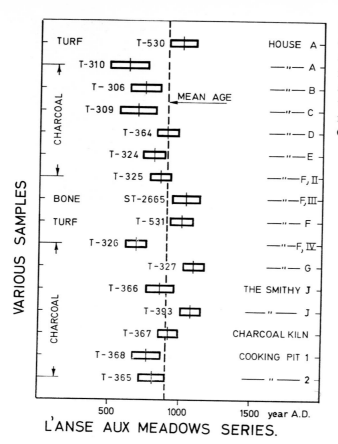

Fig. 9. Table showing the radiocarbon dates obtained by analyses at the Radiological Dating Laboratory, Trondheim, Norway, and at the Radioactive Dating Laboratory, Stockholm, Sweden. Prepared by R. Nydal, K. Løvseth and O. Syrstad.

House-site B (figs. 10–11 and pls.13–14)

House-site B lies about 4 m south of house-site A at local coordinates x= 22 m – x= 15 m, y=–9.5 m – y=–14.5 m, parallel with the latter, so that the longitudinal axis of house B also runs almost true east-west. It consists of one room only, with internal dimensions 4.5–5 m × 3.25 m. This house was clearly visible before excavation commenced, even though the remains of the walls rose only to a maximum height of 50 cm above the sterile soil after the excavation. They were built entirely of turf, and had been severely eroded by water from the brook.

During the partial excavation of this house-site in 1961, most of the floor within the walls was laid bare, but the entrance was not found until 1963, when a final investigation within and without the house was undertaken.

The cultural layer had a maximum depth of c. 45 cm by the east wall, but it diminished towards the west, where the floor sloped up to 20 cm above the level in the east (profile – 13.50 y). The top of the cultural layer was black and tough – this black layer was considerably thicker by the walls than in the centre. Obviously the turf walls had collapsed into the house, but as this tough layer was also present in the middle of the floor, we have interpreted it as including the remains of the turf-covered roof also. – At the centre, this layer was about 10 cm thick. The earth below was considerably looser – just as black as the top layer, and mixed with a large number of small pieces of charcoal. The lowest 10 cm of this layer were firm and fat, and contained charcoal and slivers of bone. This must be the actual floor of the house.

The walls of this house were considerably thinner than those of house A, but we could not ascertain why. Perhaps the brook has washed away parts of the outside of the walls in the course of the years – this is particularly likely in the case of the west and south walls. It is more difficult to find a reasonable explanation for the other two walls being so thin. The entrance to the house lies in the south wall, 1 m from the southern corner. It is marked by two flat stones and a sooted, hard-trodden patch leading through the wall. Before excavation, a depression was noted also in the north wall, indicating a possible door opening also here, but this has not been securely demonstrated.

Just inside the entrance, roughly at the centre of the west end wall, there is a hearth consisting of a flat stone slab, now cracked into many pieces (fig. 12). Part of the western edge of the hearth is aligned with the wall, so that the hearth veers towards the door, probably in order to utilize the draught. On the east side of the slab, small stones are set on edge, and in the front a shallow depression is marked by a low, torus-shaped edge of hard-burned sand. This depression is only 5–6 cm deep.

20 cm east of this hearth we found another depression in the floor, 45 cm in diameter and 25 cm deep. This was partially lined with flat stones and slates. It was full of charcoal, ashes and brittle-burned stones, and must undoubtedly have been a cooking pit (figs. 13 and 15).

About 65 cm east of the cooking pit, roughly in the middle of the floor, there was a fire patch, 65 cm wide and with a layer of charcoal and ashes 20 cm thick. It was not edged with stones, nor did it extend below floor level. The floor was ochre-yellow below the layer of charcoal, and the fill above contained some small pieces of bog ore.

At the south-east edge of this fire patch, there is a small depression in the floor, stone-lined, and 25 cm wide and 20 cm deep. It is made from slate, a beautiful piece of work, and was full to the brim with clean charcoal (fig. 14). This must be a so-called ember pit, where the glowing charcoal used to be stored at night, so that fires might be lit more easily next morning.

A 1.5 m wide section along the north side wall lacks the firm floor layer. We thought that there might well have been a bench of turf or earth here. While working here, we repeatedly encountered black, thin layers of turf. Before the bench had been excavated, it was 10 cm high. We have above stated that this may in fact have been part of the north side wall, in which case the room would have been narrower and the wall thicker – this is not, however, likely to be correct.

Fig. 10. House-site B seen from north-east, after test excavation. The entrance is marked by two stones in the south wall.

Fig. 11. House-site B seen from above east, showing the hearths.

Fig. 12. The big hearth in house-site B.

Fig. 13. The cooking pit of house-site B. The big hearth in the background.

41

At the eastern end of the house, close to the so-called bench, we found a hollow filled with black earth, but completely devoid of charcoal. This may be a post hole. It is 60–80 cm in diameter and 15 cm deep.

A radio-carbon analysis of charcoal from the cooking pit has yielded the date:
T 306: 1210 ± 110, A.D. 740, fig. 9.

Finds

1 lump of slag, LaM 3, fig. 17.
2 oval stones from the shore, with marks of pounding at the ends, LaM 37. 38, fig. 16.
1 pumice stone, LaM 46.

House-site C (fig. 19 and pl. 3 and 15)

House-site C lies 6.5 m west of B at local coordinates x = 2 m–x = 9 m, y = –9.50 m–y = –15 m, right on the bank of the brook. It showed up clearly before excavation, standing 50–60 cm above the grass. The walls were about 1.5 m thick. The site is roundish in plan, almost like a horseshoe in shape, with "arms" of turf extending on either side, to the east and to the west. The western "arm" was removed during excavation, the eastern "arm" was merely cut through. This house-site has earlier, in my preliminary article in *Acta Archaeologica,* been published without the western extension of the wall, as we, during the test excavations of the first year, did not realize the significance of this bit of wall – we then took it to be a chance accumulation of turf. The present account of the house-site is based on a drawing executed prior to all excavation here (pl. 3). The house has one room only, about 4 m long and 2.8 m wide, measured internally. The entrance showed distinctly before excavation, appearing as a depression in the northern part of the wall, so that it faced the sea and house A.

The greater part of this small house was investigated in 1961, and the excavation was completed in 1963.

As soon as the sods of grass had been removed, quite a number of slate slabs of varying sizes came to light. Below we found a c. 15 cm thick cultural layer, the topmost 5–8 cm of which proved to be tough to scrape. This layer may represent the turf roof of the house. Underneath, the earth was of a more greyish colour, almost resembling clay, and fairly fat. It showed considerable staining by rust, and contained charcoal and pieces of slate. The concentration

Fig. 14. The ember pit in house-site B.

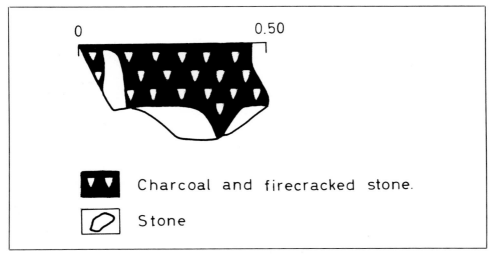

Fig. 15. Section of cooking pit in house-site B.

Fig. 16. Oval beach stone with marks of pounding at ends. LaM 37. 1 : 1.

of charcoal was greatest furthest inside the house, around a large stone. This stone has no contact with the floor, but lay on a 10 cm thick layer of earth mixed with charcoal, perhaps the remains of a hearth. No other hearth was found.

Close to the walls, in the areas where the fallen turf wall had formed a protection, the cultural layer was quite dark and contained a considerable amount of charcoal. Probably these parts were not washed out by the water from the brook to the same extent as the centre of the house. The lowest 2 cm of the floor stratum were quite dark, and contained fairly large pieces of charcoal. The sterile sub-soil here contained a great deal of gravel, but it was covered by a clay shell which had been blackened by soot on top. It seemed as though the clay had been put down here intentionally.

Outside the house, excavation revealed a small midden immediately to the north-west of the entrance door.

A radio-carbon analysis of charcoal from the cultural layer has yielded the date T–309: 1240 ± 130, A.D. 710, fig. 9.

Fig. 17. Lump of slag found in the cooking pit in house-site B, LaM 3.

Finds

2 lumps of slag, LaM 32.
1 fragmentary iron rivet, LaM 21.
1 fragment of iron, LaM 7.
2 charred slivers of bone, LaM 9. App. II and III.
1 piece of chert, LaM 156.
1 piece of red jasper, LaM 153.

House-site D I and II (figs. 20–21 and pl. 16)

House-site D lies roughly in the middle of the terrace, approximately at N6–N13, rather closer to house A than to house F, and it forms a separate complex together with house E.

The site is orientated NE/SW. It was indistinctly visible before excavation, when only the western part could be discerned. This part was partially investigated during our first year of activity here, 1961. In 1962 Rolf Petré excavated the north-eastern part, which then received the designation H, as we did not at the time realize that the two houses were connected. This designation was later changed to D III. In 1966, excavation of the south-western part was resumed, and by the autumn of that year the site had been completely excavated.

In D I and D II (the south-western part of the house) the strata were roughly similar to those found in the sites described above, except that the cultural layer was not quite as black here.

House-site D is about 18.5 m long, and may have had a maximum internal width (D III) of 3.2–5 m. It consists of three rooms, rooms I and III lying beside each other, orientated in a NE/SW direction, while room II lies north-west of room I. Rooms I and II seem to be connected by a door, but we were not able to find any door opening between I and III, even though it seems clear that there must have been such an opening. The site is aligned with the terrace, the north-western side wall running along its edge. Thus room II does not lie on the terrace, but on the slope below, so that it lies on a slightly lower level than the other two rooms. Rooms I and II together measure 7.5 m in width.

Room I

Room I is 5.5 m long and has a maximum width of 3.2 m. It is approximately rectangular, the external and internal corners being somewhat rounded. It was entered from the south–east side wall, close to the southern corner. This is probably the entrance for the whole house. It was not marked by any stones – a hard-trodden, sooted patch on the inside and outside of the turf wall was the only evidence of a passage at this point (section at y = −4.40 m, pl. 19). A narrow, sterile stripe at the centre of the wall was neither worn nor trodden down – this probably indicates the presence of a door frame or threshold, possibly wooden.

The cultural layer in this room was not as black as those found in the other house-sites on the terrace. It contained a number of pieces of charcoal, although not sufficient to suggest the presence of a hearth anywhere (pls. 17–20). The top resembled the black layer of turf described above, in connection with the other house-sites – that which we have interpreted as the turf roof; here, however, the colour was brown rather than black. We cut through the walls in this western part of the house, and the profiles revealed clearly marked stripes of brown, red and white, representing layers of turf layed on top of one another.

Room II

Room II lies north-west of room I, at a slightly lower level – c. 30 cm – than the floor of room I. The profile showed a kind of step, reminiscent of those cut out of logs in old Norwegian store-houses. There may have been primitive stairs leading down to this room, possibly made from a log split down the middle. The internal dimensions of this room are about 4 × 3 m. Three of the walls were very distinct after excavation, but the north-west wall had disappeared completely, probably as a result of the constant influx of water at work in this room. It is also possible that this fourth wall may have been of timber. The preserved walls, like those in the rest of this house-site, were of turf, and after excavation they rose 60 cm above the lowest floor level.

The top 10–15 cm of the cultural layer in this room consisted of black turf with rusty-brown stains, and it also contained a certain amount of charcoal. Right under the grass we found some fairly large slabs of slate, which had probably lain on the turf of the roof. About 28 cm below the black layer of turf we found a grey layer of sand with black stripes, giving a marbled effect – probably pigment from the eroded turf above. Pieces of charcoal occurred also in this layer, but there were fewer of them. Towards the bottom, however, the charcoal content increased greatly in some places, and straight above the sterile sub-soil we could here and there demonstrate a thin stratum of pieces of charcoal, some of them large. These patches were the remains of the original floor, most of which had been washed away. The depth of this layer varied from 1 cm to 5 cm. There is a marked difference between the layer of black turf above and the grey sand below; they differ greatly not only in colour but also in texture. The sand stratum at the bottom is thickest in the south-east, by room I, while it diminishes towards the north-west, where it finally disappears entirely. The limits of the floor in this direction could not be ascertained, but the profile of the north-east wall shows the boundary quite distinctly.

In the southern corner there was a large fire patch, with a maximum diameter of 75 cm. The layer of charcoal was 5 cm thick.

Finds

1 iron rivet head, LaM 125.
2 pieces of iron pyrites, LaM 11.

Room III lies north-east of rooms I and II. It was excavated by Rolf Petré in 1962 – his description of "Excavation No. I, The House" follows below.

Fig. 18. The meadows by Épaves Bay with Great Sacred Isle in the background.

Fig. 19. House-site C before excavation, seen from north.

II Investigations 18th–27th July 1962

BY ROLF PETRÉ

Excavation No. 1, "The House" D III (figs. 20–21 and pls. 21–23)

This was situated between house-sites D and E. Prior to excavation, it showed up as a vaguely defined, even surface of grass in the otherwise tussocky ground. A test trench revealed that there was a cultural layer containing charcoal beneath the turf. Further excavation was therefore planned, on the assumption that the smooth exterior concealed a house-site, an assumption confirmed by subsequent investigation.

A longitudinal base line was marked on the surface, the zero point at its north-eastern end. The compass bearing was 252 (new) degrees, no correction being made for magnetic variation. The base line constituted the x axis of a right-angled grid system, in which the positive x values appeared to the south-west and the positive y values to the south-east. From the base line transverse lines crossing the surface were marked at x = 3.5 m, x = 5.5 m, x = 8 m, x = 10.5 m and x = 13 m. The site was then excavated by sections between these transverse lines and the base line, and profile benches half a metre wide were reserved along the lines (pls. 22–23). These profiles were drawn and photographed, and the benches were not removed until the entire site had been exposed. All finds which came to light during excavation were plotted on the grid system, their levels being measured with a rule from the surface of the ground and later converted, so that the levels are now given according to their height above the bottom of the excavation.

The area investigated comprised the site of a house, originally rectangular and bounded by low remains of turf walls along the sides. It is possible that there were no such walls at the ends – no evidence of any remains of end walls was found. However, the remains of the other two walls were very slight, as wind and weather have eroded them and levelled them down. In only two profiles in the entire investigated area could the existence of walls be established with certainty: a thin strip of humus, marking the original level of the ground, ran from the cultural layer under what is presumably the remains of these walls. The layers other than the cultural layer, which were to a varying extent mixed with turf and humus, were extremely difficult to interpret, as

49

Fig. 20. House-site D, room III, during excavation.

they were densely permeated by roots; traces of "reshuffling", caused by frost, could also be observed in the layers. The north-west side wall seems to have been partly built of gravel.

The cultural layer lay immediately below the grass, and it was markedly loose and slack in consistency. It consisted of sand mixed with humus, with a considerable admixture of charcoal fragments, and in addition it contained charred bones, pieces of slate, and some stray, small, brittled-burned stones. There was practically no soot, except for a thin bottom layer around the hearth, and a similar layer in a clearly defined area in the south-western part of the house. Below the cultural layer there was clean, gravelly sand and abundant deposits of charcoal; the discovery of a bed of twigs or similar flooring on the site probably explains the loose consistency of the cultural layer. Many of the charcoal fragments were twigs with a round cross-section.

The cultural layer covered an irregular oblong surface, about 10 m long and 5 m wide, which must correspond to the internal dimensions of the house. In the middle of this area there was a *hearth (structure No. 1)*, which consisted of a thin layer of soot approximately 250 cm long and 100 cm wide, orientated in the longitudinal direction of the house. Some of the gravel at the bottom, under the soot, had been burned red and on it, at its south-eastern side, there was also a patch of sand which had been burned red. Along the north-western edge an irregular depression was found under the soot, burned red at the bottom and 110 cm long, 30–10 cm wide, and 5 cm deep. At the narrower north-eastern end there were a couple of brittle-burned stones. Immediately beside the south-western end of the pit there was another pit, 37 cm × 33 cm, and 18 cm deep. At the bottom of this lay a rectangular slab of slate, and a similar slab – a portion of which had broken off – stood at its north-eastern

50

Fig. 21. House-site D, room III, after excavation. In the background, the test-excavated part of room I; room II has not yet been excavated.

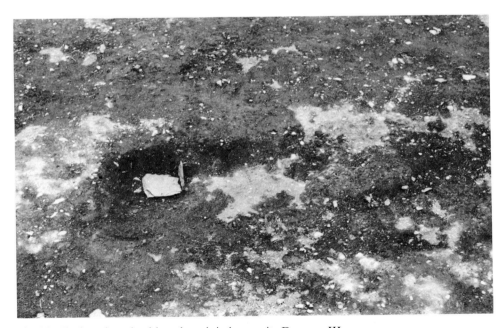

Fig. 22. The long hearth with ember pit in house-site D, room III.

Fig. 23. Copper fragment LaM 69 from house-site D, room III. c. 2⅓ : 1.

side (fig. 22). This pit was filled with soot, and the sand here was not burned;
it clearly represents the remains of an ember pit of the kind previously
encountered here at this settlement. No stones were lying directly on top of
the soot, but in the cultural layer above and around the hearth we found
scattered brittle-burned stones and slabs of slate, the latter probably from the
ember pit. By the south-eastern edge of the hearth, a small copper object was
discovered; this had been damaged by fire. In the ember pit, mixed with the
soot, we found minute fragments of thin, burned bones, one of them clearly
the vertebra of a fish, as well as a broken, burned bone needle.

No other readily identifiable structures came to light in this house. In the
north-eastern part there was a collection of *five large stones (structure No. 2)*.
They had no contact with the bottom of the excavation, and extended to the
grass sods above; like a single stone at the end of the house, they were
probably placed there in modern times in order to support a post, or for some
similar purpose. Fifty cm north-west of the hearth there was a *patch of soot
(structure No. 3)*, 20 cm × 30 cm, partly covered by a patch of sand which
had been burned red. Close to this patch we found a quartz arrow-head and
a large piece of burned bone, probably whale-bone. There were a number of
irregular pits in the south-western part of the house, the largest *(structure No.
4)* 35 cm × 30 cm, and 19 cm deep. These contained the same material as the
cultural layer, and are probably of a casual nature. The surface grass was
pitted and uneven here before excavation, and thus these depressions may well
be the result of recent disturbances.

Finds

Fragmentary iron rivet, length of shaft 2.4 cm, head 1.6 cm × 2.0 cm. Local
coordinates: x = 6.05, y = –0.24, level 4 cm above floor level, LaM 68.
Fragment of bronze or copper, damaged by fire, straight rod with round upper
surface, rounded ends, remains of ornamentation (?) on upper surface, thin
transverse lines. 1.7 cm long, 0.4 cm wide, 0.25 cm thick. Local coordinates:

Fig. 24. Bone needle from house-site D, room III. LaM 76. 1 : 1.

Fig. 25. Dorset projectile point, LaM 75. Found in house-site D, room III. 1 : 1.

x = 7.92 m, y = –0.20 m, floor level. The object was lying just outside the hearth. LaM 69, fig. 23. (See A.M. Rosenqvist below.)

Fragmentary iron nail, length of shaft 4.0 cm, head 1.8 cm × 2.2 cm. Local coordinates: x = 5.34 m, y = –1.97 m, level: 1 cm above floor level, LaM 70.

Fragment of iron (?), 1.2 cm × 1.4 cm, 0.7 cm thick. Local coordinates: x = 4.98 m, y = –2.11 m, level 8 cm above floor level. This object was lying among the stones in structure No. 2, LaM 71.

Fragment of dark grey chert, 3.4 cm long. Local coordinates: x = 10.73 m, y = 0.65 m, level 12 cm above floor level, LaM 72, fig. 27.

Biface fragment of dark grey chert, 2.2 cm long, 3.1 cm wide, 1.0 cm thick. Local coordinates: x = 10.75 m, y = 0.45 m, level 12 cm above floor level, LaM 73, fig. 27.

Chert flake, 2.8 cm long. Local coordinates: x = 10.75 m, y = 0.63 m, at floor level, LaM 74, fig. 27.

Quartzite arrowhead, two notches at the sides, 3.1 cm long, 1.8 cm wide, 0.5 cm thick. Local coordinates: x = 5.76 m, y = –0.48 m, level 6 cm above floor level, LaM 75, fig. 25.

Fragmentary bone needle, truncated triangular head, pierced, round shaft broken. 3.4 cm long, head 1.5 cm wide, 0.4 cm thick, diameter of hole 0.5 cm, diameter of shaft 0.5 cm. Local coordinates: x = 8.69 m, y = –1.25 m, level 2 cm above bottom of ember pit, LaM. 76, fig. 24.

The south-west end of Rolf Petré's Excavation No. 1 lies 2.5 m north-east of the north-east end wall of D I, at x = 2.10 m. In 1966 new trenches were cut through the untouched part between D I and Petré's Excavation No. 1, and it was then established that the layer of soot which Petré had noted at the south-western end of his area continued about one metre in the direction of house-site D I, so that these two house-sites are now separated by a turf wall about 1.5 m thick. The reason why Petré found no wall at this end of his Excavation No. 1 is that the two sites were connected, being separated by a common partition wall. We cut through this wall in several places, in the hope of finding a door opening connecting the two sites. At the middle of the wall we found a sooted patch extending some way into the wall, but it was not possible to demonstrate that there really had been a door at this point. We have therefore not shown any door on the plan, even though we feel fairly certain that there must have been one here. The wall between the rooms is very distinct, and the profile shows the old turf clearly as brownish-black lumps mixed with lighter sand and rusty-brown patches (pl. 20).* It seems probable that Petré's Excavation No. 1 was ravaged by fire, which must have deposited soot on the partition wall between the rooms, but without reaching the south-western part of the site.

A radio-carbon analysis of charcoal from the hearth in room III has yielded the date: T–364: 1050 ± 70, A.D. 900, T–817: 1300 ± 70. A.D. 650, fig. 9.

Excavation No. 2, "The Midden", Pl. 34

A layer of refuse was found on the slope from House G down to the turf in the river-bed below. This midden lay immediately below the grass sods, and consisted of a layer of sand, with a slight admixture of humus, and contained a few fragments of charcoal, a few scattered, charred bones and a few scattered, brittle-burned stones. At the top, immediately below the greensward, there were also numerous small slivers of slate. At the foot of the slope the midden merged with a layer of turf containing stray pieces of charcoal and small lumps of bog-ore. The boundaries of this layer were not clearly defined, but the pieces of charcoal occurred within an area of about 4 m × 5 m. The finds were plotted on a right-angled grid system, whose zero point lay at the edge of the trench cut for the earlier excavation of house G, while the x axis ran along the slope towards the west; the positive values of the y axis were plotted in a southerly direction. The levels were measured with a rule and converted into heights above the sterile sub-soil. Two profiles were drawn (pl. 34), one orientated toward house F (profile A–B), the other towards house G (profile B–C, coincident with the x axis).

Finds

Chert fragment, 3.0 cm long, 3.2 cm wide, 1.0 cm thick. Local coordinates: x = 2.23, y = 0.75, level: 6 cm above sub-soil, LaM 77, fig. 27.

Fragmentary iron rod with fragments of wood (?) rusted on to it, 3.0 cm long.

* See Kari Henningsmoen's assessment of the radio-carbon dating of the turf from the walls.

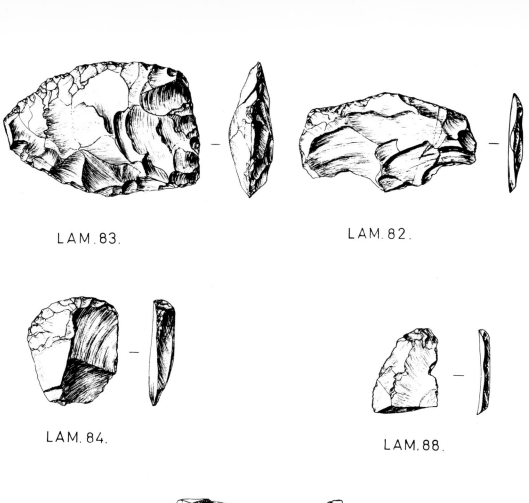

LAM.83.   LAM.82.

LAM.84.

LAM.88.

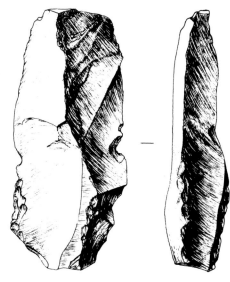

LAM.89.

T. Strenger.

0   1   2   3   4   5 cm

Fig. 26.

Local coordinates: x = 1.65, y = –0.35, level: 3 cm above sub-soil, LaM 78.

Chert fragment, 1.9 cm long. Local coordinates: x = 1.75, y = –0.35, level: 4 cm above sub-soil, LaM 79, fig. 27.

Fragmentary chert flake, 2.6 cm long. Local coordinates: x = 1.69, y = –1.35, level: 2 cm above sub-soil, LaM 80, fig. 27.

Green chert flake, 2.7 cm long. Local coordinates: x = 0.33, y = –1.06, level: 3 cm above sub-soil, LaM 81, fig. 27.

Excavation No. 3, Cooking pit II. Fig. 30 and Pls. 45–47

This site was situated north-west of house F, at N 71.5–N 66.5, E 105–E 110.5, and before excavation it appeared as a large depression in the ground, overgrown with grass and brushwood. The grass sods were stripped off, and two base lines, intersecting at right angles at the centre of the site, were plotted. One line formed the x axis of a right-angled grid system with its zero point south-east of the site; the x axis ran in a north-westerly direction, the y axis in a north-easterly direction. The finds were plotted on this grid system, levels being given in terms of height above the sterile sub-soil. The pit and its immediate surroundings were excavated square by square, and the profiles were drawn and photographed.

The structure comprised a dug pit, 290 – 300 cm in diameter and 70 cm deep. At the bottom we found a compact layer of charcoal dust, 5 cm thick and increasing to 20 cm along the edges. This layer also contained large pieces of charcoal – twigs etc., round in cross-section – up to 10 cm in diameter. It was approximately round, about 230 cm in diameter. On top, a layer of equal size contained brittle-burned stones of varying sizes, while an area at the centre, approximately 70 cm in diameter, was completely lacking in stones – it was filled with almost pure soot. On and between the stones there was a layer of sand mixed with soot, about 20 cm thick. On top of this we found a layer of soot 3 cm thick, and a second, thinner layer of brittle-burned stones. The thin top layer, covering all these, consisted of sand mixed with humus, and turfs of grass. The sand mixed with soot followed the sides of the pit and continued on the surface beyond its limits, gradually merging with a dark brown layer mixed with humus, immediately below the surface grass. The finds occurred in the layer mixed with soot, close to the edge of the pit, many of them immediately on top of the yellow sand below. South-east of the pit, at the edge of the depression, we found a small collection of brittle-burned stones, which had clearly been taken up from the pit. Practically all the finds were concentrated in a small area close to these stones. Buried in the yellow sand below, there was a polished stone axe, standing at an angle of about 45°, its cutting edge extending upwards into the cultural layer.

56

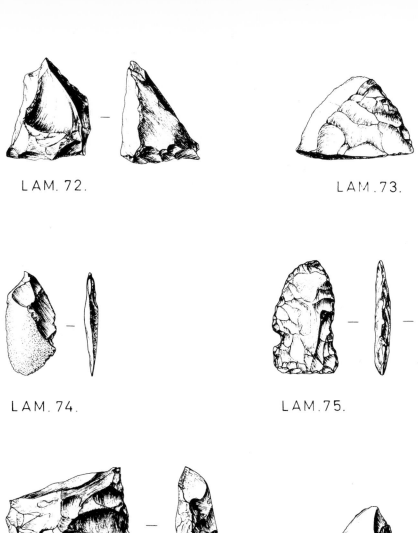

LAM. 72.

LAM.73.

LAM. 74.

LAM.75.

LAM.77.

LAM.79.

LAM. 80.

LAM.81.

T. Strenger.

Fig. 27.

0 1 2 3 4 5 cm

This was probably some kind of cooking pit, the collection of stones at the edge suggesting that heated stones had been used for cooking or roasting in or near the pit, which had clearly been used more than once, as appears not only from the two distinct layers of stone, but also from the fact that profiles showed that the outer edge of the lower layer of stones was covered by yellow sand which had slid down before the pit was taken into use once again.

A radio-carbon analysis of charcoal has yielded: T–365: 1140±90, A.D.760, fig. 9.

Finds

Chert flake, broken into two pieces, striation retouch along one edge, 4.6 cm long, 2.7 cm wide. Local coordinates of the larger fragment: x= 1.96m, y= 1.10m; of the smaller fragment: x= 2.25m, y= 1.04m, LaM 82, fig.26.

Chert biface point, 5.2 cm long, 3.7 cm wide, 1.1 cm thick, Local coordinates: x=2.8 m, y= 2.01 m, LaM 83, fig.26

Chert scraper, with rounded edge, 2.9 cm long, 2.4 cm wide, 0.6 cm thick. Local coordinates: x=2.64 m, y= 2.01 m, LaM 84, fig.26.

Polished chert axe head with knapped sides, polished upper surface and partly polished lower surface, rounded cutting edge. 10.7 cm long, 8.1 cm wide, 1.0–1.8 cm thick. Local coordinates: x=0.62 m, y= –1.55 m. The axe was standing in the gravel of the sub-soil, its cutting edge sticking obliquely upwards, LaM 85, fig.28.

Chert biface, 8.0 cm long, 5.5 cm wide, 1.6 cm thick. Local coordinates: x= 2.06 m, y= –0.92 m, LaM 86, fig.28.

Fragmentary iron plate, 2.5 cm long, 0.3 cm thick. Position: On the gravel of the sub-soil, LaM 87.

Chert flake, 2.5 cm long. Local coordinates: x= 1.23 m, y= –0.16 m. The iron fragment was lying on the gravel of the sub-soil, the chipping a few mm above it in the layer mixed with soot, LaM 88, fig. 26.

Prismatic chert flake, 7.2 cm long, 2.5 cm wide, 0.3 cm thick. Local coordinates: x= 5.06 m, y= –0.14 m, LaM 89, fig.26.

Chert block scraper, approximately 20 cm long. Plotted on the plan of the pit. Local coordinates: x= 5.75 m, y= –0.45 m, LaM 90.

23 flakes and chippings of chert, quartzite and slate varying in length from 1.8 cm to 7.2 cm. The chippings were scattered over a limited area at the southern edge of the pit, LaM 91, fig.29.

Excavation No. 4. Test trenches

As part of the investigation, a number of test trenches were dug between the bog and the slope running down to the old bed of the brook. The trenches, half

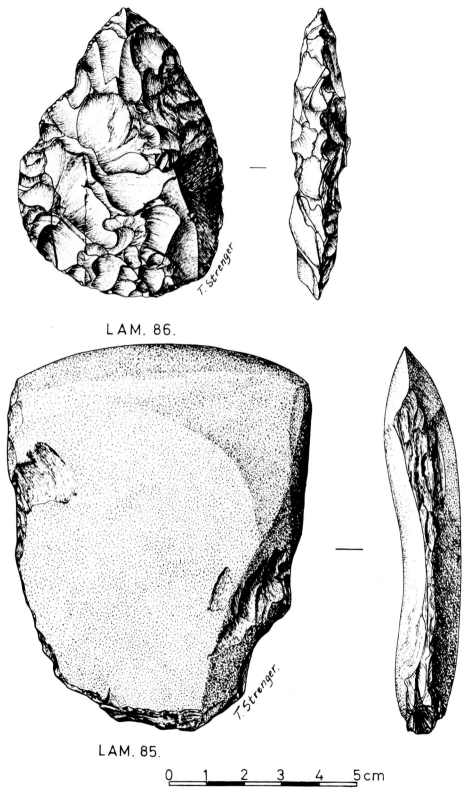

LAM. 86.

LAM. 85.

0 1 2 3 4 5 cm

Fig. 28.

a metre wide, were cut in groups and parallel to one another (see sketches), most of them at 2 metre intervals. They all showed that there was no cultural layer between the houses – the sterile sub-soil sand lay directly beneath the grass. No finds were made here. A small *hearth* was uncovered south of house F, 28 cm × 34 cm, and only 1 cm thick. A few brittle-burned stones were lying on it. The test trenches yielded no finds.

In addition, a layer of sand with a slight admixture of humus was found on the slope below house D ("Taylor's Midden") and a profile of this was drawn. It only contained scattered pieces of charcoal.*

* This was before D II was excavated, so that we did not realize at the time that this layer formed part of house D. *(Author's note)*

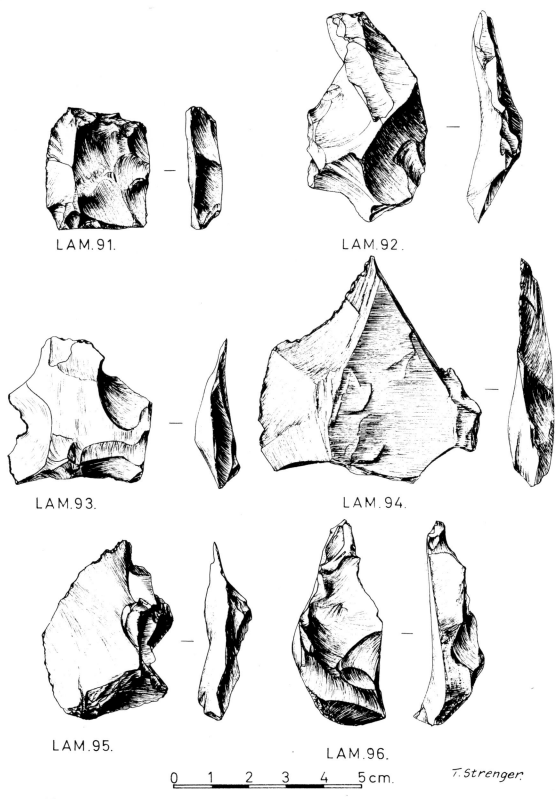

LAM.91.

LAM.92.

LAM.93.

LAM.94.

LAM.95.

LAM.96.

0 1 2 3 4 5 cm.

T. Strenger.

Fig. 29.

III Investigations

BY ANNE STINE INGSTAD

House-site E (Pls. 24–25)

House-site E lies right at the edge of the terrace, 5 m north-east of house D, at N18-N9, E113–E121. It showed up very distinctly before excavation – 1.5–2m thick remains of earth walls, covered with grass, ran around a depression on all four sides.

The external corners are rounded, so that the site appeared almost oval, but the internal corners proved to be right-angled, or at least approximately so. The floor of the house lay about 50 cm below the level of the grass outside. The site, 3.75 m long by 3.25 m wide, was orientated NW/SE. Where the entrance door had been could not be established with certainty, but it seems reasonable to suppose that it should have been in the south-eastern end wall, so that the sun could shine into the house while the cold winds from the sea would be excluded. This is, in fact, the most common position of doors in the houses on the terrace.

The cultural layer showed about the same stratification as demonstrated in the house–sites described above, but in house E the black top layer of turf was rather thicker, probably as a result of the walls having collapsed into the house. As this site is so small, the collapsed turf filled practically the entire floor. This top layer was thickest along the walls.

A number of stones were found immediately below the grass, among them a large, flat slab of slate, burned red. These had probably been used to weight down the roof, and the large slate may have covered a smoke opening. But this does not explain why it should have been burned red – somehow it must have come in contact with fire.

The layers below also contained a number of stones, apparently haphazardly scattered about except for one large, thick stone, which lay in the southern corner. This was found on top of a 10–15 cm thick cultural layer which contained more charcoal than that in the rest of the house, and it seems likely that we here have the remains of a secondary hearth. A small depression, 25 cm in diameter and 3 cm deep, was found between the south-east wall and this stone. It contained the same mixture of charcoal, sand and earth as the rest of the room – it may be of a casual nature.

Fig. 30. Cooking pit II after excavation.

Fig. 31. Hearth in house-site E.

Fig. 35. The terrace with the house-sites seen from the sea.

Fig. 36. House-site F seen from north-east during excavation.

In the eastern corner we uncovered a hearth, partly dug out of the gravel under the turf of the wall, but the bottom of the hearth lay only very slightly below the floor of the house (fig.31). In the north-west, the hearth was bounded by a 75 cm long slate, standing on edge. The hearth, 75 cm long and 30 cm wide in front, was brim-full of charcoal, ashes and brittle-burned stone. Immediately to the north-west of the slate there was a small depression, 15 cm in diameter and barely 10 cm deep. This may have housed a slender post, possibly one furnished with a support for a pan. No other post holes were found in this house-site, nor any traces of any form of wall-panelling. The hole by the south-east wall which we mentioned above may, of course, represent a central post, but it is situated slightly off centre and, moreover, no corresponding post hole was found by the opposite wall, but a flat stone, 1 m from the eastern wall and 30 cm from the northern wall, may have held a post.

The floor of this house was of hard-trodden sand, blackened by soot. The floor layer was about 10 cm thick, and it was obvious that clean sand had been spread on to the floor about three times. When we scraped this floor stratum we found that it tended to peel off in layers blackened by soot on top and clean underneath.

In the northern corner there was a small heap of nineteen stones, all of them about the size of a clenched fist – the majority were rough lime-stone. They were too light to have been used as loom weights, and none of them was pierced for attaching a cord. But the stones were so rough that a cord could certainly have been securely tied on without a hole: perhaps they were used as sinkers for fishing nets, or for some similar purpose. The fact that they lay heaped together in this way struck us as remarkable.

This house-site yielded no finds.

A radio-carbon analysis of charcoal from the hearth has yielded the date T–324: 1130±70, A.D.820, fig.9.

House-site F (fig. 32 and pls. 26–33)

House-site F lies on the north-eastern part of the terrace, furthest away from Black Duck Brook, at N67–N40.5, E106.5–E131.5. The ruin was hardly visible at all before excavation, and it took us quite a while to realize that there really was a house-site here. But it was impossible before excavation even to hazard a guess as to its type or size. Right from the beginning we therefore prepared an excavation including the use of exploratory trenches planned with a base line running NNE/SSW. The zero point thus lay about 1.40 m SE of the eastern interior corner of the house.

As soon as the grass sods of the first (easternmost) trench had been

Fig. 32. House-site F seen from the north-east. The excavated, sterile area around is re-covered with turf. In the middle, the hall with long hearth and earthen benches on either side.

removed, we were confronted with a coal-black layer full of lumps of charcoal, some of them so large that they might almost be described as logs. There was no doubt that this was a burned stratum.

The easternmost trench – which covered the north-east part of room I – was 2.5 m wide and 5.8 m long, while the other trenches, of the same width, were 11 m long. A 30 cm wide section between the trenches was reserved as profile (fig. 33, 34 and 36). The profiles were measured, drawn and partly photographed, and of some impressions were also taken.

All the trenches showed roughly the same stratification. Immediately under the grass, a coal-black layer came to light, full of pieces of charcoal, some of them of considerable size. Scattered on top of this layer we found a number of flat stone slabs and stones of varying sizes, apparently without any kind of order. This layer was of the same tough consistency as the top layer of the other houses, which we have interpreted as representing the turf of the roof. The stones on top of this layer must thus have lain on top of the roof turf, presumably in order to weight it down (see figs. 33 and 34). Practically the entire house-site was covered with this layer of tough turf, which was about 10 cm thick in most places. The layer below was just as black, and contained if anything still more charcoal, but it was considerably looser and contained more sand. As we dug down into this layer we reached more concentrated patches of charcoal, which turned out to be our first contact with hearths. The thickness of this layer varied considerably, reaching a maximum of about 45 cm.

Fig. 33. House-site F during excavation, showing the stone-packing in the upper layer of room IV.

Fig. 34. The stone-packing of room IV partly removed.

Under this looser, black layer we found the actual floor stratum, which was about 10 cm thick. This, too, was just as black as the other layers, and was indistinguishable from these in the profiles (we have therefore drawn them as one undifferentiated layer), but it was considerably fatter, with a consistency rather like that of cheese. Here the pieces of charcoal were smaller, except for a few charred pieces of wood which lay at the bottom, immediately above the sterile sub-soil. There were also some fragments of burned bone in this floor layer, and here lay most of the finds. The sterile sub-soil below consisted mostly of hard-trodden sand, burned red in some places.

The house had been ravaged by fire, but this had obviously not raged equally severely throughout. Rooms III and VI, for instance, did not contain as many large pieces of charcoal as the other rooms, nor was the sand below the cultural layer burned red here.

When we had finished excavating this site, we had before us a complex house consisting of six rooms. Three of them lie in line with each other, along an axis running NNE/SSW. Two rooms had been built on in the north-west, one of their side walls coinciding with that of the other house. Another room had been added in the south-east, and like the north-west rooms, this also has a wall in common with the three-roomed house which forms the nucleus of this complex, and which thus lies at its centre.

House F was somewhat displaced in relation to the base line, so that 17m on the base line lay 3 m SE of the interior of the wall of room III, while the zero point was 1.40 m SE of the eastern internal corner of room I.

The internal length of the house-site is about 20 m, and the total maximum width of the entire complex 15 m, also measured internally. The plan is irregular – a rectangular building, with a maximum internal width of 5 m, was added to on both sides. The walls of the central building curve slightly, so that the ends of the house are about 1 m narrower than the middle. The walls, 1 –1.5 m thick, are built of turf arranged in layers so as to form stripes (fig. 37). All the external corners are rounded. There is a door opening in the south-eastern side wall, near the eastern corner. It was not marked by any stone setting, but – as was the case with the doors of the other houses – appeared simply as a slight, sooted depression leading part of the way through the wall on both sides, while the centre was sterile. Thus it appears likely that there was some kind of door frame or threshold here, possibly wooden. Two distinct stripes of turf lay in the door opening, probably turf from the roof which had fallen down in the middle of the door. Outside the door, there was a wide midden, without distinct boundaries, hardly more than the kind of cultural layer which frequently forms outside a house. This layer was c. 5 cm deep. Several fragmentary iron rivets were found here, probably from a wooden door.

The house had a second entrance door, in the south-eastern wall of room VI. This was marked by a sooty depression leading from the central part of

Fig. 37. Section of turf wall in house-site F, showing the horizontal layers of turf.

Fig. 38. The long hearth in room II, house-site F, seen from the south-east, with the cooking pit, ember pit and large, flat stone.

69

the room, and here, too, we found a cultural layer outside the house, containing several fragmentary iron rivets. Room VI is the only room in this house which is not connected to the others by a door; there may have been another door in this room, for in the south-west end wall a down-trodden patch led to the outside, and in the corner formed by the walls of room III and room VI we found a cultural layer which contained fragments of iron and fragmentary iron rivets.

Room I

The entrance door close to the eastern corner of the house leads into room I. This is a small, rectangular room, 4.3 m × 3.45 m internally, its greatest dimension running at right angles to the longitudinal axis of the house.

Immediately inside, to the left of the door, there was a small hearth close up to the south-east wall. It was, in fact, simply a heap of brittle-burned stones, charcoal and ashes, and it did not extend below floor level. The cultural layer around was very fat and sooty.

There is another hearth, in the middle of the floor at 3 – 3.5 m on the baseline, a shallow depression in the floor without any surrounding stone setting, 75 cm in length and 50 cm in width, while the depth was only 5 cm. It was full of charcoal and ashes, and the layer of charcoal above the hearth extended to the top of the middle layer.

In the northern corner a 16 cm deep pit, with a maximum diameter of 90 cm, was found. It was full of dark earth, without any admixture of charcoal. It may possibly be a post hole, but this is very uncertain. In the eastern corner there is a small depression, only just below floor level. This cannot possibly have held a post corresponding to that which may have stood in the northern corner – the eastern depression would rather seem to have come about by chance.

In the middle of the south-west wall there is a door opening leading to room II. Another in the north-west wall leads to room IV. These openings are 80 cm and 75 cm wide respectively. They were merely marked by a hard-trodden, sooty patch running right through the wall.

Room II

The cultural layer in this room consisted largely of the same three layers as those found in room I. Immediately below the grass there were a number of stones of varying sizes, most of them flat slabs, but also some ordinary, rounder stones. We had seen these protruding through the grass before excavation – in fact, they had shown us that there was a house-site here. They lay on a layer of tough, black turf, its average thickness 10 cm, probably

70

Fig. 39. Ember pit in the long hearth in house-site F, room II.

representing the roof of the house. This contained a great deal of charcoal –
as in room I, these pieces of charcoal were very large.

Rooms II and III give the appearance of having been one large room, as
there is no partition wall between them now. But they are most likely to have
been two separate rooms – partly because the floor at the south-west end lies
at a lower level than that in the north-east, and partly because a large
depression at 15–16 m at the baseline and 3–4 m NW of this gives the
impression of having been situated in a corner.

We also have reason to believe that the long hearth of room II lay in the
middle of the floor. We therefore assume that room III was about 9 m long
and 5 m wide at the widest part, the centre – the north-east end is only 4.2 m
wide, because of the curvature of the side walls.

In the middle of the floor of room II there is a hearth (figs. 38, 39 and 40),
1.9 m long and between 40 cm and 50 cm wide. Its south-western end is a
cooking pit, 50 cm in diameter and 15 cm deep. It was full of charcoal, ashes
and brittle-burned stones. At the north-eastern end there is a large, flat stone,

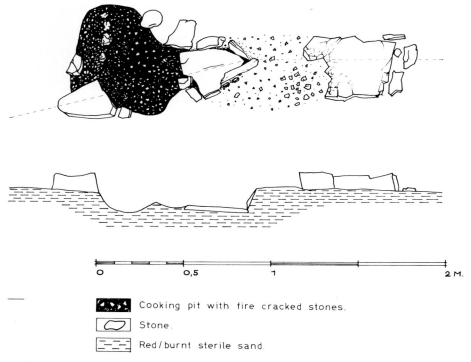

Fig. 40. Plan and section of hearth in house-site F, room II.

brittle-burned and extremely cracked – it is 40 – 50 cm wide and 50 cm long. Between the cooking pit and this stone we found a stone-lined pit, its bottom consisting of a flat stone 25 cm long, and its sides formed by 10 cm high stones, standing on edge (fig.39). This must have been an ember pit of the same type as those encountered in house B and in D III.

The floor around this hearth was very firm, sooty, and with pieces of charcoal trodden into it. This floor stratum also contained some burned fragments of bone and a great many small stones which came from the cracked stone slab in the hearth. There was no such firm floor stratum along the side walls, where a section 1.5 m wide lacked this layer. These sections were somewhat higher than the floor around the hearth (pls. 29–31). There can hardly be any doubt that there must have been benches of earth for sitting or lying down along the walls here. They may have been covered with wooden planks, for the sand here was very loose and contained a large number of fairly large pieces of charcoal. Above the centre of the hearth, the maximum depth of the burned stratum was 40 cm (pls. 30–31).

Some shallow depressions in the floor, as shown on the plan (pl. 26), may possibly be post holes, but as most of them are shallow and without any stone lining, this cannot be determined with certainty, although it seems likely that

72

at least some of them may have housed posts. A large depression by the north-west wall, north-east of the door to room V, is likely to have been a storage pit of some kind. It is 45 cm deep.

Room III

It is difficult to determine the length of room III, as there are no traces of a partition wall between rooms II and III – see p. 71 above – but it would seem most likely to have been about 6 m long. If we assume such a length, the large depression at the north-east end of this room would lie in the eastern corner. Further, at 15 m base line, the floor starts to slope down towards the south-west, so that the south-western part of the house does not seem to belong to that north-east of this point. Moreover, the fact that the so-called room III had not been ravaged by fire would also seem to indicate that there must have been a wall here, most probably a thick turf wall, so that the fire was either stopped by the wall, or burned itself out while ravaging the wall. At the north-east end, the room was 4.5 m wide, at the south-west end, 3.9 m. The cultural layer of this room was 25 cm thick and consisted of the same three layers as those found in the other rooms. The top layer was missing above part of the hearth, where three large stones, arranged in a semi-circle above the embers, took its place. It seems likely that these stones lay on the roof, around a smoke opening, perhaps in order to protect the turf from the fire below. Under these stones, roughly in the middle of the floor – if the room was 6 m long – we found embers, and below them, an oblong depression in the floor, 1.8 m long and 40 cm wide. The floor beneath was burned red. Here the two upper layers did not contain as much charcoal as those in the other rooms. The floor layer was firm, and contained small pieces of charcoal mixed with gravel and sand.

Some small hollows by the walls (pl. 26), which contained earth, may be post holes for small posts, but this is not certain.

A large pit in the eastern corner, 1 m in diameter and 1 m deep, contained only dark earth, without any admixture of stone or charcoal. Before excavation, it was clearly visible due to the fact that lush, green grass grew here, while the surface of the ground around was mostly covered by heather. This was probably a storage pit of some kind.

Room IV

Room IV lies to the north-west of room I. A door in the north-west wall of room I connects these two rooms. Room IV is small and rectangular, measuring about 3.5 m × 3 m internally; its longitudinal axis runs at right angles to that of the house.

73

Fig. 41. Hearth in house-site F, room IV. In the foreground, charred timbers, probably from the roof. In the left front corner, a round impression, probably that of a small wooden vessel.

The cultural layers of this room were the same as those described in connection with the other rooms, but here the turf from the roof was covered by a large number of stones, almost as though it had been paved. It was clearly particularly important that the roof turf above this room should be weighted down – the reason is obvious, for room IV faces the sea and the north-westerly storms. Above the floor layer we found several large, charred timbers (fig. 41), and all the layers, including the turf roof, contained a great deal of charcoal.

There is a hearth by the south-west wall, almost in the western corner. It consists of two stone-lined chambers, separated by a large slate standing on end (figs. 41–42). Total length 1.25 m, width 1.20 m. The north-western edge is bounded by a large, flat stone standing on edge. Both chambers were full of charcoal and ashes, and they also contained some brittle-burned stones, most of them small fragments of slate, possibly from the slate in the middle. We also found some pieces of slate at the bottom of the north-west chamber

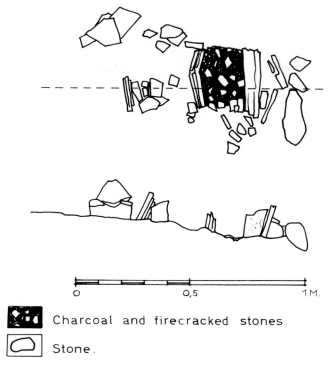

Charcoal and firecracked stones.

Stone.

Fig. 42. Plan and section of hearth in house-site F, room IV.

of the hearth, right at the centre, and it is possible that there was once a large slate at the bottom of this chamber, a slab which disintegrated after it had cracked.

Roughly at the centre of the floor a small, round depression, completely flat-bottomed, was found. It seems likely that this is the imprint of a wooden vessel which once stood here (fig. 41,1. front). It measured 40 cm × 40 cm.

Room V

Room V, north-west of room II, is connected to the latter by a door in the partition wall. Like most of the other door openings mentioned above it was merely marked by a hard-trodden depression going some way into the wall on both sides, with a sterile central part. The width of the opening cannot be determined.

The cultural layer, which was very fat in the northern corner, yielded many fragments of burned bone. The very top of the cultural layer brought us into touch with the large cooking pit here, even though this was partly concealed by the turf wall which had collapsed into the room. This cooking pit, about

75

Fig. 43. House-site F, room VI, seen from south-west, partially excavated, showing impressions of ground timbers in the floor.

1.1 m in diameter and 55 cm deep, was full of charcoal, ashes and brittle-burned stones, and it also contained some fragments of burned bone. The earth above and around it was, as stated above, extremely fat. The cultural layer of this room also was in the nature of a thick burned stratum containing large, dry pieces of charcoal and charred timbers.

There was another pit, 50–75 cm in diameter and 20 cm deep, roughly at the middle of the south-west wall. It was full of pure, dry charcoal, and it lacked the characteristics of a cooking pit – this looked more like an ember pit. But that is not an entirely satisfactory explanation either, for an ember pit would surely have lain closer to the cooking pit, which in fact lies at the opposite end of the room. Perhaps it is most likely that this is a post hole for a post which burned inside its foundation hole.

The most interesting feature of this room is the 1.5 m wide and 60 cm deep drainage ditch which starts a little way outside room V (south-west) and runs along the north-west wall to the cooking pit, after which it continues on through room IV. It was filled with stones from the shore and with gravel. It must have been dug for the purpose of leading away the melting snow from the hillock north-west of the house. We have seen with our own eyes that it still is effective. One piece of cut turf was found a little way down among the stones.

76

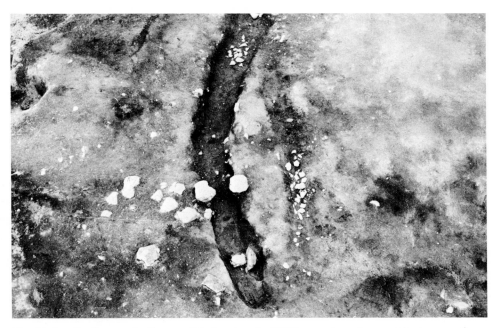

Fig. 44. Detail of house-site F, room VI, showing the NW impression of ground timber seen from south-west.

Room VI (fig. 45)

Room VI lies on the south-east side of the house, and is entered by a door in the south-east side wall. We have shown above that there may have been another door opening in the south-west end wall. This was probably a wooden wall, as indicated by the impression of planks which we found here. This impression stops short at a point where there is a small depression which seems to have been worn, rather than dug, possibly by feet. We have also pointed out above that there was a small midden or cultural layer outside the room on this side.

The internal dimensions of this room are about 8 m × 3.2 m. Three of the walls were built from turf, the fourth may have been wooden, as the narrow groove at the south-western end of the floor would seem to indicate.

Most noteworthy in this room were two narrow "channels", which run along the inside of the side walls (figs. 43, 44, 45 and 46), 6.2 m and 3 m long respectively. Their width varies from 30 to 40 cm, and they are 16 to 18 cm deep. They are quite smooth at the bottom, and as they have neither intake nor outlet, they cannot have been intended either for supplying the house with water, or for draining water away from it. At the bottom, the last vestiges of decayed timber were found. The most feasible explanation would seem to be

77

First sight of Newfoundland, when sailing in across the Strait of Belle Isle.

Cooking pit II, before excavation.

The fishing village L'Anse aux Meadows, seen from the south-east.

19th century Icelandic farm, Glaumbær, with turf houses.

Fig. 45. Room VI, house-site F, after excavation, seen from the south-west, showing impressions of ground-timbers in the floor.

Fig. 47. a–b Spindle whorl of soap-stone from house-site F, found outside the south-east wall of room VI. LaM 97.

Fig. 48. Stone lamp from house-site F. LaM 39.

Fig. 46. Detail of section through house-site F, room VI.

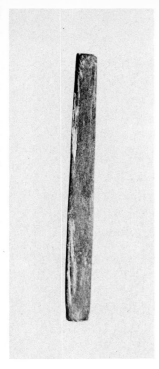

Fig. 49. Needle-hone of quartzite from house-site F, room VI. LaM 66a.

Fig. 50. Iron rivet from house-site F, room VI, in situ. LaM 60.

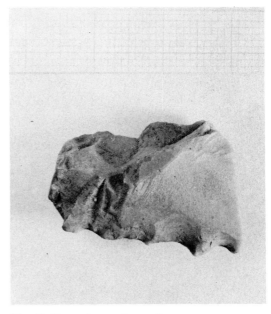

Fig. 51. Piece of red jasper from house-site F. LaM 128.

Fig. 52. Piece of green jasper from house-site F. LaM 1.

that these "channels" actually represent the remains of ground sills which may have supported internal planking. A narrow groove branches off from the south-east channel in a north-westerly direction, at an angle of almost exactly 90°. I pointed out above that this is likely to be the impression of a wooden wall which may have housed a door. If we assume that these "channels" represent traces of ground sills, objections may be raised to the effect that the longer channel is curved at one end, while a narrower and less deep groove continues in a more or less straight line from the point where the channel begins to curve. We cannot explain this shallow groove, but would add that straight timbers are very few and far between in the wind-swept forests of this part of the world.

At the north-eastern end of the room we found a cooking pit in the floor, close up to the wall. When we discovered it, it was covered by a large, flat slab of stone, under which lay charcoal, ashes and brittle-burned stones. Brittle-burned stones had also been trodden down into the floor in this part of the room. 5 small lumps of slag were found at the edge of this cooking pit.

Roughly in the middle of the floor, where there is a shallow, oval depression, the uppermost tough layer of black turf – which we have interpreted as representing the turf from the roof – was missing. In its place we found a depression full of sterile sand. It is likely that there was a smoke opening in the roof here, and that the sand blew down after the roof had collapsed into the room. The depression may, however, be of more recent date. The sand lay immediately on top of the actual floor layer which, in this room as elsewhere in the house, was about 10 cm thick. The cultural layer of this room did not contain as many or as large pieces of charcoal as those of the other rooms – in fact, it is not certain that this room actually burned together with the rest of the house, as pointed out above.

A small depression, roughly at the centre of the floor (pl. 26) may be a post hole, as may also a smaller hole at the edge of the south-east channel, at 15 m at the base line, –2 m SE of the base line.

This room, entered from the south-east, faced away from the sea and from the prevailing winds, and it must therefore have been the most pleasant and warmest room of the entire complex. Most of the finds come from room VI, a point discussed in more detail below.

Finds

1 spindle whorl of soap-stone, 3.3 cm in diameter, 1.2 cm thick, LaM 97, fig. 47 a-b.

1 stone lamp, maximum diameter 13 cm, diameter of depression 5.5 cm, 1.3 cm deep, LaM 39, fig. 48.

1 needle hone of quartzite, 7 cm long, 0.6 cm wide, LaM 66 a, fig. 49.

1 hone of sandstone, LaM 104.

14 complete and fragmentary iron rivets, the largest 7 cm long, LaM 4, 26, 29, 56, 60, 61, 62, 63, 116, 118, 119, 122, 130, 133, fig. 50.

A number of iron fragments, the largest 5.5 cm long.

1 serrated object of green jasper, 2.5 cm long, LaM. 1, fig 52.

4 pieces of red jasper, LaM 2, 50, 126, 128, fig. 51. App. IV.

1 flint chipping and other stone samples, LaM. 42.

Lumps of iron–slag, LaM 33, 49, 66 b (5), 67, 105, 112.

1 pumice stone, LaM 18.

Iron pyrite, LaM 47.

5 samples of bone, from cultural layer, App.V.

4 radio-carbon analyses were carried out, 2 of charcoal from the hearths in rooms II and IV, 1 of turf from the wall of room IV, and 1 of whalebone from the hearth in room III. The resulting dates were, respectively:

T–531 Turf wall	$950 + 50$, A.D. 1000
T–325 charcoal, room II	$1080 + 70$, A.D. 870
T–326 charcoal, room IV	$1250 + 70$, A.D. 700
St. 2665 Whalebone, room III	$925 + 100$, A.D. 1025

House-site G (figs. 53–54 and pl. 35–36)

House-site G lies 5 m from the southern corner of house F, between N34, E113 and N37, E113. Before excavation, only a 20 cm deep depression at the edge of the terrace could be seen, but after excavation we had a small room, whose floor lay 118 cm below the top of the turf of the terrace. This room had been dug out of the front of the terrace, so that the gravel of the latter formed walls on three of its sides, while the fourth, facing the sea, lay open now. There may have been a wall here, and it seems likely that this should have housed the entrance door.

The internal dimensions of this room were 2.5 m × 2 m.

No traces of posts which might have held some kind of panelling to shore up the gravel and sand of the walls have been found, nor any traces of posts which might have supported the roof. The roof of this house must have been of turf, like that of the other houses – we found the same, tough layer of old turf on top of the depression. Below this layer we found a stratum of sand mixed with charcoal, and in the middle of the room there was a large, cracked slab of slate, with two large stones on top of it (fig. 53). This slate lay on a 60 cm thick layer of sand mixed with charcoal – the 10 cm layer below this stratum

Fig. 53. House-site G during excavation. At the centre, the large, cracked slate with big stones on top, which probably served to cover the smoke opening in the roof. Under the slate, the cultural layer. In the background the large, vertical hearth stone, and the ovoid stone.

formed the actual floor layer. It seems most likely that this slate slab once covered a smoke opening in the roof, and then the stones would have served to weight it down and keep it in place. Such a slab must have been essential in a house whose roof presumably simply rose above the ground like a low mound, for otherwise people and animals alike could have fallen down the hole, and snow and sand would have blown down into the room.

Much of the fill found in this house must represent sand which had slid from the walls – most of it from the top of them – for before excavation the depression was considerably wider at the top than it can have been originally.

The floor layer, about 10 cm thick, was hard-trodden and blackened by a great deal of soot. Pieces of charcoal had been trodden down into it.

There is a small hearth by the south wall (figs. 53–54 and pl. 36), where a thick stone slab stands on edge, supported by the wall. It had been cracked by fire. On the floor in front of it we found a compact layer of charcoal, which contained a great many brittle-burned stones, a little larger than a clenched

84

Fig. 54. House-site G during excavation seen from above.

fist. 50 cm from the upright stone slab there was a large, ovoid stone from the shore. This was not cracked, and we do not know what it was used for. The great number of brittle-burned stones the size of a clenched fist and larger are characteristic of the cultural layer of this small house.

A radio-carbon analysis of charcoal from the hearth has yielded the date T–327: 870 ± 70, A.D. 1080, fig. 9.

Finds

2 iron fragments, LaM 24, 31.
1 fragment of iron rivet, LaM 30.

IV Investigations

BY KRISTJÁN ELDJÁRN

Assisted by Gísli Gestsson and Þorhallur Vilmundarson

House-site J, The Smithy (fig. 55, pls. 38–40)

Black Duck Brook runs through an oval depression, whose western bank it follows. This is comparatively high and steep, whereas the opposite bank, formed by the bottom of the depression, is low.

The western bank lies rather more than 3 m above the water-level of the brook. Along 30 m of this bank there is an arciform erosion scar, with sharp top edges. Loose sand slides down the steep slope from the top – from below, from the water, plants try to work their way up towards the sand. Apart form this erosion scar, the entire western bank of the brook is covered by vegetation, and its lines are soft and smoothly undulating.

Just at the landward end of this scar, roughly at the highest point of the bank, we noted a peculiar, horseshoe-shaped depression, its open side facing the brook. It was completely grown over, and with its smooth lines it had more or less merged into the surrounding landscape – but it was quite clear that this depression must originally have been made by human hands. Close to the seaward side of the depression there was a slight erosive scar, almost certainly a natural formation. The difference in level between the bottom and the edges of the depression, before excavation, was 105 cm.

As soon as the first sods of grass had been removed from the bottom of the depression, we saw that the surface turf lay immediately on top of sand mixed with charcoal, and we even found some small lumps of slag at quite a high level. As a first step in the excavation, a trench was dug, 50 cm wide, and running from the brook towards the dry land, extending along the full length of the cultural layer in this direction. Next, another trench of the same width was cut at right angles to the first, near the edge of the depression. This second trench also extended as far as the cultural layer, to both sides of the first one. Then the whole area was excavated section by section, and longitudinal and latitudinal profiles were drawn. (Many large and small samples were taken, including a large section which was cased without being touched. This was intended for a laboratory investigation of the stratification, from the surface turf down through the entire cultural layer to the virgin sub-soil.)

87

Fig. 55. House-site J after excavation, seen from the river. In the background, left, the kiln.

The area investigated, which covered the entire bottom of the depression was 3.75 m long (i.e. from the brook and in along the depression) and 2.75 m wide. The profiles drawn, longitudinal and latitudinal, show that the cultural layer covered the entire bottom of the depression. We caught sight of it as soon as we started to remove the surface turf; it extended down to the virgin yellow sand or sandy gravel. At the centre, the cultural layer was 25 – 30 cm thick, and it was fairly evenly distributed over the bottom of the depression. It was fairly even below, although sloping slightly down towards the edge of the depression and also from the sides towards the middle. The lowest part of the layer may surely be interpreted as representing the floor, but it was not as distinct or hard-trodden as floors usually are. In fact, the cultural layer lies on top of the sand without any clear and distinct line of demarcation – it gave the appearance of simply having accumulated without being trodden down to any great extent. The reason for this may be that the cultural layer contains a great deal of sand but comparatively little binding matter. But traces of a trodden floor were noted around the stone which stands in the middle of the floor – they were most distinct in front of it. This will be discussed in greater detail at a later stage. At the sides there was no sharp distinction between the cultural layer and the sand, the two strata more or less merging into each

88

other. The cultural layer did not extend into the two innermost corners, as it had the same arciform shape as the depression. In some places spits of coal extended a little way beyond the excavated area, and it was obvious that these tongues, which extended upwards towards the edges of the depression, contained larger pieces of charcoal than the rest of the cultural layer, apparently because they were not in the same danger of being trodden underfoot here.

The cultural layer as it appeared during excavation was remarkably black, and consisted mainly of sand, mixed with a very large amount of crumbled charcoal and pieces of coal, but some patches of clean sand and of pure charcoal were also encountered. The layer contained comparatively many small stones from the shore, but larger stones were rare and apparently without any particular significance. At the northern side of the depression, two large slabs of slate and a thick stone slab were found, and on the floor, a little to the inside of the centre, a water-ground piece of granite with a large surface of fracture came to light. Also on the floor (see below), right in front and just above the hollow, there was a big stone with a large fracture scar on one side, while the other was water-ground. All these stones gave the appearance of having accumulated accidentally; none of the other loose stones found require discussion. Here and there among the material of the cultural layer we found many small slivers of slate, just as we had at all the excavated sites at L'Anse aux Meadows. None of these can have served any significant purpose, and in fact the cultural layer of house-site J contained no evidence suggesting that this really was a house with walls and a roof.

Apart from the charcoal, the cultural layer contained a great deal of slag, mostly fairly small pieces, but some as large as a hen's egg or still a little larger also occurred. All this slag was carefully collected during excavation, and when our investigation had been completed, about half of the fill which had been dug out was sifted in order to collect the remaining small pieces of slag. The slag proved to be of different types: many of the pieces looked like ordinary bog-ore, others were more porous and resembled half-molten stone. They were highly characteristic of the entire cultural layer, and for this reason the site was from an early stage of the excavation known as "the smithy". Apart from the slag the cultural layer also contained some reddish lumps which appeared to be corroded iron, and some of them showed a strong reaction to magnets. None of these lumps of rust can be identified as the remains of any specific kind of object. Finally, we should mention the large number of fairly thin iron scales, which were also magnetic, and which are probably forge scales. We were able to collect such scales by means of a magnet throughout the cultural layer; however, their concentration was definitely greatest around the stone in the middle of the floor (see below). The cultural layer also contained some lumps of a white, clay-like material, some

Fig. 56. The earthfast stone anvil in house-site J.

of them apparently glazed on one side. The slag was distributed throughout the entire cultural layer, right up to the surface turf, but the concentration increased towards the floor. Moreover, there was much more slag in the front of the depression than at the back.

Next we must examine the "fittings of the smithy". In the middle of the cultural layer a stone was firmly, although not deeply, anchored in the floor (fig. 56). It extends 8 cm above the level of the floor, and its upper surface is quite flat and horizontal. It had been oblong originally, and of a fairly regular, rectangular shape; one end is still intact, the other is broken. Two much smaller, irregular stones, clearly broken off the main stone, lie at the broken end, both of them firmly fixed like the large stone, and at least one of them certainly seems to be in situ still. We found another piece broken off this stone in the slope in front of the smithy – this fitted the surface of fracture, and had obviously been swept out after the stone had been broken. The present length of the large stone is 25 cm at floor level (it is shorter at the top, because the surface of fracture is not straight), while the width is 15 cm. When this stone came to light, we were immediately struck by the idea that this might be an anvil, on which iron had been beaten. Many thin, glazed slivers of stone standing on edge were found near the surface of fracture of the "anvil": these appear to be half-molten splinters from this stone. Some larger, unmolten splinters of stone lay together with these slivers. To the north and the north-west of this stone a black patch of compact fire remains appeared, 30 cm × 60 cm, but fairly irregular in form; this is no doubt a hearth. The small fragments of stone were almost entirely covered by embers. As these were removed, we saw that they lay in a shallow depression, vague in shape but quite distinct, and 8 cm deep. The embers consisted mainly of crumbled charcoal and some lumps of slag. We all agreed that this was most likely to be some kind of forge; clearly the stone and the fire patch belonged together, forming the centre of activity of this smithy. A layer of a white, clay-like substance was found around the stone, extending in a fairly thin layer to the west of it (i.e. inwards along the floor). This substance which was packed around the stone must have been placed there intentionally. It was reminiscent of the whitish, semi-glazed lumps found elsewhere in the cultural layer, as pointed out above, and some such lumps were also found in the slope in front of the opening of the depression. All in all – the highest concentration of slag was found *in front* of the stone and the fire patch – *behind* these, charcoal predominated. In some places, in fact, we found layers of pure charcoal, most of them 8–10 cm thick, first and foremost in the northernmost part of the depression.

The end of the earthfast stone faces a fairly round, saucer-shaped hollow at the front of the smithy. The distance between the stone and this hollow is 40 cm, the diameter of the hollow 70 cm, and its maximum depth 40 cm. Its contents consisted mainly of sand mixed, however, with varying amounts of charcoal particles and some few lumps of slag, although there was less slag here than in the rest of the cultural layer. Immediately above the hollow, there was a large stone in the cultural layer (see above), and the bottom of the hollow was covered by a distinct 2 cm thick layer of crumbled charcoal containing some slag, similar to that found in other parts of this site. At the front of the hollow and protruding partly into it, there was a large stone of irregular shape, although the side facing the hollow – 45 cm high – is fairly vertical. The maximum dimension of this stone is about 50 cm. It appeared to be lying in its original position, bounding the opening of the hollow at one side. The cultural layer extended some way under it, however, and three lumps of natural bog-ore and some pieces of slag were found underneath the stone. As far as we could see, there is no particular reason to assume that iron was once beaten on this stone – but it may certainly have been used for this

Fig. 57. Dorset lamp of soap-stone, LaM 343, found in house-site J, upper layer. ⅓ : 1.

purpose. The side facing the hollow had traces which may possibly be a result of hammering.

The highest concentration of slag was found immediately to the north of the stone and the hollow. In front of an imaginary line drawn just north of the vertical face of the stone, the cultural layer is quite thin, and here it starts to slope markedly down towards the brook. This slope was uncovered as far down as the highest water level of the brook. Immediately under the surface turf we found scattered remains of charcoal and slag, and several pieces of unsmelted bog-ore – a relatively greater number than on the actual floor. These remains would seem to have fallen from the floor of the smithy. They formed a kind of tongue leading away from the opening of the depression, fading out on both sides.

Apart from the finds mentioned above, the following came to light: a fairly small sliver of flint (found when the fill was sifted) and a soap-stone lamp (Dorset), 19 cm long (fig. 57). The lamp was found at the northern end of the depression, just below the surface turf, at a level of 35 cm above the bottom of the cultural layer. When the earth had been scraped out of it, we saw that the lamp contained some small particles of charcoal. It is a fine piece of workmanship.

Two radio-carbon analysis of charcoal from the "forge" have yielded the dates T–366: 1090+90, A.D. 860, T–393: 890+70, A.D. 1060, fig. 9.

Finds

LaM 343, *Lamp of soap-stone,* Dorset-Eskimo type, fig. 57.
LaM 233–236, 240, 243–266, 268–280, 282–297, 301, 304, 327, 336.

The Charcoal Kiln (fig. 55, pls. 41–42)

Behind the smithy at the top of the bank of the brook, there was a distinct hole in the ground.

C. 7 m south-west of the smithy, it had obviously been dug by human hands, even though it now more or less merged with its surroundings. This assumption was confirmed when we started to dig here. We found a depression, slightly oblong in the direction of the smithy. At the top there was a 10–15 cm thick layer of reddish-brown earth, containing some turf; immediately below this, pure sand. The line of demarcation between the two layers is quite sharp. First a test trench was cut straight across the depression, and then the earth was removed from an area around it, so that the entire character of the test trench was clearly apparent. Around the depression, at the line of demarcation between earth and sand, there was a patch of charcoal about 4 m in diameter; the concentration of charcoal was highest closest to the depression, where it formed a layer with a maximum thickness of 3 cm, decreasing towards the periphery. When removing sods of grass, we frequently found pieces of charcoal adhering to the roots, including large pieces of charred twigs. The depression turned out to be a grave or pit dug out of the fairly loose sand, 1.50 m long and 80 cm wide at the bottom. The sides had originally been steep, although they sloped outwards to some extent, so that at a level of 20 cm above the bottom, the pit was 1.80 m long and 1.10 m wide. At one place, sand burned red was found in the wall of the pit. The depth of the pit, measured from the highest point by its opening down to the lowest piece of charcoal, was 75 cm. At the bottom there was a coherent layer of charcoal, with a maximum thickness of 20 cm. The lowest 5 cm consisted of charcoal only, while that of the upper part of the layer was to some extent mixed with sand. The charcoal around the pit must be considered together with that in the pit, but because of the steep slope of the walls, sand and charcoal had in several places slid and become mixed, so that no true stratification could be observed, a condition reminiscent of that observed in the smithy.

About 2 m west of this pit there was another, smaller hole, c. 30 cm in diameter at the bottom and c. 1 m in diameter at the top. It was approximately round and 40 cm deep. This hole contained no charcoal nor any other finds, but it nevertheless gave the appearance of having been dug by human hands.

Observations noted during the excavation have led the excavators to believe that the depression with charcoal was a charcoal kiln. Many large samples were taken.

Primitive Hearths (pls. 41–42)

The test trench cut across the charcoal kiln was extended in a north-westerly direction, across the old marine terrace. Several primitive hearths came to light then, about 4 m north-west of the charcoal kiln and 8 – 10 m west of the smithy.

A gentle slope led down from the charcoal kiln to a horizontal ledge, the site of the hearths. The difference in level between the top of the kiln and the hearths was about 50 cm. The position of the grass and the sand was similar to that around the charcoal kiln, but if anything the grass layer was a little thinner here. The hearths lay straight on the sand, immediately below the grass, so that some of the stones protruded into the surface turf. The stones lay at a depth of 4–8 cm. All the hearths were built from small stones from the shore, about the size of a clenched fist, although some of them were a little larger or smaller – the biggest stone had a diameter of 13–16 cm. The hearths lay in a straight line, roughly north-south, and three separate hearths may be discerned, but it may possibly be most correct to interpret them as one entity. Together they measured rather over 4 m in length, while the width varied from 40 cm to 90 cm. Most of the stones showed distinct traces of fire, several of them were burned brittle. Between them we found a thin layer of soot and charcoal, with a maximum depth of 4 cm, although it was considerably thinner in most places. A few small pieces of charcoal and patches of soot were observed in several places near the hearths, up to 50 cm away from them. Close to the southernmost hearth, a lump of slag had been trodden down into the sand; a few more lumps of slag were also found near by. 11 small flint chippings came to light in and close to the northernmost hearth – they lay close together in a patch no bigger than c 50 cm in diameter.

The present level of the hearths above the high-water line is c 4 m. The excavators interpreted these hearths as representing a native Stone Age population.

Pit near the Bridge (cooking pit I) (fig. 58, pls. 43–44)

On the west bank of the brook, about 10 m from the bridge and 6–7 m from the steeply sloping bank, we noticed an oblong, very distinct depression 45 m north-east of the smithy. It was covered by lush, green grass, which was in clear contrast to the heather around. First a 50 cm wide trench was dug across this depression, which was later uncovered on all sides. The turf-like surface layer was similar in consistency to the corresponding layers by the charcoal kiln and hearths higher up on the slope, and it was of roughly the same thickness, but the sand below was much coarser – more like gravel – and more closely packed than elsewhere, giving this site a somewhat different character.

94

Fig. 58. Cooking pit I after excavation.

It appeared that this depression was in fact an oblong pit running roughly parallel with the shore from east to west, and that it had been dug in the gravel. The pit was fairly regular in shape, almost like a rectangular box, but the corners were not sharp. The depth was 70 cm, the length at the bottom 1.70 m and that at the top 2.30 m. The width at the top was 1.10 m, and the sides were almost vertical right down to the base. At the bottom of the pit we found a layer of pure charcoal, 4–15 cm thick, which continued upwards on all sides; high up along the edges it appeared as a black line during excavation, setting off the outline of the pit. In some places, the bottom and the walls of the pit had set into a kind of hard shell; at the bottom of the layer of charcoal, we found some twigs quite uncharred below. Two of these showed traces of having been cut with a tool with rather an uneven cutting edge. Above the layer of charcoal at the bottom of the pit there was a layer of reddish-brown burned sand, not entirely coherent, containing some small pieces of turf. The thickness of this layer varied considerably, reaching a maximum of 15 cm. The sand also contained a few stones, some of them penetrating to the charcoal layer below. In fact, one must not assume an entirely regular stratification here, but the main features were regular. Above the burned sand, a thick layer of stones covered the entire pit; some of the stones penetrated the sand. These were small stones from the shore, many the size of a clenched fist, some twice as large and the rest of a size somewhere in between. These stones lay at somewhat varying levels, and their concentration was not equally high in all parts of the area. When they were found, they looked almost as though they had been wrapped in dark sand with an admixture of charcoal. At some places these stones also occurred higher up along the edges of the pit; in fact, at the western end they extended over the edge, where they met a fairly regular rectangular paved patch, 70 × 90 cm. However, the paving contained considerably less charcoal, even though the stones had been burned brittle. Most of the stones in the pit had been damaged by fire to some extent, and many of them disintegrated on being touched.

Around the pit, we found scattered stones on all sides, of the same size as the stones in the pit. Their concentration varied somewhat from place to place. In the east and the south, they were widely scattered without any semblance of order – there was also extremely little charcoal here, only a few small pieces being found. At the western end there was the paving described above, and this formed a direct continuation of the stones in the pit. But in the north, the side facing the shore, matters were entirely different – below, or north of, the western end of the pit we found an irregular patch of charcoal, 2.50 m long and 50–150 cm wide; it was longest at a point 2.50 m north of the pit. This patch, with a maximum thickness of 15 cm – although most of it was considerably thinner – may be described as a layer of charcoal. The charcoal was mixed with a great deal of sand and it contained many brittle-burned stones, particularly in the immediate vicinity of the pit. Perhaps this layer should be interpreted as being connected with the stones in the pit, in the same way as the paving at the western end? Obviously this patch of stone and charcoal must represent a hearth or a firepatch. Like the pit itself, it was surrounded by scattered stones.

No objects of any kind were found in or around the pit.

The excavators interpreted this as a cooking pit, where meat was cooked on glowing embers and heated stones.

Before the expedition left L'Anse aux Meadows late in the summer of 1962, all these excavated sites were covered up. All except the "smithy" were covered with grass turf, so that their appearance before excavation was restored. The smithy was also covered, so that it would be protected during the coming winter, but this depression was not restored to its appearance prior to excavation.

A radio-carbon analysis of charcoal from the charcoal kiln, has yielded the date T–367: 1130 + 70, A.D. 820. and a radio-carbon analysis of charcoal from the pit near the bridge (cooking pit I), has yielded the date T–368: 1170 + 90, A.D. 780, fig. 9.

V Preliminary Report of the 1963 Archaeological Excavations at L'Anse aux Meadows, Newfoundland

BY CHARLES J. BAREIS AND JON H. WINSTON

Introduction

This report summarizes the results of excavation conducted during the summer of 1963. Field work was conducted by the authors from July to September under the supervision of Dr. Helge Ingstad of Oslo, Norway. In the following pages our discussion is limited to a review of the general field procedures and a description of the archaeological features exposed at the site. All archaeological specimens recovered during the course of this work have been transferred to Norway and will be the subject of study by other specialists.

Grid System

It was necessary to establish a common grid for the whole area in order to record the archaeological work of the 1963 season.

The south-west corner of house-site J was deemed a convenient reference point for the location of the 0:0 coordinate in the new grid system. This point was 2.5 meters west and 0.5 meters south of the south-west corner of house-site J.

The grid system was orientated to magnetic north and all test trenches, features and specimens were mapped with reference to the 0:0 point, In other words, any location at the site was reckoned in terms of the number of meters north or south and the number of meters east or west of the 0:0 point. Thus, an artifact excavated 66.56 meters north and 136.06 meters east of 0:0 (iron nail) was designated N66.56E136.06; a stake set two meters west of 0:0 was designated 0W2. The location of a test trench, on the other hand, was designated by reference to the grid coordinates of the four corners of the trench such as N68–78E112–113.

Excavation Procedure

The 1963 field work was devoted to the testing of areas adjacent to the house-sites that had been exposed by previous excavations. It was hoped that additional features and artifacts of the Norse settlement would be recovered.

The testing was accomplished by utilizing a series of trenches established with a tape and compass in accordance with the grid system described above. Most of the trenches were one meter in width, but the lengths were variable (pls. 48–49). The vertical and horizontal locations of all specimens were carefully recorded, and each of these objects was bagged separately except in those instances where similar unworked items were found at the same depth within a feature.

After a feature was encountered, it was outlined by extending the exploratory trench to the limits of the aboriginal disturbance. This was usually accomplished by staking a one or two meter square adjacent to the trench where the feature was exposed and in the area where the feature was likely to continue. The square was then excavated and the outline of the feature was ascertained. Once the limits of the outline had been determined, the feature was excavated, photographed and mapped. A feature sheet (field record), which contained all the essential descriptive information pertaining to the disturbance, was also filled out.

Features

Eight features were excavated during the 1963 season. Four were associated with the Boreal Archaic component, one was associated with the Iron Age component, and the cultural affiliations of three could not be determined. In the following discussion, we have utilized (with minor modifications in terminology) the format for describing features recently presented by Binford, Schoenwetter and Fowler (1964).

Feature 1 (whale ribbon) (pl. 50)

Location: N58–59E97–100 (all feature locations given in terms of inclusive meters).

Dimensions: Length 2.07 meters east to west; width 0.115 meters north to south. The feature was located 0.18 meters below the surface and was 0.01 meters in depth.

Shape: Elongated in plan with a flat or horizontal cross section.

Defining characteristics: A large whale ribbon located within the sod.

Elements of the feature (fe) and associated elements (ae) 1. Whale ribbon (fe)

Distribution of elements: The whale ribbon was lying on a thin layer of sod.

Observations: No other archaeological specimens or natural lithic objects were located near the whale ribbon. A worn area is present near the narrow end of the ribbon. The whale ribbon probably would have decomposed if it had been lying on sand rather than on turf.

The function and cultural affiliation of the whale ribbon is unknown.

Feature 2 (pit) (pl. 51)

Location: N60–64E111–113.

Dimensions: Length 3.34 meters north to south; width 1.53 meters east to west. The feature was located 0.18 meters below the surface and was 0.175 meters in depth.

Shape: Irregular or figure 8-shaped in plan with a basin-shaped cross section.

Defining characteristics: A difference in the soil (gray sand with charcoal fleck inclusions) filling a shallow depression at the base of the sod.

Elements of the feature (fe) and associated elements (ae)

1. Gray sand (fe)
2. Charcoal flecks (ae). (R1, radio-carbon sample)
3. Four chert items (ae)

Distribution of elements: This feature was dug from the dark brown sand level into dark brown sand and gravel, and later became filled with gray sand. The charcoal flecks were scattered throughout the fill of the pit. Two of the chert items were located on top of the pit in the gray sand.

Observations: Aside from the charcoal flecks, there was no evidence of burning inside the pit and the pit had not been lined.

Interpretation: This feature was a small pit of unknown function. Although the pit was situated adjacent to house-site F, the presence of four chert items indicates an affiliation with the Boreal Archaic component.

Feature 3 (cooking hearth) (pl. 52 and fig. 59)

Location: N79–81E111–114.

Dimensions: Length 2.16 meters east to west; width 1.51 meters north to south. This feature was located at the base of the sod.

Shape: Irregularly oval in plan.

Defining characteristics: A concentration of archaeological specimens at the base of the sod.

Elements of the feature (fe) and associated elements (ae)

1. Gray sand (fe)
2. Dark brown sand (fe)
3. Fire-cracked rocks (fe)
4. Fire-blackened rocks (fe)
5. Other rough rocks and stones (fe)
6. Charcoal (ae). (R2, radio-carbon sample)
7. Thirty chert items (ae)
8. Animal bones (ae)

Distribution of elements: This feature was situated on dark brown sand and was filled with a thin layer of dark brown sand overlain by gray sand. Most of the archaeological specimens were concentrated in the south-eastern and

Fig. 59. Excavation of features 3 and 4.

north-western sections of the feature. In the south-eastern section, the upper portion of the animal bones and some of the chert items were actually located in the lower portion of the sod. This indicated that the hearth had been used after as well as before the deposition of the gray sand. Other materials consisting of fire-cracked and fire-blackened rocks, charcoal, and chert items were situated towards the north-western section of the feature.

Observations: There was no evidence of a pit.

Interpretation: This feature is a hearth that was used for outdoor cooking. The presence of chert items and animal bones near the hearth suggests that fauna were dismembered and/or cleaned in the area prior to cooking. The association of chert items with the cooking area indicated that the hearth was of Boreal Archaic affiliation.

Feature 4 (cooking hearth) (pl. 52 and fig. 59)
Location: N80–82E113–115.
Dimensions: Length 1.44 meters north to south; width 1.36 meters east to

100

west. This feature was located 0.135 meters below the surface.

Shape: Oval in plan.

Defining characteristics: A concentration of archaeological specimens at the base of the sod.

Elements of the feature (fe) and associated elements (ae)

1. Gray sand (fe)
2. Fire-cracked rocks (fe)
3. One fire-blackened rock (fe)
4. Stones (fe)
5. Charcoal (ae). (R3, radio-carbon sample)
6. Twenty-seven chert items (ae)

Distribution of elements: This feature was situated on dark brown sand and was filled with a thin layer of gray sand. Practically all the archaeological specimens were concentrated near the north-western section of the feature.

Observations: There was no evidence of a pit. Animal bones were not associated with the feature.

Interpretation: This feature, which was adjacent to Feature 3, is another hearth that was used for outdoor cooking. The presence of chert items within the feature indicated that the hearth was of Boreal Archaic affiliation.

Feature 5 (chert knapper's station) (pl. 53)

Location: N64–67E101–104.

Dimensions: Length 1.86 meters east to west; width 1.79 meters north to south. This feature was located at the base of the sod along the slope of the five meter terrace.

Shape: Irregularly oval in plan with a westward sloping cross section.

Defining characteristics: A difference in the soil (gray sand with charcoal fleck inclusions) and a concentration of chert items at the base of the sod.

Elements of the feature (fe) and associated elements(ae)

1. Gray sand (fe)
2. Dark brown sand (fe)
3. Rough rocks (fe)
4. Post hole (ae)
5. Charcoal flecks (ae). (R4, radio-carbon sample)
6. Six projectile points (ae)
7. One hundred and three chert items (ae)

Distribution of elements: This feature was originally situated in a shallow depression in the dark brown sand and gravel level of the terrace slope, and gradually built up to a thickness of 0.15 meters with the accumulation of dark brown sand and gray sand. When the feature was recognized in the gray sand, charcoal flecks were observed near the perimeter as well as in the fill. A post hole was also located near the eastern edge of the feature. Most of the chert items were concentrated in the depression, but some of them as well as one projectile point and a few rough rocks were located outside the depression along the western limits.

Observations: There was no evidence of an intentionally dug pit nor, with the exception of the charcoal flecks, any evidence of burning along the terrace slope.

Interpretation: This feature probably represents a chert knapper's station. None of the chert items was stacked or positioned at a certain location within the feature as might be the case if the intention had been to store objects for future use. The presence of chert items, particularly the six projectile points, indicated that this feature was associated with the Boreal Archaic component.

Feature 6 (hearth) (pl. 54 and fig. 60)

Location: N63–65E137–138

Dimensions: Length 0.63 meters north to south; width 0,535 meters east to west. This feature was located at the base of the sod.

Shape: Oval in plan.

Defining characteristics: A concentration of fire-cracked rocks at the base of the sod.

Elements of the feature (fe) and associated elements (ae)
1. Gray sand (fe)
2. Fire-cracked rocks (fe)
3. One fire-blackened rock (fe)
4. Other rough rocks and stones (fe)
5. Charcoal (ae). (R7, radio-carbon sample)

Distribution of elements: This feature was situated on dark brown sand and was filled with a thin layer of gray sand. The feature was entirely consolidated with the charcoal concentrated around the fire-cracked rocks.

Observations: There was no evidence of a pit. Chert items and animal bones were not associated with the feature.

Interpretation: This feature was a hearth. Although the specific function of the hearth is unknown, it probably was used either for cooking or heating purposes. Because of the absence of associated cultural debris, the affiliation of the feature is also unknown.

Feature 7 (water trench) (pl. 55)

Location: N32–35E112–117

Dimensions: Length 4.0 meters east to west; width 0.445 meters north to south. This feature was located 0.18 meters below the surface on top of the five meter terrace and along a portion of the west slope. The feature was 0.105 meters in depth.

Fig. 60. The hearth at feature 6.

Shape: Rectangular in plan with a rounded or broad u-shaped cross section.

Defining characteristics: A difference in the soil (dark brown sand and gravel with charcoal fleck inclusions) filling a trench at the base of the sod.

Elements of the feature (fe) and associated elements (ae)
1. Dark brown sand and gravel (fe)
2. Several pieces of thin slate (fe)
3. Charcoal flecks (ae)

Distribution of elements: This feature, which was recognized in the gray sand at the base of the sod, had been dug into dark brown sand and gravel. The charcoal flecks were scattered throughout the dark brown sand and gravel fill of the trench. Several pieces of slate had been placed in juxtaposition on the bottom of a small section of the feature.

Observations: Aside from the charcoal flecks, there was no evidence of burning in the trench. Cultural materials were not present in the trench.

Interpretation: This feature was a trench presumably dug (and partially lined with slate) by the Vikings to allow for the passage of rain water from the five meter terrace to a lower level at the site. The water trench was situated south of house-site F and south-east of house-site G. The trench did not connect with either of these structures, but was strategically positioned to funnel off excess rain water in order to prevent flooding.

Feature 8 (two structures) (pl. 56)
Location: N1–9W15–20.

Dimensions: Length 6.44 meters north to south; width 3.785 meters east to west. This feature was located at the base of the sod.

Shape: Two circles in plan.

Defining characteristics: A number of slate rocks located in gray sand at the base of the sod.

Elements of the feature (fe) and associated elements (ae)
1. Gray sand (fe)
2. Slate rocks (fe)
3. Two chert items (ae)

Distribution of elements: This feature was built on dark brown sand and was filled with a thin layer of gray sand. The slate rocks appear to have been arranged in two juxtaposed circles. Circle 1 is represented by the rocks between N3 and N6. Two chert items were present along the eastern margin of this circle. Circle 2 is represented by the rocks between N6 and N9.

Observations: There was no evidence of a pit nor of burning inside the two stone circles.

Interpretation: Feature 8 represents the stone walls used to anchor two structures made of hides or skins. Although there was very little information with these tent rings that can be used to assess their cultural affiliation, there is little doubt that these structures were associated with either a pre-Eskimo or an Eskimo occupation at the site rather than with the Iron Age component.

The implements found in connection with these features are listed in the catalogue of finds under Nos. 183–227, 308 fig. 61.

Soil Profiles

Pl. 57 illustrates three soil profiles recorded at the site. A typical profile consists of (from top to bottom) sod or surface turf overlying a thin layer of gray, wind blown sand, which overlies dark brown sand, which overlies dark brown sand and gravel. Moreover, in the area north of house-site F a dark organic layer was encountered at the base of the sod on top of the gray sand. The dark organic layer was mixed with sand and appeared to be composed mainly of burned or charred sod.

With the exception of those objects situated within the fills of features, specimens of archaeological significance were always located near the base of the turf in some relationship to the gray sand layer. Boreal Archaic lithic materials, for example, were found on top, within, and at the bottom of the gray sand layer. While temporal differences are obviously represented in the deposition of these items in the gray sand contexts, there do not appear to have been significant technological changes in the types of artifact produced.

104

Secondly, the only Dorset Eskimo artifact recovered during 1963 was a projectile point and it was found within the gray sand layer. Iron Age specimens, on the other hand, were usually recovered from the surface of the dark organic layer at the base of the sod. Likewise, a whale ribbon (Feature 1) was excavated within the sod. In the case of both the iron specimens and the ribbon, the underlying thin cushion of organic matter or sod apparently served to preserve the matrix of these items.

Since the culture-bearing zone in practically all cases was located at the bottom of the turf, we can conclude on *present* evidence that there is really no depth to any of the occupations. This conclusion is particularly significant for the Boreal Archaic materials in view of the stratigraphic position of such specimens at sites elsewhere in Newfoundland and Labrador. In a brief comparative analysis of soil profiles from Boreal Archaic sites in these regions, Harp (1963:248–52) has established a three-phase chronology based on the depth of Boreal Archaic specimens from the surface and their association with former turf lines. Those sites with the greatest depth are considered to represent the earliest phase; those sites with the least depth, in which cultural items were associated with the surface turf, are considered to represent the latest phase; and those sites with specimens positioned between these two extremes in the profiles are assigned to an intermediate category (Harp 1963:251–2, figs. 7–8). Furthermore, this chronology is supported in large by a typological seriation of the projectile points and other lithic artifacts found at the sites (cf. Harp 1963:254, table 1). On the basis of the soil profiles at L'Anse aux Meadows, we would assign the Boreal Archaic component to the intermediate phase of Harp's chronology. Whether or not a typological study of the specimens associated with this component will also support assignment to the intermediate phase remains to be seen.

Conclusion

The 1963 archaeological excavations at L'Anse aux Meadows were successful in recovering additional information on the multi-aboriginal occupations at the site. Although relatively little data was obtained with regard to the Dorset Eskimo and Iron Age occupations, considerable information was recovered for the Boreal Archaic component. Perhaps the major contribution to the isolation of this component was the identification of at least two activity areas (cooking and tool preparation).

Finds (cfr. catalogue of finds nos. 183–227, 308).

In the final analysis, there is little question that the site spans a long period of time and represents an important segment in the prehistory of eastern North America.

Acknowledgments. We would like to express our appreciation to James C. Hertter of the University of Illinois for preparing the accompanying illustrations.

References

Binford, Lewis R. Schoenwetter, James and Fowler, Melwin, 1964. Archaeological investigations in the Carlyle Reservoir, Clinton County, Illinois, Archaeological Salvage Report No. 17. Southern Illinois University Museum.

Harp, Elmer jr. 1963. Evidence of Boreal Archaic Culture in Southern Labrador and Newfoundland, In *Contribution to Anthropology*, 1961–1962, Pt. 1, pp. 184–261. *National Museum of Canada,* Bulletin No. 193.

Fig. 61. Projectile points from excavations outside the house-sites.

VI Test Excavation of the Boat-sheds

BY ARNE EMIL CHRISTENSEN JR.

On the west bank of Black Duck Brook, there are four roughly oval depressions in the terrace, close to the shore (fig. 62). They appeared to be man-made, and had been tentatively interpreted as boat-sheds. During the 1968 season, a test excavation was carried out, with a view to ascertaining whether these depressions really were man-made, whether they might be attributed to the Norse settlement and, if possible, what methods of construction had been employed and to what use the structures had been put. We did not aim at undertaking a complete excavation. The work, which lasted from 30th August until 25th September, was entrusted to the present author.[1]

The depressions are short and wide, and at first it was difficult to establish their dimensions exactly. When the tall grass had been cut, the area was summarily mapped. The resulting sketch map and the levels obtained indicated that the four depressions had been partly dug into the marine terrace, partly built up. There were no traces of gable-ends facing the shore (pl. 58).

The exploratory trenches were set out as shown on pl. 58. At this stage I held that if the structures we were hoping to find really were boat-sheds, they would be orientated at right angles to the shore. We therefore plotted the main trench parallel to the shore.

When the excavation was well under way, we had a day with unusually favourable lighting conditions, and then we could see that the walls actually lay at an oblique angle to the shore, a fact which should be borne in mind when studying the profiles.

After we had stripped off the thin surface turf with spades, we excavated the trenches with trowels, proceeding into the sterile layers below. All the stones found were plotted on the map and a number of levels were recorded, in order to establish whether the stones lay in any kind of order which might indicate a paving or floor (pls. 59 and 60).

Immediately below the surface turf, we encountered a layer of dark sand. Nearly all the stones were of the local, dark grey variety of slate, water-ground to a greater or lesser extent. It was extremely difficult to see or feel any differences in the soil, and later it proved necessary to keep an eye on the profiles after they had been scraped down, so that they could be photographed

109

Fig. 62. The boat-sheds seen from the north-east prior to excavation.

Fig. 63. The boat-sheds seen from the east. The trenches are laid out and the excavation is well under way.

and measured at exactly the right point of drying out, when the layers in the ground were most clearly visible.

As no full excavation was being attempted, I decided that it would be best to obtain long, continuous profiles through the depressions and the banks separating them. The main trench, which consisted of two parts, was 50 cm wide and ran parallel to the shore. In the second boat-shed from the east, larger areas – 2.50 m × 3 m and 2.50 m × 2.80 m – were excavated so that, in the event of there being a floor or paving here, we might more easily see the pattern formed by the stones. This excavation was arranged so that the faces produced a longitudinal section through one of the walls of the boat-shed. Further west, a short trench was cut at right angles to the main trench, in order to ascertain whether a couple of large stones visible above ground were in any way connected with the depressions. This turned out not to be the case – the stones lay in sterile soil in the terrace, high above the rear gable end of boat-shed 4. Finally a 5.20 m long trench, running northwards at right angles to the main trench, was cut between 22.50 m and 24.50 m, with a view to obtaining another longitudinal profile through a wall; trench A was also extended 4.50 m to the east. In this way we hoped to obtain a clearer section through boat-shed 3, for this did not show up distinctly in trench B. In the trench cut between 22.50 m and 24.50 m, and the eastward extension of trench A, the sections only were documented.

The profiles clearly revealed that the depressions were the work of man, that they had been dug into the bank, and that the loose soil had been heaped up on the sides, after which stacked turfs to form the walls were added – the same method of building as was employed in the other houses at L'Anse aux Meadows.

The soil being unfavourable for the purpose, we found no absolutely certain post holes, although two depressions filled with dark soil rich in humus, which border on the depression of boat-shed 4, may be post holes. If this is correct, they would have held posts standing in or along the interior face of the turf wall.

There were no significant small finds. In boat-shed 2, a piece of highly decayed wood was found on what is probably the floor layer. This may have formed part of a fallen-in roof or wall, but the decay was too far advanced to allow of any traces of an original surface or of constructional features. Fragments which could be lifted were numbered LaM 174 a–b, 175. Two pieces of whalebone (LaM 176) were found in or just below the floor layer, as shown on the plans. They may have been brought into the boat-sheds while these were in use, or they may be considerably older fragments of a whale skeleton washed up on land, which simply happened to be there when the boat-sheds were built.

The most important archaeological evidence resulting from this excavation

Fig. 64. Work in progress in boat-shed 3.

Fig. 65. Trench B, at the point where it cuts boat-shed 1.

112

was yielded by the profiles. I shall comment on these in some detail, with a general reference to pls. 61 and 62.

When we compare them to the turf walls of, for example, house F, the walls of the boat-sheds appear very indistinct.[2] On this part of the site, the erosive action of the water seems to have been greater. However, the remains are sufficient to give us a clear picture of walls, constructed partly from gravel excavated during building, and partly from stacked turfs. These are clearly visible in the west wall of boat-shed 2, for instance.

Below the built-up walls, the original surface could be discerned in many places, as a thin line of decayed turf. It is particularly clearly visible under the gravel bank between boat-sheds 3 and 4. In my opinion, the stripe of turf running across the depressions – also most clearly visible in boat-shed 4 – must represent the collapsed roof.

Black lines were visible in the profiles also below the walls and "floor layers", however, right down into the sterile sub-soil. These were continuous lines, running through the section. When rubbed in the hand, this material felt more gritty and less fat than the turf layers of the buildings. At first I thought that these lines were due to discolouration by minerals – iron or manganese. A small test trench cut in the sterile soil on top of the terrace above the sheds showed similar layers in the sand.

A series of samples was taken from the long profile, in order to ascertain whether the sub-soil layers differed from the turf of the walls (see pl. 61).

Analyses undertaken by Kari Henningsmoen, cand.real., of the University of Oslo, and Rolf Sørensen, cand. real., of the Geological Institute of the Norwegian Agricultural College, showed that the dark colour of all the samples was caused by their humus content.[3] Kari Henningsmoen has proposed an explanation for the high humus content of the layers in the sand below the boat-sheds: at a time when the shore still lay below the level it had reached when the boat-sheds were built, storms may have swept marine sand over the vegetation on the shore, thus producing a layer of slowly decaying organic matter below a layer of sand. If new vegetation formed on top of the sand, only to be covered by sand during a new storm, we would have the stratification we can see here. Another possible explanation is that wind-blown sand covered the vegetation several times.

To return to the profiles, starting at the eastern end of trench B: the interrupted turf stripes from 0.5 m to 4 m may best be interpreted as representing the eastern, rear wall of boat-shed 1. The boat-shed itself appears as a depression in the old turf layers at 4 m and 5 m. As the trenches do not cut the depressions at right angles, the section cuts across a corner of the boat-shed. A thin double line of turf across the boat-shed may represent the remains of a collapsed turf roof.

The next wall, common to boat-sheds 1 and 2, extends to c. 10 m. Here a

Fig. 66. Section through east wall of boat-shed 2.

fairly clearly defined line of turf continues across the depression, overlaid by some stones between 12 m and 13 m. The line of turf and the stones may represent the floor layer of the boat-shed. Between 13 m and 14 m the turf wall is relatively well preserved, and the stacked turfs are still visible in the profile. Between 16 m and 22 m the profile is difficult to interpret, as the layers are highly eroded. When drawing and interpreting the profile, I concluded that the oblique layer of stones, which starts at 18 m, represented the last remains of eroded turfs, indicating where the wall stopped and the depression began. I guessed rather than saw remains of the roof represented by the turf specks preserved in the sand at 19.50 m to 20 m.

The new trench, which runs westwards from trench A, showed the layers of the east wall of boat-shed 3 more clearly. The west wall starts fairly distinctly at 22.50 m.

The wall between boat-sheds 3 and 4 consists of more gravel and less turf than the other walls. Here the layers indicate that this wall was built by heaping up a bank of gravel and stacking turfs on top of it. The depression of boat-shed 4 is deeper than the other three, and the layers of turf are fairly well preserved. A turf layer across the depression, overlain by some gravel, probably represents the roof. The layers from 28.50 m to 29.50 m I would interpret as the remains of a turf and gravel wall which collapsed into the house. This would imply that the original excavation for the boat-shed extended to c. 29.60 m, and that the wall was built inside this excavated area instead of being constructed on the bank beside it. Such a method of

114

construction may have been necessary if the side of the bank showed a tendency to collapse under the weight of the stacked turfs.

The profiles show that shallow depressions were first dug in the bank, the soil excavated being heaped up on both sides. Here the old layer of surface turf is visible under the sand and gravel.

The turf walls were built on top of these banks of excavated material. The turfs were cut as thick as possible, and a fair amount of sand still adhered to the roots of the grass. In the relatively small area excavated and investigated by us, we found no secure evidence of posts to support the roof – no secure post-holes came to light either inside the houses or as part of the walls. Nor did we find any traces of wooden"panelling" on the interior face of the turf walls, or of the manner of construction employed for the roof. I consider that the turf layer running across the boat-sheds from wall to wall, covered by more recently deposited silt, clearly indicates that the roofs of these buildings were covered by turf, which probably rested on wooden roofs, consisting, for instance, of closely spaced thin tree-trunks or branches resting on rafters. However, we found no evidence indicating how such a wooden structure might have been made.

In boat-shed 4, the hollows containing turf, which can be seen in the profile at 26.80 m and 28.50 m, may be post-holes for roof-supporting posts set just inside the turf wall, or they may indicate a shallow groove which held the lower ends of closely arranged standing planks or timbers, forming a panelled or palisade wall lining the inner face of the turf wall.[4] However, as our excavation was comparatively limited, we have no evidence for or against either of these two theories.

In my view, the evidence of these layers visible in the profiles proves that our "boat-sheds" really were boat-sheds, built with turf walls of the same type as those known from the other houses of the Norse settlement. The turf layers covering the depressions demonstrate the presence of a turf roof, which must have rested on some kind of wooden "inner roof". The gable ends facing the sea were either open, or closed with a light, wooden wall. Even though we found no artefacts enabling us to date these structures or assign a cultural affiliation to them, I consider that the most logical explanation is that they were, in fact, the boat-sheds of the Norse settlement.

A more detailed survey of the theories concerning Scandinavian architecture during the Viking Age and earlier is beyond the scope of this paper.[5]

In spite of this, one common trait – the roof-supporting posts found in most of the houses – must be discussed. Simplifying matters somewhat, we may say that the characteristic feature of these houses is the fact that the walls are merely an insulating screen inserted under the eaves of a post-supported roof. Regardless of whether these walls are of stone, turf, timber or wattle-and-daub – they carry little or none of the weight of the roof. The resulting house

Fig. 67. Section through east wall of boat-shed 3.

Fig. 68. Details of the layers in the east wall of boat-shed 3.

116

is a structure consisting of three aisles; this is an inconvenient plan for a boat-shed, where open, unimpeded floor space is important, and where the cross-beams tying each pair of posts would be very much in the way of the tall stems and stern posts of the ships.

Thus special features of construction are to be expected in the case of boat-sheds.

As Erik Hinsch has shown, the normal roof-supporting posts of the Iron Age Norse hall would be very much in the way in a boat-shed.[6] The boat-shed he excavated had sturdy gravel banks outside the walls proper, designed to take the outward thrust of the roof. But a more recent excavation has shown that a boat-shed may in fact have the roof-supporting posts we know from the dwelling houses of the period.[7] In the boat-shed, however, the posts are placed close to the walls, thus leaving as much free floor space as possible for the ship.

Medieval Icelandic literary sources use two words to designate boat-sheds – *naust* and *hrof*.[8] The descriptions given in the sources are not very precise, but it seems clear that the *naust* was a proper building, a boat-shed, corresponding to the type of building still known as *naust* in northern and western Norway. The *hrof* must have been a structure of a more temporary nature, probably a trench or a pair of walls, where the vessel lay covered by loose boards or some other kind of temporary roofing.

When we compare them to Iron Age and Viking Age boat-sheds in Norway, the boat-sheds at L'Anse aux Meadows appear unusually short and wide. The fact that they are partly dug into the terrace and set at an oblique angle to the shore must, in my opinion, indicate that the distance from the high-water mark to the terrace was not great enough to allow of boat-sheds placed at right angles to the shore, with built-up walls only. The profile along one of the walls of boat-shed 3 shows a bank of almost pure gravel at the outer end, where the layers of the wall show damage. This may be a result of the ground having frozen in winter, or it may indicate that the original walls were longer, and that storms and high water caused this damage after the boat-sheds had fallen into disuse.

The interpretation of the depressions as representing boat-sheds is based on the analysis of the profiles and on their topographical situation. However, their use as boat-sheds presupposes a sea-level not much above the modern level (pl. 63), for with a higher sea-level the boat-sheds and the boats in them would be very vulnerable during northerly storms. The measurements taken (pl. 63) gave a mean level above high water of c. 190 cm. for the floor of the sheds. Extreme high water level could be seen on the shore as a bank of sand and seaweed, the vertical difference between the bottom of this and the floor of the sheds is c. 155 cm. The "safe distance" between high water and a boat-shed differs, of course, with the topographical situation and prevailing winds, but I do not think that the sea-level can have been much more than

Fig. 69. Nineteenth-century boat sheds, at Nordnes, Sogndalsfjord, Norway.

Fig. 70. Boat-sheds, with store-houses and dwellings in the background. Kvivik, Straumøy, the Faroes.

118

at most 1 m higher than at present when the boat-sheds were in use. For a discussion of the sea-level and the topographical situation of the site during the settlement period, see Kari Henningsmoen's contribution to this publication. Even if the original walls were considerably longer, the boat-sheds at L'Anse aux Meadows must have been built for rather small boats. Boat-sheds for four small boats reflect the kind of life which one might find along the coasts of Norway and Iceland, in the Viking Age as during the nineteenth century. The economy of such a settlement would be mixed, based on farming, animal husbandry and fishing, and some small boats would form an important part of the equipment of the people living here.

In order to gain an idea of the kind of boat for which these boat-sheds were built, we must turn to the preserved boats from the Viking Age, and also adduce material from later periods for comparison. In the Gokstad ship burial, fragments of three small boats were found, and two of these have been restored. Their maximum dimensions (length × beam) are 9.7 m × 1.8 m and 6.5 m × 1.4 m respectively.[9] The third boat seems to have been c. 8 m long. The two larger boats were rowed by three pairs of oars, the smallest by two pairs. Boat burials where the timber has decayed, but where the iron rivets lie in approximately the right position, indicate that the Gokstad boats are typical of the normal small boats of the Viking Age.[10] A Swedish Viking grave has yielded a much smaller boat,[11] but this is a shallow, delicate skiff for lake and river use, too frail even for being used inshore.

From the Middle Ages, but not dated more precisely, comes a four-oared boat found in the harbour of Kalmar, Sweden.[12] More heavily built and sturdier than the Viking vessels, it measures 4.4 m × 1.5 m, length and beam respectively.

Four and six-oared boats of roughly the same shape and dimensions as the Gokstad boats were the most common fishing boats along the coast of Norway well into the nineteenth century; we must assume that the boats housed in our L'Anse aux Meadows boat-sheds were also of this type.

Boat-sheds are known from the Pacific, where they were built for the large canoes used for war and commerce. In Europe, the Greeks built covered slipways for their triremes,[13] and boat-sheds were in use for galley-like naval vessels in various countries until well after the Napoleonic wars. Apart from these, boat-sheds are the exception rather than the rule all over Europe, except in Norway and the lands colonized by Norway during the Viking Age.

Boat-sheds, prehistoric and modern, are known from the other Scandinavian countries, but they are rare there as they are also in eastern Norway. To this day it is common practice in western and northern Norway to keep small boats in sheds, and a number of boat-shed ruins have been found along the

Fig. 71. Boat-shed with dry-stone walls, eighteenth or nineteenth century. Austre Åmøy, Rogaland, Norway.

Fig. 72. Corner-timbered boat-sheds, probably mid-19th century. Innvik, Nordfjord, Norway.

120

Fig. 73. Boat-shed in *grindehus* technique. Olden, Nordfjord, Norway.

Fig. 74. Ruins of boat-sheds, partly dug into the marine terrace. Probably of Viking Age date. Steigen, Nordland, Norway.

coast from Egersund to Tromsø. Excavated boat-shed sites range in date from the Roman Iron Age to the Middle Ages.[14]

The medieval laws contain detailed provisions governing the construction of boat-sheds for warships;[15] western and northern Norwegian boat-sheds from the eighteenth and nineteenth centuries offer interesting constructional parallels.

Ideally, the boat-shed (ON and Mod.Norw. *naust*) should lie as close to the shore as possible, preferably with a gently sloping beach in front, in order to facilitate the work of launching and landing the boats as much as possible. The building must lie sufficiently high above the high-water mark to prevent storm damage – thus on an exposed stretch of coast the boat-sheds must lie further inland than in a sheltered harbour. The original situation of an ancient boat-shed may, of course, be greatly changed as a result of regressions or transgressions.

In modern times, boat-sheds have been constructed in one of the following three ways: dry-stone walls with timber for the roof and gable-ends, or one of two different types of timber construction might be employed, either corner timbering (Norw. *laftehus*) or roof-supporting posts (Norw. *grindehus*).[16]

Corner-timbered boat-sheds are mainly found in well-forested areas, for this building method requires a great deal of timber. It is generally accepted by scholars working with architectural history in Norway that the *grindehus* is a descendant of the prehistoric building technique employing roof-supporting posts. Figs.69 to 73 show a selection of "modern" (mainly nineteenth century) *naust* for comparison. The boat-shed shown on fig. 70 lies on the Faroes, the rest are Norwegian.

Prehistoric boat-sheds most commonly seem to have had walls of stone and turf. There are examples of pure stone walls, but these are rare (fig. 75).[17] We also have several examples of boat-sheds which were partly excavated, and partly built up (fig. 74).

Apart from the numerous ruins in western and northern Norway, we also have ruins of early boat-sheds in Iceland. However, none of the latter has been excavated, so the dates are uncertain.[18] One Greenland ruin has also been interpreted as representing a boat-shed. It is rather surprising that there should only be one boat-shed ruin in Greenland – this is probably due to damage resulting from transgression.[19]

To date, only two boat-sheds are known in Denmark, both at Harrevig by Limfjorden. Their date is uncertain, but they are believed to be of Viking Age or early medieval date (fig. 76).[20]

We should stress that the main function of a Norwegian *naust* is that of housing one or more boats of the light, traditional type, boats that were – and still are – hauled up on land between fishing trips. A *naust* may also be used

122

Fig. 75. Boat-shed ruins with dry-stone walls, Viking Age or earlier. Nes, Karmøy, Norway.

Fig. 76. Boat-shed ruins, variously interpreted as *naust* and *hrof*. Harrevig, by Limfjorden, Danmark.

for storing bulky fishing gear, or as a warehouse, but these functions are secondary to that of housing the boat. The seaward gable end of the *naust* either has large doors, or it may be quite open. *Naust* built in the *grindehus* technique may even lack walls altogether (fig. 73).

Appendix

List of level readings taken in the trenches.

All readings are below a local datum point for the boat-sheds. This datum point lies 291 cm below the main datum point of the excavation.

Number of point	converted reading	Number of point	Converted reading	Number of point	Converted reading
1	102	38	127	75	84
2	96	39	142	76	70
3	95	40	144	77	67
4	101	41	138	78	68
5	102	42	124	79	108
6	89	43	132	80	68
7	117	50	106	81	108
8	116	51	117	82	111
9	119	52	123	83	108
10	124	53	130	84	116
11	117	54	131	85	116
12	116	55	134	86	112
13	111	56	132	87	108
14	112	44	119	88	106
15	111	45	108	89	105
16	108	46	111	90	103
17	106	47	105	91	96
18	106	48	104	92	87
19	104	49	104	93	86
20	118	57	118	94	78
21	120	58	123	95	79
22	122	59	118	96	77
23	126	60	112	97	86
24	119	61	114	98	77
25	122	62	111	99	74
26	128	63	110	100	74
27	127	64	108	101	133
28	110	65	109	102	130
29	121	66	106	103	132
30	126	67	109	104	128
31	133	68	114	105	122
32	127	69	105	106	122
33	134	70	96	107	118
34	133	71	90	108	121
35	130	72	91	109	110
36	124	73	85	110	131
37	128	74	87	111	130

Notes

1 I should like to thank Anne Stine and Helge Ingstad for asking me to join the 1968 expedition, and inviting me to publish the results of the test excavation of the boat-sheds.
2 E.g. Ingstad 1970, fig. 20
3 Letter of 25th May 1972, in the author's files.
4 Myhre 1973.
5 The relevant literature is listed in Ingstad 1970.
6 Hinsch 1961, p.15.
7 Myhre 1973.
8 Ellmers 1972, p.148.
9 Johannessen 1940; Christensen 1959.
10 Müller-Wille 1970, pp.33 ff., tables.
11 Arbmann 1940.
12 Åkerlund 1951, pp.55 ff. and pl. 12.
13 Shaw 1972.
14 Hinsch 1961; Rolfsen 1974.
15 The laws are discussed in detail by Hilmar Stigum in *Kulturhistorisk Leksikon for Nordisk Middelalder*, Vol.XII, under NAUST:
16 *Grindehus* is a dialect term now generally accepted by scholars of rural Norwegian architecture, but the synonymous term *stavbygning* may be encountered in the literature.
17 The best example of dry-stone walls is provided by the larger of the two boat-sheds at Nes, Karmøy, Rogaland, Norway (fig. 75). This boat-shed is about 30 m long, and walls to a height of about 2 m are still preserved. (These boat-sheds are known in the literature as "Ferkingstad-naustene", see Isachsen 1941.)
18 Eldjárn 1967.
19 Nørlund 1930, pp.130 ff.
20 Ramskou 1960.

List of Illustrations

Fig.66
Section through east wall of boat-shed 2.
Fig. 67
Section through east wall of boat-shed 3.
Fig. 68
Details of the layers in the east wall of boat-shed 3.
Fig. 69
Nineteenth-century boat sheds, at Nordnes, Sogndalsfjord, Norway.
Fig. 70
Boat-sheds, with store-houses and dwellings in the background. Kvivik, Straumøy, the Faroes.
Fig. 71
Boat-shed with dry-stone walls, eighteenth or nineteenth century. Austre Åmøy, Rogaland, Norway.
Fig. 72
Corner-timbered boat-sheds, probably mid-19th century. Innvik, Nordfjord, Norway.
Fig 73
Boat-shed in *grindehus* technique. Olden, Nordfjord, Norway.
Fig 74
Ruins of boat-sheds, partly dug into the marine terrace. Probably of Viking Age date. Steigen, Nordland, Norway.
Fig. 75
Boat-shed ruins with dry-stone walls, Viking Age or earlier. Nes, Karmøy, Norway.
Fig. 76
Boat-shed ruins, variously interpreted as *naust* and *hrof.* Harrevig, by Limfjorden, Denmark.

References

H. Åkerlund, *Fartygsfynden i den forna hamnen i Kalmar;* Uppsala 1951 (Åkerlund 1951).

S. Andersson *Finländska Båthus*, Budkavlen 3, 1943.

H. Arbmann, *Der Årby-Fund.* Acta Archaeologica XI. København 1940. (Arbmann 1940)

E. Bull, *Skipstomter eller naustetomter fra vikingetid eller middelalder*, Foreningen til Norske Fortidsminnesmerkers bevaring, Aarsberetning 1917

A.E. Christensen jr, *Færingen fra Gokstad*, Viking XXIII 1959 (Christensen 1959)

K. Eldjárn, *Naust, Island.* Kulturhistorisk Leksikon for Nordisk Middelalder vol XII. Oslo 1967 (Eldjárn 1967)

D. Ellmers, *Frühmittelalterliche Handelsschiffahrt in Mittel und Nordeuropa.* Neumünster 1972. (Ellmers 1972)

E. Hinsch, *Naust og Hall i jernalderen,* Årbok for Universitetet i Bergen, Humanistisk serie 1960 – 2. Bergen 1961 (Hinsch 1961)

A.S. Ingstad, *The Norse settlement at L'Anse aux Meadows, Newfoundland*, Acta Archaeologica XLI. København 1970 (Ingstad 1970)

F. Isachsen, *Langskips-Naustene ved Ferkingstad og landhevningen*, Norsk Geografisk Tidsskrift VIII. Oslo 1940/41. (Isachsen 1941)

F. Johannessen, *Båtene fra Gokstadskibet*, Viking IV Oslo 1940. (Johannessen 1940)

M. Müller-Wille, *Bestattung im Boot. Studien zu einer nordeuropäischen Grabsitte*, Offa 25/26. Neumünster 1970. (Müller-Wille 1970)

A. Myhre, *Nausttufter, havnivå og kulturlandskap på Jæren i eldre tider*, Ætt og Heim 1959.

B. Myhre, *Nausttuft fra eldre jernalder*, ARKEO 1973 no. 1. (Myhre 1973)

P. Nørlund, *Norse Ruins at Gardar*, Meddelelser om Grønland LXXVI. København 1930 (Nørlund 1930)

T. Ramskou, *To "Naust" ved Harrevig*, Årbøger for Nordisk Oldkyndighed og Historie 1961 (Ramskou 1961)

P. Rolfsen, *Båtnaust på Jærkysten*, Stavanger 1974.

J.W. Shaw, *Greek and Roman harbourworks,* in G. Bass: A History of Seafaring, based on underwater archaeology. London 1972. (Bass 1972)

H. Vreim, *Buer og Naust, Spiren til våre eldste byer,* Foreningen til Norske Fortidsminnesmerkers bevaring, Årsberetning 1933

Part II
Interpretation and Assessment

BY ANNE STINE INGSTAD

VII Newfoundland in Prehistoric Times

Ethnic groups

The history of Newfoundland may be said to begin in 1497, when John Cabot discovered the island. From that time on, the history of Newfoundland has undergone constant changes, lasting until our own day: the English and the French were forever contending for dominion over the land. We shall not dwell on these historical events in any detail here. In the present context we are first and foremost interested in the period which preceded Cabot's discovery. It is essential that we should try to establish which ethnic groups lived in Newfoundland, and particularly in the parts by the Strait of Belle Isle, before the advent of the Europeans. We must also investigate the methods of building employed by these people, in order to be able to decide who the builders of the houses at Épaves Bay might have been.

Two ethnic groups at least, seem to have lived here from time immemorial. It has been established by means of radio-carbon dates from Elmer Harp's extensive investigations of a Dorset Eskimo settlement site at Port aux Choix on the north-west coast of Newfoundland [8] that there were Dorset Eskimoes living in Newfoundland as early as the first centuries A.D. Tools from their culture occur sporadically along the coast of northern Newfoundland, and they appear to be of the same character, and to include the same types, as those found in arctic settlements of the Cape Dorset cultural complex. (Strait of Belle Isle series, Canada, P–682, 683, 692, 693, 676, 678A, 679, 690–696, 727, 729–737.) None of these is later than A.D. 600.

A number of settlement sites with Stone Age material different from that of the Dorset culture are also known. They belong to the so-called Boreal Archaic culture, which is thought to be of American Indian origin. [9]

When Cabot discovered Newfoundland in 1497, it was inhabited by Beothuk Indians. Of these, Elmer Harp, says: "It seems that the island shared in the boreal cultural complex of the Archaic period which has been found widespread in the north-east. Furthermore, because these traits can with considerable confidence be linked with the Beothuk Indians, these people appear to have been a last isolated outpost of the ancient tradition which they or their forebears at one time carried over from the mainland." [10]

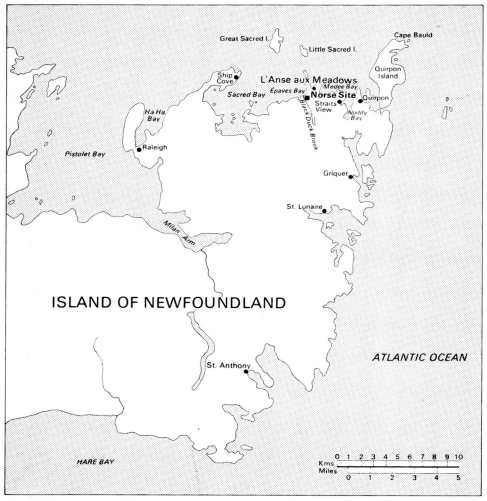

Fig. 77. North-eastern Newfoundland with L'Anse aux Meadows, the area where the Norse house-sites were discovered and excavated. Drawn by G. Furuholmen. After Canada Department of Mines and technical Surveys.

A third group may have been of some importance to the history of settlement in these regions: the Montagnais Indians from Quebec and Labrador, along the Gulf of St. Lawrence. Literary tradition, written down by early white settlers, has it that these Indians used to come to Newfoundland to hunt every year. Harp considers it unlikely, however, that such annual hunting expeditions should have taken place in prehistoric times, when these Indians were still at a Stone Age stage of culture.[11] Another group of Indians, the Micmac Indians from Nova Scotia, were to ally themselves with the white settlers in their struggle against the Beothuk Indians. We have a number of reports of their annual hunting expeditions to Newfoundland, and it is a known fact that they came as far north as White Bay and other localities along the north coast. According to Harp, such expeditions were not common before the French had begun their colonization of Nova Scotia and Cape

Breton Island in 1604, for he considers it hardly likely that the Micmac Indians should have crossed the 65 miles wide Cabot Strait regularly before this time.[12]

Of these four ethnic groups – one of which is likely to have been Eskimo and three Indian – it seems that only the Dorset Eskimoes and the bearers of the Boreal Archaic culture lived in Newfoundland in prehistoric times, according to Harp.[13]

A fifth group of people which must also be considered in a discussion about the possible builders of the houses at Épaves Bay are the Norse Greenlanders, who colonized Greenland shortly before the year A.D.1000, and who lived there until about A.D.1500. The Icelandic sagas – the Grœnlendinga Saga and Eirík's Saga – both tell of several expeditions from Greenland to unknown lands in the west and the south-west.[14] Helge Ingstad gives a detailed discussion and interpretation of these sagas in Volume II (not yet published) and therefore we do not need to dwell on them here at any length.

From the sagas it would appear that these Norse Greenlanders may have come to the north coast of Newfoundland, a view held by some scholars.[15] These Norse Greenlanders had left the Stone Age stage of culture long ago – they forged their tools from iron which they obtained from bog-ore.

Once the route to the New World was known, one would expect that more Norsemen would have travelled this way, for their community in Greenland was to endure for centuries (until about A.D.1500).[16]

The journey was comparatively short, and Vinland must have been tempting to the people from so desolate a polar land – it could offer timber for ship building, fur, walrus ivory, etc. And this new world also had plenty of fuel and bog-ore for iron production.

A few sources suggest that such journeys were undertaken later.[17] But our sources are sparse and, moreover, we have not a single document composed in Greenland, where so much happened in the course of the centuries.

The sagas say that the Norse Greenlanders met natives, and that they traded and fought with them. It is impossible to be certain whether the natives referred to were Eskimoes or Indians, or possibly both. W.W. Fitzhugh considers it unlikely that they should have been Eskimoes, for the Dorset Eskimoes, he holds, do not appear to have lived in Newfoundland at that time – the most recent radio-carbon date from the Port aux Choix settlement site is from c. A.D.600, as pointed out above. According to Fitzhugh, the *Skrælings* mentioned in the Vinland sagas must have been Indians of Algonkian linguistic affiliation – at least in Labrador, in the parts around Hamilton Inlet.[18] We shall return to this problem in a later section.

We do not know whether the Thule Eskimoes ever came to Newfoundland or not. Not a single object of their culture has been found there to date.[19]

Taylor feels that they may have visited Newfoundland in historic times, at least.[20]

The modern history of Newfoundland begins in 1497, when John Cabot rediscovered the island. In 1500 and 1501, Gaspar Cortreal from Portugal made for Newfoundland, and he probably landed somewhere in Notre Dame Bay. He called this land Terra Verde – the green country. In the wake of his and the many subsequent expeditions came a veritable stream of ships sailing for these new lands, first and foremost because of the wealth of fish and whale, but the fur trade also played an important part.

In the course of a surprisingly short time, a large fishing and whaling fleet was working off the coasts of Newfoundland. Many countries took part, the Basques, the French, the English and the Portuguese dominating.

The natives living here when the first white men came were Beothuk Indians, possibly descendants of the Boreal Archaic group. The Dorset Eskimoes had apparently disappeared.

L'Anse aux Meadows is not shown on the early maps; this may mean that it lay outside the fishing and whaling region of those days. R.E. Seary points out that the earliest mention occurs on a map published in 1862: here it is called Anse à la Medée.[21] The first white settler at L'Anse aux Meadows was of English descent, his name was William Decker, and his descendants still live there today.

George Decker, William's grandson, said that his grandfather used to tell of a French schooner which, in his youth, called at Noddy Bay from time to time, just a few miles farther south on the east coast (fig. 77), and that some French fishermen had houses at L'Anse aux Meadows, roughly at the place where the modern fishing village lies. At the outermost point of the headland, Beak Point, jutting out to the north on the east shore of Épaves Bay, there are some ruins which are said to be the remains of French fishermen's houses. The fishermen now living there occasionally find fishing hooks and fragments of clay pipes of the kind commonly found in the ruins of early fishermen's and whalers' houses, and it is possible that the ruins represent the houses of the French fishermen of whom William Decker spoke.

Why, one may wonder, was this early fishing village situated at the northern point of the headland, where there is only an old well with brackish water, when the area where our houses lie has a plentiful supply of fresh water from Black Duck Brook? The reason must be that Épaves Bay is so shallow that not even the smallest fishing boat can put ashore there, and according to Kari Henningsmoen's pollen analyses, the water is not likely to have been very much deeper here when the houses on the terrace were built (see p. 329). The water level may have been somewhere around $1/2$–1 m above the present level, while out by the headland the water is deep enough for the boats to land their

134

catch. This is a decisive point for fishermen, and it is also significant that the modern fishing village is situated on the eastern side of the headland.

The Beothuk Indians, who died out in 1829, depended on a taiga economy.[22] They were hunters and fishermen, whose nomadic way of life caused them to move from their summer settlement by the coast to the winter settlement inland. Their house was a tent-like, conical wigwam, the so-called mamateek. There were two types – a winter-mamateek and a summer-mamateek. The winter-mamateek had an octagonal base and a vertical wall, about two foot high, at the bottom. On the inside of the mamateek, earth was piled up against this wall, probably for the sake of warmth. A conical palisade roof, covered with birch bark on the outside, was erected above this earthen wall.[23] The summer-mamateek was rather lighter, and lacked the vertical base wall.[24] The Beothuk Indians are known to have had also a third type of house, a rectangular building constructed with stakes.[25] This was a store house, which was never used as a dwelling, and is probably a result of the influence of white settlers.

The Montagnais Indians, like the Beothuk, were nomads, and their dwelling was the conical wigwam.[26] The same applies to the Micmac Indians from Nova Scotia – they, too, lived in conical wigwams.[27] Under the influence of the white settlers, they also built small, rectangular palisade houses at a later date.

Harp who, as stated above, has registered a number of sites from the Boreal Archaic culture on either side of the Strait of Belle Isle, divides this material into three different categories: major occupation sites, workshop sites and camp sites. On only one of these settlements did he find the vestiges of a dwelling – a tent ring consisting of large stones.[28]

A number of different types of dwelling were used by the Dorset culture. We know of oval and of rectangular structures, some of them subterranean. Characteristic of them is the lack of any form of interior construction; thus they may have served as foundations for some kind of tent.[29]

The ruins which Eigil Knuth found on Peary Land are different from these. They are more elaborate in that some of them have a central passage marked by horizontally placed stones.[30]

The Dorset culture settlement excavated by Elmer Harp at Port aux Choix has yielded several oval foundations. These Harp assumes to be foundations for tents made from hide.

In recent years, several long, rectangular ruins of houses have been found and excavated in northern Labrador, by Ungava Bay. Some scholars consider that they represent the Dorset culture, as most of the finds from these excavations are Stone Age tools, the majority from the Dorset culture. Thomas Lee, however, who has excavated these ruins of buildings, is certain that they must be of Norse origin. He bases his assumption on the apparent similarity between some of these ruins and the Viking Age house-sites in Iceland and in Scandinavia. But as no object which may be said to be Norse has as yet been found in these house-sites, this theory must for the present be regarded as being hypothetical.[31] Without expressing any view on this hypothesis, I would here stress the fact that some features of these houses may be reminiscent of Norse building practice; these house-sites must therefore be considered in connection with an assessment of the houses at Épaves Bay and the people who built them – the same applies also to any other house-sites of this type which may in future be found in America. In connection with the discussion of house-site A below, I give a more detailed description and assessment of the sites at Ungava Bay.

The Thule Eskimoes, who may have begun their expansion southwards along the coast of Labrador around the year A.D.1350,[32] cannot have crossed to Newfoundland before the historic period, if indeed they ever did so. But the type of dwelling characteristic of their culture may in this connection be not without interest: a roundish or rectangular house half dug into the ground, whose characteristic feature was a long underground passage; there was a raised platform inside the room, and the floor was paved.[33]

Some of the more recent Eskimo houses in Labrador have many features in common with this Thule house. At Hopedale in Labrador, Junius Bird has excavated several Eskimo house-sites, the earliest of which are the remains of oval, one-family dwellings. These, too, have a long entrance tunnel. Later development favoured larger, rectangular houses, designed for several families. Some of these later houses are as long as 13 m, and many lack the long entrance tunnel. A typical feature of all these houses is the building material – turf.[34]

Finally, we have the Norsemen of the period around A.D.1000, when the Vinland expeditions took place. In the following, reference will be made to different types of house represented in Norse building practice.

Not a single trace of any more recent settlement has been found on the terrace – whalers and fishermen of historic times are not represented. There are scattered ruins from this period along the coasts of Newfoundland and Labrador, most of them are overgrown, but perfectly clear. One need not dig long before finding timber, much of it in a surprisingly good state of preservation, glazed sherds, well preserved iron fishing hooks and fragments of clay pipes. We must here add that a typical feature of the whalers' settlements are large stoves, and the remains of such stoves are found in several places along the coast. These items are listed here in order to show what the excavators might have expected to find if the ruins at Épaves Bay had represented a European settlement of historic date.

136

VIII Cultural Affinities

Eight, possibly nine house-sites have been excavated on the terrace by Épaves Bay. A charcoal kiln, two outdoor cooking pits, a number of outdoor hearths and four boat-sheds were also partially investigated (pl.2).

The house-sites differ – some of them greatly – from one another in size and shape, and a closer study of each individual house is therefore essential if we are to have any hope of establishing whether they all belong to one and the same cultural complex or, if this should prove not to be so, to which cultural complexes they should be assigned. To this end we must consider the different groups of people discussed above (see VII) and the types of houses built by them. The main intention of the present chapter is that of accounting for the cultural affinity of each house and structure. A discussion of the type of habitation is also included.

The house-sites lie at some distance from one another on the terrace within Épaves Bay; they appear to form three groups in such a way that each group consists of one large house and one or two smaller houses close by. As the excavation reports show, three of the house-sites are of quite an impressive size. A and D are aligned with the edge of the terrace; their orientation differs slightly – east/west and north-east/south-west respectively. House F, on the other hand, lies with one gable end on the western edge of the terrace, at the point where the latter curves. Thus its orientation is north-north-east/south-south-west. All three lie with one of their side walls facing the sea. One of the smaller houses, house B, is orientated in the same direction as house A. All these four houses were entered from the southern side wall, away from the ocean and facing the sun.

Houses B, C, E, G and J are all small. Their orientation varies somewhat: B, as we saw above, is orientated like A, and its entrance door lay in a corresponding position; C is orientated north/south, and E lies north-west/south-east, so that one of its end walls faces the edge of the terrace. G and J, both of which are almost as wide as they are long, were dug out of the terrace, their entrances facing the sea in the north-west, and the brook in the south-east respectively. No entrance was definitely demonstrated for house E but, as pointed out on p. 63 above, this is likely to have been in the south-eastern wall, away from the sea and facing the sun. This is undoubtedly the best and most practical position for an entrance door here in these parts, where the coldest winds blow from seaward. The entrance of house C, on the other hand, was in the northern wall, but as house A provided shelter from the cold inshore winds, no such problems arose in the case of this house. Moreover, the position of the door of house C was surely determined by that of house A just north of it – with the entrance in the northern wall of house C, one could quickly go from one of these two houses to the other.

The three large houses, as well as houses B and C, were built level with the ground, although it seems that the grass turf was removed before the walls were built. In all probability this turf was then used as part of the building materials for the walls (see p. 164). – Houses E, G and J were dug down into the ground. House E was dug down to a depth of 50 cm; it lies a little way from the edge of the terrace, so that the external face of the north-western end wall runs flush with it. Houses G and J, on the other hand, were dug into the edge of the terrace from the side. The depth of these, measured from the top of the terrace to the bottom of G and J, is 118 cm and 130 cm respectively.

The remains of the walls, as they appear after excavation, are fairly low; in six of the houses they consist of horizontal layers of turf piled on top of one another. In two of the houses – G and J – no traces of any such walls remain; it is unlikely that there ever were turf walls of this kind here, as these houses, as pointed out above, were dug down into the slope of the terrace, probably to the full height of the walls. Stone does not occur as a structural element in any of the turf walls of these houses – an occasional isolated stone may have been placed in position in order to shore up some of the turfs. In one place – in the western end wall of house A – we found some flat slabs and smaller stones under the turf wall, placed so close together that they formed a kind of low sleeper wall, but sleeper stones below the turf were mostly absent here.

In only one of the houses, house B, was the entrance marked by flat stones. Elsewhere, only a black, worn patch leading from both sides towards the centre of the wall indicated the position of the entrance. In most cases the centre of the wall was untouched, which probably means that there was a door frame or a threshold here. In several of the houses we found iron rivets near the door openings – they probably derive from wooden doors. Middens outside the entrances provided another indication of the presence of a door in this position. The roofs of the houses must have been covered with turf: in several of the house-sites we noted a top layer of tough old turf. Such layers were found in houses A, B, C, D I and II, F and G, but none was securely demonstrated in E, D III or J. Flat slabs of stone of varying sizes lay above this roof turf in several of the house-sites – they must have served to prevent the turfs from blowing off the roof. D III and J have also yielded such stones, which may show that these houses also had turf roofs, and this is, in fact, the most likely roofing material.

We attach particular importance to the hearths in the various houses. They are of different types: the most common is a so-called cooking pit. These pits, which are sunk into the floor, vary in size and depth, the largest having an upper diameter of more than two metres while the smallest do not exceed 0.5 m. Apart from charcoal, these pits contain large amounts of brittle-burned stones – this is a characteristic feature, for food was cooked on red-hot stones here. Such cooking pits were commonly placed in a corner – this was the case in house A rooms III and IV, house E, and house F room V. They might also lie up against a wall, the position of the cooking pit in house F room VI, or in the middle of the floor, frequently in conjunction with some other hearth, as was the case in house B and house F room II.

As a rule, the cooking pits were simple pits dug down into the floor, but that of house B was more elaborate – we found a stone at the bottom and stones also along the sides. It seems likely that this cooking pit was once lined with stones, most of which have disappeared in the course of the years.

The other hearths found vary in type. The simplest type is no more than a fire patch with a layer of charcoal and ashes of varying depth. In two of the houses, A II and F I, we found thick layers – almost mounds – of brittle-burned stone, clay and broken pieces of slate above these fire patches. In A II, this mound covered an oval depression in the floor, so this particular hearth should perhaps be related to a different group. The actual fire patch does not extend below floor level, and the floor below the fire patches was usually burned red and hard.

We found fire patches up against walls (A II, F I), in a corner (D II) and in the middle of the floor (B). Thus there seems to have been no hard and fast rule about the position of fire patches.

Another type of hearth, which is also very simple, consists of an oval, elongated depression in the floor, which runs in the longitudinal direction of the room, and has no surrounding stone setting. This type was found in A I – II – III – IV, D III, F I and III. One of them (A III) was close to a wall, and another (A IV) was almost round, but on the whole the above general description applies. The hearth of house B, which is stone-lined, is without parallels at the settlement site. It was described on p. 39 above.

In house F room IV we found a hearth placed up against the wall, near one of the corners of the room. As stated on p. 74 above, it consists of two chambers lined with stone, and separated by a slate slab standing on end. This hearth was also without parallels in the other houses.

Finally we must consider the hearth in F II. This elongated hearth lies in the middle of the room, and its orientation follows the longitudinal axis of the house. As pointed out on p. 71 above, it consists of three different components: a large flat slab of stone burned extremely brittle, an ember pit and a cooking pit. House D room III also had a hearth with an ember pit, but this had no stone slab and, as stated on p. 50 above, it was merely a shallow depression in the floor. The common feature of hearths of this type is that they consist of several components, including an ember pit. It is a moot point whether they are in fact composite hearths consisting of several components, or whether they should rather be regarded as several hearths with different functions. However, as they most frequently lie close together in a row, it would seem most correct to regard them as composite long hearths. This is most apparent in the hearth in F II. In connection with the first group – cooking pits – we mentioned a cooking pit in one of the corners of house-site E. This differs somewhat from the others in the same group: it is dug out of the gravel of the terrace behind, but at the front it does not extend below floor level, and at one side it is bounded by a large slab of slate standing on edge. That this hearth was used as a cooking pit appears quite clearly from the large number of brittle-burned stones found in it. In fact, this hearth is related not only to the cooking pits, but also to the two-chambered hearth in F IV, the only difference being that the hearth of house E consists of one chamber only. Both of them lie in or near a corner.

The hearths of house-sites G and J must also be mentioned. That in house G (p. 84) consists of a large, brittle-burned stone slab standing on edge, and a fire patch in front of it, while the hearth of house J was a shallow depression roughly in the middle of the room, near the edge of the so-called anvil stone (p. 90).

Above we have attempted to account for the great number of details apparently shared by these house-sites: the method of building, where turfs are stacked on top of one another in horizontal layers, is common to most of them; the hearths, although primitive in character, are sufficiently true to type to be important to the assessment of whether they all belong to the same cultural complex or not. But the hearths alone do not provide decisive evidence on this point – the building material employed, turf, forms a weighty argument, for there must in all likelihood have been sufficient timber and drift-wood for building houses here. People who nevertheless built their houses from turf must have done so simply because this was what they were used to – in other words, they must have come from a country whose natural building material was turf.

Finally we must point out that nearly all the house-sites have yielded iron rivets, fragments of iron, lumps of slag and pieces of jasper, while stone tools are not among the items found in the floor layers. True, some stone tools were found in house D III, and an arrow-head came to light in the wall of house A (see p. 163 below), but we have already pointed out that these occurred in more recent strata. This will be discussed in more detail in a subsequent chapter.

We also attach great importance to the radio-carbon analyses, which have yielded an average date of c. A.D. 920 ± 20 years (see R. Nydal), fig. 9.

We have seen that the plans of the houses vary in type. This fact we consider to be so important to our assessment of the cultural complex or complexes represented here that the houses must be considered individually.

Interpretation of house-site A (pp. 30–37)

From the excavation report above the form and size of house-site A should be clear. It seems unlikely that Indians of the ethnic groups discussed on p. 131 above should have built a house of this type, as their dwelling was the conical wigwam. True, the Beothuk Indians, as we have pointed out, also had a kind of rectangular storehouse, which was raised on close-set piles, but buildings of this kind cannot have had many features in common with our house A, especially seeing that they served as storehouses, not as dwellings.

I would here also mention another group of Indians, one which was not considered in the previous discussion, as they lived in a different region. They are the Iroquois Indians, who lived by the shores of the Great Lakes, Lakes Huron, Erie and Ontario in the interior of Canada. According to William Taylor jr., they do not seem to have built any permanent or semi-permanent settlement further east than 7 miles east of Quebec City.[35] But we must nevertheless consider them in our discussion here, for their large, long houses had curving side walls, thus being narrower at the ends than at the middle. These houses were divided into several rooms aligned along the length of the house, with primitive hearths in the middle of the floor.

These features are common to the Iroquois houses, to our house A and to Norse houses of the Viking Age and the early Middle Ages, although they differ in details. – But here the similarity ends. We have seen that house A was built of turf, even though there was presumably a plentiful local supply of timber. This can only mean that the men who built this house were accustomed to building with turf, that they came from a country where there was not sufficient timber for building houses. Further – if we consider the objects most commonly found in an Iroquois house – stone implements, pot-sherds, fragments of clay pipes etc. – all doubt must vanish: house A cannot have been built by these people.[36]

The houses built by the Dorset Eskimoes constitute a far more varied material. This cultural complex, as mentioned above, includes a number of different dwellings, but in our opinion none of the types of dwelling usually ascribed to the Dorset Eskimoes – these are given on p. 135 above – resembles house A sufficiently closely to be adduced as material for comparison.

The house-sites excavated by Thomas Lee at Ungava Bay must, however, be considered in greater detail. Lee, on the one hand, maintains that these house-sites are of Norse origin; in his view they probably derive from Norse Greenlanders who emigrated from the West Settlement in Greenland during the thirteenth and fourteenth centuries A.D. or even earlier.[37] Dorset Eskimo specialists, on the other hand, assert that these are Dorset Eskimo sites, and that this type of house occurs sporadically in the arctic regions of Canada, as far west as Victoria Island.[38]

One thing, at least, is certain – regardless of whether they prove to be Norse or Eskimo, these house-sites must be studied in some detail, for all future searches for traces of Norse remains in North America must take this type of house into consideration. We shall here try to assess these houses, basing our conclusions on the available Norse material illustrating building customs and practice.

Thomas Lee presents the material so far excavated at Ungava Bay and he concludes by stating that several long houses of Norse type have come to light, as well as a number of tent rings and other features, some of them, according to him, of Norse origin, others deriving from Eskimoes.[39]

We shall here confine ourselves to discussing a couple of the long house-sites. From a Norse point of view, we would consider the so-called Pamiok Longhouse No. 1 the most interesting – this is a long, rectangular site, rounded at the external corners, and with a passage jutting out from one of the side walls, forming the entrance. The house is divided into three rooms by means of partition walls. There may have been a second entrance in one of the end walls.[40] According to Thomas Lee, the walls appeared as low banks of stone and turf prior to excavation; only a few stones appeared to be in situ. A remarkable feature of this house-site is the presence of two parallel rows of small slate chambers – these varied somewhat in size and depth, being on the average about 18 inches deep. The bottom as well as the sides consisted of slate slabs. Here Thomas Lee adduces as parallels the ember pits in the house-sites at Épaves Bay, as well as the two at the Norse farm Brattahlið, East Settlement No. 29 in Greenland (fig. 91).[41] The method of building is largely the same, and the use of slate for small, structural details is undoubtedly a Norse feature, but might perhaps just as well have been used by Eskimoes.

I am unable to agree with Lee when he interprets all these stone boxes at Pamiok I as ember pits: an ember pit is a small pit, with or without a stone lining, and it was used for storing the glowing embers at night, and the most common position is therefore close to the hearth. In the entire Norse material, we know of not a single example of more than one ember pit per room, though rooms with more than one hearth are not uncommon. But all these slate boxes can hardly have served as hearths either. At the Dorset Eskimo settlement site Port aux Choix a stone box which may have served as a kind of hearth was found,[42] and a few of the Icelandic farm ruins also have stone box hearths, but never more than one in each room.[43] We know of no instance where so many hearths of this type occur in one and the same room, nor of such hearths being so regularly arranged. Furthermore – the stone boxes at the Pamiok I site did not contain enough charcoal to render such a theory likely.

Their function must surely have been an entirely different one. The only possible explanation, to my mind, is that the double rows of stone boxes represent stone-lined post holes, a sound method in an area with deep ground frost. The Norse material includes examples of similar post holes, but these are constructed of larger stones. In fact, post holes were commonly lined with stones in the North. As examples we may cite a Migration Age house-site, site III near Brostorp on Öland in Sweden,[44] and Lundur site III in Borgarfjarðarsýsla in Iceland. Many others might also be mentioned.[45] The slate boxes at the Pamiok house-site No. 1 may thus have served as post holes. Moreover, some later, unlined post holes near some of these boxes may indicate that some of the posts were replaced. If this is correct, the roof must have rested on two rows of posts, and such a construction is fairly similar to that of a Norse house-site. But one must bear in mind that this is a primitive method of construction, found among various people at a primitive stage of culture. Moreover, some typically Norse details are lacking at Pamiok Longhouse No. I, first and foremost the typically Norse hearths inside the house. There are many pits outside the house, and some of them may possibly be hearths, but they give an extremely un-Norse impression.

Thomas Lee describes the different strata in this house-site, which show that the house saw several phases of habitation. In his opinion the first phase was Norse – he maintains that the house was built by Norse Greenlanders. Fig. 32 in the 1966 publication shows some stone implements found in the lowest stratum. [46]Lee would have these stone implements, which are of cherty quartz, to be Norse. They are quite unlike anything we normally connect with Norse culture, but Lee finds support for this assumption in Tryggvi Olesen's hypothesis to the effect that the Norsemen must have mixed with the Eskimoes, only to revert to a pure Stone Age way of life.[47] This hypothesis carries no weight as evidence. The Norse Greenlanders represented a culture in which the use and the production of iron had roots going back more than a thousand years; their agricultural tradition was still more ancient. Only absolute necessity would make these people renounce the advantages of their way of life. On the other hand, it is quite possible that the Norsemen should have reached the Ungava Bay district in the course of the centuries, and that they should have hunted and trapped here.

It seems reasonable to suppose that Norsemen who might have been forced

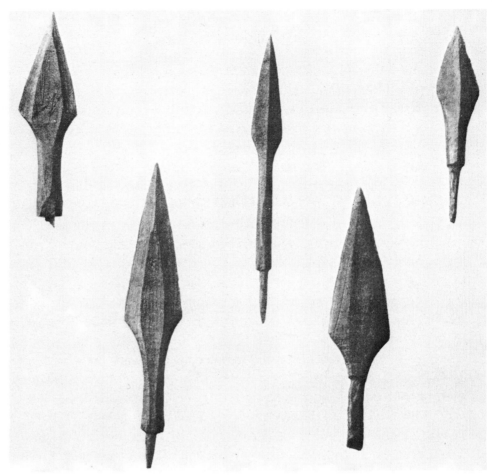

Fig. 78. Bone arrow-heads found in farm ruin at Narssaq, East Settlement, Greenland. After C.L. Vebæk.

to adopt a hunters' and trappers' culture in a country where iron was difficult to obtain, would have used bone and antler for making tools. Not only is the production of bone tools a natural development of their traditions in working wooden tools: it is also quite clear that the Norse Greenlanders actually employed bone and antler for making tools. This Birgitta L. Wallace also has pointed out.[48] Bone arrow-heads of Viking Age type have been found in ruins in Greenland (fig. 78).[49].

Pamiok Longhouse No. I would, in fact, have been of more interest to us if it had yielded no finds at all: Norse settlement sites frequently yield very few finds, even if they were inhabited for a long time. This is particularly true in countries where the natives may be assumed to have taken whatever they might have found, a circumstance of which Lee is also aware.

Another house-site of particular interest from our point of view is Cartier site, East Hall, the so-called church.[50] The latter name has been applied to this

144

site because of the apse-like, semi-circular extension at the eastern end wall.

A row of fairly large stones, double in places, marks the walls. The northern wall curves slightly. A small compartment at the southern corner may perhaps represent a small room, and the entrance is to the east of this. The south wall is straight, and at the centre there is a hearth with projecting sides built of stone. Lee is probably right in interpreting this as a hearth. In front of it, a semi-circular part of the floor is carefully paved. Two small post holes were found in the opening of the hearth.

Lee compares this hearth with one just inside the door of the hall at Brattahlíð in Greenland (fig. 88). [51] I cannot see this similarity – the "church" hearth looks entirely different to me. The Brattahlíð hearth is of a very special type, which is discussed below in connection with the large hearth of house B, and only a few specimens of which have been found in Greenland, all of them dating from the first years of settlement. Apart from that in the hall of Brattahlíð North Farm, there are two more in the so-called "Fireplace area" in the fields of Brattahlíð, out in the open. [52]

The method of construction underlying these Norse hearths has little in common with that of the hearth in the Cartier site. In fact, the only feature shared by the East Hall site hearth and the Greenland hearth in the hall at Brattahlíð is their position by a wall – and that cannot be taken as evidence of any kind of relationship.

If the semi-circular so-called apse projecting from the eastern wall really forms part of this house-site, it seems most natural to compare the East Hall site with certain houses of the medieval, Icelandic "Lundur type", especially with Lundur house-site I. [53] This is a long, rectangular building, with its entrance in one of the end walls. The walls are straight, or almost straight, and they consist of two rows of stones, which may have served as a foundation for turf walls. Part of the floor of the large room is carefully paved with stone. A circular room was built on to one of the end walls, its circular wall consisting of two rows of stones. They, too, may have served as a foundation for a turf wall.

Thus there are certain points of similarity between the East Hall site and Lundur I. The stone circle of the East Hall site is also double, "so far apart that a man may walk there", according to Lee, who assumes that this building had an external gallery, like those surrounding the Norwegian stave churches. He interprets the round annexe as an apse, and thus arrives at the conclusion that this house-site was a church-like structure – a meeting place or ceremonial house. [54] The eastern room is connected to the large main room by a door opening into a passage, which has another door on the southern side. A single row of stones separates a small room from the main building – the floor of this small room is paved with cobble-stones.

If we were to attempt an interpretation of this Ungava site in terms of Norse parallels, we would arrive at a double row of sleeper stones supporting a turf wall. This is most obvious in the so-called apse, where Lee has interpreted these stones as representing an external gallery. Voiomnaa considers the Icelandic Lundur house to have been a stable, the round annexe forming a storage lobby of some sort. A comparison with the Orcadian houses with round storage lobbies of this type shows that this is the most likely interpretation. The Lundur type is not one of the earliest types of building in Iceland.[55]

The East Hall site may be interpreted also in a different way: it may represent two buildings which happen to have been built adjacent to each other, one of them long and rectangular, the other circular. They both look more like dwellings rather than stable and storage lobby, like the Lundur 1 house. The round house-site is highly reminiscent of Eskimo houses with a platform paved with cobble-stones. All in all, the interpretation of this annexe involves so many problems that definite conclusions as to its origin seem impossible, especially for one who has not actually seen the site. Any argument in favour of a Norse origin of the house-sites at Ungava Bay must take into consideration the fact that they are typologically quite unrelated to building practice in Greenland, especially of the thirteenth-fourteenth centuries and thus cannot derive from thirteenth-fourteenth century Norse Greenlanders.[56] In fact, certain of their features are more reminiscent of the types of houses built in Iceland and in Scandinavia during the eleventh century, while the East Hall site recalls somewhat later building practice in Iceland – The West Settlement in Greenland has not as yet yielded any long houses of these types. If the settlement at Ungava Bay really had been inhabited by Norsemen from the West Settlement during the twelfth, thirteenth and fourteenth centuries – and this is what Lee claims, –[57] we should have expected to find passage houses or centralized houses of the Greenland type, instead of early Icelandic buildings.

Patrick Plumet has given an assessment of these house-sites but he does not express any conclusions as to the cultural complex they represent.[58]

Birgitta L. Wallace, who is familiar with the Norse material in question, agrees largely with the conclusions at which we have also arrived: these house-sites certainly resemble Norse houses of the Viking Age and the early Middle Ages on some points, and the choice of building materials – stone, turf and driftwood – which was dictated by local supplies and availability, adds to this appearance of similarity.[59] We must, however, bear in mind that this is a primitive type of construction employed in other cultures too. Moreover, had these houses been Norse, we should have expected to find a number of other details which are lacking here; above all, the finds which have come to light here do not support the theory which would ascribe these house-sites to Norsemen.

146

An iron axe-head, which was found in the vicinity of "Longhouse no. 2" on Pamiok Island, is thought to be of Norse origin. This assumption is based on metallurgic analyses carried out by Dr. K. Winterton of The Physical Metallurgy Division of Energy, Mines and Resources, Ottawa.[60] The method of manufacture – laminating – was undoubtedly employed in Europe during prehistory, but apart from this, the axe-head bears no similarity at all to Viking Age axes from the Norse cultural area.

In "Longhouse no. 2" an end section of bone facing for a bow was found, also assumed to be Norse, and a number of stone items of non-Dorset origin, which Lee thinks must be Norse.[61]

I am not able to take any definite standpoint as to the cultural affiliation of the bow facing, because of the absence of sufficiently close parallels in the Norse material. As concerns the stone items, they are definitely not Norse.

All in all, this material presents so many interesting problems that we can only hope that future excavations will serve to elucidate them further. I agree with Thomas Lee when he says that the Norse Greenlanders must be considered, but pressing the material beyond its capacity is detrimental to the objective assessment of it.

We have dwelt on the sites at Ungava Bay at such length because all future searches for Norse settlements in North America must take them into consideration. Space does not allow me to go into greater detail, in spite of the fact that many features from Ungava Bay would be very interesting to discuss. In our view, significant evidence would be gained if sites of this type were to be found in locations where the Norsemen are unlikely to have been, for instance on Victoria Island, as suggested by Taylor (see p. 142).

We pointed out in the excavation report above that not a single implement suggestive of whalers or fishermen of historic times was found in house A. No discussion of their dwellings is therefore required in the present context.

Eskimo implements were represented by a Dorset type arrowhead which lay on top of the turf of the western end wall. This is certainly unconnected with any habitation of this house. It was found at the outer edge of a thin burned layer which was observed immediately below the surface grass, on top of the cultural layer and above the remains of the western wall. It is just possible that it may have lain in the turf from which the walls were built.

In volume II of the present work, Helge Ingstad accounts for the Norse settlement in Greenland, which began shortly before the year A.D.1000 and lasted for almost five hundred years. The Norsemen who settled on the arctic island in the western sea came from Iceland. Danish archaeologists have found and excavated the ruins of a number of their farms, nineteen churches and two monasteries. The archaeological material from Norse Greenland is extensive – some of it has been published in comprehensive theses, some in shorter articles, and these will be referred to below.

If these Norsemen built the houses at Épaves Bay, it seems most likely that they would have employed the building methods to which they had been accustomed in their former home – at least in as far as the local supply of building materials permitted.

In a comprehensive work on the subject, Aage Roussell has listed and classified all the house-site material from the Norse settlements in Greenland which had been found by the time of publication.[62] Some more material has since come to light, but this does not seem to alter Roussell's results and conclusions to any major extent.

Roussell divides the material into three main groups:[63] the long house, assumed to be the typologically oldest, since it is represented among the earliest farm ruins in Iceland and also, as we shall see later, in Scandinavia. Its roots in the North go far back into the early Iron Age, – the periods preceding the Viking Age.

Roussell considers the passage house to be a natural development of the long house. While the long house might consist of one room, or of several rooms in a row, the passage house might also have several rooms in a row, but it also had rooms added at the rear. The rooms were connected by passages, one or more, as the case might be. Both these types, the long house and the passage house, were used exclusively as dwellings – there were separate buildings for animals, and also other out-houses.

The centralized house, still according to Roussell, is the most recent of the Greenland types. Here we have dwelling house and out-buildings built together into one complex, the rooms of which were connected by passages, so that one did not need to go out into the open in order to reach one of the out-buildings. Whether this theory is tenable, or whether the centralized house made its appearance earlier than has generally been assumed, as a result of the climate of Greenland – this Helge Ingstad maintains[64] – is hardly of consequence for our present purpose.

The closest parallell to our house A is the farm ruin at Narssaq in the East Settlement in Greenland (fig. 79). It was excavated by C.L. Vebæk in 1954, 1958 and 1962.[65] This is the earliest of all the securely dated farm ruins of Greenland. A runic inscription gives a Viking Age date (A.D. 800–1000). It has been read by Erik Moltke, who considers that certain features of the runes show that the man who cut them must have come from Norway or from one of the Norse colonies on Man, in Scotland or in Shetland.[66] The ruin at Narssaq represents a 36–37 metre long and 6.5–9 metre wide building (external measurements). It was divided into three rooms which lie in a row. The walls consisted of alternating horizontal layers of turf and stone. No post

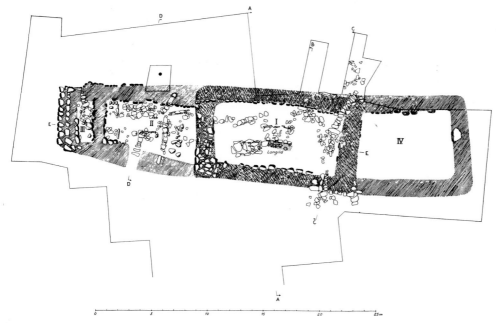

Fig. 79. House-site at Narssaq, East Settlement, Greenland. After C.L. Vebæk.

holes were found in the interior. One of the rooms – room I – must have been the first building on this site, and Vebæk points out that the interior of this room was identical with that of Viking Age halls. There was a long hearth in the middle of the floor, running along the longitudinal axis of the room, and a raised part at the eastern end, probably an earthen bench used for sitting or lying on. The external measurements of this first house (room I) were 14.5 metres in length and 6–9 metres in width – the equivalent internal dimensions were c. 11 metres and 5.5 metres. This was the house where the first settler lived. When the house became too small, additional rooms were built on. The ancient practice of extending a house in a lengthwise direction was followed, a practice known to have been employed in the North from the beginning of the Iron Age.

Our house A is also built of turf, but unlike the house at Narssaq, its walls contain practically no stone. Both houses have the same plan (pl. 3) – they were long, rectangular, with slightly curving walls, and both had several rooms lying in a row. As far as we can tell, the interior of house A room I was very similar to that of room I in the Narssaq house – a long hearth, running in a lengthwise direction, occupied the middle of the floor. There were probably earthen benches by the side walls on either side of the long hearth – the lack of a firm floor there indicates their presence. In Narssaq room I there was an earthen bench along one of the end walls, and the room was rather longer than the corresponding room of house A, measuring 11 metres as compared to the 5.5 metres of house A room I. Our house A had two rows of post holes arranged in pairs, while no traces of interior rows of posts were found in the Narssaq house. In spite of these differences, however, there can hardly be any doubt that these two rooms are of the same type – this is the so-called hall of the Viking Age, the *skáli* or sleeping-hall of Icelandic terminology – a type well known from a number of ruins of the Norse cultural complex.

The hearth of house A room I is of a simpler type than the corresponding Narssaq hearth; the latter consisted of one or more flat slabs of stone, while the hearth of house A room I was simply a long lengthwise depression in the floor. There was no stone setting or edging. Simple hearths of this kind were quite common during the earliest phase of settlement in Greenland; there was a similar hearth in the Festal Hall (room X) of the Hvalsey complex (ruin group No. 83) in the East Settlement in Greenland.[67] Another room of the same ruin complex, room IX – the oldest part of this farm ruin, according to Roussell – also had a plain hearth of this type, without any stone setting, but this one had an ember pit (fig. 81).[68]

Room IX at Hvalsey is not only the oldest part of this complex – Roussell maintains that it must be one of the very first houses built in Greenland. According to him, it was probably built by Þorkell, one of the first settlers.[69] Greenland has other houses of this ancient type, including that which is known as the Hall of Eirík the Red at Brattahlíð, ruin group No. 29, ruin 2, room I, in the East Settlement (fig. 80).[70] Poul Nørlund and Mårten Stenberger, who excavated this house-site in 1932, base their assumption that this was the hall of Eirík the Red on the extremely ancient impression conveyed by the plan of this house as well as on the form and position of its hearths.[71] However, remains of a still older building, apparently built mainly from turf resting on a row of sleeper stones, project under the hall, and thus it is clear that room I cannot have been the first building erected here.[72]

Among the most ancient buildings of Greenland Roussell also includes parts of Garðar, the episcopal seat of Greenland, ruin group No. 47, ruin 8, room I – V, in the East Settlement,[73] but the plan of this building would nevertheless seem to be somewhat more recent, for the fifth room was built on behind the others. Ruin groups No. 51 in the West Settlement and No. 20 in the East Settlement also belong to this latter type, for they also include a room built on behind the others.[74] Roussell sees this type as a natural development of the earliest long houses, and he considers it to be a transitional form from this ancient type of building to the more recent type, the passage house.[75]

It seems certain that the farm at Narssaq, room I of the Brattahlíð complex and room IX of the Hvalsey complex should all be included among the earliest buildings found in Greenland to date. We saw above that this type may be traced back to the Viking Age buildings of Iceland and Scandinavia.

150

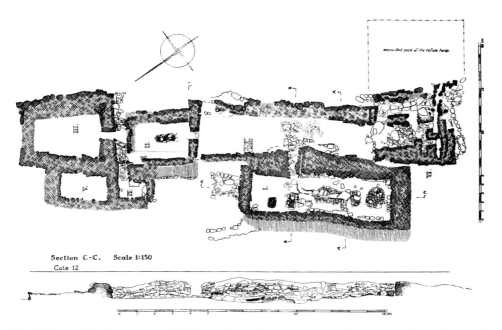

Section C-C.   Scale 1:150
    Cote 12

Fig. 80. Plan of dwelling at Brattahlið North Farm, East Settlement, Greenland. After P. Nørlund and M. Stenberger.

Fig. 81. The old hall, Hvalsey, East Settlement No. 83, 6, IX, looking west. On the right, the gravel bench along the rear wall, in the middle, the long fire trench with ember box, on the left, southern row of post-holes. After Aa. Roussell.

151

We were not able to establish whether room I is the earliest, original part of house A, and whether the other rooms were added later. Such a hypothesis might perhaps be justified by the fact that the partition walls separating this room from the adjacent rooms are as thick as the outer walls and of the same material – this would hardly have been necessary if all the rooms were built at the same time. We shall return to this point later.

The remaining rooms of house A must also be considered. Room II lies west of room I, and there is a door in the partition wall between them. This wall, as we have already pointed out, was of turf like the external walls, and it was as thick as these. There was a hearth in the middle of the floor of room II, of the same simple type as that of room I, and with parallels in the Greenland farm ruins. Further – above this hearth lay a heap of brittle-burned stones, ashes and clay, some of it burned red. Jan Petersen discusses similar heaps which he found when excavating Iron Age house-sites in Rogaland in Norway.[76] The heap or mound in room II was obviously a result of stone and clay repeatedly having been poured on to the hearth, for the clay is unburned below and burned red on top. This heap came to light at an early stage of the excavation.

There was a separate entrance in the south wall, leading to rooms III and IV, and there does not seem to have been any door connecting them with the two western rooms of the house.

In each of these two rooms we found a large cooking pit in the north-eastern corner (fig. 7), and roughly in the middle of each room there was a hearth of the same, simple type as those in rooms I and II. Cooking pits, as we pointed out above, are among the most common types of hearth found in Greenland. This particular type is very common in many primitive cultures but, as Roussell points out, its period of use has hardly been as long anywhere as in the Norse settlements in Greenland, where it continued in use as long as there were Norsemen living there.[77]

A small pit without stone lining found in room III was full of clean pieces of charcoal – this was probably an ember pit. Ember pits of this kind were very common in the Norse cultural complex, and they will be discussed in more detail below, in connection with house B.

Archaeological excavations in Iceland have yielded valuable material from farms of the time of settlement and the Middle Ages. Several different types have been classified, and they enable us to trace the development from the earliest building, the hall consisting of one room only, to the compound farm complexes of the Middle Ages.

In the present context we are concerned with the earliest type, the one-roomed hall or *skáli*. Several such buildings have been found; as examples we may cite one at Snjáleifartóttir in Þjórsárdalur (fig. 83) and one at Isleifsstaðir

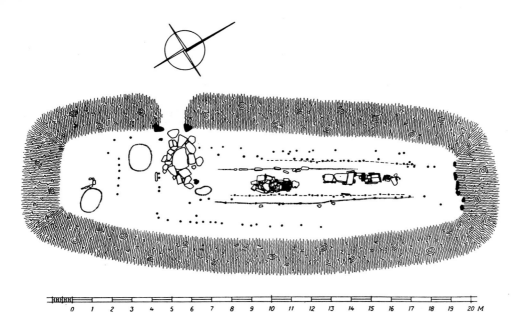

Fig.82. Ísleifsstaðir, level 2. The plan also shows the hearth of level 3 (the northernmost hearth).
After M. Stenberger.

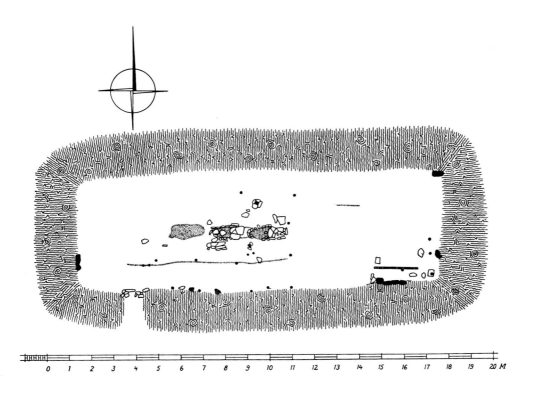

Fig. 83. The hall under Snjáleifartóttir, Iceland. After M. Stenberger.

153

in Borgarfjarðarsýsla (fig. 82), both excavated by Mårten Stenberger in 1939.[78] They have been dated to the first years of settlement, or to the years immediately afterwards.[79] Other examples are a house-site on Papey, excavated by Kristján Eldjárn in 1971,[80] and the oldest hall at Hvítárholt in Árnessýsla, which Þór Magnússon excavated during the years 1962–1967.[81] It is characteristic of all these halls or *skálar* that their side walls curve, and that the roof is normally carried by double rows of posts standing in the middle of the floor. But other roof constructions must also have been employed, especially in Greenland where we have examples of halls of this type without posts or traces of posts to support the roof, possibly due to the lack of large timbers, such as the farm ruin at Narssaq and the hall at Brattahlið.[82]

The interior of these buildings was similar throughout the entire Norse cultural sphere. There was a long hearth running along the middle of the floor; the most common form consisted of a flat slab of stone edged with smaller stones standing on end, but there are also instances of such hearths without any stones – they simply take the form of a long, shallow depression in the floor. There were usually low earthen benches along the walls. The form and position of the hearths are important criteria for this type of building, and they will be discussed in greater detail in connection with the other house-sites.

This type of house must go back to the earliest days of settlement in Iceland, around the year A.D.900. It was intended as a dwelling house for people – the animals were housed in separate out-buildings. Farms from this early phase also included a number of other buildings. We have a good example of such a farm in Hvítárholt, Árnessýsla in Iceland, which was mentioned above. This farm consisted of ten buildings, including three *skálar* or sleeping halls, the earliest of which is of the type we are considering here. It lay under one of the other buildings. There was also a barn, a cow-shed, and no fewer than five sunken-floored huts. These were the first sunken-floored huts found of the earliest phase in Iceland, and this fact adds to the particularly great interest of this excavation.[83]

These so-called halls or *skálar* were at times divided into several rooms by means of light partitions walls; if and when they became too small, new rooms were added at the end walls. The house at Narssaq and our house A are examples of long houses extended in this way.

In Norway, house-sites from the past have been investigated since the 1920ies, the excavations varying somewhat in scope; the archaeological material resulting from these investigations has grown to some considerable volume, so that we are now familiar with several different types of house-site, covering the period from the early Iron Age to the Middle Ages.

We cannot list each and every one of these excavations – such a list would

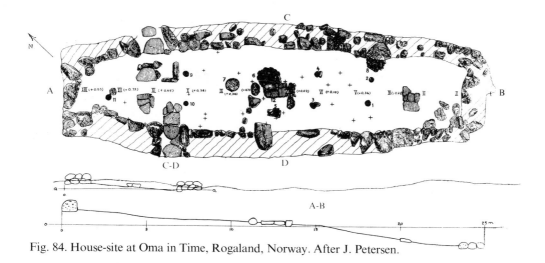

Fig. 84. House-site at Oma in Time, Rogaland, Norway. After J. Petersen.

be outside the scope of the present work, and it would also be far too space-consuming. They will be referred to below in as far as they have any bearing on our problem.

The entire material spans a very long period of time – probably from the Celtic Iron Age until some time during the Middle Ages. Unfortunately, the Viking Age is less well represented than the other periods, probably because later farms were built on the ancient sites, concealing or destroying them completely. Some good and well-preserved house-sites from this period (A.D. 800–1000) remain, however, and these we shall examine in some detail.

In the present context, we are particularly interested in the so-called long house with curving walls. The house-site at Oma in Time, Rogaland (fig. 84), is an excellent example of this type. Its internal length is 21 metres, the width varies from 5 metres at the centre to 3–4 metres at the gable ends, the difference in width being due to the slight curvature of the walls.[84]

The entrance of this house was near one of the corners of a side wall; this is the position we noted in the halls of Iceland also.

The main hearth runs along the middle of the floor. The house seems to have consisted of one room only. There was a double row of posts along the middle of the room – this type of construction was apparently used also in house A as well as in Icelandic buildings of this type. A date during the Viking Age or the early Middle Ages seems indicated.

This building does not differ from the earliest Icelandic houses in any way – it has the same plan, the same interior and the same curving walls.

The house-site at Rapstad, Årstad in the parish of Egersund also belongs to this type.[85] It has – although with certain reservations – been dated to the Viking Age. This house has one room only, 13.5 metres long and rather more than 4 metres wide at the widest point, these being internal measurements. The

155

entrance of this house was again in one of the side walls. Several hearths were found in the room, the main hearth being aligned with the longitudinal axis of the house, and lying a little way east of the centre.

The house-site at Grødheim in Time, Rogaland, probably dates from the Viking Age as well.[86] Again we have a house with only one room, this one 8.8 metres long and 3.3 metres wide. The walls were straight, the corners slightly rounded. The hearth lay a little to the south-east of the centre, and there was a small cooking pit roughly in the middle of the floor. Six post holes were found around the hearth. A paved entrance near one of the corners of a side wall led into the room.

Finally we would mention a house-site which probably dates from the Viking Age, although it may be somewhat older; this is situated at Fosse in Time.[87] It was in a particularly good state of preservation, and consisted of only one room, 16.8 metres long and 5 metres wide. It was almost rectangular, and the corners were straight. There was an entrance near the south-western corner of the western side wall, and another near the north-eastern corner of the eastern side wall. The room was divided into three aisles by parallel rows of posts standing along the middle of the floor. At the centre of the room, a paved hearth edged with small slabs of stone standing on end was found; a round cooking pit lay in line with this. The paved hearth was 1.75 metres long and 0.85 metres wide, and it lay 0.13 metres above the firm gravel ground. The cooking pit, built from pebbles, was 0.85 metres $\times$ 0.75 metres, and it lay roughly level with the gravel ground. The total length of the combined hearth/cooking pit was 2.6 metres. Immediately to the north of the paved hearth a smaller, round slab of stone was found, propped up in a horizontal position by smaller stones. It measured 25 cm in diameter and was 3 cm thick.

The Oma house-site and that at Fosse lie near each other, on either side of a river. Fosse may be the older of these buildings, but they resemble each other so closely in form and interior, and especially in the form and position of the hearth that the difference in age can hardly be great. In any case – these house-sites are in many respects more similar to the Icelandic sites of this type than any others. The form and construction of their hearths, where the cooking pit lies in line with the paved long hearth, are very similar to those at, for instance, Ísleifsstaðir in Borgarfjarðarsýsla in Iceland.[88] It is interesting to note in this connection that Rogaland is one of the districts from which particularly many emigrants are said to have left for Iceland.[89]

Although the types of house listed above differ from one another in their construction and material, there can be no doubt that they all belong to the same fundamental type.

Finally we have the house-site at Hovden, Møsstrand in Telemark, which Irmelin Martens excavated in 1962–63.[90] It is rather more than 30 metres long, and its width varies from 6 to 7 metres. This house, which lies in an east-west direction, was probably divided into seven rooms lying in a row. They are separated by low stone foundation walls, which presumably carried ground sills at one time. This house-site had hearths in the middle of the floor and also corner hearths. – Hovden has been dated to the twelfth-thirteenth century. We shall not discuss this house-site in detail – in the present context we are interested in the actual form of the house, in the fact that the rooms lie in a row, like those of house A and of the Narssaq house. It seems that in Norway people continued to build in this way; in Iceland and Greenland, on the other hand, more practical types were soon evolved, and new rooms were added to the rear wall of the long house. Anders Hagen states that it is likely that the houses were added to in the way employed in Iceland and Greenland also in parts of Norway, pointing to the house-sites Gilberg, Nygård and Skattum in Oppland excavated by Sigurd Grieg.[91] Bjørn Myhre draws attention to three Rogaland settlements included in A. Myhre's publication of material from Rogaland: Vasshodl at Håland in Varhaug, Sande-Skadberg in Sola, and Torland in Nærbø.[92] Their form is very reminiscent of that of Icelandic farms. This matter will be discussed below in connection with house-site D. The Narssaq house and our house A testify to the ancient Scandinavian method of building having been conveyed to Greenland, and thence to America.

The Norsemen took this method of building with them also to the islands of the western sea – Orkney and Shetland. A number of Norse house-sites have been found on these islands.[93] First and foremost we must consider the Viking Age farm at Jarlshof in Shetland, excavated by J.R.C. Hamilton. The investigations carried out here have revealed the various stages of development of the long house from the earliest phase, which Hamilton dates to A.D. 800–850, onwards. Naturally, the further development of the long house took a somewhat different form here than in the other northern countries, as appeared from the phases resulting from the excavation. The first phase covers the Norse hall or long house, surrounded by out-buildings like the farm at Hvítárholt in Iceland, for instance. The last phase but one (phase VI) shows a building which combines the dwelling house with the cow-shed, the practice we know from the early Iron Age in Scandinavia. This is an interesting development, which may be due to Anglo-Saxon influence, for this type of farm was found over large parts of the Germanic region during the early Iron Age, and it seems likely that it was introduced into the British Isles by the Anglo-Saxons. But recent excavations show that this type of farm was also introduced to the islands of the western sea by the Scandinavian Vikings: Alan Small has excavated a Norse house-site of this ancient type, where people and animals lived under the same roof, at Underhoull on Unst, the northernmost inhabited island of Shetland.[94] His excavation revealed the interesting fact that the development undergone by this house is diametrically opposed to that observed at the Viking farm at Jarlshof – at Underhoull the animals were moved out of the main building and into a separate cow-shed after some time, and the long house was rebuilt into a dwelling house for the people of the farm.

It appears from these two excavations, Jarlshof and Underhoull, that the Vikings brought two different types of farm-house to the islands of the western sea; in this connection it is of interest to note that Jan Petersen inferred from his rich house-site material from Rogaland that the early Iron Age type of farm, where people and animals lived under the same roof, continued in use in Rogaland into the Viking Age and the Middle Ages, in fact into modern times in places.[95]

At how early a date did the Vikings introduce this early Iron Age type of farm to the islands of the western sea? We cannot as yet be certain of the answer to this question, but it is to be hoped that future excavations will throw more light on to this interesting problem. A.W. Brøgger suggested that the latter half of the eighth century might have seen an emigration from the deserted farms of Rogaland to these islands and to Scotland.[96] But Jan Petersen demonstrates that many of these farms were deserted as early as at the end of the sixth century, and he therefore feels that if Brøgger's theory is correct, such emigration must have taken place towards the end of the Migration Age. He finds evidence in support of this assumption in the fact that Orkney and Shetland have many place names ending in -land, and his own excavation of house-sites in Rogaland show that such place names should be dated to the end of the late Roman Iron Age/Migration Age (A.D. 400 – 600).[97]

In Denmark, the large long houses at Trelleborg, Fyrkat and Aggersborg are examples of the finest, and possibly also the most nearly original form of long house.[98] These houses cannot be directly compared with Iceland's and Greenland's simple long houses of stone and turf, but we are surely justified in classifying them within the same main type, in spite of the great difference of construction.

As we have already stated, it is our view that one particular type must have been aimed at, but that the variations in construction found in these houses – many of them considerable – are first and foremost due to the material employed in each case.

The house with curving walls is not unknown in the North during the early Iron Age; but the special type which we are here considering seems to have appeared suddenly in Scandinavia during the early Viking Age, and in the course of a few centuries it spread all over the entire Norse region, to the farthest outposts. It seems likely that the type as such is the result of impulses received from northern Germany, perhaps already during the eighth century.

158

At Warendorf in Westphalia, an entire complex of farms has recently been excavated, and here the long house, almost in the form in which it appeared in Denmark during the Viking Age, was fully developed by the middle of the eighth century.[99] The excavations brought to light a group of four or five farms, lying close together. Each farm consisted of a large dwelling house and fourteen or fifteen out-houses. As regards the walls of the dwelling house, Winkelmann asserts that the transition from straight to curving walls seems to have taken place during the time of habitation at Warendorf, between the latter half of the seventh century and the year A.D.800.[100]

This farming settlement is of great interest not only because it illustrates the development of the long house from straight to curving side walls, but also because it includes a farm of the fully developed Norse Viking Age type: one or more large dwelling houses surrounded by a number of out-buildings, each of which served one of the many requirements of the farm. Winklemann points out that farms of this kind may be regarded as being common Germanic, supporting this view with evidence provided by other excavations in southern, central and north-western Europe, and with the testimony of literary sources dealing with Germanic law. The settlement at Warendorf is assumed to represent a Saxon migration which penetrated southwards shortly before the year A.D.700, and which is supported by literary sources.[101]

This brief survey of the development of the long house in the western Norse cultural region is merely intended to provide a background for the appearance of this type of house in Newfoundland – no exhaustive survey of the entire Norse material is intended.

As the Norse material includes so many close parallels for our house A, there can hardly be any doubt as to the Norse origin of this house. It is of the so-called long house type, which was in use in the Norse cultural region around the year A.D.1000.

The most important of the finds, a ring-headed bronze pin (fig. 5), is indisputably of Norse-Celtic origin. It is 10 cm long, the upper part of the shank is round in section, somewhat flattened near the head. Below mid-point, the section is square. The head is not looped over, the ring being passed through a hole drilled into the flattened end of the shank. There was no ornamentation on either shank or head.

Ring-headed pins are quite common in Viking Age Norway. Jan Petersen divided the material into three groups[102]: group a) consists of pins with rings circular in section, whose shanks are looped over. Pins of group b) have rings with a square section, while in pins of group c) the upper part of the shank is flattened and has a drilled hole through which a thin ring is passed. Below the flattened head, the shank widens into a cube or polyhedron, often with ornamentation formed by beaten small circles or dots. Our ring-headed pin

159

belongs to this third group, although it lacks the polyhedric widening and ornaments. According to Jan Petersen, twenty specimens of this type have been found in securely attested women's graves, while six were found in men's graves – from this he concludes that they were most commonly used by women. But we cannot base any definite conclusions on these circumstances of find.

There is a marked concentration of these simple ring-headed pins in Vestfold, and it would be reasonable to connect this concentration with the market-centre Kaupang at Tjølling. The Kaupang excavations have yielded several ring-headed pins of group c) as well as some of the more elaborate types.*

Two ring-headed pins from Kvassheim, Ogna, Rogaland, and one from Rivjaland, Årdal, Rogaland, are also of this simple type, although the shank of the latter is ornamented with raised and punched circles.[103]

Seven or eight ring-headed pins of this simple type, with a hole for the ring in the flattened shank, have been found in Iceland. A pin found in a man's grave at Tindar is closest in type to our specimen.[104] Two ring-headed pins, Þjms. 808 from Kálfborgará and Þjms. 7347 from Hrísar (fig. 85), as well as one found at Stöng in Þjórsárdalur also belong to this group.[105]

The remaining ring-headed pins found in Iceland are more elaborately made; many of them have a pronounced polyhedric head, as a rule ornamented with circles and dots.[106] The ring and the shank are also frequently ornamented. These pins are very close in type to some ring-headed pins in the Limerick City Museum in Ireland.[107]

Thomas Fanning has drawn our attention to the fact that ring-headed pins of group c) have been found in Ireland, Scotland, on the Hebrides, the Isle of Man, and in Iceland, whereas they are not particularly common in Norway. A close parallel to the ring-headed pin from house A came to light during the excavations under the High Street in Dublin (Reg. No. 432039).**

It thus appears that the ring-headed pin from house A represents a fairly common Norse/Celtic type of adornment. Charlotte Blindheim considers it likely that even these plain ring-headed pins were imported from Ireland, as they are as a rule found together with other imported objects.*** The distribution of these pins would also seem to indicate an Irish origin, for they are particularly common in coastal areas.[108] But we must not disregard the possibility of their being locally-made copies of Irish originals.

It should be evident from the above survey that the ring-headed pin, the type of the house itself, the form and position of the hearths and the

* Information personally supplied by Charlotte Blindheim.

** Information personally supplied by Thomas Fanning.

*** Information personally supplied by Charlotte Blindheim.

160

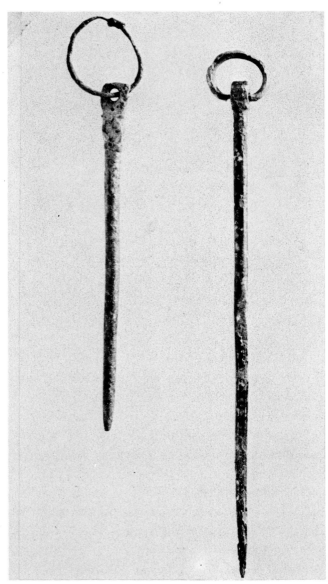

Fig. 85. Ring-headed pins of
bronze from Kálfborgará and
Hrísar. Þjms. 808 and 7347.
Photo G. Gestsson.

radio-carbon dates all add support to the theory of the Norse origin of
house A.

It is difficult to date the house precisely on the basis of the ring-headed pin:
even though this form of adornment appears first and foremost during the
ninth and tenth centuries A.D.,[109] we cannot know how long the type
remained in use in distant regions such as Iceland and Greenland.

House A also yielded four more or less fragmentary iron rivets and thirteen

161

Fig. 86. Iron nails from the house-sites.

fragments of iron which probably derive from rivets. In most cases the riveting plate and a small part of the shank are preserved; although they are highly corroded, it is still possible to determine them as clinching rivets with a rectangular riveting plate. No double rivets were found, as every specimen was broken immediately below the plate. As our type examples we have chosen some found at the excavations at Helgö in Lake Mälaren, Sweden.[110] But the type occurs throughout the Norse cultural region (fig. 86).

Most of the rivets and iron fragments were found in or near a door opening, and therefore it seems likely that they should have been used for riveting wooden doors.

House A also yielded two small fragments of red jasper. One of these, LaM 143, lay at the centre of the western hearth of room III, at floor level. Its maximum length is 1.2 cm. The other piece, LaM 151, lay 80 cm south-west of the large cooking pit of room III, at 2 cm above floor level.

Several other chippings of jasper were found in or near the hearths of some of the other houses, as we shall see below. It therefore seems likely that jasper was used for striking fire.

A small piece of flint (LaM 142) was also found in this hearth, lying at floor level.

In Iceland, various kinds of hard stone, such as jasper, flint and obsidian, were commonly used for striking fire. Fragments of jasper and obsidian were found when the farm Skjeljastaðir in Þjórsárdalur was excavated.[111] At Fiskefjorden in Greenland, there was a small piece of jasper among the finds,

162

pierced with a hole and intended to be carried on the person. This stone has been interpreted as a "whetstone or hone",[112] but it does not seem unreasonable to suppose that it was, in fact, used for striking fire. If this interpretation is correct, the small "eye" offers an interesting piece of information, for it shows that fire-stones were also carried hanging, as accessories, as it were. As fire-stones were vital equipment, one would surely take some along when setting out for a new country, so that fires might be lit immediately on disembarkation. How was one to know whether such stones existed in the new country?

Another piece of red jasper, this one from house F (LaM 50), has been analysed together with a piece of Icelandic jasper. We quote a letter from Professor T.F.W. Barth: ". . . there are typical traces of copper and nickel. Both samples contained approximately 0.1% of copper and 0.05% of nickel. This suggests, but is no proof, that the samples come from one geological region. Had there been a great difference in their content of trace elements, one could have deduced with a reasonable degree of certainty that they could not both have come from Iceland. Of course jasper from Newfoundland could have the same content of trace elements as jasper from Iceland, but as the geological formations in these two regions are so different, this seems highly unlikely."[113] (App. IV)

Another type of stone which was found in house A was probably also used for striking fire. LaM 146 is a flat piece of iron pyrites, found at floor level in room II, at the outer edge of the hard-trodden floor around the hearth. We shall see below that several of the other houses also yielded iron pyrites (see A.M. Rosenqvist and K. Henningsmoen below).

It seems likely that a special bag, which formed part of the daily dress, was used for carrying iron pyrites and flint or jasper.

A small fragment of bone, LaM 182, which derives from the domestic pig (Sus scrofa), was also found in the house.

There were also a few lumps of slag in and outside house A.

LaM 140 is a flint arrow-head (fig. 8), 4.6 cm long and 2.3 cm wide at the base, and it is furnished with large notches for attachment. This is a Dorset arrow-head of the same type as Elmer Harp jr. 1964, Pl. III, No. 1.[114] It was found just below the surface grass, on top of the western end wall of room II. Near the arrow-head there was a fire-patch, also right up under the grass, on top of the heap of brittle-burned stones which constituted the hearth of room II. This fire-patch gave the impression of being quite unconnected with the hearth below; it seemed, in fact, to have been made after the house had collapsed completely. It is tempting to connect the arrow-head with this fire-patch, but we must also take into consideration the possibility that it may have lain in the turf used for the top layer of the wall. The arrow-head lay a

163

mere 4.5 cm below the surface grass. We shall return to this problem later in connection with other Stone Age items found on the terrace (p. 228).

Finally we must note that the small, charred fragment of a pig's bone (Sus scrofa) found in house A proves that the people who lived in the house must have had domestic animals: the inhabitants can therefore have been neither Indians nor Eskimoes.

The finds from house A lend additional support to the conclusion inferred above from the actual house – this is a Norse house. The ring-headed pin, as we saw there, does not enable us to date the house securely, but its evidence, combined with that of the radio-carbon dates, the type of the house and the form and position of the hearths, gives us good reason to stipulate a comparatively early date. Early in the first half of the eleventh century seems most likely.

The earliest radio-carbon date derives from charcoal; it is considerably earlier than one of those derived from the turf of the walls, and a number of circumstances which might lead to errors must be taken into consideration. For an account of the various radio-carbon dates from the house-sites I refer to Reidar Nydal's report below and to Kari Henningsmoen's assessment of the radio-carbon datings of turf from the walls, p. 335 below.

We have not attempted to discuss the construction of the house in any detail, concentrating instead on the plan of the house, and on details such as the form of the hearths and their position in the rooms. It is very unfortunate that so relatively few structural features illustrating the construction in more detail came to light as a result of the excavation. This is largely due to the brook, which floods its banks every year, and which has repeatedly washed over the house-site. But some information, at least, we do have: we know that the foundation walls of the house were of turf, but we cannot tell how tall these turf walls were, whether they extended all the way up to the eaves or not. As there are no traces of any wooden walls, it seems most likely that no material other than turf was used. Kari Henningsmoen has examined samples of the turf layers, and in one single sample she found at least twenty layers of turf, highly compressed and lying on top of one another. If we assume that each layer was about 5 cm thick – this is somewhat less than the normal thickness of the surface turf here – twenty layers would result in a height of 1.00 m. We cannot today establish whether this was the original height of the walls, or whether there were other layers of turf above, washed away by the brook over the years. The average thickness of the walls, external as well as partition walls, was 1.5–2 metres. The south wall is somewhat thicker than the others, probably as a result of the house having collapsed in this direction.

Where any details could be discerned, the walls proved to consist of horizontal layers of turf, laid on top of one another. This is the technique known as the *strengur* technique in Icelandic terminology: the firmest grass-turf available is cut into strips, c. 5 cm thick, 20–25 cm wide and 70–130 cm long.[115] This technique was employed especially in houses which were to be particularly well-built, such as dwelling houses. As it requires a large area of turf per house, the people were compelled to find other ways of using turf for building. The *strengur* technique would seem to be the most ancient of the building methods employing turf. One of the oldest buildings in Greenland, for instance, Þjóhildr's church, was built by this method.[116] Among the late medieval buildings of Greenland, several ruins built in the so-called *klömbruhnaus* technique have been excavated.[117] By this method, the turf was as a rule cut in rhomboids measuring 25 cm × 30 cm × 10–20 cm. As the turfs were so much thicker, this method meant a real saving of material.[118]

In Iceland, turf walls were always built on top of a row of sleeper stones or on a low stone wall; this was not the case in our house A. During the earliest period in Greenland, stone was also used under and between the turfs, but turf walls without sleeper stones may also have been used, for instance in Þjódhildr's church. In south-western Norway, a kind of frame-wall technique was employed, utilizing stone and earth or turf.[119] In more northerly parts of Norway, turf seems to have been the most common building material of prehistoric times. The houses of the so-called ring-formed farms of northern Norway were constructed of turf only, without any sleeper stones below.[120]

Thus we see that turf walls might be built with or without sleeper stones – which of these two methods was chosen must presumably have depended on the local supply of stone and the local traditions. There were very few stones below and in the walls of the houses at Épaves Bay, and this is probably due to the fact that there is practically no stone suitable for building here. Down by the beach, there is some stone, but none really suitable for building.

Whether the end walls of house A were built of turf all the way up to and including the gables, it is impossible to say. If they consisted entirely of turf, there would presumably have been more turf here than along the side walls, but this is not the case. It therefore seems likely that the house had a hip roof.

A double row of post holes along the middle of the floor in a lengthwise direction indicates that the roof rested on posts. This was the building method normally employed in early Icelandic houses of this type, while the Greenland houses frequently lack traces of any posts.

These are the only certain facts at our disposal concerning the construction of the roof. A curved roof and stepped gables seem indicated by the curving side walls.

Roar Tollnes has devoted special attention to the construction of these houses, basing his arguments on the interesting excavations of house-sites at Kaupang in Tjølling, Norway, where a number of wooden remains were preserved.[121] Unfortunately neither the Kaupang houses nor the Danish houses of the Trelleborg type provide true parallels with which to compare

165

Fig. 87. Interior of a *gamme* from Trollbukt, Lebesby, Finnmark. Showing framework of birch with twigs, birch bark, and a thick layer of turf. After H. Vreim.

our house A, which apparently had a different and considerably simpler form of construction. This is an outcome of the local supply of materials – turf, driftwood and bent, crooked fir-trees. It seems reasonable to suppose that some of the primitive out-houses which still exist in some places in the countryside of Norway and Iceland provide a better illustration of the appearance of house A, and it may perhaps have been rather similar to the simple huts which the Fjord Lapps built in Finnmark, Norway, until recent years. They were built of bent trees, and covered with twigs, brushwood, bark and a thick layer of turf.[122] This ancient type of building remained in use among these Lapps until very recently (fig. 87).

House A lay low in the landscape, almost merging into the terrace surrounding it. A modest turf house, not unlike a bowl turned upside down in appearance, may perhaps have inspired the Icelandic term for these ancient houses, *skáli,* as suggested by Valtýr Gudmundsson.[123]

In the countryside of Iceland we also find certain simple types of building whose construction adds to our understanding of that of house A. The most important literature on this subject is: Valtýr Guðmundsson "Privatboligen på Island i Sagatiden", various articles on the subject by K. Eldjárn in Kulturhistorisk leksikon for Nordisk middelalder, *Island*, Albert Nilsson "Den sentida bebyggelsen på Islands landsbygd", "Forntida Gårdar i Island" 1943, Arnheirður Sigurðardóttir "Híbýlahættir á miðöldum" 1966, and

166

Fig. 88. The large hearth opposite the doorway in room I, Brattahlið North Farm, East Settlement, Greenland. After P. Nørlund and M. Stenberger.

Hórður Ágústsson "Islandsk byggeskik i fortiden" 1968. We cannot here discuss the various methods of construction in detail, and would instead refer the interested reader to these works.

Interpretation of house-site B (pp. 38–42)

In the interior of this house-site, we found a row of hearths, some of them very well constructed. One of these hearths lies at the middle of the western end wall (fig. 12). At the bottom of it there was a large, cracked slab of stone, bounded in the east by small, upright stones. At the front there was a shallow depression bounded by a low torus of hard-burned sand or clay. This hearth veers towards the door, probably in order to make the fire draw better.

The closest parallel for this hearth is that in the hall (room I) at Brattahlið North Farm, No. 29, ruin 2, in the East Settlement in Greenland (fig. 88). This also lies by a wall, immediately opposite the door; and these two hearths were made in the same way – a large stone slab at the bottom, and smaller, upright stones marking the edges. Furthermore, both are bounded by a shallow depression in front.

Hearths of this type are not common in Greenland, and it almost looks as though they belong to the years immediately after the Norsemen settled there.

Nørlund and Stenberger conclude from their excavations of the farm complexes at Brattahlið that the hearths became smaller and fewer as time went on; this, they consider, is due to a lack of fuel, which forced the people to save wood, and perhaps to use seal blubber and turf as fuel instead of wood.[124]

Roussell has also taken a particular interest in the Greenland hearths, and he states that the fine, stone-edged hearths of the type we are here discussing are rare in Greenland.[125] As an example he mentions the long hearth in the farm ruin Ánávik in the West Settlement.[126] Others have been found in the outfield of the Brattahlið farm, in the so-called "Fireplace area".[127] These are not placed up against a wall – they lie out in the open, but apart from this difference, their construction is the same as that of the hearths we are discussing here: that of our house B, and that in the hall at Brattahlið. Poul Nørlund and Mårten Stenberger have found no remains of any building above the hearths of the so-called "Fireplace area", but there were sites of sheds without hearths in the immediate vicinity. The excavators have interpreted this area as the site of the first Thing in Greenland – it lay on Eirík the Red's property, and it seems natural to think of him as the chieftain of this pioneer society.[128] Another interpretation may also be possible: these sheds combined with hearths in the open air may represent the provisional camp where Eirík the Red and his people lived while they were building the farm. They must have lived somewhere, and there must surely have been quite a large number of people requiring food and shelter as soon as they had disembarked.

Even though Greenland has few hearths of this type, Iceland has yielded a considerable number. Many stone-edged hearths have been found here, many of them combined with ember pits and cooking-pits. As examples we would mention the hearths at Ísleifsstaðir levels 2 and 3 (figs. 89–90), and those at Snjáleifartóttir (fig. 83).[129] Two similar hearths were also found in one of the dwelling houses at the farm Hvítárholt in Árnessýsla,[130] which was probably built when Iceland was settled. These hearths lie in houses which were presumably built during the time immediately following the settlement of Iceland, c. A.D. 900.

The hearth of house-site B is of the same type as the above, except in that it lies up against a wall. Of our comparative material, that which it resembles most closely is, as pointed out above, the large hearth in the Hall at Brattahlið, in the East Settlement in Greenland. Here the position in the room and the construction of the hearth are identical with those of our hearth in house-site B, except that larger stones were used at Brattahlið.

The cooking pit in the floor (fig. 13), which lies east of the hearth, was probably lined with slate slabs originally. Some of these lay in situ when the cooking pit was excavated, while the rest were found as innumerable fragments among the fill at the bottom of the pit. We have a close parallel to this

168

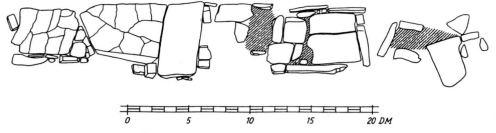

Fig. 89. Hearth at level 3, Ísleifsstaðir, Borgarfjarðarsýsla, Iceland. After M. Stenberger.

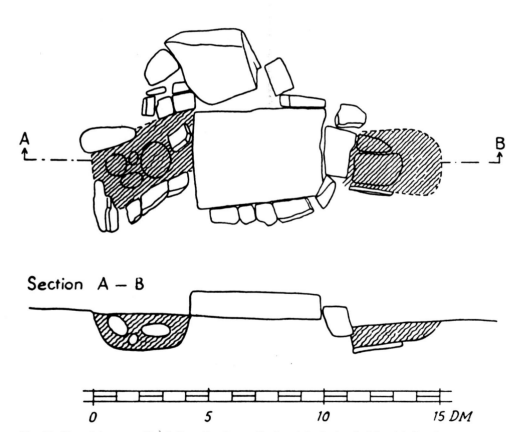

Section A — B

Fig. 90. Hearth in room V, Ísleifsstaðir, Borgarfjarðarsýsla, Iceland. After M. Stenberger.

169

Fig. 91. Ember pit in "The Fireplace Area" close to the farm ruins "Brattahlið North Farm", East Settlement, Greenland. After P. Nørlund and M. Stenberger.

cooking pit in one which lay in the south-eastern corner of room IX in the Hvalsey complex, East Settlement No. 83, ruin No. 6.[131]

In the middle of the floor of this hall there was also a long hearth, of the same simple type as those of our house-site A.[132] This simple type extended only slightly below floor level, but it was not bounded by stones, and thus it differs only insignificantly from the fire patch in the middle of the floor of house-site B (see p. 39). It contained thick layers of charcoal and ashes, and the soil below was burned very red. We found some pieces of burned turf containing small pieces of bog-ore above the embers. The pronounced ochre yellow colour of the floor below the layer of charcoal may be due to these. The turfs may represent part of the collapsed roof – but turf may also have been used as fuel here.

At the south-western end of this fire patch we found a small ember pit (fig. 14), built of slate and filled to the brim with clean charcoal. The extension of the simple hearth in room IX in the Hvalsey complex also held an ember pit; this room in the Hvalsey complex provides a parallel also for the well-made cooking pit, and thus these two hearths are very similar indeed. Ember pits occur sporadically in the Norse material from Greenland. Most similar to ours in house-site B are two from the so-called "Fireplace area" in the outfields of Brattahlið (fig. 90), close to the two hearths discussed above.[133]

170

Another ember pit is that found in the farm ruin Ánávik – this site was mentioned above in connection with the hearths with a stone setting,[134] and we have yet another in the smithy (room VIII) in ruin group 47, in the vicinity of Brattahlíð.[135]

In Iceland ember pits are more common than in Greenland – they frequently occur together with hearths, for example in Ísleifsstaðir.[136]

Seeing that ember pits are so common in Iceland and Greenland, one would also expect them to have been commonly employed in Norway and in the rest of Scandinavia, that the glowing embers should there, too, have been stored in special pits at night, in the floor and close to the hearth. But here a difficulty arises: in the course of time, so many different terms have been applied to charcoal pits in the floor that it is impossible to be quite certain to what kinds of pit they apply. In his book about Vallhagar, Mårten Stenberger speaks of "emberpits" in the Vallhagar houses,[137] but these seem to be cooking pits. And when Jan Petersen writes about ash pits, we cannot know whether these are the same as the Icelandic *feluholur* or ember pits, night repositories for glowing embers.[138]. Thus one can hardly tell to what use all these pits were put, without examining each of them personally. In his unpublished probation lecture of 1920, "Vestnorske hustufter fra Jernalder" (Western Norwegian Iron Age House-sites), Helge Gjessing proposes an explanation of an assumed post hole, which was full of black, charred earth and pieces of charcoal – that this could have been an ember pit, corresponding to the Icelandic *feluholur*.[139]

There seems to be no doubt that some of these pits were ember pits in the true sense of the word; it can hardly have been easy to light a fire in prehistoric Scandinavia either, and therefore an ember pit for storing the glowing embers at night, to facilitate the lighting of the next day's fires, would seem to have been just as essential here.

Grettis Saga contains an interesting piece of information on the difficulty of obtaining fire: we hear that when Grettir, who had been outlawed, had lived for two winters at Drangey in Skagafjörður, the fire went out one night; Grettir then grew angry with the bondsman who had not looked after the fire with enough care. He then conferred with Illugi as to what they were to do; as a result, Grettir swam to the mainland, a matter of six miles, in order to fetch fire at a farm, even though he was an outlaw.[140] This story really brings home to us the difficulties connected with the lighting of fires, and the importance of looking after the fire, so that it did not go out.

When we are in this small room, house B, we are struck by the great care with which even the smallest details here were carried out – how different from house A, where everything was as simple as possible. House B must be interpreted as a small hall of the same type as room I in house A, and room I in the farm ruin Narssaq in Greenland, room I in Brattahlíð and room IX in Hvalsey, all of which have been discussed above in connection with house A.

171

– House B has a row of hearths running along the middle of the floor, and a bench along one wall, while the entrance was in one of the side walls.

There was only one securely attested post hole (p. 42), and thus it is very uncertain how the roof of this house was supported. Of course, the annual flooding of the river may have wiped out all traces of posts, but it seems most likely that this house had no rows of posts. Nor did all the earliest Greenland buildings have posts to support their roofs – there were no traces of rows of posts in Brattahlíð room I[141] or in the house-site near Narssaq.[142]

Little can be said about the construction of house B. The walls, which were of turf, were thinner than those of house A; the annually recurring flooding of the brook, which affects this part of the site most severely, may well be the explanation. Sections cut through the walls did not reveal whether *strengur* were employed also in the construction of this house, as the turf was very highly eroded. We found no row of sleeper stones below the walls – just an occasional stone occurred here and there in the turf; probably these were intended to support the layers. During excavation we noted thick layers of turf inside the room, representing the collapsed walls – there was relatively more such turf here than in house A. From this fact we infer that the end walls of house B may have consisted exclusively of turf, including the gable, right up to the ridge of the roof. If this assumption is correct, the gables must have been straight, unlike those of house A.

There was, as pointed out above, a large post hole at the eastern end of the room, approximately on the central axis – no traces of a corresponding hole at the western end of the house were found, however. Besides, the row of hearths covers the greater part of the floor here. The post at the eastern end of the room may have carried a central purlin, but the excavation did not reveal how such a purlin might have been supported at the other end of the room (figs. 10–11). Even though not a single trace of any internal wooden construction along the walls remains, the room may nevertheless have had internal wooden walls or posts supporting a *vegglægja* which carried the rafters, for we must remember that this house-site was subjected to the constant action of flood water from the brook. Albert Nilsson points out that in old farm houses in Iceland today the rafters of a purlin roof and the spars of a simple roof truss are invariably supported by the inner part of the wall, which thus acquires the function of a bearing member of the structure. This applies first and foremost to stone walls – in the case of turf houses, whose walls are built entirely of turf, as those of house B presumably were, the rafters were most often supported by a *vegglægja*.[143]

We have reason to believe that the roof of this house was covered with turf, and the house may possibly not have been unlike the barn from Gilhagi in Skagafjörður, Iceland, as shown on fig. 92.

The entrance, marked by two flat stones, lay in the southern side wall

172

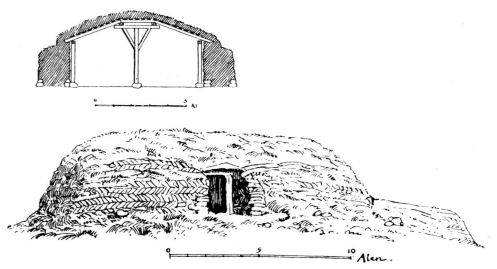

Fig. 92. Perspective and section of barn from Gilhagi in Skagafjörður, Iceland. After Johs. Klein.

(fig. 10). No other house on the terrace has its entrance marked by flat slabs of stone; probably the reason for their presence in house B is the entirely practical one of the conditions here being wetter than in the other parts of the terrace.

In conclusion, we may thus infer that the construction and fittings of house B include features which relate this building closely not only to house A but also to a great number of early house-sites in Greenland, Iceland and Scandinavia; these, which date from the time before and around A.D. 1000, were discussed in connection with house A above. At present, special features such as the stone-lined hearth which is placed up against a wall are known only from this house and from the hall of the Brattahlið North Farm complex, room I. It thus appears likely that these two houses should have been built at approximately the same time. Further – the closest parallels for the cooking pit and the ember pit are found in room IX of the Hvalsey complex and in the "Fireplace area" at Brattahlið. Roussell maintains that the old hall, room IX, of the Hvalsey complex must be of the same date as room I at Brattahlið; this statement is founded not only on the great similarity of these two halls, but also on a soap-stone fragment from Hvalsey whose ornamentation is identical with that of one found in the hall at Brattahlið. We have already pointed out that both these buildings convey the impression of extremely great age, and Roussell includes them among the earliest of the buildings excavated in Greenland.[144]

The finds deriving from house B provide no information either about the age of the building or about its inhabitants. Two quite ordinary stones from the shore, with marks of pounding at the ends, were found, one in the hearth

173

at the western end of the room, the other just beside it (LaM 37 and 38) (fig. 16). The stone which lay in the hearth was burned brittle and had broken into two pieces, which were found at 2 cm above floor level and at floor level respectively. Both these stones must undoubtedly have been used during the preparation of food, for crushing or some similar purpose. But we can derive no further information from them, and they may represent almost any of the ethnic groups mentioned above.

Only one secure statement can be made with regard to these stones: such stones from the shore were in use in Scandinavia from the Stone Age onwards, until far into the Iron Age. Jan Petersen repeatedly found such pounding stones during his excavations of early Iron Age farms in Rogaland in Norway.[145]

A lump of slag was also found in house B (LaM 3 fig. 17). This lay at the bottom of the cooking pit, among a large amount of brittle-burned stone, ashes and charcoal. This find gives us an Iron Age setting, and thus we can eliminate Indians and Eskimoes from the list of possible builders of this house, for these people had not learned to extract iron. Thus this lump of slag lends support to the impression of Norse origin conveyed by the type of construction and by the hearths.

A particularly interesting feature of this lump of slag is the fact that it contains a piece of charcoal which was revealed when a section was cut through the slag (fig. 93). (See also A.M. Rosenqvist below.)

Interpretation of house-site C (pp. 42–45)

This small round or horse-shoe shaped house cannot be immediately ascribed to any definite culture, for few structural details have come to light. The house was built of turf, like A and B, and parts of the walls – some very thick – are clearly visible. The tough, black stratum which covered the cultural layer must be the collapsed turf roof of the house. An interesting feature connected with the shape of this house is an "arm" of turf projecting from the east wall, in the direction of house B. Another "arm" projects in the direction of house A (pl. 3).

Of the two lumps of iron slag found in the house, one was inside the turf wall, 40 cm above sterile ground. It would seem that it might have lain in the turf before this was cut for building, presumably an indication of this not having been the first house to be built here.

A small midden outside the door yielded an iron rivet and a fragment of iron. Both were in the same poor state of preservation as the iron found in house A, and the types they represented could no longer be determined. As it is practically a rule for the houses on the terrace that all middens lie

Fig. 93. Microscope photograph of a section of a lump of slag, LaM 3, from the cooking pit in house-site B, showing a fragment of charcoal in the central part.

immediately outside the door of the house to which they belong, we may assume that this midden was used by the people who lived in house C. The iron rivet, the fragment of iron and the lumps of iron slag all indicate that the people who lived here belonged to an Iron Age culture.

We must, however, be careful in basing definite conclusions exclusively on these finds, for we know that iron has sometimes been found in Eskimo settlements representing a pure Stone Age culture. Such a possibility should therefore not be ignored. Iron is found on two Dorset settlements, on Hall Land and Inglefield Land. Therkel Mathiassen has described the find from Hall Land as a small piece of iron, apparently beaten from meteoric iron.[146]

Erik Holtved found a complete tool at Inglefield Land, a knife blade of meteoric iron.[147]

The early Thule culture in Greenland was not a pure Stone Age culture, for these Eskimoes learned the use of iron from the Norsemen who came to Greenland during the tenth century. Before the Thule Eskimoes, the Dorset Eskimoes had lived in Greenland, and they may also have been in contact with the Norsemen.[148] Henry Collins suggests that the polar Eskimoes probably used meteoric iron not as a substitute for or an improvement on stone as a material for tools, but rather as a substitute for wrought iron.[149]

The Eskimoes probably acquired iron other than meteoric iron occasionally, in the form of iron attachments on drift-wood.[150]

According to Bird, it is possible that this was the source of iron employed

175

by the Labrador Eskimoes as late as during the seventeenth century.[151] An interesting piece of information derives from one of Martin Frobisher's journeys: in 1576 Frobisher found one of the Eskimoes at Frobisher Bay in possession of a box of iron nails.[152] Bird is of the opinion that these nails may have been acquired by way of trading in Greenland, since the Eskimoes had so many that they could even afford to use them as arrow-heads.[153]

Before it was excavated, house C was not entirely unlike some Eskimo ruins which have been investigated along the coast of Labrador. Those excavated by Junius Bird, near Hopedale (p. 136) are of interest in this context. Particularly Bird's types I a, b, c bear a superficial resemblance to house-site C.[154] Before excavation, these sites appeared merely as shallow depression in the ground, surrounded by low banks of turf. However, excavation brought great differences to light.

The most striking feature of these houses is the long entrance tunnel, characteristic of Eskimo houses of this type, but lacking in house C. One may perhaps object that the "arm" which projects from the east wall of house C may superficially resemble an entrance tunnel, but in fact this "arm" is merely a turf bank, or possibly the remains of a wall. Moreover, the structural details characteristic of the Hopedale houses are without parallel in house-site C. Thus we have little reason to believe that house C should be traced back to the recent Eskimo culture. As for the Thule and Dorset cultures, their houses resemble house C still less. This view is supported by the complete lack of tools deriving from any of these cultures.

Nor have any finds come to light here to suggest that any of the Indian groups which might be considered could have built this house and lived here. It is just about conceivable that the winter mamateek of the Beothuk Indians might have left a site like that of house C, but the possibility is remote (see p. 135). The walls of house C must have been considerably higher than two feet, which is the height of the vertical wooden wall at the base of the mamateek. Even though house C has subsided considerably, it still stands 40–60 cm above ground level today.

Whalers and fishermen of historic times must also be considered as possible inhabitants of the house, but such a theory is practically without any support. True, fragments of iron have been found in the midden, but all that remains of them is a rusty crust, an indication of a far greater age than is commensurable with a historic date. Iron from such settlements is always in a far better state of preservation than our fragments. The early date resulting from the radio-carbon analysis of the house – A.D. 710 – points in the same direction.

Thus only one possibility remains: that house-site C belongs to the Norse culture.

From Iceland we know of a small, round building, the *fjárborgir*. Built entirely of turf, it had a dome-shaped roof.[155] Valtýr Guðmundsson states that such buildings were still in use during the 1880s, and that they probably represent a very ancient tradition.[156] They were not true domes but corbelled structures, with pieces of turf as the building material. Thus the width of the room decreased as the height increased, and all that was left when one reached the top was a round hole in the middle of the roof. This hole was commonly covered by a flat stone.[157]

At Keldur, a farm in the south-east of Iceland, small houses of a similar type are still in use as out-houses (fig. 93). Thv. Krohn-Hansen also discusses such houses – they were still in use in Jæren, Norway, during the 1880s (fig. 95).[158]

Such a house, built entirely of turf, would in all probability leave a site like C, but this is purely hypothetical.

The situation of house-site C, in the immediate vicinity of A and B, is important from the point of view of its cultural context (pl. 2). The largest of these houses must in all probability have been the main building, where most of the members of the household lived.

The two "arms" of turf extending from the east and west of this house-site may represent the remains of a turf bank serving as a fence, connecting this house with B and A in such a way that it enclosed a yard.

The latter may either have been open in the east, between houses A and B, or it may have had a gate of some kind in this position, although no traces of any such gate remain today. The flooding river, which breaks its bank in the west and runs between houses B and C, has partly washed away these "arms". We should here note that the south wall of house A was thicker between 14.50 m and 18 m – the part immediately facing house B – than elsewhere; this may indicate that a wall had been raised between these two houses in this position.

We have already mentioned a lump of slag which was found in the turf of one of the walls, at 40 cm above floor level. There can hardly be any doubt as to this having lain in one of the turfs from which the walls were built.

The other lump of slag was a piece of flown slag – this was found in the floor layer of the house. Unfortunately, this piece was accidentally discarded, and it was not found again, in spite of a most thorough and energetic search.

An iron rivet was also found – this lay in a midden immediately to the west of the entrance of the house. This was in the same poor state of preservation as the rivets from house A, and as far as it was possible to tell, it was of the same type as these.

On analysis, the iron fragment proved to be iron precipitate.

Above we have discussed the possibility of iron occurring in Eskimo cultures, pointing out that it would here occur either in the form of meteoric iron or as attached to drift-wood. On p. 174 above we also showed that iron slag can never be interpreted as representing Indian or Eskimo tribes, as these people were not acquainted with the art of extracting iron. Therefore the iron

177

Fig. 94. Out-houses at the farm Keldur, Iceland. The farm is still in use.

Fig. 95. Out-houses at the farm Tjøtta, Rogaland, Norway. The farm was abandoned in 1894. No. 1: cow-shed; No: 2: tool-shed; No. 3: drying-shed; No. 4: privy; Nos. 5–6: potato cellars. After Thv. Krohn-Hansen.

178

rivets and the lumps of slag show that house C cannot have been built by either Indians or Eskimoes; in fact, they support our prior conclusion regarding this house – together with houses A and B it belongs to the Norse cultural complex.

Strangely enough, the most interesting of the finds from house C is a small fragment of bone (LaM 9), which was found in the midden outside the house, near the iron rivet. Rolf W. Lie of the Zoological Museum in Bergen has kindly analysed this fragment, and he concludes – with reservations – that it forms part of the scapula of a domestic pig (sus scrofa). He states: "I am somewhat in doubt as concerns the fragment of a scapula (LaM 9). The coracoid process has disappeared, and this is the best means of determining the species from this part of the pig's scapula. It may thus resemble the scapula of a sheep or a goat (two species which cannot be distinguished from each other). However, the remaining characteristic features indicate the pig as the source of the fragment. We may disregard the possibility of it deriving from a wild animal – there has never been any wild boar in Newfoundland, nor any representative of the most closely related Tayassuidea. Wild sheep and goats occur exclusively in the mountain regions of the mainland, from Alaska southwards. Furthermore, the distribution of some of the wild breeds of sheep seems to have been affected by the activity of man. On Soay (sauøy = sheep island?) in the Hebrides, for instance, there is a local breed of sheep which is highly reminiscent of the "bronze sheep' which were common during the Bronze Age. Tradition has it that these sheep are descended from sheep brought here by Scandinavian Vikings. St. Kilda, also in the Hebrides, has a similar breed."*

It thus appears that this fragment of bone is most likely to derive from a pig, although the possibility of its representing a sheep or goat must also be borne in mind. Be that as it may – the important aspect in the present context is that it cannot possibly derive from a wild animal. This fragment must therefore represent a domestic animal. This matter will be discussed in greater detail in a later chapter, where it will be related to a wider context.

* Letter from Rolf W. Lie, keeper at the Zoological Museum of the University of Bergen. (App. III)

Interpretation of house-site D (pp. 45–54)
House-site D lies roughly in the middle of the terrace, the north wall aligned with its edge. Because of the slight curvature of the terrace, the orientation of this house diverges somewhat from that of house-site A (pl. 2).

Like the houses described above, house D was built of horizontal layers of turf, stacked on top of one another. The external corners are rounded off, as a result of which the house-site is oval in shape.

If we consider room III of this house-site (fig. 21), we shall find that its interior is strikingly similar to that of room I of house A, of room I of the ruin near Narssaq (p. 150), and also of Hvalsey room IX – all these have a long hearth running more or less along the middle of the floor. Around the hearth, the floor has been trodden hard and firm, and it is black with soot, but along the walls, the floor is neither trodden down nor black. This looser part of the floor has yielded a great number of small, charred pieces of twigs; these may well indicate that these parts of the floor were covered with twigs and served as benches. In plan, they appear to be far too wide for this purpose, but judging from the photograph of this house-site, (fig. 21), it would seem that the width of the excavated area exceeds that of the original room; the interior face of the walls would thus lie further inside the room, particularly in the case of the north wall. As appears from the plan in fig. 21, this wall is very thin. As it coincides with the edge of the terrace in the north, any additional thickness must surely have lain in the south, so that its inner face extended further into the room than the present southern limit. The assumed original inner face is indicated by a broken line on the plan.

The two hearths, one along the north-western end of the hard-trodden floor in the middle of the room, the other at the south-eastern end, are both without any stone setting. At the western end of the northern hearth, we found the remains of a small ember pit lined with slate (fig. 22). This must have been practically identical with that found in house B, and consequently also with those in the so-called "Fireplace area" of northern Brattahlið in Greenland (fig. 91). The hearths are simple in type, merely a shallow depression in the floor, without any surrounding stone setting, of the type encountered in house A and in the Norse farms of Greenland. We have an exact parallel for the simple hearth with ember pit in room IX, the old hall of the Hvalsey complex, East Settlement No. 83, 6.[159] This hall we have discussed several times above, in connection with houses A and B; we noted then that Roussell regards it as one of the earliest Norse buildings in Greenland (fig. 80).

Thus the Norse material includes close parallels for house D room III, and the method of construction, with turf walls without sleeper stones at the base, as well as the hearths and the ember pit indicate a close connection between this house and houses A and B.

The ground plan of the house, which is long and approximately rectangular and comprises two rooms, is not unlike that of house A. But house D differs from house A in that a small room was built on to the rear wall of the house. Plans of this type are unknown in the material deriving from those Indian and Eskimo tribes which might be considered here, nor are fishermen and whalers

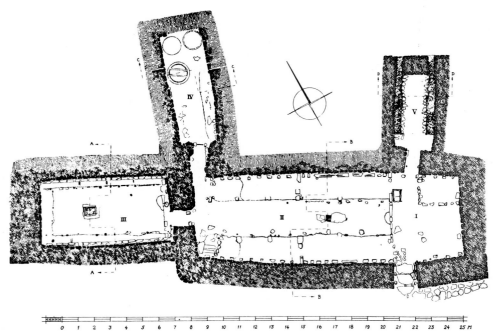

Fig. 96. The house-site Stöng in Þjórsárdalur, Iceland. After Aa. Rousell.

of more recent times known to have built such houses. It seem most likely that the origin of this type of building should be sought in the Norse cultural complex, where it was evolved as a natural development of the long house. The closest parallels are to be found in Iceland. A typical example, in a very good state of preservation, is the farm ruin Stöng in Þjórsárdalur (fig. 96). In plan this is a long house complete with a "lobby", a sleeping hall and a living room, *stofa,* built in a row, to which two rooms were added at the back. This type of house, known as the "Þjórsárdalur type", may have been developed in Iceland; no such house has as yet been securely demonstrated in Scandinavia. The dwelling houses of some farms excavated by Sigurd Grieg in Oppland, Norway, as mentioned above, seem to have been added to at the sides. In Grieg's opinion they have the same plan as the dwellings known from farms in Iceland and Greeland.[160]

A similar farm has been excavated at Gran, Hadeland, Norway.[161] Anders Hagen also compares this "Þjórsárdalur type" with these ruins excavated in eastern Norway, and he apparently thinks that the type may well have been developed in Norway.[162] Bjørn Myhre holds the same view, as pointed out on p. 157 above. In our opinion these farm ruins are not sufficiently typical of the "Þjórsárdalur house"; therefore I prefer not to take a stand on this matter.

As was the case in Stöng, the entrance of house D lies near one of the corners of what we have interpreted as the "lobby" (room I). From this room, an

181

assumed door-opening leads into room II. We have found no door-opening leading from room III into room I; this must be due to the difficulties involved in locating such an opening. We have no doubt whatsoever that one must have been able to enter room III and that this room must, moreover, have been connected to room I by a door. After all, room III cannot have been completely isolated from the outside world. Everything point to this room having been the sleeping hall *(skáli)* of the house. In Stöng there was also another room built on to the sleeping hall – the living room, *stofa,* which was a little narrower than the sleeping hall (fig. 96). This room is lacking in house D. According to Kristján Eldjárn, the *stofa* did not make its appearance in Iceland until some time during the eleventh century, and it represents in his opinion the first significant change of the Icelandic farm.[163] It appears from the farm ruins excavated in Iceland that the earliest *stofar* formed lengthways extensions of the *skáli,* being added to the end farthest removed from the entrance as, for example, at Stöng.

In its classic form, the "Þjórsárdalur type" has not been found in Greenland, for we cannot draw a direct parallel between Garðar I–V, East Settlement No. 20 and West Settlement No. 51 on the one hand, and Stöng on the other.[164] These Greenland farm houses are not long halls with the entrance near one corner, and with the interior divided into several rooms by means of partition walls: the entrance door of the Greenland houses lay in the middle of one of the side walls and led into a kind of vestibule, which gave access to the other rooms. Each of these may well have been in the form of a small house with its own, individual roof. Thus in actual fact there is a considerable difference between the Greenland houses with an annexe at the rear, and the Icelandic houses of the "Þjórsárdalur type". The "Þjórsárdalur type" also includes Bær in Gjáskógar, Áslákstunga innri and Sámsstaðir, as well as a number of others.[165] All these differ from the Greenland type just discussed in that they consist of a long hall or sleeping hall with a long hearth in the middle of the floor; one or more rooms were added at the gable ends, and one or more at the back wall. The entrance was in the front wall, near one of the gable ends, and there were doors connecting the rooms.

Thus it seems to be quite clear that the closest parallels to the actual plan of house D are to be found in the Icelandic material, whereas simple hearths of the type found in room III were most commonly employed in Greenland, the hearth of Hvalsey room IX providing the closest parallel for the combination of simple hearth and ember pit which we find in room III (fig. 80).

The excavations yielded few structural details and thus the methods of construction here employed are difficult to ascertain. Only two reasonably certain post holes have come to light, one in room II and one in room III. Some flat slabs of stone were found in the layers, but as none of these was in contact with the floor, they cannot have been used for supporting posts. It seems more likely that they should have lain on top of the turf covering the roof, in order to keep it in place – this practice we noted also in several of the other houses on the terrace. – The walls were built from turf arranged in horizontal layers. They were about 1.5 m thick. We found no traces of an interior panelling, with the possible exception of room III, where a carbonized stripe was noted on the inside of the partition wall dividing rooms I and III: in several places along this wall we found a black stripe of charcoal which may represent burned panelling.

Rooms I and III may have formed one long building with one roof covering both rooms. The small room, II, must have had a separate roof, even though it was joined to the other house by a party wall. This is all we know about the construction of house D – we have so little information that it would be wrong to hazard any speculative hypothesis as to its construction.

Some of the finds from this house-site emphasize the impression of a Norse cultural background conveyed by the house itself. As the finds occurred at different levels, two periods of habitation could be distinguished. A fragment of a bone needle was found right down at floor level – this was preserved as a result of having been burned (LaM 76, fig. 24). The eye of the needle was broken, but even so it was quite obvious that it had been drilled. This is a feature of great importance, for it shows that this needle cannot have been made by the Dorset Eskimoes, a people not familiar with the drill.[166] Nor does our needle in any way resemble the bone needles with gouged eyes which have been found in Newfoundland, and which probably derive from the culture of the Dorset Eskimoes. Some of these needles are quite small, while others measure up to nine inches in length.[167] LaM 76 is also quite different from any of the various types of "bone pendant" of the Beothuk culture.[168]

In the Norse cultural sphere, on the other hand, needles of the type we found here are very common. The Norse farm ruins in Greenland have yielded a great number (fig. 97),[169] and one specimen, very similar indeed to ours, has come to light in the ruins of the Viking farm at Freswick in Caithness, Scotland,[170] while others were found when the Norse farm at Jarlshof in Shetland was excavated.[171] The excavations of the early medieval strata of the ancient city of Lund in Sweden yielded similar needles,[172] and such finds have also occurred as a result of excavations of the medieval cities of Norway.[173] Northern Norway, too, is represented by a specimen, which was found in the Viking Age strata of the mound at the farm Grunnfarnes.[174] A great many more could be listed, but the above should surely be enough to show how common such needles were in the Norse cultural sphere. Moreover, bone needles of the same type have also come to light in the sunken-floored house at Wezinge, Groningen, Holland.[175]

A small fragment of copper (LaM 69, fig. 23) was found among the

Fig. 97. Bone pins from Umiviarssuk, Farm ruin No. 52 a, West Settlement, Greenland. After Aa. Rousell.

charcoal in the ember pit in room III. When the fragment was analysed, it appeared that the copper had been smelted, and that it contained a number of other minerals (see A.M. Rosenqvist p. 401). From this we may infer that

184

this piece of copper cannot derive from any native population, for we know that those natives of Canada who used copper for making tools worked the cold metal, without smelting it, and copper in its natural state is practically a hundred per cent pure.

A small flint chipping (LaM 74), which was also found at floor level, is probably a fragment of a flint used for striking fire.

Two iron rivets (LaM 70 and 68) were also found approximately at floor level. They lay at 2 cm and 4 cm above sterile ground respectively, and are of the same type as those found in house A. They are also just as highly corroded as these. Most of the rivets from the houses at Épaves Bay are of this type. Their state of preservation is so poor that most of them were broken immediately below the clinch; they are, moreover, so highly corroded that practically bo iron remains (see A.M. Rosenqvist below). A small fragment of iron (LaM 71) lay 8 cm above the floor.

J. Winston and C. Bareis' report states that an iron rivet was found immediately outside the eastern gable-end (LaM 318). This may indicate the presence of an entrance to D III at this end, but no such opening has been found. – All these items clearly represent the first phase of habitation, and there can be no doubt as to their Norse origin. Room II also yielded a fragmentary iron rivet at floor level, again of the same type.

Higher up in the cultural layer, at a level of between 6 cm and 12 cm above the floor, we found four stone implements (see pp. 54–55), one of which may be securely identified as representing the Dorset culture: an arrow-head of quartzite (LaM 75, figs. 25 and 27). These stone items will be discussed later, together with other stone implements found on the terrace.

All in all, the cultural layer is about 30 cm thick; this means that objects found at between 6 cm and 12 cm above the floor must presumably have got there while room III was still under cover. They were found close to a secondary hearth which did not extend down to floor level. The room probably burned down some time later, and it was never rebuilt. It is possible that the natives who left these stone tools behind were responsible for the fire which destroyed the room.

Interpretation of house-site E (pp. 63–65)

Before excavation, this small house-site, dug half-way down into the ground, was not unlike some semi-sunken Eskimo ruins of the type excavated by Junius Bird at Hopedale, Labrador.[176] The walls of these Eskimo huts were also of turf. Not a single object of Eskimo origin was found in house E, but neither did this house yield any other objects which might have suggested a possible cultural affinity.

As for the type of house here represented, a constantly increasing number of such small, semi-sunken huts has in recent years come to light in the countries of Norway, Sweden, Denmark and Iceland – as well as on the Continent. By now these houses – the so-called *Grubenhäuser* (sunken-floored huts) – are quite common in the archaeological material from these countries. Southern Sweden has yielded more such houses than any other part of Scandinavia.

During the extensive investigations at Hagestad and Valleberga in Scania, Sweden, Märta Strömberg excavated a number of house-sites of this type.[177] Sunken-floored huts of several types were found here – some were round, others rectangular. Most of them were small, 3–4 metres long, and the difference between the length and the width was very slight. The depth to which they were cut into the ground was as a rule difficult to ascertain, since no more than the base of the hut remained in many cases, and since the ancient surface of the ground had changed as a result of cultivation. Most probably a depth of 40 cm was the most common, but 90 cm also occurred. The method of construction included the use of posts – posts at the centre of the end walls were most common, but there were also huts with corner posts. – At other excavations in Scania, too, the type with posts at the centre of the end walls seems to predominate.[178]

A settlement of sunken-floored huts was found at Löddeköpinge.[179] Here the largest houses measured 3–4 metres in diameter, and they were 0.6 metres deep; the smaller ones had a diameter of 2.3 metres and a depth of 35–40 cm. They varied in shape – some were round, others oval or square. The floor consisted of stamped earth. One of the houses had a separate lean-to containing a large hearth; the remaining hearths and cooking pits seemed to have been arranged without any system at all. The entrance doors faced south. Several post holes were found, possibly representing larger houses constructed with posts. The entrances were difficult to find throughout, and at Valleberga the entrance of only one house could be demonstrated with certainty. It lay on the south side of the house. Some of the houses at Hagestad had their entrances in the east wall.[180]

In Sweden, sunken-floored huts apparently made their first appearance during the Migration Age/Viking Age. But there is one exception – at Gårdlösaåsen in Scania, Berta Stjernquist has demonstrated continuous habitation in sunken-floored huts lasting for several centuries from the transition Roman Imperial Age/Migration Age onwards. The earliest house on this site measured 2 × 2.5 metres, and it had a hearth.[181]

On the island of Helgö in Lake Mälaren in Sweden, Wilhelm Holmqvist found several small houses of this type.[182] It appears that traces of sunken-floored huts were found in both settlement group 1 and settlement group 2.[183] In four of these houses a primitive hearth was found in one corner. One of the sunken-floored huts of settlement group 2 had been dug down into the ground to a considerable depth. Settlement group 1 also included a house of a similar type: this had a hearth in its north-western corner, with a flat slab of stone at the base. No trace of any wall construction was found in any of these sunken-floored huts, but in the first of them a stone paving was noted, ending 20–25 cm from the outer edge of the house. This fact has led Holmqvist to believe that the walls may have been 20–25 cm thick, but nothing is known of the material used.[184]

Berta Stjernquist deals with various problems concerning these sunken-floored huts, their construction and function, in several of her books. She discusses the question of whether they might in fact have been dwelling houses, pointing out several counter-arguments to this theory, however, such as the fact that only some of them are equipped with hearths, and that several are far too small to have housed a large family, especially bearing in mind the large looms then in use in the homes.[185] She therefore concludes that these huts cannot have served as independent dwelling houses, but that they appear to have been combined with other buildings, of different form and construction.[186]

The extensive investigations on the island of Helgö have prompted Holmqvist to maintain that these sunken-floored huts must have served several domestic purposes essential to the life of the farm, functions such as that of bake-house, weaving-shed, bath-house and pottery. On Helgö, the sunken-floored huts occur together with large long houses of timber, constructed in different ways (log houses and houses of post construction).[187] According to Holmqvist, the long houses of timber are the most recent, for they show no signs of intersection by buildings of a later phase.[188]

In Märtha Strömberg's view the finds indicate that these huts were also used as dwelling houses.[189] Loom weights and spinning whorls are among the items most commonly found. Hearths are not as common, but most of those found lie in a corner of the room.

Several scholars have pointed out that the area near the sunken-floored huts contains a great many post holes – these may represent houses constructed with posts. Berta Stjernquist noted many such post holes during the excavation at Gårdlösa in Scania.[190] According to her, Gårdlösa represents several farms, each consisting of two or three sunken-floored huts and several long houses of post construction. The long houses have not been found, but the post holes and remains of parts of buildings which have come to light may well represent such houses.

Tischler appears to be certain that the sunken-floored huts were secondary buildings, always associated with larger houses – this, in his view, holds true also of locations which have yielded sunken-floored huts only, such as Ezinge in Groningen, Holland.[191,192] He points out that the size of this area is

187

sufficient for larger houses also; these, which must have lain at a level higher than that of the sunken-floored huts, have now disappeared.

The small sunken-floored huts at Hedeby in Slesvig lie close to larger, rectangular houses, the latter constructed in various different ways.[193] J. Jankuhn has demonstrated that these huts were always built and rebuilt on the same sites, and that there are several floor strata above one another. Some of the huts were sunk to only a slight depth. The method of construction most common here was that with posts at the centre of the end walls, the method also noted in Scania, but corner posts were also found.[194]

Below the Viking Age fortress at Aggersborg by the Limfjord in Denmark, C.G. Schultz uncovered an earlier settlement, village-like in character, which consisted of long houses of post construction, with curving walls; close to these there were a number of depressions, to all appearances the remains of sunken-floored huts.[195]

Quite a number of sunken-floored huts were also found when the ancient city of Århus in Denmark was excavated. These were also small, some were oval, others more nearly rectangular, and some had a corner hearth. Several of these huts must have been weaving-sheds, including one with wattle walls. In Andersen's view, only sunken-floored huts were built here during the first phase of habitation, around A.D. 900.[196]

Until recently Norway had yielded not a single house of this type from prehistoric or medieval times, but two have come to light in recent years as a result of the excavations of the ancient city of Oslo, conducted by the Inspectorate of Ancient Monuments and Historic Buildings.[197]

Perry Rolfsen has excavated nine sunken-floored huts – two secure, seven not securely attested – at Oddernes near Kristiansand in Norway. These have been dated to the late Roman Iron Age/Migration Age (A.D. 300–600). The two secure huts – A and B – measure 4.15 × 3.1 m and 4.05 × 3.3 m respectively, and they are 0.45 m and 0.30 m deep.[198]

In hut A, there was a post at the middle of each of the short walls; most of the Scandinavian prehistoric huts of this type have such central posts at the end walls. This hut is highly reminiscent of our house E in both shape and size, and also by the fact that it was dug down into the ground instead of being cut into the terrace from the side. House E has not, however, yielded any securely demonstrable traces of posts which might have supported the roof.

The sunken-floored huts at Oddernes also occur together with houses of a different type – rectangular houses, built on the level ground. Here, too, the question thus arises as to whether the sunken-floored huts were out-houses, serving one or more of the many functions of the farm, or whether they may also have served as dwelling houses. Rolfsen is of the opinion that these two interpretations need not necessarily be mutually exclusive – a plausible theory, in our view, when applied to buildings found in a country as cold as Norway.

Sunken-floored huts are warm in winter, and might therefore make admirable dwellings during that season. One may raise the objection that such sunken-floored huts are as a rule too small to house a family with many children, but then we can hardly apply our modern requirements as to space and comfort to the people of prehistoric times. As Rolfsen says – the function of sunken-floored huts must be assessed and interpreted in the light of the other monuments found on the same site.[199]

Sunken-floored huts must have been quite common in Norway, for they are still found in the countryside to this day. Being sunk into the ground they offer insulation from frost and are therefore extremely well suited for a variety of purposes. These more recent sunken-floored huts in Norway are dug into the ground from the side, so that one of the gable-ends is visible.[200] Thus they should be regarded as a variant of the normal prehistoric type, that dug down into the ground. But this variant also goes back to prehistory, as we saw above. It will be discussed in greater detail below, in connection with house-sites G and J. Vreim states that sunken-floored huts of this type are most common in western Norway, where they occur as fire houses, fishermen's shanties, smithies and boat sheds. As outfarm buildings and cowsheds they are also used in northern Norway.[201] There can be no doubt that such houses have very ancient roots in Norway.

In Iceland such houses remained in use until very recently. The small *dyngja* or women's house is an example. These were the women's living quarters, where they busied themselves with weaving and needlework. Valtýr Guðmundsson states that these huts were without any form of hearth, and that they in the past seem to have been built at a distance from the other houses, or at least without any direct connection with these. But the distance was never very great – the *dyngja* usually lay south of the dwelling houses so that it might be warmed by the sun, while it was at the same time protected from the prevailing winds.[202]

Iceland also had sunken-floored huts other than the *dyngja* – the bath house was frequently semi-sunk, or it might form a cellar under another building.

As huts of this type were apparently common in Iceland during the Saga Age, it would seem most probably that their roots should be still more ancient also here. Strangely enough, however, not a single example from the time of settlement or the early Middle Ages was known until very recently. When Þór Magnússon excavated a farm near Hvítárholt in Arnessýsla in the 1960ies, he found five such sunken-floored huts, all of them with a corner hearth.[203] They lay together with long houses of an early type, with curving sides and large, separate cowsheds. This excavation has provided valuable information about the Norse farms of the time when Iceland was settled. It was rebuilt several times, and the buildings are not all contemporaneous. This is the first excavation in Iceland to yield a farm apparently complete with all its buildings.

Tacitus writes that the Germanic tribes used houses of this kind as winter houses, as store rooms, or as a refuge in case of enemy attacks. He says that these houses were sunk into the ground, and that only the earth-covered roof was visible above ground.[204] Pliny, too, writes of houses of this kind, where Germanic women used to sit at their needlework.[205]

No isolated sunken-floored huts of early medieval date are known from Greenland, but there are a great many farms here which have not as yet been investigated. Our knowledge of Greenland buildings is largely confined to the late Middle Ages when, as we pointed out above, large farm complexes with corridor or central plans were in use.[206] In a centralized house complex, all the buildings of a farm are fused into one, each of whose rooms corresponds to an earlier separate house. Some of these complexes include rooms sunk into the ground in the same way as the sunken-floored huts. As an example, we may cite the ruin group West Settlement No. 16, whose room III has been identified as the fire house. This room is dug into the ground to a depth of 55 cm.[207] Another example is offered by the ruin group West Settlement No. 35 – here both room V and room X are sunk far down into the ground, and according to the description, the floor of room X lies at a considerably lower level than that of the adjoining room. Room X has been identified as the cowshed – and this is one of the very buildings still sunk into the ground today as a protection from frost in some places, including parts of Norway.[208]

At Warendorf in Westphalia such sunken-floored huts occur together with long house-sites of various shapes and sizes.[209] The sunken-floored houses here served various purposes, and it is clear that they were all designed for work. Some of them had hearths, and post holes at the outer edge of the floor show that the walls were supported by timber walls. These sunken-floored huts form part of a complex which includes several houses with curved walls practically identical with the Viking Age houses of Denmark. According to Winkelmann the Warendorf settlement comprised independent farms, each with its own houses and out-houses fulfilling various functions – the farm, he states, consisted of eight to ten houses above ground, two hexagonal houses and three or four sunken-floored huts. Each farm had its own smithy.[210]

The hearth at the eastern corner of house E (fig. 31) is constructed in a manner well known in the Norse cultural sphere, perhaps most especially in Greenland. Roussell points out that corner hearths are very common there.[211] Hearths of our type occur, for instance, at Anavik, West Settlement No. 7, West Settlement No. 53 c, and Austmannadal No. 4.[212] Corner hearths occur among the prehistoric material from Scandinavia. They apparently made their first appearance in the sunken-floored huts, where they have been demonstrated as early as the early Iron Age.[213] Probably a lack of space led to their adoption – a hearth in the middle of the floor of a sunken-floored hut would take up far too much room. And corner hearths are most frequently found in these small houses; all the sunken-floored huts at Hvítarhólt in Iceland have corner hearths.[214] We would also draw attention to the corner hearths of the Hovden house-site at Møsstrand in Norway, discussed above in connection with house A (p. 156).[215] From the early Middle Ages, we have several examples of hearths of this type in other houses also. Lidén, for instance, discusses corner hearths in connection with houses dating from the twelfth century,[216] and Asbjørn Herteig has demonstrated a corner hearth in one of the early medieval houses at Kaupangen in Borgund, Sunnmøre.[217] All these hearths bear a striking resemblance to that of our house E. The type is not known from Eskimo houses – normally the Eskimoes heated their homes with lamps.

It appears clearly from the above that our sunken-floored hut – the small house E – fits naturally into the Norse cultural complex, as part of the Norse farm. The thick turf banks at the edge of the depression must be interpreted as proof of a built-up wall of turf, consisting of layers arranged on top of one another in the so-called *strengur* technique.

The construction of the roof is impossible to determine – it may have rested on an interior wooden structure, or it may have sloped up from the edge of the walls, the method of construction we noted in connection with house C (p. 177). We should here point out that houses of this type still in use in western Norway – for storing potatoes, for instance – have slate roofs without any interior timber support. At Sotra near Bergen, potato cellars were until very recently sunk into the ground – they had flagged roofs. These cellars might measure up to 5 metres in diameter, although some were smaller, and they were high enough for a man to stand upright. The walls were built of stone, with layers of earth in between. The roof consisted of stone slabs laid first from the corners, then from the sides, and so on until a dome was formed. Finally the stone slabs were covered with earth and turf. The door was of wood.[218] If we compare the domed turf roofs from Saga Age Iceland with the flagged roofs from Sotra, we shall find the same principle underlying both. These Icelandic roofs were also without timber support.[219] I consider it very likely that the roof of house E should also have been constructed in this manner.

The position of house-site E, near house D and isolated from the other houses on the terrace, suggests that it must in some way or other have been connected with house D. Above we have several times discussed the functions of the sunken-floored huts in relation to those of the larger long houses; most scholars agree that these huts must have had specified functions, but that they were not used as dwelling houses. In the case of our house E the great number of brittle-burned stones found in the hearth may well indicate that this was a fire house. There is also a slight possibility of house E having been a weaving-shed – this is supposing that the fist-sized stones found heaped up in the northern corner were loom weights. All of them are limestone, and personally I think they are too light and too few in number to represent loom weights. It would seem more likely that they had been used to weight down a fishing net, for instance – they are so irregular in shape that they could easily be tied on. There are no other finds from this house.

We have reason to believe that the simple type of house here discussed may turn out to be one of the most ancient types of building in the North, and that it may, moreover, have been a common European phenomenon. In spite of its primitive character, it has so many features to recommend it – it was easy to build, required a minimum of building material, and offered excellent insulation from heat as well as from cold – that it would seem reasonable to suppose that this would be one of the first types of dwelling to suggest itself when people had learned to build, and that it later became a secondary building.

The purely technical step from the cave to the sunken-floored hut is not great, but such houses could be built successfully only when the ground into which they were sunk provided good insulation and drainage. A sand and gravel terrace would provide the best possible site for this purpose.

Interpretation of house-site F (pp. 65–83)

This house is surely far too large to have been spanned by one roof; it seems most likely that this site actually represents several houses built together in such a way that each shared a party wall with its neighbour. The rooms built on to the main house are of particular interest.

To the best of my knowledge, none of the Eskimo or Indian cultures in question has ever yielded a complex house of this kind. On the other hand this complex shares many features with house D, and thus it would seem that farm ruins of the "Þjórsárdalur type" provide the closest parallels for house F. Typical also of a "Þjórsárdalur" house is the fact that it forms a complex consisting of a main house – which is frequently divided into several rooms in a row, according to the ancient Norse pattern – and one or more rooms or houses built on the rear wall. The latter are connected to the main house by doors. The complex was entered by way of a door near one of the corners of the front wall. House F deviates from this pattern by the additional room built on to the front wall, but it must nevertheless be regarded as being of the "Þjórsárdalur type". We would add that it would seem quite natural to add a room to the front wall of house F, for such a room would lie in the sun at the same time as it would be protected from the cold winds from the sea. There

192

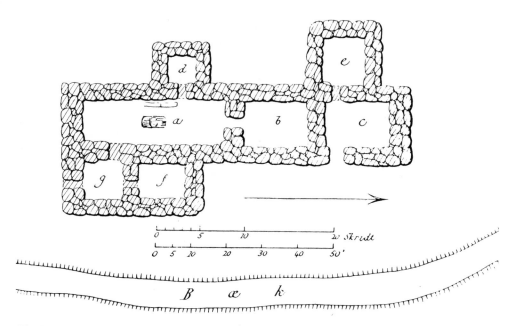

Fig. 98. Plan of house-site at Hraunstunga, Óðaðahraun, Iceland. After D. Bruun.

may have been farm ruins with rooms built on to the back and the front also in Iceland – Daniel Bruun mentions a house-site with annexes on both sides, at Hraunstunga near Òdaðahraun (fig. 98).[220]

A more detailed account of the various rooms of house F seems called for at this point. The long house in the middle, which comprises room I, II and III, must be regarded as the centre of the complex. This central house is c. 20 metres long, and its maximum internal width is 5 metres; the gable ends are about 1 metre narrower, and as a result of this difference, the side walls curve. The end walls are also curved (fig. 32). The curvature of the walls lends an appearance of unity and completeness to the house, and it is possible that these three rooms were built at one and the same time. But the sturdy partition wall dividing room II from room I, which is as thick and of the same material as the external walls, might indicate that room I was added at a later date, and that rooms II and III form the original building. These rooms, probably once divided by a now lost partition wall, form a building of the earliest Viking Age type – this was discussed in detail in connection with house A room I. There is a striking resemblance between room II and a Norse hall of the period preceding A.D. 1000. The interior is identical, with its long hearth in the middle and earthen benches along the walls – like, for instance, house A room I, house D room III, Narssaq room I,[221] Hvalsey room IX,[222] and many others. The long hearth in this room is of a special type, which occurs in several Icelandic farms (fig. 38). The best examples are the hearths of the farm ruin Ìsleifsstaðir in Borgarfjarðarsýsla (figs. 89 and 90), excavated by Mårten Stenberger in 1939.[223]

Room III also has a long hearth in the middle of the floor, but no benches along the two side walls have been securely demonstrated here. The hearth is simple in type, a long depression in the floor; it is similar to the hearth in house A and to several of the Greenland hearths which are discussed in some detail below.

These two rooms, house F rooms II and III, may be compared with rooms II and III in Stöng in Þjórsárdalur.[224] It appears that farms of the "Þjórsárdalur type" retained, as their centre, the ancient sleeping hall with a hearth along the middle of the floor and benches along the walls.

This central building of house F lacked the pairs of post holes running along the middle which are so common in Norse houses of this ancient type. We know, however, that other methods of construction were also employed: sometimes the roof was supported by sturdy corner posts, or by several posts standing just inside the turf walls.

In house F we found depressions which may be post holes in several of the corners not only of the central building, but also in some of the added rooms. There were also depressions of varying size here and there by the walls – these may also represent post holes. Here we must also mention the depressions at the corners of the sunken patch surrounding the hearth. They may have held posts standing in the corners of the patch of floor around the hearth. If this is correct, there must have been four post holes originally, but only two of the existing depressions give the impression of being post-holes. The sand here is extremely loose, and it was difficult to locate post holes. Four such post holes in the middle of the room are not really exceptional in the Norse material – Stenberger draws attention to a similar arrangement at a house-site at Kallberga in Happsta, Alunda, Sweden,[225] investigated by Oscar Almgren and dated to the late Iron Age. According to Almgren, they represent four sturdy posts which supported the roof. Stenberger, on the other hand, interprets them as the remains of posts which supported the frame around the smoke bonnet in the roof.[226] An early Iron Age house-site near Kraghede in Vendsyssel, Jutland, has posts in an identical position to those of the Happsta house,[227] and similar post holes were observed in one of the house-sites of the Danish Iron Age town Ginderup in Thy, north-western Jutland.[228] Aage Roussell also points to three post holes on the edge of the hearth of room I in the farm Sandnes, ruin group No. 51 in Greenland. He refrains from discussing the possible function of these posts, pointing out, however, that the site shows no traces of any other structure to support the roof.[229]

It seems likely that there was a small wooden house within the turf walls of the central building of house F; the presence of such a structure is suggested by the thick, burned stratum and by the great amount of burned timber. It would seem reasonable to assume that the raised parts of the floor, by the walls, were also covered with planks, for here the sand was loose, and not as it would have been had people sat or lain either immediately on it, or on some loose covering. In this connection I would refer the readers to the reconstruction drawing made by Roussell of a wooden building within the turf walls of Stöng in Þjórsárdalur.[230] The earliest Icelandic sources call these raised parts of the floor *set* or *flet;* they were used as sitting and sleeping places. Valtýr Guðmundsson apparently holds the view that these platforms were as a rule covered with planks.[231] Interior panelling has been observed in several Norse houses of the Viking Age and the late Iron Age – on excavation, such panelling is represented either by charred or decayed remains of poles or planks, or by rows of stones whose only possible function would seem to be that of supporting a wooden wall. The latter was the case at Stöng in Þjórsárdalur;[232] similar rows of stones have also been observed in Migration Age houses in Norway.[253]

We have noted that house F room I may have been a kind of lobby or corridor giving access to rooms II and IV. Room II must have been the sleeping hall of the house – there can hardly be any doubt about this.

The earliest addition to the sleeping hall of Icelandic houses was the living hall, the *stofa,* which was built on to one of the gable ends of the house. Room III would seem to be such a living hall, but it appears to have been built at the same time as the sleeping hall. Kristján Eldjárn does not think that the living hall came to Iceland before the eleventh century.[234] If we compare house F room III to the corresponding room of Stöng in Þjórsárdalur, we shall find that the hearth of our room III differs from the corresponding hearth at Stöng: that at Stöng is like a stone box sunk into the floor,[235] while the hearth of house F room III is of the simple Greenland type, a long depression in the floor, without any stone setting, The hearth of room III at Stöng – and, for that matter, also that of room II at the same site – is typically Icelandic; to the best of my knowledge, no such hearth has been encountered in Greenland.

Rooms IV and V have not yielded as much factual information. Both these rooms had hearths – that of room V is a large cooking pit, while room IV had a corner hearth of a different type (fig. 41). These rooms were fire houses, where food was prepared – this is the only information we can derive from the remains. Room VI (fig. 45), on the other hand, has more information to offer: it lies south-east of room II, with which it shares a party wall. The most remarkable feature of this room are the two "channels" which run along the inside of the side walls in the south-western part of the room. They obviously did not serve as channels such as, for instance, that of Stöng room V, which was a privy.[236] Both of them are smooth and even at the bottom, and they lack both intake and outlet. Decayed timber was found in both, and it seems most likely that they are actually impressions of ground sills bearing panelled walls. True, one of them – the north-western one (figs. 43 and 44) – is not entirely straight, but we must bear in mind that it cannot have been easy to find straight timbers in these parts. – Another possible objection: why should one dig a ground sill down into the ground, where it would decay all the more quickly? The answer to this may be that it would thus be more securely fixed in the loose sand – the Norse material includes several examples of such a practice. The impression of a ground sill sunk into the ground has been found in a Migration Age house-site at Mogen, Møsstrand, Telemark, Norway; it lay at one of the end walls, on either side of the entrance.[237] – It is, of course, possible that the sills were not dug down at all, but that the great weight of the roof pressed them down into the loose sand in the course of time.

At the south-western end of the room, between the two assumed ground sills, a shallow groove was observed – this must surely represent traces of a wooden wall. There was no turf bank outside this wall; a trodden-down patch of ground beyond the shallow groove can be interpreted as representing a door. In Iceland, end walls of this type, still in use today, have been built since the Viking Age, as Aage Roussell has also pointed out.[238] On the outside, there was a slight cultural layer, which yielded some burned bones and fragments of whale bone.

This room had another door leading out, in the south-eastern side wall. A cooking pit was found by the north-eastern end wall.

Most of the finds come from this room, including the soapstone spindle whorl, which lay immediately outside the south-eastern door (fig. 47a–b), and a small needle hone of quartzite (fig. 49). These two finds would seem to indicate that this was the women's room, and this may be the explanation of the position of room VI in front of the house. This would give the women a more pleasant room in which to work, facing the sun and sheltered from the coldest winds. The room must have been divided into two parts, but it is not likely that they were separated by a partition wall. The south-western part was probably panelled, while the rest of the room had panelling on the north-western wall only.

Valtýr Guðmundsson states that panelled alcoves were common in various rooms, for instance in the fire house.[239] In ninth and tenth-century Iceland the fire house was panelled, and the floor between the panelling was raised and covered with wood. This is what the earliest sources call a *flet* or *set,* a platform which served as a place for sitting and sleeping. During the Saga Age, only the word *set* was used to describe such a raised sleeping platform in the fire house. During the early periods the fire house was thus used for sleeping and for preparing food, and in winter the women might sit here with their needlework.[240] The finds from room VI accord well with this.

During the early Middle Ages the fire house was usually the largest and finest building on the farm, with one or two outer doors; such fire houses served as kitchens, and all the people of the farm slept there. Such combined kitchens/sleeping quarters must have been normal at early medieval Icelandic farms. But there must have been a tendency even then to separate these two functions of the house, to build separate kitchens and sleeping houses. The former was then known as *eldhús,* fire house, and the latter as *skáli,* sleeping hall. Such a separate fire house might stand on its own, isolated from the other buildings, but this does not seem to have been common practice.[241]

Above we noted that to all appearances room VI must have had two outer doors. One of these led from the south-east into the partially unpanelled part, which probably served as kitchen; the other led from the south-west into the panelled section, probably the alcove. This is in agreement with Valtýr Guðmundsson's observation to the effect that early Icelandic fire houses of the type which served as a combined sleeping alcove and kitchen sometimes had two doors, so that each section had its own entrance.[242]

When assessing the cultural complex here represented, the hearths of house F, which are of four different types, are of particular importance.

The simplest type is merely a long depression in the middle of the floor, running in a longitudinal direction. It is barely 10 cm deep, and has neither stone setting nor stone slabs at the bottom. Hearths of this simple type were found in rooms I and III. There was nothing in these hearths, nor in their surroundings, to suggest that food had been prepared here, and thus it seems most probable that they served exclusively as sources of heat and light.

All the rooms of house A had hearths similar to these. Further – there was a hearth of this type in house D III, this with an ember pit at one end. On pp. 150 and 180 above, in connection with houses A and D, we accounted for the Norse parallels for hearths of this type, and therefore no such account is required here.

The second type, the cooking pit, which occurred in three rooms in house F – II, V and VI – was also encountered in houses A and B. In our description of these houses we pointed out that hearths of this type were not only common in primitive cultures – they also occur regularly in the Norse houses.

The long hearth of room II, which consisted of a cooking pit, an ember pit and a stone slab (figs. 38, 39 and 40) is of particularly great significance in our cultural assessment of house F. This is a typically Norse kind of hearth, one that is so common in the Norse archaeological material that there can hardly be any doubt that the long hearth of house F room II must, in fact, be a Norse hearth. The closest parallels are to be found in some of the Icelandic farm ruins discussed above; there appears to be a particularly striking similarity between this hearth and those at levels 1 and 2 at Ísleifsstaðir in Borgarfjarðar-sýsla. Figs. 89 and 90[243] show the hearths at Ísleifsstaðir – here we find the cooking pit, the little box-like ember pit of stone – the *feluholar* of Old Norse terminology – and the flat stone slab. The only difference between this hearth and that of house F room II is the position of the flat stone slab – at Ísleifsstaðir this lies in the middle, with the cooking pit and the ember pit on either side. The other hearths at Ísleifsstaðir appear to have been of the same type. – The earliest stratum at Snjáleifartóttir in Þjórsárdalur has also yielded a hearth which must be of this type, even though it lacks the ember pit; it has a cooking pit next to the stone slab, however.[244] Unlike the others, this hearth was edged with small stones standing upright, and thus it is somewhat closer to the fine Greenland hearths of the type discussed above in connection with the hearth of house B. The long row of hearths in the farm ruin Ánávik in the West Settlement in Greenland must also be included here.[245] It had a cooking pit and an ember pit, but instead of the stone slab there was a long, narrow depression edged with small stones standing on edge. As in our house B, these different components lay close to one another, but here they did not form one continuous hearth.

Hearths of this type may be traced back to the Viking Age and the periods preceding it in the Scandinavian region, including those districts from which particularly many people emigrated to Iceland. Several of the hearths in the excavated house-sites of Rogaland are of this type.[246] We may mention the hearth in the farm ruin Fosse in Time, Rogaland, which we described above p. 156, and which consisted of several stone slabs ending in a cooking pit.[247] The entire hearth was 2.6 metres long. Nor must we omit the house-site at Oma in Time, Rogaland, whose hearth consists of a slab of stone and a cooking pit.[248] Jan Petersen has demonstrated the difference between the hearths of houses of the early Iron Age and those dating from the Viking Age. In the older houses, the so-called *åregrue* or sunken hearth seems to have been the normal type: this is merely a depression in the floor like the simple Greenland hearths. The hearths of the more recent houses consist of one or more flat slabs of stone, frequently edged with smaller stones. In a few of the older houses a large, flat slab of stone, burned brittle, was found in the vicinity of the sunken hearth. The function of this slab was generally assumed to be that of a drying place for corn – the so-called *tussa*. However, Jan Petersen does not exclude the possibility of a different function also, basing his arguments partly on the fact that they were burned so very brittle. These stone slabs were frequently edged with smaller stones extending above the edge of the slab. Petersen points out that many of the Migration Age house-sites at Utsira have no hearth at all except for a stone slab of this kind. He further shows that this stone slab seems, in the more recent house-sites on the mainland – those dating from the Viking Age and the early Middle Ages – to have developed into the hearth proper of the house.[249]

As a result of Mårten Stenberger's excavations of early Iron Age house-sites on Öland, Sweden, several hearths came to light, in many ways reminiscent of the above. In house-site I at Brostorp there was a hearth running along the middle of the floor, consisting of a flat slab of stone 1.4 metres long and 1.25 metres wide, and a cooking pit 1.1 metres in diameter at the end of the slab.[250]

Similarly, in house I at Övetorp two hearths consisting of stone slabs with cooking pits came to light.[251] The cooking pit was probably used mainly for cooking meat and fish on red-hot stones. This is what Old Norse calls *seyðir*– the cooking fire.

The stone slab may have been used for baking a kind of unleavened bread – the slab would have to be heated first by a fire burning on top of it. The embers from this fire were then swept down into the cooking pit or the ember pit, and the bread was baked on the stone. It is also possible that bread was baked in the cooking pit. In Norway, bread of this kind is known as *glohoppe* (*glo*=ember) or *oskestomp* (New Norw. *oske*=ash), and Hildmar Stigum writes that bread of this kind was used in the countryside until fairly recently. He also states that in Old Norse this kind of bread was called *öskubakað brauð* = bread baked in the ashes.[252] In the nineteenth century it was known as *oskestump* in Setesdalen in Norway. On the Faeroes, a similar kind of bread was baked–this was known as *drýlur* (unleavened bread baked in the embers). Stigum suggests that this was the daily bread of prehistoric Norway.

This primitive method of baking bread was widespread in large parts of Europe. The Greeks baked their bread in this way; the French called theirs *brassier*. – Other types of unleavened bread which were probably baked already in prehistoric Norway are so-called *skoroleg* (a flat barley bread) and *takkekake* or *hellekake*,[253] which were baked on a griddle (*takke*) or slab (*helle*).[254] It is quite possible that this is the kind of bread which was baked on the stone slabs of our hearths.

If we are right in assuming that the flat stone was used for baking bread, one may wonder if the fact that such a stone occurs in the Greenland hearths only during the first years of settlement might perhaps indicate that bread was not baked there later, probably because grain was in so short supply.

The third component, the ember pit or *feluholur,* is discussed in some detail in connection with house B above. In my opinion there is no doubt that the hearth in house F room II belongs to the special type here discussed: it must be a Norse hearth, whose individual components, as well as the practice of arranging them close to one another, may be traced back to the Scandinavian region, to the centuries preceding the Viking Age.

The only hearth not yet discussed is that of room IV (figs. 41–42). As pointed out on p. 74 above, this hearth lies in the western corner of the room. It consists of two stone-lined chambers, separated by a slate slab standing on edge. Hearths of this type were observed in Greenland for the first time in 1896, when Daniel Bruun noted such a hearth in the corner of a room in a ruin near Tingimiut, ruin group No. 2, just a few kilometres from Brattahlið.[255] Later a similar hearth was found in the corner of one of the so-called "thing booths" in the northern fields of Brattahlið (fig. 99), excavated by Poul Nørlund and Mårten Stenberger.[256] Hearths of this type have been found

Fig. 99. Hearth found below the mound of No. 38, in the home field of Brattahlið North Farm, East Settlement, Greenland. After P. Nørlund and M. Stenberger.

Fig. 100. Drawing of the kitchen at the farm Glaumbær, Iceland, showing the double hearth in the background. After D. Bruun.

200

quite a number of times since, and Aage Roussell points out that they are common in Greenland; he states that they might have as many as three compartments, each of which probably corresponds to a cooking vessel.[257]

Such hearths must have been very convenient, otherwise they would hardly have remained in use as long as they apparently did. In old farm kitchens in Iceland they seem to have survived almost down to the present day, the only innovation being that they were raised on a stone platform. On fig. 100 we see a hearth from the farm Glaumbær in Skagafjörður. I think this is a good illustration of the use of hearths of this kind.

There is not really any intrinsic difference between this hearth and the corner hearth of house E, which had one compartment only. Both contained brittle-burned stone, charcoal and ashes, and it was quite obvious that food had been prepared in both.

Corner hearths were discussed in some detail in connection with house E, and no repetition of this discussion is required here.

Some depressions in the floor should be studied in some detail:

In the northern corner of room I we found a depression measuring 90 cm in diameter and 16 cm in depth. At the top it was covered with the same burned stratum as the rest of the room, but further down it contained a black stratum of humus mixed with sand; this had no clearly defined boundary.

As there is no corresponding depression in the opposite corner, it is not certain that this should be interpreted as a post hole. A similar, but somewhat larger depression was found in room II, just north-east of the door opening leading from room II into room V. Its upper diameter was 90 cm, and its depth 60 cm. It extends some little way into the wall. Here, too, the top layer of fill consisted of charcoal, below which we found only sand with a darker "marbelling", undoubtedly a result of the action of the water washing at the turf wall nearby. The Icelandic farm ruins at Þjórsárdalur contain several examples of depressions of this kind just inside a door – Ísleifsstaðir I,[258] Skallakot,[259] Skjeljastaðir[260] and Stöng.[261] Even though these depressions in the Icelandic farms were lined with stone, it seems likely that those of house F may have served the same purpose as their Icelandic counterparts.

Another depression, this one in the door opening between rooms I and II, has an upper diameter of 1.50 metres and is 30 cm deep. This almost looks like two pits merging into each other, and it may be the impression of wooden vessels which stood here. Such vessels were often used for storing water or a thirst-quenching drink known as *skyr,* a kind of curdled milk.

Finally, there is a pit in the eastern corner of room III, 1 metre in diameter and 1 metre deep. Here, too, only the top layer of the fill, at floor level, consisted of charcoal, while below we found a mixture of sand and brownish-black earth. It gives the appearance of having been a kind of storage pit, perhaps for food – no other explanation suggests itself. It may be of interest

201

to note that this pit stood out clearly even before excavation: there was heather growing all around, but the pit was covered with lush, green grass.

A small depression roughly at the middle of the south-western end wall of room V, close up to the wall (p. 76), differed somewhat from the other, for it was filled with charcoal throughout. It is, of course, possible that it served as a kind of ember pit, but this explanation seems unlikely as the hearth lies at the opposite end of the room. A more feasible explanation would seem to be that it held a post which burned while it was still standing in the hole.

Finally we should mention the shallow, roughly circular depression almost in the middle of the floor of room IV (fig. 41): this would seem to be the impression of a small wooden vessel.

The other pits and depressions found in house F require no discussion – as we pointed out above, they are so small as to make it uncertain whether they represent post holes or not. No other explanation suggests itself.

The finds from house F fully confirm our above conclusion regarding the type of house here represented – this complex belongs to the Norse cultural sphere.

True, this house yielded comparatively few finds in relation to its size; but the conditions of preservation here are extremely poor, for the sharp, sandy soil has preserved no objects of wood, antler or bone which may once have lain here – even the iron rivets were in so poor a condition that only one of all the rivets and iron fragments analysed still contained a little iron, the remainder consisting exclusively of rust (see A.M. Rosenqvist below).

The majority of objects found in the Norse farm ruins of Greenland are of bone, antler and wood; apart from these, only stone and iron objects were found: stone lamps, whet-stones and spinning whorls, as well as iron rivets and a few other iron objects. This fact must be borne in mind when we assess the finds from the houses at Épaves Bay.

Apart from the poor conditions of preservation, there is also another aspect to be considered. We know that Eskimoes and Indians sporadically lived on this marine terrace, and we may be sure that they went over the houses with a tooth-comb, taking with them anything of use to them. This is a common enough phenomenon in Greenland, where Norse objects have turned up even in far distant Eskimo settlements.[262] We also know that the Beothuk Indians helped themselves to whatever they could lay hands on of objects belonging to the white settlers.[263]

As for the individual finds, we should first note that house F rooms I, II, III and IV yielded scattered finds, while rooms IV and V were empty. Furthermore, outside both the entrance doors and outside the south-eastern wall of room III, some discarded objects were found lying in shallow middens.

The small stone lamp, LaM 39, which was found in the upper layer of room I together with stones which must come from the roof, is made from a natural beach stone, roundish in form and flat below, which was furnished with a small depression (fig. 48).

This was undoubtedly a lamp designed to burn fish-oil or seal-oil. It has the simplest possible shape; it is so primitive that it might well be expected to occur independently in several different cultures. And in fact identical lamps were used by the Incas of Peru,[264] and they are also known from Polynesia.[265] Obviously these cultures cannot be adduced here. As for the Dorset culture, we know that this cultural complex had various different lamps and cooking vessels. They were worked into round or square vessels, and the majority of them are of soap-stone.[266] Wintemberg has a lamp said to be made from a beach stone, but if we are to judge from his illustration, it has no feature at all in common with our specimen.[267]

The more recent Eskimo culture, the so-called Thule culture, used bowl-shaped soap-stone vessels as lamps and for cooking, just like the Dorset culture. Theirs were large, open vessels, quite unlike our lamp. There are a number of soap-stone lamps of various kinds in the museum at St. Johns, Newfoundland, all ascribed to the Beothuk Indians. Jennes maintains that the Indians' use of soap-stone vessels is a loan from the Eskimo cultures.[268] Howley gives an example of soap-stone lamps found in a Beothuk grave,[269] but Harp is of the opinion that there is not sufficient proof to support the assumption that the Beothuk Indians used soap-stone lamps, and he prefers to think that the Beothuk Indians did not use such lamps.[270] He considers it most likely that these Indians used various kinds of container made from birch bark, and as an example he cites the following account, quoted by Howley: Lieutenant Buchan, who travelled up the Exploits River in the winter of 1810–11 in an attempt to establish friendly relations with the Indians, visited one of their settlements near Red Indian Lake. His description of the cultural elements he observed includes the following: "all their household vessels were made from birch or fir bark . . .," and further "There were iron boilers which must have been plundered from our settlers."[271]

In the archaeological material from Iceland, primitive stone lamps of this kind, there known as *kolur,* are very common. In the ruins of Stöng in Þjórsárdalur, three specimens of this kind, made of tuff or basalt were found: a bowl-shaped depression had been formed in oval pebbles (fig. 102).[272] There are many such lamps in the National Museum in Reykjavik, including the two shown on fig. 101. Another stone lamp of this type was found at Gröf in Öræfum, Iceland.[273]

The houses which have yielded such *kolur* are not among the earliest Icelandic farm ruins, and thus they provide no evidence of the earliest use of such lamps in Iceland. But the National Museum in Reykjavik has a primitive lamp of this type, found in the Ingólfsstaðir house-site, the farm said to have been built by Ingólfr, the first settler in Iceland. The circumstances under

203

which this lamp was found are somewhat uncertain, and thus one can hardly base definite conclusions on the evidence of this one find. It does, however, indicate that such lamps may have been in use in Iceland from the first days of settlement – the material required for making them was readily available everywhere.

No such lamps have as yet been found in Norway, and it seems unlikely that the type should have originated here, for most lamps were made from soap-stone in Viking Age and early medieval Scandinavia, although iron was also used for this purpose. There are rich deposits of soap-stone in Norway, but Iceland has none, and thus all the soap-stone to be used there had to be imported. This would presumably render it not only costly but also rare.

In Greenland as in Norway, soap-stone was the most commonly used material for lamps as well as for cooking vessels, at least during the later phases of settlement. But as some time is bound to pass before settlers are likely to find a soap-stone deposit in their new country, one might have expected to find primitive stone lamps such as this one from house F in the oldest farm ruins in Greenland, those from the time of settlement. But to the best of my knowledge not a single specimen has as yet come to light in Greenland.

We can hardly be certain whether stone lamps of this type originated in Iceland as a substitute for soap-stone lamps, or whether they came to that country from some region outside the Nordic sphere. In this connection we must note that a stone vessel found in a broch near Bowermadden, Caithness, Scotland, is very close to our type.[274]

In his list of objects found at Jarlshof (phase V), Hamilton has a small lamp of sandstone with a depression ¾ inch deep on one side. The sides of this depression are blackened by soot.[275] As there is no illustration showing this lamp, we cannot know whether it is of the same type as ours, but this seems likely.

While ploughing, a farmer found a stone lamp of this type at Fairygreen, Collace, Perthshire.[276] Stone vessels, cups and lamps of stone occur commonly in the local Iron Age culture stone industry from the brochs of Scotland. Many of the objects are of soap-stone, which was imported from Shetland, but a great deal of ordinary stone was also used.[277] The type specimen from Bowermadden, Caithness, was made from an ordinary beach stone, just like the lamp from house F. Thus we cannot exclude the possibility of this particular type of lamp having come to Iceland from Scotland or Orkney and Shetland.

In this connection it is particularly interesting to note that the small soap-stone spindle whorl which was found immediately outside the door of room VI is, in fact, the only soap-stone object of Norse origin found at L'Anse aux Meadows (figs. 47a–b). It was quite obviously made from a fragment of

Fig. 101. Three stone lamps: the upper from house-site F, LaM 39, the two below from house-sites in Iceland, now in the National Museum at Reykjavik. Photo: G. Gestsson.

Fig. 102. Stone lamp from the Icelandic farm Stöng. Photo: G. Gestsson.

205

Fig. 103. The spindle whorl from house-site F (bottom) together with a spindle whorl from a Norse farm in Greenland (top). Scale 1 : 1. Photo: P. Maurtvedt.

a soap-stone pot, for the bottom is concave and blackened by soot. The soot must have been there before the spindle whorl was made – the edges, which were rounded when it was turned into a spindle whorl, showed no traces of soot.

There can be no doubt whatsoever as to the type represented by this spindle whorl – it was the most common type during the Viking Age throughout the entire Nordic region, and it remained in use far into the Middle Ages. It is also very common in the Norse settlements of Greenland (fig. 103).[278]

Jan Petersen's survey of the spindle whorls of Norway, although no longer up-to-date, shows this to be the most common type – of a total of 450 specimens, 300 are of this type. The majority are made from soap-stone – this is the raw material of almost half the total number found, but there are also spindle whorls of sandstone, slate, fired clay, and even iron and glass. The slate spindle whorls seem to have been most common in northern Norway, while those of fired clay predominate in eastern Norway and Trøndelag. In western Norway and in Oppland, on the other hand, soap-stone was the most common material.[279]

Several of the excavated farms in Þjórsárdalur in Iceland have also yielded spindle whorls. A few of these were made from soap-stone, others are of tuff, slate and palagonite.[280] This is due to the fact that soap-stone does not occur naturally in Iceland, but had to be imported. Soap-stone must surely have been preferred as a raw material, for it was easy to work; this we may infer from the fact that in Iceland spindle whorls were often made from fragments of soap-stone vessels. Even in Norway, where soap-stone is plentiful, old potsherds were used for making spindle whorls. A soap-stone sherd found in a house-site in Ulsrud, Skattum, Gran, Hadeland had clearly been subjected to an attempt at turning it into a spindle whorl.[281]

The same has been observed at Jarlshof in Shetland. In house-site No. 2, phase II, a spindle whorl made from a fragment of a soap-stone pot was found.[282]

In the cultural layer of house F and in shallow middens outside, a number of highly corroded small fragments of iron were found: we were able to identify 11 of these fairly securely as fragments of rivets. They appear to be of two types: 1) a rivet with a large, rectangular head or clinch and a comparatively thin shaft (fig. 86); 2) a rivet with a comparatively small head and a longer and thicker shaft (fig. 50). Type 1 appears to have been a clinch rivet with a rectangular head. Most of the specimens of this type were found in the vicinity of the entrance doors, and it seems reasonable to suppose that they had been used on wooden doors. Type 1 is very common throughout the Norse region. The rivets found in houses A and D would also appear to be of this type.

Type 2, with its comparatively small head and thicker shaft, looks like a nail rather than a rivet. It may perhaps be of the same type as a nail found at Lundur in Iceland.[283] A large specimen of this type was found in room VI (fig. 50).

A number of smaller iron fragments, which could not be determined, were also found, including one which looks like half a ring, except that one end is thicker than the other. For more information about the iron objects, I would refer the reader to A. M. Rosenqvist below.

A small needle hone of quartzite was found in the lowest, 10 cm thick cultural layer of room VI (fig. 49). Needle hones of this type are very common in the Norse cultural complex. Most of them are furnished with a hole at one end,[284] but specimens without a hole are also common. The earliest parts of Lund in Sweden have yielded such needle hones – of slate – with as well as without holes.[285] Another example, from "Vesle Hjerkinn", a house-site in Dovre, Norway, was excavated by Bjørn Hougen. This house-site has a secure date *non ante quem,* provided by a coin minted during the reign of Olav III, and most probably dates from the 1070s.[286]

In the Norse farm ruins of Greenland small hones of this type are also common.[287] The National Museum in Reykjavik has several specimens, and others were found at Jarlshof in Shetland.[288] In other words – this is a very common item in the Norse cultural sphere.

Of course it is not impossible that the Dorset culture, or any of the Indian cultures which might be considered here, should also have had an implement of this type, since the form of the hone is so simple and so highly functional, but I have been unable to trace any such hone within these cultural complexes. It is important to note that small needle hones of this type are typical of the Norse cultural complex, and that this find thus supports our above conclusions.

Four chippings of red jasper were found, one in a hearth, two near a hearth, and one in a midden outside the house. The largest measures 1.9 cm, and it is blunt at one end. There can hardly be any doubt that these chippings derive from fire lighting stones. I would also refer to the letter from Professor T. Barth, App. IV.

In this context we must also mention the small piece of flint found in the lowest layer in room VI. As this was found at floor level, it can hardly derive from native tool manufacture – it is most likely to be a chipping from a fire flint. For further information, I would refer to the discussion on p. 162 above.

Among the stones found in a heap on top of the cultural layer of room IV – those which are assumed to have lain on top of the turf roof – a fragment of a sandstone hone was found, LaM 104. It is 16 cm long, 10.4 cm wide and 2–3 cm thick. The upper surface, which is smooth and concave, has three deep grooves, the result of grinding sharp objects. In my view, it is impossible to assign this fragment to any particular cultural complex.

Some lumps of slag were found in various places in and outside the house. For more information about these, I would refer to A.M. Rosenqvist, below.

Right down on sterile ground, a fragment of a green jasper tool, 2.5 cm long, was found. One side of this tool has retouch with clearly marked serrations; the spine is 2–3 mm thick. The piece is broken at the fourth tooth (fig. 52).

Serrated implements of this kind occur in the Dorset culture where they, however, appear to have been shorter.[289] To the best of my knowledge, no survey of tools of this kind in the Beothuk culture is available. What we do know, however, is that the Norse people had a tool known in literature as "smoothing sticks"; but these were made from bone, and appear to have been somewhat larger than that found in house F is likely to have been.[290] Thus we do not know whether this really was a "smoothing stick" or not. A similar implement was found during the excavation at Jarlshof in Shetland, but its Norse origin is doubtful.[291] – No more archaeological information is as yet available on this subject. An analysis of the stone from which our implement was made may perhaps supply additional evidence.

A few slivers of charred bone were found in house F. Håkon Olsen of the

Zoological Museum in Bergen has kindly analysed these. Apart from some fragments of whalebone, it was impossible to determine the species represented by these bones (App. V).

The above discussion of the material seems to make it quite clear that house F must be of Norse origin. This conclusion is first and foremost based on the house itself – a long house of the so-called "Þjórsárdalur type". As we pointed out above, house F differs slightly from the standard "Þjórsárdalur" houses in that a room has here been added also to the front wall of the long house. We showed on p. 192 above that this is a likely extension of the type, and in the case of house F it was an obvious and practical proposition to build the room which apparently served as the women's quarters on to the front of the house.

Further, we showed that the different hearths of this house belong to types which were common in the Norse cultural sphere during the Viking Age and the centuries preceding this period. In addition, it appears that the finds – several of which, such as rivets, slag and jasper also occur in several other houses on the terrace – clearly belong to the Norse cultural complex. This is true not least of the spindle whorl. However, no secure dates can be derived from any of these finds, but the form of the house, as well as the types of hearths and their position in the rooms, give a fairly good indication of the time when the house must have been inhabited: the closest parallels for the house itself are to be found in some of the farm ruins in Þjórsárdalur, as we saw above. It was formerly held that this valley was laid waste when Hekla erupted in A.D. 1300,[292] but Sigurður Thorarinsson has recently arrived at the conclusion that the valley was laid waste and the farms with which we are here concerned were buried as a result of the eruption in A.D. 1104.[293]

Thus houses of this type were still in use in Iceland in A.D. 1104, but we do not know when the first ones were built. The radio-carbon analyses of material from this house have yielded the following four dates: A.D. 870, A.D. 700, A.D. 1025 and A.D. 1000, the first two of these derive from charcoal from the hearths of rooms II and IV respectively, the third derives from turf from the walls of room IV, while the last derives from a piece of whalebone which lay at the bottom of the hearth of room III.

The dates deriving from whalebone must be more secure than those deriving from charcoal from the hearths, for driftwood may have been used as fuel. Épaves Bay is, after all, a typical driftwood bay. I would here also refer the reader to Reidar Nydal, L.M. Paulssen and Kari Henningsmoen below. If we therefore consider A.D. 1000 to be the most correct of these dates, we find ourselves well within the period during which houses of this type are known to have been built. The hearths, their form and their position in the rooms, offer further support for this early date. Poul Nørlund, Mårten Stenberger[294] and Aage Roussell[295] have all devoted special attention to the

Greenland hearths, and their results show that several of the types of hearth discussed above were built only during the first years of settlement; later, small hearths and cooking pits were taken into use.

All in all, it seems most likely that house F was in use at some time during the first part of the eleventh century.

Interpretation of house-sites G and J (p. 83 and p. 87)

Like house E, houses G and J are sunken-floored huts, but they differ from E in that they were dug out of the sloping side of the terrace. Thus the gravel of the terrace forms three of the walls of each house, while the fourth has disappeared. The entrance must presumably have been in this fourth wall, in which case the door of house G faced the bay and that of house J the river – north-west and south-east respectively.

These small house-sites were cut deeper down into the ground than house E – 118 cm and 135 cm respectively. No traces of any wall which might have shored up the gravel and prevented it from sliding into the house – and which might perhaps also have supported the roof – remained either along the edge of the depression or at the edge of the cultural layer within these houses. We shall return to this point at a later stage.

House-site G gave a fairly clear picture. We were able to differentiate between three different strata. The uppermost was tough and resisted scraping, and it stood out clearly from the loose, greyish sand and gravel below. As stated on p. 83 above, a large, cracked slab of slate, with two large stones from the shore on top of it, was lying immediately below the grass sod (figs. 53 and 54). For quite a while we were mystified by the function of the slate and the stones, which had obviously been put there intentionally. As we dug our way down into the loose sand, we found a distinct floor layer at a depth of c. 60 cm, with a hearth up against the wall. Now the depression assumed the appearance of a small room, sunk deeply down into the terrace. The tough layer on top must represent the turf roof of the house, and the slate slab must have covered a smoke hole in the roof. Now the function of the two large stones from the shore also appears: they must presumably have weighed down the slate in order to prevent it from being blown off the roof. It seems most likely that the loose sand between the upper, tough layer of earth and the floor layer at the bottom represents the gravel and sand of the walls which must have caved in, subsiding into the room. This must have been the first part of the house to collapse, presumably followed by the wall which held the door. We showed on p. 84 above that one iron rivet and two fragments of iron were found at 25 cm, 40 cm and 30 cm above floor level respectively, and in the light of the finds from the other houses we would interpret these as deriving from a door.

210

Finally the turf roof collapsed, taking with it the slate slab and the stones; now grass started to grow, covering the remains of the house. This is the most likely explanation of the origin of the shallow depression at the edge of the terrace.

House-site J did not provide us with as much information as to the construction. Kristján Eldjárn did not note any tough upper layer of earth, which might be interpreted as the roof of the house (p. 87). Immediately below the surface grass, the Icelandic archaeologists found a layer of sand mixed with charcoal. This circumstance led Eldjárn to infer that house J could not have been a proper house with walls and a roof. We find this difficult to believe, for in a climate as rainy as that of northern Newfoundland one would hardly instal a smithy – and this was the function of house J – without covering it with a roof of some kind. Nor should one encounter any difficulty, for turf and other materials were readily available. The layer of charcoal which was still lying at the far end of the room would quickly become wet through and quite useless if it were not under cover. High up in the cultural layer there were some fairly large slabs of slate – like those found in some of the other houses on the terrace, they may have lain on top of the roof turf; as, however, no tough layer was found below the slate of house J but lots of charcoal, the smithy may perhaps have burned down. The fact that such large amounts of charcoal occurred throughout the fill, right up to the top of the depression, may mean that the turf which once covered the roof was completely devoured by the flames. On the other hand – the heap of charcoal which lay at the far end of the smithy might presumably have burned together with the house, if the smithy really was destroyed by fire. Some of the other houses on the terrace, such as F and D III, were also burned down, but on comparison we see that the roof turf of house F does not seem to have been destroyed completely by the conflagration. It may perhaps have been wet as the result of rain. There we were able to distinguish a clearly marked tough, black top layer, full of pieces of charcoal.

This room must also have been without any internal walls to shore up the gravel and prevent it from subsiding into the room, Kristján Eldjárn gives a very graphic description of this: "There was no sharply defined limit at the sides of the cultural layer; it followed the edges of the depression upwards, like irregular tongues, while tongues of sand stretched down along the edges, so that the sand and the cultural layer intertwined, as it were."

A comparison of house-sites G and J before as well as after excavation reveals so many points of resemblance that we would seem to be justified in assuming that these two houses must have been built by the same methods, at least as far as their principal features are concerned. I consider it most likely that houses G and J were small, domed houses sunk deeply into the edge of the terrace, and that their front walls must have held the door. It would seem that there must have been smoke holes in the domed roofs. Buildings of such a primitive type may well have their origin in various cultures.

We know that certain American Indian tribes built sunken-floored huts,[296] but the fact that not a single item of Indian origin has been found either in house G or house J makes it seem unlikely that these sunken-floored huts should derive from them. Moreover, these Indians tribes never came to Newfoundland. True, the midden NE of house G yielded some stone implements of Archaic Indian origin, but items indicative of Norse occupation of house G were also found there (see p. 54); inside the house, rivets and fragments of iron in the same corroded state as iron from the other houses were found. Further – the water trench which runs down the slope of the terrace immediately SE of house G would appear to be connected with this house, and if house G was a bath-house – which is what we believe – such a water trench would have a natural function. This trench was partially lined with slate, a feature frequently observed in Greenland, for instance in the Hall at Brattahlið and in the Narssaq house.[297]

Any function other than that of a smithy would seem to be out of the question for house J. In that case, no North American Indian tribes can be considered in connection with this house at the time it was occupied, according to the evidence of the radio-carbon dates.

Certain Eskimo houses, on the other hand, resemble G and J on some points, although the resemblance is superficial. We need not take the Dorset Eskimoes into account here. As Elmer Harp has stated, they lived in round or oval tents in their Newfoundland settlements,[298] and the traces left by these take the form of shallow, saucer-shaped depressions in the ground, surrounded by a grass-covered ridge of earth.

But there are more recent groups of Eskimoes whose houses might leave traces superficially resembling those of house-sites G and J. I am here thinking particularly of houses of the type investigated by Junius Bird at Avertok near Hopedale in Labrador.[299] The ruins which he excavated here had appeared merely as slight depressions in the ground prior to excavation. Bird's types I a, b and c are of particular interest in the present context. They had an irregular, almost oval plan, and were furnished with a long entrance tunnel. Characteristic of them are their turf walls; the walls of the tunnel, on the other hand, were of stone, as a rule. There was a raised platform of gravel and sand along the rear wall. The floors were paved, and a timber structure formed the roof of the tunnel.[300]

The above shows that the resemblance between these houses and our house-sites G and J is confined to their appearance prior to excavation, which is due to their having been sunk in the ground. G and J lack the long entrance tunnel, and they have neither stone floors nor platforms – all these are typical

Eskimo features. The more recent houses at Avertok also lack the long entrance tunnel, but they do not resemble G and J in the slightest: they are large, rectangular, and have stone floors and sleeping platforms along three of the walls.[301] Another important point – none of these houses has a hearth, whereas G and J both have open hearths, by the wall and in the middle of the floor respectively.

Bird assumes that the houses of types I a, b and c were in use in the mid or late sixteenth century.

We noted above that no traces of any more recent habitation have been found on the terrace at Épaves Bay, but we must nevertheless consider the possibility of G and J deriving from a settlement of whalers or fishermen of historic times.

Along the coast of Labrador, Quebec and Newfoundland there are a number of places with ruins of houses built by early colonists. Many of these places have French names. The majority of the ruins appear as thick banks of earth, frequently densely overgrown. Some of these houses had cellars, and the woodwork and posts supporting the floor of the house may be in a surprisingly good state of preservation. Test digs in these ruins have brought to light iron nails – also in a very good state of preservation – fragments of clay pipes, fishing hooks and glazed pot-sherds. Sometimes such a settlement also includes a large brick oven, probably used for baking bread. Nearby, there are depressions in the ground, filled with very fat, black earth – this is probably where the vessels used for smelting whale and seal blubber stood. All in all – these historic whalers' and fishermen's settlements are just about as different from the settlement at Épaves Bay as possible.

We pointed out in connection with house E that small, sunken-floored huts of this type are common in the Norse cultural sphere, from prehistory until modern times. In prehistoric days, the type represented by house E would appear to have been the most common. As a rule, such houses were dug down into the ground to a depth of about 40 cm below ground level. G and J represent a variant, for houses of this type are dug into a terrace or a slope from the side. – Both these types of sunken-floored hut occur in prehistoric Scandinavian settlements. As an example we may mention the two huts of the same type as G and J which Wilhelm Holmqvist has excavated on the island of Helgö in Lake Mälaren in Sweden (the cellar buildings).[302] One of these lay 90 cm below ground level. He found no traces of any wall construction, but in one of the houses paving came to light, stopping 20–25 cm beyond the outer edge of the house. Holmqvist interprets this as showing that the walls may have been 20–25 cm thick, but nothing is known about the material from which they were made. One of the Helgö houses had a corner hearth with a flat stone slab at the bottom – Holmqvist regards this as being a baking house. This baking house, as well as several of the other sunken-floored huts on

Helgö, would seem to belong to the early phase of settlement here. Several large house-sites are dated to the same phase.[303]

Sunken-floored huts of this type, dug into the ground, seem to have remained in use longer in Scandinavia and Iceland than elsewhere, and they are still used as fire houses, potato cellars, smithies, cow-sheds, boat-sheds, etc. In Norway they are particularly common in the western part of the country and in the county of Nordland, but they also occur in eastern Norway.[304]

Bearing in mind how common these small sunken-floored huts are in the Norse cultural sphere, and considering the radio-carbon dates yielded by houses G and J, together with the evidence of the iron rivets, iron fragments, iron slag etc. found in these houses, we arrive at a prehistoric date of habitation, around A.D. 1000, by a people no longer at a Stone Age stage of culture, a people who apparently forged their tools from iron which they must presumably have extracted from bog-ore.

At this early date none of the Indian or Eskimo groups who lived in these parts can be responsible for the houses. Not only are the houses of a type different from theirs, but, moreover, these people were still at a Stone Age stage of culture. The Beothuk Indians were unfamiliar with iron when they first came into contact with the white settlers. The laborious process of extracting iron from bog ore was completely unknown to all these people. On p. 175 above, in connection with house-site C, we discussed the Eskimoes' use of iron. It appeared then that their use of iron must have been highly sporadic – they used either iron which they found attached to driftwood, or meteoric iron.

At one time Samuel E. Morison claimed that house J (the smithy) at L'Anse aux Meadows had been built and used by French whalers.[305] Later, however, he arrived at the conclusion that this house must form part of the settlement on the terrace, and that it must be contemporary with the other houses here.[306]

The white settlers in America were familiar with the art of extracting iron from bog-ore. In 1645 John Winthrop jr., later governor of Connecticut, established an iron works at Saugus near Lynn. Here iron was extracted from bog-ore which was smelted with charcoal made from oak. Other foundries were later established, and they are the forerunners of the modern iron industry of the United States.[307] But house J cannot possibly be in any way connected with the French settlement on the headland, which is discussed on p. 134. In addition to the facts cited above, we must also note that the iron found in house J was in so poor a state of preservation that no more than a crust of rust remained; iron found in white settlements, on the other hand, is in a good state of preservation. Moreover, we have two radio-carbon dates deriving from house J: A.D. 1060, and A.D. 860. These dates accord well with

214

most of the radio-carbon dates obtained from the other houses on the terrace, and they lend support to the assumption that house J forms part of this settlement. Furthermore, not a single implement or fragment suggestive of whalers, fishermen or other early white settlers has been found; there are, for instance, no fragments of clay pipes, and these are very frequent at such settlements.

There is a small earthen house probably of early colonial type at L'Anse aux Meadows, still in use as a potato cellar. It may have been built as a sunken-floored hut, or it may have had turf walls, and its domed roof is made from turf. In appearance, this house is strikingly similar to the probable original appearance of houses G and J, but, as should have been clearly demonstrated above, it is quite out of the question that these two houses should have been used for storing potatoes.

The small potato cellar at L'Anse aux Meadows merely shows that houses of this simple type may occur spontaneously in different cultures. It is also possible that the English emigrants who settled here during the eighteenth century might have built such earthen huts in a way with which they had been familiar in England. We discussed the distribution of this type of house in prehistoric Europe above, and in fact it is not impossible that our sunken-floored huts E, G and J should have the same cultural background and ancient roots in Europe as the potato cellar at L'Anse aux Meadows!

It thus appears that the closest parallels for our small sunken-floored huts are to be found within the Norse cultural complex.

There can be no doubt that house J was a smithy. Norse farms usually had their own smithy, most often some way away from the dwelling houses, because of the danger of fire, and often on the bank of a river, like house J.

Several prehistoric Norse smithies have been found. Aage Rousell has excavated an unusually fine smithy at the farm Stöng in Þjórsárdalur in Iceland.[308] This farm was laid waste by an eruption of Mt. Hekla, probably in A.D. 1104. The thick layer of ash and pumice under which it is buried has helped to preserve the ruins in an incomparably fine state of preservation.

The ruins of another smithy were found when the Norse farm at Jarlshof in Shetland was excavated.[309] This consists of one room only. In the middle of the floor there is an open hearth made from four large stones. One of these, a little smaller than the others, had served as an anvil. This smithy is more primitive than that at Stöng, and more reminiscent of house J at L'Anse aux Meadows.

The smithy at Sandnes, ruin group No. 51 at the West Settlement in Greenland, is also primitive, and very similar to house J. Here the hearth is in a corner, and a large stone formed the anvil.[310]

The smithy at the ancient bishop's farm at Garðar in the East Settlement

215

Fig. 104. The smithy at the Icelandic farm Keldur, seen from behind, with the smoke-opening in the roof.

in Greenland also consists of one room only. It is built of stone. There was a large stone "forge" at the eastern end of the room.[311]

Further examples could be cited, but the above should suffice to show how primitive these smithies often were, and how common the presence of a smithy on a farm was in the Norse cultural complex.

None of the above examples was a sunken-floored hut. We should here also mention the great number of small sunken-floored huts excavated at Warendorf in Westphalia; according to Winkelmann they were workshops serving various farm purposes, and some of them must have been smithies. If this is correct, they are our closest parallels for house J.[312]

The oldest farm of Iceland, Keldur in Sydlandet, has a smithy which is still in use today (fig. 104). It stands on the bank of the river, and has a domed roof with a smoke opening. This is surely what house J must once have looked like! Today the smithy at Keldur lies quite deeply in the edge of the terrace, but it is impossible to say whether it was built in this way, or whether its present level is a result of drifting sands. The interior of this smithy has stone walls and roof, and thus it is a more advanced kind of structure than house J. But

216

apart from this, the two smithies must have resembled each other closely.

Regarding the iron fragments, slag etc. found in the smithy, I would refer to Anna M. Rosenqvist below. No identifiable objects were found in the cultural layer, but above this, just below the surface grass, a soap-stone lamp (LaM 343) was found at the far western end of the depression, its opening facing up (fig. 57). This is an Eskimo lamp, of the Dorset culture, and so far it is the only such lamp found in Newfoundland. The extensive excavations of a Dorset site at Port aux Choix have not yielded a single lamp of this type. Farther north, however, in polar regions and in Greenland similar lamps have been found.[313]

Jim Tuck (Dept. of Anthropology, Memorial University of Newfoundland) has personally informed me that it is quite possible that the Norsemen might have brought this lamp along from Greenland. The circumstances of the find indicate that the lamp must have lain on the roof.

A radio-carbon analysis of roots and turf from inside the lamp has yielded a twentieth-century date.

The rootlets inside the lamp presumably come from the grass covering the site prior to excavation.

The finds from house G do not give a clear indication of the purpose of this house. But one feature was remarkable – the very great amount of brittle-burned stone in the fill, and the hearth with the cracked stone slab which shows that big fires must have been lit here. The function of this hearth we cannot determine today, but as it is typologically entirely different from those of the other houses, it seems likely that it should also have had a different function. One may, of course, raise the objection that the stone slab in house G was put in an upright position in order to make more room in this small house, where the hearth might otherwise have occupied too large a part of the available floor space; but this can hardly be the whole explanation. Most of the brittle-burned stones found in the hearth and elsewhere were larger than cooking stones tend to be, and thus they may well have been used for purposes other than cooking and baking. The stone slab, which was burned extremely brittle, has been subjected to great differences of temperature.

We discussed sunken-floored huts of this type in the Norse cultural sphere in connection with house E. According to Valtýr Guðmundsson, nineteenth-century Iceland still had a small sunken-floored house, the *dyngja,* as mentioned above on p. 189, where the women used to sit at their needlework.[314] This must be the house in which, according to Pliny, the Germanic women used to weave.[315] The walls of the *dyngja* were apparently low, as it was most often sunk into the ground for the sake of warmth and comfort. There were earthen benches but, according to the sagas, no fires were ever lit in this house.[316]

Thus our house G, whose most characteristic feature was the fact that large fires must have burned there, can hardly be a *dyngja*. It would seem more natural to interpret it as a bath-house. Bath-houses usually had a stone stove and loose stones which were heated before bathing; then cold water was poured on the stones, quickly producing steam. The large slate slab (figs. 53 and 54), which probably covered the smoke opening in the roof, is described in the excavation report. If house G really was a bath-house, this slate slab had an important function, for by covering the smoke opening, one could prevent the steam from escaping. Probably water was also poured on to the hearth and the heated stones from the hole in the roof.[317]

While excavating an Icelandic farm, Gröf in Öræfum – which appears to have been laid waste when Mt. Öræfajökull erupted in 1362 – Gísli Gestsson was able to demonstrate that one of the rooms (room V) of the complex must have been a bath-house.[318] Here, too, a great number of brittle-burned stones were found, as well as a hearth, even though the room was small. The finds suggest that this bath-house was used for other purposes too, and that it also served as a working room for the women – this, however, is a result of conditions peculiar to Iceland. When, as a result of a fuel shortage, one had to stop lighting fires on the floor of the living room, the bath-house – the only room which had a stove – was sometimes used as living quarters, particularly by the farmer's own family; it was at times used also at night. Later, when stone stoves were installed in the living rooms, the name bath-house was transferred to these.[319] It seems evident that in a country such as Iceland, which is so short of fuel, one would make a point of utilizing the warmth of the bath-houses as long as ever possible, and not only while bathing, even though the other rooms of the farm were equipped with hearths.

Gísli Gestsson points out that the bath-house at Gröf had distinct traces of benches along the walls[320] – these house G lacked. But that does not necessarily mean that house G had no such sitting or lying benches, for here the conditions of preservation were far less favourable than in the bath-house at Gröf, and thus traces of such benches may well have disappeared.

Valtýr Guðmundsson discusses a number of bath-houses, some of them sunk into the ground, others built as cellars under other houses.[321] Such bath-houses usually had stone stoves. In the Eyrbyggja Saga we read that Styr had a bath-house built on his farm Hraun, and that this was sunk into the ground. There was an opening in the roof, above the stove, so that water could be poured on from outside. This bath-house had a small lobby, which was connected to the bath-house proper by a door.[322]

The Icelandic sagas make occasional mention of bath-houses, and they appear to have been quite common there during the thirteenth century, but there are very few mentions referring to the first part of the Saga Age. This has led some authors to believe that bath-houses were not in use in Iceland during

218

the early phases, but Valtýr Guðmundsson states that there is a great deal of evidence showing that bath-houses were in common use also during the early years of settlement, especially on the larger farms.[323] Arnheiður Sigurðardottir appears to share this view.[324] The many sunken-floored huts excavated by Þór Magnússon at Hvítarholt in Arnessýsla are clear evidence in favour of this theory.[325] They belong to a farm complex whose oldest phase to all appearances would seem to date from an early period, possibly from the time of settlement. Þór Magnússon interprets these huts as bath-houses.

At Umìviarsuk (ruin group No. 52a) in the West Settlement in Greenland, Aage Roussell has identified one of the ruins as a bath-house.[326] There was a stove in one corner, and the wooden platform which had been used for sitting or lying on was in an unusually good state of preservation. Roussell also points out that the fill contained a remarkably great number of brittle-burned stones. This house dates from the thirteenth or fourteenth century, and there can be no doubt whatever that it was a bath-house. In this context we should also mention the Viking Age settlement at Freswick in Caithness, Scotland, one of whose ruins was a bath-house.[327] This one had a lobby, like Styr's bath-house at Hraun.

Bath-houses were very common in the North throughout the Middle Ages, and they are still in regular use in Finland today. The interior of the medieval bath-houses of Scandinavia was very similar to that of the bath-houses described above.[328] As yet we have no evidence of bath-houses in prehistoric Norway.

Wilhelm Holmqvist thinks that he may have identified one of the sunken-floored huts excavated on the island of Helgö in Lake Mälaren in Sweden as a bath-house.[329] If Holmqvist is right in his assumption, this is the earliest bath-house as yet found in Scandinavia.

The only finds from house G were one fragmentary iron rivet and two fragments of iron which probably also derive from rivets. These fragments were found at a depth of 40 cm, 25 cm and 30 cm in the fill. It seems reasonable to assume that they were once attached to a wooden door which must have fallen into the room when the sand from the disintegrating walls had reached a certain height within the house. As far as it was possible to tell, this rivet did not differ typologically from several of those found in the other houses on the terrace at Épaves Bay, and it was in an equally poor state of preservation.

We should be justified in inferring from the above that house G was a bath-house; the radio-carbon date derived from charcoal found in the hearth and the fragments of iron found in the fill provide clear evidence to show that this bath-house forms part of the Norse settlement on the terrace.

Feature 7 (p. 102), which was excavated by Charles J. Bareis and Jon H. Winston, is probably a water trench, running down the slope of the terrace immediately south-east of house-site G. If this interpretation is correct, it underlines our assumption that house G is a bath-house, because one needs water for producing steam and this house lies quite a way from the brook.

Interpretation of the Charcoal Kiln (p. 93)

The charcoal kiln, 7 metres south-west of the smithy (house J), appears as a deep depression in the ground. Its upper diameter is 1.5 metres and it is 0.75 metres deep (fig. 55). A radio-carbon analysis yielded the date A.D. 820 + 70 years; we thus have good reason to assume that it forms part of the settlement on the terrace (cf. R. Nydal below).

Charcoal kilns are common in the Norse cultural complex; in some places they were still in use in living memory, for instance in the valleys of Norway. To the best of my knowledge we have no secure evidence of their earliest date, but the fact that they are frequently found at a fairly low level during ditching operations renders it likely that their use may be traced back to a prehistoric date.

In the past, charcoal burning formed an important part of the farmer's work. Charcoal was used in the smithy – and most farms had their own smithy – and the extraction of iron from bog-ore required a great deal of charcoal.

Several methods were employed. One of them, possibly the most ancient in the Norse cultural complex, used a pit in the ground, the kind of pit we found here on the terrace at Épaves Bay. We also know of charcoal kilns above ground; these could lie level with the surface, or raised on a small mound. Kilns of this kind were for instance used for the production of charcoal for the copper works at Røros in Norway. These kilns undoubtedly could produce more charcoal than those in a sunken pit, but the men attending them must have had to exercise a great deal of care and attention, for the slightest breath of wind might make the fire blaze up, thus burning up all the charcoal. The pits are most likely to have been used by farmers for their own requirements, for one could not produce much charcoal at a time by this method. In Dølaminne 1971, Asle Kirkedalen has a description of charcoal burning in Hallingdal, Norway, during the 1880s.[330] Deep pits were used here. They had one great advantage as compared to the kilns above ground – they were easier to attend to, because the draught from below did not reach the fire as easily. This must have been of particular importance in a windy climate such as that of Épaves Bay.

Thus the charcoal kiln at Épaves Bay, situated close to the smithy, must have formed an important link in the process of forging iron. It seems likely that charcoal produced here must also have been used for extracting iron from bog-ore – there were large quantities of such ore in the bog just south of the houses. The extraction of iron also required pits, the so-called smelting pits; no such pit has as yet come to light, but it would be most surprising if these

220

Norsemen, who not only were familiar with the art of extracting iron from bog- ore, but who also relied on iron as an essential material, had not extracted iron here at Épaves Bay, where there was an ample supply of bog-ore and plenty of forest for fuel. In fact, Épaves Bay would seem to be the ideal spot for this process. The smelting pit has not been found, it is true, but that does not mean that no iron was extracted on the terrace. We may compare this with the finds from Greenland, where slag and smithy have been found, but no smelting pit. Niels Nielsen (1930) has analysed this slag. Basing his arguments on fifteen lumps of slag from two different localities – Igaliko and Qagssiars- suk – he arrives at the conclusion that the Greenland Norsemen must have produced iron from bog-ore in Greenland, for he feels that all the necessary pre-requisites were present here – there was bog-ore as the raw material, and wood for fuel.[331]

If Nielsen considers that conditions in Greenland were favourable enough for the extraction of iron, in spite of the poor supply of wood there, conditions in Newfoundland must be considered extraordinarily good. Keeping in mind the conditions to which the Norsemen were accustomed in Greenland and Iceland, where the production of iron must have been restricted by the amount of fuel available, they must surely have extracted iron on the terrace at Épaves Bay. For the first time, they had an ample and ready supply of both bog-ore and fuel at their disposal.

I would here also refer to Å.M. Rosenqvist's article below.

Interpretation of the out-door hearths and cooking pits

Ten metres west of house J and four metres north-west of the charcoal kiln, the Icelandic archaeologists, led by Kristján Eldjárn, uncovered some primi- tive hearths in 1962. They were situated on a horizontal ledge about 50 cm below the level of the charcoal kiln and about 4 metres above the modern high-water line. The excavators considered that these hearths formed one entity, as they lay in a straight line running north-south. Because of their primitive character they were interpreted as native hearths. Eleven small flint chippings which were found close to the northernmost hearth lend support to this view. But close to the southernmost hearth a lump of slag was found, trodden into the sand, and there were also a few other lumps of slag in the vicinity of the hearths. Thus the finds from these hearths do not provide evidence for any conclusion except that the lumps of slag and the flint chipping must presumably be roughly contemporary with the hearths. The hearths are stated to have lain immediately above the sand.

These hearths are made from small beach stones, some of which have been burned brittle (pls. 41 and 42). Nothing either in their form or in any other feature is suggestive of any particular cultural complex.

We should here like to consider the presence of hearths at this particular spot in rather more detail. They lie on the terrace, a little way south of and above the only place where a boat could possibly land, the spot where the boat-sheds were found. It seems that the Norsemen must have landed here, and they can hardly have wasted much time before lighting fires, preparing food, and warming themselves after the long, cold crossing. From that point of view it seems likely that these hearths should date back to the very earliest days of the Norse settlement, that they were used while the people were still busy building their turf houses. It also seems likely that they should have pitched their tents somewhere around here.

Nor must we reject the idea of native use – it seems quite likely that they used the hearths, perhaps at a later date, for they would also find this an ideal spot for camping. We know that Eskimoes and also Indians were on this site – but unfortunately the cultural context of the chippings found close to one of the hearths could not be determined.

These hearths out in the open are in many ways comparable to the so-called "Fireplace area" which Poul Nørlund and Mårten Stenberger excavated in the fields of North Brattahlið farm in the East Settlement in Greenland, even though the Greenland hearths were far less primitive than ours.[332] They interpreted the hearths of the "Fireplace area" and the sheds nearby as Greenland's first Thing site – this explanation is self-evident, for they lie on the fields of Eirík the Red's own farm. But there is another possibility also: might not these hearths and sheds represent the first, temporary home of Eirík and his household, where they lived while building the house on the farm? In support of such an assumption we may adduce the fact that hearths of this type are common in Iceland, while they were probably used in Greenland only during the first years of settlement. As we have already pointed out, a similar hearth was also found in the house interpreted as Eirík's own hall.

In 1963, when excavating in the area, Charles Bareis and Jon Winston interpreted feature 8 (see pl. 56), which consists of two stone circles, as tent rings, i.e. as stones which once lay on top of the hide or other fabric of a tent, weighing it down. These circles of stone are close to the row of hearths, but as circle No. 1 yielded 2 chert items (LaM 212–213), it is likely that they derive from a native population. Tent rings like these are very common in North America, and may be ascribed either to the Indians or to the Eskimoes.

Apart from feature 8, Charles Bareis' and Jon Winston's report covers seven other features excavated in 1963.

Feature 2 (p. 99) may possible be a sunken hearth or cooking pit. Four chert items were found here, lying in grey sand on the top of the pit (LaM 184a–d). Two of the four chert items from this feature have been identified as scrapers (LaM 184 a and b). In the following, I refer to the excavation report

222

and catalogue of finds with regard to the coordinates and analyses of the items found in connection with these features.

Feature 3 (p. 99 pl. 52 and fig. 59) is also undoubtedly a hearth, 2.16 metres long and 1.51 metres wide. It was not sunk into the ground. This hearth yielded brittle-burned stones found together with charcoal, animal bones and 30 chert items (LaM 189 a–b).

The excavators suggest that these items are of Boreal Archaic affiliation, but according to William Taylor they defy identification.

A radio-carbon analysis of charcoal from the fill has yielded the date A.D. 1500 ± 90 years. T–410.

Feature 4 (p. 100) is a hearth, level with the ground. It yielded brittle-burned stones, charcoal and 27 chert items (LaM 185 and 214).

The excavators suggest that the presence of chert items indicates that the hearth derives from the Boreal Archaic culture. It is not impossible that specimen LaM 185 could belong to the Archaic, whose assemblages do include prismatic flakes, but its particular attributes, and the incidence of microblades in Dorset sites suggest the possibility of a Dorset affiliation for this object. A radio-carbon analysis of charcoal from the feature yielded the date A.D. 1060 ± 90 years. T–411.

Feature 6 (pl. 54, fig. 60, p. 102) is a hearth, oval in shape, measuring 0.63 m north to south and 0.53 m east to west. There was no evidence of a pit. A concentration of fire-cracked stones was found at the base of the sod. The feature was entirely consolidated with the charcoal concentrated around the firecracked stones. No animal bones or chert items were found in this feature.

Approximately 2.5 metres NW, and 3.5 metres and 4 metres W respectively of the hearth two iron fragments and one iron rivet were found (LaM 310, 313, 314).

I consider it most probable that a small turf house once stood here, up against the low rocky knoll about 10–15 metres east of house F. The rivets probably come from a wooden door in the western wall of this assumed house, facing house F and half facing the sea.

A profile of the layers of earth cut roughly where these iron objects were found clearly reveals a depression in the ground, corresponding exactly to those which were left by the other turf houses (pl. 57). At this spot the cultural layer was c. 10 cm thick, and the excavators described it as "dark brown turf". It seems likely that this profile cuts through a turf wall, or through the edge of the cultural layer, cutting the wall itself at E36.5; this wall was c. 1.5 m thick, and could be traced for 0.5 m above the bottom of the depression. Very few of the walls of the other houses have left higher traces than this. Taking all factors into consideration, it seems likely that there was a turf house here, and that the hearth is connected with this house.

Finally we have the two *out-door cooking pits* (p. 56 and p. 94. See also fig. 30 and fig. 58).

It is difficult to say whether they form part of the Norse settlement on the terrace, or whether they represent a different culture. No archaeological evidence at all was obtained from *cooking pit I* (pls. 43 and 44, fig. 58), but the radio-carbon date from this pit – A.D. 780 ± 90 years – accords well with the earliest dates from the house-sites and with some of the other dates obtained.

Cooking pit II (pls. 46 and 47, fig. 30) was in use during two distinct periods; their levels are separated by a 20 cm thick layer of sand and soot. A small fragment of iron was found in the gravel at the bottom of the pit, but as there were also several flint chippings and items there, we cannot be certain who the builders and first users of this hearth were. The stone specimens are uncertain evidence as to their cultural affiliation. (LaM 82, 83, 85, 86, 88, 89, 90, 91 11–15, 91 16–32.)

All the stone items found in connection with these hearths will be discussed below together with other stone implements from the terrace, where we shall concentrate especially on the strata at which they lay and their cultural affiliation as seen in relation to the Norse occupation of the terrace.

The radio-carbon analysis of charcoal from the pit yielded the date A.D. 810 ± 90 years, a date which agrees well with those obtained from several of the houses on the terrace.

As mentioned above, Aage Roussell has made it clear that cooking pits are a form of hearth commonly used for primitive cooking[333] in many parts of the world by various primitive cultures, so we must beware of drawing any rash conclusions from the cooking pits here. What is certain, however, is that cooking pit II was used by natives; but it is quite possible that only the upper layer should be ascribed to them. The sheet iron found at the bottom may be an indication of the cooking pit having been constructed and first used by Norsemen. The radio-carbon date supports this assumption.

Although comparatively rare, out-door cooking pits are known in the Norse cultural sphere, while indoor cooking pits are among the most common hearths of this culture.

Poul Nørlund draws attention to a large pit, with an upper diameter of 5 metres and a depth of 2 metres, which was found in the south-western corner of the home field at Garðar in the East Settlement in Greenland. This he interprets as a cooking pit.[334] He also draws attention to other pits in the Norse material, which have so far defied any explanation other than that of refuse pits. One of these, at the farm Hofstaðir in Iceland, lay a short distance away from the gable end of the ruin which, although with some doubt, is assumed to be that of a pagan temple.[335]

Out-door cooking pits of this kind must have been extremely useful, especially in view of the shortage of large cooking utensils. In fact, they must

224

have been essential when food for a large gathering was prepared, or a large animal, such as a whale, was to be cooked.

Interpretation of other features

Feature 5: The chert knapper's station.

This feature is situated about 10 m NW of house-site F at N64–67E101–104. (See report p. 101).

It was located at the base of the sod along the slope of the terrace. It is oval, measuring 1.86 m by 1.79 m. A little charcoal was found in connection with this feature, and a concentration of chert items lay at the base of the sod (LaM 190a–b, 192, 193a–b, 216–221).

The projectile points, LaM 217, 219, 220 and 221, and the oval biface blades, LaM 216 and 218, found in feature 5, make it seem likely that the chert knapper must have been a man of Boreal Archaic affiliation.

Feature 7 (pl. 55, p. 102). This feature, which is located close to house-site G, on the south-western side of the latter, is a 4 m long and 0.44 m wide trench running down the sloping terrace in an east-westerly direction. It was partly lined with slate, and there can hardly be any doubt as to its having served as a water trench. This is the opinion also of the excavators, but their statement that this water trench should have been made exclusively for the purpose of draining off rain water from the upper terrace seems to be an insufficient explanation. Its location near house-site G surely indicates its close connection with the assumed function of that house – that of a bath-house. The necessity of a supply of water for the purpose of obtaining steam for the bath-house is obvious, and as the brook is a long walk away, this trench must have had a very important function in leading water from the bog down to the bath-house. In fact, this water trench supports the assumption that house G must have been a bath-house.

Midden NW of house-site G (pl. 35, p. 54)

Several items were found when Rolf Petré excavated this midden NW of house-site G in 1962 (LaM 77, 79, 80, and 81). Apart from these stone implements, an iron fragment was found at local coordinates $x = + 1.65$, $y = - 0.35$, level: 3 cm above sub-soil (LaM 78). The fragment is 3 cm long, and there were fragments of wood rusted on to it.

A number of samples for analysis were taken from this midden, including:
LaM 229 (sample 138) 2 round stones resembling rust
LaM 230 (sample 138.1) 1 piece red jasper

LaM 232 (sample 38.3) glazed slag, blue
LaM 237 (sample 40) charred bones
LaM 238 (sample 38.7) shale
LaM 239 (sample 138.6) ground pyrites.

Of these, we attach particular importance to the small piece of red jasper and the piece of ground pyrites. Such items were repeatedly found in and outside the house-sites, and in our view the Norsemen used such jasper and pyrites for striking fire.

The analyses of these samples have been carried out by A.M. Rosenqvist, see below. It is impossible to say whether the small flint chippings found in this midden should also be interpreted as fire-stones, or whether they form part of LaM 77, a fragmentary lance-point of flint. The latter certainly does not belong to the Norse cultural complex, and it cannot with any certainty be ascribed to any other specific cultural complex either. It seems likely that these flint objects came into this midden quite by chance, for the pieces of slag, the jasper and pyrites, and not least the iron rod clearly indicate a Norse origin for the midden. They must be discarded objects thrown out of house G.

In the test trenches dug by Charles J. Bareis and Jon Winston in 1963 and in house-site D III, a number of stone items and a few iron fragments came to light (LaM 187, 194, 196–210, 215, 223–225, 227 cf. catalogue below).

These finds shows that people of at least three different cultures lived on the terrace, first and foremost the Norsemen who built the houses and lived here for some years around the year A.D. 1000. It also seems likely that an Indian group, the Boreal Archaic, sporadically stayed here.

LaM 216–223, 227, 83 (fig. 26), 85 and 86 (fig. 28) can securely be ascribed to this culture.

A group of Eskimoes, the Dorset culture, is also represented by some finds: LaM 75 (fig. 27), 140, 185, 225 and 343.

The remaining Stone Age implements cannot be securely ascribed to any specific culture, as they are so simple in form that they may just as well represent one culture as another. William Taylor jr. has subjected all of them to a thorough analysis, and his results are included in the catalogue below. My own conclusions are based on his provisional draft, for which I am extremely grateful to him.

This account is first and foremost an attempt at elucidating the chronological relationship between the various ethnic groups in question. A serious difficulty immediately confronts us: only one of these groups – the Norse – can be securely dated. The Norse occupation of the houses on the terrace seems to date to the time around the year A.D. 1000, and we must therefore base our attempt at relating these groups to one another on this date as our point of departure.

As none of the stone implements can be dated exactly, our only chance of shedding light on these chronological relationships is provided by those stone items which were found together with Norse objects. The natural soil on the terrace lies in a very thin layer – in most places a 5 cm thick layer of new sod covers an old zone of vegetation, 5–10 cm thick, which in turn overlies sterile sand. Bareis and Winston account for these layers (p. 104) and, as their report shows, most of the stone implements were found "on gray sand", "below top of gray sand", "below sod on gray windblown sand", etc. The four specimens deriving from the Norse culture brought to light by Bareis and Winston during their excavations, on the other hand, lay "at the base of the sod", "below base of sod", "below surface and base of turf". It thus appears that the stone implements lay at a somewhat lower level than the Norse objects – but we must keep in mind the problems involved in making deductions from the stratigraphy of a settlement site. It is my personal opinion that in a settlement, where people – and perhaps also their animals – are constantly moving about, sharp objects such as flint will tend to work their way down through the soil in the course of the centuries. Another possible factor must also be taken into consideration – the fires lit on the terrace may have burned right through the thin layer of turf, down to the sand below.

The stratigraphy of the terrace thus shows such thin layers that we must beware of basing definite conclusions exclusively on the evidence it provides.

We are on firmer ground as far as the objects found in close contact with the Norse culture are concerned.

Unfortunately only a few of these stone implements can with certainty be ascribed to any specific culture, but a stone tool found in house D III – a projectile point – certainly belongs to the Dorset Eskimo culture (LaM 75, fig. 25). It was found close to a secondary hearth which was not in contact with the floor of the house, and lay at 6 cm above floor level. The other stone implements found here (LaM 72, 74), which cannot be securely identified, lay at between 6 and 12 cm above floor level.

This room also yielded several Norse objects, which were found between floor level and 4 cm above floor level; an uncertain iron fragment (LaM 71) lay at 8 cm above the floor (see pp. 52–53).

There can be no doubt that these stone implements were deposited here after the Norse objects, but before the roof of the house had collapsed – in other words, not more than some twenty years after the house had been built for, as pointed out below (p. 243), this is the span of life of turf houses. If these objects had been in the turf from which the roof was made, they would have lain at a higher level, as the turf of the roof, which is highly compressed, is barely ten cm thick, thinner in many places. The total thickness of the cultural layer of this house is c. 30 cm. Of course the objects may have worked their way down through the soil, but it seems unlikely that they should have been buried so very much deeper.

These observations, we feel, permit of the assumption that these Eskimoes of the so-called Dorset group were on the terrace at approximately the same time as the Norsemen, probably during the first half of the eleventh century. Before discussing this problem in more detail, we shall consider some of the other implements of the Dorset culture found on the terrace.

LaM 140 is a fine arrow-head of flint, type Harp 1964 Pl. III, No. 1 (see catalogue p. 256).[336] This arrow-head was found immediately below the sod, above the western end wall of house A. It is not impossible that this item could have been buried in the top layer of turf on the ground, which was cut and used for constructing this house, but we must note that there was a fire-patch in the immediate vicinity, above the cultural layer, and extending a little into the surface sod. This fire-patch extended right up to the western wall, and when we were digging here, we had a definite impression that the fire-patch and the arrow-head belonged together.

Thus here, too, we have a Dorset object at a level higher than that representing the Norse culture. If we are right in assuming that this arrow-head is connected with the fire-patch, then it must have been deposited after the house had collapsed entirely, for the fire patch apparently lay entirely above the turf of the roof and, moreover, the arrow-head lay on top of the wall, which it would hardly have done if it had been left here while the house was still covered by a roof.

LaM 343 is a soap-stone lamp of Dorset type.[337] It was found while house J was being excavated, and lay immediately below the new turf. The opening of the lamp faced up, and the depression was filled with rootlets. These were radio-carbon analysed, and found to be of twentieth-century date. Obviously the date of these roots tells us nothing about the age of the lamp.

We pointed out on p. 217 above that no other such lamp has as yet come to light in Newfoundland, not even at the extensive Port aux Choix excavations. But this type has been found further north, especially in the polar regions and in Greenland. A discussion of this lamp was given on p. 217 above, and it should not be necessary to repeat it now.

If the Norsemen brought it here, it could have been buried in the position where it was found only if they had left it standing on the roof of the smithy before this collapsed. If, on the other hand, Dorset Eskimoes brought it along to Newfoundland, it may either have stood on the roof – and thus be approximately contemporary with the Norse settlement – or it may have been left in its position at the far end of the depression after the house had collapsed, but before the new grass had established itself. In the latter case it would be more recent than the Norse settlement, but not necessarily much more recent. The lamp was found at a level definitely higher than that representing the Norse culture.

LaM 225 is a projectile point of Dorset type, found in a grey sand layer, at a spot filled practically to bursting point with Stone Age items – the area between house-site F and cooking-pit II.

This object lay below the level of the Norse objects which were found outside the houses – but here again we encounter the problem of the reliability of the stratigraphy in an area constantly frequented by people and animals.

LaM 214 includes 26 culturally unassignable small flakes and chips of grey-greenish chert refuse, and these were found together with a large core or core scraper (LaM 185), tentatively assigned by William Taylor jr. to the Dorset culture. The specimens LaM 214 and 185 were found in Feature 4, a hearth which was situated on dark brown sand, and filled with a thin layer of grey sand. Charcoal from this hearth, which has been analysed, has yielded the radio-carbon date A.D. 1060 $\pm$ 90 years.

It was previously assumed that the Dorset culture endured in polar regions until about A.D. 1350,[338] and that its duration must have been similar, or perhaps somewhat longer, in Newfoundland. William Fitzhugh argues against this assumption, maintaining that the Dorset culture of Labrador can hardly have survived the first centuries of the Christian Era, while lasting until about A.D. 600 in Newfoundland; the latter date is based on the radio-carbon analyses from Port aux Choix, none of which shows a date more recent than A.D. 600.[339,340]

As for the stone implements, one of which we have identified as being of Dorset type (LaM 75), it seems incomprehensible that they should lie above the Norse implements if the Dorset culture really had died out by about A.D. 600 in Newfoundland. We have already mentioned the possibility of their having lain in the turf which was used to cover the roof of the house – but this, too, is unlikely. The difference in time between these two phases of habitation cannot, in fact, have been great. It would seem most likely that the natives decided to live in this house while it was still covered by a roof. Taking into consideration the short time turf houses can survive without collapsing, we must visualize the natives living in this house fairly soon after its builders and first inhabitants had abandoned it.[341] The above may mean that the Dorset culture endured beyond c. A.D. 600 in Newfoundland as previously asserted by Harp.[342]

As for the Indian group in question, the Boreal Archaic, our material includes quite a number of securely identifiable objects from this culture. Unfortunately in only one place – cooking pit II – do we feel convinced that securely identifiable objects of this group occur together with Norse finds. Rolf Petré has accounted for the stratification of this pit on p. 56 above, and we need not repeat his description here. From the stratification it appears that this pit saw two distinct periods of use, divided by a layer of sand (pls. 45–46). The lower of these two layers yielded an iron fragment and a piece of flint (see p. 58), while the upper layer yielded stone implements, most of them lying by the sides and around the edges of the pit.

There can hardly be any doubt that this cooking pit was constructed and first used by the Norsemen, as we saw on p. 224 above. This assumption is supported by the result of a radio-carbon analysis, A.D. 810 + 90 years. It is unfortunately impossible to establish the length of time during which the natives used this pit.

It is to be hoped that experts in this field will take up this matter for a more comprehensive discussion than I am able to here, as a more detailed discussion would fall outside the scope of the present paper.

House D, as far as I know, offers the first find of Dorset objects in conjunction with those from a different culture, one which may be dated with a high degree of certainty. It is to be hoped that future excavations of Dorset settlement sites will shed more light on the problem of dating this culture; this is of interest also in connection with the question of the ethnic identity of the natives whom the Norsemen met in America.

A number of problems arise from these finds: problems connected not only with the relationship between the Stone Age people and the Norsemen who lived in these houses, but also, and not least, with that between these different ethnic groups. The two radio-carbon dates obtained from the hearths which yielded stone tools cover a long period of time. It seems beyond doubt that the more recent of these dates – A.D. 1500 – must represent the Beothuk Indian occupation of the settlement.

Interpretation of the cairns (fig. 105)

Finally we have the four ancient cairns on the low ridge west of the terrace. They had collapsed almost completely, and they were overgrown with black lichen. Two of them were only 5 metres apart, while the other two lay about 100 metres to the north-west, at a distance of about 50 metres from each other.

The two cairns which stood close together were still easily visible in 1961, as up to four courses of stone were still in situ, and a fair amount of stone lay at the base. Later we used these stones to rebuild the cairns, which are now 1.5–2 metres high. The other two cairns must have been smaller, and in 1961 they were only barely visible. – All the cairns were built in the same way, carefully put together of flat, preferably long stones, which were arranged in a circle around an open space at the centre.

Various possibilities as to the functions of these cairns have been considered over the years. Cairns occur in many parts of the world, and their functions

230

Fig. 105. Ruins of cairn at the hill-top west of the terrace at Épaves Bay.

vary. Some served as beacons, to guide ships and sailors. Others were of service to hunters, for instance the owl-cairns which are still used by the fishermen at L'Anse aux Meadows. In the culture of the Norsemen cairns were used not only as beacons, but also in order to mark roads and paths. They had another important function as well, serving to divide the day into parts – a kind of clock, in fact. Cairns along mountain ridges, often several of them close together, are a very common sight in Scandinavia and Iceland, and also in the Norse settlement of Greenland.[343] The so-called "tourist cairns", which are raised on the peaks of mountains, and which apparently serve only to mark the highest point, are probably of recent date, and they seem to be without any connection with the farmers' society of the past. – The Norse cairns are constructed in exactly the same way as those at Épaves Bay, with courses of stone surrounding an open space at the centre. An entirely different method of construction was employed for the so-called owl-cairns at L'Anse aux Meadows, and also for some of the cairns which Thomas Lee found at

231

Ungava Bay – the latter would seem to be of Eskimo origin. But other cairns, one of which is similar to ours, were also found at Ungava Bay;[344] quite clearly we should not base any definite conclusions exclusively on the method of construction employed.

It is a characteristic feature of the Épaves Bay cairns that they are not visible from the sea, and thus they cannot have served as beacons. We must note that the two large cairns, which stand close together nearest the house-sites, do not lie on the highest point of the ridge, although they would have been most easily visible in that position. Instead, they lie in a slight depression in the mountain ridge. But when one stands by the houses on the terrace, one can see them as a silhouette against the sky – and only from this aspect does it seem possible to explain their existence. It appeared that the sun was immediately above these cairns at 3 p.m. Did they perhaps serve to mark the divisions of the day? – The two cairns farther away on the ridge, to the north-west of the two large ones, are more problematic. They are in such a state of disintegration and so low that they are difficult to see from a distance now – but they, too, would have appeared as a silhouette from down on the terrace, and they seem to have been positioned just there intentionally. One of them lies near the front of the ridge, the other further back, but neither of them marks the highest point in the vicinity. Thus the only reasonable explanation of these cairns also would seem to be that they marked a certain point of time which was important for the people living on the terrace.

Such time cairns are by no means unknown in the culture of the Norsemen – it is ancient practice, in fact, to tell the time from the position of the sun above certain points in the landscape, the "ancient marks", as they were called. This was the way in which the Norsemen from times immemorial marked the hours into which their day was divided.

It would seem reasonable to connect these cairns with the Norse settlement on the terrace, for a consistent division of the day must have been of importance in the daily life of these people.

IX Conclusion

We have above dealt with a number of significant features of the various house-sites at Épaves Bay. In our opinion, an assessment of the archaeological material provides sound reasons for concluding that the settlement is of Norse origin, and that it appears to date from first part of the eleventh century A.D.

This conclusion is supported by twenty-one radio-carbon dates obtained from the different sites. Most of them derive from charcoal from the hearths, but four come from the turf of the walls, and one from whale-bone.

The earliest date is A.D. 640 + 130 years, the most recent A.D. 1080 + 70 years. Quite a few of the dates are close to the year A.D. 1000, and the mean date is A.D. 920 + 30. We refer the reader to the table fig. 9, and to Reidar Nydal's account below.

The earliest dates derive from house-sites A, B and C, and also include two from house F. They all come from charcoal from the hearths.

We pointed out on p. 177 above that house A represents the earliest type of dwelling house on the terrace, and that it seems likely that houses B and C are contemporary with house A. It also seems likely that these were the first houses built on the terrace. Their position so near the river supports this assumption, for a good supply of fresh water must have been one of the reasons for settling on the terrace.

The early radio-carbon dates obtained from houses A, B and C are due to various factors, as shown by Nydal, including the fact that driftwood was used for fuel, for these dates are not in entire agreement with the archaeological evidence. Épaves Bay being a typical driftwood bay, as pointed out on p. 22 above, where considerable quantities of driftwood must have accumulated through the ages, we may assume that the people who lived here must have made extensive use of this material for fuel and for building purposes, particularly during the first years of their stay, when there was surely plenty of dry wood amongst the driftwood lying on the shore. Thus the dates deriving from charcoal from these houses must naturally pre-date the time of settlement somewhat. The charcoal from the hearths has been analysed by L.M. Paulssen, and I refer the reader to his article below.

We have also two radio-carbon dates from house A, deriving from turf from the walls – A.D. 1000 + 90 years and A.D. 630 + 80.

Our archaeological assessment is largely based on the plans of the different house-sites, on the form and position of the hearths, and not least on the objects found. Certain negative conclusions have also been considered, and especially important to the assessment of the date of settlement was the complete absence of Norse soap-stone objects, with the exception of the soap-stone spindle whorl. The reason, we feel, must be that the settlement is of so early a date that the Norse Greenlanders, who seem to be the most likely settlers, had not yet lived long enough in Greenland to discover the soap-stone deposits there, before they sailed to Newfoundland. Soap-stone objects, or fragments of such objects, are common in the late medieval farms ruins of Greenland. But Iceland has no soap-stone deposits; the Icelanders had to import this material, but most often they used other kinds of stone as a substitute.

A find of particularly great importance to our understanding of the pattern of settlement at Épaves Bay is the ring-headed pin of bronze, discussed on p. 159 above. It was found in house A. This type has been dated to the ninth and tenth centuries, but in outlying places such as Greenland and America it may still have been in use somewhat later.

As to the types of houses here represented, we shall give a brief summary of our description above: the long house A is a further development of the simple hall or *skáli* of the Viking Age, as it occurred in Iceland and Scandinavia just before and around the year A.D. 1000. We interpret house A room I as such a hall, and this is one of the factors which we regard as evidence of the great age of house A. Another feature of this house, also indicative of great age, is the fact that it was extended lengthways – this was common practice in Norway from the early Iron Age until far into the Middle Ages. The farm ruins at Narssaq in the East Settlement of Greenland may serve as an example of a house extended in this way.

The Narssaq farm, which we consider to be the closest parallel of house A, has been dated to the Viking Age or to the first years of settlement (c. A.D. 1000) by means of a runic inscription.

Thus the date assigned to house A on an archaeological basis is in agreement with the most recent of the radio-carbon dates, that obtained from turf from the walls.

The closest parallels to house B are to be found among the earliest Greenland ruins, as we saw on p. 168 above, e.g. Hvalsey room IX (East Settlement No. 83.6). The early date of house B appears not only from the radio-carbon analysis of charcoal from the cooking pit, which yielded the date A.D. 740 + 110 years – but first and foremost from the hearth and the ember pit.

The type of house represented by house-site C forms a natural part of the Norse farm complex. Houses of this type have remained in use until our own times, and they served many different purposes.

That A, B and C formed one farm complex is indicated not only by their situation close to one another, but also by the fact that A and B, at least, are typologically contemporary. The typological age of house C is more difficult to assess securely, but the situation of this house, whose door faces house A, and the radio-carbon date derived from it, A.D. 710 + 130, which agrees with the earliest dates obtained from houses A and B, indicate that these houses must be contemporary. But the most decisive indication of a contemporaneous farm complex consisting of these three houses is provided by the two fragments of walls projecting from house-site C. One of these runs in the direction of house B, the other westwards, towards the western part of house A: it thus appears that these three houses were once linked into a complex enclosing a yard, which must have had an opening in the east, for no traces of any turf wall were found on this side.

Various functions may be suggested for these walls: they may, for instance, have served as dams to protect the houses from the waters of the flooding brook in the spring, when Black Duck Brook is full of drifting ice (p. 30). A wall between houses B and C may have protected house A from the water, for this house, whose doors face the brook, must have been particularly exposed to the danger of being flooded completely. The wall between C and A ran parallel with the brook in the west, and it may have served as a barrier against the water from that direction.

Another interpretation is also possible: the walls, together with the houses, may have formed an enclosure where one could confine the animals at night. In this connection we would remind the reader of the bone fragments, probably deriving from the domestic pig, possibly from sheep or goats, but in any case from domestic animals, which were found in the midden outside the door of house C and also in house A (p. 179 and p. 164).

The above should be sufficient to show that houses A, B and C must be contemporary, and that they probably represent the first phase of settlement on the terrace, in all likelihood shortly after the year A.D. 1000 (cf. R. Nydal below).

We do not know how long these houses were inhabited. We saw on p. 152 above that house A may have been extended after a while, so that room I may form the earliest part, possibly together with room II. But whether rooms III and IV were built while the older part was still intact, or whether they were added after rooms I and II had collapsed can no longer be determined. There is no indication of any of the rooms having been rebuilt at any stage. Now – if we assume that a turf house would hardly last for more than twenty or thirty years in the humid climate here at the northern point of Newfoundland, we get some idea of the length of the period of habitation. The shallow middens, and the comparatively thin floor layers (lower strata) inside the houses also suggest a fairly brief period of habitation. Moreover, the waters from the flooding brook must have been a constantly recurring danger threatening the houses each spring in spite of the walls which probably linked them together. The ground water is likely to have been a nuisance also – the floor of house B was probably always damp. This house lies closest to the bog, and as soon as we had excavated it, the ground water rose, filling the cooking pit and the post hole. This problem would presumably not have been so serious if there had been forest growing on the bog behind the terrace during the Norse period, but Kari Henningsmoen considers it unlikely that there should have been many trees there then (see p. 324). All in all, it seems reasonable to suppose that the period of habitation in houses A, B and C was brief, in spite of the fact that the complex lay conveniently near the brook and a good supply of fresh water.

Certain features of houses A, B and C indicate Greenland as the land of origin of the people who built these houses and lived there. In this connection particular interest attaches to the long hearths without flat stone slabs and without an edging of stones standing on end – simply shallow, elongated depressions in the floor. They are absolutely identical with certain long hearths found in some of the oldest farm ruins of Greenland. Further – the closest parallel to the hearth by the western end wall of house B is to be found in the hall of Brattahlið North Farm, and the little ember pit in house B is identical with two found in the so-called "Fireplace area" in the fields of this farm, as we showed above.

We should also note that the type of house represented by house-site A points to Norway and Greenland as possible countries of origin rather than to Iceland.

House D is an extended long house, reminiscent of the so-called "Þjórsárdalur type". When we described this house on p. 181 above, we saw that no example of the classic form of this type has come to light in Greenland, where the long house underwent a different form of development. Thus house D represents a further development of the long house, one probably characteristic of Iceland. In Scandinavia, it seems, the ancient method of extending houses in a lengthwise direction was retained, as we saw above.

We do not know for certain when houses of this type were first built in Iceland, but it seems likely to have been early in the eleventh century. Maybe it became too cumbersome to have to run to and fro the long house, and to have to go out of doors in order to reach the other houses. Or perhaps it was considered desirable that as much grass and turf as possible should be saved, and a turf house consumes turf from a large area. By building several houses together into one, one could at least save some material and labour.

How long houses of this type remained in use is not known for certain, but we do know that they were still in use in Þjórsárdalur when the valley was laid waste by the eruption of Mt. Hekla in A.D. 1104. House D is hardly as late as this.

It seems most likely that house D represents an early stage of the "Þjórsárdalur type", in spite of two rooms having been added to the main building, but no *stova* as yet.[345]

A radio-carbon analysis of charcoal from the hearth of room III has yielded the date A.D. 900 + 70 years.

The long hearth in house D room III is practically identical with that of room IX of the Hvalsey complex in the East Settlement in Greenland. The position confronting us here is this: while the type of the house indicates Iceland as the country of origin of the people who built this house, the hearth points towards Greenland during the earliest phase of settlement.

The small, semi-sunken house E was probably the fire-house of house D, as we saw above. As a type, this house cannot be dated, but we showed on p. 191 that the hearth in the one corner is of a type which was very common in the Norse settlements of Greenland from the earliest years of settlement onwards. A radio-carbon analysis of charcoal from this hearth has yielded the data A.D. 820 + 70 years. This date agrees with others deriving from charcoal, and the same reservation applies also here: driftwood, or other factors, may have influenced the analysis, resulting in too early a date (cf. R. Nydal below).

Thus we find that houses D and E display features which connect them to the Norse cultural complex of Iceland as well as that of Greenland; the period of habitation may have been roughly contemporary with that of houses A, B and C, or possibly a little later.

House F may be regarded as a variant of the "Þjórsárdalur type", with rooms built on in front and behind. As we saw it has at least one parallel in Iceland, but our house-site F may possibly be due to impulses received from Greenland, where the long house, as we saw above,was extended in a more haphazard fashion than in Iceland, as far as we are able to tell today. We saw on p. 192 above that practical reasons may also have influenced the plan of house F: by building room VI on to the front wall of the house, one obtained a room which was warmed by the sun, while the house was at the same time protected from the prevalent on-shore winds.

The radio-carbon dates derived from charcoal from house F are, respectively, A.D. 870 + 70 years and A.D. 700 + 70 years. These dates agree with those obtained from charcoal from the other houses, but again they apparently do not entirely agree with the archaeological results, for house F represents the most recent of the types of house found on the terrace. The same factors and sources of error may apply to this house as to the others, including the use of driftwood for fuel. A radio-carbon analysis of turf from the walls of house F yielded the date A.D. 1000 + 50 years, while a piece of whale-bone from the hearth gave the result A.D. 1025 + 100 years. The last date accords well with the archaeological results; for all the dates deriving from turf I refer the reader to Kari Henningsmoen and R. Nydal below.

The hearths of house F combine, as we have seen, Icelandic features with those from Greenland. Those in rooms I and III are of the simple Greenland type of long hearth, lacking the flat stone as well as the surround of stones standing on edge. This is the type which also occurs in houses A and D. The hearth of room IV, which consists of two stone-lined chambers, also has its closest parallels in Greenland. On the other hand, there can hardly be any doubt that the long hearth of room II belongs to a type peculiar to Iceland, where it is represented in a number of farm ruins, and whose roots go far back into the early Iron Age in Scandinavia. The hearth in room I of the farm ruin at Narssaq in the East Settlement of Greenland, the earliest known farm ruin there, also comes very close to this type.

The construction of the houses, whose walls consist entirely of turf, indicate Iceland rather than Greenland as the background of the people who settled at Épaves Bay, but we have reason to believe that the earliest Greenland farms had walls containing more turf than was the case at a later date. This is true of, for instance, the farm at Narssaq. Þjóðhildr's church had turf walls around a small wooden building, and room I of Brattahlíð North Farm was partly built over a still earlier building, which seems to have had turf walls resting on a low row of sleeper stones.

The primitive stone lamp from house F is of a type peculiar to Iceland, which seems to occur nowhere else in the Norse sphere. We pointed out on p. 205 above that this type of lamp may well be a cultural loan from Orkney/Shetland.

All in all, it would seem that the settlement at Épaves Bay suggests Iceland as its cultural source, but a number of features also indicate the first phase of settlement in Greenland.

This is the background on which we base our conclusion that the settlement derives from Norse Greenlanders and is of an early date, probably of the first half of the eleventh century. The builders of these houses, their inhabitants in fact, still had their roots in the Icelandic culture of the tenth and eleventh centuries, but they had also developed new features, independent of the culture of Iceland. These recall the earliest Norse period in Greenland. It was in the year A.D. 986 that the first Icelanders settled in Greenland; our houses at Épaves Bay must have been built shortly afterwards, probably by people who came from Greenland. At that time the Norse culture of Greenland had not yet developed into the independent culture to which a number of medieval farm ruins of the East and the West Settlement – the so-called passage houses and centralized houses – testify. – Our dating of the settlement is also supported by the most recent of the radio-carbon dates and by the ring-headed pin, which is a Viking Age form of jewellery.

Concerning the finds from the houses at Épaves Bay we must point out that conditions of preservation are extremely unfavourable here. The sharp, sandy soil has destroyed all remains of organic material, with the exception of a few burnt slivers of bone and a burnt fragment of a bone needle. We must remember that a great many of the tools and objects used by these people must have been of wood, bone and antler, as was the case on the Norse farms of Greenland. Moreover, the natives probably picked up any iron and other useful objects which they might have found; and the Norsemen presumably could not afford to leave any useful objects behind when they left these houses – no wonder, then, that so few objects have come to light. Many wooden objects have been found at Kaupang in Tjølling, Norway, and Charlotte Blindheim considers it most likely that wooden implements played an important part in the daily life of Viking Age Norway.[346]

The Oseberg Find has also yielded a great number of wooden implements, evidence showing that wooden objects were in common use even by members of the upper social strata.[347]

The material found during the excavation of the Icelandic farm Stöng in Þjórsárdalur is of interest in this context. This farm was in all likelihood built during the eleventh century and inhabited until A.D. 1104; the finds include stone lamps, spindle whorls, iron rivets and a ring-headed pin – all of the same types as the corresponding finds from the houses at Épaves Bay. We should note that in Iceland, too, the finds from house ruins are rather sparse.

There are lush meadows all around Épaves Bay and the inlets and firths nearby, and this must be one of the main reasons inducing the Norsemen to settle here. These meadows are so typical of the bay that they have, in fact, given it its modern name – freely translated, L'Anse aux Meadows means "the bay with the meadows".

Kari Henningsmoen has found the ratio between herbaceous pollen and tree pollen dating from the time of the Norse settlement to be more or less identical with that of today. We therefore have every reason to believe that there must have been large meadows in this part of Newfoundland also during the period around A.D. 1000.

Even though fishing, hunting and catching at sea were important features of their economy, their way of life was first and foremost based on stock-keeping. In this context the two fragments of bone, which probably derive from the domestic pig, are important, and the little soap-stone spindle whorl assumes much greater importance in view of this background than would have been the case if it had been found elsewhere in the Norse cultural complex. It proves that the people who built these houses and who lived in them had their cultural roots in a stock-keeping economy, and that spinning –and probably also weaving – of wool for their garments formed part of their daily round. This, in fact, is the basic difference between the Norse culture and those of the Eskimoes and Indians of Newfoundland, for neither of the latter ever became familiar with the arts of spinning and weaving.

Samuel E. Morison has drawn attention to some spindle whorls said to be of Eskimo origin, which were found when David Sanger and his wife excavated an Indian settlement site in British Columbia.[348],[349] Morison points out that these "spindle whorls" are quite unlike that found at L'Anse aux Meadows – they measure 10 cm in diameter, and it is not even certain that they were used for spinning.

Kari Henningsmoen states that the pollen material contains no evidence to show that the Norsemen had taken domestic animals along to Newfoundland She found no traces of the "culture flora" which would have followed in the van of extensive stock-keeping or of any agricultural activities (cf. Kari Henningsmoen below). A comparatively brief period of pasture, however, would probably have had only a slight or no effect on the pollen diagrams. Thus it is perhaps possible that the two fragments of bone from a pig may derive from cured or salted pork which formed part of the provisions on board ship, and the wool which was spun at L'Anse aux Meadows may have been brought along from Greenland.

But in spite of all this, it still seems most likely that the Norsemen should have kept domestic animals here at L'Anse aux Meadows. Why would they choose to settle at a place with such excellent pasture as Épaves Bay if it were not for their stock? Two irregular, round enclosures, marked by low turf walls, a few hundred metres north-east of house F may possibly have been used as folds, and the walls connecting houses A, B and C may have served the same purpose, as we pointed out above. But none of the houses on the terrace, and none of the rooms of any house have been identified as sheep cotes or cowsheds. House C may have been intended for sheep, but we have no proof of this. But it seems quite possible that sheep, at least, could graze most of the winter long in northern Newfoundland, roughly on the same latitude as London. Even in modern Greenland the sheep are out in the open all the year round, and it seems likely that the same practice should have been observed, at least to some extent, in Norse Newfoundland. The annual mean temperature recorded for the years 1921 – 1950 is 1° C.

People now living at L'Anse aux Meadows can recall some winters so mild that no snow fell before February, and during such winters, the cows graze out in the open. Other winters can be hard, with very deep snow and frequent, strong blizzards.

The great variations in climate are characteristic of these parts today, and there is no reason to think that it should have been so very different during the Norse period. Some changes have occurred during the last thousand years, but they cannot have been very great, for Kari Henningsmoen has found no traces of them in the composition of the local flora (cf. Kari Henningsmoen p. 326 below). Thus it is quite possible that the Norsemen let their cows and sheep graze out in open if the winter was mild.

Apart from the pasture land around all the bays of this, the northernmost part of Newfoundland, this land must have been attractive to the Norse Greenlanders also for other reasons: there was forest here, plenty of forest for building and for fuel, perhaps also for ship-building. Kari Henningsmoen infers from her pollen-analytical investigations of these parts that the vegetation a thousand years ago cannot have differed much from today's (p. 324). Paulssen arrives at the same conclusion on the basis of his analyses of charcoal from the hearths of these house-sites (p. 369).

Moreover, there was a considerable amount of bog-ore in the bogs around the terrace. For the first time in their lives these people could revel in fuel – in Iceland and Greenland one had to use fuel sparingly, for the only wood available there was scattered birch of poor quality and some driftwood. But on the terrace at Épaves Bay they could extract all the iron they wanted, and this must have been of great importance to people whose tools and weapons were largely made of iron.

Some rust-brown stripes are to be seen in the turf-layers of some of the walls. Kari Henningsmoen has shown that they in fact consist of rust – thus iron precipitation must already have occurred at the time when the Norsemen built the houses on the terrace, cf. Kari Henningsmoen below.

The country offered yet other advantages – there was salmon in the river, and the sea held all kinds of fish as well as larger animals, such as seal and whale. One of the main breeding grounds of the Greenland seal lies off the coast of Labrador, just north of the settlement at Épaves Bay; and the annual passage to and from the other main breeding ground, in the Bay of St. Lawrence, leads through the narrow Strait of Belle Isle, which lies only a short distance to the west of Épaves Bay. Moreover, at different times of the year these animals make for several parts of the coast of northern Newfoundland, including a spot just off L'Anse aux Meadows. The finds from the houses include fragments of bones from both seal and whale, see app. I, II, III, V.

Épaves Bay is so shallow that not even a fishing boat can land there, and Kari Henningsmoen's pollen analyses show that the bay is hardly likely to have been much deeper at the time when the Norsemen settled on the terrace

– the difference may amount to 0.5–1.00 metres. But these people were used to pulling their boats up on land, unlike the Newfoundland fishermen of our days, who make theirs fast in deep water. The boat-sheds should be proof good enough – they lie at the very point where a boat drawing little water could have landed in those days, when the water-level was a little higher.

Arne Emil Christensen has stated on p. 119 above that boat-sheds were very common in Norway and the lands colonized by Norway during the Viking Age. Apart from this, boat-sheds are the exception rather than the rule all over Europe.

We have good reason to believe that there were bears, reindeer and fur-bearing animals living in the northern parts of Newfoundland a thousand years ago, and the economy of the Norsemen depended on such animals to quite a considerable extent.

Last, but hardly least – during good summers, there is any amount of wild fruit to be found here: strawberries, raspberries, bilberries, cranberries, currants, red as well as black, not to forget cloudberries, which grow in incredible quantities – a veritable Garden of Eden for the Norse Greenlanders, who had probably never tasted some of these before.

As far as one can tell, these berries, which thrive at L'Anse aux Meadows today, must also have grown there during the eleventh century. Hans W. Ahlmann, the Swedish glaciologist, is of the opinion that the climate of the eleventh century was not very different from today's, although there was a deterioration lasting from the latter part of the thirteenth century until some time during the fifteenth. The results of the pollen investigations carried out in the West Settlement of Greenland are among the most important evidence available on this matter. They show that the climate of Greenland must presumably have been relatively mild and humid during the eleventh century. The thirteenth and fourteenth centuries saw a change to a dryer, more continental climate. In spite of this, Ahlmann assumes at least that the summer temperature of Greenland has remained fairly unchanged for a thousand years.[350]

Others have arrived at a similar climatic deterioration. I would here especially mention W. Dansgaard, S.J. Johnsen, J. Møller and C.C. Langway's studies of how the long-term variations in the isotopic composition of the Greenland ice sheet reflect the climatic changes during the past nearly 100,000 years.[351]

It would seem most likely that the variations in the climate of Newfoundland should have been fairly similar to those of Greenland.

It would be wrong to try to visualize stock-keeping and farming in Newfoundland in terms of our knowledge of eleventh-century farm life in

Greenland and Iceland, without bearing in mind that the Épaves Bay settlement was built by and for people taking part in an expedition, most of them members of the crew of one or more ships. Certain features of the houses, at first seemingly inexplicable, make sense when we remember that ships with perhaps as many as thirty or forty men landed here, all of whom had to be provided with food and shelter. It is typical that there are hearths in all the rooms of the large houses A and F, and that food was prepared at several places in the same house appears from the great number of cooking stones found in some of these hearths. In this our houses differ from, for instance, Stöng in Þjórsárdalur, where each room had its specific function, but Stöng was the permanent home of a farmer, his family and his hands.

How long did the Norsemen stay on the terrace at Épaves Bay? This we can hardly be certain of, but there are features indicating a comparatively brief stay. We found no indication of any of these turf houses having been rebuilt after it had collapsed. When we consider that a turf house could hardly endure for more than twenty or thirty years in a climate as humid as that of Newfoundland, it seems very unlikely that the period of habitation should have lasted for as long as a century or more. Moreover, the middens and the floor layers in the houses were barely 10 cm thick.

Furthermore, we do not know whether all the houses were inhabited at one and the same time, or whether the buildings represent successive habitation. The typological development from A to F may, as we have seen, indicate a period of habitation exceeding twenty or thirty years; if this were so, there would be no reason why people should not have lived here around the year A.D. 1050: this statement is based entirely on the archaeological evidence, whereas that of the radio-carbon dates would seem to show that there cannot be a great difference in time between the period of habitation of house A and that of house F.

Reidar Nydal has re-examined the radio-carbon dates obtained from material from L'Anse aux Meadows, and he concludes by saying: "The discussion of agreement between the radio-carbon age and the assumed historical age must necessarily be limited because of the uncertain magnitude of systematic error due to the presence of driftwood, and also to charcoal derived from various tree-ring layers. Altogether we find that there is a reasonable agreement between the radiocarbon age and the assumed historical age. One must, however, be aware of the fact that agreement would have been found satisfactory also if settlement had occurred somewhat before A.D. 1000."

This view is supported by the ring-headed pin, a ninth-tenth century specimen, although the type may have remained in use for longer in a faraway country like Greenland.

H.T. Waterbolk has arrived at a later date for the settlement on the terrace – A.D. 1030 – and according to him, habitation here may have lasted for almost 60 years.[352]

Our comments to this are that the date A.D. 1030 would seem to be too late: we noted above that the houses have several features – and, above all, details – which show that they must have been built during a brief period around the year A.D. 1000. As for Waterbolk's statement that habitation lasted beyond the middle of the century, we can only say that this is certainly possible from an archaeological point of view, provided that the houses were not all occupied at the same time, that the settlement in fact represents successive habitation. But as even house F has so many details which are suggestive of the year A.D. 1000 rather than of a later date, the archaeological facts would seem to render Waterbolk's theory unlikely.

Further, the four boat-sheds down by the shore may also indicate that all the houses were occupied at one and the same time, for otherwise one would hardly have required so many boat-sheds. Probably each shed represents one boat, every one of which belonged to one of the houses on the terrace.

Why, then, did the Norsemen leave this land, promising in so many respects?

It seems likely that they met natives with whom they came into conflict. We know from Eirík's Saga that Þorfinnr Karlsefni's expedition returned to Greenland for this very reason: they did not think that the natives would let them live in peace. Natives and Norsemen alike had simple weapons, neither much more effective than the other; but the natives probably outnumbered the Norsemen by far. And as their weapons were of stone, they could easily make new ones, unlike the Norsemen, who must have fashioned most of theirs from iron – a difficult and laborious process. Probably they only had a limited supply of arrow-heads for hunting, although they may also have used arrow-heads of bone. It therefore seems most likely that the natives were superior in various ways.

We have seen that the natives must have occupied house D III fairly shortly after the Norsemen had left it. The great number of undatable stone tools found in various parts of the terrace may, however, be contemporary with the houses and with the Norse settlers. The two radio-carbon dates – A.D. 1050 and 1500 – show that the natives must have lived here at least sporadically for no less than five hundred years.

If the terrace at Épaves Bay was a site favoured by various ethnic groups also before the arrival of the Norsemen – and this we have reason to believe – it seems obvious that the latter may have come into contact with natives who were largely dependent on the same resources, the same facilities for hunting and trapping. And if the Norsemen had cattle, and perhaps also other domestic animals, the natives may well have hunted these. In that case the

Norsemen would with good reason to defend their property – and the conflict was under way. Further, we know from the sagas that the Norsemen must have looked upon the natives as a kind of dangerous supernatural beings, and that they on occasion killed them as soon as they set eye on them. In other words – there were reasons enough for a conflict between the Norsemen and the natives, and it is easy to see that one would not feel safe staying in a country where the natives were so greatly superior in number.

Several of the houses – house D room III, house F, and possibly also the smithy – were burned down, and they were never rebuilt.

As to the reason for the fire, we can no more than hazard a guess. The possibilities are legion. We saw on pp. 185 above that natives lived in house D after the Norsemen had left it, but before it collapsed entirely. Did they set fire to this house?

The settlement at Épaves Bay, with all its houses, large and small, its smithy and its charcoal kiln, its boat-sheds and probably also its bath-house, whose closest parallels are to be found in the farm ruins of Iceland, Greenland and Scandinavia, provides a varied picture of many aspects of eleventh-century Norse life.

X Catalogue of Finds

LaM
No.

Group 1 – Iron and objects of iron

a) Rivets, nails and rivet heads

4   *Iron rivet head*. Found in profile at 8.70 m (13 on plan), 4.37 m NW of base, at a depth of 30 cm. House F, room II. 2.5 × 3 cm.

21   *Iron rivet*. Local coordinates: x = 5.65, y = –9.25. 5 cm above sterile ground, in a small midden outside house C, immediately below the sod.

26   *Iron rivet*. Found in house F, room II, at centre of layer at the profile 5 m NW of 14.20 m base. Head 1.8 cm, shank 1 cm.

27   *Iron fragments*. 8.70 m base, 4.37 m NW. House F, room II. These four small fragments probably form part of the shank of LaM 4.

29   *Iron rivet*. Found in house F, room I, in hearth which also yielded LaM 2 (see below). L: 2.4 cm, diam. of head: c. 2 cm.

30   *Iron rivet*. 0.50 m at the base 2.40 m NW of it. Found at a depth of 25 cm above sterile ground in house G, in sandy soil containing charcoal. Shank and part of plate preserved. Max. l.: 1.9 cm, w: 0.7 cm, diam. of head: 1.3 cm.

56   *Rivet head*. 10.75 m base, – 2.30 m SE, 8 cm deep in old turf. House F, room VI.

60   *Large iron rivet*. 8.70 m base, – 25 cm SE, 10 cm deep in soil mixed with charcoal. House F, room VI. Magnetic. L: 6.1 cm, weight: 18.8 g. Head comparatively small, diam.: 2.8 cm, thickness: 0.4–0.7 cm. Shank 0.8 cm thick. Fig. 50.

61   *Large rivet head of iron*. 10.80 m base, – 4 m SE, 5 cm above floor level. House F, room VI.

62   *Rivet head of iron*. 13.50 m base, – 1.50 m SE, 10 cm deep in old turf. House F, room VI. L: 2.3 cm, w: 2.7 cm, thickness: 0.8 cm.

63   *Rivet head of iron*. 10.80 m base, –0.9 m SE, at bottom of cultural layer. House F, room VI. L: 1.7 cm, thickness: 1.2 cm, diam. of head: 2.6 cm, thickness: 0.8 cm. Weight: 13.1 g.

65   *Iron rivet*. Local coordinates: x = 13.25 m, y = 2.66 m, 10 cm under modern surface. House A. Found 6th August 62 by Kristján Eldjárn at the eastern end of the long test trench L–M, which ran under the test excavation of house A. The rivet lay near the cooking pit in room III, the finds from which area included the ring-headed pin. L: 5.7 cm, thickness: 0.4 cm.

68   *Fragmentary iron rivet*. Local coordinates: x = 6.05 m, y = –0.24 m, level 4 cm above floor. House D, room III. L. of shank 2.4 cm, head 1.6 × 2.0 cm.

70   *Fragmentary iron nail*. Local coordinates: x = 5.34 m, y = –1.97 m, level 1 cm above floor level. House D, room III. L. of shank 4.0 cm, head 1.8 × 2.2 cm.

116   *Iron nail*. 2.30 base. –0.15 m SE. Found immediately outside entrance of house F, room I, at the bottom of a 3 cm thick cultural layer containing some scattered charcoal, 8 cm below turf. L: 2.6 cm, w. of head 1.7 cm, l. of shank 1.6 cm.

118   *Iron rivet*. 2.20 m base, –0.50 SE. Found outside NE entrance of house F, room I, at bottom of a 3.5 cm thick cultural layer. Magnetic, highly corroded, shank broken. Diam. of head: 1.5 cm, l. of shank: 1.9 cm.

119   *Iron rivet head.* 2.10 m base, 0.10 m NW. House F. Found at same depth, layer and trench as LaM 118 above. Magnetic. Max. diam.: 2.9 cm, weight: 5 g. Fig. 6, bottom.

122   *Iron rivet.* 1 m base, 0.50 m NW. House F, at the bottom of slightly dark earth containing a little charcoal, almost on sterile ground, 12 cm below present surface sods. Magnetic. L: 2.7 cm, max. diam. of head: 1.6 cm, weight: 5 g.

125   *Iron rivet head.* Local coordinates: x = –1.40 m, y = 1.35 m. Found in house D, room II, at bottom of sand layer containing a great deal of charcoal. Max. diam.: 2.2 cm, weight: 2.5 g.

130   *Iron rivet.* Found when sifting earth from a field between 8.10 and 16.70 m base, and 0.35 m NW and –0.20 m SE, in house F. Magnetic. Max. diam. of head: 1.7 cm, 1. of shank: 1 cm.

133   *Large iron rivet.* Found when sifting earth from the same field as also yielded LaM 130 above and LaM 131 below. Max. diam. of head: 1.8 cm.

158   *Iron rivet.* Local coordinates: x = 17.27 m, y = –2.30 m, level: 7 cm above sterile ground. Found in house A, in profile at y = –2.30 m. Many small fragments, max. 1.: 2.6 cm, max. w.: 2.3 cm.

160   *Iron rivet head.* Local coordinates: x = 18.95 m, y = –2.48 m, level: floor. House A. Max.w.: 2.8 cm.

168   *Iron rivet head.* Local coordinates: x = 16.70 m, y = –2 m. House A. Max.w.: 3.1 cm.

279   *C. 2 g rusted iron. Rivet head?* House J.

302   *Rivet head.* House J. Found in two fragments.

310   *Iron rivet.* Location: N 66.56 E 130.06. Found in feature 6, at base of turf, 15 cm above grey sand.

b) other objects of iron

78   *Fragmentary iron rod.* Local coordinates: x = 1.65 m, y = –0.35 m, level 3 cm above bottom. Midden outside house-site G. Remnants of wood rusted on to object? L: 3 cm.

c) indeterminable iron fragments

5   *Piece of magnetic iron.* Found under the sod in house F, room VI.

15   *Small fragment of iron.* Magnetic. Found in house F, room II, in the cultural layer 10 cm above floor level. L. 2 cm, w: 0.8 cm.

24   *Iron fragment.* Located at 0.15 m at the base, 1.90 m NW of it. Found at 40 cm above sterile ground in house G, in sandy soil containing charcoal. In 2 pieces, total 1: 5.4 cm, max.w: 0.6 cm.

31   *Iron fragments.* Location: 0.50 m at the base, 2 m NW of it. Found 30 cm above floor level of house G, in sandy soil containing charcoal. 3 small fragments, the largest 2.1 cm.

41   *4 g magnetic iron.* Found by sifting in house F, room II. 2 pieces, the larger measures 3.6 cm.

51   *Small piece of iron.* Found in house F, room VI, 12.54 m base, –3.72 m SE. 7 cm deep in cultural layer. Weakly magnetic, holes and blisters of rust. L: 2.6 cm, w: 0.3–0.8 cm.

52   *1 fragment of iron.* 12.74 m base, –3.58 m SE, 7 cm deep in cultural layer. House F, room VI. L: 3 cm, w: 1 cm.

53   *Iron fragment.* 13.15 m base, –3.90 m SE, 5 cm above floor level. House F, room VI.

54   *Iron fragment.* 14.79 m base, –3.85 m SE, floor level. House F, room VI. Magnetic, sickle-shaped. L: 3.5 cm, w: 1–1.5 cm, weight: 1 g.

55   *Iron fragment.* 8.95 m base, –4.10 m SE, 5 cm deep in cultural layer. House F, room VI. Rusty lump of iron, very blistered, magnetic. L: 2.7 cm, w: 1.2 cm, weight: 6.5 g.

57   *Iron fragment.* 9.11 m base, –4.10 m SE, 5 cm deep in cultural layer. House F, room VI. L: 2 cm, w: 1.4 cm.

58   *Iron fragment.* 10.56 m base, –4.40 m SE, 5 cm deep in sterile sand. House F, room VI. L: 2.7 cm, w: 1.2 cm.

59   *Iron fragment.* 16.30 m base, –1.50 m SE, 10 cm deep in cultural layer (at bottom of this). House F, room VI.

64 a   *Two pieces magnetic rust.* House F. Weight: 9.5 g.

  b   *Two pieces magnetic rust.* House F. Weight: 1.7 g and 2.35 g.

71   *Iron fragment?* Local coordinates: x = 4.98 m, y = –2.11 m, level: 8 cm above floor level. House D, room III. 1.2 × 1.4 cm, thickness: 7 cm.

87   *Fragmentary iron plate.* Cooking pit II. L: 2.5 cm, thickness: 0.3 cm.

98   *Iron fragment.* 12.08 m base, –5.62 m SE. Found in trench outside the SE wall of House F, room VI. Indeterminable, magnetic. Weight: 0.1 g.

99   *Iron fragment.* 12.05 m base, –5.75 m SE. House F, trench SE of house F, room VI. Indeterminable, magnetic. L: 3 cm.

100 *Iron fragment.* 12.95 m base, –5.70 m SE. House F. Indeterminable. Weight: 5 g.

101 *2 small, indeterminable lumps of iron.*

  a   12.87 m base, –5.31 m SE. House F, in thin layer of dark cultural earth containing a little charcoal. Weight: 5 g.

  b   12.77 m base, –5.31 m SE. In thin layer of dark cultural earth containing a little charcoal.

102 a *Iron fragment.* 11.62 m base, –5.62 m SE. House F, in dark cultural earth containing charcoal. Weight: 1 g.

103 *Iron fragment.* 12 m base, –5.60 m SE. House F, in dark cultural layer containing a little charcoal. Weight: 0.5 g.

106 *12 g non-magnetic iron.* House F.

108 *1 piece magnetic iron.* 11.87 m base, –6.55 m SE. House F, 3 cm above sterile ground. Indeterminable.

110 *1 piece magnetic iron.* 15 m base, –6.55 m SE. House F, 30 cm above sterile ground. Weight: 0.5 g. Indeterminable.

111 *2 "lumps", possibly iron.* 9.80 m base, –7.30 m SE. House F, in black cultural earth. Non-magnetic.

117 *2 pieces magnetic iron.* Found immediately outside entrance of house F, room I, at the bottom of a 3 cm thick cultural layer containing some scattered charcoal, 8 cm below surface of turf, same level and trench as LaM 116 above. Indeterminable. Apart from charcoal, the layer also contained brittle-burned stones. Weight: 1 g and 4 g respectively.

120 *1 piece magnetic iron.* House F, found when sifting earth from the trench which also yielded LaM 118 and 119 above. Max. diam. 1.8 cm.

121 *1 piece magnetic iron.* House F, found when sifting earth from the trench which also yielded LaM 118, 119 and 120 above. Weight: 1.5 g.

123 *Magnetic iron.* Found when sifting earth from the same field as also yielded LaM 122 above. Weight: 1 g.

129 *Lump of magnetic iron.* 19.50 m base, –0.25 m SE, found in house F, at 2 cm above sterile ground, in black layer containing charcoal. May possibly be a small rivet head. Diam.: 1.4 cm.

131 *2 pieces magnetic iron.* Found when sifting earth from the field in which LaM 130 above was also found. Total weight: 5 g.

132 *2 pieces magnetic iron.* Found when sifting earth from a trench 2 m SW of SW wall of house F. Total weight: 1 g.

134 *Iron fragment.* Found when sifting earth from the same field as also yielded LaM 130, 131 and 133 above. L. of shank: 2.5 cm, weight: 1 g.

137 *Lumps of iron.* Found when sifting earth from a shallow midden SE of house F, room III. Weight: 12 g.

138   *Iron fragments.* Found when sifting earth from the same field as also yielded LaM 137 above. Indeterminable. Total weight: 7 g.

141   *Iron fragment.* Local coordinates: x = 13.38 m, y = –7.23 m, level: –118.5, bottom –126.5. House A. May possibly be a rivet. L: 3.2 cm, "head" 1.5 cm, thickness of "shank": 0.9 cm.

147   *1 piece magnetic iron.* Local coordinates: x = 15.15 m, y = –3.30 m, level: 11 cm above bottom, House A. Max.w.: 1.5 cm.

148   *1 piece magnetic iron.* Local coordinates: x = 15.30 m, y = –3 m, level: 11 cm above bottom. House A. Max.w: 1.5 cm.

154   *1 piece magnetic iron.* Local coordinates: x = 12.30 m, y = –17.70 m, level: 11 cm above bottom. Max. dimension: 2.5 cm.

155   *1 piece magnetic iron.* Local coordinates: x = 15.30 m, y = –5 m, level: 4 cm above bottom. Max. dimension: 2 cm.

157   *3 pieces magnetic iron.* Local coordinates: x = 16.42 m, y = –3.70 m, level: 15 cm above bottom. House A. The largest piece measures 1.9 cm.

163   *Lump of magnetic iron.* Found in midden S of house A, room III. Max. w: 1.1 cm.

165   *Small piece magnetic iron.* Local coordinates: x = 21.40 m, y = –1.30 m, level: 5 cm above bottom. House A. Max.w: 2 cm.

167   *1 piece magnetic iron.* Local coordinates: x = 16.70 m, y = –2 m, level: 10 cm above floor level of house A. Max.w: 2.5 cm.

179   *2 pieces magnetic iron.* Local coordinates: x = 13.30 m, y = –7.75 m. Found in midden S of house A, room III, 7 cm above sterile ground..

233   *Iron fragments.* Found at surface of charcoal heap, field B, house J. K.E.

247   *Lumps of magnetic iron.* From house J.

313   *Iron fragment.* Location: N 65.58 E 133.715. Found at top of dark, organic layer, 21.5 cm below surface.

314   *Iron fragment.* Location: N 66.68, E 133.53. 2 pieces (broken). Found at top of dark organic layer, at 21 cm below surface.

318   *Iron fragments.* Location: N 5.115, E 110.40. Found at 10 cm below base of sod, 13.5 cm below surface.

      d) crude iron

7   *Iron?* (crude iron), house C. Natural formation.

22   *6 pieces non-magnetic crude iron.* House F, room II.

23   *Samples of crude iron.* House B.

28   *6 lumps, probably crude iron.* Found in the cultural layer of house F.

35   *Crude iron.* House F. Natural formation.

46   *1 small pumice stone and some flakes of crude iron.* See group 9.f below.

48   *Crude iron.* House G.

136   *Small lumps, probably crude iron.* Found when sifting earth from a shallow midden SE of house F, room III, which also yielded LaM 137 above. Weight: 12 g.

Group 2 – Slag and forging scales.
      a) slag.

3   *Large lump of slag.* Local coordinates: x = 17.30 m, y = –12.25 m, found at bottom of cooking pit of house B. Cut into two pieces. There is a piece of charcoal inside the lump. See photograph, fig. 17.

32   *Slag.* Local coordinates: x = 5.25 m, y = –14.10 m. From house C.

33   *Slag.* House F, II–III. Found in a depression (post hole?) between rooms II and III, on sterile ground, 5 cm below floor level.

49   *Slag.* Found when the earth from house F was sifted.

66 b   *5 pieces slag.* House F, room VI. Found at edge of cooking pit at NE end of room VI, 5 cm above floor level. Originally 5 pieces, now 3.

67   *Slag and 2 other objects.*

102 b   *1 piece of slag.* Same position as 102 a above. Found when sifting earth.

105   *Slag?* Found outside SE wall of house F, room VI, in shallow midden near LaM 97 below. Weight: 9 g.

112   *1 piece of slag.* 12.87 m base, −6.12 m SE. Found outside house F, in shallow midden containing a little charcoal. Weight: 1.5 g.

149   *1 lump of slag.* Local coordinates: x = 15.10 m, y = −0.15 m, level: 88, height of wall: 0.76. House A. Max.w: 2.4 cm.

150   *Magnetic lump* (slag?) Local coordinates: x = 13.90 m, y = −4 m, level: 13 cm below top of wall. House A. Max.dimension: 3.2 cm.

159   *Lump of slag,* in 2 fragments. Local coordinates: x = 12 m, y = −7.10 m. Found in midden S of house A, room III. Max.w:2.8 cm.

161   *Lump of slag?* Local coordinates: x = 12 m, y = −7.55 m. Found in midden S of house A, room III.

162   *Lump of slag.* Local coordinates: x = 12.25 m, y = −7.80 m. Found in midden S of house A, room III. Max.w: 4.3 cm.

164   *Lump of slag.* Local coordinates: x = 12.80 m, y = −7.75 m. Found in the innermost, 10 cm thick layer in the midden S of house A, room III. Max.w: 2.6 cm.

172   *Slag.* Local coordinates: x = 8 m, y = −12 m. From trench between house B and ditch.

181   *Slag.* Found when sifting earth from the lowest layer of house J.

232   *Glazed slag, blue.* Found in cooking pit II.

243   *Slag.* From floor of house J.

245   *160 g magnetic slag.* From house J.

250   *147 g non-magnetic slag.* From house J.

251   *Slag with clay.* See group 8 below.

254   *Magnetic slag.* House J.

261   *850 g blistered, light, glassy slag.* From slope S of house J.

263   *15 g slag with clay.* See group 8 below.

265   *360 g slag.* From slope S of house J.

266   *Slag.* From 1st profile in house J.

268   *415 g non-magnetic, heavier slag.* From area N of large stone in house J.

271   *Slag with clay-lining.* See group 8 below.

276   *Blistered, light slag.* From profile cut across house J (0.5 m).

280   *Compact slag.* partly with bog-ore. See group 3 below.

282   *Slag.* From 25 cm wide belt from the northern edge E of section DN. House J.

283   *Slag, charcoal and bog-ore.* See group 3 below.

284   *2.1399 kg slag.* Unusually red (remains of bog-ore?) Area N of large stone in house J.

286   *Slag with burned clay.* See group 8 below.

288   *Remnants of magnetic slag.* Cultural layer. House J.

289   *280 g compact, heavy slag.* Cultural layer. House J.

291   *Light, glassy, blistered slag.* Cultural layer. House J.

292   *2 pieces of slag.* From slope S of house J.

296   *Slag.* From slope S of house J.

297   *Slag with clay.*

301   *Slag.* Cultural layer. House J.

303   *Pulverized slag.* Cultural layer. House J.

309   *Slag.* In front of house J, at base of sod.

327   *Blistered slag.* Cultural layer. House J.

341   *Slag.* Location: 14.25 m base, 4.12 m NW. House F, room II.

LaM
No.

b) forging scales.

180   *Forging scales*. From floor of house J. Max.dimension: 2.5 cm.

234   *Magnetic scales*. Cultural layer. House J.

304   *Scales from anvil*. Cultural layer. House J.

Group 3 – Bog-ore.

241   *Bog-ore*. From midden NW of house G.

252   *Bog-ore*. Cultural layer. House J.

260   *47 g bog-ore*. From slope S of house J.

267   *Bog-ore*. From test trench in southern area, about 10 m south of house B.

269   *95 g bog-ore*. From area N of large stone in house J.

274   *Bog-ore*. Cultural layer. House J.

280   *Compact slag, partly with bog-ore*. See group 2 above.

281   *Bog-ore*. Found under sod when digging at the N edge of the cloudberry marsh for the purpose of making a drainage ditch S of houses B and C.

283   *Slag, charcoal and bog-ore*.

293   *80 g bog-ore*. House J.

Group 4 – Metals other than iron.

69   *Fragment of bronze or copper*. Local coordinates: x = 7.92 m, y = –0.20 m, floor level. House D, room III. The object lay at the outer edge of the hearth. Damaged by fire, straight shaft with round upper surface, rounded ends, remains of decoration? on upper surface, thin, transverse lines. L: 1.7 cm, w: 0.4 cm, thickness: 0.25 cm. Fig. 23.

169   *Ring-headed pin of bronze + fragment*, Jan Petersen type C. For details, see group 7 below. Fig. 5.

Group 5 – Stone and stone implements.
a) scrapers

74   *Chert flake scraper*. Local coordinates: x = 14.81 m, y = 0.63 m, level: on gravel. House D, room III. Minute, unifacial, steep, irregular use scars on two margins and the rounded tip of this roughly ovate flake indicate its casual use as a random flake scraper. L: 2.8 cm. Fig. 27.

79   *Chert fragment, scraper*. Local coordinates: x = 1.75 m, y = –0.35 m, level: 4 cm above gravel. Midden NW of house-site G. This is a small, nearly pyramid-shaped fragment of coarse, black chert. Unifacial use scarring for distance of 1.8 cm along one long edge of this object suggests its casual employment as a scraper. Measurements: 1.9 × 1.8 × 1.1 cm. Fig. 27.

80   *Chert fragment, scraper*. Local coordinates: x = 1.69 m, y = –1.35 m, level: 2 cm above gravel. Midden NW of house G. This broken fragment of a flake of reddish-brown chert shows slight use scarring along two edges, indicating brief use as a random flake scraper. Measurements: 2.6 × 2.7 × 0.3 cm. Fig. 27.

82   *Two fragments of chert flake composite tool*. Local coordinates: larger fragment x = 1.96 m, y = –1.10; smaller fragment x = 2.25 m, y = –1.04 m, level: on the gravel. Cooking pit II. This is a thin, random form flake of fine-grained, reddish-brown chert, and shows steep, delicate, uniface retouch along one of its long, convex edges. This sharp edge, showing the best retouch of any specimen from the pit, probably served as a scraper or a flake knife. The bulb of percussion is well-pronounced on the under side, which is unaltered except for the distal end. There delicate retouch occurs along the edge for a distance of 1.2 cm. That, in conjunction with similar chipping on the edge of the upper surface, combines to produce a sharp yet delicate beak or point, for incising or perforating. Such artifacts, delicate composite flake tools, do occur in Dorset, but comparable tools occur in prehistoric Indian stone inventories as well. Measurements: 4.6 × 2.7 × 1.2 cm. Fig. 26.

LaM	
No.	

84   *Chert scraper*. Local coordinates: x = 2.64 m, y = 2.01 m, level: on the gravel. Cooking pit II. This is a culturally undiagnostic, snub-nosed end scraper of coarse black chert. It has a roughly sub-rectangular plan, a plano-convex cross-section, a plane flake under surface, a slightly flaked upper surface, and a steeply retouched, convex scraping edge which shows signs of being dulled through use. No certain cultural identification is possible. Measurements: 2.9 × 2.4 × 0.6 cm. Fig. 26.

88   *Chert flake scraper*. Local coordinates: x = 1.23 m, y = –0.16 m, level: a few mm above sterile ground. Cooking pit II, in layer mixed with charcoal. This item lay in close association with the rusted iron fragment LaM 87 above. It is a small, irregular, incomplete flake of grey-brown chert. The under side is unaltered, but the slightly convex upper surface shows some shallow flaking and, along one edge, the small, steep, irregular chipping scars usually considered to be use flaking. Probably this specimen served briefly as a random flake scraper. Measurements: 2.5 × 1.7 × 0.3 cm. Fig. 26.

90   *Chert block scraper*. Local coordinates: x = 5.75 m, y = –0.45 m. Cooking pit II. Battered block of very dark, grey-green slatey chert. Its plan is crudely oval and its cross-section markedly triangular. Several large, random-form flakes have been struck from the block and, further, abundant, steep, irregular flake scars extend unifacially along a 10 cm length of one slightly convex and slightly dulled edge of the object. Thus it seems to have served, not only as a crude core, but also as a crude block scraper. Measurements: 18 × 10.5 × 5.7 cm.

91   *Group of 23 flakes and chippings*. In the gravel of cooking pit II. These items were scattered over a limited area by the southern edge of the pit. The group includes 1 quartzite scraper, 5 random flake scrapers, and 17 flakes and fragments. For details of the latter, see group 5 k below.

91,10   *Quartzite scraper*. This is a mottled, grey quartzite piece, which seems to be part of a crude blade or prismatic flake, for it has a rectangular plan, triangular cross-section and a slightly concavo-convex longitudinal section. Its bulb of percussion is barely discernible. Its lateral edges show slight use scarring. More significant, however, is its straight end which has been steeply chipped to serve as end scraper. Considered as a crude end-of-the-blade scraper, this specimen is of a type that occurs in the Dorset culture but which might also occur in prehistoric Indian collections. Measurements when found: 3.3 × 2.8 × 0.8 cm. Fig. 29.

91,11–   *5 flake scrapers*. These five sturdy flakes show steep, unifacial flaking along a small part
15   of one of their irregular edges, reflecting casual use as random flake scrapers. One is of grey-green slate, another of banded, dark grey, slatey chert, and three are of mottled grey-green to near-purple chert. Max.1: from 4.5–6.3 cm.

185   *Core and 22 chert flakes and chips*. Location: N 89–82, E 113–115. This find, from the fill of feature 4, includes 22 culturally unassignable, small flakes and chips, described under group 5 k below. Also included is a large core or core scraper of mottled greenish-grey chert. This specimen has a triangular plan, subtriangular longitudinal section, and roughly quadrangular cross-section. Its edges and surface are extensively chipped and show the scars of removal of at least three microblades, or prismatic flakes, from the specimen's convex edge; irregular bifacial retouch on it suggests that edge served both as striking platform and heavy scraper. Measurements: 6 × 3.8 × 3.1 cm.

189 a   *Chert flake scraper*. Collected from the fill of feature 3. Location: N 79–81, E 111–114 at the base of the sod together with 27 unreworked flakes and another worked piece. This thin, pale grey chert flake shows minute, steep, unifacial retouch along one edge for a distance of 0.9 cm, which reflects its brief use as a random flake scraper. Measurements: 2.7 × 3.4 × 0.3 cm.

189 b   *Fragmentary chert scraper*. Location: N 79–81, E 111–114. From the fill. An incomplete, mottled grey-green chert fragment which has been heavily chipped and worn for a length

of 2.8 cm on one edge; this suggests considerable use as a scraper. Its fragmentary condition precludes the assumption that the item belonged to a side scraper. Measurements: 2.7 × 3.4 × 0.3 cm.

190 *55 flakes.* Collected from feature 5. Location: N 64–67, E 101, 104 in grey sand. This specimen number contains 42 random-form flakes, described under group 5 j below.

Also included here are an additional 13 flakes which, unlike the first 42, have been worked. The materials are grey-green slate, slatey chert, dark grey chert and banded grey-beige chert. 11 of the 13 show restricted unifacial edge scarring from their casual employment as flake scrapers. Measurements range up to a maximum of 8 × 8.4 cm.

a The remaining two items deserve special mention. The first, LaM 190 a, is a quadrangular chert fragment which shows diligent steep unifacial chipping along one slightly convex edge; that edge has been subsequently dulled through use. Clearly the specimen was fashioned and used as a scraper. Measurements: 4.9 × 3.5 × 1 cm.

b The second, LaM 190 b, a thin, irregular chert flake, shows steep minute unifacial chipping about its rounded end, indicating use as a tiny end scraper. Measurements: 2.9 × 1.8 × 2 cm.

The absence of microblades in this sample of 55 flakes from feature 5 hints faintly that these objects are not of Dorset culture origin.

192 *39 flakes.* Collected from Feature 5. Location: N 64–67, E 101–104, in grey sand. This specimen number, which was recovered from the grey sand layer before feature 5 was outlined, refers to 27 unreworked flakes, described under group 5 j below, as well as 12 reworked flakes of grey-green slate, cherty slate, black chert and banded black-beige chert. These 12 flakes exhibit casual use scarring, or very rarely delicate intentional retouching, unifacially along one or more edges, reflecting their brief use as scrapers.

199 *Chert flake scraper.* Location: N 69.49, E 112.38. Found 1 cm below the top of the grey sand, this mottled grey chert flake shows a few use scars along one edge that reflect its very brief use as a flake scraper. Measurements: 3.3 × 4.2 cm.

203 b *A pale beige chert flake.* Within grey sand layer. This, and the following three items (LaM 203 c, d and e), come from a group recovered from the grey sand layer between coordinates N69, N70, E111 and E112. Its longest straight edge is entirely covered with neat, steep, unifacial retouching to enhance its use as a flake side scraper. Measurements: 3.7 × 2.4 × 0.3 cm.

203 c *Fragmentary chert scraper.* Location: 69.70, E111–112. Within grey sand layer. This dark grey chert fragment is the battered remnant of a convex-edged, snub-nosed end scraper; only a small part of its steeply retouched scraper edge remains. Measurements: 3.5 × 3.4 × 7 cm.

203 d *Flake end scraper.* Location: N69,70, E111–112. Within grey sand layer. This complete flake end scraper is formed on a flake of dark grey chert; steep retouch occurs along the non-bulbular edge of this flake. Measurements: 3.7 × 2.9 × 0.6 cm.

203 e *Chert flake scraper.* Location: N69,70, E111–112. Within grey sand layer. The fourth flake tool of this group is à dark grey chert flake; irregular scars along one of its thinner edges reflect its brief use as a random scraper. Measurements: 3.4 × 2 × 0.5 cm.

204 *Group of artifacts.* This group of nine items, five of them refuse flakes and four scrapers, was found between coordinates N69, N70, E111 and E112, within the dark brown sand layer from the bottom of the grey sand to a depth of 2 cm in the brown sand.

a *Snub-nosed end scraper,* small, mottled grey-green chert flake. Identified because its convex distal edge is entirely trimmed with neat, steep, unifacial retouch which shows slight wear from use. Measurements: 2.8 × 2.7 × 0.4 cm.

b *End scraper.* A coarse, dark grey chert flake with a convex, distal edge showing irregular unifacial scarring, indicating its use, without being specially shaped, as an end scraper. Measurements: 3.9 × 2.9× 0.6 cm.

c,d   *Casual quartzite scrapers.* Both these specimens are random-form quartzite flakes with unifacial use scars along one edge which suggest their casual use for scraping. Measurements: 204c: 4.6 × 2.4 × 0.3 cm; 204d: 3.7 × 2.2 × 0.3 cm.

205   *Group of artifacts.* This group of 16 flakes was found in the grey sand layer between coordinates N69, N70, E112 and E113. It includes:
four dark grey and dark brown chert flakes showing unifacial retouch or use scarring along one edge reflecting their brief use as flake scrapers; and

205 a   *Chert flake scraper.* This is a banded grey chert flake, which has been well-retouched along 2 cm of one of its straight edges from scraper use; further, that retouched edge has been dulled by use. Measurements: 3.7 × 2.4 × 0.5 cm.

216   *Chert scraper, chopper or knife,* dark grey chert. Found in the fill of feature No.5. Oval biface blade, similar to LaM 223 below, but smaller, it seems safely classified as an Archaic pattern specimen. Measurements: 7.6 × 4 × 1 cm.

218   *Chert scraper, chopper or knife,* dark grey chert. Found in feature No.5. Location N64–67, E101–104. Pointed ovate biface with biconvex cross and longitudinal sections, it seems safely classified as an Archaic pattern specimen. Rounded base. Both sides show sure, shallow, overall chipping; the steeper, more delicate edge retouch scars are restricted almost entirely to one surface where they appear along both margins and seem quite fresh and unworn. Measurements: 8.1 × 5.1 × 1.7 cm.

222   *Chert scraper, chopper or knife,* of nearly black slatey chert. Location: N66.02 and E124.39, in grey sand, 6.2 cm below the turf. This well-made biface of nearly tear-drop shape and biconvex cross and longitudinal sections seems safely classified as an Archaic pattern specimen. There is impressively shallow, sure, overall chipping on both surfaces and steeper edge retouch along the edges. The latter is especially seen on the two long sides of the object and there the edge retouch is mostly unifacial but on a different surface for each of these two edges. Measurements: 10.9 × 4.9 × 1.1 cm.

223   *Chert scraper, chopper or knife,* of pale grey-green mottled slatey chert. Location: N69.10, E132.46, on top of a dark organic layer, 1 cm above the grey sand and 38 cm below surface. This well-made biface blade of pointed ovate form with bi-convex cross-sections, bold overall chipping and shallow secondary retouch on much of the edges of both its surfaces seems safely classified as an Archaic pattern specimen.
Measurements: 10.2 × 6.2 × 1.7 cm.

224   *Fragmentary slate flake knife or scraper.* Location: N73.18, E 124.56. This item occurred in the dark brown sand, 6.5 cm below the top of the grey sand and 16.4 cm below present surface. This sub-rectangular fragment of grey-green slate has a flattened biconvex cross section. One end is broken off and the other is roughly rounded. The object is generally smooth-surfaced but it has not been intentionally ground or polished. One of its long margins was irregularly chipped then subsequently worn dull. The other edge has more abundant flake scars and these appear almost exclusively on one surface of that edge. Also this edge is not quite as dull as the other. The object might have been naturally formed, but it seems more likely to be a natural slate flake which was slightly chipped to facilitate its use as a knife or scraper. Measurements: 8.6 × 3.5 × 0.7 cm.

b) Projectile points

73   *Biface fragment of dark grey chert,* knife blade or weapon point? Local coordinates: x = 10.75 m, y = 0.45 m, level: 12 cm above gravel. A dark grey chert biface fragment with shallow, overall retouching, this piece could be the stem or blunt tip of either a knife blade or weapon point. Its biconvex cross-section is 0.9 cm thick; the fragment is 3.1 cm wide and 2.2 cm long. House-site D III. Fig. 27.

75   *Quartzite knife blade or weapon point.* Local coordinates: x = 5.76 m, y = –0.48 m, House D, room III, level: 6 cm above floor. Pale grey, translucent quartzite, an asymmetric,

straight-based, side-notched, biface knife blade or weapon point. It shows overall shallow retouch, and a general dulling of the edges, especially in the notch concavities. Maximum dimensions: 3.1 × 1.8 × 0.4 cm. This is quite a typical occurrence in Dorset assemblages. Figs. 25 and 27.

77   *Chert fragmentary weapon point or knife.* Local coordinates: x = 2.23 m, y = 0.75 m, level: 6 cm above the gravel. Midden NW of house G. This is a black chert biface fragment of a knife or weapon point. The base is nearly straight and, as far as can be determined, the lateral edges seem to have been parallel and approximately straight. Both surfaces are covered with shallow flake scars and, in addition, slight, steeper retouch occurs sparingly on the edges of the object. It is 3.2 cm wide and has a biconvex cross-section, 0.9 cm thick. Originally it was much longer than its present 3 cm. Fig. 27.

83   *Chert biface point.* Local coordinates: x = 2.80 m, y = 2.62 m, level: on the gravel. Cooking pit II. Straight-based, biface, triangular point of Archaic origin. It is an asymmetric, triangular biface of coarse, slatey chert, mottled grey-green and reddish-brown in colour. It shows biconvex cross and longitudinal sections, a slightly convex slanted base and converging, convex lateral margins. Both surfaces show shallow, overall flaking and incomplete edge retouch. On one side the base has been thinned by the removal of at least six shallow flakes. There is no appreciable edge dulling. L: 5.2 cm, w: 3.7 cm, thickness: 1.1 cm. Fig. 26.

140   *Flint arrow-head.* Local coordinates: x = –0.40 m, y = –0.80 m. This specimen is entirely intact. Similar in type to E. Harp jr. 1964, Pl. III, No. 1. Found in the upper layer of turf of the western end wall of house A, where the turf was highly eroded. A little way N and E of the spot where this item was found, there was a fire-patch which extended up to the underside of the surface sod. The arrow-head may be associated with this fire-patch. Level: 153.5, upper limit of sod: 149.0. Fig. 8.

217   *Chert blade or projectile point.* Location: N64–67, E101–104. From the fill of feature 5. This is a straightbased, triangular chert blade or projectile point, probably the tip of a spear or lance. It reflects a general tendency to slight asymmetry in plan view. Further, it shows converging, convex margins, basal thinning, biconvex cross and longitudinal section, extensive shallow overall retouch and skilled, steeper, secondary retouch along the margins. Max. measurements: 5.9 × 3.4 × 1 cm. Of Archaic origin.

219   *Chert blade or projectile point.* Location: N64–67, E101–104. From the fill of feature 5. Dark grey chert; as LaM 217 above. Max. measurements: 8.2 × 4.3 × 1.5 cm. Fig. 61.

220   *Chert blade or projectile point.* Location: N69–67, E101–104. From the fill of feature 5. Dark bluish-grey chert; as LaM 217 above. Max. measurements: 6.7 × 4.3 × 1.1 cm.

221   *Chert blade or projectile point.* Location: N69.67, E101–104. From the fill of feature 5. Dark grey chert; as LaM 217 above. Max. measurements: 6.4 × 4 × 1.1 cm.

225   *Dorset projectile.* Found in the grey sand layer, location: N96.32, E113.26. This is a diagnostic Dorset culture type, the tip-fluted chipped stone end blade. It is a very carefully made biface of mottled black-and-white quartzite with an elongated triangular plan, concave base, symmetrical, gently convex sides converging to a sharp point, and biconvex cross-section and longitudinal sections. On both surfaces the base has been thinned by the removal of longitudinal flakes; both surfaces show delicate, shallow, skilled, overall flaking. On one surface a thin, 2.5 cm long sharpening flake has been driven off, from the tip of this point, to produce the flake scar and medial ridge of this artifact that pronounce it to be of Dorset origin. This was an isolated find, which occurred c. 15 m N of features 3 and 4. Max. measurements: 4 × 1.7 × 0.5 cm.

227   *Chert blade or projectile point.* This item, of dark grey chert, comes from an area of wind-blown grey sand, location: N64.49 and E107.87. It is a straight-based, triangular biface end blade or projectile point, which probably once tipped a spear or lance. It shows converging convex margins, basal thinning, biconvex cross and longitudinal sections,

256

extensive shallow overall retouch and skilled, steeper, secondary retouch along the margins. It is not of Dorset origin, reasonably assigned to the Archaic Indian pattern. Measurements: 5.4 × 3.9 × 1 cm.

c) Perforators, incising tools, cutting tools

1   *Tool of green jasper, serrated edge.* 14.25 m base, 4.37 m NW, floor level. The object was found at the middle of a patch between rooms II and III of house F, where a wall is assumed to have stood. L: 2.5 cm. Fig. 52.

73   *Biface fragment of dark grey chert.* Knife blade or weapon point? For details, see group 5 b above. Fig. 27.

75   *Quartzite knife blade or weapon point.* See group 5 b above. Fig. 27.

77   *Chert fragmentary weapon point or knife.* See group 5 b above. Fig. 27.

81   *Green chert flake perforator or incising tool.* Local coordinates: x = 0.33 m, y = –0.06 m, level: 3 cm above the gravel. Midden NW of house G. This small, ovate flake of fine-grained, green chert was struck from a larger piece marked by broad, shallow flake scars. Concavo-convex in section. This item would belong with the stone refuse except that, on its upper or convex surface where the two longer of its three edges converge to a broad point, those two converging edges show steep, very delicate retouch for a distance of 1 cm. Thus the point of this flake has been minutely retouched to serve as a perforator or incising tool. Measurements: 2.7 × 1.7 × 0.3 cm.

82   *Two fragments of chert flake composite tool.* See group 5 a above. Fig. 26.

86   *Chert biface blade knife.* Local coordinates: x = 2.06 m, y = –0.92 m, level: on the gravel. Cooking pit II. This large ovate biface, sturdy, and of banded black and brown chert in an asymmetric broad oval plan with biconvex cross and longitudinal sections, seems safely classified as an Archaic pattern specimen. There is generally shallow, overall flaking of both surfaces and, on one edge, a pair of distinct notches set about 1 cm apart and formed by steep, unifacial chipping. As these notches are slightly dulled and the specimen's edges are otherwise quite sharp, one may suspect that this object was hafted as some kind of skinning knife rather than as an adze. It measures 8 × 5.5 × 1.6 cm.

193 a   *Chert flake perforator or incising tool.* Location: N64–67, E101–104. One of a group of artifacts from the excavated black dirt pile from feature 5. A carefully retouched flake of fine-textured, glassy, translucent, grey chert. It has a strong bulb of percussion and platform and a concavo-convex longitudinal section. Its irregular edges show sporadic use scarring and, across its distal end, minute unifacial retouch that has shaped the natural beak-like tip of the flake into a delicate perforator or incising tool. Measurements: 4.1 × 3 × 5 cm.

198   *Chert flake perforator or incising tool.* Found at 1 cm below the top of the grey sand at coordinates N69.14, E112.42. This banded grey chert flake shows delicate retouch on its beak-shaped tip, suggesting its use as a perforator or incising too. Measurements: 3.7 × 2.1 × 0.4 cm.

222   *Chert scraper, chopper or knife.* For details, see group 5 a above.

223   *Chert scraper, chopper or knife.* For details, see group 5 a above.

224   *Fragmentary slate flake knife or scraper.* Location N73, 18 E124, 56. This item occurred in the dark brown sand, 6.5 cm below the top of the grey sand and 16.4 cm below present surface. This sub-rectangular fragment of grey-green slate has a flattened biconvex cross section. One end is broken off and the other is roughly rounded. The object is generally smooth-surfaced but it has not been intentionally ground or polished. One of its long margins was irregularly chipped then subsequently worn dull. The other edge has more abundant flake scars and these appear almost exclusively on one surface of that edge. Also this edge is not quite as dull as the other. The object might have been

257

naturally formed, but it seems more likely to be a natural slate flake which was slightly chipped to facilitate its use as a knife or scraper. Measurements: 8.6 × 3.5 × 0.7 cm.

d) Axes, choppers and celts.

85   *Polished chert axe head.* Local coordinates: x = 0.62 m, y = –1.55 m. Cooking pit II. This chipped and polished axe head lay in the gravel of the pit. It is made of pale green to olive drab slatey chert. The gently convex bit is fully polished, quite sharp and of moderately biconvex cross-section and a concavo-convex longitudinal section. Excepting the bit, its margins have been crudely chipped, then dulled by incomplete polishing. The convex surface is quite well polished overall, but polishing is incomplete on the concave side, except, as noted, about the bit. It is reasonably, if not certainly ascribed to the Archaic pattern. Measurements: 10.7 × 8.1 × 1.8 cm. Fig. 28.

222   *Chert scraper, chopper or knife.* For details, see group 5 a above.

223   *Chert scraper, chopper or knife.* For details, see group 5 a above.

e) Hones

66 a   *Small needle hone of quartzite.* 11.10 m base, –4 m SE, at floor level. House F, room VI. Traces of fine tools having been ground. Rectangular cross-section. L: 7.3 cm, section: 0.7 cm. Fig. 49.

104   *Flat fragment of hone.* Found among a large amount of stones from house F, room IV, upper layer. Red sandstone. Ground on both sides, clear traces of having been used for grinding a sharp tool on one side. L: 16 cm, W: 10.4 cm.

f) Lamps

39   *Stone lamp.* 4.50 m base, 4 m NW, among stones in the upper layers below the sod. This is a natural beach stone, flat above and below. It has an oval depression on one of the flat surfaces. Max.diam. of depression: 5.5 cm, depth: 1.3 cm; max.diam. of stone: 13 cm. Fig. 48.

343   *Dorset lamp, soap-stone.* Found in top layer at the far NW end of house J, immediately below the sod. The opening of the lamp faced up. It is oval, like G. Rowley 1940. L: 19.2 cm, max.w: 10.7 cm, h (exterior): 4 cm. Fig. 57.

g) Pounding stones

37   *Oval beach stone,* broken into two pieces which match exactly. Local coordinates: x = 16.90 m, y = –12.20 m. Found in hearth at SW end of house B, 2 cm above floor level. Pounding marks at ends. Glued together. L: 12 cm, w: 10 cm. Fig. 16.

38   *Oval beach stone,* with pounding marks at ends. Local coordinates: x = 16.75 m, y = –11.90 m. Found in same hearth as LaM 37 above, at floor level. L: 17.9 cm, max.w: 10.3 cm.

214 a   *Fire-blackened, granitic hammerstone.* Location: N89–82, E113–115. From LaM 214, a group from the fill of feature 4. The hammerstone, very roughly spheroidal in form, shows the usual battering scars on its smaller end. Measurements: 11 × 8 × 7.5 cm.

215   *Large slate flake.* Found below the turf, location: N70.55, E122.50 in house D, room III. This is a huge flake of grey-green slate with smooth surfaces and large, irregular chipping scars which occur sporadically about its edges. The cross-section is biconvex, but the plano-convex longitudinal section tapers to a rounded point where the chipping scars tend to be concentrated. Probably this tool served in such coarse tasks as breaking bones and beheading fish. Although a crude, generalized form, it is not the kind of thing that suggests Dorset culture, but is an item one might reasonably expect in Archaic assemblages. Measurements: 17.9 × 3.3 cm.

h) Cores

72   *Fragment of dark grey chert.* Local coordinates: x = 10.73 m, y = 0.65 m, level: 12 cm
     above the gravel. House D, room III. This thick little fragment of dark grey chert is the
     diligently battered remnant of a random-form core. It has a roughly triangular plan and
     measures 3.4 × 2.5 × 2 cm. Fig. 27.

196 *Chert core.* Location: N4.18, E62.43. Found at the base of the sod. It is a non-descript
     random-form core of pale beige chert, measuring 3.5 × 2.6 × 1.6 cm.

j) Random flakes.

89   *Prismatic chert flake.* From the midden NE of house G, level: on the gravel. This large,
     sturdy prismatic flake of nearly black coarse chert shows an irregular sub-rectangular
     plan and triangular cross-section. The striking platform, adjacent to a strong bulb of
     percussion, measures 1 × 1.1 cm. The inner main flake surface shows slight and
     irregular use scarring along one edge but is otherwise unaltered. The upper surface,
     which has an irregular medial ridge, shows a 4.2 cm long scar of a prismatic flake struck
     from the platform end and also slight, very irregular signs of use scarring. Measure-
     ments: 7.2 × 3 × 1.3 cm.

187 *Chert flake.* Location: N66,73, E111,46, on top of the sand layer. It is a coarse, black
     chert flake struck off in the process of fashioning an artifact and not subsequently
     worked. Measurements: 3.2 × 2.8 cm.

189 *Group of chert flakes.* Location: N79–81, E111–114. This group, collected from the fill
     of feature 3, includes 27 unworked grey, green, grey-green, black and near white chert
     as well as two worked pieces. The two latter are described under group 5 a above.

190 *55 flakes.* Location: N64–67, E101–104, feature 5. In grey sand after feature was
     outlined. This number contains 42 random-form flakes of grey-green slate, cherty slate
     and banded, green, grey and near purple chert. These tend to be elongated flakes with
     frequently pronounced striking platforms and bulbs of percussion. Size range from very
     small flakes to one with a max. 1: 8.5 cm.

     Also included here are an additional 13 flakes which, unlike the first 42, have been
     worked. These are described under group 5 a above.

192 *39 flakes.* This specimen number, which was recovered from the grey sand layer before
     feature 5 was outlined, refers to 12 reworked flakes, described under group 5 a above,
     as well as 27 unreworked flakes of grey-green slate, cherty slate and black chert.

193 *Stone items from feature 5.* Location: N64–67, E101–104. This group came from the
     excavated black dirt pile from the feature, and includes a spall from a water-worn
     pebble (see group 8 d below), four subsequently unaltered flakes of grey-green slate, and
     item LaM 193 a, a carefully retouched chert flake perforator or incising tool (see group
     5 c above).

194 *Chert flake.* Location: S5.31, W8.85, level: 9 cm below present surface. This is an
     unaltered flake of grey chert. Measurements: 2.3 × 1.6 cm.

197 *Chert flake.* Location: N69.08, E112.36. Found 1 cm below the top of the grey sand,
     this is simply an unaltered flake of coarse, dark grey chert, measuring 3.7 × 2.7 × 4
     cm.

200 *Chert flake.* Location: N69.30, E112.28. Found 1 cm below the top of the grey sand,
     this elongated flake of pale grey chert has a pronounced bulb of percussion and
     measures 5.8 × 3.4 × 6 cm.

201 *Chert flake.* Location: N77.66, E112.20. Found on grey, wind-blown sand below the
     sod, this is a tiny refuse flake of grey chert. It measures 1.2 × 1.1 cm.

202 *Chert flake.* Location: N77.71, E112.39. Found below the sod on the grey, wind-blown
     sand, this is a reject flake of coarse grey chert. It measures 3 × 2.2 cm.

203 *Flakes and fragments.* Location: N69–70, E111–112. This group, recovered from the

area between these coordinates, includes one slate and six chert flakes of no consequence, four flake tools and one biface fragment.

203 a   The banded green, chert biface fragment *203 a* has generally a shallow overall retouch, unretouched edges, a biconvex cross-section, rounded base and slightly diverging convex sides. L: 2.6 cm, w: 3.4 cm, thickness: 0.8 cm.

203 b, c and d are described under group 5 a above.

204   *Group of artifacts*. Location: N69–70, E111–112. This group includes nine items found in the area between these coordinates, the area which also yielded the LaM 203 group of artifacts, which lay within the grey sand layer. The *204* group of artifacts lay within the dark brown sand layer from the bottom of the grey sand to a depth of 2 cm in the brown sand.

The group includes three dark grey chert and two quartzite flakes of stone refuse. Two chert end scrapers and two used quartzite flakes, *LaM 204 a–d*, also included in the group, are described under group 5 a above.

205   *Flakes*. Group of 16 flakes found in the grey sand layer, location: N69, N70, E112 and E113. It includes 5 reworked flakes, described under group 5 a above, and three quartzite and eight chert and slatey chert unretouched flakes.

206   *Chert flakes and fragment*. This group, found in the area between coordinates N69, N70, E112 and E113, within the dark brown sand layer from the bottom of the grey sand to a depth of 2 cm within the brown sand, comprises 3 small flakes and one small fragment of chert (listed under group 5 k below), dark grey, and grey-green in colour.

207   *Chert flake*. Location: N70.25, E117.63. This single, unretouched flake of banded grey-green slatey chert was found at the base of the grey sand layer.

208   *Slate flake*. Location: N64.55, E108.10. Found on top of the grey sand layer, this single grey-green slate flake shows no retouch. Measurements: 8.4 × 4 × 0.5 cm.

210   *Chert flake*. Location: N67.12, E110.675. From the grey sand layer, this pale green chert flake without retouch measures 3.2 × 2.5 cm.

212   *Chert flake*. Location: N4.30, E16.95. This nearly white chert flake, a unifacially scarred fragment of chipping refuse, lay below the sod in feature 8. Measurements: 2.7 × 1.8 × 0.7 cm.

k) Fragments and chippings

91,16–   *Seventeen flakes and fragments*. Part of a group of 22 flakes and chippings, LaM 91,
32   which lay scattered over a limited area by the southern edge of cooking pit II, on the gravel of the pit. These flakes and fragments, of nearly black, grey and purplish chert and greenish-grey slate and slatey chert represent the usual detritus of a stone-chipping industry, and echo a brief aboriginal occupation.

142   *1 piece of flint*. Local coordinates: x = 12.60 m, y = –0.50 m, level: bottom. House A. Fragment of a chipping block with rectangular section. L: 2.4 cm, w: 1.7 cm.

156   *1 piece of chert*. Local coordinates: x = 8.60 m, y = –11.50 m. Found outside house C, level: 0.89, top of wall of house C: 0.69. Max. dimension: 3.5 cm.

184   *4 flint chippings*. From the midden S of house A.

185   *Core and 22 chert flakes and chips*. Location: N89–82, E113–115. These are the 22 culturally unassignable, small flakes and chips found together with a core scraper, described under group 5 a above, in the fill of feature 4. These flakes and chips are of grey and greenish-grey chert refuse.

206   *Chert flakes and fragment*. See group 5 j above.

209   *Slate*. Location: N64.04, E105.16. Excavated from the dark brown sand layer, 2.5 cm below the bottom of the grey sand, this longitudinal, grey-green slate shows a pronounced bulb of percussion but no subsequent chipping. Measurements: 7.3 × 4.4 × 0.7 cm.

213   *Chert fragment*. Location: N4.875, E16.64. Found below the sod in feature 8. It is a

214   grey-blue chert fragment devoid of retouch. Measurements: $3 \times 1.4 \times 0.5$ cm.

214   *Group from fill of feature 4.* Location: N89–82, E113–115. The group includes unworked cobble fragments, a slate flake and a fire-blackened, granitic hammerstone. The latter is described under group 5 g above.

226   *Stone chippings.*

336   *Part of anvil from house J.* Found in slope S of house J, c. 3 m from the anvil.

344   *Chert chip.* Location: N67.12, E110.15, in grey sand layer.

Group 6 – Stones used for striking fire

2   *1 piece of red jasper,* blunt at one end. 2.62 m base, 2.12 m NW, house F, room I. Found in a shallow pit, in fat earth containing charcoal, which also held some slivers of bone and a great number of burned bones. Used for striking fire. 1.9×1.5 cm.

50   *Small piece of red jasper.* Found in the long hearth of house F, room II. Analysed by Professor Tom Barth. Fig. 51.

67   *Slag and 2 other objects.* For details of this find, which includes a round stone of syenitic type and a pyrite, see group 9f below.

113   *Stone.* 14.06 m base, –6.55 m SE. House F, sterile soil. Possibly a block of flint or green jasper, long scars of flaking, especially on one side. L: 3.4 cm, w: 2.3 cm. Used for striking fire?

126   *1 piece of red jasper.* 18.60 m base, –1.30 m SE. Found in house F, in soil containing charcoal. L: 1.3 cm.

128   *1 piece of red jasper.* 19.60 m base, 0.55 m NW. Found in house F, in soil containing charcoal. L: 1.8 cm.

143   *1 piece of red jasper.* Local coordinates: x = 12. 35 m, y = –1.60 m, Level: bottom. House A. Found in a hearth, together with LaM 142 above. Max. 1: 1.2 cm.

146   *I flat, oblong piece of pyrite.* (3 fragments). Local coordinates: x = 8.05 m, y = –0.90 m. House A, room I, 15 cm below turf.

151   *1 piece of red jasper?* Local coordinates: x = 15.42 m, y = –2.60 m, level: 118, bottom: 120. House A. Max. dimension: 0.9 cm.

153   *1 piece of red jasper.* Local coordinates: x = 7.60 m, y = –12.20 m. Found outside house C, level III, top of E wall of house C 0.99. Max. dimension: 1.5 cm.

230   *1 piece of jasper.* Midden NW of house G.

239   *Polished pyrites.* From midden NW of house G.

Group 7 – Textile tools and dress ornament

76   *Fragmentary bone needle.* Local coordinates: x = 8.69 m, y = –1.25 m, level: 2 cm above bottom of ember-pit. House D, room III. Broken, triangular head, pierced with drill, needle round, broken. L: 3.4 cm, w. of head: 1.5 cm, thickness: 0.4 cm, diam. of hole: 0.5 cm, diam. of needle: 0.5 cm. Fig. 24.

97   *Soap-stone spindle whorl.* 10.0 m base, –5.50 m SE. Found in house F, outside SE entrance to room VI, in a 5 cm thick layer of old turf. Convex and sooty under surface, made from a cauldron sherd. Some more recent cuts along the edge. Upper surface rounded. Diam: 33 – 33.4 mm, max. thickness: 11.6 mm. Fig. 47 a–b.

169   *Ring-headed pin of bronze + fragment.* Local coordinates: x = 16.10 m, y = –1.90 m. Base: 103.5, level: 180, floor level: 186. Jan Petersen type C. L: 10 cm. Fig. 5.

Group 8 – Clay from forge, house J

235   *Samples of white clay around anvil.*

240   *Sample of white clay from around anvil stone.*

248   *5 g clay-like material.*

251   *Slag with clay.* See group 9f below.

256	*Burned clay.*
263	*15 g slag with clay.* See group 9f below.
271	*Slag with clay lining.* See group 9f below.
286	*Slag with burned clay.* See group 9f below.
297	*Slag with clay.* See group 9f below.

Group 9 – Various samples

a) Charcoal

Samples of charcoal:

- a   *1 bag* from midden S of house A, room III, all layers. Weight: 260 g.
- b   *1 bag of charcoal* from house A, room I, SW field, collected from a hard-trodden floor layer, c. 10 cm thick, which was full of small, brittle-burned stones and pulverized, charred bones. Weight: 245 g.
- c   *1 bag of charcoal,* collected from all layers of hearth at W end of house A, room II. Weight: 320 g.

Samples of charcoal:

1 bag of charcoal collected in 1966, in the floor layer of house D, room II, at 2 cm above sterile ground.

177	*Sample of charcoal.* Bottom layer of hearth of house A, room II.
231	*Charcoal.* Midden NW of house G.
242	*Charcoal.* From midden NW of house G.
246	*Charcoal.* House J.
249	*8.5 g charcoal.* House J.
253	*Charcoal.* House J.
262	*4 g charcoal.* From slope S of house J.
270	*Charcoal.* From area N of large stone in house J.
277	*Sand with small slivers of charcoal.* See group 9f below.
278	*70 g charcoal.* House J.
283	*Slag, charcoal and bog-ore.* See group 9f below.
285	*Small pieces of charcoal.* From house J.
311	*Charcoal.* Location: N67.30–68, E134. Found in dark, organic layer.
312	*Charcoal.* Location: N67.70–68, E134. Found in dark, organic layer.
325	*Sample of charcoal.* Location: N68, E131.
326	*Sample of charcoal.* Location: N79–81, E111–114. From base of feature 3, 29th July 63.
328	*Sample of charcoal.* Location N64.67 E101–104. Found in feature 5, 30th. july 63.
330	*Charcoal.* Location: N67.82, E31.41. 9th August 63.
331	*Charcoal.* Location: N63–65, E137–138. From base of feature 6.
333	*Charcoal.* From trench SE of house F.
334	*Charcoal from cooking pit.* House F, room VI.
338	*Charcoal.* From old drainage ditch under NW wall of house F room V.
339	*Charcoal.* House F, room VI, 20 cm from the large rivet LaM 60 above.
340	*Charcoal* House F, room II.
345	*Sample of charcoal.* Location: N63–65, E137–138. Found in feature 6, E of house F.

b) Bones

115	*1 bag of whale-bone.* Found between 16.80 m base and 17.20 m base, –1 m SE. House F, on sterile soil under a thin layer of old turf.
127	*Bag of whale-bone.* 18.20 m base, –2.50 m SE. Found in house F, in soil containing charcoal. Weight: 415 g.
135	*Bag of whale-bone.* Found at 17–17.25 m base, –0.50– –1 m SW of it, house F, room VI, in thin cultural layer. Weight: 340 g.

139 *Small pieces of whale-bone*. 18–18.50 m base, –1.50 –2 m. SW of it. Found in a shallow midden, SE og house F, room III. Total weight: 8 g.

170 *Fragment of a whale-bone*. Local coordinates: x = 13.10, y = –7.62. From midden S of house A.

176 *Whale-bone?* from area near boat-sheds. Local coordinates: x = 23.85, y = 4.60, level: 143.

182 *Charred bone from domestic pig*. Local coordinates: x = 16.75, y = –3.50. House A.

317 *Whale-bone*. Location: N6.25, E108.90. Found at base of sod, on sand and gravel.

319 *Whale-bone*. Location: N4.18, E106.13. Found in turf wall, 21 cm below surface.

320 *Whale-bone*. Location: N71.26, E112.13. Found on top of grey sand.

337 *Whale-bone and unidentified bones*. Found by sifting SE of house F, room III in a shallow midden.

8 *Unidentified bones*. Found in and near the long hearth in house F, room II, in fat earth containing charcoal.

9 *2 fragments of charred bone,* one from domestic pig. Local coordinates: x = 5–5.50, y = –9.60. Found at the bottom of a small midden outside house C.

12 *Unidentified bones*. Found immediately below the sod in house F, room III.

19 *1 fragment of charred bone*. House F, room II, near hearth.

20 *Fragment of bone*. Found close to the long hearth of house F, room II, in fat soil containing charcoal, at floor level.

107 *3 charred bones + small snail shell*. Found in trench SE of house F, room VI.

144 *1 piece of charred bone*. Local coordinates: x = 12.56, y = –7.20, level: 112.5. Found S of house A, among a large amount of charcoal in a midden.

145 *1 piece of charred bone*. Local coordinates: x = 1.55, y = –2.3, level: 150, bottom: 161.5. Found in profile cut at this spot. House A.

152 *1 piece of charred bone*. Local coordinates: x = 14.30, y = –11.70. Max. dimension: 1.5 cm.

166 *2 pieces of charred bone*. Found in the middle profile cut in house A, at 10 cm above floor level, c. 0.5 m from LaM 169, the ring-headed pin, at the upper edge of the cooking pit. Dimensions: 1.8 cm, 1.9 cm.

171 *1 piece of charred bone*. Local coordinates: x = 14.60, y = –2.60, level: 20 cm above floor level. House A. Max. dimension: 1.6 cm.

237 *Charred bones*. From midden NW of house G.

308 *Animal bone*. Location: N79–81, E111–114. Found in fill of feature 3, 29th July 63.

321 *Bone fragment*. Found by sifting in shallow midden SE of house F, room III.

322 *Bone fragment*. Found by sifting in shallow midden SE of house F, room III.

323 *Bone fragment*. Found by sifting in shallow midden SE of house F, room III.

324 *Bone fragment*. Found by sifting in shallow midden SE of house F, room III.

c) Stone

6 *Sample of stone*. From the bottom layer of house G.

11 *2 iron pyrites,* non-magnetic. House D, room I, in cultural layer containing charcoal. 24 g.

17 *Stone*. From house G. Found in the lowest 20 cm of cultural layer.

18 *1 pumice stone*. House F, room II.

25 *2 samples of stone*. From house B.

34 *2 stones*. House E.

36 *2 stones*. House G.

42 *Samples of stone* from house F. Various places.

43 *Heavy stone*. House F, room II.

44 *Samples of stone*. From house D.

45   *Limestones*. From house G.

46   *1 small pumice stone* and some flakes of crude iron. See group 9 f below.

47   *Pebble*. House F.

109   *Stone tool?* 11.37 m base, –7.12 m SE. House F. Good point, pointed and flattened at base. L: 5.7 cm, w: 2.9 cm. Proved to be natural formation.

114   *1 piece of glazed stone*. 14.84 m base, –5.55 m SE. House F, sterile soil. Bluish-black glaze.

173   *Small black stone, soft*. Area near boat-sheds.

183   *Rough stone*. Location: N80, W2.05. From surface on grey sand, 16th July 63.

186   *Rough stone*. Location: N98, W2.20.

188   *Rough stones*. Found in feature 3, 29th July 63.

191   *Rough stones*. Found in feature 5, in grey sand, after feature was outlined. 31st July 63.

193   *Stone items from feature 5*. This group came from the excavated black dirt pile from the feature, and includes a spall from a water-worn pebble, four subsequently unaltered flakes of grey-green slate (see group 5 j above), and item LaM 193a, a carefully retouched chert flake, perforator or incising tool (see group 5 c above).

195   *Rough stone*. Location: N65.2, E130.8. Found in dark organic layer on 9th August 63.

211   *Rough stone*. Location: N61.80, E108.10. From grey sand layer.

229   *2 round, rust-like stones*. Midden NW of house G.

238   *Shale*. From midden NW of house G.

244   *Half-molten stones from near anvil*. House J.

257   *Stone*. House J.

258   *Stone or iron*. House J.

264   *40 g stone*. From slope S of house J.

272   *Stone*. From area N of large stone in house J.

275   *Stone*. House J.

287   *50 g stone*. House J.

294   *Stone*. From slope S of house J.

316   *Rough stone*. Found in feature 6, on top of grey sand, 10th August 63.

332   *Stone*. Found in a trench 1.50 m E of house C.

335   *Stone*. Found on top of cultural layer. House F, room IV.

336   *Part of anvil from house J*. Found in slope S of house J, about 3 m from the anvil.

e) Wood

13   *Sample of bone or wood?*

14   *Small piece of birch bark*. 7 m base, 2 m NW. House F, room II.

174 a–b *Samples of wood*, from area near boat-sheds.

175   *Samples of wood*, from area near boat-sheds.

315   *Rotted log*. Location: N71.51, E139.61. Found at top of dark, organic layer, 64.5 cm below surface.

340   *Charcoal or wood?* See group 9 a above.

e) Earth and sand

10   *Sample of red earth*. Local coordinates: x = 18.50, y = –12. Taken at SW end of ember-pit in house B, under a small firepatch.

16   *Sample of earth* from NW part of house E. Cultural layer.

40   *Sample of earth* from wall of house A, room IV. Local coordinates: x = 21.10, y = 5.

124   *Small lump of earth* or clay, with hole at centre. 2.75 m base, 1.50 m NW. Found as a result of scraping the dark, hard-trodden layer in the entrance to house F, room I. Not burned. Diam.: 2.2 cm. Natural formation.

178   *Samples of earth* from area near boat-sheds.

259   *82 g sand* with small particles of all other categories. From slope S of house J. See group 9 f below.

LaM
No.

273   *Sand and small pieces of all the other categories of sample 23.*
277   *Sand with small slivers of charcoal.* See group 9 f below.
295   *Small glass containing fine sand.* From slope S of house J.
306   *Sand* in which ring-headed pin, LaM 169 above, was found.
329   *Surface* at N68, E31. 9th Sept. 63.
342   *Soil sample.* From below iron fragment from feature 3, LaM 314 above.

f) Mixed samples.

46   *1 small pumice stone and some flakes of crude iron.* Local coordinates: x = 17.75–18.50, y = –12.20. From house B. The crude iron lay at a depth of 20 cm in the cultural layer, 10 cm above sterile ground, at the centre of the fire patch. These items lay immediately below old turf.
67   *Slag and 2 other objects.* House F, room VI. The two objects were a round stone of syenitic type and a pyrite, weighing 24 g. Weight of slag: 5.1 g.
236   *Finds from sifting.* From house J.
251   *Slag with clay.* House J.
256   *"Various".* House J.
259   *82 g sand* with small particles of all other categories. From slope S of house J.
263   *15 g slag with clay.* From slope S of house J.
271   *Slag with clay-lining.* From area N of large stone in house J.
273   *Sand and small pieces of all the other categories of sample 23.*
277   *Sand with small slivers of charcoal.* House J.
280   *Compact slag, partly with bog-ore.* From the section across house J.
283   *Slag, charcoal and bog-ore.* Slope S of house J.
286   *Slag with burned clay.* From house J.
297   *Slag with clay.* From profile cut across house J, where the two large samples were taken, and where the Dorset lamp was found.
298   *Sample 45.* From southern area.

App. I

Determination of Species, Bone, Cat. No. LaM 182

We acknowledge receipt of a fragment of bone, sent to us for a determination of the species it represents. Our investigations show that it derives from the species Sus scrofa, the pig.

Yours sincerely,
(sign.) Rolf W. Lie
cand.real.

Encl.: 1 fragment of bone
Cat. No LaM 182

App. II

Material of Bones from L'Anse aux Meadows, Newfoundland

Results of investigations.

LaM 8
Whale, species indeterminable. Several fragments.

LaM 9

Pig, *Sus scrofa*. Scapula (shoulder-blade) 1 fragment.

LaM 20

Common Seal, *Phoca vitulina*. Toe phalanx. 1 fragment, (two fragments glued together.)

Whale, species indeterminable. Several fragments.

The remainder of the find defies determination.

Material of Bones from L'Anse aux Meadows, Newfoundland

I am enclosing the result of our investigations regarding the species represented by the bones submitted to us for determination. I very much regret having to inform you that the greater part of the material submitted defied determination, but experience shows that charred bones are very difficult to identify. In any case, I hope that our work may be of help to you.

I am somewhat in doubt as concerns the fragment of a scapula (LaM 9). The coracoid process has disappeared, and this is the best means of determining the species from this part of the pig's scapula. It may thus resemble the scapula of a sheep or a goat (two species which cannot be distinguished from each other). However, the remaining characteristic features indicate the pig as the source of the fragment. We may disregard the possibility of it deriving from a wild animal – there has never been any wild boar in Newfoundland, nor any representative of the most closely related Tayassuidea. Wild sheep and goats occur exclusively in the mountain regions of the mainland, from Alaska southwards. Furthermore, the distribution of some of the wild breeds of sheep seems to have been affected by the activity of man. On Soay (*sauøy* = sheep island?) in the Hebrides, for instance, there is a local breed of sheep which is highly reminiscent of the "bronze sheep" which were common during the Bronze Age. Tradition has it that these sheep are descended from the sheep brought here by Scandinavian Vikings. St. Kilda, also in the Hebrides, has a similar breed. All this simply for your information.

Today the common seal occurs along the coasts of the northern Atlantic and Pacific, and it is numerous around Newfoundland.

Whale occurs in all oceans. It is difficult to say which species, one or more, might be represented by your fragments.

. I hope this information may be of some use to you in your further work on the L'Anse aux Meadows finds. I should like to take this opportunity of thanking you for asking me to determine the material, which I am returning separately by registered mail.

Yours sincerely,
(sign.) Rolf W. Lie
dep. keeper

Samples of jasper.

1. L'Anse aux Meadows.
2. Icelandic jasper.

Microscopic examinations of specimens prepared from the above samples showed that both had a compact crystalline basic mass of jasper (SiO_2), densely impregnated with iron hydroxides; the red colour of the samples derives from this. The sample from Iceland shows a far greater degree of iron impregnation than that from Newfoundland. I would estimate the iron content of the

Icelandic sample at 10%, while that from Newfoundland contains only 1%. This difference is not likely to be of any significance, for the iron impregnation of jasper may vary considerably: jasper from one vein frequently shows variations of this magnitude.

There are typical traces of copper and nickel. Both samples contained approximately 0.1% of copper and 0.05% of nickel. This suggests, but is no proof, that the samples come from one geological region. Had there been a great differnce in their content of trace elements, one could have deduced with a reasonable degree of certainty that they could not both have come from Iceland. Of course jasper from Newfoundland could have the same content of trace elements as jasper from Iceland, but as the geological formations in these two regions are so different, this seems highly unlikely.

In my opinion, we can do no more than this with these samples. I only hope that you will be able to make some use of my result.

Yours sincerely,
(sign.) T.F.W. Barth

Bones from Newfoundland.

Your letter of 3rd Jan. 1962.

The five bags contained fragments of:

No. XV Whalebone, medium-size whale.
No. XVI Scapula socket, species undeterminable.
No. XX Undeterminable, 1 small sliver.
No. XXXII
     XXII Whalebone, 3 small slivers.
No. XXXVI Whalebone and 3 stones (in brown bag)

I presume that No. XXII in your letter corresponds to the label on the bag with the number XXXII.

The scapula socket, No. XVI, comes from an animal the size of a deer-hound, or somewhat larger. I am sorry to say that it did not prove possible to determine it. Any discussion as to the species from which it derives must be hypothetical, as the species cannot be determined. Had the fragment been 1 cm longer, so that it had included the beginning of the shoulder-blade ridge, I would have been able to determine the species from which it derives. The species of whale from which the whalebone fragments derive cannot be determined.

Yours faithfully,
(sign.) Haakon Olsen

I am returning the bones, as they may perhaps be used for isotope dating.

List of Illustrations

Fig.

to Iceland, to the Norse settlements in Greenland and thence to North America. Drawn by G. Furuholmen. After Canada Department of Mines and technical Surveys.

3 Aerial photograph of the marine terrace at Épaves Bay, showing the partially excavated house-sites. In the foreground, Black Duck Brook; in the background, Great and Little Sacred Isles.

4 House-site A, seen from east. The curving south wall continues into the excavated area in the background; there are two door openings in that part of the wall.

5 The ring-headed pin of bronze from house-site A in situ. LaM 169.

6 Western end of house-site A, room II, showing impression of a post in the clay.

7 The cooking pit in house-site A, room III. The ring-headed pin of bronze was found on the edge of this pit. At the right side of the pit, a post-hole may be seen.

8 Dorset projectile point, found in the west wall of house-site A, LaM 140.

9 Table showing the radio-carbon dates obtained by analyses at the Radiological Dating Laboratory, Trondheim, Norway, and at the Radioactive Dating Laboratory, Stockholm, Sweden. Prepared by R. Nydal, K. Løvseth and O. Syrstad.

10 House-site B seen from north-east, after test excavation. The entrance is marked by two stones in the south wall.

11 House-site B seen from above east, showing the hearths.

12 The big hearth in house-site B.

13 The cooking pit of house-site B. The big hearth in the background.

14 The ember pit in house-site B.

15 Section of cooking pit in house-site B.

16 Oval beach stone with marks of pounding at ends. LaM 37.

17 Lump of slag found in the cooking pit in house-site B, LaM 3.

18 The meadows by Épaves Bay with Great Sacred Isle in the background.

19 House-site C before excavation, seen from north.

20 House-site D, room III, during excavation.

21 House-site D, room III, after excavation. In the background, the test-excavated part of room I; room II has not yet been excavated.

22 The long hearth with ember pit in house-site D, room III.

23 Copper fragment LaM 69 from house-site D, room III.

24 Bone needle from house-site D, room III. LaM 76.

25 Dorset projectile point, LaM 75. Found in house-site D, room III.

26 Stone implements from the terrace by Épaves Bay.

27 Stone implements found at the terrace by Épaves Bay.

28 Stone implements found at the terrace by Épaves Bay.

29 Stone implements found at the terrace by Épaves Bay.

30 Cooking pit II after excavation.

31 Hearth in house-site E.

32 House-site F seen from the north-east. The excavated, sterile area around is recovered with turf. In the middle, the hall with long hearth and earthen benches on either side.

33 House-site F during excavation, showing the stone-packing in the upper layer of room IV.

34 The stone-packing of room IV partly removed.

35 The terrace with the house-sites seen from the sea.

36 House-site F seen from the north-east during excavation.

37 Section of turf wall in house-site F, showing the horizontal layers of turf.

38 The long hearth in room II, house-site F, seen from the south-east, with the cooking pit, ember pit and large, flat stone.

39 Ember pit in the long hearth in house-site F, room II.

40 Plan and section of hearth in house-site F, room II.

41 Hearth in house-site F, room IV. In the foreground, charred timbers, probably from the roof. In the left front corner, a round impression, probably that of a small wooden vessel.

42 Plan and section of hearth in house-site F, room IV.

43 House-site F, room VI, seen from south-west, partially excavated, showing impressions of ground timbers in the floor.

44 Detail of house-site F, room VI, showing the NW impression of ground timber seen from south-west.

45 Room VI, house-site F, after excavation, seen from the south-west, showing impressions of ground-timbers in the floor.

46 Detail of section through house-site F, room VI.

47 a–b Spindle whorl of soap-stone from house-site F, found outside the south-east wall of room VI. LaM 97.

48 Stone lamp from house-site F. LaM 39.

49 Needle-hone of quartzite from house-site F, room VI. LaM 66a.

50 Iron rivet from house-site F, room VI, in situ. LaM 60.

51 Piece of red jasper from house-site F. LaM 128.

52 Piece of green jasper from house-site F. LaM 1.

53 House-site G during excavation. At the centre, the large, cracked slate with big stones on top, which probably served to cover the smoke opening in the roof. Under the slate, the cultural layer. In the background the large, vertical hearth stone, and the ovoid stone.

54 House-site G during excavation seen from above.

55 House-site J after excavation, seen from the river. In the background, left, the kiln.

56 The earthfast stone anvil in house-site J.

57 Dorset lamp of soap-stone, LaM 343, found in house-site J, upper layer.

58 Cooking pit I after excavation.

59 Excavation of features 3 and 4.

60 The hearth at feature 6.

61 Projectile points from excavations outside the house-sites.

62–76 see Arne Emil Christensen jr. above. pp. 125–126.

77 North-eastern Newfoundland with L'Anse aux Meadows, the area where the Norse house-sites were discovered and excavated. Drawn by G. Furuholmen. After Canada Department of Mines and technical Surveys.

78 Bone arrow-heads found in farm ruin at Narssaq, East Settlement, Greenland. After C.L. Vebæk.

79 House-site at Narssaq, East Settlement, Greenland. After C.L. Vebæk.

80 The old hall, Hvalsey, East Settlement No. 83, 6, IX, looking west. On the right, the gravel bench along the rear wall, in the middle, the long fire trench with ember box, on the left, southern row of post-holes. After Aa. Roussell.

81 Plan of dwelling at Brattahlið North Farm, East Settlement, Greenland. After P. Nørlund and M. Stenberger.

82 Ísleifsstaðir, level 2. The plan also shows the hearth of level 3 (the northernmost hearth). After M. Stenberger.

83 The hall under Snjáleifartottir, Iceland. After M. Stenberger.

84 House-site at Oma in Time, Rogaland, Norway. After J. Petersen.

85 Ring-headed pins of bronze from Kálfborgará and Hrísar. Þjms. 808 and 7347. Photo G. Gestsson.

86 Iron nails from the house-sites.

87 Interior of a *gamme* from Trollbukt, Lebesby, Finnmark, Showing framework of birch with twigs, birch bark, and a thick layer of turf. After H. Vreim.

88 The large hearth opposite the doorway in room I, Brattahlið North Farm, East Settlement, Greenland. After P. Nørlund and M. Stenberger.

89 Hearth at level 3, Ísleifsstaðir, Borgarfjarðarsýsla, Iceland. After M. Stenberger.

90 Hearth in room V, Ísleifsstaðir, Borgarfjarðarsýsla, Iceland. After M. Stenberger.

91 Ember pit in "The Fireplace Area" close to the farm ruins "Brattahlið North Farm", East Settlement, Greenland. After P. Nørlund and M. Stenberger.

92 Perspective and section of barn from Gilhagi in Skagafjórður, Iceland. After Johs. Klein.

93 Microscope photograph of a section of a lump of slag, LaM 3, from the cooking pit in house-site B, showing a fragment of charcoal in the central part.

94 Out-houses at the farm Keldur, Iceland. The farm is still in use.

95 Out-houses at the farm Tjøtta, Rogaland, Norway. The farm was abandoned in 1894. No. 1: cow-shed; No: 2: tool-shed; No. 3: drying-shed; No. 4: privy; Nos. 5–6: potato cellars. After Thv. Krohn-Hansen.

96 The house-site Stöng in Þjorsárdalur, Iceland. After Aa. Roussell.

97 Bone pins from Umiviarssuk, Farm ruin No. 52 a, West Settlement, Greenland. After Aa. Roussell.

98 Plan of house-site at Hraunstunga, Ódaðahraun, Iceland. After D. Bruun.

99 Hearth found below the mound of No. 38, in the home field of Brattahlið North Farm, East Settlement, Greenland. After P. Nørlund and M. Stenberger.

100 Drawing of the kitchen at the farm Glaumbær, Iceland, showing the double hearth in the background. After D. Bruun.

101 Three stone lamps: the upper from house-site F, LaM 39, the two below from house-sites in Iceland, now in the National Museum at Reykjavik. Photo: G. Gestsson.

102 Stone lamp from the Icelandic farm Stöng. Photo: G. Gestsson.

103 The spindle whorl from house-site F (bottom) together with a spindle whorl from a Norse farm in Greenland (top). Scale 1 : 1. Photo: P. Maurtvedt.

104 The smithy at the Icelandic farm Keldur, seen from behind, with the smoke-opening in the roof.

105 Ruins of cairn at the hill-top west of the terrace at Épaves Bay.

List of Plates

Pl. 1. Topographic Survey Map of L'Anse aux Meadows, Newfoundland.
Pl. 2. Sketch map showing the excavated house-sites at Épaves Bay.
Pl. 3. Plan of house-sites A, B and C.
Pl. 4. Plan of test-trenches in the SW area.
Pl. 5. Longitudinal section of the western part of house-site A.
Pl. 6. Cross section of the western part of house-site A.
Pl. 7. Plan of SE and SW area and parts of house-sites A, B and C.
Pl. 8. Section at y = –2.30 m.
Pl. 9. Section at x = 21.10 m.
Pl. 10. Section at x = 17.30 m.
Pl. 11. Section at x = 14.60 m.
Pl. 12. Section at x = 12.60 m.
Pl. 13. Plan of house-site B.
Pl. 14. Sections of house-site B (3).
Pl. 15. Sections of house-site C.
Pl. 16. Plan of house-site D.
Pl. 17. Section at y = 0.
Pl. 18. Section at x = –5.35 m and y = + 1.8 m.
Pl. 19. Section at y = –4.40 m and y = 0.65 m.
Pl. 20. Section at x = 0 and x = –1.9 m.
Pl. 21. Plan of room D III.
Pl. 22. Sections of room D III.
Pl. 23. Sections of room D III.

270

Notes

1. Helge Ingstad 1959 and 1966.
2. H.P. Biggar 1911, p. 64.
3. J. Howley 1915. D. Jennes 1934, pp. 265–267.
4. J. Howley 1915, pp. 231–232.
5. D.R. Grant 1975. See also L.M. Cumming 1975.
6. Helge Ingstad 1965 and 1969.
7. Uddrag af Professor Dr. philos. H.P. Steensby's Dagbog om Rejsen til "Vinland" v/Ad. Jensen. Medd.o. Grld. LXXVII 1931.
8. E. Harp jr. 1964 pp. 140–156.
9. Idem.

10. Idem.
11. Ibid.
12. Ibid.
13. Ibid. Chaps. 9 and 10.
14. Grœnlendinga Saga. Islendinga sógur, Reykjavik 1953; Eiriks saga rauða, Islendinga sógur, Reykjavik 1953.
15. H. Ingstad 1959 and 1967, A.H. Mallerey 1951, J. Meldgaard 1961, W.A. Munn 1929, V. Tanner 1941.
16. Poul Nørlund, 1935, 1936.
17. Islandske annaler, indtil 1778, Utg. for Det Norske Kildeskriftfond ved Gustav Storm, Christiania 1888.
18. W.W. Fitzhugh 1972, pp. 135 and 191–195.
19. E. Harp jr. 1964, p. 168.
20. W.E. Taylor jr. 1964, p. 205.
21. Private information given to Helge Ingstad by Dr. R.E. Seary, Memorial University, St. John's, Newfoundland. See H. Ingstad 1965, p. 173.
22. J. Howley 1915.
    D. Jennes 1934, pp. 265–267.
23. J. Howley 1915, p. 245, Sketch VI.
24. Ibid., p. 245, Sketch VI.
25. Ibid., p. 245, Sketch VI.
26. D. Jennes 1934, pp. 270–274.
27. op. cit. pp. 267–279.
28. E. Harp jr. 1963, p. 245.
29. Idem. 1964, p. 125.
30. E. Knuth 1952, pp. 28–30.
31. Th. E. Lee 1965, 1966, 1967, 1968, 1970.
32. W.E. Taylor jr. 1964, pp. 203 and 205.
33. Th. Mathiassen 1936, p. 116, fig. 24.
34. J. Bird 1945, p. 131.
35. W.E. Taylor jr. 1964, p. 191. J.V. Wright 1966.
36. J.V. Wright 1966, Plate I–XIX.
37. Th. E. Lee 1965, pp. 98–100.
38. Personal information from W. Taylor jr.
39. Th.E. Lee 1965–1970.
40. Idem. 1966, pp. 69–83.
41. Ibid., p. 152, P. Nørlund and M. Stenberger 1934, fig. 75.
42. E. Harp jr. 1964.
43. Aa. Roussell 1943, figs. 42–44; K. Eldjárn 1961, fig. 12.
44. M. Stenberger 1933, figs. 79–81.
45. J. Voionmaa 1943, fig. 132.
46. Th.E. Lee 1966, fig. 32, 10–16.
47. T. Oleson 1964, pp. 59–61.
48. B.L. Wallace 1969, no. 2.
49. Aa. Roussell 1941, p. 262
    C.L. Vebæk 1964, pp. 223–224.
50. Th.E. Lee 1965, fig. 7.
51. P. Nørlund and M. Stenberger 1934, fig. 34.
52. Ibid., figs. 77–78
53. J. Voionmaa 1943, figs. 118–119.
54. Th.E. Lee 1965, p. 74.
55. J. Voionmaa 1943, p. 178.
56. Th.E. Lee 1965, p. 99.

57. Idem., pp. 140.
58. P. Plumet 1969.
59. B.L. Wallace 1969, no. 2.
60. Th.E. Lee 1970, fig. 26.; K. Winterton 1971, pp. 1–9.
61. Th.E. Lee 1970, fig. 20.
62. Aa. Roussell 1941.
63. Ibid.
64. H. Ingstad 1959, pp. 93–94, English version 1966, pp. 57–59.
65. C.L. Vebæk 1964.
66. E. Moltke 1961, pp. 401–409.
67. Aa. Roussell 1941, fig. 118.
68. Ibid., fig. 88.
69. Ibid., p. 147.
70. P. Nørlund and M. Stenberger 1934, fig. 26.
71. Ibid., pp. 48–61.
72. Ibid., fig. 26.
73. Aa. Roussell 1941, pp. 147–149, fig. 91.
74. Ibid., figs. 92 and 93.
75. Ibid., pp. 202–213.
76. J. Petersen 1933, p. 86.
77. Aa. Roussell 1941, p. 200.
78. M. Stenberger 1943, figs. 63 and 104.
79. Ibid., pp. 164–167.
80. Personal information from Kristján Eldjárn.
81. Þ. Magnússon 1973, pp. 1–80.
82. C.L. Vebæk 1964, pp. 202–203; P. Nørlund and M. Stenberger 1934, fig. 26.
83. Þ. Magnússon 1973, pp. 1–80.
84. J. Petersen 1933, pp. 66–68, Pl. LIII.
85. Ibid., fig. XLV.
86. H. Egenes Lund 1938/39.
87. Ibid.
88. M. Stenberger 1943, figs. 103, 107 and 108.
89. J. Johannesson 1969, p. 17.
90. I. Martens 1973, pp. 33–52.
91. A. Hagen 1953, pp. 190–191; S. Grieg 1938 and A. Helmen 1953.
92. B. Myhre 1972, p. 170; A. Myhre 1962, p. 58.
93. J.R.C. Hamilton 1956; S. Hillern-Hansen Kaland 1973; A.O. Curle 1939; A. Small 1968.
94. A. Small 1968, pp. 62–70.
95. J. Petersen 1933, p. 106.
96. A.W. Brøgger 1929, pp. 92–93, 1930 No. 3, p. 270.
97. J. Petersen 1933, pp. 118–119; 1954, p. 11. See also O. Møllerop 1957, pp. 23–54.
98. O. Olsen 1965, 4, pp. 18–27; P. Nørlund 1936, 1938.
99. W. Winkelmann 1954, pp. 189–213, 1958, pp. 492–517.
100. Idem, 1958, p. 499.
101. Idem, 1954, pp. 116–117.
102. J. Petersen 1928, p. 197.
103. E. Bakka 1973, Tafel XVI, 53 and XVII, 57.
104. K. Eldjárn 1956, fig. 28, p. 101, see also fig. 139.
105. Aa. Roussell 1943, fig. 52, No. 41.
106. K. Eldjárn 1956, fig. 140.
107. T. Fanning 1969, figs. 1.3.4.5.
108. J. Petersen 1928, p. 197.
109. Ibid., p. 197.

110. W. Holmqvist 1961, fig. 43, 9–10.
111. M. Þorðarson 1943, p. 133.
112. Gr.Hist.min. 1845, Bd. II, p. 835.
113. Letter from Professor T.F.W. Barth, Geological Institute, University of Oslo, app. IV.
114. E. Harp jr. 1964, Pl. III No. 1.
115. A. Nilsson 1943, p. 292.
116. K. Krogh 1967, p. 25.
117. Aa. Roussell 1941, fig. 85.
118. A. Nilsson 1943, p. 292.
119. J. Petersen 1933.
120. Th. Sjøvold 1971, p. 27.
121. R.L. Tollnes 1969, pp. 41–74.
122. H. Vreim 1947, pp. 1 and 5.
     E. Klein 1926, pp. 187–221.
123. Valtýr Gudmundsson 1889, p. 207.
124. P. Nørlund and M. Stenberger 1934, p. 78.
125. Aa. Roussell 1941, pp. 196–200.
126. Ibid., fig. 121.
127. P. Nørlund and M. Stenberger 1934, figs. 77–78.
128. Ibid., pp. 114–115.
129. M. Stenberger 1943, figs. 107 and 108.
130. Þ. Magnússon 1973, figs. 14 and 27.
131. Aa. Roussell 1941, fig. 89.
132. Ibid., fig. 88.
133. P. Nørlund and M. Stenberger 1934, fig. 75.
134. Aa. Roussell 1941, fig. 121.
135. P. Nørlund and M. Stenberger 1934, fig. 62.
136. M. Stenberger 1943, figs. 107–108.
137. Idem, 1955 No. II, pp. 1049–50, and Vol. I, p. 216 b.
138. J. Petersen 1933 and 1936.
139. S. Grieg 1934, pp. 55–6.
140. Soga um Grette Aasmundsson p. 190.
141. P. Nørlund and M. Stenberger 1934, fig. 26.
142. C.L. Vebæk 1964, pp. 202–203.
143. A. Nilsson 1943, fig. 176, p. 296.
144. Aa. Roussell 1941, p. 147.
145. J. Petersen 1933, p. 91.
146. T. Mathiassen 1928, p. 215.
147. E. Holtved 1944, Pt. I, p. 241, Pt. 2, p. 63.
148. E.Harp jr. 1964, p. 126.
149. H. Collins 1951, pp. 32–39.
150. T.A. Richard 1934, pp. 525–543.
151. J. Bird, 1945, pp. 127–128.
152. V. Stephansson 1938.
153. J. Bird. 1945, p. 126.
154. Ibid., fig. 3.
155. V. Gudmundsson 1889, fig. 13.
156. Ibid., p. 107.
157. Ibid., p. 107.
158. T. Krohn-Hansen 1944, pp. 170, 187, fig. 4.
159. Aa. Roussell 1941, fig. 88.
160. S. Grieg 1938, p. 106.
161. A. Helmen 1953.

162. A. Hagen 1953, pp. 180–195.
163. K. Eldjárn 1972, pp. 248–250.
164. Aa. Roussell 1941, pp. 138, 151.
165. Th. Erlingsson 1899; K. Eldjárn 1961.
166. E. Harp jr. 1964, p. 127.
167. Ibid., Pl. XXXIV, and p. 122.
168. J. Howley 1915, Pl. XXV–XXVII.
169. Aa. Roussell 1936, fig. 194, 1–2.
170. A.O. Curle 1939, Pl. XLVIII.
171. J.R.C. Hamilton 1956, fig. 59, p. 126, Nos. 5–6 from left.
172. R. Blomquist 1963, II, figs. 184–185.
173. S. Grieg 1933, figs. 207–211, pp. 241–243.
174. G. Stamsø Munch 1965, pp. 13–17, fig. 5.
175. A.E. van Giffen 1936, Abb. 2, 1079, Beilage 3.
176. J. Bird 1945.
177. M. Strömberg 1963, pp. 1–25; 1967, pp. 117–122; 1973, pp. 192–265.
178. B. Stjernquist 1970, pp. 144–152.
179. Idem 1965 nr. 3, p. 37.
180. M. Strömberg 1971, p. 249.
181. B. Stjernquist 1965, no. 2, pp. 18–19.
182. W. Holmqvist 1968, pp. 188–199; 1970, pp. 139–140.
183. Ibid., Abb. 3–4 and 1970, pp. 139–140.
184. Idem. 1964, p. 14, Pl. 9–10.
185. B. Stjernquist 1970, p. 149.
186. W. Holmqvist 1968, p. 146.
187. W. Holmqvist 1961, 1964, 1968, 1970.
188. W. Holmqvist 1968, p. 199.
189. M. Strömberg 1971, p. 250.
190. B. Stjernquist 1970, p. 151.
191. F.T. Tischler 1954, pp. 136–137.
192. A.E. van Giffen 1936, p. 42.
193. H. Jahnkuhn 1936, pp. 96–149.
194. Idem 1963, p. 122.
195. C.G. Schultz 1949, p. 103.
196. H.H. Andersen 1965, no. 2, pp. 3 and 7.
197. H.E. Lidén 1972.
198. P. Rolfsen 1976, pp. 65–82.
199. Ibid.
200. H. Vreim 1947, p. 3.
201. Ibid., pp. 2–3.
202. V. Gudmundsson 1889, p. 244.
203. Þ. Magnússon 1973.
204. Tacitus, C. Germania (Pandora 7) 1920.
205. Pliny, Hist.Nat. XIV, 1.
206. Aa. Roussell 1941, pp. 151–189.
207. Ibid., p. 163.
208. Ibid., p. 167.
209. W. Winkelmann 1958, pp. 497–99.
210. Ibid., p. 499.
211. Aa. Roussell 1941, p. 196.
212. Ibid., figs. 124, 143.
213. W. Holmqvist 1968, 1970 Pl. 10.
214. Þ. Magnússon 1973, figs. 16–17.

215. I. Martens 1973, fig. 31.
216. H.E. Lidén 1972, p. 19.
217. A. Herteig 1957, p. 430, fig. 6.
218. Personal information from Rigmor Monsen, Institute of Comparative Cultural Research, Oslo.
219. V. Gudmundsson 1889, p. 197, Fig. 13.
220. D. Bruun 1928, pp. 168–70.
221. C.L. Vebæk 1964, pp. 200–214.
222. Aa. Roussell 1941, fig. 88.
223. M. Stenberger 1943, figs. 107–108.
224. Aa. Roussell 1943, fig. 37.
225. O. Almgren 1910–12, Bd. 6, p. 342.
226. M. Stenberger 1933, p. 160.
227. G. Hatt 1928, p. 254, fig. 25.
228. H. Kjær 1935.
229. Aa. Roussell 1936, p. 34.
230. Idem 1943, fig. 144.
231. V. Gudmundsson 1889, p. 203.
232. Aa. Roussell 1943, p. 85.
233. O. Møllerop 1962, 2, p. 148.
234. K. Eldjárn 1972, pp. 248–250.
235. Aa. Roussell 1943, figs. 37 and 42.
236. Ibid., fig. 37.
237. I. Martens 1973, p. 11.
238. Aa. Roussell 1943, fig. 143, p. 210.
239. V. Gudmundsson 1889, p. 209.
240. Ibid.
241. K. Eldjárn 1958, pp. 558–559.
242. V. Gudmundsson 1889, pp. 200–206.
243. M. Stenberger 1943, figs. 103, 107, 108.
244. Ibid., fig. 64.
245. Aa. Roussell 1941, figs. 120–121.
246. J. Petersen 1933 and 1936; O. Möllerop 1957.
247. H. Egenes Lund 1938/39, p. 37.
248. J. Petersen 1933, pp. 85–87.
249. Ibid., pp. 85–87.
250. M. Stenberger 1933, p. 114, fig. 73.
251. Ibid., pp. 132–133, fig. 90.
252. K. Visted and H. Stigum 1952, Vol II, pp. 43–44.
253. Ibid. p. 43.
254. Ibid. p. 44.
255. D. Bruun 1895, Mo.Gr. XVI, p. 218.
256. P. Nørlund and M. Stenberger 1934, fig. 73.
257. Aa. Roussell 1941, p. 197.
258. M. Stenberger 1943, fig. 106.
259. Aa. Roussell 1943, fig. 29.
260. M. Þorðarsson 1943, fig. 82.
261. Aa. Roussell 1943, fig. 39, p. 81.
262. Th. Mathiassen, 1936, pp. 116–117.
263. J.P. Howley 1915, p. 86.
264. Peabody Museum, Yale University, New Haven, Conn. U.S.A.
265. Personal information from Thor Heyerdahl.
266. E. Harp jr. 1964, pp. 68–72.

267. W.J. Wintemberg 1940, p. 309, Pl. XV 2:1.
268. D. Jennes 1934, Bull. 65, pp. 267–269.
269. J. Howley 1915, p. 336.
270. E. Harp jr. 1964, p. 169.
271. J. Howley 1915, p. 86.
272. Aa. Roussell 1943, p. 97.
273. G. Gestsson 1959, p. 72.
274. A.W. Brøgger 1930 fig. 54; J. Anderson 1886, p. 232.
275. J.R.C. Hamilton 1956, p. 168.
276. A. Small 1962, pp. 221–222.
277. J. Anderson 1883, p. 241.
278. Aa. Roussell 1936, fig. 120, nos. 1, 5, 6, 7, 13, 14, 16, from top left.
279. J. Petersen 1951.
280. M. Stenberger 1943, fig. 113, nos. 1 and 2 from top left.
281. A. Helmen 1953, p. 46.
282. J.R.C. Hamilton 1956, p. 135.
283. J. Voionmaa 1943, fig. 135, no. 2.
284. J. Petersen 1951, fig. 140.
285. R. Blomqvist och A.W. Mårtensson 1963, fig. 186, nos. 1 and 2 from left.
286. B. Hougen 1944, fig. 4, and Plate XXXIV.
287. Aa. Roussell 1941, fig. 160, 7–8.
288. J.R.C. Hamilton 1956, p. 142, 17–18.
289. E. Harp jr. 1964, p. 56, Pl. XIII, 5 and Pl. IX, 7.
290. Aa. Roussell 1936, fig. 87.
291. J.R.C. Hamilton 1956, Pl. XVII, b.
292. S. Thorarinsson 1943, p. 51.
293. Idem 1967, p. 153.
294. P. Nørlund and M. Stenberger 1934, pp. 110–115 and 78.
295. Aa. Roussell 1941, pp. 196–200.
296. H.E. Driver 1961, fig. 8.
297. P. Nørlund and M. Stenberger 1934, fig. 33.
298. E. Harp jr. 1964, p. 22.
299. J. Bird 1945, fig. 3.
300. Ibid. p.131.
301. Ibid., fig. 4.
302. W. Holmqvist 1964, p. 14; 1970 pp. 139–140, Pl. 9–10.
303. Idem 1968, pp. 197–198.
304. H. Vreim 1947, pp. 3–4.
305. S.E. Morison 1965, p. 20.
306. Idem 1971, p. 49.
307. Idem 1965, p. 73.
308. Aa. Roussell 1943, figs. 50 and 51.
309. J.R.C. Hamilton 1956, p. 110, fig. XIC b.
310. Aa. Roussell 1936, pp. 54–56.
311. P. Nørlund 1930, pp. 110–112, fig. 58.
312. W. Winkelmann 1958, pp. 513–516; 1954, pp. 208–209.
313. G. Rowley 1940.
314. V. Gudmundsson 1889, pp. 244–245.
315. Pliny, Hist. Nat. XIV, 1.
316. V. Gudmundsson 1889, 244–245.
317. M. Gislason 1956, pp. 387–388.
318. G. Gestsson 1959, pp. 25–28.
319. V. Gudmundsson 1889, p. 243.

320. G. Gestsson 1959, p. 26.
321. V. Gudmundsson 1889, p. 241.
322. Eyrbyggjasaga, 1935, Bd. 4, pp. 1–186.
323. V. Gudmundsson 1889, p. 240.
324. A. Sigurðardottir 1966, pp. 69–70.
325. Þ. Magnússon 1973.
326. Aa. Roussell 1936, pp. 74–81.
327. A.O. Curle 1939, Plate XXXVIII; fig. 3, pp. 77–79.
328. A. Sandvig 1928.
329. W. Holmqvist 1970, pp. 127–128, Pl. 49.
330. A. Kirkedalen, see K. Svarteberg 1934, pp. 77–79.
331. N. Nielsen 1930.
332. P. Nørlund and M. Stenberger 1934, figs. 77–79.
333. Aa. Roussell 1941, p. 200.
334. P. Nørlund 1930, fig. 2 no. 39.
335. D. Bruun 1929, 40, 46 and 182.
336. E. Harp jr. 1964, Pl. III, No. 1.
337. G. Rawley 1940.
338. W.E. Taylor jr. 1964, pp. 203–205.
339. W. Fitzhugh 1972, p. 192.
340. Strait of Belle Isle series, Canada: 682, 683, 692, 693, 676, 678A, 679, 694–696, 727, 729–737.
341. A. Nilsson 1943, p. 293.
342. E. Harp jr. 1964, p. 165.
343. H. Ingstad 1960, pp. 172, 174.
344. Th.E. Lee 1966, fig. 6b.
345. K. Eldjárn 1972, pp. 248–250.
346. Ch. Blindheim 1969, p. 23.
347. S. Grieg 1928.
348. S.E. Morison 1971, p. 69.
349. D. Sanger 1968, pp. 34–39, figs. 14 and 16.
350. H.W. Ahlmann 1951/52, pp. 56–75.
351. W. Dansgaard, S.J. Johnsen, J. Møller and C.C. Langway jr. 1969.
352. H.T. Waterbolk 1971.

References

Águstsson.H. 1968 Islandsk byggeskik i fortiden. Nordisk byggedag X. Reykjavik
Ahlmann, H.W:son 1951–1952 Glaciärer och klimat i Norden under de senaste tusentalen år. Norsk geografisk tidsskrift 13/1951–52
Almgren, O. 1910/12 Alunda sockens fornminnesförenings tidskrift, Bd. 6 (XXVI-XXVIII)
Andersen, H.H. 1965 Fra det gamle voldkvarter. Skalk 1965, nr. 2
Andersen, H.H. and Madsen, H.J. 1966. Nygade i Århus. Bidrag til teorien om det ældste Århus. Kuml.
Anderson, I. 1955 A Contribution to the Problem of Transitional Forms between the Primitive Hut and the House Proper. Vallhagar II, pp. 1008–1032. Copenhagen.
Anderson, Joseph 1883 Scotland in Pagan Times. The Iron Age. Edinburgh.
Bakka, E. 1965 Ytre Moa. Eit gardsanlegg frå vikingtida i Årdal i Sogn. Viking 1965, Oslo.
  1973 Goldbrakteaten in norwegischen Grabfunden: Datierungsfragen Frühmittelalterliche Studien. Jahrbuch des Instituts für Frühmittelalterforschungen der Universität Münster. 7. Band.
Bersu, G. and Wilson, D.M. 1966 Three Viking Graves in the Isle of Man. Society for Medieval

Archaeology. Monograph series No. 1. London.

Biggar, H.P. 1911 The Precursors of Jacques Cartier, 1497–1534. A Collection of Documents Relating to the Early History of the Dominion of Canada. Canadian Archives Publications. no. 5. Ottawa.

Bindford, L.R. 1962 Archaeological Investigations in the Carlyle Reservoir Clinton Country, Illinois, 1962. Southern Illinois University Museum Archaeological Salvage Report Number 17.

Bird, J. 1945 Archaeology of the Hopedale Area, Labrador. Anthropological Papers of The American Museum of Natural History. Vol. 39.

Blindheim, Ch. 1969 Kaupangundersøkelsen avsluttet. Kort tilbakeblikk på en lang utgravning. Viking 1969. Oslo.

1975. See Herteig, A. Lidén, H.E. and Blindheim, Ch.

Blomqvist, R. och Mårtensson, A.W. 1963 Thulegrävningen 1961. En berättelse om vad grävningen för Thulehuset i Lund avslöjade. Gårdsbebyggelse i det äldste Lund. Archaeologica Lundensia II. Lund.

Bruun, D 1895 Arkæologiske Undersögelser i Julianehaabs Distrikt. Meddr. Grønland XVI. København.

1906 Gammel Bygningsskik paa Færøerne. Aarsb. til Norske Fortidsmin. Bevaring, Oslo.

1907 Gammel bygningsskik paa de islandske Gaarde. Arkæologiske Undersøgelser. Aarsb. Foreningen til Norske Fortidsmin. Bevaring.

1917 Oversigt over Nordboruiner i Godthaab- og Fredrikshaab-Distrikter. Meddr. Grønland LVI. København.

1928 Fortidsminder og Nutidshjem paa Island. København.

1929 Fra de færøske Bygder, Samlede afhandliger om gammeldags sæd og skik. København.

Brøgger, A.W. 1929 Ancient Emigrants. Oxford.

1930 Den norske bosetningen på Shetland-Orknøyene. Skrifter utg. av Det Norske Videnskaps Akademi i Oslo, II, Hist. -filos. Klasse nr. 3

Brønsted, J. 1957 Danmarks Oldtid. B.1.B. 3–1960

Christensen, A.E. jr. 1967 Naust. Kulturhistorisk leksikon for nordisk middelalder. Bd. 12. Oslo

1977 Test excavation of the boat-sheds. The Discovery of a Norse Settlement in America, Vol. I. Oslo.

Collins, H.B. 1951 Recent Developments in the Dorset Culture Area. Mem. Soc. Amer. Arch. nr. 9

Cumming, L.M. 1975 Geology of the L'Anse aux Meadows National Historic Park, Northern Newfoundland. Geol. Surv. Can. Paper 75–1 Part A.

Curle, A.O. 1939 A Viking Settlement at Freswick, Caithness; Report on excavations carried out in 1937 and 1938. Proc. Soc. Ant. Scot. Vol. 73, 7th series, I

Dansgaard, W. Johnsen, S. J. Möller, J. and Langway, C.C. 1969. One Thousand Centuries of Climatic Record from Camp Century on the Greenland Ice Sheet, Science, Vol. 166.

Driver, H.E. 1961 Indians of North America. Chicago.

Egenæs Lund, H. 1938/39 Undersøkelser av jernalders gårdsanlegg på Fosse og Grødeim i Time prestegjeld, Høg-Jæren. Stav. mus. Årsh. Stavanger 1939

Eiriks saga rauða. Islendinga sógur. Bd. I. Reykjavik 1953

Eldjárn, K. 1941–42 Skálarústin i Klaufanesi og nokkrar aðrar svarfdælskar fornleifar. Árbók hins Islenzka fornleifafélags. Reykjavik 1952

Eldjárn, K. and Gestsson, G. 1951–52. Rannsóknir a BergÞórsvoli. Árbók hins Islenzka fornleifafélags. Reykjavik 1952

Eldjárn, K. 1958 Report on the Third Viking Congress. Reykjavik.

1956 Kuml og Haugfé. Reykjavik.

1958 Eldhus. Island. Kulturhistorisk leksikon for nordisk middelalder. Bd. III. Oslo.

1960 Gård. Island. Kulturhistorisk leksikon for nordisk middelalder, Bd. V, Oslo.

1961 Bær i Gjáskógum i Þjórsárdal. Árbok hins Islenzka fornleifafélags (English Summary) Reykjavik.

1967 Naust. Island. Kulturhistorisk leksikon for nordisk middelalder. Bd. XII, Oslo.

1972 Stóve, Island. Kulturhistorisk leksikon for nordisk middelalder. Bd. XVII. Oslo.

Erixon, S. 1918 Några bidrag till det nordiska husets historia. Fataburen 1917. Stockholm.

1932. Eldhus. Svenska kulturbilder. Del XI. Stockholm.

Erlingsson, T. 1899 Ruins of the Saga time. London.

Eyrbyggja saga. Edited by Sveinsson, E.O. Islenzk fornrit. Bd. 4. Reykjavik 1935.

Fanning, Th. 1969 The Bronze Ringed Pins in the Limerick City Museum. North Munster Antiquarian Journal. Vol. XII.

Fitzhugh, W.W. 1972 Environmental Archeology and Cultural Systems in Hamilton Inlet, Labrador. A Survey of the Central Labrador Coast from 3000 B.C. to the Present. Smithsonian. Contributions to Anthropology. No. 16.

Forntida Gårdar i Island. Medd. från den nord. arkeolog. undersökn. i Island sommaren 1939. Edited by Stenberger, M. København 1943

Gestsson, G. 1951–52 See Eldjárn, K. and Gestsson, G. 1951/52

Gestsson, G. 1959 Gróf i Óræfum. Árbók híns Íslenzka fornleifafélags. Reykjavik.

van Giffen, A. 1936 Der Warf in Ezinge, Provinz Groningen, Holland, und seine westgermani-schen Häuser. Germania 1936. Jahrg. 20. Berlin.

Gíslason, Magnus 1956 Bastu. Island. Kulturhistorisk leksikon for nordisk middelalder. Bd. I. Oslo.

Gjessing, H. 1925 Vest-Agder i forhistorisk tid. Norske Bygder II, Bergen

Grant, R. 1972. Postglacial Emergence of Northern Newfoundland. Geological Survey of Canada, Paper 72–1, Part B.

1975. Surficial Geology and Sealevel, L'Anse aux Meadows National Historic Park, New-foundland. Geological Survey of Canada. Paper 75–1, Part A.

Grieg, S 1928 Kongsgaarden. Osebergfundet Bd. II. Utg. av Den Norske Stat under redaksjon av A.W. Brögger, Haakon Shetelig. Oslo.

1933 Middelalderske byfund fra Bergen og Oslo. Utg. av Det Norske Videnskaps-Akademi i Oslo.

1934 Jernaldershus på Lista. Instituttet for sammenlignende kulturforskning, Ser.B. Skr. 27. Oslo.

1938 Listas jernalder. Bidrag til Vest-Agders Eldste Kulturhistorie. Universitetets Oldsaksam-lings Skrifter I. Oslo.

1938 Vikingetidshus i Gudbrandsdalen. Årbok for Dølaringen.

Grænlendinga saga. Islendinga sógur. Bd. I. Reykjavik 1953

Gudmundsson V. 1889 Privatboligen paa Island i Sagatiden, samt delvis i det øvrige Norden. København.

Hagen, A. 1953 Studier i jernalderens Gårdssamfunn. Universitetets Oldsakssamlings Skrifter IV Oslo.

Hamilton, J.R.C. 1956 Excavations at Jarlshof, Shetland, Edinburgh.

Harp, E.Jr. 1950–51 An Archaeological Survey in the Strait of Belle Isle Area. Amer. Ant. Vol. 16, nr. 3

1963 Evidence of Boreal Archaic Culture in Southern Labrador and Newfoundland. Nat. Mus. Canada. Bull. 193. Contributions to Anthropology, 1961–1962, Ottawa.

1964 The Cultural Affinities of the Newfoundland Dorset Eskimo. Nat. Mus. Canada. Bull. 200, Ottawa.

Hatt, G. 1928 To bopladsfund fra ældre jernalder fra Mors og Himmerland. Aarb. f. Nord. Oldk. Hist.

1935 Jernalderbopladsen ved Ginderup i Thy. Fra Nationalmuseets Arbejdsmark 1935

Helliesen, G. 1901 Vikingetidsgaard paa Jæderen. Stav. mus. Aarsh. 1901.

Helmen, A. 1953 Den første bosetning og husbygging på Hadeland. Bygdebok for Hadeland, Bd. IV, Oslo.

Henningsmoen, K.E. 1977, Pollen-Analytical Investigations in the L'Anse aux Meadows Area Newfoundland. The Discovery of a Norse Settlement in America, Vol. I, Oslo.

Herteig, A. 1957 Kaupangen i Borgund. Borgund og Giske I Bergen.

Herteig, A., Lidén, H.E., Blindheim, Ch. 1975. Archaeological contributions to the early history of urban communities in Norway. Oslo, Bergen, Tromsø.

Hillern-Hansen Kaland, S. 1973 Westnessutgravningene på Rousay, Orknøyene. Viking 1973

Holmqvist, W. 1961 Excavations at Helgö I. Report for 1954–56. Stockholm.

1964 Excavations at Helgö II. Report for 1957–59. Stockholm.

1968 Frühgeschichtliche Haustypen auf Helgö. Studien zur europäischen Vor- und Frühgeschichte. Neumünster.

1970 Excavations at Helgö III Report for 1960–1964 Stockholm.

Holtved, E. 1944 Archaeological Investigations in the Thule district. I: Descriptive part, II: Analytic part. Meddr. Grønland Bd. 141, 1–2 København.

1954 Archaeological Investigations in the Thule district. III: Nûgdlit and Comer's midden – Meddr. Grønland Bd. 146.3 København.

Hougen, B. 1944 Gamle fjellstuetufter. Viking.

Howley, J. 1915 The Beothucks or Red Indians. The aboriginal inhabitants of Newfoundland, Cambridge.

Ingstad, A.S. 1970 The Norse Settlement at L'Anse aux Meadows, Newfoundland. A preliminary Report from the Excavations 1961–1968 Acta Archaeologica Vol. XLI.

Ingstad, H. 1959 Landet under Leidarstjernen, en ferd til Grønlands norrøne bygder, Oslo.

1965 Vesterveg til Vinland. Oppdagelsen av norrøne boplasser i Nord Amerika. Oslo.

1966 The Land under the Pole Star. London–New York.

1969 Westward to Vinland. London–New York.

Islandske Annaler indtil 1578. Edited by Gustav Storm, Christiania 1888

Jankuhn, H. 1936 Die Ausgrabungen i Haithabu 1935/36 Offa. Neumünster.

1963 Haithabu, ein Handelsplatz der Wikingerzeit. 4. ergänzte Auflage. Neumünster.

Jennes, D. 1934 The Indians of Canada. Nat. Mus. Canada. Bull. 65. Ottawa.

Jensen, Ad.S. 1931 Uddrag af Professor Dr. phil. H.P. Stensby. Dagbog om Rejsen til "Vinland". Meddr. Grønland LXXVII

Jóhannesson, J. 1969 Islands Historie i Mellomalderen. Fristatstida. Overs. av H. Magerøy, Oslo.

Johnsen, S.J. 1969 See Dansgaard, W., Johnsen, S.J., Møller, J., and Langway, C.C.Jr.

Jones, G. 1964 The Norse Atlantic Saga. Being the Norse voyages of discovery and settlement to Iceland, Greenland, America. København, London, New York, Toronto.

Kirkedalen, A. (se Svarteberg, K. 1971).

Kjær, H. 1928 Oldtidshuse ved Ginderup i Thy. Fra Nationalmuseets Arbejdsmark. København.

Klein, E. 1926 Den lappiske torvkåtan som nordisk husform. Fataburen. Stockholm.

Klindt-Jensen, O. 1955 The General Character of The House Types of Vallhagar. Vallhagar II. København.

Knuth, E. 1952 An Outline of the Archaeology of Peary Land. Arctic. Vol. 5.

Krogh, K. 1967 Erik den Rødes Grønland. Sagatekster ved H. Bekker-Nielsen. Nationalmuseet. København.

Krohn-Hansen, Thv. 1944. Jord- og Steinhus på Jæren. Stav. mus. Årsh. 1942/43. Stavanger 1944

Langway, C.C.jr. 1969 See Dansgaard, W., Johnsen, S.J., Møller, J. and Langway, C.C.jr.

Lee, Th.E. 1965 Excavations at Fort Chimo and Paine Lake, Ungava. Archaeology 1965. Centre d'Études Nordiques. Traveaux divers 16, Université Laval, Quebec. 1965

1966 Payne Lake, Ungava Pensinsula. Archaeology 1966, Centre d'Études Nordiques. Traveaux divers 12. Université Laval, Quebec. 1966

1968 Archaeological Findings, Quebec. Gyrfalcon to Eider Islands, Ungava 1968. Centre d'Études Nordiques. Traveaux divers. Université Laval. Quebec 1968.

1970 Archaeological Investigations of a Longhouse. Pamiok Island, Ungava 1970. Centre d'Études Nordiques. Université Laval, Quebec 1970

Lidén, H.E. 1975 See Herteig, A., Lidén, H.E. and Blindheim, Ch.

Løvset, K. 1970 See Nydal, R., Løvseth, K. and Syrstad, O.

Madsen, H.J. 1966 See Andersen, H.H. and Madsen, H.J.

Magnússon, Þ. 1973 Sogualdarbyggd i Hvítárholti. Árbók hins Islenzka fornleifafélags. 1972. Reykjavik 1973.

Mallerey, A.H. 1951 Lost America. The Story of Iron-Age civilization prior to Columbus. Washington.

Martens, I. 1972 Møsstrand i Telemark. En jernproduserende fjellbygd før svartedauen. Viking. Oslo.

Martin, P.S., Quimby, G.I., Collier, D. 1962 Indians before Columbus. Twenty Thousand Years of North American History.

Mathiassen, P. 1928 Eskimo Relics from Washington Land and Hall Land. Meddr. Grønland, Bd. 71, nr. 3, København.

1936 The Eskimo Archaeology of Julianehaab District. Meddr. Grønland. B. 118, nr. 1. København.

Meldgaard, J. 1961 Fra Brattahlid til Vinland. Naturens Verden 1961. København.

Moltke, E. 1961 En grønlandsk Runeindskrift fra Erik den Rødes tid. Narssaq-pinden. Tidsskriftet Grønland Nov. 1961.

Morison, S.E. 1961 The Oxford History of the American People. Oxford.

1971 The European Discovery of America. The Northern Voyages A.D. 500-1600. Oxford.

Munch, J. Storm 1965 Greipstad. Trekk av en nordnorsk gårds historie. Ottar, nr. 46. Tromsø.

Munch, G. Stamsø 1965. Gårdshauger og tuftegrupper. Fra utgravningen i gårdshaugen på Grunnfarnes. Ottar, nr. 43. Tromsø 1965.

Munn, W.A. 1929 Wineland voyages; location of Helluland, Markland and Vinland. St. John's.

Myhre, A. 1962 Gard-Øydegard. Utrykt manuskript for Instituttet for sammenliknende kulturforskning.

Myhre, B. 1972 Funn, fornminner og ødegårder. Jernalderens bosetning i Høyland Fjellbygd. Stav. mus. skr. Bd. 7.

Møller, J. 1969 See Dansgaard, W., Johnsen, S.J., Møller, J. and Langway, C.C.jr.

Møllerop, O. 1962 Gårdsanleggene på Vaule, Mosterøy. Frá Haug ok Heiðni, 2.

1964 Utgravningene ved Risavik sommeren 1964. Et gårdsanlegg fra vikingetid. Frá Haug ok Heiðni, 3, Stavanger.

Mårtensson, A.W. 1963. See Blomqvist, R. och Mårtensson, A.W.

Nielsen, N. 1930 Evidence on Extraction of iron in Greenland by the Norsemen. Meddr. Grønland Bd. 76. nr. 4. København.

Nielsen, E.L. 1968 Pedersstræde i Viborg. Købstadarkeologiske undersøgelser 1966/67 Kuml

Nilsson, A. 1943 Den sentida Bebyggelsen på Islands Landsbygd. Forntida gårdar i Island. Meddelanden från den nordiska Arkeologiska Undersökningen i Island Sommaren 1939. København.

Nydal, R., Løvseth, K. and Syrstad, O. 1970. Trondheim Natural Radiocarbon Measurements V. Radiocarbon, Vol. 12 No. 1, 1970. pp. 205–223

1972 Trondheim Natural Radiocarbon Measurements V, Vol. 14. No. 2, 1972, pp. 418–451.

Nydal, R. 1977. Radio-carbon Dating of Material from L'Anse aux Meadows, Newfoundland. The Discovery of a Norse Settlement in America, Vol. I, Oslo.

Nørlund, P. 1929 Norse Ruins at Gardar. The episcopal seat of mediaeval Greenland. Meddr. Grønland, Bd. LXXVI nr.1, København.

1935 De gamle Nordbobygder ved Verdens Ende. København. Ny. ed. 1967

1936 Viking Settlers in Greenland and Their Descendants during Five Hundred Years. London.

Nørlund, P. and Stenberger, M. 1934 Brattahlid. Meddr. Grønland, Bd. 88.1. København.

Ohlsson, T. 1965 Grophusbebyggelse. Ale. Hist. tidskr. för Skåneland. Lund.

Oleson, T. 1964 Early Voyages and Northern Approaches. 1000–1632. Toronto.

Olsen, O. 1965 Typehuset på Trelleborg. Skalk 1965, nr. 4.

Paulsen, L.M. 1977. Identification of Charcoal Finds. The Discovery of a Norse Settlement in America, Vol. I, Oslo.

Petersen, J. 1928 Vikingetidens Smykker. Stavanger.

1933 Gamle Gårdsanlegg i Rogaland fra forhistorisk tid og middelalder. Inst. sammenlikn. kulturforskn. Ser B. Skr. 23. Oslo.

1936 Gamle Gårdsanlegg i Rogaland. Fortsettelse. Utsira, Lyngaland, Håvodl, Birkelandsstølen, Hanaland. Inst. sammenlikn. kulturforskn. Ser. B. Skr. 31. Oslo.

1937/38 Et gårdsanlegg fra folkevandringstiden i Helleland i Dalene. Stav. mus. Årb. 1937–38. Stavanger.

1943 En gård fra 1500 årene på Fjøløynå. Stav. mus. årh. 1942/43. Stavanger.

Pliny Hist. nat. XIV.I.

Plumet, P. 1969 Archaeologie de l'Ungava: Le problème des maisons longues à deux hemicycles et separations interieure. École Pratique des Hautes Études-Sorbonne. Contributions du Centre d'Études Arctiques et Finno-Scandinaves. No. 7. Paris.

Quimby, G.I. 1960 Indian Life in the Upper Great Lakes. 11,000 B.C. to A.D. 1,800. A Contribution to Chicago Natural History Museum. The University of Chicago Press, Chicago & London

Reeves, A.M. 1895 The Finding of Wineland the Good. The History of the Icelandic discovery of America. London.

Rickard, T.A. 1934 Drift Iron, a fortuitous factor in primitive culture. Geogr. Rev. Vol. 24

Rolfsen, Perry 1976 Hustufter, grophus og groper fra eldre jernalder ved Oddernes Kirke, Vest Agder. Universitetets Oldsaksamlings årbok 1972–74, pp. 65–82, Oslo.

Rosenqvist, A.M. 1977. Material Investigations. The Discovery of a Norse Settlement in America, Vol. I. Oslo.

Roussell, Aa. 1934 Norse Building Customs in the Scottish Isles. London.

1936 Sandnes and the Neighbouring Farms. Meddr. Grønland, Bd. 88, nr. 2. København.

1941 Farms and Churches in the Mediaeval Norse Settlements of Greenland. Meddr. Grønland Bd. 89, nr. 1. København.

1943 Komparativ avdeling: Det nordiske hus i Vikingetid. Forntida gårdar i Island, pp. 193–200. København. Edited by M. Stenberger.

1943 Stöng: Þjórsárdalur. Forntida gårdar i Island pp. 72–97. København. Edited by M. Stenberger.

1943 Skallakot: Þjórsárdalur. Forntida gårdar i Island, pp. 55–71. København. Edited by M. Stenberger.

1943 Islands tomter, pp. 201–214. Forntida gårdar i Island. København. Edited by. M. Stenberger.

Rowley, G. 1940 The Dorset Culture of the Eastern Arctic. Amer. Anthrop. New Ser. Vol. 42. pp. 490–499

Sandvig, A. 1928 De Sandvigske Samlinger i tekst og billeder. Fra ættegården til husmannsplassen. Et bidrag til Gudbrandsdalens kulturhistorie.

Sanger, D. 1968 Seven thousand years prehistory in British Columbia. The Beaver. Spring 1968. Hudson Bay Company, Winnipeg, Canada.

Schultz, C.G. 1949 Aggersborg. Vikingelejren ved Limfjorden. Fra Nationalmuseets Arbejdsmark. København.

Shetelig, H. 1909 En ældre jernalders gaard paa Jæderen. Bergens museums årbok 1909. Bergen.

Sigurðardottir, A. 1966 Híbylahættir á midøldum. Reykjavik.

Skjølsvold, Arne 1970 To keltertids hustufter fra Ogna i Rogaland. (English Summary) Viking. pp. 47–72. Oslo.

Sjøvold, Th. 1971 Åse-anlegget på Andøya. Et nord-norsk tun-anlegg fra jernalderen. Acta Borealia Humaniora. No. 12. Tromsø–Oslo–Bergen.

Small, A. 1962 Two Pictish Symbol Stones. II: Fairygreen, Collace, Perthshire. Proc. Soc. Ant. Scot. Vol. 95, p. 221–222

1968 A Viking Longhouse in Unst, Shetland. The Fifth Viking Congress, Torshavn.

Soga um Grette Aasmundsson. Umsett fraa gamalnorsk ved Ola Røkke. utgjevne av Det Norske Samlaget (Landsmålslaget) 1912

Stenberger, M. 1933 Öland under äldre järnåldern, en bebyggelsehistorisk undersökning. Akad. Avh. Uppsala. Stockholm.

1934 See Nørlund, P. and Stenberger, M.

1943 Snjáleifartóttir. Þjórsárdalur. Forntida gårdar i Island. pp. 98–112. København.

1943 Áslákstunga fremri: Þjórsárdalur. Forntida gårdar i Island. pp. 113–120. København.

283

1943 Ísleifsstaðir: Borgarfjárðarsýsla. Forntida gårdar i Island. pp. 145–170. København 1943

1943 Vollmoen och Island. Fornvännen. B. 38. Stockholm.

1955 Vallhagar I–II. A Migration Period Settlement on Gotland, Sweden. København.

Stephansson, V. 1938 The two Voyages of Martin Frobisher. In Search of a Passage to Cathay and India by the North-West, A.D. 1576–78. From the original 1578 text of George Best. 2 vols. London.

Stigum, H. 1952 (see Visted, K. and Stigum, H.)

Stjernquist, B. 1961 Gårdlösaundersökningen. Ale. Hist. tidskr. för Skåneland. Lund.

1965 Gårdslösaundersökningen. Ale nr. 2, 1965. Historisk tidskrift för Skåneland

1970 Jahrbuch des Römisch-Germanischen Zentralmuseums. Mainz. 14. 1967 Jahrgang Mainz.

Strømberg, M. 1961 Untersuchungen zur jüngeren Eisenzeit in Schonen. Acta Archaeologica Lundensia, Ser. nr. 40, 4, Lund.

1961 Eine siedlungsgeschichtliche Untersuchung in Hagestad, Südost-Schonen. Vorläufiger Berich. Medd. Lunds. Univ. Hist. Mus. Lund.

1963 Handelsstråk och vikingabygd i sydöstra Skåne. Om Hagstad undersökningen. Ale. nr. 3 Hist. tidskr. för Skåneland. Lund.

1966 Nya fynd i Valleberga. Skånes hembygdsförbunds Årsbok.

1967 Undersökningarna rörande Hagestad i Skåne. Kuml.

1971 Grubenhäuser in Valleberga. Untersuchungen 1965/70. Medd. Lunds univ. hist. mus. Lund.

Sundt, E. 1900 Bygningsskik paa bygderne i Norge. Kristiania

Svarteberg, K. 1971 Asle Kirkedalen. Samlaren og granskaren. Kolbrenning, Dölaminne s. 62–65. Årbok for Hallingdal. Ål.

Syrstad, O. 1970 See Nydal, R., Løvseth, K. and Syrstad, O.

1972 See Nydal, R., Løvseth, K. and Syrstad, O.

Tacitus, Germania. (Pandora, 7) Leipzig 1920.

Tanner, V. 1941 De gamla nordbornas Helluland, Markland och Vinland. Ett försök att lokalisera Vinlandsresornas huvudetapper i de islandska sagorna. Budkavlen, nr. 1. Åbo.

Taylor, W.E.Jr. 1959 Review and assessment of the Dorset problem. Anthropologica New Ser. Vol. I

1964 The prehistory of the Quebec-Labrador Peninsula. Le nouveau Quebec, contribution à l'étude de l'occupation humaine. Paris.

Thorarinsson, S. 1943 Þjórsárdalur och dess förödelse: läge och naturförhållanden. Forntida gårdar i Island, pp. 11–16. København. Edited by M. Stenberger.

1967 The Eruptions of Hekla in Historical Times. Societas Scientiarium Islandica. Reykjavik

Thordarson, M. 1943 Skeljastaðir: Þjórsárdalur. Forntida gårdar i Island, pp. 121–136. København. Edited by M. Stenberger.

Thordeman, B. 1920 Forhistoriske hustyper i Norden. Rig. III. Lund.

Thun, E. 1965 Archäologische Untersuchungen in Vä in den Jahren 1962/63 Lunds Univ. Hist. mus. Medd. 1964/65

Tischler, F. 1954 Der Stand der Sachsenforschung archäologisch gesehen. 35. Bericht der Römisch-Germanischen Kommission. Berlin.

Tollnes, R.L. 1969 Bygningsrester fra Kaupang. Viking. Oslo.

Vebæk, C.L. 1941 Middelalderlige bondegaarde paa Grønland. En sommers Udgravninger i Nordboernes Østerbygd. Fra Nationalmuseets Arbejdsmark, København.

1943 Inland Farms in the Norse East Settlement. Meddr. Grønland Bd. 90, nr. 1. København

1964 En landnamsgaard i nordbobygderne i Grønland. Naturens Verden. Juli. pp. 200–214.

Viking Congress. Proc. 3 1956. Edited by Kristján Eldjárn. Reykjavik 1958

Visted, K. and Stigum, H. 1952. Vår gamle Bondekultur II, Oslo.

Voionmaa, J. 1943 Lundur: Borgarfjarðarsýsla. Forntida gårdar i Island, pp. 171–190. København. Edited by M. Stenberger.

Vreim, H. 1947 Norsk trearkitektur. Ny utvidet utgave. Oslo 1947

284

Wallace, B.L. 1969 American Antiquity, Vol. 34, nr. 2, Washington.

Waterbolk, H.T. 1971 Working with Radiocarbon Dates. Contributions to Prehistory Offered to Graham Clark. Proceedings of the prehistoric Society, Vol. XXXVII, December 1971

Wilson, D. 1966 See Bersu, G. and Wilson, D. 1966

Winkelmann, W. 1954 Eine westfälische Siedlung des 8. Jahrhunderts bei Warendorf, Kr. Warendorf. Germania 32. Die Römisch-Germanische Kommission. Berlin.
1958 Die Ausgrabungen in der frühmittelalterlichen Siedlung bei Warendorf (Westfalen). Neue Ausgrabungen in Deutschland. Berlin.

Wintemberg, W.J. 1939 Eskimo Sites of the Dorset Culture in Newfoundland. Am. Antiquity, Vol. 5, pp. 83–102. Menasha
1940 Eskimo Sites of the Dorset Culture in Newfoundland. Am. Antiquity, Vol. 5, pp. 309–333 Menasha

Wright, J.V. 1966 The Ontario Iroquois Tradition. Nat. mus. Canada. Bill 210, Ottawa.

Part III

Pollen-analytical Investigations in the L'Anse aux Meadows Area, Newfoundland

BY KARI E. HENNINGSMOEN

Introduction

A number of problems which could hardly be solved by archaeological means alone were encountered in connection with the excavations at L'Anse aux Meadows. The name "Vinland", for instance, did it imply that grapes really did grow here a thousand years ago? Or could there perhaps be some different explanation of the name? Sven Söderberg's theory (summarized by H. Ingstad, 1965) suggests that the name refers to the Old Norse meaning of the term *vin*, i.e. a meadow, grassland. This explanation may be just as sound as the grape theory (cf. H. Ingstad, op.cit.).

The name problem is closely connected with the question of the natural conditions in the area around the year A.D.1000. What were the climate and the vegetation like? It is generally assumed that the climate was more favourable at that time than it is today, but was it so favourable that plants as profoundly alien to the recent vegetation of the area as grapes could grow here? Today, the northern limit of wild grapes in eastern North America lies in the northern U.S. and southern Canadian region, a distance from the L'Anse aux Meadows area of about a thousand km.

Did the Norsemen find a country fairly similar to what we see today, or was the general vegetation conspicuously different? Have their own activities left any recognizable traces in the vegetation at or near the site? And where was the sea-shore level, compared to today's? A somewhat higher sea-level would undoubtedly facilitate sailing on the shallow Épaves Bay, as well as landing and disembarkation on the shore below the houses. On the other hand, as the site lies only 4 – 5 m above today's shoreline, the difference could hardly be more than a couple of metres; in fact, it was almost certainly less.

Pollen analysis has been employed as the main instrument in trying to find an answer to at least some of these questions. Radiocarbon datings were indispensible in combination with the pollen investigations. Diatom analyses were tried, but with limited success: only one locality yielded diatoms well enough preserved to be of informative value.

General description of the area
Geography/geology

The investigated area is a lowland, most of it reaching less than 60 m above sea-level, with only the highest points (on Quirpon Island) going up to about 150 m. The uplands and hills are rugged and uneven, bare or sparsely covered with glacial deposits. The lower-lying parts, up to 20 – 30 m, have extensive infillings of marine sediments, deposited when the relative sea-level was higher than at present. The Quaternary geology of the area has been studied by Grant (1970, 1972, 1975); he suggests a marine limit of up to 425 feet in northern Newfoundland (cf. p.327).

The marine sediments often take the form of terraces and beach ridges. The Norse site is situated on the edge of rather a conspicuous terrace, which lies about 4 to 6 m above sea-level. Another prominent terrace lies behind the site, at about 12 to 14 m elevation.

The area contains innumerable lakes and peatlands, the latter consisting of minerotrophic as well as more ombrotrophic peat complexes.

The bedrock around L'Anse aux Meadows has been investigated by Cumming (1975). East of the site, around Noddy Bay and eastwards, he has found Ordovician limestones and clastic sediments of the Table Head and Goose Tickle Formations.

West of the site, the Maiden Point Formation, the age of which is doubtful, dominates. Gillis (1966) suggests Ordovician (?), and Williams, Smyth and Stevens (1973) suggest Lower Cambrian (?) or older. The Maiden Point Formation consists of greywacke, quartz conglomerate, sandstone and shale. The site itself is situated within a zone of "mélange", a bedrock consisting of a mixture of blocks of varying sizes and lithologies, and with structures of greatly discordant orientation. They are set in a matrix of intensely deformed black shale.

Basaltic volcanic rocks are found on Cape Onion and on some of the islands west of the site. They are part of a north-east trending belt of Lower Ordovician volcanic rocks extending from Milan Cove to Cape Onion (Cumming, 1975; Williams, Smyth and Stevens, 1973).

The Maiden Point Formation/mélange contact is easily recognizable as a conspicuous escarpment to the west of the site (cf. A.S. Ingstad, fig. 36 this volume). The mélange underlying the settlement site probably had a significant influence on the life conditions of the Norse inhabitants. Slag, lumps of bog-iron, and a smithy have come to light at the site (cf. A.S. Ingstad's and Rosenqvist's papers 1977, this volume), indicating iron production from bog ore at the site. As pointed out by Cumming (1975): "Disseminated pyrite cubes and nodules are common in the matrix for the mélange, and provide a ready source of iron for transportation by ground-waters, which by biological

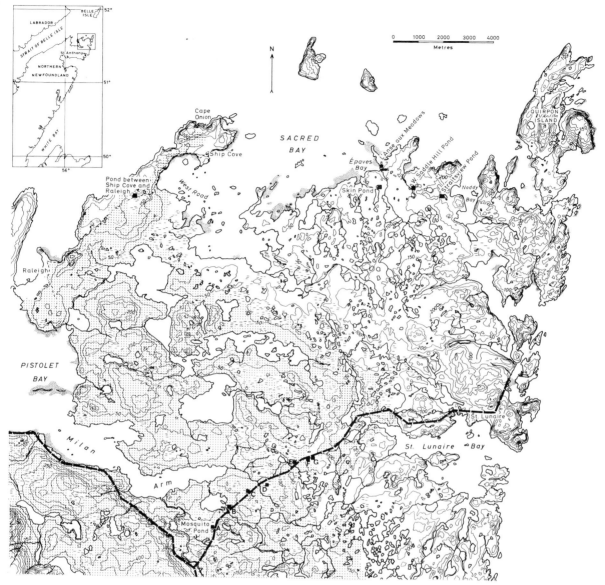

Fig. 1. Map of the investigated area (redrawn from maps published by Canadian Mines and Technical Surveys 1965). Black squares = sampling localities. Dotted land areas = forested ground. Heavy line = road.

precipitation produced bog-iron concentrations in the lowland areas under-lain by mélange."

Climate

Situated on the eastern edge of North America, Newfoundland is influenced all the year round by continental air masses, causing a great difference between summer and winter temperatures. On the other hand, the island is encircled by the cold waters of the Labrador Current, which have a domina-ting influence on the climate, moderating both summer and winter tempera-tures. Sea-ice, which normally reaches its greatest extent in March, retards the advent of spring, not least on the very northern tip of the island (The Climate of Newfoundland, 1964).

According to Hare (1952), the vegetative season (the beginning of which is defined as the date in spring when mean air temperature rises above 43° F) starts as late as between 15th and 20th June in the investigated area, whereas Montreal and Ottawa, for instance, reach this temperature about 10th April. The vegetative season is rather short in the area, lasting only 100 to 110 days, and the summer temperatures are not very high. Belle Isle and St.Anthony, the two nearest meteorological stations, have registered mean temperatures for the warmest month (August) of 50.4° and 55.7°F respectively (Tempera-ture and Precipitation, 1941–1970).

Nor are the winter temperatures very favourable, the corresponding tem-peratures for the coldest month (January at Belle Isle, February at St. Anthony) are 14.9° and 15.7° F, and the annual mean temperatures for the two stations are 32.1° and 35.5° F.

Hare (1952) describes the climate of the shores of the Strait of Belle Isle at the northern Newfoundland peninsula as near-Arctic, as a result of the constant presence of the Labrador Current water, often ice-laden well into July. "Nowhere else on earth," he says, "does the Arctic verge drive so far south into middle latitudes," the latitude being about the same as that of London.

The frequent flow of warmer, humid air across the cold waters of the Labrador Current and the Gulf of St. Lawrence results in the well-known fogginess of the Newfoundland coasts. At the Strait of Belle Isle it has a pronounced summer peak (over 30% of all July observations in the actual strait), decreasing somewhat in the autumn. However, fog does occur at all times of the year, and the "fog risk" never falls below 5%.

Precipitation is evenly distributed throughout the year. The St.Anthony station shows a slight spring minimum; at Belle Isle this is hardly noticeable. Total annual precipitation at the two stations amounts to 36.05 and 35.16 inches respectively, 22.79 and 25.79 inches of this being rainfall. The rest falls as snow, and St. Anthony registers measurable mean snowfalls throughout the year except in June to September. At Belle Isle, only July and August are without measurable mean snowfall.

Outline of the present vegetation

The northern tip of the northern peninsula lies within the transitional zone between sub-arctic forest and tundra, the "Forest-Tundra section" of Rowe (1959). This consists of a pattern of tundra "barrens" and patches of more or less stunted forest.

In the area north-east of a line from the head of St. Lunaire Bay to West Road, Sacred Bay (cf. map, fig. 1, where the forest limit is indicated), small forested parts occur only in those places where hills and ridges provide shelter. The height of the trees greatly depends on that of the shelter; occasionally the trees may reach a height of a few metres. More common is a low, shrubby vegetation, often very dense and very difficult to traverse. Most of the wind-swept land is, however, covered by grassy herbaceous and/or heath vegetation, or by peatland. More or less extensive barren rock knolls occur commonly, mostly in the uplands.

South-west of the same line, the forest is more predominant. The primary arboreal species on the northern tip of the island are *Picea mariana* and *Abies balsamea*. *Picea glauca* occurs on fairly well drained ground, and *Larix laricina* is frequent in moist localities. *Alnus crispa, Betula papyrifera, B. pumila* and *B. glandulosa* are common, as are also *Salix* spp., *Sorbus decora* and *Juniperus communis. J. horizontalis* occurs here and there, and *Populus balsamifera* and probably also *P. tremuloides* are seen occasionally.

It may also be of informative value to review some trees *not* growing in the area. Hare (1952) and Damman (1965) have recorded some trees with more or less southern affinities occurring elsewhere in Newfoundland, which do not, however, reach as far north as the northern peninsula. *Pinus strobus* and *P. resinosa* belong to this category, the former being more widespread than the latter. *Corylus cornuta* and *Acer rubrum* are common in the central and southern parts, and some other *Acer* species, viz. *A. spicatum* and *A. saccharum,* occur locally. The genus *Fraxinus* just about reaches the island, being represented by *F. nigra* which is restricted to warm, favourable localities on the west coast, where it appears only as a small tree or shrub (Hare, op.cit.). *Ulmus americana* has been recorded in south-western Newfoundland, according to Native Trees of Canada (1963).

However, most of the more exacting broad-leaved tree genera are not indigenous to Newfoundland at all: this applies, for instance, to the genera *Fagus, Tilia, Quercus, Juglans, Carya, Ostrya, Carpinus, Castanea* and *Celtis*. The same is true of some more exacting gymnosperms such as *Tsuga* and *Thuja*.

In spite of their absence from the northern peninsula – or from the entire island – most of these genera occur more or less sporadically in the pollen diagrams, obviously as a result of long-distance pollen transport (cf. p.324 and p.325).

The archaeological site and its immediate surroundings lack genuine forest, but shrubby specimens of the tree species common in the area are found, often taking the form of dense shrub thickets. Heath and herbaceous vegetation are, however, rather more predominant.

Kuc (1975) has published a detailed environmental map of the historic site. This shows that the site itself lies within a mosaic of different vegetation types, xeric-heathy areas, mesic areas with grass-herbaceous growth, atlantic meadows and peatland, the house-sites being situated on the more xeric-heathy parts.

No detailed vegetation analyses were carried out during my investigation, and thus no complete vegetation tables or flora lists can be given, although some main features may be mentioned. *Empetrum* may be the most common representative among the dwarf shrubs, but *Vaccinium uliginosum, V. angustifolium, V. vitis-idaea, V. oxycoccus* and *Rubus chamaemorus* are also frequent; and during the flowering season, parts of the area are covered with a white carpet of *Ledum groenlandicum* flowers. *Myrica gale, Chamaedaphne calyculata, Lonicera villosa, Kalmia polifolia, Andomeda glaucophylla, Potentilla fruticosa* and *P. palustris* are more or less frequently seen, while *Potentilla tridentata* occurs locally in large quantities.

The herbaceous vegetation is dominated by grasses and graminids, the genera *Calamagrostis, Poa, Festuca, Deschampsia, Carex, Eriophorum, Scirpus, Eleocharis, Luzula* and *Juncus,* for instance, being abundantly represented. More conspicuous flowering herbs are also common in the area. *Sanguisorba canadensis* and *Thalictrum polygamum* are common on fairly moist soils, *Cornus canadensis* is frequent, *Smilacina trifolia* and *Coptis groenlandica* are seen here and there. *Fragaria virginiana* produces a tasty crop in the autumn, and *Habenaria* sp. may be spotted by its scent. *Heracleum maximum* also occurs, and it is difficult to overlook *Iris hookeri* either in the meadows or by the shore.

Other sea-shore plants in the area may also be mentioned, such as *Potentilla anserina, Mertensia maritima, Arenaria lateriflora* and *Lathyrus japonicus.* The most interesting, perhaps, is the large grass *Elymus arenarius* var. *villosus* = *E. mollis,* which is rather common in the area. As several authors, including Fernald (1910), have pointed out, this plant is very likely to be the "wild wheat" of the sagas. It looks rather like wheat, and it was used by the Icelanders as a source of grain for centuries.

Several European weeds grow in the L'Anse aux Meadows area today, such as *Plantago major, Rumex acetosa, R. acetosella* and *R. domesticus,* to mention just some of the taxa which may be of special interest from a pollen-analytical point of view. *Trifolium repens, Ranunculus acris, Stellaria media, Capsella bursa-pastoris, Thlaspi arvense, Achillea millefolia* and *Carum carvi* also grow at and around the settlement.

Sedges and grasses are abundant at and around the site, and the area could undoubtedly offer pasture for domestic animals. As H. Ingstad (1965) and A.S. Ingstad (1977, this volume) have pointed out, this part of the country is certainly deserving of the name Vinland in the Old Norse sense of the term *vin* – meadow or grassland. The present name, L'Anse aux Meadows, also indicates a large quantity of this type of vegetation.

Several trees and shrubs with juicy fruits are also more or less frequent in the area. As Fernald pointed out as early as in 1910, the Norsemen would have had no difficulty in finding "wineberries" other than genuine grapes. *Viburnum edule* (squashberry), *Amelanchier bartramiana* (mountain-juneberry), *Ribes* spp. (red and black currants, gooseberry), and *Rubus idaeus* (raspberry) are all easy to find. In addition, various dwarf shrubs with tasty berries grow plentifully, for instance *Vaccinium* spp. (blueberry, bilberry, cowberry, cranberry) and *Rubus chamaemorus* (cloudberry). These dwarf shrubs are probably less likely to be "wineberries", since we must assume that the Norsemen knew them so well that they would hardly be likely to misname them. But some of the shrubs and trees might very well have been interpreted as grapes, not least the squashberry and the currants, as earlier pointed out by H. Ingstad (1965). (The use of currants in wine procuction is well known in the northern countries. "Red and black wineberries" are the common Swedish terms for red and black currants, and "red wineberries" are also known in some Norwegian and northern English dialects.)

Thus the vegetation today does not render either of the two above interpretations of the name Vinland unlikely from a botanical point of view, provided that one accepts the possibility of berries other than genuine grapes being designated "wineberries". The vegetation of the past is described below, being based on the information derived from the pollen diagrams.

With a few minor exceptions, the botanical nomenclature employed in this paper is in accordance with Fernald (1950).

Methods

Field work

During the first field summer, 1962, I spent a little more than two weeks at L'Anse aux Meadows, from 24th June to 10th July. In 1968 I was so fortunate as to get an opportunity of returning to the field in order to carry out additional sampling; the field work lasted three weeks on this occasion, from

6th to 28th August. Being able to experience the early as well as the later summer floral aspect of the area proved to be of great advantage. Plants that were quite inconspicuous in June could predominate in August, and vice versa.

Sample series for pollen analysis were collected from eight pond and bog localities, three of which were situated at the site itself or in its immediate vicinity (L'Anse aux Meadows Pond, Palsa Bog, and "C. 30 m East of House F"). Three localities are situated within 3 km of the site, and in more or less the same vegetational surroundings (Straitsview Pond, W. Saddle Hill Pond and Skin Pond). The last two (Pond between Ship Cove and Raleigh, and Mosquito Pond) lie, respectively, on the border of the forested area and in the forest. These two localities lie somewhat further away from the site, at a distance of c. 10 km and c. 14 km respectively, as the crow flies.

The pollen series were collected in order to investigate the vegetational development in the area, including both the shrub-heath-meadow area around the site and the forested area situated not far from it (cf. map fig. 1). Any substantial vegetational change would presumably be reflected in pollen diagrams from either the heath-meadows or the forested area, or probably from both.

In order to support the interpretation of the pollen diagrams, surface samples from different vegetation types in the area were collected. Seven of these samples were taken along a transect from the Mosquito Pond – near the head of Milan Arm – and eastwards in the direction of St. Lunaire.

Four sample series were collected from the house walls in order to study the origin of the wall material: two from house A, and one each from houses F and D, the last has not been analysed, but radiocarbon dated.

Most of the sample series were collected by means of a Hiller sampler with chamber length 50 cm. To avoid contamination, all the samples were taken from the central parts of the core, the diameter of which is 2.5 cm. No obvious contamination of the samples was recorded, and no samples had to be rejected owing to suspected contamination. A Livingstone piston core sampler was used to collect some of the samples from L'Anse aux Meadows Pond; unfortunately this sampler was damaged by the very hard sediments of the pond bottom, so that we had to return to the Hiller sampler for the rest of the field work. The samples from the house walls were cut directly from the cleaned profiles, knife and forceps being employed. The same technique was employed for the Palsa Bog series, where a trench was dug almost to the bottom of the bog. The bottom 40 cm were collected by the Hiller sampler. Surface samples were taken from the top of the living moss/peat.

Samples for radiocarbon dating were collected at the same time and by the same methods as the pollen samples.

The main features of the living vegetation were registered, in the entire area as such as well as at the actual sampling localities (cf. the chapters on vegetation and on localities and pollen diagrams). Pollen material (flowers with ripe anthers) from the living vegetation was collected during both the field seasons for the purpose of making a "pollen herbarium" for comparison during the analyses.

The sampling localities were selected at different altitudes – from 1.4 m to about 50 m above sea-level – in order to obtain some information about the shore-line displacement during the last thousands of years in this way. The elevation was measured partly with a levelling tube and partly with a Pauline altimeter. In the latter case, the results were controlled by repeated readings. The normal high water level, in as far as this could be established, was used as the basis for the elevation measurements. This was no problem as far as the Norse site was concerned, as a detailed map of the site had been made by the Department of Northern Affairs, Newfoundland, in 1962. This map was very useful to us in our work. (Cf. A.S. Ingstad, 1977, this volume pl. 1. The reference datum for the contour lines is mean low water.) A metal bolt at elevation 24.34 feet above mean low water served as starting point for my levellings here. According to the map, average high water is at elevation 5.5 feet = 1.67 m. The altimeter measurements, which *per se* are rather inaccurate and are used only for the higher localities, are not seriously affected by this difference between high and low water. The lower-lying Straitsview Pond had to be levelled from an estimated high-water line, and the result, 1.4 m above sea-level, is not necessarily absolutely accurate. One must allow for an error of some cm in this case.

Further details concerning the field work are included in the description of the localities.

Laboratory work

The samples for pollen analysis were acetolyzed and – when necessary – treated with HF, as described by Fægri & Iversen (1964). Coarser organic material was removed by sieving; this material was in many cases used as an information source employed for a description of the sediment. In other cases, a small portion of the entire sample was boiled in KOH and investigated for this purpose. The pollen samples were stained with basic fuchsin and embedded in glycerol. Diatom samples were boiled in perhydrol and mounted in Hyrax.

The pollen diagrams

Most of the pollen analyses were carried out by myself; Dr. Kerstin O. Griffin rendered valuable help, however, by analysing fourteen samples. Four to five hundred pollen grains were normally counted per sample, but in a few cases the material was so poor in pollen that such a number was unattainable. In some of the more pollen-rich samples, on the other hand, it was exceeded.

First an attempt was made – in the traditional manner – to include only the arboreal pollen (=AP) and the pollen of the anemophilous non-arboreal plants (=NAP) in the basic 100% pollen sum (cf. Fægri & Iversen 1964). It soon proved necessary to include the pollen of entomophilous herbs (=EP) also. In this largely forestless area the entomophilous herbs form too important a part of the plant cover to be omitted from the pollen sum. Cyperaceae pollen is included in the 100% sum in all samples, in spite of its often very local occurrence. As stated by Lichti-Federovich and Ritchie (1968), species of this family are important and widespread components of the vegetation in both upland and lowland habitats in the subarctic and arctic regions. Field observations from northern Newfoundland support this view. Aquatic plant pollen (= AqP) and spores are not included in the pollen sum, the spores being excluded perhaps more for traditional than for logical reasons. The calculation basis for the aquatic pollen percentages is the sum of AP+NAP +EP+AqP. Correspondingly, the spores, algae and other counted microfossil categories have been calculated separately on the basis of the pollen sum + the taxon in question.

The diagrams are constructed in a traditional manner, depth and stratigraphy being indicated to the left. Sediment and peat symbols are in accordance with the principles put forward by Fægri & Iversen (1964). Next comes the "total diagram" (cf. Fægri & Iversen 1964, p. 88), which expresses the ratio between the AP, EP and NAP groups, and the percentages of the most important AP and NAP constituents. The other pollen types are given in the next part, mainly as individual curves, but sometimes written in the diagrams. The taxa included in AP, NAP and EP are expressed in separate groups. In AP, gymnosperms are listed before angiosperms. The most frequently occurring taxa of each group are generally shown on the left, while the others follow alphabetically. This rule is broken occasionally in order to save space, and for the same reason some of the curves are shown only in parts of the diagrams.

Two different scales are used in the individual curves, the normal scale being shown in black; the other, a quintuple scale, is horizontally hatched, and is used to express the lower pollen percentages. The curves for aquatic pollen, spores and other microfossils are drawn in the same way.

Pollen corrosion is recorded to the right in some of the diagrams, expressed as corroded pollen of deciduous arboreal plants as percentage of the total number of the same category. Where corrosion is not quoted, it is negligible.

Most of the arboreal pollen comes from taxa growing in the area, but lesser amounts of obviously long-distance transported pollen occur in all diagrams and in almost every sample. The individual curves for long-distance transpor-

298

ted arboreal taxa are to be found in the AP group, but in many diagrams a combined curve for these taxa has been added in order to give a clearer record of the extent of this group taken as a whole.

No pollen numbers have been recalculated or omitted in order to correct either for differential pollen production or for local over-representation. Any correction would, in my view, have been very tentative in this case, and the resulting diagrams would hardly have been more representative of the vegetational development than the original ones.

Indisputable limits between the AP, NAP, EP and AqP groups can hardly be established. In the present report, pollen of all tree and shrub species is included in AP, without regard to origin in tree, shrub or field layer, the only exceptions being some insect-pollinated more or less dwarfy shrubs. Ericales, for instance, is included in NAP in the traditional manner (cf. Fægri & Iversen 1964). *Lonicera villosa* and *Potentilla* type, including *P. fruticosa,* are included in EP, together with other dwarf shrubs of the Rosaceae. The NAP/AqP limit may certainly also be questioned in many cases, many Cyperaceae and Gramineae, for instance, being more or less aquatic. In this paper, all Cyperaceae and Gramineae are included in NAP.

Remarks on some plant taxa in the diagrams

Picea mariana and *P. glauca,* both of which grow in the area, have not been separated pollen-analytically. It seems difficult to me to find reliable criteria for distinguishing between the two species, not least in the present material where a number of the *Picea* pollen grains were fragmented.

Betula papyrifera, B. pumila, B. glandulosa and *B. michauxii* are common in the area. Size-statistics for *Betula* pollen are not very promising for material assumed to contain a mixture of these species. Leopold (1956) gives a size range of New England *Betula* species, including the four in question. *B. glandulosa* has the smallest pollen grains, with a mode from 20 to c. 23 μ, while *B. michauxii, B. pumila* and *B. papyrifera* have mode values of about 28, 30 and 33 μ respectively, the modes being measured on acetolyzed material. Considering the intraspecific overlapping in size, it seems hazardous to attempt to differentiate between the three latter taxa. It may be possible to separate the small *B. glandulosa* type, and size-statistics were experimentally carried out on material from L'Anse aux Meadows Pond and from W. Saddle Hill Pond. The only result was a relatively stable percentage of 5 – 10 of small pollen grains, probably of *B. glandulosa* type, calculated as a percentage of the total *Betula* number. Neither this result, nor the general impression of the *Betula* material in the other series, encouraged me to carry out further *Betula* statistics.

Populus pollen occurs in very low percentages. Some of these pollen grains could be referred to *P. balsamifera* type, but most of the *Populus* pollen has not been identified below the genus level.

No attempt has been made to differentiate between different *Salix* pollen types.

Pinus pollen is found in small quantities in the majority of samples. Both *P. strobus* type and the smaller *P. banksiana/resinosa* type are seen, in addition to some more or less indeterminable *Pinus* pollen. The *Pinus* types are combined in one curve on the diagrams.

A large Gramineae pollen type occurs in many of the pollen spectra. It is referred to *Elymus arenarius* var *villosus*. The pollen is distinguished from other Gramineae by its size, which exceeds 50 µ, and by the regularly scattered *punctae* (cf. Fredskild 1967 p.23). The species is common on sea-shores in the area today, and according to the pollen diagrams, it has been so for at least four thousand years.

Most of the *Thalictrum* pollen is ascribed to *T. polygamum,* a species which grows commonly in the area. *T. alpinum* is also present, but its pollen is more distinctly michroechinate than most of the observed *Thalictrum* pollen, the morphology thus indicating *T. polygamum* as the main source of this pollen type. The similar, but smaller and clearly echinate pollen of *Coptis* occurs in some diagrams; reliable identification kindly confirmed by Dr. Bent Fredskild.

Rumex sect. *Acetosa* is found in small frequencies only, exclusively in some of the uppermost samples. The *Rumex* pollen generally seen undoubtedly belongs to the indigenous *R. fenestratus/orbicularis* type. In addition, the *Oxyria* pollen type is also found.

The *Sparganium/Typha angustifolia* pollen type is assumed to originate from *Sparganium* rather than from *Typha angustifolia* which, according to Fernald (1950), does not grow in Newfoundland today. Previous occurrence of this species cannot be precluded, but is not very probable, cf. the chapter on results.

The term *Dryopteris* is used for all monolete spores of *Dryopteris* type.

The spore type designated as "*Tilletia*" occurs in many of the diagrams. Such spores have long been recognized as spores of a fungus parasitizing in sporangia of *Sphagnum* spp. It has been referred to different genera; according to Eckblad (1975), *Hymenoscyphus schimperi* is the correct name of the fungus.

Radiocarbon datings

The age determinations have been carried out by Dr. Reidar Nydal, Radiological Dating Laboratory at the Norwegian Institute of Technology, Trondheim. All ages are given in uncorrected conventional radiocarbon years before

300

A.D. 1950, and the applied half-life is 5570 years (cf. Nydal 1977, this volume, and Nydal et al. 1970 and 1972).

Localities and pollen diagrams
Mosquito Pond (locality 1)

C. 20 m above sea-level (Measured by altimetre)
Pollen diagram fig. 2.

The locality (see map fig. 1) is one of the thousands of unnamed ponds in the area, and the name used here is quite unofficial – it was assigned for reasons obvious while sampling was in progress. This pond is situated about 2 km south of the head of Milan Arm, the south-eastern arm of Pistolet Bay. Of all the investigated localities, this is the only one surrounded by genuine forest in all directions, the distance from the boring point to the edge of the forest varying from about 50 m to about 300 m. *Picea mariana* is the dominating tree in the vicinity; other forest constituents noted at the locality are *Abies balsamea*, *Betula papyrifera*, *Larix laricina* and *Sorbus decora*. The trees reach a height of 5 – 10 m, thus forming a well developed forest from the point of view of this area.

The sample series was taken at the southern shore of the pond, about 3 m from open water. The pond is situated in the southern part of a *Sphagnum* peatland with several small ponds. The following plant taxa were recorded in the immediate vicinity of the sampling point: *Myrica gale*, *Betula michauxii*, *Andromeda glaucophylla*, *Ledum groenlandicum*, *Kalmia angustifolia*, *Rubus chamaemorus*, *Vaccinium* spp., *Sarracenia purpurea*, *Empetrum*, *Eriophorum*, *Scirpus caespitosus*, *Drosera rotundifolia* – plant taxa indicative of oligotrophic to weakly minerotrophic conditions (cf. Pollett 1972).

The lowest organic layers of the series have been radiocarbon dated to 5680 ± 120 years B.P. (T–816). The surface sample was taken from living *Sphagnum* moss, and the sample series is assumed to cover the period from about 5600 B.P. to the present.

The pollen diagram shows an extremely monotonous vegetational development. The *Picea*, *Betula*, *Alnus* and *Abies* curves run almost parallel through most of the diagram, indicating a rather unchanged composition of the forest in the area. The Cyperaceae and Ericales curves are low and fairly constant, and most of the other NAP and EP constituents are negligible. The ratio between AP, NAP and EP is almost constant, which indicates that the relation between forested and unforested areas has remained largely unchanged for the last 5600 years.

The only changes in the diagram curves probably reflect the local development of the basin. This development is also reflected in the stratigraphy

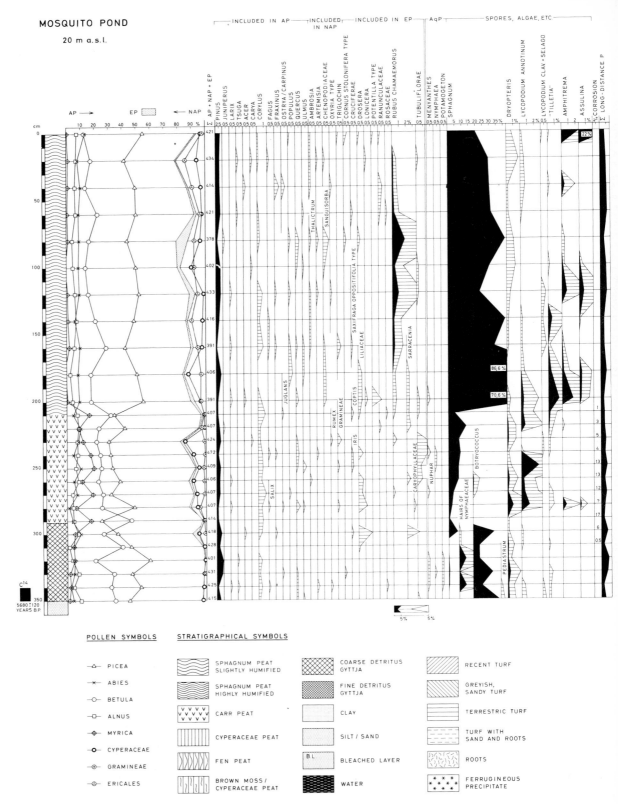

MOSQUITO POND

20 m a.s.l.

Fig. 2. Pollen diagram from locality 1.

302

column. The lowest samples, consisting of coarse gyttja, contain lacustrine indicators: pollen of some aquatic plants, hairs of Nymphaeaceae and cells of the freshwater algae *Botryococcus* and *Pediastrum*. A development from open water to a moist brushwood may be observed in the stratigraphy column, the deposit changing to a rather highly humified carr peat containing not only various roots and rootlets, but also fragments of twigs, bark and leaves of conifers and deciduous trees/shrubs. Corrosion is noticeable in this peat.

A transition to less humified *Sphagnum* peat at about 2.10 m depth indicates a change to wetter conditions: this may be due to local events in the basin, or to a deterioration of climate. The pollen curves give no clue in this matter. Fluctuations in the *Picea* and *Betula* curves occur predominantly near the levels showing changes in the stratigraphical column, which indicates that the fluctuations are due to very local, developmental changes. A *Myrica* maximum and a corresponding *Picea* minimum during the brushwood stage, as well as a maximum of *Rubus chamaemorus* during parts of the *Sphagnum* stage, obviously also reflect the local plant succession rather than regional changes.

Pond between Ship Cove and Raleigh (locality 2)

C. 52 m above sea-level (Measured by altimetre)
Pollen diagram fig 3.

This locality is situated within an extensive peatland crossed by the path leading from Ship Cove to Raleigh (cf. map fig. 1). There are several shallow ponds in this peatland; test borings in many of them showed depths varying from 1 m to almost 3 m. A pond in the higher part of the peatland was finally chosen; here it was possible to obtain an uninterrupted sample series of 2.65 m. The borings were made from *Sphagnum* peat, less than 1 m from the shore of the pond. The peatland is surrounded by forested areas, but the trees are lower and the forest less dense than around the Mosquito Pond; the distance to the edge of the forest is some hundred metres in all directions. The following tree species were recorded in the forest: *Picea mariana, Abies balsamea, Betula payrifera, Alnus crispa, Larix laricina* and *Sorbus decora*. At lower altitudes the following were seen: *Ribes* sp., *Viburnum edule, Amelanchier bartramiana*, and one single specimen of *Populus balsamifera*. *Empetrum* grew abundantly near the sampling point, together with *Ledum groenlandicum* and *Rubus chamaemorus*. Other taxa noted are *Scirpus caespitosus, Kalmia angustifolia, Andromeda polifolia, Chamaedaphne calyculata, Eriphorum spissum, Myrica gale, Juniperus communis* and *Salix* spp., indicating slightly more oligotrophic conditions than those obtaining in locality 1.

A radiocarbon dating (T–502) of 6420 ± 130 years B.P. gives the age of the

303

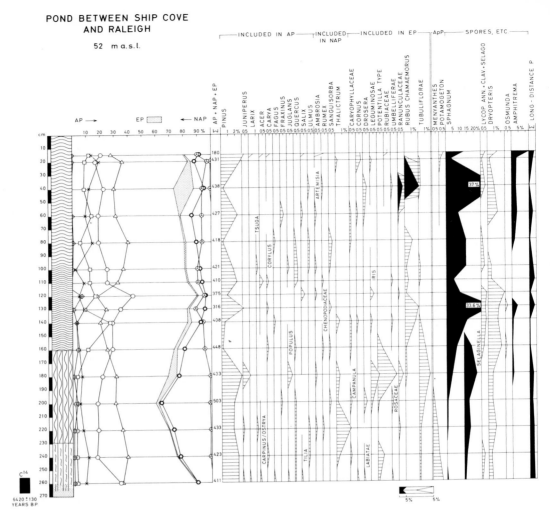

Fig. 3. Pollen diagram from locality 2. Legend, see fig. 2.

lowest layers, and the top sample is probably fairly recent, being taken at only
15 cm below the living *Sphagnum* surface (cf. the upper radiocarbon dating
from the Palsa Bog and the dating from L'Anse aux Meadows Pond II).

The stratigraphy column shows a development from wet brown moss peat
(*Scorpidium scorpioides*, det. P. Størmer) through Cyperaceae-fen to *Sphagnum* peat. Judging from the degree of humification, there was a change from
drier to moister conditions in the basin at a depth of about 0.95 m, where there
is a transition from rather highly to slightly humified *Sphagnum* peat. Whether
this should be ascribed to a deterioration in climate or to changes in the local
conditions obtaining in the peatland is uncertain. The pollen curves do not
provide conclusive evidence on this point. They do not reveal any great
vegetational changes in the area during the c. 6500 years covered by the
diagram. The most striking feature, a Cyperaceae maximum in the lower part,
is obviously connected with the local Cyperaceae-rich fen peat formation. The
slight *Betula* maximum connected with the drier part of the *Sphagnum* peat
may be tentatively interpreted as representing bog birches which invaded the
drier peat surface, and which retreated towards the end of the drier period –
whether this period is due to local or to climatic changes. Another possible
interpretation is that a slight *Betula* increase occurred more generally in the
surrounding forests in connection with a climatic somewhat drier/warmer
period.

With the exception of the – probably locally conditioned – Cyperaceae
maximum, the ratio AP:EP:NAP is fairly constant throughout the diagram,
indicating a fairly stable arboreal cover throughout the entire period dealt
with.

W. Saddle Hill Pond (locality 3)

C. 32 m above sea-level (Measured by altimetre)
Pollen diagram fig. 4.

According to what inhabitants of L'Anse aux Meadows told me, the hill
between this village and Straitsview is known as Saddle Hill, while the pond
near the hill pass and a few neighbouring ponds are collectively known as
Saddle Hill Ponds. As the sampled locality is situated west of the pass, it is
designated "West Saddle Hill Pond" for the purpose of the present paper.

The pond is situated less than 2 km from the archaeological site, within the
same forestless area. A shrubby vegetation near the pond consists of the
following arboreal taxa, all common in the area: *Picea mariana*, *Abies
balsamea*, *Juniperus communis*, *Betula papyrifera*, *B. pumila*-type, *Alnus
crispa*, *Larix laricina*, *Salix* spp., *Sorbus decora*, *Amelanchier bartramiana*,
Viburnum edule and *Ribes* spp. At the *Sphagnum* peatland surrounding the
pond the following were noted: *Empetrum*, *Eriophorum*, *Scirpus*, *Ledum*

W. SADDLE HILL POND

32 m.a.s.l.

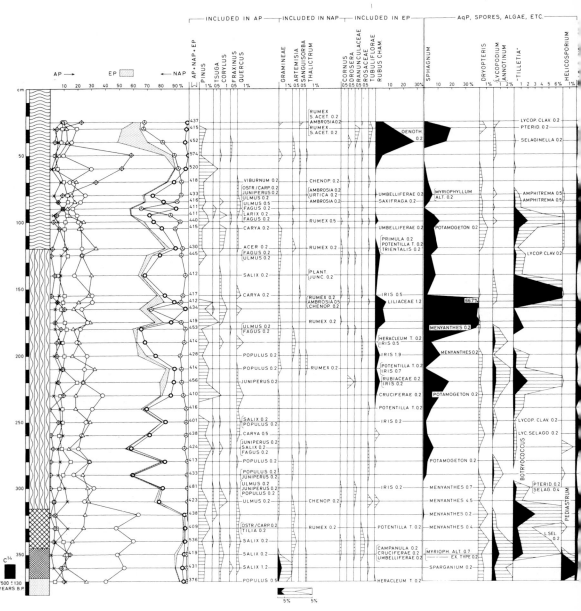

Fig. 4. Pollen diagram from locality 3. Legend, see fig. 2.

groenlandicum, Rubus chamaemorus, Andromeda glaucophylla, Drosera rotun-difolia, Chamaedaphne calyculata, Kalmia angustifolia and *Vaccinium* spp.

The boring was made in *Sphagnum* peatland some metres south of the pond, in order to avoid the floating *Sphagnum* mat near the shore.

The lowest layers of this basin were radiocarbon dated (T–501) to 7500 ± 130 years B.P., the highest age of any dated sample covered by the present paper. It is assumed to represent roughly the time when the sea level had fallen below about 32 m, the altitude of the basin. Cf. the chapter dealing with the shore-level displacement.

According to the stratigraphy column, development at the sampling point was quite regular – from open water – represented by fine and coarse gyttja – through a lengthy stage of *Sphagnum*/Cyperaceae-fen to peatland with slightly humified *Sphagnum* peat.

The *Betula* pollen curve shows a distinct maximum in the lowest half metre of the series. Tentative *Betula* statistics showed rather unchanged *Betula* sizes throughout the entire sample series, 90–95% of the *Betula* pollen having mode values of 28 – 32 μ. As pointed out earlier (p.299), only *B. glandulosa* could be expected to be distinguished by its size in this area, and the *Betula* maximum is obviously not due to this species. The *Betula* maximum occurs during the lacustrine stage of the series. It may very well be an entirely local phenomenon, representing *Betula* brushwood – or forest – near the former shore. On the other hand, one cannot preclude the possibility of the *Betula* maximum being a more regional occurrence. None of the other diagrams included in this material goes far enough back in time to be definitely contemporaneous with the *Betula* maximum in W. Saddle Hill Pond. The two earliest of the other sample series, from Skin Pond and from the Pond between Ship Cove and Raleigh, go back to about 6500 years B.P. Since we have no radiocarbon dating indicating the date of the termination of the *Betula* maximum, we do not know whether or not these series could be expected to show the *Betula* maximum, if it were regional. Thus the absence of the maximum in these two series is not conclusive as either positive or negative evidence.

Other published diagrams from Newfoundland provide little help in this matter. Wenner's (1947) two diagrams from the St. Anthony area show no *Betula* maximum comparable to the present find, but being from 1947, they lack radiocarbon datings, and their contemporaneity with the W. Saddle Hill *Betula* maximum is questionable. Terasmae (1963) has three radiocarbon dated diagrams from south-eastern Newfoundland; two of them show *Betula* maxima possibly comparable in age to that in question. However, the *Betula* top in Terasmae's diagrams consists of an unchanged curve of "normal-sized" *Betula* with an additional amount of small-sized *Betula*. This is not the case in the W. Saddle Hill diagram, and thus there is reason to believe that the

Betula maximum from the south-eastern area had different causes than that from W. Saddle Hill Pond. In addition, considering the distance of about 500 km between the two areas, a direct comparison between the diagrams does not seem justified.

The other pollen curves of the W. Saddle Hill Pond diagram show mainly local variations, more or less connected with the stratigraphical development. The AP curves are comparatively stable, with the maximum of the very local *Myrica* in the *Sphagnum* stage as the main exception. At the transition from gyttja to fen peat, the *Betula* maximum is replaced by a Cyperaceae maximum which certainly is of local origin; rootlets and epidermis fragments of Cyperaceae type are common in the fen peat. The Cyperaceae forms the dominating NAP constituent for most of the diagram. This curve fluctuates greatly in the long fen stage, but it has not been possible to find any connection between the Cyperaceae curve fluctuations and the small variations in the fen deposits. The *Sphagnum* peat stage shows a succession of maxima of Cyperaceae, *Myrica, Rubus chamaemorus* and, finally, of Ericales, reflecting main features of the local vegetational development near the boring point.

Two short-lived Ericales maxima and corresponding Cyperaceae minima are seen at 0.90 m and 1.65 m depth, respectively. At first glance, the Ericales maxima seem to represent contaminations from the upper, Ericales-rich layers. As to the lower sample at least, this explanation is obviously wrong. Most of the sample consists of *Sphagnum majus* (det. A. Pedersen), a species growing in very wet habitats, and which is lacking in the upper *Sphagnum* peat layers. A substantial contamination of Ericales pollen from above would probably have occurred together with remains of *Sphagnum fuscum,* the species constituting the bulk of the upper *Sphagnum* peat layers.

The Ericales maximum and the contemporaneous maximum of *Rubus chamaemorus* are probably due to a very local and short-lived occurrence of these plants in the vicinity of the sampling point – probably not *at* the actual point, since *Sphagnum majus* grows in habitats too wet for most Ericales species, and also for *Rubus chamaemorus.* A lowering of the water level in the basin may be the reason for this occurrence, giving growing conditions for Ericales and *Rubus chamaemorus* closer to the boring point than before and after the actual period, and to an increased quantitiy of *Sphagnum majus* in the wet fen at the boring point. The contemporaneous maximum of *Sphagnum* spores in the diagram may be due to *Sphagnum majus* and /or other *Sphagnum* species. A climatic reason for such a water level fluctuation is possible, but not proved.

The upper Ericales maximum lies within the *Sphagnum fuscum* peat stage, and contamination cannot be precluded. A very local occurrence of Ericales plants at the boring point is another possible explanation; Ericales may very well grow in *Sphagnum fuscum* peat. A climatic fluctuation is rather difficult to assert in this case, although it cannot be completely precluded.

The ratio AP:NAP fluctuates, mainly as a result of the fluctuating Cyperaceae curve. Apart from the *Rubus chamaemorus* maxima, the EP amounts are negligible.

Six seeds of *Najas flexilis* (det. K.O. Griffin) were found in the small gyttja sample (collected for pollen analysis) from 3.20 m depth, providing evidence of the former presence of the plant here. According to Hultén (1958, map 194), the species grows in the south-western, but not in the northern part of Newfoundland today. *Najas flexilis* is the only species in this material known to have grown previously in the area, but lacking now. The reason for its disappearance is, however, rather uncertain. The similar disappearance of *Najas flexilis* from a series of Fennoscandian localities has been discussed by for instance Sandegren (1920, 1932), Backman (1935), Samuelsson (1934) and Pedersen (1976). They all tend to assume changes in biotope rather than in climate as resposible for the disappearance.

The main trend of the stratigraphical development in the series gives no indication of climatic changes. The deposits show the normal development, from wetter to drier conditions, and no reversion like those observed in localities 1 and 2 is found.

The implication of the *Betula* maximum is uncertain; the changes in the other pollen curves are probably results of normal plant succession in the basin, perhaps with the exception of the above-mentioned fluctuations in the Ericales and *Rubus chamaemorus* curves.

Skin Pond (locality 4)

C. 20 m above sea-level (Measured by altimetre).
Pollen diagram fig. 5.

This locality lies only about 1 km south of the village of L'Anse aux Meadows, and the name refers to the fact that seal skins were soaked here to get the fur off before tanning.

The vegetation is very similar to that around W. Saddle Hill Pond, with the same arboreal taxa in the thickets. In the peatland the following taxa were noted: *Empetrum, Eriophorum, Rubus chamaemorus, Myrica, Ledum, Chamaedaphne, Andromeda, Equisetum, Coptis groenlandica, Sarracenia purpurea, Vaccinium* spp.

A wet peatland at the northern end of the lake was finally chosen as sampling point. The transition inorganic/organic sediments occurred 1.80 m below the surface. The radiocarbon age of the lowest organic layers proved to be 6610 ± 150 years B.P. (T–532); this is assumed to correspond approximately to the date of the withdrawal of the sea from the 20 m level.

SKIN POND

20 m a.s.l.

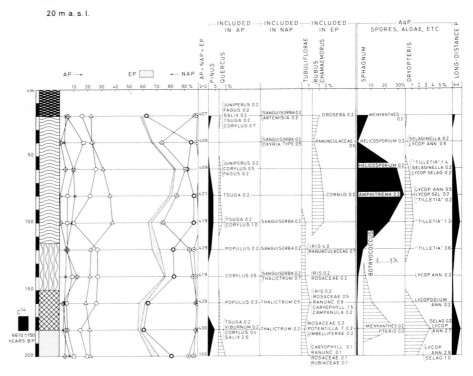

Fig. 5. Pollen diagram from locality 4. Legend, see fig. 2.

STRAITSVIEW POND

1.4 m a.s.l.

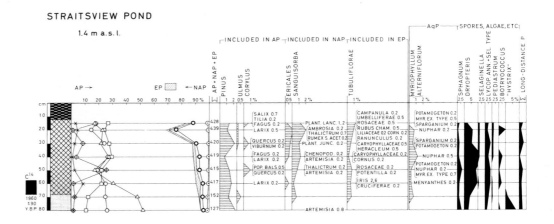

Fig. 6. Pollen diagram from locality 5. Legend, see fig. 2.

310

There are no irregularities in the stratigraphy column, the development passing from open water through a fen peat stage to a *Sphagnum* peat stage. The upper part of the series was too wet for sampling. Also this locality is rather monotonous from a pollen-analytical point of view. The pollen curves show very little vegetation change through the diagram. The *Picea* and Ericales curves increase where the deposits change from fen to *Sphagnum* peat, probably a direct result of the local successional development.

The uppermost sample shows an increase of Cyperaceae at the expense of *Alnus* and *Betula*. This is probably a result of the shrubs having been cut for fuel in modern times. Extensive fields of stubs in the area clearly indicate the recent exploitation of the arboreal material.

Straitsview Pond (locality 5)

1.4 m above sea-level (Measured by levelling).
Pollen diagram fig. 6.

This pond is situated near the village of Straitsview, about 3 km from the archaeological site and about 1 km from W. Saddle Hill Pond. Thickets of the type mentioned previously are found in sheltered places. The boring point lies at the west side of the pond, where *Myrica gale* is rather dominant in the vegetation. The occurrence of *Potentilla palustris* and *Triglochin maritimum* confirms the rather minerotrophic character of this locality. In the vicinity there are field and meadow patches, where weeds and other herbs grow in plenty; this is reflected in the two uppermost samples in the diagram, where weed pollen occurs.

The sample series was collected from shallow water close by the shore, and the deposit – coarse gyttja with sand – shows lacustrine conditions throughout the organic part of the series. The same evidence is also provided by the presence of pollen of aquatic plants. The bottom clay contains marine diatoms such as *Grammatophora oceanica*, *Cocconeis scutellum*, *Rhabdonema arcuatum* and *Coscinodiscus* sp. This is the only locality of the present material which has yielded marine diatoms, and even here they were none too well preserved. The "*Hystrix*" type (probably cysts of dinoflagellates) from the bottom layers supports the interpretation of the clay being of marine origin.

The radiocarbon dating of the bottom gyttja – 1960 ± 90 years B.P. (T–503) – indicates the time when the basin was finally isolated from the sea.

The pollen diagram, which is assumed to cover the two last millennia, does not show any unambiguous change in the vegetation. The *Picea* maximum in the marine layers may represent the vegetation near the shore, or perhaps a more general change. The pollen diagrams are not conclusive in this matter.

Palsa Bog (locality 6)
Palsa surface 6.50 m above sea-level (Measured by levelling).
Pollen diagram fig. 7.

The samples were collected from the central area of an extensive peatland covering most of the terrace just behind the archaeological site. Several long, grey lichen-covered ridges cross the peatland; test borings carried out on these ridges showed them to be palsas with frozen peat 30–40 cm below the surface. The palsas are quite low, rising less than half a metre above the general peatland surface.

According to Brown's map of permafrost in Canada (1968), the investigated area lies south of the limit of discontinuous permafrost. However, according to information I received locally, such palsas are found in many peatlands in the northern peninsula of Newfoundland.

The sample series was taken from the top of one of the most conspicuous palsas and downwards. The uppermost 35 cm were easily sampled from a hole dug through the unfrozen peat. It proved impossible, however, to penetrate the frozen peat with a spade or with the Hiller borer, and we therefore used a small portable paraffin stove to melt a hole through the peat, a process which took several days. The frozen layer at the sampling point proved to be 1.10 m thick, and was underlain by 30 cm of unfrozen peat.

The peat wall of the hole was cleaned thoroughly before samples were taken directly out of the wall down to 1.35 m below the surface. The layers at about 1.40 m were too wet to be sampled, but further down the unfrozen peat was dense and easily sampled with the borer. The burning paraffin from the melting process represented a risk of contamination in samples for radiocarbon dating. The upper dated sample was taken from unfrozen peat, i.e. the stove had not been used before this sample was taken. Before the lower sample was collected, melt-water was carefully baled out of the hole, in order that possible contamination from above might be avoided. Thus the radiocarbon sample, taken from the bottom of the dense, unfrozen peat, is assumed to be clean.

The radiocarbon analysis of the bottom sample (T–820) yielded an age of 5320 ± 60 years B.P. At that time the terrace had obviously risen above sea-level, but it is difficult to fix an exact level corresponding to that date. The palsa surface was levelled at 6.50 m, thus the bottom lies 4.75 m above sea-level. This represents the lower – or lowest? – part of the terrace, which was evidently covered by wet fen as soon as the sea had receded from the terrace. It is uncertain whether or not there was a threshold here, damming up a basin where this wet fen existed. The pollen in the lower fen samples is badly corroded, indicating oxygen-rich conditions at the beginning. The fen may quite possibly have been caused by a brook running slowly across the terrace, without any threshold at all. In that case, the date c. 5300 years B.P.

312

refers to the lowest possible level, 4.75 m. Considering the thickness of the fen peat, however, I tend to assume that there was a threshold. Unfortunately it was not possible to ascertain where such a threshold lay, or what level it reached, since *Sphagnum* peatland covers the possible threshold area today. The present peat level of the terrace represents the maximum value, but this is probably too high. More likely is a threshold at about the level where the fen peat changes to *Sphagnum* peat, viz. 5.85 m. This value has been used in constructing the curve for shoreline displacement (fig. 13), although I am well aware that this level may be too high. This means that the regression during the last 5300 years may have been slower, but hardly any quicker than indicated by the curve.

Among the recent vegetation around the sampling point the following taxa were noted: *Empetrum, Vaccinium* spp., *Ledum, Rubus chamaemorus* (very common), *Andromeda, Drosera rotundifolia, Carex* spp., *Scirpus, Eriophorum, Smilacina trifolia, Kalmia polifolia* and some *Betula pumila* and *Picea mariana*.

Towards the house-sites, the peatland becomes shallower and definitely more minerotrophic. At the border peatland/dry ground near the house-sites, the following were noted i.a.: *Betula glandulosa, B. michauxii, Lonicera villosa, Equisetum silvaticum, Potentilla tridentata, Iris hookeri, Sanguisorba canadensis, Rhinanthus borealis, Rubus acaulis, Scirpus hudsonianus, Clintonia borealis, Cornus canadensis, Galium palustre*.

In the east, this terrace ends in a slope which connects it with the higher terrace. This slope is covered with a very dense thicket, consisting of all the common arboreal species mentioned previously. In addition, *Rubus idaeus, Ribes* spp. and *Potentilla fruticosa* are also found here.

Situated only about 100 m east of the nearest house-site (House F), this locality is assumed to register possible vegetational changes at the site. The top sample consisted of living green *Sphagnum* moss, and it probably registers the pollen rain of recent years. The uppermost radiocarbon date (T–905), 460 ± 80 years B.P., does not contradict this assumption, and the entire series probably covers the last 5300 years.

A gradual oligotrophication process is obvious in this series. The lowest peat reveals minerotrophic conditions near the sampling point. *Sherpherdia canadensis*, with a 14% occurrence in the bottom sample, undoubtedly grew in the immediate vicinity. *Selaginella* is common up to 1.35 m below the surface, and brown mosses are common in the lowest peat.

Most of the AP:EP:NAP fluctuations are obviously directly connected with the local development of the peatland – as revealed by the stratigraphy – and the plant succession at the boring point.

The deposit changes from Cyperaceae peat to Cyperaceae-*Sphagnum* peat at about 1.27 m. The samples from 1.20 m and 1.15 m, just above this level,

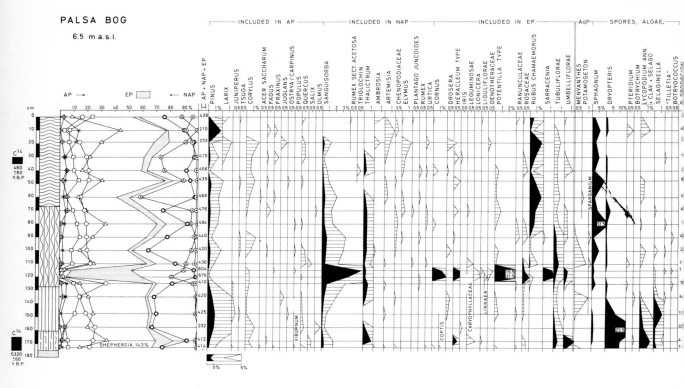

Fig. 7. Pollen diagram from locality 6. Legend, see fig. 2.

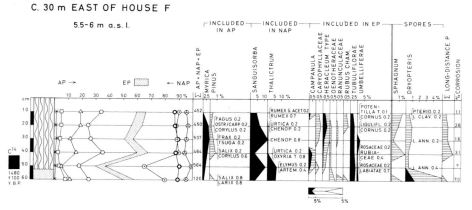

Fig. 8. Pollen diagram from locality 7. Legend, see fig. 2.

314

reflect the transition stage quite conspicuously; very local herb pollen dominates completely. *Sanguisorba canadensis* pollen occurs in amounts of about 20%, and *Potentilla* type is just as frequent. This *Potentilla* is referred to *P. palustris*–type (cf. Fredskild 1973 p.29). Other herbs also occur in considerable quantities. Pollen of *Heracleum* type, probably *H. maximum,* occurs in about 5%, *Cornus canadensis* type in 6% to 10%, and *Sarracenia purpurea* in 6% to 7%. Above this level the EP sum quickly decreases to a few per cent again, and the fen peat, consisting of *Sphagnum* and Cyperaceae, takes over. In the *Sphagnum* peat, Ericales plays a more important part than in the fen peat.

The changes in the AP group are not very striking, apart from the pronounced local AP minimum, reflecting the herb maximum at 1.20 m – 1.15 m. A slight minimum is seen at 60 cm, reflecting a maximum in Ericales and *Rubus chamaemorus,* probably connected with the change fen peat/ *Sphagnum* peat.

Small *Picea* maxima and corresponding EP+NAP minima occur at 10, 50 and 80 cm. It is tempting, of course, to suggest short-lived climatic changes as the reason for these fluctuations, but in my opinion such conclusions would be far from convincing, Temperature curves published in recent years (for instance Dansgaard et al. 1975 and Bryson 1974) show several small temperature fluctuations during the last two millennia, but it seems hazardous to connect any of them with the mentioned small *Picea* maxima as long as these maxima are not radiocarbon-dated. More detailed pollen analyses combined with series of close radiocarbon datings would be required if one were to trace climatic reasons for such small fluctuations in pollen diagrams, so I prefer to leave this question open.

The obvious *Picea* decrease in the surface sample is undoubtedly a result of recent felling of wood, judging from the arboreal stubs in the area.

Unambiguous traces of the Norsemen's activities have not been found. Some of the small fluctuations in the pollen curves at, say, 0.50 m – 1.00 m depth may be ascribed to them, but this would be a mere guess. European weeds are not found in the samples that could possibly be of "Norse age", the only representative of this category, a single pollen of *Rumex* sect. *Acetosa,* being found in the topmost sample.

The palsas in this peatland provide obvious testimony of a rather arctic climate. Their age is a matter of interest, not least in connection with the Norse habitation. University lecturer Karl-Dag Vorren at the University of Tromsø has studied the plant remains from the upper unfrozen peat layers at locality 6 in order to investigate the age of the palsa. He has stated (Vorren 1972) that dating of the formation of palsas is probably best effected by dating the uppermost hydrophilous layers in an uneroded palsa, but below its summit area. Vorren concludes from his investigation that the dated sample from

0.30 m to 0.33 m below the surface – 460 $\pm$ 80 years B.P.(T–905) – which contains *Sphagnum lindbergii* peat, is definitely older than the palsa development at the sampling point. This indicates that the permafrost in this area is quite recent a phenomenon, which developed fully first after the Norsemen had left the site. Presumably, permafrost started to develop some time during the "Little Ice Age", a cold spell which culminated between A.D. 1550 and 1700 according to Lamb (1965).

A similar age of palsa development in Finnmark, northern Norway, has also been found by Vorren (1972).

C. 30 m East of House F (locality 7)

Peat surface is estimated at 5.5 m –6 m above sea-level.
Pollen diagram fig.8.

The boring point is situated on the same terrace and near the margin of the same peatland as the Palsa Bog locality. The vegetational description of the border between this peatland and dry ground also applies to locality 7. In addition, there are several grasses and graminids.

The deposit throughout the whole series is highly humified fen peat with decayed remains of *Sphagnum* as well as of herbs and arboreal taxa.

The radiocarbon dating from the lowest layers (T–533), 1480 $\pm$ 100 years B.P., indicates the time when peat had transgressed to this peripheral part of the terrace.

As this locality is situated approximately *at* the archaeological site, we expected it to reveal vegetational traces of Norse activity, perhaps more clearly than what might be expected from the Palsa Bog locality. The radiocarbon dating, nearly 1500 years B.P., shows that the pollen diagram covers the time in question. The diagram does not, however, reveal any traces of the Norsemen, no traces of either agriculture of any kind or of any exploitation of the arboreal vegetation. The Gramineae maximum in the bottom peat is about 500 years earlier than the time in question, and cannot be due to the Norsemen. It probably implies a Gramineae-rich vegetation at the beginning of the peat stage. Above the Gramineae maximum, the curves of the diagram change very little. Arboreal vegetation from this part of the terrace obviously did not supply the Norsemen with fuel – driftwood logs were probably more attractive.

European weeds are here represented by one single pollen grain of *Rumex* sect. *Acetosa,* found in the sample at 10 cm depth, showing that this agricultural indicator is of fairly recent origin.

L'Anse aux Meadows Pond (locality 8)
3.90 m above sea-level (Measured by levelling).
Pollen diagrams figs. 9, 10 and 11.

This small pond is situated on the outer, lower part of the terrace on which the house-sites lie, less than 150 m north of House F. The distance to the boring point on the Palsa Bog locality is also less than 150 m.

To the east of the pond there is the same peatland as that described under locality 6, but the pond vicinity has a more minerotrophic character than the area around the boring point at the Palsa Bog. Among the plant taxa noted at the east side of L'Anse aux Meadows Pond, the following may be mentioned: *Sanguisorba canadense, Potentilla palustris, Rubus acaulis, Myrica gale, Lonicera villosa, Dryopteris spinulosa, Betula pumila, Vaccinium angustifolium, V. uliginosum* var. *alpinum* and – of course – large quantities of *Ledum groenlandicum* and *Rubus chamaemorus.*

To the west of the pond there is a meadow/heath vegetation with grasses and graminids, *Potentilla tridentata, Iris hookeri, Campanula rotundifolia, Euphrasia* spp., *Lathyrus palustris, Cornus canadense, Empetrum, Vaccinium* spp. and *Fragaria virginiana.*

There is a very dense stand of *Carex aquatilis* around the pond, particularly luxuriant on the north side.

The pond is very small, less than 15 m across. The first boring (diagram I, fig. 9) was made in 1962, from a small boat which was carried up to the pond for this purpose. The samples were taken a metre or two from the shore; the upper 50 cm was water, the organic deposits were fine gyttja, and the inorganic bottom deposit was silt.

The radiocarbon dating from the bottom gyttja (T–500), 3890 ± 110 years B.P., probably represents the time shortly after this basin was isolated from the sea.

A pronounced Cyperaceae maximum at the expense of AP starts between 1.10 m and 1.00 m in the diagram; at first glance this may give the impression of being a result of human activity – and if so, why not of Norse life? Additional sample series were collected in 1968, first and foremost for the purpose of radiocarbon dating this vegetational change.

One sample series (fig. 10) collected by a Livingstone piston core borer was taken from approximately the same boring point as series I; this time a raft was used instead of a boat. But as the Livingstone sampler was damaged by the very hard bottom silt, the rest of the sampling again had to be carried out by the Hiller borer.

The upper part of the gyttja was too loose for successful sampling with either Hiller or Livingstone borer, and there was no way of telling how much gyttja was lost here, nor the length of time it represented. Therefore a second Hiller borer sample series (diagram II, fig. 11) was collected from the eastern shore of the pond, about 40 cm from the edge of the water.

The radiocarbon analysis (T–906) of the Livingstone series dates the middle part of the Cyperaceae increase to 2010 ± 100 years B.P., a date which obviously precludes the Norsemen as the possible cause of this vegetational change. This finding is corroborated by the radiocarbon dating (T–819) from the termination of the Cyperaceae increase in the Hiller II series, 1290 ± 80 years B.P. If any human activity caused or influenced this process, the people responsible cannot have been the Norsemen.

The pollen curves from the L'Anse aux Meadows Pond locality fluctuate more than those from any of the other localities included in the present material.

Diagram I (fig. 9.) has two AP maxima corresponding to two EP+NAP minima, and vice versa. The lower of the AP maxima occurs in the two lowest samples, which represent the vegetation just before and after the basin was isolated from the sea. At that time the basin was situated very near the sea-shore, and the shore vegetation probably produced only small amounts of pollen. Therefore pollen from arboreal vegetation – shrubs? – a little further inland plays an important part in these spectra. Above the two lowest samples follows a stage with mass occurrence of *Sanguisorba canadense,* together with a maximum of *Thalictrum polygamum,* and with *Heracleum* and other Umbelliferae, Tubuliflorae, and several other herbs being well represented. At the next stage, AP takes over parts of the neighbouring area, together with ferns and club-mosses, but there is still a fair amount of EP present. *Hippuris* and *Menyanthes* grow in shallow parts of the pond, and *Myriophyllum, Potamogeton* and *Sparganium* still occur.

Next follows a pronounced Cyperaceae maximum, which starts between 1.10 m and 1.00 m and lasts for the remainder of the diagram. Its local character is indicated by the stratigraphy in diagram II (fig. 11), where Cyperaceae/*Sphagnum* fen peat starts contemporaneously with the Cyperaceae pollen increase; rootlets of various Cyperaceae types are the main constituents of this peat. Obviously the Cyperaceae increase demonstrates a mass invasion of Cyperaceae at the pond, and at least part of the increase is probably due to the occurrence of *Carex aquatilis,* which still grows plentifully both in the pond water and on land. The Cyperaceae pollen, being predominantly of *Carex* type (cf. Fægri & Iversen 1964), does not refute this, and seeds of *Carex aquatilis* type (det. K.O. Griffin) were found as deep as about 0.50 m in the Cyperaceae peat, diagram II. A lack of suitable material for seed analysis prevented us from determining how far down this seed type actually occurs. The disappearance of *Hippuris* and *Menyanthes* as well as of other aquatics at the Cyperaceae increase may indicate that *C. aquatilis* replaced them in shallow water. On the shore, *C. aquatilis* and other Cyperaceae species may have replaced ferns and club-mosses as well as some AP constituents and herbs.

318

ANSE AUX MEADOWS POND I

3.9 m a.s.l.

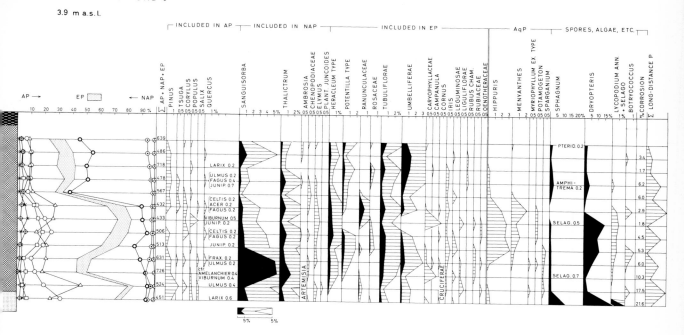

Fig. 9. Pollen diagram from locality 8. Legend, see fig. 2.

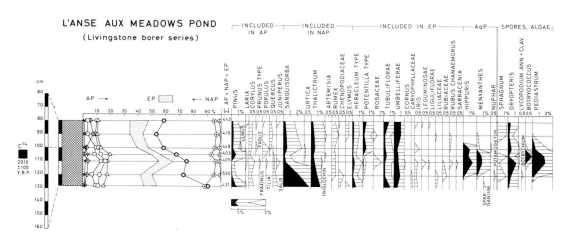

Fig. 10. Pollen diagram from locality 8. Legend, see fig. 2.

319

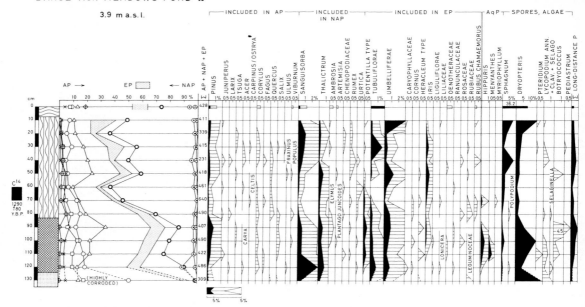

Fig. 11. Pollen diagram from locality 8. Legend, see fig. 2.

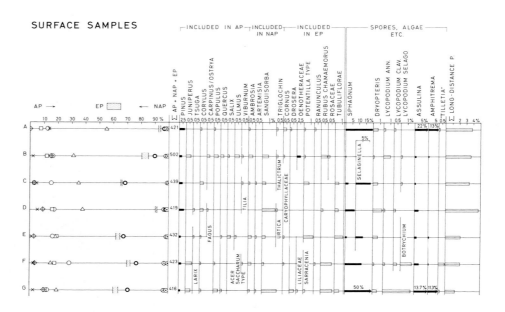

Fig. 12. Pollen diagram from locality 9. Legend, see fig. 2. For details, see text.

The local character of the Cyperaceae maximum in the pond is corroborated by the Palsa Bog diagram. In spite of the short distance between these two localities – less than 150 m – the Palsa Bog has no counterpart to the conspicuous and long-lasting Cyperaceae maximum of L'Anse aux Meadows Pond.

The local nature of the maximum does not, however, explain the rather sudden invasion of Cyperaceae here. We can neither preclude nor prove the influence of a human population earlier than the Norsemen.

Oligotrophication is to be expected, not least in such a cool, moist climate as prevails in northern Newfoundland today. An oligotrophication process in the course of time is demonstrated in the Palsa Bog series, and such a process is possible, although not unambiguous, in the Pond. *Carex aquatilis,* hardly an indicator of oligotrophic conditions (cf. Pollett and Bridgewater 1973), still grows abundantly at the locality, and the pollen curves do not provide a clear picture of the degree of minerotrophy in the past, as compared to present conditions.

The radiocarbon dating indicates that the Cyperaceae increase started somewhat before 2000 years B.P. This age may indicate that the increase occurred more or less contemporaneously with the climatic deterioration which occurred in North America prior to 2000 years B.P. (cf. Nichols 1969a and b,. Denton and Karlén 1973, Wendland and Bryson 1974, and others). The Cyperaceae increase may very well be connected with such a deterioration, for instance through a rise in the ground water level. If this is correct, the preceding AP maximum may represent a drier period with more favourable climatic conditions.

The Livingstone borer series was collected as close to the first boring point as possible without the risk of collecting samples disturbed by the first boring.

The gyttja sediments from the Hiller boring were nearly 1.20 m thick. In spite of several attempts we did not succeed in sampling a core of similar length with the Livingstone borer. Obviously, considerable compression took place during the process of boring, and the longest core obtained measured only 48 cm. Pollen analysis of the core allowed of a high degree of correlation to the Hiller series, and confirmed the compression of the core, cf. the diagrams figs. 9 and 10. The bottom samples are evidently lacking in the Livingstone series, but the *Sanguisorba-Thalictrum* maximum, the *Hippuris-Menyanthes* maximum, and the Cyperaceae increase are all easily recognized in the series. It is uncertain whether the top samples of the two series are contemporaneous. Schneider (1974) demonstrates that Livingstone borer cores in addition to compression may also be subject to loss of material during the sampling process. Apart from the bottom samples, such loss cannot be demonstrated in the L'Anse aux Meadows series; if present, it is not of a significant order.

The Hiller series II from the peripheral part of the Pond is easily correlated to the first series. The main trend in the pollen curves corresponds in the two series, as appears in the diagrams figs. 9 and 11. Since the age of the top sample in series I is very uncertain, we are safer in reading the vegetational development up to the present from diagram II. The Cyperaceae maximum is unchanged up to the 10 cm level, the highest possible level for sampling the wet Cyperaceae fen peat. The surface sample was taken from living *Sphagnum* near the boring point. The decrease in Cyperaceae and increase in *Myrica* in this sample probably do not indicate any sudden vegetational change in recent years; they are more likely to result from this sample having been collected closer to the *Myrica* zone and farther from the Cyperaceae belt than boring point II is.

No European weeds were found in the samples from this locality.

Surface sample transect (locality 9)

Pollen diagram fig. 12.

This analysis covers seven surface samples from the area between Milan Arm and St. Lunaire Bay, viz. from a transect starting in forest-covered land and continuing in the transitional zone between the forested and the unforested area, cf. map fig. 1. Surface samples from the unforested area are represented by the topmost samples from localities 4, 5, 6 and 8.

The surface samples, which were taken from living moss/peat, are assumed to represent approximately an average of the pollen rain of recent years. The purpose was to provide a basis for comparison between the pollen diagrams and the recent vegetation, especially with a view to the changes in the AP:EP:NAP ratio as compared to the degree of forest cover.

Samples A, B and C are taken from localities within the most densely forested part of the area. Around the sample D locality, the trees were markedly lower and the forest somewhat more sparse. Sample E was collected in an area with approximately 50% forest cover, which decreased to less than 40% at localities F and G.

Sample A, the topmost sample from the Mosquito Pond series, shows *Picea* dominance and negligible amounts of EP and NAP.

Sample B was taken from a fen area bordering a river, only 10–20 m away from the forest.

The herbaceous vegetation, including Cyperaceae, is subordinate, and local *Myrica* is well represented in the pollen spectrum.

Sample C was taken from a Cyperaceae-covered fen near a small pool, and the local dominance of Cyperaceae is obvious in the pollen spectrum.

322

Sample D, from a less dense forest than that surrounding the above localities, is an example of local dominance of a coniferous species. Dense *Picea mariana* shrub, less than half a metre high, covered most of the immediate surroundings of the sampling place; the spectrum indicates a far better developed *Picea* forest than that which in fact occurred at the locality.

Samples E, F and G were all taken from fair-sized peatlands within more thinly forested areas. Cyperaceae of local – and probably also extra-local – origin is well represented in the pollen spectra.

The surface samples seem to be markedly influenced by local pollen, perhaps with the exception of sample A. In the other surface samples it is clear that the AP:NAP ratio *per se* is not very conclusive as to forest coverage. (The EP amounts are negligible in the surface samples dealt with here.) Sample C, from a forested area, has just as high a Cyperaceae percentage as samples E, F and G, which come from a less forested area, and sample D indicates a densely forested area, although the nearest "forest" is a mere 30–40 cm high.

Lichti-Federovich and Ritchie (1968) have investigated recent pollen assemblages from the western interior of Canada. At stations within the tundra zone they find NAP values (including EP) varying from 13% to 32% of total pollen. The forest-tundra zone, the zone which is assumed to be comparable to the surface sample area of the present material, gives NAP values from 4% to 49% of total pollen sum. Terasmae (1967), in his study of recent pollen deposition in the tundra zone of north-western Canada, gives NAP values (including EP) varying from 36% to more than 300% of arboreal pollen (exclusive values). From forested areas near Nichicum Lake, Quebec, Terasmae and Mott (1965) have corresponding values of from 5% to 50% of arboreal pollen sum.

The NAP + EP values from locality 9 vary from 8% to 40% of total pollen sum, while the corresponding values from the top samples from localities 3 – 8 vary from c. 20% to c. 50%. Thus it seems clear that the local vegetation allows of a great deal of variation in the amount of NAP + EP within more or less the same vegetation type, and a certain degree of overlapping in the AP:EP:NAP ratio takes place between localities situated within differently forested areas. Because of this, one should be careful when drawing general inferences as to forest coverage from the AP:EP:NAP ratio here; instead one must judge the vegetation development of every locality in order to get an idea of the local development, and then try to synthesize a more general idea of the vegetational development of the northern Newfoundland area.

The above-mentioned authors all find high percentages of long-distance transported *Pinus* pollen in samples from forested and from unforested localities outside the area of this genus. In this respect there is an evident difference between the present investigation and theirs. *Pinus* is present in nearly all the northern Newfoundland samples, but only in small quantities, cf. the diagrams. The reason for this difference may lie in varying proximities to extensive pine forests and/or in the direction of the prevailing winds. Other long-distance transported pollen types occur in very low percentages in all the above works, as in the present study.

Results

Vegetation

The vegetational development is very monotonous in most of the diagrams (cf. descriptions of localities and diagrams). Most of the pollen curve fluctuations are recognized as the result of local vegetational succession. Possible indications of more regional changes are found, for instance the *Betula* maximum in W. Saddle Hill Pond and, although less likely, the *Picea* maximum in Straitsview Pond, but the material available can hardly supply any corroboration. Nor can these indications be controlled by other available pollen diagrams. As pointed out above (p. 307), Wenner's (1947) and Terasmae's (1963) diagrams can hardly be compared directly to those submitted here. Pollen-analytical investigations from Nova Scotia (Livingstone 1968, Hadden 1975, and others) give valuable information on vegetational and climatic development in that area, which is, however, too far distant from that of northern Newfoundland and comprises types of vegetation too different from those with which we are concerned to permit of detailed correlations.

Pollen diagrams from Quebec (Potzger 1953, Potzger and Courtemanche 1956) provide evidence of vegetational changes as results of climatic changes in the southern part of the area with which they deal, but here, too, the pollen curves give no basis for direct comparison with the northern Newfoundland material. Potzger and Courtemanche's northern localities are assumed to be rather young, radiocarbon datings indicating an age between 2000 and 3000 years, and consequently they reflect the vegetation of, at most, the last three millennia. These localities, like those of Newfoundland, show rather a monotonous vegetational development.

The present study demonstrates that no profound vegetation change has taken place during the last c. 7½ millennia. Apart from *Najas flexilis* (see p. 309) there is no indication of other plant taxa having grown in the area than those present today. The arboreal taxa listed as not growing in or near the area today (see p. 293) show no sign of having been present – or even of having grown closer to the area than they do today – throughout the span of time covered by the diagrams. They occur sporadically as long-distance transported pollen not only in the younger and surface samples but also in the older ones. Their percentages are not significantly higher during the presumably warmer periods than during the cooler ones. It seems clear that more

324

demanding arboreal taxa *(Tilia, Fraxinus, Quercus* etc. – cf. p. 293) did not grow in the area, and even *Pinus,* the "exotic" tree genus most likely to have grown more closely to our localities during warmer periods, gives no indication of actually having done so. Consequently it is highly improbable that any *Vitis* species – grapes – should have existed in the area a thousand years ago, and genuine grapes as the origin of the name Vinland must thus be ruled out as far as this area is concerned. Other berries, however, are very probable as "grapes", not least the squashberry – *Viburnum edule* (cf. p. 295).

The impression of a rather unchanged flora in the area is not refuted by Paulssen's investigation of charcoal from the site (Paulssen 1977, this volume). The majority of his samples proved to have come from indigenous arboreal species, only very few are referred to species not growing in the area today. Presumably, at least some of the charcoal comes from driftwood fuel, and it seems quite reasonable to assume that some of the driftwood logs originated in other vegetation zones and were transported over longer distances. As pointed out by Nydal (1977, this volume), the action of the Labrador Current and of winds may bring wood from both northern and southern regions to L'Anse aux Meadows.

Another question is the degree of forest cover around the L'Anse aux Meadows area when the Norsemen arrived. We had almost expected an abrupt change in the quantity of arboreal vegetation near the ruins, but found no evidence of this. As stated above, the vegetation at localities 7 and 8 has remained almost completely unchanged during the last 1–2 millennia, and the implications of the small changes at locality 6 are extremely ambiguous. The parts of the diagrams just prior to "Norse time" give no evidence of a higher degree of forest cover than the surface samples do. Consequently, the total amount of arboreal coverage was probably not very different from that obtaining today, but the pollen diagrams do not, of course, give any indication of the size of the arboreal plants. Shrubby specimens produce pollen just as the tree-formed ones do, and the pollen diagrams do not differentiate between these two types, provided that both belong to the same species. The arboreal cover at L'Anse aux Meadows a thousand years ago may well have consisted of tree-formed specimens instead of the present shrubs, but the pollen diagrams do not suggest that the area was densely forest-covered. The amount of EP+NAP – local and/or extra-local – roughly corresponds to that found today; this allows of considerable areas of meadow/heath vegetation, certainly enough to justify the name Vinland meaning "Meadow-land".

The pollen diagrams from the other localities give the same indication as to the former forest cover. Locality 1, forested today, shows very slight changes over the years. Locality 2, situated near the border of forested land today, shows no change in the forest limit. The same applies to localities 3, 4 and 5, all of them situated outside the forest today.

Mott (1975) carried out pollen-analyses from peat monoliths from the archaeological site. His conclusions accord well with those of the present study. He finds no drastic change in the vegetation through the last 2000 years, the only prominent changes being among the non-arboreal pollen, and they indicate only local changes in the habitats.

European weeds – *Rumex* sect. *Acetosa* and *Plantago lanceolata* – are very sparsely represented in the diagrams. They occur only in the topmost samples, where they are found in very small quantities, and must clearly be connected with the recent habitation.

Other possible weeds, such as *Artemisia* and *Ambrosia,* appear in small quantities on many of the diagrams, *Ambrosia* with a slight tendency to increase in the uppermost samples (localities 1, 6 and 8).

Thus, although we looked for a conspicuous "landnam" phase, as seen in the pollen diagrams from Greenland (Iversen 1934, Fredskild 1973) and Iceland (Einarsson 1963), we did not find any such evidence. Obviously the Norse settlement was too small and too short-lived to leave its mark on the vegetation. Besides, there were probably driftwood logs on the shore, which were used as fuel, so that it was not necessary to cut fresh material at the site. Great quantities of driftwood logs were observed by the author in the southern part of Pistolet Bay as recently as in 1968, so it seems quite probable that driftwood was available as a ready source of fuel near L'Anse aux Meadows a thousand years ago (see also A.S. Ingstad 1977, this volume p. 22).

As to the "self-sown wheat" of the sagas, I agree completely with the view of Fernald (1910), that this probably was *Elymus arenarius* var. *villosus,* certainly present at the site when the Norsemen arrived (cf. p. 300).

Climate

The pollen curves in the present material give no more than weak indications of climatic changes, cf. localities 3 and 8. The stratigraphical sequences at the localities provide somewhat clearer indications on this matter. Localities 1 and 2 have both yielded stratigraphical evidence demonstrating a change from drier to wetter conditions. The contemporaneity of these events has not been proved, as no radiocarbon datings from the levels in question are available. In my opinion, this change corresponds to the climatic deterioration prior to 2000 years B.P. (cf. p. 321), but no proof of this theory can be deduced from the material.

A more recent climatic change is indicated by the age determination of one of the palsas in the Palsa Bog (p. 316). This palsa, which developed rather recently – after 430 years B.P. or A.D.1500 – was probably initiated during the "Little Ice Age". Indirectly this may indicate that climatic conditions were better at the "Norse" time than later, when palsas were able to form.

During recent years, several authors have put forward evidence suggesting that climatic conditions were favourable at that time. Thorarinsson (1958), Lamb (1965), Dansgaard et al. (1969), Nichols (1969 a and b), Fredskild (1973), Miller (1973), Bryson (1974), Dansgaard et. al. (1975) all find evidence of a climatically favourable period in the North Atlantic-North American area during the period of settlement in Iceland and Greenland, and of the Vinland expeditions. It is worth bearing in mind, however, that the published climate curves indicate a climate similar to today's a thousand years ago, and not a warmer climate like that of the Postglacial Hypsithermal period. The favourable period about a thousand years ago was followed by periods of fluctuating temperatures, none of them as favourable as those of the past few decades.

Shore-line displacement

It has long been assumed that an upwarping of the coasts of northern Newfoundland took place during Postglacial time. Daly (1921) suggests a marine limit of 423 feet at Quirpon Island off the very northern tip of Newfoundland. Flint (1940) and Jenness (1960) indicate a marine limit of 250 feet further south on the northern peninsula, and thus the corresponding limit in the investigated area exceeds this value. The results of the most recent shore-line studies by Grant (1972) show that the maximum elevation of the former marine inundation varies from 425 to 225 feet above the present sea level in northern Newfoundland, the variation being due to differences in the time and rate of deglaciation and to two glacial readvances which removed all evidence of earlier, higher sea levels. The lower part of his shore-line displacement curve corresponds fairly well to the results of the present study, especially in view of his most recent publication (Grant 1975), where he suggests a high tide level a thousand years ago of 1.5 m or less above the present mean sea level.

For the purpose of the present study radiocarbon analyses of the bottom organic sediments from localities 1 to 8 were undertaken, in order to provide age determinations of the pollen material and in order to obtain information about the shore-line displacement during the last millennia.

The age of the bottom of Mosquito Pond provided clear evidence of the presence of a hiatus between inorganic and organic deposits, and therefore the locality had to be rejected for the purpose of constructing a shore-line displacement curve. The same was the case with the Pond between Ship Cove and Raleigh and with the locality c. 30 m East of House-site F.

The remaining five localities – W. Saddle Hill Pond, 32 m, Skin Pond, 20 m, Palsa Bog, 5.85 m (surface 6.5 m, cf. description of locality), L'Anse aux Meadows Pond, 3.9 m, and Straitsview Pond, 1.4 m above sea-level – were

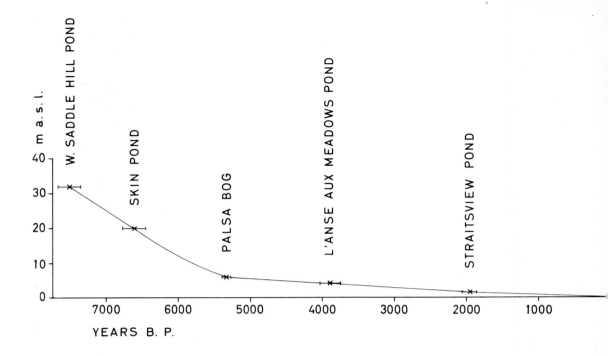

Fig. 13. Shore-level displacement curve.

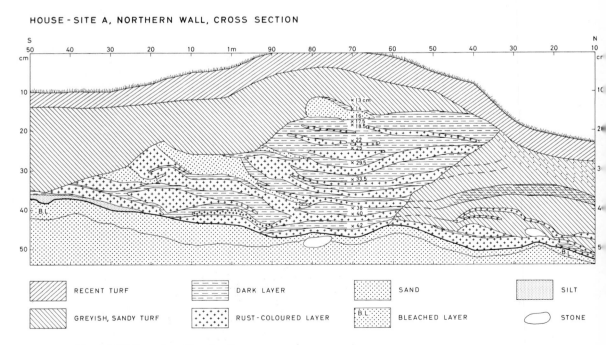

Fig. 14. Wall section. For details, see text.

328

used to construct the curve fig. 13. The radiocarbon dated material represents the organic layers deposited just after the isolation from the sea, and thus the indicated ages are minimum values for the isolation.

The localities were chosen primarily for the purpose of pollen analysis, and although the presence of rock thresholds was desirable, it was not crucial. Thus the elevation above sea-level is in most cases connected with more unstable thresholds, and the elevations must be considered as approximate values.

The curve gives only the main trend of the shore-line displacement in the area during the last 7500 years. There are few age determinations, and between the dated levels of the curve there is room for possible details not revealed by this investigation. The pronounced terrace 4 – 6 m above sea-level (cf. p. 290) is probably connected with the very slow regression which took place between c. 5400 and 3900 radiocarbon years B.P. A flattening of the curve, corresponding to the distinct upper terrace at 12 – 14 m level, might be expected, but does not appear from the evidence of this study, possibly as a result of too few fixed points on the curve at the height interval in question.

The curve shows a very slow regression during parts of the Postglacial time. Transgressions are not indicated, but can hardly be rejected as non-existent on the evidence of this study. More detailed information can only be obtained from further investigations.

One fact which is clearly evidenced, however, is that the sea-level during "Norse time" was not much higher than the present level. Judging from the curve, it was some $1/2$ to 1 m above today's sea-level: this would give the Norse ships somewhat better landing conditions than those obtaining today, but no better than in accordance with the shallow waters described in the sagas. The indicated sea-level also accords well with the position af the boat-shed sites found at the settlement, at almost 2 m above high water level measured on a calm summer day with low wave activity (cf. A.E. Christensen 1977, this volume).

One cannot, on the evidence of the present material, exclude the possibility of a hiatus near the transition marine/lacustrine (or telmatic) deposits in one or more of the series forming part of the background of this curve. If so, the real age of the organic bottom layers would be higher, and the curve would be lower than shown. In that case, the "Norse-time" sea-level may have been even more similar to the present level than assumed above.

The turf walls

The low walls of the houses were conspicuously stratified. Layers of dark turf alternated with lighter, sandy layers, and in some of the walls rust-coloured layers were very distinct. The walls had clearly been built by piling sods of various types of turf on top of one another. It was not possible to determine, however, whether or not the builders had used the method common in Iceland, where every other sod layer is turned upside down in building. (In Norway it is still common practice to construct turf roofs with two layers, the lower layer with the sods turned upside down.)

Sample series were collected from the northern and southern walls of house-site A, from the north-eastern wall of house-site F and from the wall dividing rooms I and III in house-site D. Pollen analyses were carried out on the first three of these series, and one radio-carbon age determination was made from each of the four.

The investigation of the layers showed that the wall material consisted predominantly of terrestric turf of various kinds, as was to be expected. The turf is generally rather highly humified, with or without more or less easily recognizable plant remains such as roots, rootlets, pieces of epiderms etc. Pollen preservation varied, from layers with no corrosion at all, to layers where practically nothing was left of the pollen exines. Obviously parts of the underlying sandy soil had adhered to the turf before it was cut, probably as a result of roots penetrating down into the mineral soil. Layers of sand, generally interspersed with plant roots, are frequently seen as parts of the wall material.

Fig. 14 is a cross-section of the northern wall of house-site A at $x = 12.4$, $y = 0$ in Ingstad's system of coordinates, showing the alternating layers. Being one of the best preserved house-walls at the site, it was sketched and used in an attempt to illustrate the appearance of the walls. The most conspicuous feature in this section was the great number of rust-coloured layers alternating with dark, turfy ones. The wall was underlain by sand with a weakly developed podzolization. The bleached sand layer was distinctly whitish grey, but the sand below was only slightly brownish, and no hardpan was observed.

In the north there was a distinct sloping limit between coloured layers and more greyish, weathered (?) parts of the wall. The coloured layers could be traced through parts of the greyish deposits, most clearly in the lowest-lying parts; this probably indicates a gradually decreasing degree of weathering towards the bottom of the wall. The wall has obviously subsided a great deal since it was in use, and the sloping limit in the north may indicate an incline in this direction.

The whole wall was overgrown by vegetation after the site had been abandoned; it is covered by a thick, turfy layer containing plant remains and considerable amounts of sand. The top 4 – 6 cm consist of a mat of fresh plant material, predominantly roots, evidently the recent turf.

In fig. 14 the same symbol is used for the greyish, weathered turf in the northern part of the wall as well as for the greyish, younger turf covering the

330

house-site, This was done because it was impossible to establish the limit between the two greyish turf types on the northern side of the wall.

As pointed out by Grant (1975), the spring floods of Black Duck Brook have a destructive effect on the site; at present this applies especially to house-site A, which is situated on the east bank of the brook, near the point where it cuts through the terrace. Flood deposits were found in this house-site during the excavation (cf. A.S. Ingstad 1970, and 1977, this volume), which is highly suggestive of the flood waters having found their way into at least parts of the house also during earlier times. The thick sand lenses in the south side of the wall are probably also a result of the flooding brook having invaded the house before the walls were overgrown by more recent vegetation. We do not know whether the Norsemen actually experienced such floods in the house.

The pollen sample series was collected through the central parts of the cross-section; pollen analysed samples are indicated by cross marks, and levels below the top of the present surface are given. The layers of the cross-section (fig. 14) were measured and drawn from the visual impression in the field, whereas the pollen sample series was microscopically investigated in greater detail as to type of material. Therefore it was possible to draw the stratigraphy column of the pollen diagram (fig. 15) with more details than was the case with the entire cross-section.

The investigation showed that the rusty parts were due to a ferrugineous precipitate occurring in varying quantities in the wall layers. Some of the most conspicuously coloured samples proved to contain very little organic material, and no pollen at all. The bulk of these samples was an amorphous-looking, rust-coloured material. Treatment with dithionite-citrate according to the method described by Mehra and Jackson (1960) dissolved this material completely, thus showing that it consisted of a precipitate of iron oxide compounds. The same treatment was also applied to several other samples with varying contents of coloured precipitate: in all cases, the rust-coloured part of the material disappeared, thus confirming the first results.

Thus the wall was obviously built of sods taken from an area where ferrugineous compounds were precipitated in the organic layers. Puustjärvi (1952) has investigated precipitation of iron in peat soils, and states that "The pH of the peat which contains an iron precipitate is at least 5.4 but usually over pH 5.5." He also finds that "As the oxygen content increases, the solubility of ferrous hydroxide decreases and vice versa." Consequently, one would consider oxygen-rich and slightly acid to alkaline environments essential to the presence of such ferrugineous precipitates. No vegetational observations – of present or past vegetation – refute the indicated pH values on minero-trophic localities at the site. The layers richest in precipitate (samples at 27, 32 and 34.5 cm) contain no pollen, and this accords well with the fact that

331

HOUSE - SITE A,
NORTHERN WALL

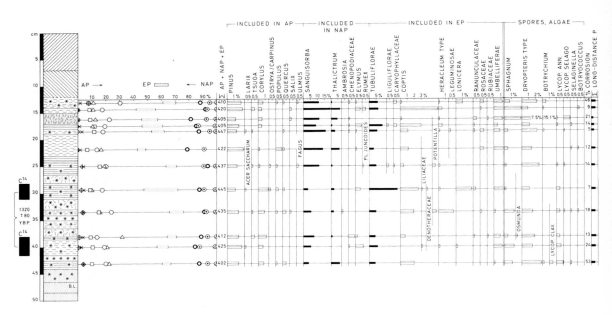

Fig. 15. Pollen diagram from the wall section in fig. 14. Legend, see fig. 2.

oxidation is one of the few chemical processes apt to destroy the pollen exines.

A present-day parallel to the suggested organic layers containing ferrugineous precipitates was found in living turf less than 50 m south of house-site A. The organic layers were nearly 30 cm thick here, and consisted of roots and other plant remains, with the amount of ferrugineous precipitate increasing downwards. The bottom layer, close to the mineral soil, consisted almost entirely of such precipitate. Nodules of bog ore (ill. in H. Ingstad, 1964) were found near this locality, in somewhat moister environments.

The presence of bog ore at the site today is quite evident, and the finds of slag lumps, the smithy etc. all provide strong evidence of such material having been at hand also during the time of the Norse settlement. (Cf. Cumming 1975.) The wall layers described above also provide support for the view that bog ore and similar compounds existed in the vicinity of the site when the Norsemen arrived. The ferrugineous precipitate was obviously present in turf and peat at the site, and was then deposited in the walls by pure chance, as part of the building material. As far as could be seen, it was most plentiful in the walls of house A, the house-site closest to the known occurrences of bog ore today, but smaller amounts of rust-coloured material have also been found in other house-walls, for instance in the sample series from house-site F.

A comparison of the chemical composition of the precipitate on the one hand, and of the slag lumps and iron fragments found at the site on the other, would have been highly desirable. But such analyses were out of the question, as the archaeological material had been returned to Canada when evidence of the ferrugineous character of the precipitate was found.

The pollen diagram from the northern wall of house-site A indicates that the wall material must have come from different habitats on and near the site. No remains of *Sphagnum* moss were found in these samples, and *Sphagnum* spores occur in very low percentages only. Arboreal pollen is present in varying amounts. Gramineae and Cyperaceae are well represented, indicating that the material is Gramineae/Cyperaceae turf, some of it with considerable quantities of *Sanguisorba canadense*, Tubuliflorae, *Coptis* and *Botrychium*. Corrosion percentages are very high in many of the samples, indicating oxygen-rich conditions.

The diagram (fig. 16) from the southern wall of the same house-site gives a similar impression. *Betula* pollen and fern spores dominate the bottom sample, *Myrica* and Tubuliflorae occur in quantity in another sample, while *Sanguisorba* is very well represented in a third.

The bottom sample of the house-site F series (diagram fig. 17) is dominated by AP, and it also contained small amounts of charcoal. This may represent the original, shrubby vegetation which was burnt before this wall was raised. The three following samples consist of highly humified Cyperaceae turf with no pollen corrosion, whereas the analysis of the upper sample shows a Gramineae turf with a higher degree of pollen corrosion.

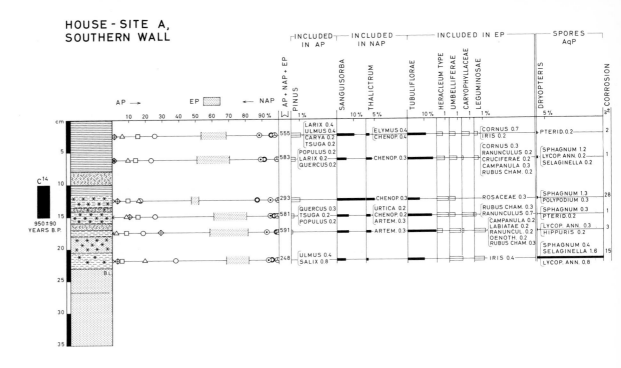

Fig. 16. Pollen diagram, House-site A. Legend, see fig. 2.

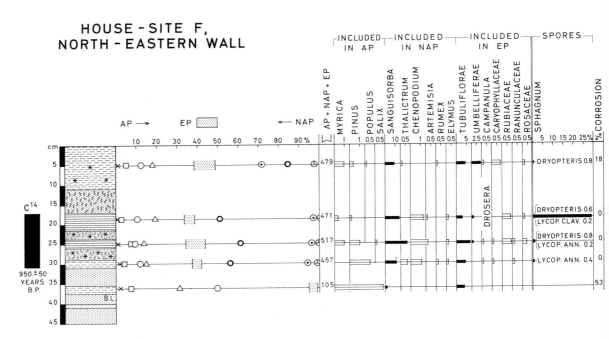

Fig. 17. Pollen diagram, House-site F. Legend, see fig. 2.

334

The more recent organic layers covering the house-sites have not been subjected to pollen analysis. In the diagram from the southern wall of house A they are not even indicated, as they had been removed prior to sampling for pollen analysis. In the house-site F series, the transition between more recent turf and genuine wall material was rather diffuse, and is not shown on the diagram. The uppermost pollen analysed sample is assumed to form part of the wall material.

The radiocarbon analysis of material from the southern wall of house-site A (T–530) yielded the result 950 ± 90 years B.P., almost identical with the age obtained at house-site F, 950 ± 50 years B.P. (T–531). These ages are slightly younger than one might have expected. As suggested by Kuc (1975), the dated material is likely to include material from the vegetation living at the time when the sods were cut and, in addition, considerable quantities of older, decomposed humus. The low age may have been caused by roots from more recent vegetation having penetrated downwards into the collapsed walls. All roots of any size were removed from the samples prior to radiocarbon dating, but smaller, younger rootlets may have remained and influenced the result of the analysis.

Two samples from the northern wall of house-site A were dated together, and their combined age, 1320 ± 80 years B.P. (T–818) is in better agreement with the age one might have expected. The same applies to the dated sample from house-site D, taken at 24 – 26 cm below the top of the wall (T–817), whose radiocarbon age is 1300 ± 70 years B.P.

There is every reason for assuming that the building material must have come from the immediate vicinity of the walls. Sods are heavy, and would certainly be cut as nearby as possible, so that they would not need to be transported over a long distance.

Thus the pollen analyses of the wall material provide information about the vegetation at and near the site at the time of the Norse habitation and/or the preceding centuries. The pollen spectra vary, indicating different habitats, but taken as a whole, they agree well with the other pollen diagrams from the site (localities 6, 7 and 8), and with the diagrams published by Mott (1975). They all indicate that the vegetation at the site during the Norse period did not differ much from that obtaining today.

Acknowledgements

First and foremost my thanks are due to Anne Stine and Helge Ingstad for giving me the opportunity to take part in the L'Anse aux Meadows investigations, and for helping me to have my field work financed. For unforgettable field days – in sunshine and rough weather – for collaboration and friendship, my sincere thanks.

I owe a number of persons a debt of gratitude for help during the preparation of this paper.

To Prof. Knut Fægri, Prof. Jul Låg, and not least to Dr. Anders Danielsen I am greatly indebted for valuable discussions and suggestions. Sincere thanks go to Dr. Kerstin O. Griffin for help with pollen analyses and seed determination, to Prof. Per Størmer and cand.real. Arne Pedersen for moss determinations, and to Dr. Bent Fredskild for help with pollen identifications. Further, my sincere thanks are due to University lecturer Karl-Dag Vorren for his investigation of samples from the Palsa Bog, in order to date the palsa formation, and to the late Curator Johannes Lid for help with identification of the plant material collected. I also want to express my thanks to the Radiological Dating Laboratory, Trondheim, and Dr. Reidar Nydal for carrying out the radiocarbon datings.

To my field assistants, Nicolay Eckhoff, Hans Hvide Bang, Job Anderson, and Sam Decker I owe my heartfelt thanks, and also to Mrs. Annin Rydning, Mrs. Leena Klaveness and Mrs. Gerd Torjussen, who helped me with preparation of samples and typing of manuscript, to Mrs. Kirsten Gran who drew the map and diagrams, and to Mr. Odd Brynildsrud and Miss Marit Moen for photography.

Last, but not least, I am grateful to Elizabeth Seeberg for her valuable help with the English text of my manuscript, and for her personal interest in the work.

LIST OF PLANT TAXA
Vascular plants
Abies – Fir
Abies balsamea – Balsam fir
Acer – Maple
Acer rubrum – Red or Scarlet maple
Acer saccharum – Sugar-or Rock-maple
Acer spicatum – Mountain maple
Achillea millefolium – Milfoil
Alnus – Alder
Alnus crispa – Green alder
Ambrosia – Ragweed
Amelanchier bartramiana – Mountain-juneberry
Andromeda glaucophylla – Bog-rosemary
Arenaria lateriflora – Grove-sandwort
Artemisia – Wormwood

Betula – Birch
Betula glandulosa – Dwarf birch
Betula michauxii – Newfoundland dwarf birch
Betula papyrifera – White or Paper-birch
Betula pumila – Low or Swamp-birch
Botrychium – Moonwort, Grapefern

Calamagrostis – Reed-bentgrass
Campanula – Bellflower
Campanula rotundifolia – Harebell, Bluebell
Capsella bursa-pastoris – Shepherd's purse
Carex – Sedge
Carex aquatilis – Species of sedge
Caryophyllaceae – Pink family
Carpinus – Hornbeam
Carya – Hickory
Castanea – Chestnut
Carum carvi – Caraway
Celtis – Hackberry
Chamaedaphne calyculata – Leather-leaf
Chenopodiaceae – Goosefoot family
Clintonia borealis – Corn-lily, Bluebead-lily
Coptis groenlandica – Canker-root
Cornus – Cornel
Cornus canadensis – Dwarf cornel
Cornus stolonifera – Red osier
Corylus – Hazel
Corylus cornuta – Beaked hazel
Cruciferae – Mustard family
Cyperaceae – Sedge family

336

Deschampsia – Hairgrass
Drosera – Sundew
Drosera rotundifolia – Round-leaved sundew
Dryopteris – Woodfern
Dryopteris spinulosa – Spinulose woodfern

Eleocharis – Spike-rush
Elymus arenarius var. *villosus* – *(E. mollis)* – Strand wheat, Sea lyme-grass
Empetrum – Crowberry
Equisetum – Horsetail
Equisetum silvaticum – Wood-horsetail
Ericales – Order including i.a. Heath family and Crowberry family
Eriophorum – Cotton-grass
Eriophorum spissum – Hare's tail
Euphrasia – Eyebright

Fagus – Beech
Festuca – Fescue-grass
Fragaria virginiana – Strawberry
Fraxinus – Ash
Fraxinus nigra – Black ash

Galium palustre – Marsh bedstraw
Gramineae – Grass family

Habenaria – Fringed or Rein-orchis
Heracleum – Cow-parsnip
Heracleum maximum – Masterwort
Hippuris – Mare's tail

Iris – Iris, Flag
Iris hookeri – Beachhead-iris or -flag

Juglans – Walnut
Juncus – Bog-rush
Juniperus – Juniper
Juniperus communis var. *depressa* – Ground-juniper
Juniperus horizontalis – Creeping savin

Kalmia angustifolia – Sheep-laurel, Lambkill
Kalmia polifolia – Bog-laurel

Labiatae – Mint family
Larix laricina – Tamarack, American or Black larch
Lathyrus japonicus – Beach-pea
Lathyrus palustris – Vetchling
Ledum groenlandicum – Labrador-tea
Leguminosae – Pulse family
Liguliflorae – Subfamily of Composite family
Liliaceae – Lily family
Linnaea – Twinflower
Lonicera villosa – Mountain-fly-honeysuckle
Luzula – Woodrush
Lycopodium – Club-moss
Lycopodium annotinum – Stiff or Bristly club-moss

Lycopodium clavatum – Common or Running club-moss
Lycopodium selago – Mountain- og Fir-club-moss

Menyanthes – Buckbean
Mertensia maritima – Oysterleaf, Sea-lungwort
Myrica gale – Sweet gale
Myriophyllum – Water-milfoil
Myriophyllum exalbescens – Species of water-milfoil

Najas flexilis – Naiad
Nuphar – Yellow pond-lily
Nymphaea – Water-lily
Nymphaeaceae – Water-lily family

Oenotheraceae – Evening-primrose family
Osmunda – Flowering fern, Interrupted fern, Cinnamon fern
Ostrya – Hop-hornbeam
Oxyria – Mountain-sorrel

Picea – Spruce
Picea glauca – White spruce
Picea mariana – Black spruce
Pinus – Pine
Pinus banksiana – Jack-pine
Pinus resinosa – Red pine
Pinus strobus – White pine
Plantago juncoides – Sea-side plantain
Plantago lanceolata – Ribgrass, Ribwort
Plantago major – Common plantain, Whiteman's foot
Poa – Meadow-grass
Polypodium – Polypody
Populus – Poplar, Aspen
Populus balsamifera – Balsam poplar
Populus tremuloides – Trembling aspen
Potamogeton – Pondweed
Potentilla – Cinquefoil, Five-finger
Potentilla anserina – Silverweed
Potentilla fruticosa – Shrubby cinquefoil
Potentilla palustris – Marsh-five-finger
Potentilla tridentata – Three-toothed cinquefoil
Primula – Primrose
Pteridium aquilinum – Bracken

Quercus – Oak

Ranunculaceae – Crowfoot family
Ranunculus – Crowfoot, Buttercup
Ranunculus acris – Common buttercup
Rhinanthus borealis – Yellow-rattle
Ribes – Currant, Gooseberry
Rosaceae – Rose family
Rubiaceae – Madder family
Rubus acaulis – Plumboy, Dwarf raspberry
Rubus chamaemorus – Cloudberry, Baked-apple

Rubus idaeus – Raspberry
Rumex – Sorrel, Dock
Rumex sect. *Acetosa* – Sorrel
Rumex acetosa – Garden-sorrel
Rumex acetosella – Sheep- or Common sorrel
Rumex domesticus – Dock
Rumex fenestratus – Species of dock
Rumex orbiculatus – Water-dock

Salix spp. –Willow
Sanguisorba canadensis – Canadian burnet
Sarracenia purpurea – Pitcher-plant
Saxifraga oppositifolia – Purple mountain-saxifrage
Scirpus – Bulrush
Scirpus caespitosus – Species of bulrush
Scirpus hudsonianus – Species of bulrush
Selaginella – Spikemoss
Shepherdia canadensis – Soapberry
Similacina trifolia – False Solomon's seal
Sorbus decora – Mountain-ash
Sparganium – Bur-reed
Stellaria media – Common chickweed

Thalictrum – Meadow-rue
Thalictrum alpinum – Alpine meadow-rue
Thalictrum polygamum – Muskrat-weed, Tall meadow-rue, King-of-the-meadow
Thlaspi arvense – Field-penny-cress
Thuja – Arbor vitae
Tilia – Linden, Basswood
Trientalis – Star-flower
Trifolium repens – White clover
Triglochin – Arrow-grass
Triglochin maritima – Sea arrow-grass
Tsuga – Hemlock
Tubuliflorae- Subfamily of Composite family
Typha angustifolia – Cat-tail

Ulmus – Elm
Ulmus americana – American elm
Umbelliferae – Parsley family
Urtica – Nettle

Vaccinium – Blueberry, Bilberry, Cranberry, Cowberry
Vaccinium angustifolium – Low sweet blueberry
Vaccinium oxycoccus – Small cranberry
Vaccinium uliginosum – Alpine bilberry
Vaccinium vitis-idaea – Mountain-cranberry, Cowberry, Lingen
Viburnum edule – Squashberry
Vitis – Grape

Bryophytes
Scorpidium scorpioides – Species of brown moss
Sphagnum – Peat moss
Sphagnum fuscum – Species of peat moss
Sphagnum lindbergii – Species of peat moss
Sphagnum majus – species of peat moss

Fungi
Helicosporium – Fungus spore (conidium)
Hymenoscyphus schimperi – Species of fungi
"*Tilletia*" – Fungus spore

Algae
Pediastrum – Genus of green algae
Botryococcus – Genus of Heterocontae
Cocconeis scutellum – Species of diatoms
Coscinodiscus – Genus of diatoms
Grammatophora oceanica – Species of diatoms
Rhabdonema arcuatum – Species of diatoms
"*Hystrix*" – cysts of dinoflagellates

Addendum: Animal taxa
Amphitrema – Genus of rhizopods
Assulina –Genus of rhizopods

References

Backman, A.L. 1935: Die nördlichsten Fossilfunde von *Najas flexilis* und *Carex pseudocyperus* in Finnland. Soc. Sci. Fenn. Commentat. Biol., 3.

Brown, R. J. E. 1968: Permafrost map of Canada. Can. Geogr. J., 76 No. 2.

Bryson, R. A. 1974: A perspective on climatic change. Science, 184, p. 753.

Christensen, A. E. 1977: Investigation of the boat-sheds. In: A. S. Ingstad: The Discovery of a Norse Settlement in America, Oslo.

Cumming, L. M. 1975: Geology of the L'Anse aux Meadows National Historic Park, northern Newfoundland. Geol. Surv. Can., Paper 75 – 1, Part A.

Daly, R. A. 1921: Post-Glacial warping of Newfoundland and Nova Scotia. Am. J. Sci. (5. Ser.), I No. 5.

Damman, A, W. H. 1965: The distribution patterns of northern and southern elements in the flora of Newfoundland. Rhodora, 67 No. 772.

Dansgaard, W., S. J. Johnsen, J. Møller 1969: One thousand centuries of climatic record from Camp Century on the Greenland ice sheet. Science, 166, p. 377.

Dansgaard, W., S. J. Johnsen, N. Reeh, N. Gundestrup, H. B. Clausen & C. U. Hammer 1975: Climatic changes, Norsemen and modern man. Nature, 255, May I 1975.

Denton, G. H. and W. Karlén 1973: Holocene climatic variations – their pattern and possible cause. Quaternary Research, 3.

Eckblad, F.-E. 1975: *Tilletia sphagni, Helotium schimperi,* or what? Pollen et Spores, 17 No. 3.

Einarsson, Th. 1963: Pollen-analytical studies on the vegetation and climate history of Iceland in Late and Post-Glacial times. In: A. and D. Løve (Eds.): North Atlantic Biota and their History. Oxford.

Fægri, K. & J. Iversen 1964: Textbook of Pollen Analysis (Second edition). Copenhagen.

Fernald, M. L. 1910: Notes on the plants of Wineland the Good. Rhodora, 12 No. 134.

Fernald, 1950: Gray's Manual of Botany (Eighth edition). New York.

Flint, R. F. 1940: Late Quaternary changes of level in western and southern Newfoundland. Geol. Soc. Am. Bull., 51 No. 11.

Fredskild, B. 1967: Palaeobotanical investigations at Sermermiut, Jakobshavn, West Greenland. Medd. Grønland, 178 No. 4.

Fredskild 1973: Studies in the vegetational history of Greenland. Medd. Grønland, 198 No. 4.

Gillis, J. W. 1966: Great Northern Peninsula. Geol. Surv. Can., Paper 66–1.

Grant, D. R. 1970: Surficial deposits, geomorphic features, and late Quaternary history of the terminus of the Northern Peninsula of Newfoundland and adjacent Quebec-Labrador. Maritime Sediments, 5 No. 3.

Grant, D. R. 1972: Postglacial emergence of northern Newfoundland. Geol. Surv. Can., Paper 72–1, Part B.

Grant D. R. 1975: Surficial geology and sea-level changes, L'Anse aux Meadows National Historic Park, Newfoundland. Geol. Surv. Can., Paper 75–1, Part A.

Hadden, K. A. 1975: A pollen diagram from a postglacial peat bog in Hants County, Nova Scotia. Can. J. Bot., 53 No. 1.

Hare, F. K. 1952: The climate of the island of Newfoundland: A geographical analysis. Can. Dep. Mines Tech. Surv., Geogr. Bull. No 2.

Hultén, E. 1958: The amphi-atlantic plants. K. Sven. Vetenskapsakad. Handl., 4. Ser., 7 No. 1.

Ingstad, A. S. 1970: The Norse settlement at L'Anse aux Meadows, Newfoundland. A preliminary report from the excavations 1961 – 1968. Acta Archaeol. 41.

Ingstad, A.S. 1977: The Discovery of a Norse Settlement in America. Oslo.

Ingstad, H. 1964: Vinland ruins prove Vikings found in the New World. Natl. Geogr. Mag. 126 No. 5.

Ingstad H. 1965: Vesterveg til Vinland, Oslo.

Iversen, J. 1934: Moorgeologische Untersuchungen auf Grönland. Medd. Dan. Geol. Foren., 8 H. 4.

Jenness, S. E. 1960: Late Pleistocene glaciation of eastern Newfoundland. Geol. Soc. Am. Bull., 71.

Kuc, M. 1975: Paleoecological investigations of the Norse settlement site at L'Anse aux Meadows, Newfoundland. Geol. Surv. Can., Paper 75–1, Part A.

Lamb, H. H. 1965: The early medieval warm epoch and its sequel. Palaeogeogr., Palaeoclimatol, Palaeoecol., 1.

Leopold, E. B. 1956: Pollen size-frequency in New England species of the genus *Betula.* Grana Palynol., 1 No. 2.

Lichti-Federovich, S. and J. C. Ritchie 1968: Recent pollen assemblages from the Western Interior of Canada. Rev. Palaeobot. Palynol., 7.

Livingstone, D. A. 1968 Some interstadial and postglacial pollen diagrams from eastern Canada. Ecol. Monogr., 38.

Mehra, O. P. and M. L. Jackson 1960: Iron oxide removal from soils and clays by a dithionite-citrate system buffered with sodium bicarbonate. In: Clays and Clay Minerals. Proc. 7th Natl. Conf. Clays and Clay Minerals, Wash. D. C. 1958. Int. Ser. Monogr. Earth Sci., 5, London.

Miller, G. H. 1973: Late Quaternary glacial and climatic history of northern Cumberland Peninsula, Baffin Island, N. W. T., Canada. Quaternary Research, 3 No. 4.

Mott, R. J. 1975: Palynological studies of peat monoliths from L'Anse aux Meadows Norse site, Newfoundland. Geol. Surv. Can., Paper 75–1, Part A.

Native Trees of Canada (Sixth edition), 1963: Can. Dep. For. Bull. 61.

Nichols, H. 1969 a: Chronology of peat growth in Canada. Palaeogeogr., Palaeoclimatol., Palaeoecol., 6.

Nichols, H. 1969 b: The late Quaternary history of vegetation and climate at Porcupine Mountain and Clearwater Bog, Manitoba. Arctic and Alpine Research, 1 No. 3.

Nydal, R. 1977: Radiocarbon dating of material from L'Anse aux Meadows, Newfoundland. In A.S. Ingstad: The Discovery of a Norse Settlement in America. Oslo.

Nydal, R., K. Løvseth, and O. Syrstad 1970: Trondheim natural radiocarbon measurements V. Radiocarbon, 12 no. 1.

Nydal, R. S. Gulliksen, K. Løvseth 1972: Trondheim natural radiocarbon measurements VI. Radiocarbon, 14 no. 2.

Paulssen, L. M. 1977: Identification of charcoal finds. In: A. S. Ingstad: The Discovery of a Norse Settlement in America. Oslo.

Pedersen, A. 1976: Najadaceer, Potamogetonaceer, Ruppiaceer, Zannichelliaceer, Zosteraceer i Danmark. Bot. Tidsskr., 70 H. 4.

Pollett, F. C. 1972: Classification of peatlands in Newfoundland. In: Virgin peatlands. Proc. 4th Int. Peat Congr., Otaniemi, Finland, 1972, 1.

Pollett, F. C. and P. B. Bridgewater 1973: Phytosociology of peatlands in central Newfoundland. Can. J. For. Res., 3.

Potzger, J. E. 1953: Nineteen bogs from southern Quebec. Can. J. Bot., 31 No. 4.

Potzger, J. E. and A. Courtemanche 1956: A series of bogs across the St. Lawrence valley to James Bay. Can. J. Bot., 34 No. 4.

Puustjärvi, V. 1952: The precipitation of iron in peat soils. Acta Agral. Fenn., 78.

Rosenqwist, A. M. 1977: Material investigations. In: A. S. Ingstad: The Discovery of a Norse Settlement in America. Oslo.

Rowe, J. S. 1959: Forest regions of Canada. Can. Dep. North. Aff. Natl. Resour., For. Branch, Bull. 123.

Samuelsson, G. 1934: Die Verbreitung der höheren Wasserpflanzen in Nordeuropa. Acta Phytogeogr. Suec., 6.

Sandegren, R. 1920: *Najas flexilis* i Fennoscandia under postglacialtiden. Sven. Bot. Tidsk., 14.

Sandegren, R. 1932: Einige neue Funde von fossilen *Najas flexilis* in Schweden. Abh. Naturwiss. Ver., Bremen, 28.

Schneider, R. 1974: Vergleich der Bohrmethoden Hiller und Livingstone. Pollen et Spores, 16 no. 4.

Temperature and Precipitation 1941 – 1970. Atmos. Environ. Serv., Dep. Environ., Can.

Terasmae, J. 1963: Three C-14 dated pollen diagrams from Newfoundland, Canada. Adv. Front. Plant Sci., 6.

Terasmae, J. 1967: Recent pollen deposition in the northeastern District of Mackenzie (Northwest Territories, Canada). Palaeogeogr., Palaeoclimatol., Palaeoecol., 3.

Terasmae, J. and R. J. Mott 1965: Modern pollen deposition in the Nichicun Lake area, Quebec. Can. J. Bot., 43.

The Climate of Newfoundland. Can. Dep. Transp., Meteorol. Branch, 1964.

Thorarinsson, S. 1958: Iceland in the Saga period. Mus. Nat. Hist., Dep. Geol. Geogr. Misc. Pap.No. 21.

Vorren, K.-D. 1972: Stratigraphical investigations of a palsa bog in Northern Norway. Astarte, 5, Nos. 1–2.

Wendland, W. M. and R. A. Bryson 1974: Dating climatic episodes of the Holocene. Quaternary Research, 4.

Wenner, C.- G. 1947: Pollen diagrams from Labrador. Geogr. Ann., 29.

Williams, H., W. R. Smyth, and R. K. Stevens 1973: Hare Bay allochton, northern Newfoundland. Geol. Surv. Can., Paper 73–1.

Radiocarbon Dating of Material from L'Anse aux Meadows, Newfoundland

BY REIDAR NYDAL

Introduction

The first question concerning the radiocarbon dating of material from L'Anse aux Meadows was received by the Radiological Dating Laboratory in Trondheim in July 1961. At that time the Ingstad expedition has just started to excavate a settlement site which was assumed to be of Norse origin, and to date from about A.D. 1000. The first sample received (T–306) consisted of charcoal from a cooking pit in a house-site (House B, A.S. Ingstad, 1970). The dating of this charcoal was completed in August 1961, and the preliminary result of A.D. 650 $\pm$ 100 was sent to the expedition by telegram. This preliminary result, which was corrected to A.D. 740 $\pm$ 110 after a spectrometric analysis had subsequently been performed, seemed rather early, but was sufficiently interesting to stimulate further excavation. In the course of the following months, and during several seasons of excavation, more material was dated, and the programme of dating was finished in December 1965. Sixteen samples had then been dated, thirteen of them consisting of charcoal from various hearths and cooking pits, two of turf from a wall, while one was a sample of whale bone (fig. 1). The whale bone (St–2665) was dated at the Radioactive Dating Laboratory in Stockholm.

Important works dealing with the accuracy of the radiocarbon dating method have appeared during recent years, and as a result we are now able to undertake corrections of the dates assigned to the Newfoundland samples. Fortunately these corrections only slightly changed (10–30 years) the dates already published (A.S. Ingstad, 1970; Radio-carbon, 1970, pp. 221–227). In the present paper we intend to describe the dating procedure and also to discuss the possible correlation between the radio-carbon age and the assumed historical age, which is based on the Icelandic sagas.

Pretreatment of samples

Two samples of turf (T–530 and T–531), classified as *gyttja* in the date list, (Nydal et al., 1970) were boiled with 1M HCl in order to remove any possible contamination of carbonate in the sample. The samples were further boiled

341

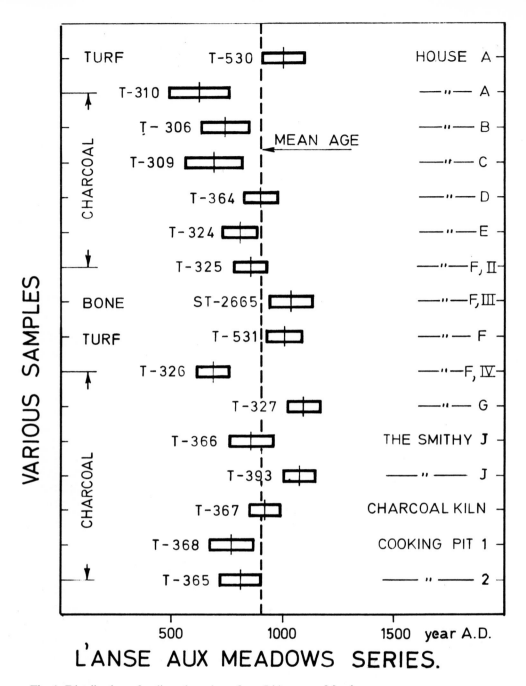

Fig. 1. Distribution of radiocarbon dates from L'Anse aux Meadows.

Table 1

Samples	Previous dates Years A.D.	Corrected dates (Damon et al., 1972) years A.D.	Corrected dates (Ralph et al., 1973) years A.D.
T–530	1000 ± 90	1020 ± 100	1020 ± 100
T–310	640 ± 130	670 ± 140	660 ± 140
T–306	740 ± 110	760 ± 120	(760–730) ± 120
T–309	710 ± 130	740 ± 140	(730–700) ± 140
T–364	900 ± 70	920 ± 80	940 ± 80
T–324	820 ± 70	850 ± 80	850 ± 80
T–325	870 ± 70	900 ± 80	910 ± 80
St.–2665	1025 ± 100	1040 ± 110	1040 ± 110
T–531	1000 ± 50	1020 ± 60	1020 ± 60
T–326	700 ± 70	730 ± 80	(720–700) ± 80
T–327	1080 ± 70	1090 ± 80	1090 ± 80
T–366	860 ± 90	890 ± 100	(910–890) ± 100
T–393	1060 ± 70	1080 ± 80	1070 ± 80
T–367	820 ± 70	850 ± 80	850 ± 80
T–368	780 ± 90	820 ± 100	(820–800) ± 100
T–365	810 ± 90	840 ± 100	(850–830) ± 100

in distilled water, and then dried. After combustion to CO_2, the CO_2 gas was dissolved in ammonia, and precipitated as $CaCO_3$. The precipitated $CaCO_3$ was washed and dried before further combustion to CO_2 by acid treatment. The purification process via $CaCO_3$ was necessary in order to remove completely all traces of SO_2 which appeared in the CO_2 gas after the primary combustion. Even very slight traces of SO_2 severely reduce the sensitivity of the counter used for dating.

Charcoal has the property of being able to withstand drastic chemical treatment applied in order to remove various organic contamination. Most of the thirteen charcoal samples submitted contained rootlets. The larger fragments of charcoal from each sample were selected for dating. All visible rootlets were carefully picked out, and the surface of the charcoal fragments was cleaned mechanically. After this, the charcoal was crushed and examined for enclosed rootlets and then boiled with 1M HC1 in order to remove any possible carbonate fraction of contamination, and with 1M NaOH in order to remove introduced humic acid, peat and other soluble organic compounds. Afterwards the samples were treated with HC1, washed and dried, before combustion to CO_2. No further treatment was applied as the CO_2 was found to be completely pure without passing through a calcium carbonate stage.

Calculation and measurements

The principle of radiocarbon dating derives from Libby (W. F. Libby, 1955), who postulated and partly verified that the concentration of radioactive C^{14}

atoms in living organisms is nearly constant all over the world, and has only shown slight variation during several thousands of years. Libby based his assumption on the fact that C^{14} is generated by the cosmic rays in the atmosphere. He assumed that the intensity of the cosmic rays had been fairly constant for many thousands of years, and consequently also production rate of C^{14}. An equilibrium between production and disintegration of C^{14} in nature was thus established far beyond the maximum age limit for the C^{14} dating method. In living plants, the uptake of C^{14} occurs by way of photosynthesis, and after death, a pure decay of the C^{14} atoms takes place. In other living organims, the uptake of C^{14} occurs through vegetative food. According to the law of radioactivity, the number of C^{14} atoms (dN) which decay during each time unit (dx) is proportional (λ) to the number (N) of C^{14} atoms present, and thus $dN/dx = -\lambda N$.

This simple first order differential equation has the solution

$$(1) \qquad N = N_0 e^{-\lambda x}$$

This formula can be applied only from the moment when death occurs in a living organism. N_0 is the C^{14} concentration when death occured, and N is the concentration at a later time x. In practice we are measuring radioactive intensities I_0 and I (number of radioactive atoms which decay during each time unit) in living and dead organic material respectively. I_0 and I are proportional to the C^{14} concentrations in the samples, and thus we obtain the time formula:

$$(2) \qquad x = \frac{I}{\lambda} \cdot \ln\left(\frac{I_0}{I}\right)$$

Where ln = natural logarithm.

Instead of applying the decay constant λ, it is more convenient to use the halflife T, which is defined as the time during which an intensity (I_0) is reduced to one half. If we replace I by $I_0/2$ for x = T in the above formula, the decay constant (λ) is expressed by the halflife ($\lambda = \ln2/T$), and the formula is changed to.

$$(3) \qquad x = \frac{T}{0.69} \cdot \ln\left(\frac{I_0}{I}\right)$$

According to this formula, the age before present (B.P.) of a sample can be determined if we know the halflife of C^{14} (T), the radioactive intensity (I_0) of a living organism, and the intensity (I) of a dead organism. The previously published dates from Newfoundland (Radiocarbon, 1970) were calculated according to the Libby halflife of 5570 years. The C^{14} intensity I_0, which represents the normal radioactivity in a living organism in the year A.D. 1950, is measured in a sample from an NBS oxalic acid standard. This activity is based on nineteenth-century wood, and has been corrected for age up to A.D. 1950.

344

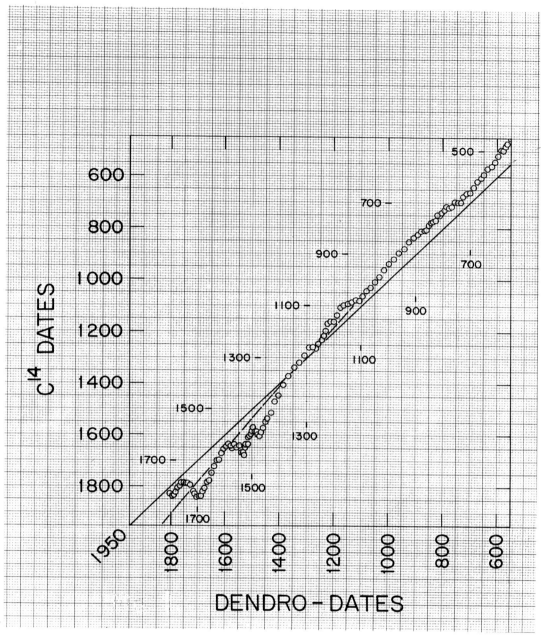

Fig. 2. C¹⁴ calibration curve (kindly provided by Elisabeth K. Ralph, University of Penn-sylvania).

——— (full curve) corrected agreement between C¹⁴ dates and Dendro-dates (A.D. scale).

– – – Measured agreement.

The main work involved in dating samples is concerned with measuring the C^{14} activity (I) of the unknown samples. The samples from Newfoundland were measured in one of two CO_2 proportional counters which were in operation during the period in question (Nydal,1962; and Nydal,1965). Counter 2 was built in September 1958. It was considerably improved in 1962, and the working conditions were very stable for most of the time when the datings of material from Newfoundland were performed. This counter, which is capable of dating samples back to 50,000 years, had in 1962 an effective volume of 1.2 litres, background and recent standard net count of 1.1 counts/min and 16.0 counts/min respectively. The counter worked at 2 atmospheres CO_2, and a sample amount of about 2 g pure carbon was required for each measurement. Eight samples (T–306, 309, 310, 324, 325, 326, 327, 531) were measured in counter 2. The seven other samples were measured in counter 3. This counter was put into operation in 1962, with effective volume (1.1 litres) slightly smaller than that of counter 2. Background and recent standard net count were 3.3 counts/min and 14.2 counts/min respectively.

The limit of error given for all dates is one standard deviation (1σ) which is calculated from the counting statistics. The limit of error in the halflife ($\pm$ 30 years) is not included in this result. It appeared that the samples dated in 1961 (T–306, 309 and 310) had greater limits of error than the other samples, due to the fact that they had been dated before an improvement of the counting apparatus. The age of all samples except T–393 and St–2665 was corrected for fractionation error based on measurement of the C^{13}/C^{12} ratio in the samples. These measurements, which were carried out by Ragnar Ryhage, K.T.H., Stockholm, show whether there is a normal ratio between the carbon isotopes in the samples. In three cases, the corrections amounted to more than 50 years, but in all others they were less.

The method of dating samples by radiocarbon analysis has the disadvantage that it does not yield an exact age. A limit of error is always included, and consequently the age is given not as an exact figure, but within a range with a certain degree of probability. Very often it is extremely difficult to decide whether one sample is older than another, or whether they are equal in age. In fig. 3 the dating of two samples is illustrated by histograms. These two samples were selected because they represent the two extremes of age among the material investigated. For these histograms the age of the two samples was calculated for sixteen counting periods, each with a counting time of one hour. The height of the columns in the histograms represents the number of dates found in the respective age intervals. It will be seen that both these histograms tend to agree with a normal distribution, and that the age is to be found with the highest degree of probability around the middle of the histograms, where the columns are highest.

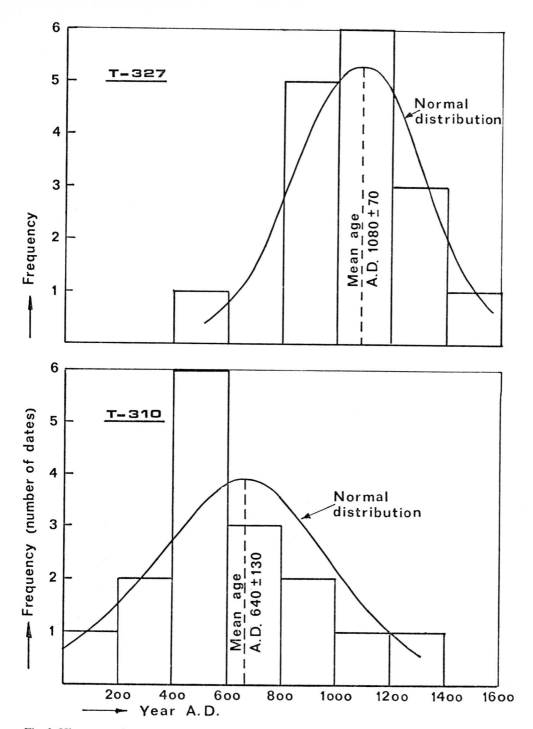

Fig. 3. Histograms from radiocarbon dating of samples T-310 and T-327.

The mean age ($\bar{x}$) and the standard deviation (σ) of the mean are, respectively, found according to the following formuae:

$$(4) \quad \bar{x} = \frac{x_1 + x_2 + \ldots x_k}{k}$$

and

$$(5) \quad \sigma^2 = \frac{(x_1-\bar{x})^2 + (x_2-\bar{x})^2 \ldots + (x_k-\bar{x})^2}{k(k-1)}$$

where k is the number of dates, and x_1, x_2 ... represent the individual measurements. If the age is given with a limit of error of $\pm$ 1σ, the probability that the age is to be found within these limits, amounts to 68%. If the age is given with $\pm$ 2σ there is a 95% probability that the age will fall within these limits.

The age distributions shown in fig.2 yield the following mean age of the samples:

T–310: x = A.D.640 $\pm$ 130 years
T–327: y = A.D.1080 $\pm$ 70 years

Now the question arises whether these samples really differ in age or not. For this purpose we use Student's t statistics (Spiegel, 1961, pp.189–190), and apply the formula

$$(6) \quad t = \frac{\bar{y} - \bar{x}}{\sqrt{\sigma_x{}^2 + \sigma_y{}^2}}$$

where σ_x and σ_y represent the standard deviation for the respective measurements.

Substituting the dates for T–310 and T–327 in the above formula, we obtain t = 3.0. According to a t-distribution table we find that the probability of the samples really differing in age amounts to 99%. This is a convincing degree of probability, and the divergence may be ascribed to the use of firewood differing in age.

The difference in age between various other samples is not equally convincing. If, for instance, we compare the ages of the two charcoal samples, T–366 and T–393, which derive from the same building, (Smithy, house-site J, fig.1):

T–366: Age A.D. 860 $\pm$ 90 years
T–393: Age A.D.1060 $\pm$ 70 years

we find that the probability of sample T–366 being older than sample T–393 amounts to only 80%. In this case we are less certain that T–366 really is older than T–393.

Further corrections of data

When the radiocarbon dating conference was held in Cambridge in 1962, there had for several years been some doubt about the accuracy of the Libby halflife of $5570 + 30$ years. At the conference, three new values of the halflife were presented (Godwin, 1962). A combination of these led to the new halflife of $5730 + 40$ years, which was in 1962 accepted as the best obtainable value. At the Cambridge conference it was decided to continue the use of the old halflife until further studies not only of the halflife, but also of other uncertainties concerning radiocarbon dating, have been performed. As a result, all dates published are calculated according to the Libby halflife, and are thus slightly too young. Dates given in the B.P. scale can be multiplied by a factor of 1.03 for purposes of correction. Thus samples dated to around A.D. 1000 should in fact be about 30 years older.

The situation in 1975 is this: the new halflife of $5730 + 40$ years is the best value available, but the old halflife is still used for purposes of radiocarbon dating. The study of other sources of error has progressed considerably since 1962. For several years a number of scientists, such as Hans E. Suess, University of California, La Jolla (H.E. Suess, 1970), Paul E. Damon, University of Arizona (P.E. Damon et al., 1972), and Elizabeth K. Ralph, University of Pennsylvania (E. K. Ralph et al., 1973), have been working on an important project, relating dendrochronological dates to C^{14} measurements. The principal material for their studies is the bristlecone pine found on The White Mountains, on the border between California and Nevada. Some of these trees have lived for more than 4000 years. A calibration curve going back to about 8000 years B.P. has been established, showing that the assumed constant C^{14} activity (I_0) in fact varied somewhat with time during different periods. There are at least three sources for this variation, the main source being the variation in the magnetic field of the earth (H.E. Suess, 1970). As the magnetic field has a deflecting influence on the cosmic rays, any variation in the magnefic field must result in a variation of the C^{14} production in the atmosphere.

The calibration curve in fig.2, showing the correspondence between the C^{14} age (based on the new halflife) and the treering age, was kindly made available by Elizabeth K. Ralph, University of Pennsylvania. This curve, which covers the last 2000 years, clearly shows how the C^{14} dates, when calculated according to a halflife of $5730 + 40$ years, are too old during the period A.D.600 to A.D.1200. The reason for this is that the C^{14} concentration in the atmosphere was lower than normal during this period. As regards the Newfoundland samples, we are now able to make corrections for the halflife (T) as well as for the recent standard (I_0). Referring to formula (3), we find that these corrections are opposed to each other: the new halflife makes the

349

samples older (about 30 years), while the correction of recent activity (I_0) makes them younger (about 50 years).

In Table 1 we show all the dates corrected according to two independent correction tables (E.K. Ralph et al., 1973; P. Damon et al., 1972), which are in close agreement with each other. Corrections are very small, and may well be omitted when individual samples are being discussed. The mean value of the series is, however, corrected in the final section of this paper, where the agreement between radiocarbon and historical age is discussed. We use the correction table given by Damon et.al. (1972) for this purpose.

Systematic error in the samples

Trees grow in such a way that a new outer cylinder of wood is annually added in the layer of growth. The number of cylinders – the tree rings – act as a calender showing how long the tree has been growing. The rings are more pronounced at high latitudes, where the climate is marked by distinct seasonal variations.

It has been verified that the radiocarbon assay for each ring approximately represents the atmospheric activity of the year during which the ring was formed. The outer rings date the last growth preceding the death of the tree. When dating periods of human history, we therefore try to select the outer rings of the wooden material, hoping that the tree was cut shortly before being used by man. It is also of importance that one should ascertain whether the sample in question derives from young trees, twigs or branches, as the time of growth for such material certainly must be relatively small. While errors introduced by dating inner rings of trees normally constitute only a few decades, experience in radiocarbon dating shows that the most serious source of error when dating wood is the possible lapse of time between the death of the tree and its application by man. Material other than contemporary wood may well have been employed: it may have been of sub-fossil origin, or it may have been taken from an older building. Massive beams, we know, were often re-used (Godwin, 1969). As regards the use of sub-fossil wood, it is a fact that the Lapps of Swedish Lappland still prefer dry fir for their camp fires today (G. Östlund and L. Engstrand, 1960). In such cases the C^{14} age may be hundreds or even thousands of years greater than the time when the camp fire was lit.

For dating purposes, charcoal derived from wood has all the limitations of wood, but in addition it is usually impossible to ascertain whether the charcoal fragments found in hearths derive from the outer or the inner part of a tree. Tree-analysis based on charcoal is often very useful in order to exclude species with a long life-time, or particularly resistant to bacterial action. As the

350

majority of the Newfoundland samples consist of charcoal, all these possible sources of error affect the question of how accurately they date the settlement at L'Anse aux Meadows. Does most of the charcoal derive from trees cut by the settlers, or does it mainly derive from driftwood? Helge Ingstad states that there is driftwood to be found everywhere along the coast. He points out that Épaves Bay at L'Anse aux Meadows is a typical driftwood bay where driftwood would accumulate in great quantities (comment by Helge Ingstad, Radiocarbon, 1970).

The Labrador Current is mainly responsible for the transport of driftwood along the coast in this region. This current flows southward along the coast of Labrador, and when it reaches the northern point of Newfoundland, it is divided into two parts. One part flows through the Strait of Belle Isle, passing L'Anse aux Meadows, and along the west coast of Newfoundland. The other part turns east along the coast, and after passing the southern point of Newfoundland it turns north, flowing along the west coast until it meets the other current. The action of the current and of winds may bring wood from both northern and southern regions to L'Anse aux Meadows. A series of tree-analyses of the charcoal samples, carried out by Leif M. Paulssen, Institute of Pharmacy, University of Oslo, is of great importance in this connection (Table 2). He also discussed the posible origin of various trees (Hough, 1965; Native trees of Canada, 1950). The analyses were performed on excess material from the charcoal samples used for dating, and they show a mixture of various species of trees in each sample. It thus seems likely that this should apply also to the material used for dating.

Paulssen studied 636 fragments of charcoal from L'Anse aux Meadows: 62.7% of these derived from conifers, 35.7% from deciduous trees and 1.6% from shrubs. Of these, 268 fragments, all deriving from conifers, were either in too poor a condition or too small in size to permit of identification. Of the remaining 368 fragments, which include many deciduous trees, 90% were identified; 85% of these derive from trees still growing in Newfoundland today. However, one of the conifers identified *(Pinus strobus)*, which accounts for only a small percentage of the total, is found only in the southern part of Newfoundland, at a considerable distance from L'Anse aux Meadows. The deciduous trees included a small fraction of *Tilia* and *Quercus,* species which apparently grow no closer to L'Anse aux Meadows than Nova Scotia. The presence of these three species, *Tilia, Quercus* and *Pinus strobus,* is convincing proof of the use of driftwood for fuel here. As the tree analysis was performed on the material which remained after fragments had been selected for purposes of dating, it cannot be employed as a direct criterium for judging any possible systematic errors in the dating. A few comments may, however, be made.

Among the deciduous trees, a large fraction of *Betula* was identified. *Betula* has a normal life-time of maximum 60 years, and decomposes quickly, even in a cool climate. Consequently, the systematic error in dating charcoal from *Betula* must be small, and therefore it is relatively unimportant whether the *Betula* identified represents driftwood, or trees cut by the settlers. As concerns several of the other trees identified from the charcoal fragments, varying systematic errors may be expected, although it is reasonable to assume that smaller trees and branches should have been preferred as fuel. The storage time of driftwood on the shore, however, is still a highly uncertain source of error.

Table 2.
(Prepared by Leif M. Paulssen)

Deciduous trees	Nearest locality	CONIFERS		Nearest locality
Betula 42.0%	Newfoundland	Larix laricina	8.5%	Newfoundland
Alnus 16.0%	Newfoundland	Picea mariana	8.0%	Newfoundland
Salix 2.0%	Newfoundland	Abies balsamea	7.5%	Newfoundland
Populus 1.5%	Newfoundland	Pinus strobus	2.0%	(southern part)
Ulmus 0.3%	(southern part)	Unknown:		
Tilia 0.3%	Nova Scotia	Group 1	6.0%	
Quercus 0.3%	Nova Scotia	Group 2	2.5%	
		Group 3	1.0%	
Shrubs 2.5%		Group 4	0.3%	

Possible agreement between the radiocarbon age and the historical age

The histogram fig.4 shows a compilation of all the sixteen C^{14} dates obtained from L'Anse aux Meadows. These dates do not have equal standard deviations, and therefore it is necessary to calculate a weighted mean value for the age. The dates are thus given weights (p_k), according to their standard deviation $p_k = 1/\sigma_k^2$, and the mean value (x) and the standard deviation of the mean (σ) are calculated according to the formulas:

$$(7) \quad \bar{x} = \frac{p_1 x_1 + p_2 x_2 + \ldots + p_k x_k}{p_1 + p_2 + \ldots + p_k}$$

and

$$(8) \quad \sigma^2 = \frac{p_1(x_1 - \bar{x})^2 + p_2(x_1 - \bar{x})^2 + \ldots + p_k(x_k - \bar{x})^2}{N(N-1)}$$

352

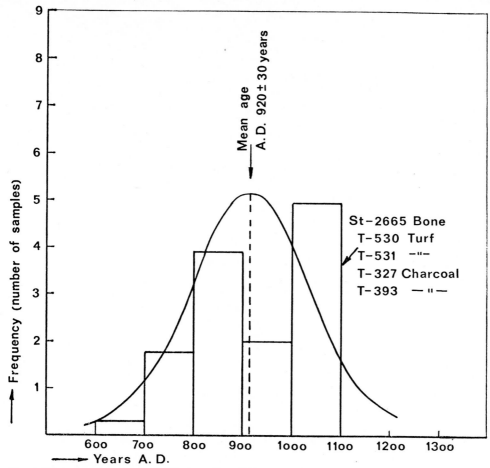

Fig. 4. Histogram based on 16 C^{14} dates from L'Anse aux Meadows.

where $N = p_1 + p_2 + \ldots + p_k$, and k represents the number of samples (k=16). Samples with a greater limit of error will contribute less than other samples to the heights of the columns in the diagram, and also to the mean value of all the samples.

The calculated mean age of all the samples is A.D.920 + 30, a very slight change from the previously obtained result (A.D. 910 + 20, Radiocarbon, 1970). If all samples were free from systematic error, they would point to the same age, thus giving a normal distribution. It is therefore of interest to see how well the histogram reflects such a distribution. For this purpose we use a chi-square test (Spiegel, 1961, p.20), thus calculating

$$(9) \quad \chi^2 = \frac{(o_1-e_1)^2}{e_1} + \frac{(o_2-e_2)^2}{e_2} + \ldots + \frac{(o_r-e_r)^2}{e_r}$$

where o and e are, respectively,– observed and estimated frequency derived from the diagram (fig.4), and r is the number of columns (r=5), The value obtained for χ^2 is 3.5. Referring to a χ^2 distribution table (Spiegel, 1961, p.345), we find that the accordance between a normal distribution and the histogram is only 50%. One weakness of this calculation is that the frequency in each column is rather low. However, we have reason to believe that some of the samples yield systematic errors which upset a more normal distribution. We are here referring to the tall column which appears just above A.D.1000 in the histogram. This column includes 2 samples of turf (T–530 and T–531), a sample of whale bone (St–2665) and two samples of charcoal (T–327 and T–393). We must bear in mind the possibility that we are here dealing with two groups of samples, differing in age; this difference may well be due to the presence of driftwood.

According to the histogram, however, there is little evidence indicating that we should have dated charcoal with a systematic error of several centuries. We would suggest that the mean systematic error for the entire series of charcoal samples is not very great, hardly more than 50–100 years.

The radiocarbon age (x = A.D.920) and the assumed historical age (m = A.D.1000) can be compared satisfactorily when a t-statistics (Spiegel 1961) is applied, according to the formula

$$(10) \quad t = \frac{m-\bar{x}}{\sigma_x}$$

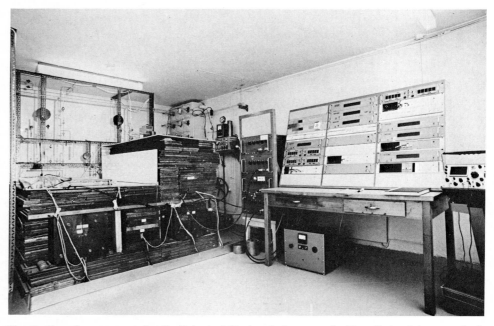

Fig. 5. Counting room at the Radiological Dating Laboratory in Trondheim (photographed 1975). The C^{14} datings were performed in two of the four iron chambers seen on the left. The electronic equipment is on the right.

354

where σ_x is the standard deviation (30 years) of the mean radiocarbon age. If we in the above formula put $m = A.D.1000$, $\bar{x} = A.D.920$ and $\sigma_x = 30$ years, and disregard any systematic error in the radiocarbon age, we arrive at $t = 2.7$.

From a t-distribution table (Spiegel, 1961, p.344), we find that there is only a 1% probability of the radiocarbon age being in agreement with A.D.1000 or a later date. The systematic error due to driftwood may, however, change this figure considerably. If we, for instance, assume a systematic error of 50 years in the entire series ($\bar{x} = A.D. 970 + 30$), we obtain $t = 1.0$. In this case, we find that the probability of agreement with the date A.D. 1000 is about 15%. For a systematic error between 50 and 100 years, the agreement will be still better.

The discussion of agreement between the radiocarbon age and the assumed historical age must necessarily be limited because of the uncertain magnitude of systematic error due to the presence of driftwood, and also to charcoal derived from various tree-ring layers. Altogether we find that there is a reasonable agreement between the radiocarbon age and the assumed historical age. One must, however, be aware of the fact that agreement would have been regarded even more satisfactory if settlement had occurred somewhat before A.D.1000.

References

Damon, P.E. et al., 1972, Dendrochronology calibration of the carbon-14 time scale: Proceedings of the 8th international conferance on radiocarbon dating, v. 1, A29-A43, Wellington, New Zealand 18–25 October, 1972.

Godwin, H. 1969, The value of plant material for radiocarbon dating: Amer.J. Bot., v.56 (7), pp.723–731.

Godwin, H. 1962, Letter to Nature, v. 195, no.4,845, p.984.

Hough, R.B., 1965, Handbook for the trees of the Northern States and Canada: New York, 1965.

Ingstad, A.S. 1970, The Norse settlement at L'Anse aux Meadows, Newfoundland: Acta Archaeologica v. XLI, pp.109–154, Copenhagen.

Libby, Willard F. 1955, Radiocarbon Dating: The University of Chicago Press, (2nd edition).

Native trees of Canada, 1950: Department of Resources and Development. Forestry Branch. Bulletin 61, Canada 1950.

Nydal, R. 1962, Proportional counting technique for radiocarbon measurements: Rev.Sci.Instr., v.33, no. 12, pp.1,313–20.

Nydal, R. 1965, Ten years trial and error with the CO_2 proportional technique in Trondheim: Sixth internatl. conf. radiocarbon and tritium dating, Proc. Pullman, Washington, June 7–11, 1965, pp.1–16.

Nydal, R. et al., 1970: Radiocarbon, v.12, pp.205–237.

Spiegel, Murry R. 1961, Theory and problems of statistics: Schaum Publishing Co., New York.

Ralph, E.K. 1973, Radiocarbon dates and reality: Masca Newsletter, v.9, no.1, pp.1–20.

Suess, H.E. 1970, The three causes of secular C–14 fluctuations, their amplitudes and time constants, pp.595–605 in: Nobel symposium 12, Radiocarbon variations and absolute chronology, edited by Ingrid U. Olsson, Printed by Almqvist and Wiksells Boktrykkeri A.B., Uppsala 1970.

Suess, H.E. 1970, Bristle-cone pine calibration of the radiocarbon time-scale, 5,200 B.C. to the present, pp.304–311: ibid.

Table 3
(prepared by Leif M. Paulssen)

	T-306	T-309II	T-309I	T-310	T-324	T-325	T-326	T-327	T-364	T-365	T-366	T-367	T-368	T-393II	T-393I	T-410	T-411	TOTAL	
Number of fragments in the sample	66	25	44	42	44	68	21	58	18	14	39	20	11	9	36	71	50	636	
Folifers																			
Betula	22	4	6	26	3	8		18	1		22			2	13	29		154 (in 12 samples)	42.0%
Alnus	7	6		8	2			1			12				10			58 (in 7 samples)	16.0%
Salix		1	1					1							3	1		7 (in 5 samples)	2.0%
Populus						5												5 (in 1 sample)	1.5%
Quercus																1		1	0.3%
Tilia	1																	1	0.3%
Ulmus						1												1	0.3%
Heather															2	8		10 (in 2 samples)	2.5%
Conifers *)	36	20	37	8	39	54	21	38	17	14	5	20	11	7	8	14	50	399 (in 15 samples)	
Conifers **)	15	6	14	0	8	20	17	10	6	0	0	10	3	2	0	7	13	131	
Larix laricina	1	3	6			3	17	1										31 (in 6 samples)	8.5%
Picea mariana	2	1	1			8		3	1								13	29 (in 7 samples)	8.0%
Abies balsamea	4	3	1			5		3	2			10						28 (in 7 samples)	7.5%
Pinus strobus	1				1	3			2									7 (in 4 samples)	2.0%
Unknown:																			
Group 1	5		6					1	1				2			7		22 (in 6 samples)	6.0%
» 2	2				6									2				10 (in 3 samples)	2.5%
» 3					1			2										3 (in 2 samples)	1.0%
» 4						1												1	0.3%

*) Number of coniferous fragments in the sample.
**) Number of fragments which of a quality high enough to permit of identification.

Identification of charcoal finds

BY LEIF M. PAULSSEN*)

Fifteen plastic bags, each containing a sample of charcoal fragments, were submitted. These have been subjected to microscopic examination, in order to establish the origin of the charcoal. The charcoal fragments derive from forges and hearths in the excavated house-sites at L'Anse aux Meadows, northern Newfoundland.

Material investigated

The samples of charcoal are marked:

T–306	T–324	T–364	T–393
T–309	T–325	T–365	R 2 T–410
T–310	T–326	T–366	R 3 T–411
	T–327	T–367	
		T–368	

The fifteen samples of charcoal consist of a mixture of charcoal fragments and sandy soil, apart from T–367, T–368 and R 3 T–411, which consist of charcoal fragments only. In addition to the charcoal fragments (and sandy soil), the plastic bag of sample T–309 contained an extra plastic bag of charcoal fragments, T–366 contained three such extra bags, and T–393 one extra bag.

Before the microscopic examination, all the samples were subjected to a radio-carbon analysis, for which purpose the largest fragments of charcoal were removed from the samples, so that the microscopic examination was largely based on the smaller fragments of charcoal included in the original samples.

*) The Department of Pharmaceutical Chemistry, Institute of Pharmacy, University of Oslo, Blindern, Oslo 3, Norway.

1. The individual samples of charcoal

1. T–306   1 bag, marked: "No. 3 House B. Coal from hearth."
   The sample consists of fragments of charcoal and of sandy soil.
   66 fragments were taken from the sample.

2. T–309   2 bags, marked: "House C. Coal No. 4."
   The samples consist of large and small fragments of charcoal and of sandy soil. The surface of the fragments is partially brownish.
   Small bag: 25 fragments were taken from the sample.
   Large bag: 44 fragments were taken from the sample.

3. T–310   1 bag, marked: "T–310 (House A)."
   The sample consists of fragments of charcoal and of sandy soil.
   The fragments are black and covered with earth.
   42 fragments were taken from the sample.

4. T–324   1 bag, marked: "D.F. 107 Meadow E (House E. From hearth)."
   The sample consists of large and small fragments of charcoal and of sandy soil. The surface of some of the fragments is brownish.
   44 fragments were taken from the sample.

5. T–325   1 bag, marked: "D.F. 107 Meadow F.1. (House F. From hearth 1)"
   The sample consists of relatively large fragments of charcoal and of sandy soil. The surface of the fragments is brownish.
   68 fragments were taken from the sample.

6. T–326   1 bag, marked: "D.F. 107 Meadow F. 2. (House F. From hearth 2)."
   The sample consists of small and relatively very large fragments of charcoal and of sandy soil. Thin root fibres could be observed as streaks in the large fragments. The fragments are black, but the surface of the small fragments appears to be brownish.
   21 fragments were taken from the sample.

7. T–327   1 bag, marked: "D.F. 107 Meadow. Pit G. (House G (Pit) From hearth)."
   The sample consists of relatively small fragments of charcoal and of sandy soil. Loose, thin root fibres can be discerned. The surface of some of the fragments is brownish.
   58 fragments were taken from the sample.

8. T–364   1 bag, marked: "Rolfsbod" Long hearth with bronze from Rolf Petré. L'Anse aux Meadows 1962. R. Petré "House 1 Excavation 1"
   The sample contained relatively small fragments of charcoal and of sandy soil. The surface of some of the fragments is brownish.
   18 fragments were taken from the sample.

9. T–365   1 bag, marked: "L'Anse aux Meadows 1962. R. Petré "Pit 2"
Coal sample (Cooking pit in front of large house. Petré.)"
The sample consists of small as well as relatively large fragments
of charcoal (as T–326) and of sandy soil. The surface of the large
fragments has brownish incrustation.
14 fragments were taken from the sample.

10. T–366   4 bags, three of which are marked: "L'Anse aux Meadows Fill
from the forge to the inside of the two small stones 4.8.'62.
Cleaned to some extent (Smithy)."
All the three bags contain sandy soil. Among the contents of one
of the bags, some fragments of charcoal can be seen with the
naked eye, but among those of the other two bags, such fragments
can be discerned only with the aid of a magnifying glass. (One of
the two latter bags also contained a small bag of iron slag.) We
must point out that all the samples of charcoal, except R 3 T–411,
were first subjected to a radio-carbon analysis, when the largest
fragments were removed from the samples.
The fourth bag is marked: "Charcoal removed from the sample.
Fill from the forge to the inside of the two small stones. 4.8.62."
This bag contained a sample of charcoal fragments and sandy
soil, and the material utilized for the microscopic examination
derives from this bag.
39 fragments were taken from the sample.

11. T–367   1 bag, marked: "Southernmost charcoal pit lower layer (lowest
layer near smithy)." It contains fairly large fragments of charcoal,
entirely black and without any trace of brown incrustation.
20 fragments were taken from the sample.

12. T–368   1 bag, marked: "Cooking pit by the bridge. Coal from the
bottom. L'Anse aux Meadows."
The contents consist of large and small fragments of charcoal
brownish on the surface.
11 fragments were taken from the sample.

13. T–393   2 bags, one large and one small, marked: "Fill from the forge in
front of the two small stones 4.8.62."
Both bags contain samples of charcoal fragments which can be
seen with the naked eye, even though they are very small, and
coarse, sandy soil.
36 fragments were taken from the larger bag, and 9 fragments
were taken from the smaller bag.

R 2 T–410   1 bag, marked: "R 2 T–410 Charcoal sample, North of large
house."
The sample consists of small fragments of charcoal and sandy

soil. Only with the aid of a magnifying glass was it possible to find sufficient material for a microscopic examination.

71 fragments were taken from the sample.

R 3 T–411   1 bag, marked: "R 3 T–411 Charcoal sample North of large house."

The sample consists of c. 60 large and small fragments of charcoal, black with brown surface portions.

50 fragments were taken from the sample.

Identification of charcoal samples

Principles

The identification of the material being investigated here is based on a comparison of the characteristic anatomical features of charcoal prepared from known species of woods with those of the material investigated. The method is described in detail in Paulssen (1964, p. 38), and a brief description will therefore suffice here.

A small piece of charcoal from the sample is coarsely crushed in a mortar, after which the resulting coarse powder is sieved, preferably through a sieve with 28 meshes to the inch (= U.S. Sieve Series No. 30, i.e. 590 microns). The coal dust which has passed through this sieve is then sieved off through a sieve with 48 meshes to the inch (= U.S. Sieve Series No. 50, i.e. 297 microns). From the coarse powder remaining, slides for microscopic examination are prepared as follows:

A small piece of plasticine is rolled into a ball which is placed between two slides, which are then pressed together by means of a hand press. One of the slides is then carefully removed, preferably by sliding it off in a plane parallel to the other slide – it must not be *lifted* off.

The charcoal powder is placed on a slide in a single layer, and the slide with the plasticine is pressed gently on to the particles of charcoal. In this way these are transferred to the plasticine, which, covered by another slide, is again placed under the hand press and subjected to slight pressure. Now the charcoal particles will be pressed down into the plasticine, so that they are in a plane which is perpendicular to the optic axis. With regard to the material used for comparison, available literature dealing with species of wood found in, among other places, North America, was consulted. (See list of references, p. 372).

Material used for comparison

The material used for comparison was obtained from Syracuse University, N.Y. (67 samples), from the Forest Products Laboratory, Madison, Wis. (7 samples) and from Norsk Treteknisk Institutt, Oslo (18 samples), making a total of 92 samples. In addition I employed my own samples of known species of woods, so that the total material used for comparison comprises over a hundred samples.

An important aspect in the selection of samples of wood to be used for comparison was that as many of these samples as possible should represent species of woods which are found on Newfoundland and on the east coast of America as such.

The material being investigated may be expected to derive from 1) species of woods which grew on Newfoundland in the past, and which may still grow there, or from 2) species of woods which grow (possibly grew in the past) in the adjacent parts of America (and possibly in countries further away), and which were washed ashore in the immediate vicinity of L'Anse aux Meadows, as a result of wind and prevailing currents, and which were used as fuel etc. here. (The material being investigated may also be expected to include fragments from species of woods of Norse origin – defective household objects or boat equipment, which were thrown on the fire when they were discarded.)

To small samples of the material used for comparison which were placed into an electrically heated crucible furnace, nitrogen was introduced during the carbonization process for one hour at a temperature of 600°C. From the charcoal thus obtained, slides for microscopic examination were prepared according to the method described above.

The microscopic examination

Individual microscopic slides were prepared from every fragment included in the fifteen samples received, provided that the fragments were of such a size as to make the preparation of slides possible in practice. Thus the identification arrived at is not based merely on random samples, although this would have been the simplest way, requiring least time; the result of such testing would, however, have been less reliable.

A total of 636 fragments were taken from the samples received. From these, c.2,000 microscopic slides were prepared. From the material used for comparison, c.600 microscopic slides were prepared.

The charcoal samples investigated must be described as varying in quality. A few of them are of superior quality, while others may be of inferior quality. One of the reason for this must be the fact that these charcoals had been lying in *sandy soil* for so long, c. 1,000 years. During all this time, air has had access to the charcoals and affected their surface adversely from the point of view of identification. Moreover, the surface of many of the fragments had a dark-coloured film consisting of iron oxide; this renders the microscopic detection of characteristic details, which might be important in identifying the charcoal fragments, difficult. (Parts of all the samples were treated with hydrochloric acid, and in every case the extract proved to contain iron (III). The above-mentioned brownish incrustation observed in most of the material investigated proved to consist of ferriferous ash – the carbon was burned away but the ash retains the structure of the wood.

The different characteristic features of the slides investigated, which were demonstrated microscopically, were compared to slides included in the material used for comparison, and to the photographs, drawings and descriptions published by Greguss (1955, 1959) and others in the literature referred to above. In those cases where we have reason to assume that a charcoal fragment represents a certain species of wood, the measurements of the various characteristic features given by Greguss for the species in question agree with the measurements found in the fragment being examined. The measurements given by Greguss apply to wood; experience shows that wood "shrinks" some 20–25% during carbonization, and this fact has been taken into account when comparing the material being investigated with that used for purposes of comparison.

An objection may be raised to Greguss's measurements – he does not state whether his figures apply to the summerwood zone or the springwood zone. Within the same species, the characteristic features of the summerwood zone may differ considerably from those of the springwood zone. However, the measurements given by Greguss can be controlled by means of the photographs and drawings which accompany his descriptions of each species of wood.

The result of the investigations

Table I, comments

T–306   66 fragments, 30 of which derive from deciduous trees (hardwoods). Of the remaining 36 fragments, all of which derive from coniferous trees (softwoods), 21 could not be identified, owing to their inferior quality, while 7 could not be identified because material for comparison was not available.

Of the hardwood fragments, 22 appear to derive from *Betula*, 7 from *Alnus* and 1 from *Tilia* (pl. I, Nos.2, 4, 6).

Of the softwood fragments, 4 appear to derive from *Abies*, 2 from *Picea*, 1 from *Pinus* and 1 from *Larix* (pl. II, Nos.14, 16, 18, 20).

T–309   25 fragments, 5 of which derive from hardwoods and 20 from
Small bag softwoods. Of the latter, 14 fragments could not be identified owing to their inferior quality. Of the remaining 6 fragments, 3

Table 1

Number of fragments from sample	T-306	T-309 Small bag	T-309 Large bag	T-310	T-324	T-325	T-326	T-327	T-364	T-365	T-366	T-367	T-368	T-393 Small bag	T-393 Large bag	R2 T-410	R3 T-411	Sum:	
	66	25	44	42	44	68	21	58	18	14	39	20	11	9	36	71	50	636	
Deciduous trees																			
Betula	22	4	6	26	3	8		18	1		22			2	13	29		154 (12 samples)	42.0%
Alnus	7			8	2			1			12				10	18		58 (7 samples)	16.0%
Salix		1	1					1							3	1		7 (5 samples)	2.0%
Populus						5												5 (1 sample)	1.5%
Quercus																1		1	0.3%
Tilia	1																	1	0.3%
Ulmus						1												1	0.3%
Heather															2	8		10 (2 samples)	2.5%
Conifers*	36	20	37	8	39	54	21	38	17	14	5	20	11	7	8	14	50	399 (all 15 samples)	2.5%
	15	6	14	0	8	20	17	10	6	0	0	10	3	2	0	7	13	131	
Larix laricina	1	3	6			3	17	1										31 (6 samples)	8.5%
Picea mariana	2		1			8		3	1				1				13	29 (7 samples)	8.0%
Abies balsamea	4	3	1			5		3	2			10						28 (7 samples)	7.5%
Pinus strobus	1				1	3			2									7 (4 samples)	2.0%
Unknown																			
Group 1	5		6		6			1	1				2			7		22 (6 samples)	6.0%
» 2	2													2				10 (3 samples)	2.5%
» 3					1			2										3 (2 samples)	1.0%
» 4						1												1	0.3%

* The upper line represents the number of softwood fragments in the sample: the lower line the number of such fragments of a quality high enough to permit identification.

363

appear to derive from *Abies* and 3 from *Larix*.

4 of the hardwood fragments appear to derive from *Betula*, and 1 from *Salix* (pl. I, No.8).

T–309
Large bag
44 fragments, 7 of which derive from hardwoods and 37 from softwoods. Of the latter, only 14 fragments were of sufficiently high quality to permit of a more detailed microscopic examination. 8 of these 14 fragments could be identified; 6 of them appear to derive from *Larix*, 1 from *Abies* and 1 from *Picea*, while the remaining 6 fragments could not be identified because material for comparison was not available.

6 of the hardwood fragments appear to derive from *Betula* and 1 from *Salix*.

T–310
42 fragments, 34 of which derive from hardwoods and 8 from softwoods. Owing to their inferior quality, none of the softwood fragments could be identified.

26 of the hardwood fragments appear to derive from *Betula*, and 8 from *Alnus*.

T–324
44 fragments, 5 of which derive from hardwoods and 39 from softwoods. Of the latter, only 8 fragments were of sufficiently high quality to permit of identification. 1 of the fragments appears to derive from *Pinus*, while the remaining 7 could not be identified because material for comparison was not available. 6 of these appear to derive from the same type of tree, probably a species of *Juniperus*.

3 of the hardwood fragments appear to derive from *Betula* and 2 from *Alnus*.

T–325
68 fragments, 14 of which derive from hardwoods and 54 from softwoods. Of the latter, only 20 fragments were of sufficiently high quality to permit of a more detailed microscopic examination. 19 of these fragments have been identified, while 1 fragment could not be identified because material for comparison was not available.

8 of the softwood fragments appear to derive from *Picea*, 5 from *Abies*, 3 from *Larix* and 3 from *Pinus*.

All the hardwood fragments have been identified. 8 of these appear to derive from *Betula*, 5 from *Populus* and 1 from *Ulmus* (pl.I, II, Nos.10, 12).

| T–326 | All 21 fragments derive from softwoods. 4 fragments could not be identified owing to their inferior quality, while 17 fragments appear to derive from *Larix*. |

| T–327 | 58 fragments, 20 of which derive from hardwoods and 38 from softwoods. Of the latter, 28 fragments could not be identified owing to their inferior quality. Of the remaining 10 softwood fragments, 3 appear to derive from *Picea*, 3 from *Abies* and 1 from *Larix*, while 3 fragments could not be identified because material for comparison was not available.
18 of the hardwood fragments appear to derive from *Betula*, 1 from *Alnus* and 1 from *Salix*. |

| T–364 | 18 fragments, one of which derives from hardwood *(Betula)*, while the remaining 17 derive from softwoods. 2 of these fragments appear to derive from *Abies*, 2 from *Pinus* and 1 from *Picea*, while 11 fragments could not be identified, owing to their inferior quality, and 1 fragment could not be identified because material for comparison was not available. |

| T–365 | All 14 fragments derive from softwoods. However, none of them could be identified, owing to their inferior quality. |

| T–366 | 39 fragments, 34 of which derive from hardwoods and 5 from softwoods. Owing to their inferior quality, none of the softwood fragments could be identified.
Of the hardwood fragments, 22 appear to derive from *Betula* and 12 from *Alnus*. |

| T–367 | All 20 fragments derive from softwoods. 10 of these appear to derive from *Abies*, while 10 fragments could not be identified, owing to their inferior quality. |

| T–368 | All 11 fragments derive from softwoods. 1 of these appears to derive from *Picea*, while 8 fragments could not be identified, owing to their inferior quality, and 2 fragments could not be identified because material for comparison was not available. |

| T–393 Small bag | 9 fragments, 2 of which derive from hardwoods and 7 from softwoods. The 2 former fragments appear to derive from *Betula*. 5 of the softwood fragments could not be identified, owing to their inferior quality, while 2 fragments could not be identified because material for comparison was not available. |

PLATE I

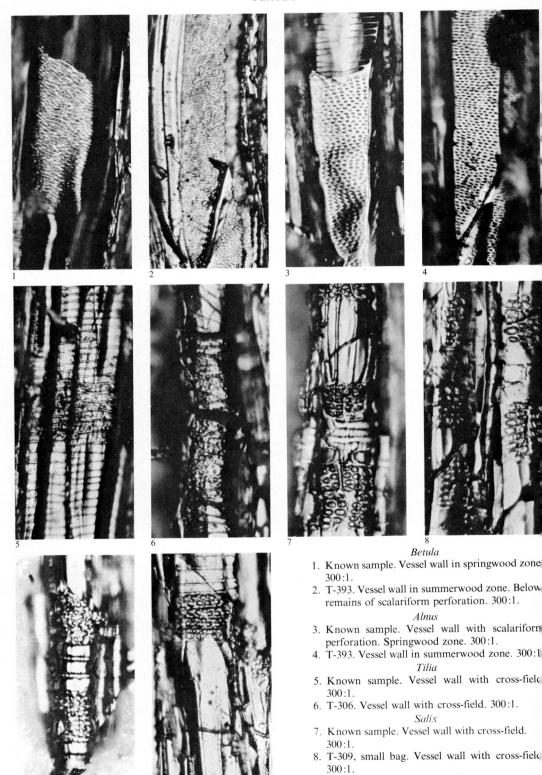

Betula
1. Known sample. Vessel wall in springwood zone. 300:1.
2. T-393. Vessel wall in summerwood zone. Below remains of scalariform perforation. 300:1.

Alnus
3. Known sample. Vessel wall with scalariform perforation. Springwood zone. 300:1.
4. T-393. Vessel wall in summerwood zone. 300:1

Tilia
5. Known sample. Vessel wall with cross-field. 300:1.
6. T-306. Vessel wall with cross-field. 300:1.

Salix
7. Known sample. Vessel wall with cross-field. 300:1.
8. T-309, small bag. Vessel wall with cross-field. 300:1.

Populus
9. Known sample. Vessel wall with cross-field. 250:1.
10. T-325. Vessel wall with cross-field. 300:1.

All photographs by J. Basberg.

366

PLATE II

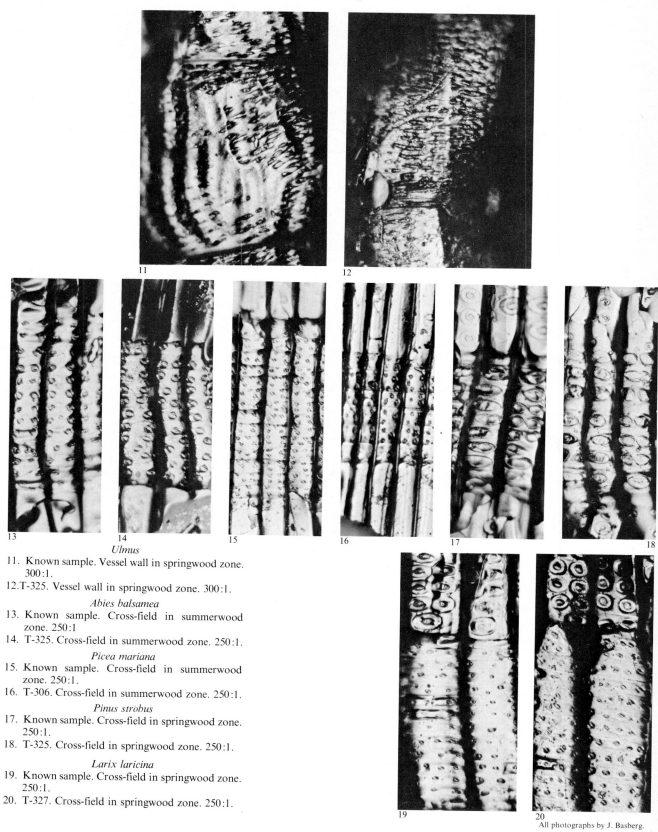

Ulmus
11. Known sample. Vessel wall in springwood zone. 300:1.
12. T-325. Vessel wall in springwood zone. 300:1.

Abies balsamea
13. Known sample. Cross-field in summerwood zone. 250:1
14. T-325. Cross-field in summerwood zone. 250:1.

Picea mariana
15. Known sample. Cross-field in summerwood zone. 250:1.
16. T-306. Cross-field in summerwood zone. 250:1.

Pinus strobus
17. Known sample. Cross-field in springwood zone. 250:1.
18. T-325. Cross-field in springwood zone. 250:1.

Larix laricina
19. Known sample. Cross-field in springwood zone. 250:1.
20. T-327. Cross-field in springwood zone. 250:1.

All photographs by J. Basberg.

367

T–393
Large bag

36 fragments, 26 of which derive from hardwoods, 2 from heather and 8 from softwoods. None of the softwood fragments could, however, be identified, owing to their inferior quality.

Of the hardwood fragments, 13 appear to derive from *Betula,* 10 from *Alnus* and 3 from *Salix.*

No attempt has been made at establishing the origin of the fragment of heather.

R 2 T–410

71 fragments, 49 of which derive from hardwoods, 8 from heather and 14 from softwoods. Of the softwood fragments, 7 could not be identified, owing to their inferior quality, while 7 fragments could not be identified because material for comparison was not available; they appear, however, to have the same origin.

Of the hardwood fragments, 29 appear to derive from *Betula,* 18 from *Alnus,* 1 from *Salix* and 1 from *Quercus.* The latter was in such a position on the slide, however, that it was impossible to obtain a photograph which could be reproduced.

R 3 T–411

All 50 fragments derive from softwoods. Only 13 of them were of a sufficiently high quality to permit of identification. They appear to derive from *Picea.*

All the *hardwood* fragments among the material investigated have been identified, even though their quality is in some cases as inferior as that of the remaining fragments comprising the samples. We were not, however, able to determine the *species* of the wood from which the fragments derive, merely the *genera* – this is due to the small size and, in some cases, to the inferior quality of the fragments. (Species of wood belonging to the same genus are frequently difficult to distinguish from one another, because clear and certain characteristic anatomical features are lacking. This is true of, for instance, *Betula verrucosa* and *Betula odorata.* When confronted with a carbonized specimen of inferior quality, it is not merely difficult – it is impossible to determine which of these two species one has before one.) The characteristic features of the *genus,* however, could be securely determined even under the unfavourable conditions encountered here.

The *softwood* fragments which have been identified appear to derive from the species stated. In these cases the fragments could be referred to definite species because the material used for comparison included several samples deriving from *several species* of the same *genus:* the differences between the characteristic features of the different species appeared quite clearly. Moreover, these fragments come from samples of fairly high quality. The characteristic features of the specimens representing these species included in the

368

material used for comparison, as well as photomicrographs of such specimens, were microscopically measured and compared with the measurements given by Greguss for these particular species. The attribution of identified softwood fragments to given species is based on this comparison.

Five of the fifteen samples constituting the material being investigated consist exclusively of softwood fragments – T–326, T–365, T–367, T–368 and R 3 T–411. The other ten samples comprise hardwood and softwood fragments, two samples also include fragments deriving from heather – T–393 (large bag) and R 2 T–410. (No attempt has been made at determining the species of heather represented.)

Examples of measurements referring to the characteristic
features of:
Abies balsamea (Balsam fir)

			T–325 (Slide 47 a)	Greguss gives:
Bordered pits on tracheid walls, rad.	c. 15 μ	10–16 μ
Bordered pits on tracheid walls, tang.	c. 5 μ	5–8 μ
Ray tracheids in cross-field : width	c. 45 μ	30–45 μ
Ray tracheids in cross-field : height	c. 20 μ	15–20 μ
Simple pits in cross-field up to	8 μ	5–6 μ
Number of pits in cross-field	1–2(3)	1–2(6)

Picea mariana (Black Spruce)

T–368 (Slide 8 a)			Greguss gives:
Bordered pits on radial walls	15–20 μ	15–18 μ
Bordered pits on tangential walls	c. 8 μ	5–10 μ
Ray cells in cross-field: width	25–30 μ (40) c. 30 μ	
Ray cells in cross-field: height	c. 20 μ	16–20 μ
Simple pits in cross-field	4–6 μ	3–6 μ
Number of pits in cross-field	2–4–5	1–4(6)

The softwood fragments which could not be identified because material for comparison was not available have been arranged in four groups, each group representing one species of wood. Each species may be represented in one or more samples.

The material investigated includes amongst others, fragments which appear to derive from *Ulmus, Pinus strobus, Tilia* and *Quercus*. According to the literature referred to above (Hough 1950), the two former species grow in the southern part of Newfoundland, while the two latter grow in Nova Scotia. The remaining fragments of charcoal appear to derive from species which grew at L'Anse aux Meadows, as well as north of Newfoundland, along the coast of Labrador. The map of Newfoundland and adjacent regions (fig. 1)* shows that the Labrador stream passes through the Strait of Belle Isle, passing L'Anse aux Meadows, while another arm flows southwards along the

* Simplified reproduction of a pilot-map from 1970, the sea-currents only being shown on our sketch-map.

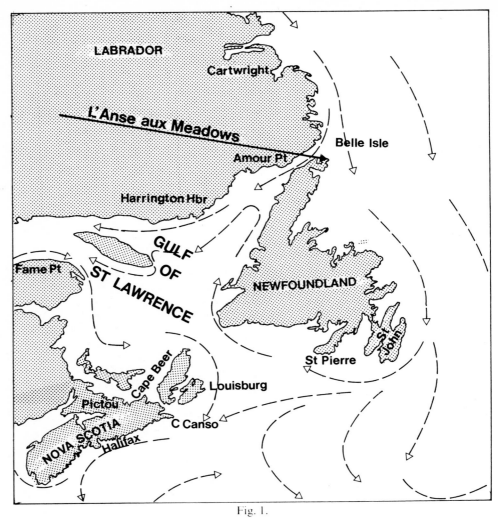

Fig. 1.

east coast of Newfoundland, following the coast westwards, after which it turns north and runs into the Gulf of St. Lawrence; here it turns when it meets the Strait of Belle Isle current, which comes from the north – at this point a back eddy is formed.

The tidal differences in the Strait of Belle Isle are stated to be very slight, pursuant to several authorities – the largest difference given is five foot.

It appears likely that the species of woods which grew in the southern part of Newfoundland and in Nova Scotia should have been carried to L'Anse aux Meadows, as driftwood, through the Strait of Belle Isle, as a result of prevailing winds and currents.

The photomicrographs

After the microscopic examination of the material investigated had been completed, eleven different species of wood had been identified as the source of the charcoal fragments examined. Photographs of charcoal fragments were

370

taken, each of these species of wood being represented, with one exception: the fragment in charcoal sample R 2 T–410, which appeared to derive from *Quercus*, was in such a position on the slide that it was impossible to obtain a photograph which could be reproduced because of a lack of sharp focus when the microscope was focused on the fragment. Photographs were also taken of specimens prepared from charcoal samples of the same species occurring in the material used for comparison – these were employed not only for purposes of comparison, but also as evidence supporting the identification of the material investigated.

The photographed fragment is an identification particle, i.e. the fragment displays features characteristic of the species of wood in question. However, *all* the identification particles which may be observed during the microscopic examination may demonstrate different characteristic features corroborating one another: *their sum* justifies the assumption that the charcoal fragment in question derives from the species of wood stated.

The photographs were taken in vertical illumination.

A modified Carl Zeiss, Jena, vertical 9×12 cm camera was used, together with a Polaroid Land filmholder No.500, and Polaroid film, type 52 (in one case type 57, high speed).

Microscope employed: Zeiss Standard Universal with vertical illumination equipment. Source of light: 100W–230V microscope lamp. Objectives: Zeiss Epiplan HD 16/0.35; in a few cases 8/0.2. Eye piece: Zeiss KPL 8 x.

Conclusion

Some of the material comprising the fifteen charcoal samples of the material investigated was of inferior quality. Of the total number of fragments selected from the samples – 636 – 62.7% were softwood fragments, 35.7% were hardwood fragments and 1.6% were fragments of heater. 268 of these fragments defied identification (c. 42%, all of them softwood fragments), owing to their very inferior quality and extremely small size. The remaining 368 fragments, or c. 58% of the total, were of a sufficiently high quality to permit of identification; they appear to derive from the genera of deciduous trees and species of coniferous trees listed below, and also from heather.

C. 90% of these 368 fragments were identified: 85% derive from species of trees which grow in the region where they were found. (A lack of material for comparison was responsible for the fact that the remaining 10% could not be identified.)

371

Deciduous trees			Coniferous trees		
		Habitat:			Habitat:
Betula	42.0%	Newfoundland	*Larix laricina*	8.5%	Newfoundland
Alnus	16.0%	Newfoundland	*Picea mariana*	8.0%	Newfoundland
Salix	2.0%	Newfoundland	*Abies balsamea*	7.5%	Newfoundland
Populus	1.5%	Newfoundland	*Pinus strobus*	2.0%	southern part
Ulmus	0.3%	southern part			of Newfoundland
		of Newfoundland			
Tilia	0.3%	Nova Scotia	Group 1	6.0%	
Quercus	0.3%	Nova Scotia	Group 2	2.5%	
			Group 3	1.0%	
Heather	2.5%		Group 4	0.3%	

References

Critchfield, W.B. and Little, E.L. Jr.: Geographic Distribution of the Pines of the World. U.S. Department of Agriculture. Forest Service. 1966.

Greguss, P.: Xylotomische Bestimmung der heute lebenden Gymnospermen. Budapest 1955. Holzanatomie der europäischen Laubhölzer und Sträucher. Budapest 1959.

Hough, R.B.: Handbook of the Trees of the Northern States and Canada. New York 1950.

Native Trees of Canada. Bulletin 61. Department of Resources and Development. Forestry Branch. Canada 1950.

Paulssen, L.M.: Identification of Active Charcoals and Wood Charcoals. Scandinavian University Books. Universitetsforlaget. Oslo 1964.

Sargent, C.S.: Manual of the Trees of Northern America. (2 Vols.) New York 1965.

Silvics of Forest Trees of the United States. Agriculture Handbook No.271. U.S. Department of Agriculture. Forest Service. 1965.

Material Investigations

BY ANNA M. ROSENQVIST

Report concluded 1971

Remains of iron objects
Description (Catalogue)

The methods employed in the identification of the remains of iron were: ordinary microscopic investigation, testing for ferro-magnetism, and X-ray radiography. The latter was carried out at a voltage of 100 KV, a current of 5 mA, and an exposure time of 1 minute; no filter was employed, and the distance between the object and the Andrex X-ray tube was 57 cm. Remains of metal, being particularly absorbant, will by radiography blacken the positive of the film, relative to the amount of corrosion products, rust in this case. For purposes of comparison, X-ray radiographs were taken of corroded, dated rivets from the following places, the same conditions being applied:

Catalogue number	Provenance	Date
C. 30088 × 14	Mogen, Telemark	Migration Age
XXII e	Kaupang, Vestfold	Viking Age
	Kongsgården, Oslo	Middle Ages, 13th century
	Ladegården, Oslo	16th century

Figs. 1 and 2 show photographs of the remains of iron objects, while positives of the X-ray films, showing the same objects, appear in figs. 3 and 4.

The texts accompanying the objects are given as they appear in the list of finds.

LaM 51 (Sample No.1): "Found in house F, room VI, 12.54 m base, –3.72 m SE of this. L.: 2.6 cm, w.: 0.3 – 0.8 cm, 7 cm deep in old turf. Weight 6.4 g."

This unidentified object showed only weak ferro-magnetism. There is a hole in it, and it consists of sandy rust with blisters. The X-ray picture did not help to identify the object, but revealed that it contained no metal. Fig. 5, r., shows a polished section of this object.

LaM 52 (Sample No.2): "House F, room VI. 12.74 m base, –3.58 m SE of this. 7 cm deep in old turf.L.: 3 cm, w.: 1 cm." The object weighed c. 0.3 g, and it was weakly ferromagnetic. Microscopic investigation showed that it consisted of the pseudomorphosis of wooden fibres in rust.

LaM 53 (Sample No.3): "House F, room VI. 13.15 m base, –3.90 m SE of this, floor level – 5 cm above this." Unidentified object, l.: 1.4 cm, w.: 0.7 cm, weight 2 g. The object was ferro-magnetic, but the X-ray picture showed that it contained no metal, but consisted of sandy iron oxides.

LaM 54 (Sample No.4): "House F, room VI, 14.79 m base, –3.85 m SE of this, floor level. Weight 1 g, magnetic, sickle-shaped, l.: 3.5 cm, w.: 0 – 1.5 cm." The ferro-magnetism was weak, and the X-ray picture showed that the object consisted of sandy iron oxides.

LaM 55 (Sample No.5): "House F, room VI. 8.95 m base, –4.10 m SE of this, 5 cm deep in old turf. Rusty lump of iron, very blistered, magnetic, weight 6.5 g, l.: 2.7 cm, w.: 1.2 cm." This tube with blisters of rust was ferro-magnetic, but the X-ray picture, fig.4, shows that it contains no metal. It may represent the remains of the shank of a rivet.

LaM 56 (Sample No.6): "House F, room VI. 10.75 m base, –2.30 m SE of this, 8 cm deep in old turf." This find consisted of several fragments of rust with sand. They were weakly ferro-magnetic, and had a total weight of 11 g. We were able to identify with great probabilty the head of a rivet, diameter 2.6 cm, maximum thickness 0.9 cm. Fig.5, top 1., shows a polished section, and fig.3 shows the positive of the X-ray picture of this sample, demonstrating the absence of metal.

LaM 57 (Sample No.7): "House F, room VI. 9.11 m base, – 4.10 m SE of this. 5 cm deep in old turf. L.: 2 cm, w.: 1.4 cm." The object, which weighed 2.2 g, was ferro-magnetic, and the X-ray picture revealed that it must have been the small head of a rivet which, however, now consists entirely of iron oxides.

LaM 58 (Sample No.8): "House F, room VI, 10.56 m base, – 4.40 m SE of this. 5 cm deep in sterile sand. L.: 2.7 cm, w.: 1.2 cm." This unidentified object, which weighed 2.3 g, was ferro-magnetic, but consisted essentially of iron oxides with burned wood.

LaM 60 (Sample No.10): "House F, room VI, 8.70 m base, – 25 cm SE of this. 10 cm deep in soil containing charcoal. Magnetic, weight 18.8 g, l.: 6.1 cm. Head diameter 2.8 cm, thickness 0.4 – 0.7 cm, thickness of shank 0.8 cm. "The length of the rivet includes the head, the maximum thickness of which includes a blister of rust. The rivet was ferro-magnetic. The X-ray picture, fig. 4, showed that this rivet contained metal, iron in this case, the only investigated object with a metal content. A polished section is shown in fig.6.

LaM 62 (Sample No.12): "House F, room VI, 13.50 m base, –1.50 m SE of this, 10 cm deep in old turf. L.: 2.3 cm, w.: 2.7 cm, thickness 0.8 cm." This object, which weighed 6.5 g, was ferro-magnetic. It had a square hole, c. 0.5 cm $\times$ 0.5 cm, and there were impressions of wood fibres in the rust. Small pieces of charcoal in sand were also found. This may be a small mounting. The X-ray picture showed no metal. A polished section is shown in fig.7, top.

374

LaM 63 (Sample No.13): "House F, room VI, 10.80 m base, –0.09 m SE of this. At bottom of cultural layer. L.: 1.7 cm, thickness 1.2 cm, diameter of head 2.6 cm, thickness of head 0.8 cm, weight 13.1 g." This is the head and upper part of a rivet. The dimensions given include rust and sand (original thickness c. 0.6 cm). The rivet was ferro-magnetic. The X-ray picture revealed no metal, fig.4. A polished section is shown in fig.7.

LaM 64a (Sample 14a): "Two pieces of magnetic rust, weight 9.5 g." Hollow nail (?), not ferro-magnetic, possibly natural formation.

LaM 64b (Sample 14b): The X-ray investigation showed two objects, fig.4, both ferro-magnetic. Small arrow-head (?), weight 1.7 g, l.: 3.2 cm, w.: 1.1 cm, thickness 0.6 cm. No metal was observed. Rivet head (?), diameter 2.1 cm, thickness 0.8 cm, with impressions of wood fibres in the rust.

LaM 65 (Sample No.15): "House A, 1.70 m to the inside of the side of the house, 11 cm from profile, 10 cm under modern surface. Found 6th August 62 by Kristján Eldjárn at the eastern end of the long test trench L-M, which ran under the test excavation of house A. The rivet lay near the cooking pit in room III, the finds from which area included the ring-headed pin. L.: 5.7 cm, thickness 0.4 cm." The rivet consisted of four fragments, which could be put together to form a rivet 5.7 cm long, with a blister of rust, c. 0.3 cm, at the top. The shank was c.0.4 cm thick and the head measured 1.2 cm in diameter. The total weight was 4.3 g, and the fragments showed ferro-magnetism. The X-ray picture may possibly reveal some metal in the head of the rivet, see fig.4.

LaM 29 (Sample No. I): "Found in House F, room I, in the same hearth as LaM No.2, fig. 7b. L.: 2.4 cm, diameter of head c. 2 cm." Completely rusted rivet, fig.4, top, shows the X-ray picture. The head was blistered. Another small piece of rust, measuring 1.2 cm × 0.4 cm, is rusted on to the head. Neither the X-ray picture nor the polished section, fig.9, shows any content of metal.

LaM 30 (Sample No.II): "Found in the cultural layer of house G, at a depth of 25 cm, in sandy soil containing charcoal (see plan). Shank and part of plate preserved. Greatest l.: 1.9 cm, w.: 0.7 cm. Diameter of head 1.3 cm." Fig.10 shows a polished section, and reveals that there is a hole in the head of the rivet. The rivet showed ferro-magnetism, but neither the X-ray picture, fig.4, nor the polished section showed any metal.

LaM 26 (Sample No.III): "Found in house F, room II, at centre of layer, base 14.20 m, 5 m NW of this. Head 1.8 cm, shank 1 cm." Completely rusted rivet, fig. 4 r. L.: 1.3 cm, thickness 0.5 cm, diameter of head 1.8 cm. Neither polished section, fig.7, nor X-ray picture showed any metal.

LaM 233 (Sample No.34): "Pieces of iron found at surface by the heap of charcoal in house J. K.E."

LaM 236 (Sample No.36): "Finds from sifting soil from house J." Completely rusted, headless nail (?), 3.3 cm × 0.3 cm. The object was not ferro-magnetic, and the X-ray picture, fig.4, showed no metal.

The following objects were subjected to X-ray examination in 1971:

LaM 118: "Found outside NE entrance of house F, room I, at bottom of a 3.5 cm thick cultural layer, at 2.20 m base, –0.50 m SE of this. Magnetic, highly corroded, shank broken. Diameter of head 1.5 cm, length of shank 1.9 cm." Examination showed this to be a small rivet.

LaM 158: "Found in house A, in profile at x = 17.27 m, y = –2.3 m. Level 108, bottom 111. Many small fragments, maximum l.: 2.6 cm, maximum w.: 2.3 cm." Examination showed that this was a rivet.

LaM 130: "Found in house F, by sifting earth from a field between 8.10 m and 16.70 m base, and 0.35 m NW and –0.20 m SE of this. Magnetic. Maximum diameter of head 1.7 cm. Shank 1 cm long. Fig.6." Examination showed that this object was a hook.

LaM 68: "Found in house D, at x = 6.05 m, y = –0.24 m, level 4 cm above floor. L. of shank 2.4 cm, head 1.6 cm x 2.0 cm." Examination showed that this was a rivet.

LaM 116: "Found immediately outside entrance of house F, room I, at 2.30 m base, –0.15 m SE, at the bottom of a 3 cm thick cultural layer containing some scattered charcoal, 8 cm below the turf. L.: 2.6 cm, head 1.7 cm wide, shank 1.6 cm long." Examination showed this object to be a nail.

LaM 162: "Found in the midden south of house A room III." Examination showed this to be slag.

LaM 133: "Found when sifting earth from the same field as also yielded Nos. 130 and 131. Max. diam. of head: 1.8 cm." On examination this object proved to be a rivet.

LaM 160: "House A. Found at x = 18.95 m, y = –2.48 m, level: 117. Maximum width 2.8 cm." Examination showed that this object was the head of a rivet.

LaM 123: "House F. Found when sifting earth from the same field as also yielded No.122. Weight 1 g." This object could not be identified on examination.

LaM 70: "House D, room III, at x = 5.34 m, y = –1.97 m, level 1 cm above floor. Length of shank 4.0 cm, head 1.8 x 2.2 cm." This object was identified as a nail.

LaM 125: "Found in house D, room II, at bottom of sand layer containing a great deal of charcoal. Weight 2.5 g, maximum diameter 2.2 cm. It may possibly be a rivet head." This object could not be identified upon examination.

LaM 119: "House F, found at 2.10 m base, 0.10 m NW. Same depth, layer and trench as No.118. Maximum diameter 2.9 cm. Magnetic, 5 g. Fig 6, bottom."

376

Examination showed that this object was the head of a rivet.

LaM 71: "House D, room 3, position x = 4.98 m, y = –2.11 m, level 8 cm above floor. 1.2 x 1.4 cm, 0.7 cm thick." This object could not be identified on examination.

LaM 120: "House F, found when sifting earth from the trench which also yielded Nos. 118 and 119. Maximum diameter 1.8 cm." On examination this object was identified as a fragment of the square head of a rivet.

Metallographic investigations

As a result of the X-ray examination it was possible to identify some of the lumps of rust, and they also enabled us to give a more precise description of the rusted objects. However, only one specimen contained sufficient metal, i.e. iron, to enable us to carry out a metallographic examination. This was the rivet LaM 60, found in house F, room VI.

Polished sections were prepared of all the large, ferro-magnetic, heavy and solid remains of iron, but microscoping revealed that they no longer contained sufficient iron to make possible an examination of the structure even under considerable magnification. Figs. 5 – 11 show macrophotographs of the sections of the objects. Polished sections were also prepared from the rivets used for comparison in the radiographic examination. Figs. 12 – 15 show macrophotographs of these sections in vertical illumination. Microscoping of the polished section of the metal of rivet LaM 60 revealed hammered, non-metallic inclusions. A microprobe was used in order to determine these inclusions. This analysis was carried out by cand.real. Svein Erik Næss, at the Central Institute for Industrial Research, with the financial support of the Norwegian Research Council for Science and the Humanities.

Fig.17 shows an electron-picture, magnified 500 x. The bright field is metal, the dark a non-metallic phase. Fig.18 shows the same area, exposed with Si-K_σ rays. Here the parts containing silicium are bright. The non-metallic phase is seen to consist mainly of silicium. Optic spectrographic analysis of the metal in the rivet showed a silicium content of 0.04% Si. This amount of silicium is concentrated in the hammered slag, which consists largely of silicates of iron, calcium and aluminium.

Fig.18 also indicates that the silicium content increases along the grain boundaries of the ferrite. When iron is extracted by primitive methods involving the direct reduction to metal, remains of slag will usually be left in the iron or mild steel as streaks elongated by hammering, or as small globular inclusions. Piaskowski (1969) found different types of such slag inclusions in prehistoric iron and steel found in Poland. He dates these types, and assigns them geographically to Poland and eastern Europe, and suggests that they represent different stages of technology. Without discussing this method in any detail, we may point out that when the polished section of the rivet LaM 60 was microscoped, most of the slag was found to be of a black single-phase type, like Piaskowski's type A, but some smaller streaks of type D_{21}, with small, bright particles, and others of type F, with fayalite crystals, were also observed.

The slag inclusions in the metal of the material used for comparison – rivets from different periods – were also microscoped.

In the earliest sample, dating from the Migration Age and found at Mogen, Telemark, the inclusions consisted chiefly of a single-phase black slag with a few bright particles of wüstite, FeO (see fig. 22).

In the Viking Age sample, from Kaupang, Vestfold, dark, single-phase slag was observed as well as two-phase slag, see fig.23. Two more samples from the Viking Age were examined: one of four well-preserved nails, 6–8 cm long and weighing 7–10 g, from the Oseberg ship burial, Vestfold, No.O 294bb, fig. 16; and a rivet from the same find, 2.5 cm long and weighing 5 g, No.O 294 g. Both were found together with the sledge of the Oseberg Find known as "the fourth sledge", Cat.No.O 294.

Both these objects were found in the ground, and they had not been subjected to fire. They therefore represent metal which may be regarded as being unchanged, apart from the action of ground water.

The nail contained two-phase slag with circular, bright inclusions, and in the rivet one could observe slag with distinct, bright dendrites in a dark matrix, as well as small amounts of dark, single-phase slag.

For comparison an iron bar, type Rygh No.438, usually dated to the Viking Age, was also included. The find as such has not been dated. It comes from a field at Sørum, Hedmark, and consisted of 273 bars of iron, 27 cm to 29.8 cm in length and 45 g to 160 g in weight. Some of the bars were highly corroded. The find bears Cat. No. C 26 208.

The bar which was examined contained few slag inclusions, of a type with bright dendrites of wüstite in a dark matrix (see fig. 25).

The Middle Ages were represented by a rivet from Kongsgården, Oslo, dating from the thirteenth century. Multiphase slags with dendrites of wüstite in a dark matrix were observed (see fig.26).

The most recent sample, dating from the sixteenth century, was found in Ladegården, Oslo. It contained more slag inclusions than the other samples examined. The slag consisted of many bright grains of similar size and shape in a black matrix, with a small amount of fayalite crystals (grey) (see fig. 27).

Varying amounts of the dark, single-phase glassy type of slag were found in all the samples. This was also the case in the samples examined by Piaskowski. The bright dendrite phase observed is FeO, wüstite, which has not been reduced to metal. The different types of slag inclusion were formed as the result of variation in the rate of cooling from variable temperatures and under different reducing conditions in the gas phase. Thus the technique of production is decisive for the formation of the slag type. The slag in the metal of rivet LaM 60 from L'Anse aux Meadows does not differ from slag in similar objects known to have been produced by primitive reduction from iron oxides.

The metal usually produced by such reduction was a nearly pure iron, or a mild steel with varying amounts of carbon and phosphorus, depending on the ore, the temperature and the reducing conditions during the process. Subsequent working by forging with charcoal will also influence the structure of the metal, but if the steel is later exposed to high temperatures, for instance in a fire, these structures will change.

Thus many factors must be taken into account when we compare the structure of, for instance, rivet LaM 60 with that of the Norwegian rivets. Fig.6 shows that the rivet from L'Anse aux Meadows consists mainly of rust. Metal is preserved only in the inner, upper parts of the shank.

According to R.Knox (1963) and others, e.g. J.Piaskowski (1969) and O.Schaaber (1963), it is possible to observe cementite and pseudomorphous pearlite in completely rusted objects of iron. During the examination of the objects from L'Anse aux Meadows very small amounts of cementite were observed. In one case, No.I (LaM 29), a rivet found in house F room I, the forms were elongated and their pattern could be interpreted as suggesting the outline of grains.

Similar lines of cementite were observed in the rivet from Kaupang, Vestfold, dating from the Viking Age, and also completely rusted. The carbon content was too low to allow for the formation of appreciable amounts of cementite in the material. The presence of martensite in these objects is of low probability.

Fig.19 shows a macrophotograph of a polished section of the rivet LaM 60, etched with 2% alcoholic HNO_3. The central part of the head is pure ferrite, fig.20, while pearlitic areas can be seen further down towards the dark tip, fig.21.

In the same way, fig.12 shows a macrophotograph of the Migration Age rivet from Mogen, Telemark, etched with 4% alcoholic HNO_3. The carbon content occurs mainly in the shank and the middle of the head. The micro-photograph fig.28 shows the transition from the coarse-grained, bright, ferritic part on the left to the finer pearlitic part on the right. Carburization may have taken place during the manufacture of the rivet, when it was forged from a billet, or during a later fire, when the object came into contact with carbon at a high temperature. The manufacture of rivets and nails – whether it is performed in a hole in the anvil or in a separate nail iron – is a process which includes forging at high and low temperatures, and as a result the original structure of the steel will be changed, either by carburization or by decarburization. Moreover, the size of the grains is also an outcome of the reducing conditions and the temperature in the smithy. Slag inclusions may even consume carbon.

Fig.13 shows a macrophotograph of an etched section of the rivet from the Viking Age, found at Kaupang in Vestfold. Only a small part of the top of the shank, immediately below the head, is preserved. Small amounts of carbon are present, and the structure is ferritic with even grains, see fig.29.

Fig.16 shows macrophotographs of the etched sections of the other Viking Age samples. The nail, O 294 bb, has a low carbon content; etching with alcoholic HNO_3 produced a weak blackening only in the head and at the centre of the shank. Under the microscope the carbon content was seen to decrease from the surface, where pearlite was observed, inwards, to pure ferrite at the centre, see fig. 31a. The size of the grains is least at the transition to the head. – This nail was made by forging together several pieces of very mild steel. The point shows ferrite of varying grain size, the smallest dimensions occurring at the outermost part, as a result of forging. The rivet O 294 g is also made from pieces of steel of varying carbon content, see fig.16. Microscoping showed a distinct border between a material where carbide is present along the outlines of the grains simultaneously with a high slag content, fig.31c, and a more coarse-grained, ferritic material which is lower in carbon and phosphorus, fig.31b, and contains less slag. Etching with Stead I in order to identify phosphorus produced a marking of the borderline by a needle-like precipitation, which may possibly indicate nitrides.

The polished section of the bar from Sørum, Hedmark, was blackened by etching with alcoholic HNO_3, see fig.16, without any great or sharp variations in the carbon content. Microscoping showed ferrite with small amounts of slag and some pearlite, enriched quite near the surface, in the dark parts, a possible result of forging and heat treatment, see fig.30.

The thirteenth-century rivet from Kongsgården, Oslo (fig.14), was in a very good state of preservation. It contained much slag and was forged together from several pieces. The etching with alcoholic HNO_3 was even and weak, and microscoping showed only ferrite, see fig.32.

The most recent of the rivets examined, that found in Ladegården, Oslo, dates from the sixteenth century. It is highly corroded, and only the inner part is left (see fig. 15).

This rivet is made from several pieces of mild steel, with some variation in their content of carbon. Close to the surface, pearlite was found, with streaks of more coarse-grained ferrite in the inner part. Fig.23 shows details of the structure of the pearlite. There is a triangular field of ferrite at the centre of the shank, immediately below the head; in the direction of that corner of the triangle which points towards the tip of the rivet, ferrite can be traced along the shank.

380

The entire material was also examined under the microscope after having been etched with the reagent Stead I, which causes areas rich in phosphorus to show up bright (white) by vertical illumination.

Rivet LaM 60 from L'Anse aux Meadows contained phosphorus in varying concentration in streaks and spots without any pronounced lamination, see fig.34. It appears to have been forged from a piece of ferritic steel with a carbon content of less than 0.2%, containing phosphorus. Fig.41 shows a microphotograph of a polished section of LaM 60, etched with Stead I. The structure resembles most closely that of the Viking Age bar from Sørum, Hedmark (see fig. 42).

A comparison with the macrophotographs of the other material from the Viking Age, also etched with Stead I as well as with alcoholic 4% HNO_3, reveals a different type of structure (see figs.13, 16, 37 and 38). The material from the Oseberg Find shows particularly clearly that the objects were manufactured by forging together lamellae of mild steel with varying contents of carbon and phosphorus. The boundaries between the different parts can be traced along the entire length of the objects, running parallel with the edges.

In the rivet from Kaupang, only very thin, bright lines rich in phosphorus were observed – these were parallel in the shank, but spread near the rivet head, illustratative of the work of forging. No slag or oxidation products were observed in the lines.

According to R.F. Tylecote (1962), the P_2O_5 content of wood-ashes may amount to 16%, and phosphorus in the form of a phosphate, e.g. calcium-phosphate, may, according to I.Rosenqvist and G. Taraldrud (1950), dissolve in iron at temperatures which were certainly reached in the primitive forge – 950°.

The Migration Age rivet from Mogen, Telemark, also has a markedly piled structure, see fig.43. The very well preserved thirteenth-century rivet from Kongsgården, Oslo, was made by forging together several pieces with no essential variation in their content of carbon or phosphorus, see figs.14 and 39.

The sixteenth-century rivet found in Ladegården, Oslo, consists of several pieces of mild steel with a low content of phosphorus (see fig.40). At a greater magnification, areas varying between pearlite and phosphorus-richer ferrite appear, with slag in the weld-seams separating them. Fig.33 shows a pearlitic area, etched with alcoholic HNO_3, and in fig. 44 we see the variation in the phosphorus content as it appeared as a result of etching with Stead I.

The distribution of phosphorus in the examined objects varies considerably. The actual phosphorus content in the metal of the rivets from Norway and the rivet LaM 60 has been spectrographically determined by S. Rutlin M.Sc. (Eng.), The Central Institute for Industrial Research. It was not possible to prove with absolute certainty the presence of phosphorus in any of the rivets by the method employed, whose accuracy for phosphorus was less than 0.05%. The results of these analyses give the average values of the phosphorus content in the bored samples, and the content will accordingly be higher in those areas of the metal which appear bright as a result of etching the polished section with Stead I. Several blooms and bars have been microscoped, and the pattern of variation of the phosphorus distribution found in the bar from Sørum, Hedmark, seems to be representative for iron (mild steel) produced from bog-ore. One cannot, however, overlook the fact that a possible content of phosphorus in the charcoal and the ash of charcoal will, by the forging of the bloom, influence the variation of the structures, possibly exemplified by the cases without any distinct welds between the distinctly phosphorus-rich and the phosphorus-poor parts. The effect of the phosphorus on the carburization is clearly demonstrated by the material.

As a result of the metallographic examination we may state that the metal in the single rivet preserved from L'Anse aux Meadows, LaM 60, represents a primitive form of mild steel. In its content of phosphorus and of carbon, as well as in the distribution of these elements, it resembles the iron bar of type Rygh 438, from Sørum, Hedmark, closely. The latter seems to be representative for blooms and bars made from bog-ore by primitive, direct reduction in Norway.

Spectrographical and chemical analyses

While a great number of analyses of copper and its alloys and of gold in prehistoric artefacts has been carried out, for instance in order to determine the origin of the ores used, few analyses of iron exist. In the copper-based alloys and in gold, the determination of elements of very low concentrations, the so-called trace elements, is of particular interest; the iron analyses so far carried out, on the other hand, are concerned with the determination of more common elements such as carbon, phosphorus, sulphur and manganese. Tylecote (1970) shows the material analysed and the possibly significant elements affecting the study of iron in a table reproduced as Table 1. The most characteristic elements are underlined, and the methods of analysis are given.

Table 1, from Tylecote (1970), Table 6

Material	Chemical analysis	Spectrographical analysis
Ore	Fe, Si, Ca, Mg	As, Cr, Cu, Ni, Pb, Ti, U, Zn, Co
Slag	P, Al, Mn, S, Cu	As, Ba, Bi, Cr, Cu, Mo, Co, Ni, Pb, Sb, Sn, Ti, U, Zn
Metal	P, Si, Mn, S, Ni, Cu	Al, As, Ba, Bi, Ca, Co, Cu, Mg, Ni, Pb, Sb, Sn, Ti, U, Mo, Zn

382

Table 2. Optical spectrographical analysis of remains of iron objects and of bog-ore from Newfoundland.

Results shown in %.

Analysis No.	Rest of ignition	Cr	Na	Mg	Al	Si	P	Ca	V	Mn	Fe	Co	Ni	Cu	Zr	Mo	Ti	Ba	B
6 I 1 Fragment (LaM51) ……				< 1	< 4	< 4		~ 1			~50	≲0.01	0.01	≲0.001					
9 I 6 Head of rivet (LaM56) 4	84			< 3	< 4	~ 5	~ 2			<0.2	~75	0.04	0.02	0.002			0.02		Traces
10 I 10 Rivet (LaM60) ………	84			< 5	~10	~20				<0.4	~50	0.03	0.01	≲0.001			0.05		
12 I 12 Mounting? (LaM62) ..				~10	~20	~25				>0.1	~75	0.03	0.03	0.001			0.05		
13 I 13 Head of rivet (LaM63) .	83		0.5	~25	~20	~25	~ 1	~ 2		>0.4	~75	0.02	0.02	0.002	0.04		0.10		
15 I I Rivet (LaM29) ………				< 2	~ 5	~20?		<0.2	~0.1	>0.2	50	0.10	0.05	0.004		0.02	0.05	0.20	
16 I II Rivet (LaM30) ………			0.1	~ 5	~10	~20		<0.1	~0.01	<0.4	50	0.04	≲0.01	≲0.001			0.02		
17 I III Rivet (LaM26) ………				< 4	< 2	< 5				<0.1	~50	0.10	0.01	0.003			0.04		
20 I 3 Fragment (LaM53) …÷						~ 5					~25?	≲0.01	≲0.01	0.001					
27 J34, I Fragment (LaM233) .			0.4	~25	~ 5	~25		~ 2	~0.01	<0.4	~50	0.02	0.01	0.001	0.01		0.04		
28 J34, II Fragment (LaM233)		~0.01	0.4	~25	~10	~25		~ 2	~0.01	<0.4	~50	0.02	0.01	0.002	0.01		0.05	0.04	
14 I 43 Bog-ore (LaM281) ….				~25	~ 5	~ 1				>1–2	~50	0.03	0.01	0.001			0.01		
25 I 22 Bog-ore (LaM293) ……				< 5	~ 5	~10				>1–2	~50	0.02	≲0.01	≲0.001			0.01		
11 I 12 Sand with rust (LaM62)			0.4	~20	~20	~50	~ 5	~10	0.04	>0.4	~25	0.02	0.02	0.004	0.04		0.10		Traces

383

In many cases the iron ores which were worked in prehistoric times no longer exist, but analyses of slags in conjunction with metallographic examinations of the structure of the remains of slag in the iron may provide some information concerning their origin. On the other hand, the abundance of iron ores, and the fact that they are found over such extensive territories, render it less likely that one should be able to determine the place of origin of the ore used in the production of a given artefact.

Very often, prehistoric iron objects were manufactured by forging together smaller pieces which may be of different origin. One must also take into consideration the influence of the forging-process on any surface of the different parts constituting the total object, and the change in the surface of this caused by the process of forging the smaller parts together (Coghlan, 1956). By repeated heating during forging, the iron will be oxidized and removed from the metal phase, which will be enriched on the more noble metals which may be present, such as Cu, Ni, and, further, on As, P and other elements which are less easily oxidized. By the analysis of an object formed in the way described, the result will be an average value, of rather small significance in most cases. In these cases, and also when the slag in the metal is to be examined, the use of the microprobe will be extremely helpful. Samples of the material from L'Anse aux Meadows, as well as of the material for comparison, were analysed with an optical spectrograph by S. Rutlin M.Sc. (Eng.) of the Central Institute for Industrial Research. The results are given in appendix I, 1 in extenso.

Table 2 shows the results of these analyses as applied to the remaining iron objects and the bog-ore from Newfoundland. The analyses were carried out before the objects had been examined by X-rays. The X-ray radiography, as we have pointed out above, proved the existence of more than a microscopic amount of metallic iron for only one rivet, LaM 60. Accordingly, new analyses were later carried out on the metal in the rivet LaM 60 and on the material for comparison, samples being taken by boring in the metal. These analyses were carried out by the same method as the first series, and the results shown in Table 3 were obtained.

**Table 3. Optical spectographic analysis of the
rivet LaM 60 (1970)**

Major constituent: Fe

Co:	0.015%
Cu:	0.08%
Al:	0.02%
Ni:	0.06%
Si:	0.04%
Mn:	$< 0.005\%$

384

Table 4. Optical spectrographic analysis of the dated
rivets from Norway (1970)

Major constitutent: Fe

	No.1	No.2	No.3	No.4
%Co	0.06	<0.005	0.06	0.02
%Cu	0.02	$\lesssim 0.005$	0.01	0.01
%Al	0.025	<0.005	0.01	0.01
%Ni	(0.005)	<0.005	0.15	<0.005
%Si	0.1	~ 0.03	0.05	0.07
%Mn	0.01	<0.005	$\lesssim 0.05$	$\lesssim 0.05$

Phosphorus in concentrations above 0.05% was not found. Analysis no.1 in Table 4 represents the thirteenth-century rivet from Kongsgården, Oslo; no.2 represents the sixteenth-century rivet from Ladegården, Oslo; no.3 the Viking Age rivet from Kaupang, Vestfold; and no.4 the Migration Age rivet from Mogen, Telemark.

A sample of bog-ore from Mogen was also analysed, analysis no.5, Appendix I,1. Phosphorus was not found in this case either. The accuracy of the method employed for this analysis is 0.05%.

Table 5. Optical spectrographic analysis (no.5) of bog-ore from Mogen, Møsstrand, Telemark, found together with the rivet (analysis no.4 above).

Major constituent: Fe

%Co	0.02
%Cu	0.004
%Al	20
%Ni	0.03
%Si	25
%Mn	1-2

Two Norwegian rivets have been analysed by T. Dannevig-Hauge (1946, p.180 and p.200), by the optical spectrographic method. All the 76 samples of prehistoric iron from Norway analysed by Dannevig-Hauge yielded less than 0.001% phosphorus.

The earlier of these two rivets, Cat.No. C 16898, dates from the Migration Age, and was found in Bø, Telemark. The carbon content was 0.67%. The more recent rivet, Cat.No. C 6734d, dates from the Viking Age, and comes from Nord Aurdal, Oppland. It contained 0.62% carbon. Co, Cu, Ni and Mn were also determined, with the following results:

Cat.No. C 16898: Co. 0.003%, Cu: 0.030%, Ni: not determined, Mn: 0.010%.
Cat no. C 6734d: Co: 0.214%, Cu: 0.007%, Ni: 0.022%, Mn: 0.186%.

C.A.Zapfe (1955) has analysed a rivet from the Oseberg ship with the following result:

C: 0.22%, Si: 0.02%, Mn: 0.04%, S: 0.005%, P: 0.075%, N: 0.003%. This is the highest content of phosphorus so far found (1971) in prehistoric Norwegian iron, in contrast with the much higher values observed in the Swedish,

385

Table of detected elements with estimate of their relative concentrations.

	Cr	Na	Mg	Al	Si	P	Ca	V	Mn	Fe	Co	Ni	Cu	Zr	Mo	Ti	Ba	B	Rest of ignition
1			II+	IV+	V+				1+	4+(?)	10+	5+	5+		1+				
2			V+	IV×	X+					4+(?)			3+						
3									1+	4+	5+	5+	4+		4+				
4			2+	1+	1+				1+	4+	4+	3+	3+		1+				97%
5		4+	1+	4+	5+		2+		10–20+	3+	2+	3+	4+		1+	5+			
6					IV+		1+			2+		1+							
9			III+	IV+	1+	2+			II+	3+	4+	2+	2+			2+		1+	84%
10			V+	2+	4+				IV+	2+	3+	1+				5+		1+	84%
11		4+	4+	4+	10+	5+	10+	4+	4+	1+	2+	2+	4+	4+		10+			
12			2+	4+	5+				1+	3+	3+	3+	1+	3+		5+			83%
13		5+	5+	4+	5+	1+	2+	10+	4+	3+	2+	2+	2+	4+		10+			73%
14			5+	1+	1+				10–20+	2+	3+	1+	1+			1+			
15			II+	1+	4+(?)		II+	1+	2+	2+	10+	5+	4+		2+	5+	2+		
16		1+	1+	2+	4+		1+		IV+	2+	4+					2+			
17			IV+	II+	V+				1+	2+	10+	1+	3+			4+			
18			1+	1+	4+		2+	2+	10–20+	2+	1+		1+	1+		5+	1+		
19		4+	4+	4+	5+		5+		4+	1+(?)	3+	1+	3+			10+	4+		
20					1+					1+			1+						
21		2+	3+	1+	4+		4+		4+	2+	1+		2+	1+		4+	2+		
22	1+	4+	5+	2+	5+		5+	4+	4+	2+	4+	1+	3+	2+		5+	4+		
23	1+	4+	5+	1+	4+		5+	2+	5+	2+			1+	1+		5+	5+		
24	1+	5+	5+	2+	5+		10+	4+	4+	1+		1+	1+	2+		10+	5+		72%
25			V+	1+	2+				10–20+	2+	2+					1+			
26	2+	2+	5+	2+	4+		4+	5+	10+	2+			2+	1+		10+	2+		
27		4+	5+	1+	5+		2+	1+	IV+	2+	2+	1+	1+	1+		4+			
28	1+	4+	5+	2+	5+		2+	1+	IV+	2+	2+	1+	2+	1+		5+	4+		

Estimated %

1+ ~1/100% x/10% ~5% ~5% ~5% ~1% ~1% >1/10+ ~25%

1+   <1% <1% <1% <1% <1/10% <1/10% <1/10%

Estimated %

1/100% 1/100% 1/100% x100% 1/1000% x100% 1/100% 1/100% 1/100% traces

In charge
Betty Dirdal

Order No.
FS 1752

Page

Danish and northern German material from the same period, see e.g. O.Arrhenius (1959) and R. Thomsen (1967 and 1972).

Samples of the slag from house J were subjected to chemical analysis: LaM 303 (No. I 20), Lam 283 (No. I 21), and LaM 284 (No. I 31). Bog-ore found near house J, LaM 293 (No. I 22), was also analysed chemically. For comparison, a sample of slag from the smithy at Jan Mayen, probably from the seventeenth century, was also analysed. These chemical analyses were carried out by Turid Malthe-Sørensen, cand. mag., Institute for Geology, University of Oslo. Her report is given in extenso in appendix I, 2. She also determined the MgO content of a sample of sand from the excavation site, which proved to contain between 1.85% and 2.05% of MgO. This analysis was carried out with a view to finding an explanation of the high Mg content resulting from the spectrographic analyses made in 1964. All these analyses must be contaminated by sand from the site, a fact which is confirmed by the content of Ti, Zr and V which, apart from the major constituents, were common to the excavated samples and the sand.

Sand from the rivet head, LaM 62, was analysed spectrographically, analysis No.11, table 2. It seems to be a calcium-magnesium-aluminiumsilicate with manganese and titanium, and c. 5% phosphorus, as well as rust. Two more of the iron remains contained phosphorus in concentrations of the same order of magnitude, viz. LaM 56 and LaM 63, analyses No.9 and No.13 in table 2. LaM 56, LaM 62 and LaM 63 were all found in the same room, house F room VI. The high phosphorus content must be a result of habitation – bone was also found in this room.

Below we have used the analytic material in an attempt at finding a correlation between the chemical composition of the rivet LaM 60, the slag found in house J and the samples of bog-ore: The bog-ore LaM 293 (No.I 22) was found in house J, while bog-ore LaM 281 (No. I 43) was taken from under the turf beyond the area excavated.

The low yield of the primitive methods of reducing iron practised during the Viking Age and the early part of the Middle Ages is reflected by, among other factors, the high iron content of the slags. The impurities, consisting of Si, Al, Ca, Mg, Mn and the alkalis will normally all be included in the slag, except where exceptionally reducing conditions obtain.

In all cases, at least 99% of the manganese in the ore finds its way into the slag, where it plays a very important part in replacing some of the iron. The phosphorus in the ore can be reduced and taken up by the iron, although part of it goes into the slag. According to Tylecote (1962, p.253) there is evidence of a partition of the phosphorus, $\frac{1}{4}$ to $\frac{1}{2}$ of the phosphorus present in the ore entering the slag, although this will depend on the composition of the actual slag. Usually 100% of the Cu and Ni will be found in the metal-phase, possibly also the Co.

A dated slag from the Viking Age, which forms part of a find consisting mainly of smiths' tools, Cat.No. C 27454, from Morgedal, Telemark, was examined by microprobe by William L. Griffin, Ph.D., of the Mineralogical-Geological Museum of the University of Oslo. In one sample, metallic blebs from 10–40μ were analysed with the following result:

Table 6.

Metallic blebs 10–40μ in slag from Cat.No. C 27454, Morgedal, Telemark, Viking Age, analysed by microprobe by W.L.Griffin.

Bleb No.	Fe%	Cu%	Ni%	Sum
1	5.4	83.2	0.4	89.0
2	98.6	0.7	–	99.3
3	100.9	0.2	0.2	101.3
4	100.8	0.3	1.1	102.2
5	98.1	1.2	–	99.3
6	99.8	0.4	–	100.2
7		8.4	–	–

One of the seven blebs analysed consisted of copper with 5.4% Fe and 0.4% Ni; the other constituents were not determined. It will be seen that the copper content of some of the other blebs was also considerable, and we must assume that the temperature was so low that the copper, the first metal to be reduced, could not be taken up in solution in the iron.

In another sample from the same lump of slag, the reduced metal consisted exclusively of iron with Cu, Ni and Mn, all below 0.05%. Here the temperature must have been sufficiently high for an even distribution by solution in the iron of Cu, Ni and Mn to take place. If this is generally applicable, the significance of the fact should be noted when slags are analysed.

A lump of slag from L'Anse aux Meadows, weight 120 g, LaM 284 (No. I 31), which was found in house J, has been analysed by W.L. Griffin. No copper blebs were found in the slag, and only one bleb (< 5μ) with a Ni-concentration in Fe. All the other Fe-blebs contained less than 0.05% of Cu, Ni and Mn.

The slag will be in contact with the material of the lining of the smelting hearth or furnace, and take up silicates from this. The ash from the fuel may influence the contents of alkaline metals and of metals of alkaline earths, and possibly also the content of phosphorus. A calculation of the yield obtained if the ore I 22 had been reduced, producing the slags I 20, I 21 and I 31, gives an indication of the probability of this being the case. Correspondingly, a calculation of the yield based on the Cu and Ni-contents of rivet and ore might be employed. Usually the yield obtained is estimated at about 20%, and this was also the result obtained by Wynne and Tylecote (1958) from experimental reductions carried out in the laboratory. Table 7 shows the results of the analyses of the 3 slags and the bog-ore, I 22. It appears from appendix I, 1 that the bog-ore gave a rest of ignition of 72%. The slags were not ignited. In none of the samples was Al determined.

Table 7. Chemical analyses of slags and bog-ore from L'Anse aux Meadows (T. Malthe-Sørensen)

	LaM, 303 I 20 Slag	LaM 283 I 21 Slag	LaM 284 I 31 Slag	LaM 293 I 22 Bog-ore	LaM 293 I 22 Recalculated
%SiO_2	18.9	18.1	15.7	1.4	1.9
%FeO	59.0	53.4	64.1	11.4	15.8
%Fe_2O_3	9.8	16.1	9.35	57.4	79.5
%MnO	3.3	2.1	1.1	0.5	0.68
%CaO	1.4	2.0	1.8	0.5	0.68
%MgO	1.6	1.4	1.4	0	
%Na_2O	0.4	0.5	0.4	0.09	0.12
%K_2O	0.5	0.7	0.8	0.1	0.14
%P_2O_2	0.59	0.52	0.47	0.26	0.38
Sum	95.49	94.82	95.12	Rest of ignition 72%	99.18
%Z:Fe_2O_3	75.4	75.4	80.6		97.0
%Z:FeO	67.8	67.8	72.5		87.2

These analyses show that the chemical composition of the slags is similar to that found in slags occurring in connection with the prehistoric production of iron. The results of chemical analyses of such slags are given by i.a. M. Bartuska and R. Pleiner (1965, p.20), who list the results obtained from 25 different European slags (see table 8). The low alkali and alkaline earth content suggests that no flux had been added, and that the slags had been essentially produced by the ore and the fuel-ash. The alkalis may also have been leached out by the ground water.

Table 8. Chemical analyses of slags from prehistoric ion production in bloomeries (M. Bartuska and R. Pleiner, 1965)

	Range	Average	Molecular%
%SiO_2	13.20–34.93	23.2	27.2
%FeO	39.20–65.42	52.8	51.5
%Fe_2O_3	0.44–24.29	7.0	3.1
%MnO	0.35–13.00	5.5	5.5
%CaO	Traces- 7.24	3.0	3.8
%MgO	Traces- 9.20	1.8	3.1
%P	0.06- 1.48	0.37	0.8
%S	Traces- 0.37	0.05	0.1
%Al_2O_3	0.8- 19.63	5.8	4.0
%Fe	0.23- 3.68	0.71	0.9

In cases where bog-ore was used, the phosphorus content tends to be higher than that given in table 8, especially in analyses of Swedish material, by O. Arrhenius (1959). Analyses of Norwegian reduction slags carried out by R. Falck-Muus (1931), on the other hand, fall within the range given in table 8, but the material analysed is unfortunately undated. The reason for this difference is probably the essential use of bog-ore in Norway on the one hand, and the exploitation in Sweden of the very rich lake-ores on the other; these occur in abundance in the southern half of that country. We still do not have a sufficient number of analyses of the Norwegian material, but the problem is at present being investigated.

On the basis of the content of SiO_2, MnO and CaO in the slags and ore from L'Anse aux Meadows, table 7, the eventual yield has been calculated on the assumption that the slags were produced by the reduction of the bog-ore No.I 22. The sample of ore gave a rest of ignition of 72%, and the values of the analyses were recalculated, the ore being considered as roasted.

Table 9, $\text{Yield}\,\% = \dfrac{C_{Fe_2O_3/ore} - C_{Fe_2O_3/slag} \cdot C_{MeO/slag} \cdot \dfrac{C_{MeO/ore}}{}}{C_{Fe_2O_3/ore}} \cdot 100$

Slag	Yield calculated on basis of MeO=%SiO_2	Yield calculated on basis of MeO=%MnO	Yield calculated on basis of MeO=%CaO
LaM303 – I 20	92.0%	84.4%	62.2%
LaM283 – I 21	91.8%	76.0%	73.4%
Lam284 – I 31	90.1%	43.5%	68.8%

Contaminations by the above oxides from the environment on the slag will give the effect of a "false" increase in the yield, but even when this is taken into consideration, the calculated yield is far too high, implying that the slag was not produced by the reduction of the bog-ore I 22.

Schürmann (1958) shows the yield of iron as a function of the loss of iron oxydul at varying content of iron oxydul in the ore. This curve is reproduced in fig.45.

Table 7 shows the iron oxide content expressed as iron oxydul in slags and ore. The slags I 20 and I 21 both contain 67.8% FeO, expressed in this way, and will according to Schürmann's curve produce a maximum yield of c. 70% by the reduction of the ore I 22, which contains 87.2% FeO, whereas the slag I 31, with a content of 72.5% FeO, will produce a yield value of 65%. As stated above, such high yields are improbable, and the result confirms our earlier assumption that the slags cannot have been produced from the ore I 22.

Calculations of the yield, $y = \dfrac{C_{metal/ore}}{C_{metal/iron}} \cdot 100$, on the basis of the content of the elements copper, nickel and cobalt in the ore and metal may also be of interest for the evaluation of the possibility of producing iron from the ore found at L'Anse aux Meadows. Unfortunately only one of the remains of iron

390

still contains metallic iron, LaM 60; and this as well as all the other objects originally of iron may have been brought here as finished objects.

For purposes of comparison, we shall now turn to the spectrographic analyses of the Norwegian rivet from the Migration Age, found at Mogen, and of the bog-ore found together with this, tables 4 and 5. On the assumption that 100% of Cu, Ni and Co enter the metal, the yield of the production of the Mogen rivet would be: according to the Cu content, 40%, to the Ni content 600%, and to the Co content 100%. This must mean that the rivet was produced from an ore of a different composition than that found together with it. At this point one should bear in mind the results obtained by Griffin when analysing the blebs of reduced metals in the slag, which show a certain degree of heterogenity.

Table 10 shows the yield calculated from the spectrographic analysis of the rivet LaM No.60, and of the samples of bog-ore, one of which, I 22, was found inside house J, while the other comes from beyond the site of excavation. The values employed are taken from table 2.

Table 10.

	Cu%	Ni%	Co%	Yield acc. Cu content	Yield acc. Ni content	Yield acc. Co content
Rivet LaM 60	0.08	0.06	0.015			
LaM 293 Ore I 22	0.001	0.01	0.02	1.25%	16.6%	135%
LaM 281 Ore I 43	0.001	0.01	0.03	1.25%	16.6%	200%

The fact that the calculated yields accord so badly may be due to the assumption that Cu, Ni and Co will go over into the metal to the extent of 100%; but the low value of yield obtained from Cu as compared to the extremely high values obtained from Ni and Co shows that neither of these ores can have been exploited. Here we should again refer to the observations of Coghlan (1956) on the local increase in the concentrations of these metals as a result of forging.

S. Ektorp (1963) reduced analysed bog-ores, and analysed the metal obtained, before and after forging. He observed that the content of Cu and Co in the metal was high. His Co content in the ore was 0.020%, that in the metal 0.31%, which produces a yield of c. 66%, whereas the Cu content in the ore was less than 0.002%, and that of the metal less than 0.005%, which gives a caculated value of yield of c.40%.

II The Slags

Samples containing slag, collected at the excavation, were submitted for examination. Those deriving from house J, the Eskimo settlement and the southern area had been taken by Kristján Eldjárn. His list of these collections of samples is included in the main catalogue, pp 250–2. Further, three more samples of slag were received. Two of these, found in house B, were examined by Sveinung Bergstøl, and his report appears in extenso in Appendix II.2. The third of these samples was marked "Lump of slag(?), house B, cooking pit". The author has not herself visited the site.

The collections of samples weighed up to 4 kg. They were examined under a binocular microscope, and polished sections and thin sections were prepared and observed under the special microscopes at high magnification. X-ray powder diagrams were taken, and chemical and optic-spectrographic analyses carried out.

All the samples with slag contained light slag, glassy with bubbles, and of a whitish colour, and many of them were contaminated with stones and sand. These were the major consitituents of each of the collections of samples, but apart from these, they also held up 20% dark, dense, heavier slag; in some cases there were also small pieces of tap-slag. Fig.46 is a representative picture of the heavier, dark slag, and fig.47 shows an example of the dark slag which has flown, i.e. tap-slag.

Nearly all the collections of samples contained bog-ore in varying amounts. Most of them also contained a light, clay-like, burnt material in contact with slag, very similar to the burnt clay used for lining the hearths and furnaces known from iron bloomeries in Scandinavia.

The remains consisted of burnt and unburnt stone, charcoal, rust and sand which, together with the light slag with bubbles, is what one would expect to find on the site of a house which had burned down. On the other hand, the presence of the heavy type of slag and the bog-ore, the objects found near the anvil-stone, and the charcoal kiln which was discovered close by, would all seem to show that forging, and probably also the production of iron were carried out here, even though the bloomery has not been found.

The primitive reduction carried out in a bloomery produces a characteristic type of slag. On the basis of the chemical analyses, chapter I, table 7, different diagrams of constitution can be constructed for the slags. Morton and Wingrove (1969), for instance, have used the three-component system of FeO, Fe_2O_3 and SiO_2, recalculating these values in the analyses of the slags to 100% for the purpose of constructing the diagram. Table 11 shows the values of the slags from L'Anse aux Meadows, recalculated according to this method.

Table 11. Analysis of slags from L'Anse aux Meadows, expressed in FeO + Fe_2O_3 + SiO_2 = 100%

Slag	FeO	Fe_2O_3	SiO_2
LaM 303 I 20	67.25	11.25	21.50
LaM 283 I 21	60.90	18.40	20.70
LaM 284 I 31	72.00	10.50	17.50

On fig. 48 the diagram is shown, with the addition of the point representing the average values of the 25 analyses of European slags given by Bartuska and Pleiner (1965) (see table 8). Recalculated, these values are: FeO–63.6%, Fe_2O_3 – 8.4%, and SiO_2 – 28.0%; the point is indicated by the letters B–P. In order that low-melting slags, which are essential if the production is to succeed, may be formed, the composition of the slags must be close to that of fayalite. It may be seen on the diagram that outside the area of fayalite the melting point rises steeply, and small changes in the composition may have the effect of producing non-running slag. This argument is based on the assumption that the present Fe_2O_3 content of the slag is the same as that when it was tapped, and that it is not the result of later oxidation.

The average value of the European slags lies within the fayalite area, where the melting point is below 1200°C. Although the slags I 31 and I 21 lie outside this area, their melting point is fairly close to 1200°C, and I 20 lies within the fayalite area. The temperature which is generally held to have been obtained in the primitive iron bloomeries was a maximum of 1300°C, and the composition of the slags shows that they could have worked, i.e. they could have been fluid.

The constitution of the slags can also be studied by determining the mineralogical phases present, again on the assumption that no oxidation has taken place. For this examination samples were taken from the inner part of the slag specimens. X-ray powder diagrams, thin sections and polished sections were prepared. For purposes of comparison, slag from known Norwegian iron bloomeries was subjected to a corresponding examination.

Figs. 49–54 show thin sections of samples of slag. All of them contain more or less fayalite, opaque minerals and glass. On the inside of the bubbles hematite occurred, probably as a product of oxidation. This also appears on fig.55, which shows a slag from Rogne, Slidre, Oppland, dating from A.D. 500, and on fig.56, an undated slag from Laurvik, Ustevann, Buskerud.

Figs. 57 – 63 show the polished sections. It appears from these that the slags consist of wüstite (FeO), light grey, in dendrites; a small amount of metallic iron, quite white particles; these are in a matrix of fayalite and glass. The amount of wüstite present shows that the reduction did not proceed far, i.e. the slag is a result of a not entirely successful process. Most of the slags from early periods which have been examined give pictures like this, for instance those shown by Bartuska and Pleiner (1965), and by Morton and Wingrove (1969).

X-ray powder diagrams of the Norwegian slags and of those from L'Anse aux Meadows confirmed the presence of the phases wüstite, some magnetite and fayalites.

Four of the slags, Nos. I 20 and I 22 from house J, and IV and V from house B have been analysed by optical spectrograph, see table 2 and appendix I,1. The two latter samples were analysed twice, and the results are shown in table 12.

Table 12: Optical spectrographic analysis of slags from L'Anse aux Meadows

No.	Provenance	Co%	Ni%	Cu%	Mn%
LaM 49 IV	House B	0.01	≲0.01	0.001	1–2
LaM 49 IV	House B	0.01	≲0.01	0.002	0.4
LaM 3 V	House B	0.03	0.01	0.003	0.4
LaM 3 V	House B	0.04	0.01	0.003	0.4
LaM 303 I 20	House J	≲0.01	≲0.01	0.001	0.5
LaM 301 I 22	House J	≲0.01	0.01	0.001	0.4

By the method employed for these analyses in 1964, phosphorus in concentrations less than c. 1% could not be detected. The content of Co and of Cu seems to be somewhat higher in the two samples from house B than in those from house J. Ba, Ti, Zr, V and Cr were found; of these elements, Ba and Cr were not found in the sand. If these slags had been formed as a result of the reduction of the bog-ores found on or near the site (Nos. I 43 and I 22, analyses Nos.14 and 25, table 2), one would have expected at least the Cu content of the slags to be lower than the corresponding content of the ores which was, for No.I 43, found outside the site, 0.001%, and for No.I 22, found in house J, still less.

Comparison with dated, prehistoric slags from Europe has shown that the investigated slags from L'Anse aux Meadows have a constitution which corresponds chemically, and also with regard to the phases present, to those formed by the primitive direct reduction to iron in the bloomery. There is, however, also a possibility of formation of slags of the type found by the process of forging, Usually when forging operations are carried out at a comparatively low temperature (1000°–1100°), hammer-scale consisting of iron oxides is formed. But the primitive wrought iron was not pure, and almost always contained inclusions of slag. This had to be removed by forging at a temperature higher than the melting point of the slags, i.e. at least above 1100°. Such slag inclusions are shown in figs. 22–27. By the hammering carried out when forging, the slag is pressed out to the surface, and slag of the same composition as the smelting slag may be produced.

It was common practice in prehistoric times to weld together small pieces of iron, or iron and steel, when manufacturing objects. This was a process

394

requiring a high temperature. Near the stone which forms the anvil of the smithy magnetic flakes (No I 32) were found. These were shown to consist of FeO and Fe_3O_4 with small amounts of fayalite, as appeared from the presence of these phases in the X-ray powder diagrams. The flakes are hammer-scale, which is frequently observed on the surface of early iron, and has been described by, for instance, R.F. Tylecote (1962, p.254). When welding, the hammer–scale must be removed, in order that the metal parts will combine; sand may have been employed as flux, which would give a low-melting iron silicate and, accordingly, a smithing-slag of a composition like that of the reduction-slag. It is highly probably that the slags from L'Anse aux Meadows should include such smithing-slag, but the size of the lumps of the heavy type of slag and the tap-slag found must with a high degree of probability be interpreted as evidence of iron production.

A material was found in contact with the slag, which was luted together of whitish-pink, fine grains and a clay-like substance. Fig.62 shows a thin section, prepared by sawing through a sample, No.I 33. This substance was, together with a piece of the slag with the clay-like layer, No. I 22, examined by I. Th. Rosenqvist. His report is given in appendix II.3. According to this investigation, the white clay-like substance, No.I 33, contained so much clay that it may have been formed plastically and dried without loss of form, at the same time as it contains a high amount of quartz, which gives the material a good refractoriness. Sample No. I 22 may have been formed from sample No. I 33, by heating the latter to a temperature above 550°C, as is shown by the fact that the clay minerals have broken down, and below 1150°C, shown by the presence of unmelted plagioclase.

It appears from Eldjárn's report above and from information personally given by Gísli Gestsson, Keeper of the National Museum of Iceland, that a fine-grained white substance, similar in appearance to sample No. I 33, was used in Iceland – at least during the nineteenth century – for the construction of forges. In Icelandic this is known as *deigul-mór* or *smiðju-mór*. But no such substance has been found in Saga Age smithies in Iceland. Few smithies from this period have as yet been found. – The substance known as clay in Iceland is never a true clay, but silt. This cannot be heated to form a solid ceramic mass, turning instead into a powder on being heated. This powder, which looks like sand, may have escaped the attention of the archaeologists. – In Norway, clay linings of the type found at L'Anse aux Meadows are known from smelting hearths and forges, and also from furnaces, all periods of early iron being represented.

III The Ore

Microscoping and X-ray powder diagrams showed that the ores found inside house J contained the same minerals as those sampled outside the excavation site, and that both consisted of geothite, $HFeO_2$, and lepidocorcite, $FeO(OH)$.

The samples analysed by the optical spectrographic method, Nos.I 22 and I 43, had a rest of ignition of 72% and 73% respectively, while the chemical analysis of No. I 22 showed a rest of ignition of 72.65%, see table 7. It also showed that the SiO_2 content of I 22 was very low, 1.4%, and the iron oxide content, expressed as Fe_2O_3, very high, 69.8%, which means that the ore consists of nearly pure iron oxide. By optical spectrographic analysis the SiO_2 content was found to be 10 – 20%, and the Fe_2O_3 content c. 75%. Manganese was present in concentrations from 0.5 – 2%, and the sample analysed by the chemical method showed a concentration of phosphorus of 0.26% P_2O_5. By optical spectrography, both samples were found to have a phosphorus content of less than 1% P by the method employed.

The content of trace elements varied in the two samples. The ore found in the smithy contained 0.02% Co, but no Cu or Ni were detected by the method employed, while the sample of ore collected outside the excavation site contained 0.03% Co, 0.01% Ni and 0.001% Cu. The author has observed similar variations in analyses of bog-ores from adjacent occurrences at Møsstrand, Telemark, Norway. These analyses were carried out by spark-scorce mass-spectroscopy by O. Christie, Ph.D., Institute of Geology, University of Oslo, as part of an investigation of analytical methods for bog-ores. The results were given at the second Scandinavian conference on trace-elements, which was held in Århus in September 1971(unpublished). The sample of ore from the smithy at L'Anse aux Meadows, No.I 22, was also analysed by this method, resulting in a Co content of only 0.00079%, and a Cu content of 0.00032%, while Ni was not determined.

We may conclude from the investigation of the bog-ore from L'Anse aux Meadows that this may be said to be a good exploitable ore under the given conditions, being low in content of organic material, silica, lime and magnesia, and very high in iron oxides.

Final conclusions

The above investigations of the material excavated at L'Anse aux Meadows show that it is highly probable that iron production should have been attempted during an early period on the site, or close to it. Even though some of the iron slag must be interpreted as smithing slag, the presence of 1) larger, individual pieces of the same type of slag as that found in bloomeries of the Migration and Viking Ages on the continent of Europe, 2) the clay lining in contact with slag, in sherd-like pieces, of a thickness of 1–3 cm, 3) charcoal and the presence of a charcoal kiln nearby, 4) the bog-ore of good quality found

396

both with the slags and elsewhere in the area, should be sufficiently ample evidence of such attempts, even though the bloomery itself has not been found. The slags may even have been brought to the place where they were found, for instance in the rubble forming as a result of the breaking down of a used bloomery for the construction of a forge. Most of the pieces of slag seem to be broken fragments. As the author has not visited the site, this problem will not be discussed in more detail.

We do not know whether the production of iron here was successful or not, for the only find still containing iron was the inside of one single rivet. The metal is a very mild and pure steel, essentially ferritic, with a small amount of pearlite. The phosphorus content is less than 0.005%.

Most of the remains of iron objects found were rivets and nails excavated together with the houses, and they were probably used during building. If tools were manufactured here, they may have been taken away when the settlement was abandoned, or they may have rusted away completely, while metal which was in contact with wood is better preserved.

Miscellaneous

The following finds have been analysed:
LaM 67 (Sample No. I 17): "Slag and two other objects, house F, room VI." The two objects were a round stone of syenitic type and a pyrite, weighing 24g.
LaM 228, 230, 239 (Sample No. I 38): "House G, 1962, Rolf Petré. 3 finds from midden by house G." This sample includes a small piece of jasper, 28 mm $\times$ 23 mm $\times$ 6 mm, and 2 pyrites, weighing 10.24 g and 8.65 g respectively. If they were found lying together, they may have been used for striking fire.

In house A, room III, a bronze ring-headed pin of type Jan Petersen C was found. The ring was completely corroded, so that no metal remained, but the shape was quite clear in the form of the corrosion products, which consisted mainly of stannic acid. The semi-quantitative optical spectrographic analysis gave the following result:
Sn: $\sim$ 50%, Cu $\sim$ 20% Ag $\sim$20%, Pb $\sim$ 10%, with small amounts of Si, Al and Mg, probably contaminations from the soil. Corrosion removes Zn and also Cu, thus enriching Sn, Ag and Pb. Zn was not found, and one may thus assume that the original material was a bronze containing Ag and Pb.

Appendix I, 1

Central Institute for Industrial Research   REPORT
For: Mr. Helge Ingstad
Spectrographic analysis and comparison of 28 samples

Department	Order No.	Our ref.	Date
FS	FS 1,752	SR/bf	25th November 1964

We have received:

Samples for comparison, marked:
1. Kongsgården, Oslo. Middle Ages. 13th century.
2. Ladegården, Oslo. 16th century.
3. Kaupang, Vestfold. No. XXIIe. Viking Age.
4. Mogen, Telemark. Cat. No. C30088,x,14. Iron rivets. Migration Age.
5. Mogen, Telemark 1961. Cat. No. C30088,x, 14 – bog-ore.

Samples from America, marked:
6. No.1. LaM 51. Small piece of iron. House F room VI, 12.54 base, – 3.72 SE of this. 7 cm deep in old turf.
7. No. 3. Identical with analysis No.20.
8. No.4. LaM 54. Iron fragment, sickle-shaped. House F room VI. 14.79 m base, – 3.85 m SE, at floor level. Not analysed.
9. No.6. LaM 56. Rivet head. House F room VI. 10.75 m base, – 2.30 m SE. 10 cm deep in old turf.
10. No.10. LaM 60. Large iron rivet. House F room VI. 8.70 m base, – 25 cm SE. 10 cm deep in soil containing charcoal.
11. No.12. LaM 62. Rusty sand. House F room VI. 13.50 m base, – 1.50 SE. 10 cm deep in old turf.
12. No.12. LaM 62. Iron rivet head, found together with No.12, analysis No.11.
13. No.13. LaM 63. Iron rivet head. House F room VI. 10.80 m. base, – 0.09 m SE. At bottom of cultural layer.
14. No.43. LaM 281. Bog-ore found under turf S of houses B and C.
15. I. LaM 29. Iron rivet. House F room I.
16. II. LaM 30. Iron rivet. House G. At 25 cm depth in cultural layer, in sandy soil containing charcoal.
17. III. LaM 26. Iron rivet. House F room II, at centre of layer.
18. IV slag. LaM 49. Slag. Found when sieving soil from house B.
19. V slag. LaM 3. Large lump of slag, cut into two. Found at bottom of cooking pit, house B.
20. No.3. LaM 53. Iron fragment. House F room VI. 13.15 m base, – 3.90 m SE. Floor level – 5 cm above this.
21. IV slag. LaM 49. As analysis 18 above.
22. V slag, LaM 3. As analysis 19 above.
23. No.20. LaM 303. Slag. From house J.
24. No.22. LaM 301. Slag. From house J.
25. No.22. LaM 327. Bog-ore. From house J.
26. No.30. LaM 304. Flake from anvil. House J.
27. No.34 I. LaM 233. Piece of iron or rust. From house J.
28. No.34 II. LaM 233. Piece of iron or rust. From house J.

Preliminary treatment

In order to avoid all possible damage to the samples, we have not crushed down any great part of them, although this is required if a representative specimen for analysis is to be obtained. Our small specimens (a few mg) were taken from the surface or close to it, at a point where the material seemed to have undergone least change.

However, in order to obtain a specimen as representative of the average as possible, we have taken our specimens from different places on the objects (lumps), and in those cases where the sample consisted of more than one lump, a little material was taken from each. For some of our analyses we have spectrographed specimens derived from different lumps (of the same sample) individually, for others a magnetic separation was undertaken, and both fractions spectrographed. As these spectrograms (from the same main sample) show the same elements, although in some cases with a shift of concentration (e.g. the magnetic fraction contains more Fe and more

398

of the metals of the Fe group, while the non-magnetic fraction contains a greater proportion of the rock-forming elements), the table gives only a middle range of concentration. In most cases part of the outer layers was removed before specimens were taken.

All the specimens taken from the American samples could be pulverized, but they were more or less magnetic (magnetite?), and may consist of oxidized iron.

Commentary

Our analysis Nos. 18 and 21, 19 and 22 are similarly marked, IV and V respectively. We consider that the same sample was sent us twice, but as they showed a slight difference, both analyses are given in the table. Because of difficulties experienced in spectrographing some of the American samples, among others the bog-ores (analyses Nos. 14 and 25), these were ignited, and the rest of ignition spectrographed. The percentage of rest of ignition is given in the last row in the table.

In spite of repeated attempts, our analysis No.20 yielded only weak spectra. Because of this, the sample *may* contain elements which have not been detected. For some of the elements (Mg, Al, Si and MN) the concentration is given in two series, the lower concentrations being shown in Roman proportional figures, the higher in Arabic.

Appendix I, 2

Turid Malthe-Sørensen,
Institute of Geology,
University of Oslo.

Mr. Helge Ingstad,
Vettaliveien 24,
Oslo 3.

The following analyses of slag and bog-ore from Newfoundland have been carried out on the instructions of Anna Rosenqvist.

Five samples, marked as follows, were analysed:

    Ingstad 20 – LaM 303
    Ingstad 21 – LaM 283
    Ingstad 31 – LaM 284
    Bog-ore (22) – LaM 327
    Smithing slag from Jan Mayen

SiO_2 and total iron, calculated as Fe_2O_3, have been determined by atomic absorption. The sample was dissolved in hydrofluoric acid under pressure and analysed.

CaO, MgO and MnO were determined by atomic absorption. K_2O and Na_2O were determined by flame-photometer, and P_2O_5 was determined spectrophotometrically.

SiO_2 was removed by hydrofluoric acid, after which the solution was analysed by atomic absorption, flame-photometer and spectro-photometer.

Results:

	I 20	I 21	I 31	Bog-ore 22	17th-century smithing slag Jan Mayen
% SiO_2	18.9	18.1	15.7	1.4	32.6
% Fe_2O_3	75.4	75.4	80.6	69.8	30.1
% MnO	3.3	2.1	1.1	0.5	0.2
% CaO	1.4	2.0	1.8	0.5	6.2
% MgO	1.6	1.4	1.4	0	5.7
% Na_2O	0.4	0.5	0.4	0.09	1.15
% K_2O	0.5	0.7	0.8	0.1	0.9
% P_2O_5	0.59	0.52	0.47	0.26	0.36

Analysis of MgO in sand from L'Anse aux Meadows:

The MgO was determined by complexometric titration with EDTA. Results:

Sample 1.　Marked:........ under the turf (black)　......................2.05% MgO

Sample 2.　Marked: 15 m S of house J under the turf (brown) 1.83%MgO

Turid Malthe-Sørensen

(Sign.)

FeO determinations in Ingstad's samples:

	% Fe
I 20	59.0
I 21	53.4
I 31	64.1
Bog-ore I 22	11.4
Smithing slag, Jan Mayen	18.0

Central Institute for Industrial Research REPORT

Appendix I.3.

For: The University Museum of National Antiquities, Oslo, A.M. Rosenqvist, M.Sc.

Spectrographic Analysis of 4 Iron Rivets

Department	Order No.	Our ref.	Date
512	512 – 112	BD/1b	24th June 1970

Result:

	No.1 Kongsgården	No.2 Ladegården	No.3 Kaupang	No.4 Mogen
% Co	0.06	<0.005	0.06	0.02
% Cu	0.02	⪝0.005	0.01	0.01
% Al	0.025	<0.005	0.01	0.01
% Ni	⪝0.005	<0.005	0.15	<0.005
% Si	0.1	~0.03	0.05	0.07
% Mn	~0.01	<0.005	⪝0.005	⪝0.005

The samples remain at the Institute until further notice.

In charge	Approved	Enclosures	No. pages
B. Dirdal	S. Rutlin	1 X-ray photograph. Report No. FS 1753	1

Central Institute for Industrial Research REPORT

For: A.M. Rosenqvist,
　　　The University Museum of National Antiquities, Frederiksgt.2, Oslo 1.

Spectrographic Examination of an Iron Rivet, from Helge Ingstad (LaM 60).

Department	Order No.	Our ref.		Date
512	512 – 123	BD/1b		24th June 1970

Result:

	Co	0.015%
	Cu	0.08%
	Al	0.02%
	Ni	0.06%
	Si	0.04%
	Mn	$<0.005\%$

In charge	Approved	Enclosures	No. of pages
B. Dirdal	S. Rutlin		1

Central Institute for Industrial Research REPORT

For: The University Museum of National Antiquities, Oslo, A.M. Rosenqvist.
Determination of P in 5 Iron Rivets from the University Museum of National Antiquities.

Department	Order No.	Our ref.	Date
512	153	SR/gbs	3rd September 1970
inst.anal.			

Result:

P has not been securely demonstrated in any of the rivets
$P < 0.05\%$

Grindings from the following rivets were examined:
No. 2 Ladegården, Gamlebyen, Oslo. 16th century
No. 3 Kaupang, Vestfold, Norway. Viking Age
No. 4 Mogen, Telemark, Norway, C 30088 × 14
     – iron rivets + 2 sections from Helge Ingstad

In charge
Sigurd Rutlin

Appendix II.1.
6th July 1963.

Mr. Helge Ingstad,
Lance aux Meadows via Strait View,
Northern Newfoundland.

Dear Helge Ingstad,
    I now have the result of the analysis of the piece of metal, which shows that the piece consists of impure copper.

Copper (Cu)	95%
Zinc (Zn) order of magnitude	1%, possibly up to 5%
Iron (Fe) order of magnitude	1%
Lead (Pb) order of magnitude	$0.1 – 1\%$
Tin (Sn) order of magnitude	0.1%
Silver (Ag) order of magnitude	$0.01 – 0.1\%$

Traces: Antimony (Sb), bismuth (Bi), arsenic (As), gold (Au).
Impurities: Silicium (Si), aluminium (Al), magnesium (Mg), manganese (Mn), titanium (Ti)

All in all, we get the impression not of an alloy, but of a piece of copper made from ore which contained other metals also, and that these were not removed during the process of reduction. It seems most likely that a primitive method

401

was employed. In this connection it would be most interesting to know whether there are ores rich in zinc in Newfoundland – this would explain the comparatively high zinc content. This content is not high enough to suggest that this is an attempt at producing a brass alloy. The piece cannot represent a natural occurrence of metallic copper, for such copper is always extremely pure. I have not been able to find any references in literature to analyses with such a high content of zinc, lead and iron in metallic copper from a natural occurrence.

When you return to Norway we might perhaps discuss the possibility of taking a section from this piece of copper, so that we can find out how it was worked.

Anna M. Rosenqvist

Appendix II,2.
6th July 1962.

Mr. Helge Ingstad,
Vettaliveien,
Skådalen, Oslo.

Re: *Investigation of Samples of Slag*, submitted by Helge Ingstad from find in house-site in Newfoundland.

The lumps of slag had diameters of 2–10 cm. There were a number of pieces of charcoal in the slag, measuring up to 2 cm.

Microscoping of thin sections of the slag showed typical slag structures; polished sections examined under the metallographic microscope also showed typical slag structures. There are two phases of silicates, as well as iron oxide minerals, which chiefly consist of magnetite (Fe_3O_4) in the fresh samples; in the less fresh samples, an oxidation of the magnetite to other iron oxides had taken place. The polished sections also showed small grains of elementary iron (metallic iron).

All the above observations are proof of the samples being slag deriving from iron production. We were not able to establish with certainty whether this is slag deriving from the smelting of bog-ore or from iron production utilizing other kinds of ore.

Some photographs of polished sections, taken under the microscope, are enclosed.

Sveinung Bergstøl.

X-Ray Diphractometric Investigation of Samples I 22 (LaM 293) and I 33 (LaM 240) from the Excavations of Helge Ingstad in Newfoundland.

The two samples, submitted to us for investigation by A.M. Rosenqvist of the University Museum of National Antiquities, have been studied at our X-ray laboratory by the method normally employed for the analysis of the fine-fractions of fills and clay sediments.

The method consists of recordings made by the Siemens diphractometer with CuKαradiation, at a goniometer speed of 1°/min. Specimens were prepared by sedimenting the fine fraction of the samples on to glass holders, producing an orientation of the material which will give a maximum of intensity for the 001 reflections of material with a layered lattice structure.

Sample I 22 was a lump measuring c. $2 \times 2 \times 2$ cm, which consisted of fused, dark slag material on one side, and of lighter, coherent, brick-like, reddish material on the other. The specimen we investigated was taken from the latter.

Sample I 33 consisted of numerous earthy lumps which could be crumbled between the fingers. The material was light grey to brown. When reduced to powder, the colour was the same reddish-brown as the powder from I 22.

The X-ray diphractograms showed that I 22 contained mainly quartz, with some acid plagioclase-felspar (albite). In the range of 2θ between 4° and 15°, where the strongest refraction lines of the common clay minerals occur, no reflections were found. Sample I 33 gave reflection of quartz, acid plagioclase (albite), illite, chlorite, amphibole, potassium felspar (?) and kaolin (?). It may be described as a silt of low clay content, with a domination content of quartz.

If sample I 22 had been produced from I 33 by heat treatment, the temperature would have to have been sufficiently high to dehydroxylate (i.e. decompose) the clay minerals completely, i.e. higher than 550°C, but lower than the melting point of plagioclase, which is 1150°C.

Sample I 33 probably contains sufficient clay for it to be shaped plastically and dried out without any collapse, at the same time as the dominationg quartz content will give the material a high degree of refractoriness.

I.Th. Rosenqvist

Geological Institute, University of Oslo.

References

Arrhenius, O.: Die Grundlagen Unserer Älteren Eisenherstellung. Antikvarisk Arkiv 13, 1959, Stockholm

Bartuska, M. and Pleiner, R.: Untersuchung von Baustoffen und Schlacken aus den frühgeschichtlichen Rennöfen Böhmens und Mährens. Technische Beiträge zur Archäologic II Mainz 1965.

Coghlan, H. H.: Notes on Prehistoric and Early Iron in the Old World, p. 152. Occasional Papers on Technology, 8, Oxford 1956.

Dannevig-Hauge, T.: Blesterbruk og Myrjern, Universitetets Oldsaksamlings skrifter Bind II, 1946, Oslo

Eggers, R.: Die Ausgrabungen auf dem Magdalensberg 1960–61 Carinthia I/153 Jahrg., 1963.

Ektorp, S.: Några metallurgiska observationer vid reduksjonsforsök. Älvdalen 1965. Helgöundersökningens rapport, stensil.

Falck-Muus, R: Jernvinneslaggenes konstitusjon. Norsk Geologisk Tidskrift B. XII, pp. 193–217, Oslo 931

Haldane, W.: A study of the chemical composition of pre-Roman iron-work from Somerset. Bulletin of the Historical Metallurgy Group, Vol. 4, No. 2, 1970, pp. 53–66.

Knox: R.: Detection of iron carbide structure in the oxide remains of ancient steel. Archeometry 6, 1963 pp. 44–45.

Morton, G. R. and Wingrove, Y.: Constitution of bloomery slags Part I: Roman. Journal of Iron and Steel Institute. 1969. December pp. 1556–1564.

Nielsen, N.: Evidence of the Extraction of Iron in Greenland by the Norsemen, pp. 193–212. Meddelelser fra Grönland BC LXXVI. København 1930.

Oelsen, W. and Schürman: Untersuchungsergebnisse alter Rennfeuerschlacken. Archiv für das Eisenhüttewesen, 25 Jahrg. 1959.

Piaskowski, J.: Metallkundliche Untersuchungen an archäologischen Eisengegenständen der vorrömischen Eisen- und der römischen Kaiserzeit aus dem Nordosten der DDR. Etnogr. Archäl. Zeitschr. 10., pp. 301–332, Berlin, 1969.

The achievements of research carried out in Poland on the history of early technology of Iron. Méthodes et Méthodologie. Archaelogia Polana XII, pp. 187–215.

Classification de la structure des inclusions des scories et son application pour la determination de l'orgine des anciens objects de fer. (French summary), pp. 61–71. Kwartalnik Historie Kultury Material B. RXVII, nr. 1, 1969.

Pleiner, R. and Bartuska, M.: Untersuchung von Baustoffen und Schl.u.s.

Rosenqvist, I. and Taraldrud, G.: Noen undersøkelser over reaksjoner mellom jern og kobolt med Thomasslagg i fast fase. Tidsskrift for kjemi, bergvesen og metallurgi, nr. 1. January 1950, Oslo.

Schaaber, O.: Beiträge zur Frage des nordischen Eisens: Metallkundliche Grundlagen und Untersuchungen an Funden vom Magdalensberg in Die Ausgrabungen auf dem Magdalensberg 1960–61 Carinthia I/153 Jahrg., 1963 pp. 129–206.

Schürman, E.: Die Reduktion des Eisens im Rennofen. Stahl und Eisen 78, 1958, nr. 19, pp. 1307.

Schürman, E.: Untersuchungsergebnisse alter Rennfeuer Schlacken Archiv für das Eisenhüttewesen, 25 Jahrg. 1959 pp. 507–514.

Thomsen, R: Forsøg på rekonstruksjon av en fortidig jernudvindingsprocess. Kuml. 1963, pp. 60–74

Thomsen, R.: Undersögelse av jernalderslagger og jerngjenstander fra Hagestad i Skåne. Kuml, 1967, pp. 124–142.

Thomsen, R.: Untersuchungen zur Technologie des Eisens. Berichte über die Ausgrabungen in Haitabu, Berichte 5, 1972.

Thälin, L.: Svensk förhistorisk jarn – ett forskningsprosjekt. Jernkontorets annaler 151, 1967, pp. 305–324.

Tylecote, R., F.: Metallurgy in Archeology, London 1952, pp. 348.

Wingrove, Y. and Morton G. R.: Constitution of bloomery slags Part I: Roman. Journal of Iron and Steel Institute, 1969, December pp. 1556–64.

Wynn E. Y.: An Experimental Investigation into Primitive Ironsmelting-technique. Journal of the Iron and Steel Institute, December 1958, pp. 339–348.

Wynn E. Y.: The composition of metal artifacts: A Guide to Provenance, Antiquity XLIV, 1970, pp. 19–25.

Wynne, E. Y. and Tylecote, R. F.: An Experimental Investigation into Primitive Ironsmelting-technique. Journal of the Iron and Steel Institute, December 1958, pp. 339–348.

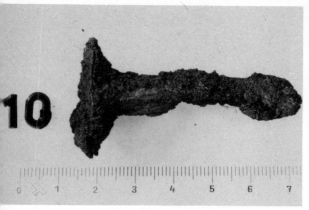

LaM 60 (Sample No. 10).

LaM 65 (Sample No. 17).

LaM 56 (Sample No. 6).

LaM 67 (Sample No. 17).

LaM 52 (Sample No. 2).   LaM 55 (Sample No. 5).

LaM 62 (Sample No. 12).

Fig. 1. Remains of Iron Objects.

LaM 244 (Sample No. 30).

LaM 51 (Sample No. 1).

LaM 66a, LaM 66b (Sample No. 16).

LaM 57 (Sample No. 7).
LaM 58 (Sample No. 8).

LaM 64a (Sample No. 14a). LaM 64b (Sample No. 14b).

Fig. 2. Remains of Iron Objects.

LaM 53 (Sample No. 3).
LaM 54 (Sample No. 4).

Mogen, Migration Age.

Kaupang, Viking Age.

Kongsgården, Oslo 13th century.

Ladegården, Oslo, 16th century.

LaM 51 (Sample No. 1),
LaM 56 (Sample No. 6).

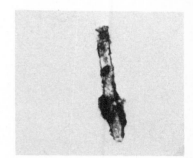

LaM 236 (Sample No. 36).

Fig. 3. X-ray radiographs of the remains of iron objects.

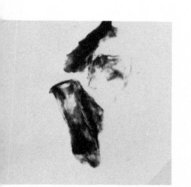

LaM 55 (Sample No. 5).

LaM 60 (Sample No. 10).

LaM 62 (Sample No. 12).
LaM 63 (Sample No. 13).

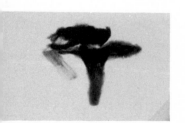

LaM 29 (Sample No. I).

LaM 30 (Sample No. II).

LaM 26 (Sample No. III).

LaM 65 (Sample No. 15).

Fig. 4. X-ray radiographs of the remains of iron
objects.

LaM 64 a and b (Sample No. 14 a
and b).

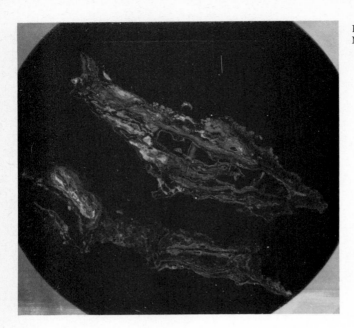

Fig. 5. Polished sections of unidentified objects: LaM 51 (Sample No. 1) on right, LaM 56 (Sample No. 6) on left.

Fig. 6. Polished section of LaM 60 (Sample No. 10).

Fig. 7. Polished section of LaM 62 (Sample No. 12) at top, and LaM 63 (Sample No. 13) below.

Fig. 8. Photographs of iron remains LaM 29 (Sample No. I), LaM 30 (Sample No. II) and LaM 26 (Sample No. III).

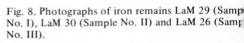

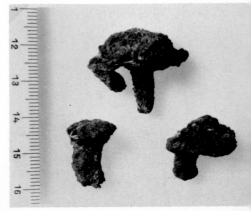

Fig. 9. Polished section of LaM 29 (Sample No. I), 3 x.

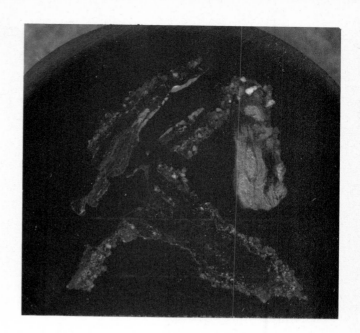

Fig. 10. Polished section of LaM 30 (Sample No. II), 3 x.

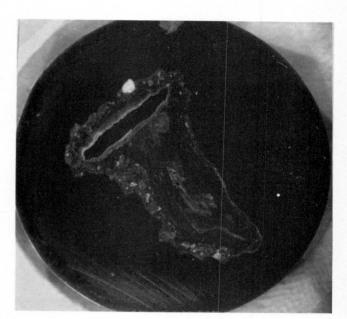

Fig. 11. Polished section of LaM 26 (Sample No. III), 3 x.

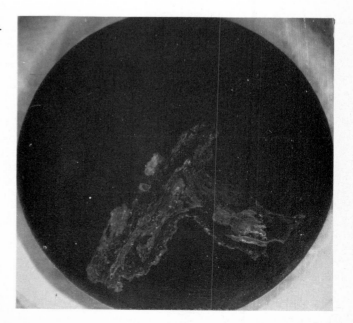

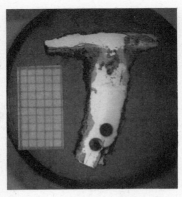

Fig. 12. Polished section of rivet,
Cat. No. C 30088, x,14, from
Mogen,Møsstrand, Telemark,
Norway. Migration Age. Etched
with 2% alcoholic HNO_3.

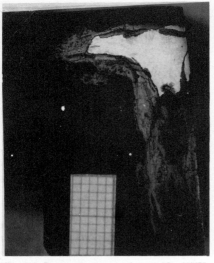

Fig. 13. Polished section of rivet, No. XXII e,
from Kaupang, Tjølling, Vestfold, Norway.
Viking Age. Etched with 2% alcoholic HNO_3.

Fig. 14. Polished section of rivet from Kongsgården, Gamlebyen, Oslo. 13th century.
Etched with 2% alcoholic HNO_3.

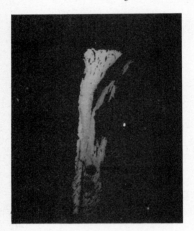

Fig. 15. Polished section of rivet from Ladegården, Gamlebyen, Oslo. 16th century.
Etched with 2% alcoholic HNO_3.

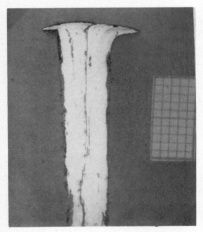

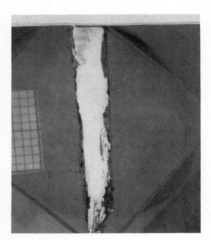

Top and bottom third of O 294 bb.

O 294 g,

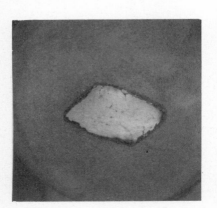

Fig. 16. Polished section of 2/3 of nail and of complete rivet from Oseberg, Slagen, Vestfold, Norway, Cat. No. O 294 bb and O 294 g, and of bar, Cat. No. C 26208, Sørum,
Veldre, Hedmark, Norway. All from Viking Age. Etched with 4% alcoholic HNO_3.

C 26208.

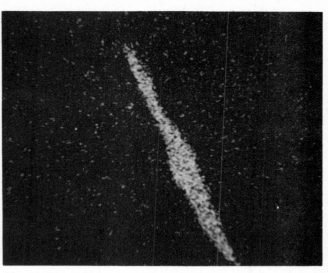

Fig. 17. Electron picture of polished section of rivet LaM 60 from 'Anse aux Meadows, taken with microprobe. The black areas are on-metallic. 500 x.

Fig. 18. The same area as in Fig. 17, taken with SiK_α - rays. The white areas consist of Si. 500 x.

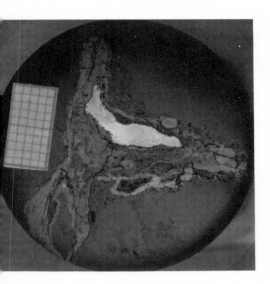

Fig. 19. Macrophotograph of polished section of rivet LaM 60. Etched with 4% alcoholic HNO_3.

Fig. 20. Microphotograph of polished section of rivet LaM 60, etched with 4% alcoholic HNO_3. Ferritic area with single-phase slag. 125 x.

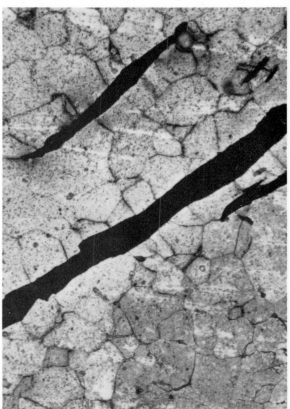

Part of same microphotograph, 200 x.

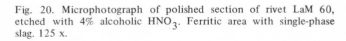

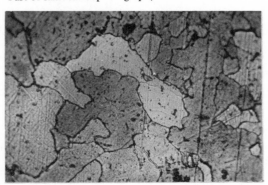

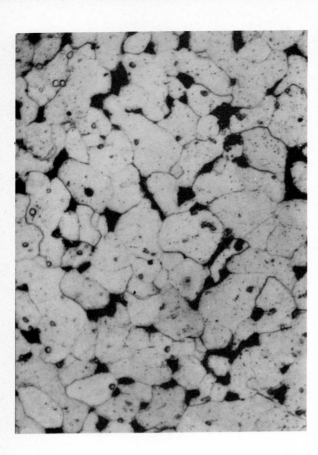

Fig. 21. Microphotograph of polished section of rivet LaM 60. Area with pearlite. Etched with 4% alcoholic HNO_3. 125 x.

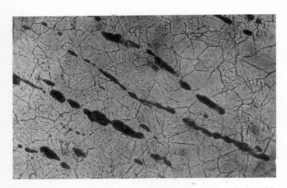

Fig. 22. Polished section of rivet, Cat. No. C 30088, x,14, Mogen, Møsstrand, Telemark, Norway. Migration Age. Etched with 2% alcoholic HNO_3. 200 x. Inclusions of single and two-phase slag.

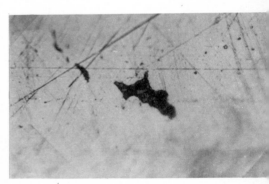

Fig. 23. Polished section of rivet, No. XXIIe, Kaupan Tjølling, Vestfold, Norway. Viking Age. Unetche 200 x. Inclusions of single and multi-phase slags.

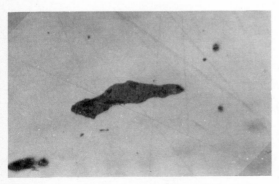

Fig. 24. Polished section of rivet, No. O 294g, Oseberg, Vestfold, Norway. Unetched. 200 x. Inclusions of multi-phase slags.

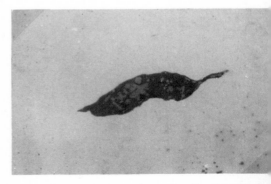

Fig. 25. Polished section of bar, Cat. No. C 26208, S rum, Hedmark, Norway. Viking Age (?). Unetche 200 x. Inclusions of multi-phase slags.

Fig. 26. Polished section of rivet, Kongsgården, Oslo. 13th century. Unetched. 200 x. Inclusions of multi-phase slags.

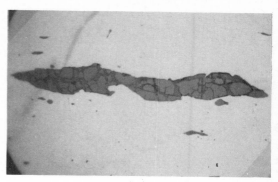

Fig. 27. Polished section of rivet, Ladegården, Oslo. 16th century. Unetched. 200 x. Inclusions of multi-phase slags.

Fig. 28. Polished section of rivet, Cat. No. C 30088, x, 14, Mogen, Møsstrand, Telemark, Norway. Migration Age. Etched with 4% alcoholic HNO_3. Transition in grain sizes. 200 x.

Fig. 29. Polished section of rivet, No. XXIIe, Kaupang, Tjølling, Vestfold, Norway. Viking Age. Etched with 4% alcoholic HNO_3. 200 x. Ferritic area.

Fig. 30. Polished section of bar, Cat. No. C 26208, Sørum, Veldre, Hedmark, Norway. Viking Age (?). Etched with 4% alcoholic HNO_3. 200 x. Transition from ferrite to pearlite.

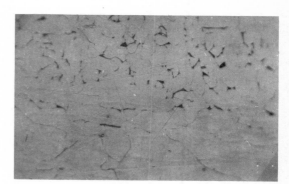

Fig. 31. a. Polished section of nail, No. O 294 bb, Oseberg, Vestfold, Norway. Viking Age. Etched with 4% alcoholic HNO_3. 200 x. Transition from ferrite to pearlite.

Fig. 31. b. Polished section of rivet, No. O 294 g, as above. Etched with Stead I. 200 x. Ferrite with clear boundary lines.

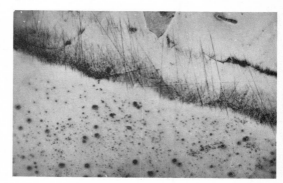

Fig. 31. c. A different area of section as above, etched as above. Transition from ferritic area (fig. 31b) at top, to carbon and phosphorus-richer smaller grains with unclean boundary lines dividing them, possible cementite. In the lower part the slag content is lower. The boundary between upper and lower part is marked by a needle-like precipitation by the etching with Stead I. (Nitride?)

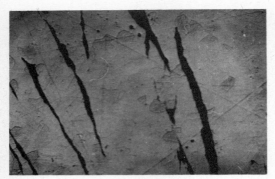

Fig. 32. Polished section of rivet from Kongsgården, Oslo. 13th century. Etched with 4% alcoholic HNO_3. 200 x.

Fig. 33. Polished section of rivet from Ladegården, Oslo. 16th century. Etched with 4% alcoholic HNO_3. 200 x. Pearlitic area.

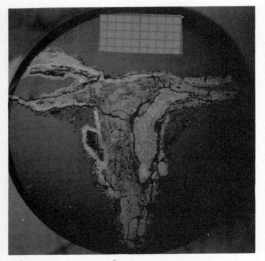

Fig. 34. Macrophotograph of polished section of rivet LaM 60, etched with Stead I.

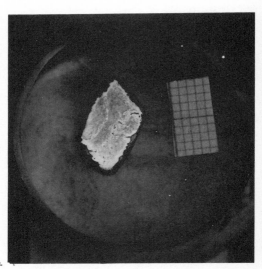

Fig. 35. Macrophotograph of polished section of bar, Cat. No. C 26208, Sørum, Veldre, Hedmark, Norway. Viking Age (?). Etched with Stead I.

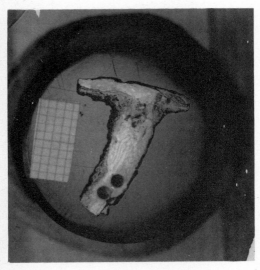

Fig. 36. Macrophotograph of polished section of rivet Cat. No. C 30088, x, 14, Mogen, Møsstrand, Telemark, Norway. Migration Age. Etched with Stead I.

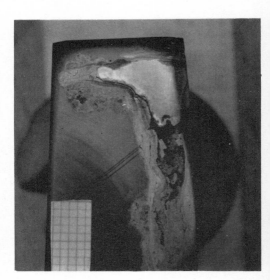

Fig. 37. Macrophotograph of polished section of rivet No. XXIIe, Kaupang, Tjølling, Vestfold, Norway. Viking Age. Etched with Stead I.

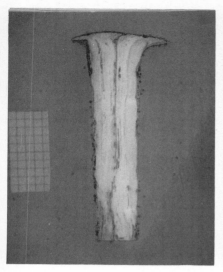
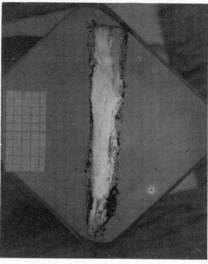
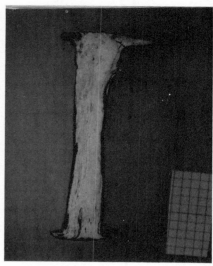

Fig. 38. Macrophotographs of polished section of upper and lower thirds of nail No. O 294 bb, and rivet No. O 294g, Oseberg, Vestfold, Norway. Viking Age. Etched with Stead I.

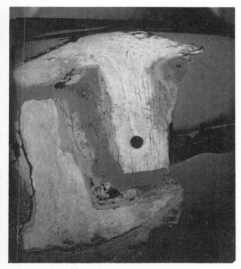

Fig. 39. Macrophotograph of polished section of rivet from Kongsgården, Oslo. 13th century. Etched with Stead I.

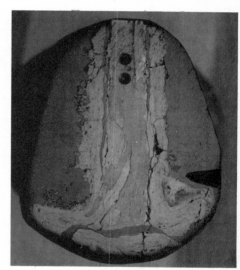

Fig. 40. Macrophotograph of polished section of rivet from Ladegården, Oslo. 16th cetury. Etched with Stead I.

Fig. 41. Microphotograph of polished section of rivet LaM 60. Etched with Stead I. 70 x.

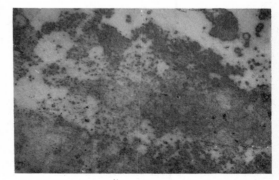

Fig. 42. Microphotograph of polished section of bar, Sørum, Veldre, Hedmark, Norway. Viking Age (?). Etched with Stead I. 70 x.

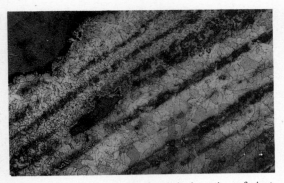

Fig. 43. Microphotograph of polished section of rivet Cat. No. C 30088, x, 14, Mogen, Møsstrand, Telemark, Norway. Migration Age. Etched with Stead I. 70 x.

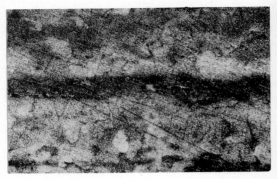

Fig. 44. Microphotograph of polished section of rivet from Ladegården, Oslo. 16th century. Etched with Stead I. 70 x.

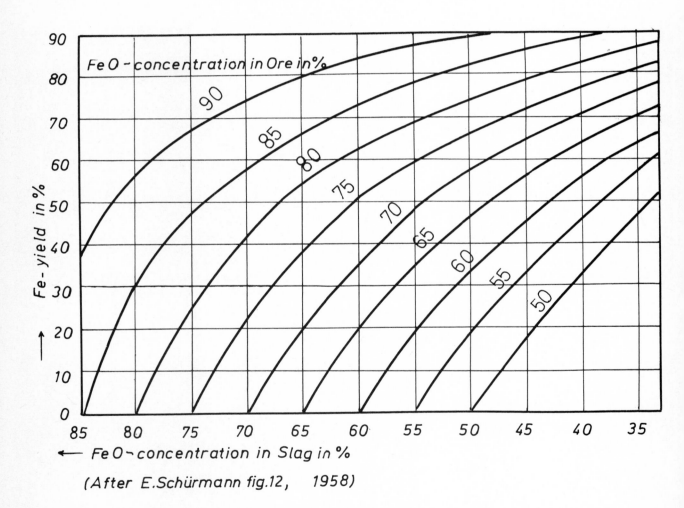

(After E.Schürmann fig.12, 1958)

Fig. 45. Yield of iron as a function of the loss of iron oxydul, FeO, at varying concentrations of iron oxydul in the ore.

Fig. 46. *a*. Slag of dark, heavy type, sawn over, from house B, No. IV, weight 190 g.

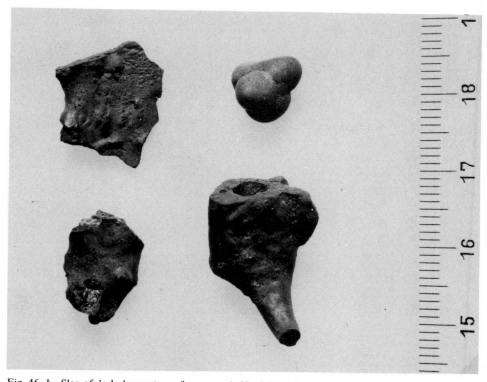

Fig. 46. *b*. Slag of dark, heavy type, from sample No. I 21, which has been melted: tap-slag.

Fig. 47. Slice of slag from cooking-pit in house B, LaM 3, No. V, probably fragment, seen from below.

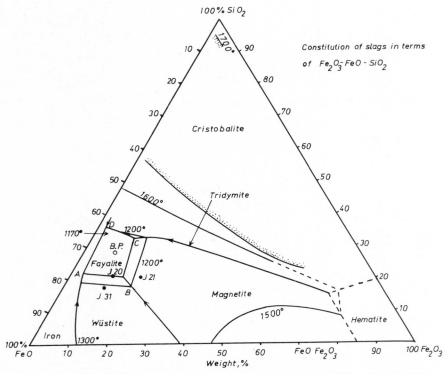

Fig. 48. The constitution of slags, expressed in terms of their content of FeO - Fe_2O_3 - SiO_2.

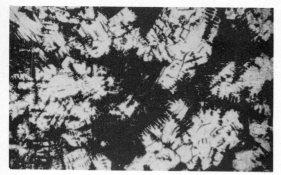

Fig. 49. Thin section of slag No. I 20, X Nicols (10 x 6.3). Wüstite, fayalite and glass.

Fig. 50. Thin section of slag No. I 21, X Nicols (10x6.3). Wüstite, fayalite and glass.

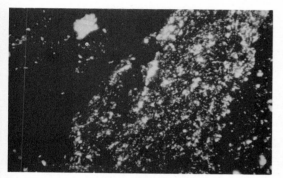

Fig. 51. Thin section of slag No. I 22, X Nicols (10x6.3). Wüstite, fayalite and glass.

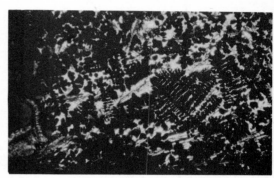

Fig 52. Thin section of slag No. I 50, house C, X Nicols, (10x6.3). Wüstite, fayalite and glass.

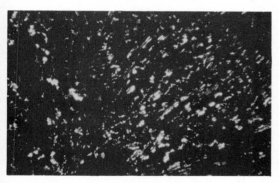

Fig. 53. Thin section of slag No. I 31, X Nicols (10x6.3). Wüstite, fayalite and glass.

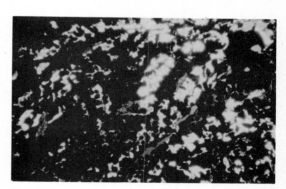

Fig. 54. Thin section of slag No. IV, X Nicols (10x6.3). Fayalite, wüstite, glass and Fe_2O_3.

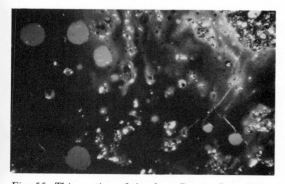

Fig. 55. Thin section of slag from Rogne, Østre Slidre, Oppland, Norway, A.D. 500. Fayalite, wüstite and glass.

Fig. 56. Thin section of undated slag from Laurvik, Ustevann, Buskerud, Norway.

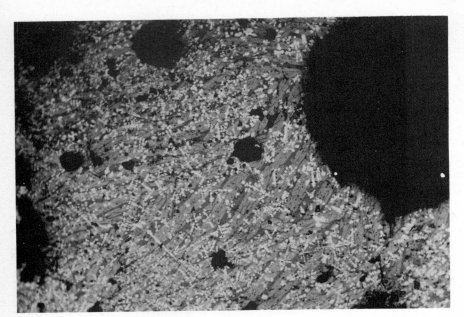

Fig. 57. Polished section of slag LaM 303 (No. I 20), 70 x. Wüstite in a glass-fayalite matrix.

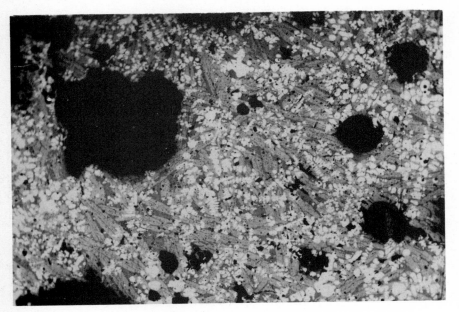

Fig. 58. Polished section of slag LaM 283 (No. I 21), 70 x. Wüstite and iron in a glass-fayalite matrix.

Fig. 59. Polished section of slag LaM 284 (No. I 31), 110 x. Wüstite and iron in a glass-fayalite matrix.

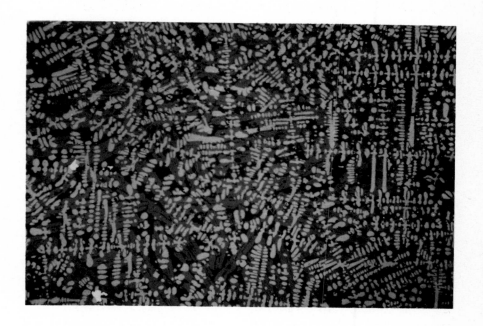

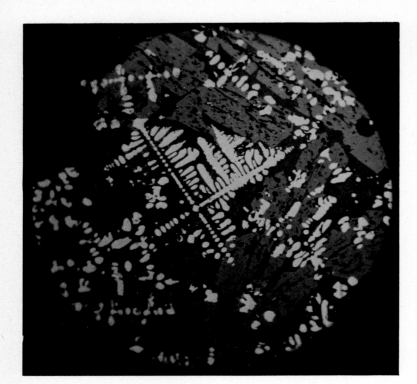

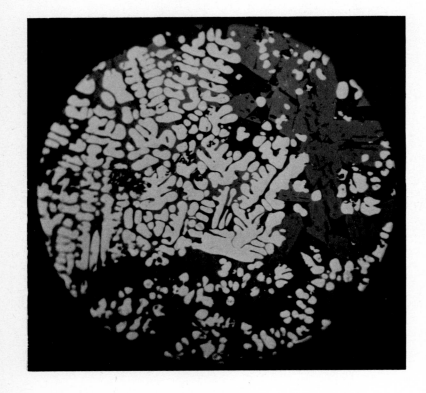

Fig. 60. 1 and 2. Polished sections of slag, No. V house B, 70 x (Bergstøl, appendix II,2). White: magnetite, grey and dark grey: silicates.

Fig. 61. 3 and 4. Polished sections of slag, No. IV, house B, 70 x (Bergstøl, appendix II,2). This slag shows the magnetite oxidized into other iron oxides. At the centre of No. 4, metallic iron may be seen as a small, irregular white and striped spot. White: magnetite; light grey: other iron oxides; grey and dark grey: silicates.

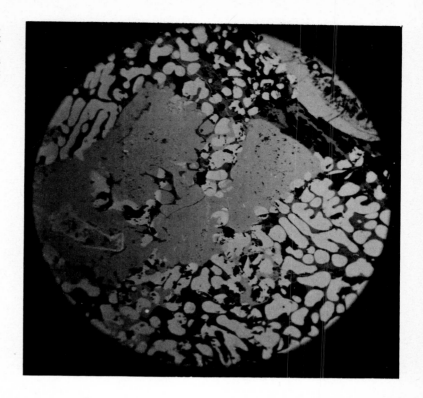

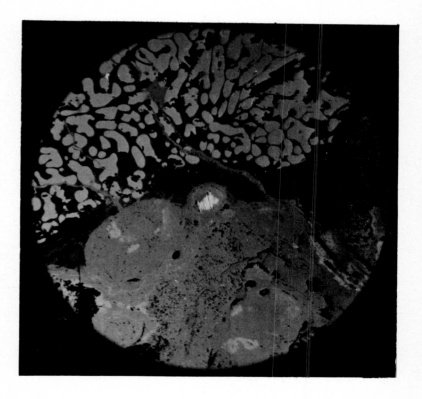

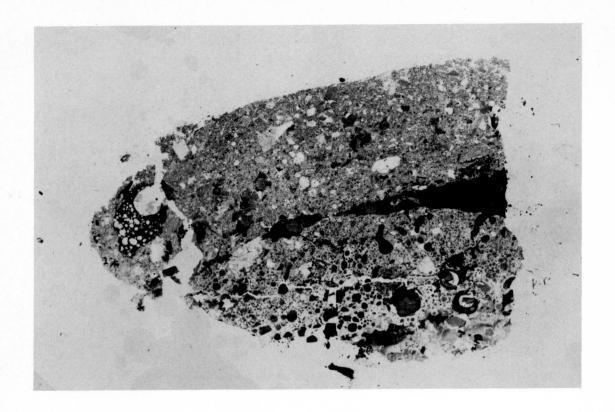

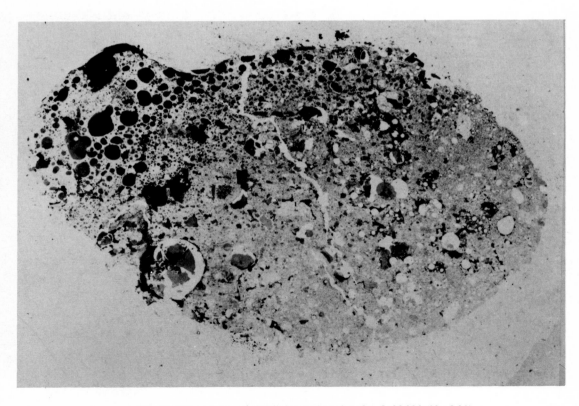

Fig. 62. Thin section of clay lining against slag. 6 x. LaM 293 (No. I 22).

Index

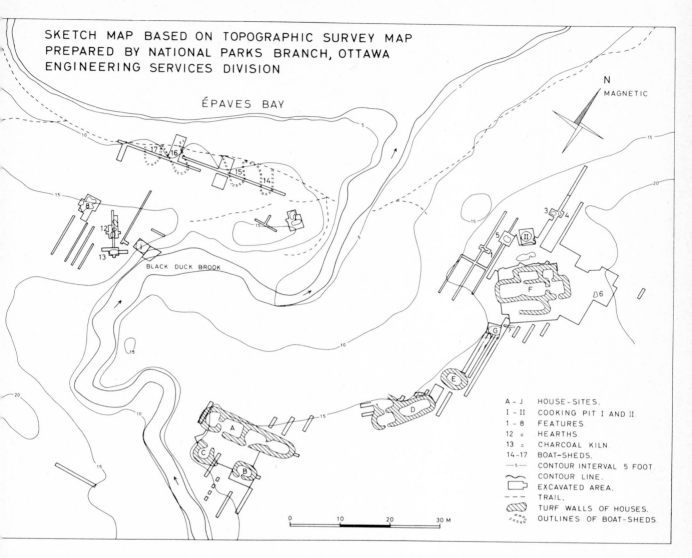

SKETCH MAP BASED ON TOPOGRAPHIC SURVEY MAP
PREPARED BY NATIONAL PARKS BRANCH, OTTAWA
ENGINEERING SERVICES DIVISION

ÉPAVES BAY

N
MAGNETIC

BLACK DUCK BROOK

A – J   HOUSE-SITES.
I – II   COOKING PIT I AND II.
1 – 8   FEATURES.
12 =   HEARTHS.
13 =   CHARCOAL KILN.
14-17   BOAT-SHEDS.
—5—   CONTOUR INTERVAL 5 FOOT.
        CONTOUR LINE.
        EXCAVATED AREA.
- - -   TRAIL.
        TURF WALLS OF HOUSES.
        OUTLINES OF BOAT-SHEDS.

0   10   20   30 M

Pl. 2

HOUSE-SITE A SURROUNDED BY B AND C.
L'ANSE AUX MEADOWS,
NEWFOUNDLAND.

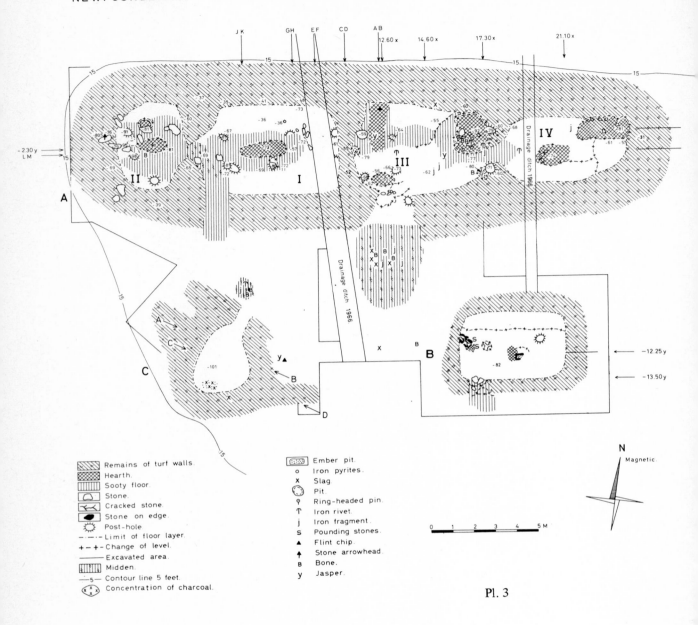

Remains of turf walls.
Hearth.
Sooty floor.
Stone.
Cracked stone.
Stone on edge.
Post-hole.
─·─·─ Limit of floor layer.
+─+─ Change of level.
──── Excavated area.
Midden.
──5── Contour line 5 feet.
Concentration of charcoal.

Ember pit.
o   Iron pyrites.
x   Slag.
    Pit.
φ   Ring-headed pin.
⊤   Iron rivet.
j   Iron fragment.
s   Pounding stones.
▲   Flint chip.
↑   Stone arrowhead.
B   Bone.
y   Jasper.

0 1 2 3 4 5 M

N
Magnetic.

Pl. 3

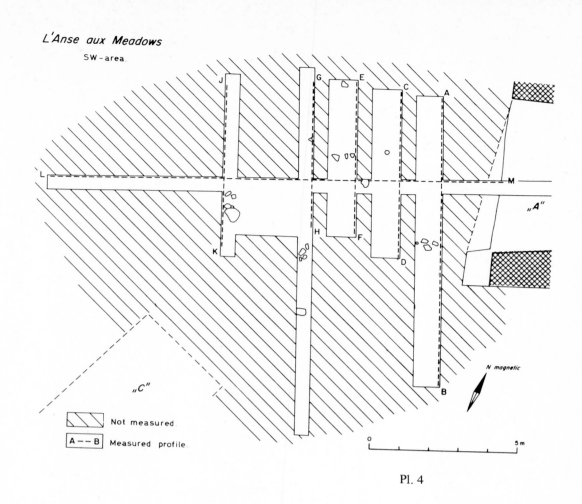

L'Anse aux Meadows
SW–area.

J G E C A

L ———————————————————————————————————— M

"A"

K

"C"

N magnetic

▨ Not measured.

A — B Measured profile.

0 5m

Pl. 4

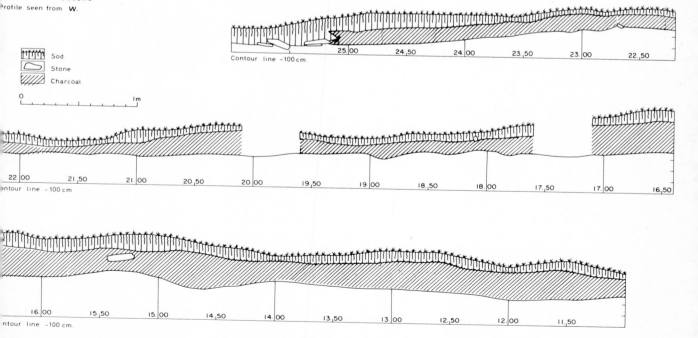

L'Anse aux Meadows
Profile seen from W.

▥ Sod
▱ Stone
▨ Charcoal

0 1m

25.00 24.50 24.00 23.50 23.00 22.50
Contour line –100 cm.

22.00 21.50 21.00 20.50 20.00 19.50 19.00 18.50 18.00 17.50 17.00 16.50
Contour line –100 cm.

16.00 15.50 15.00 14.50 14.00 13.50 13.00 12.50 12.00 11.50
Contour line –100 cm.

Pl. 5

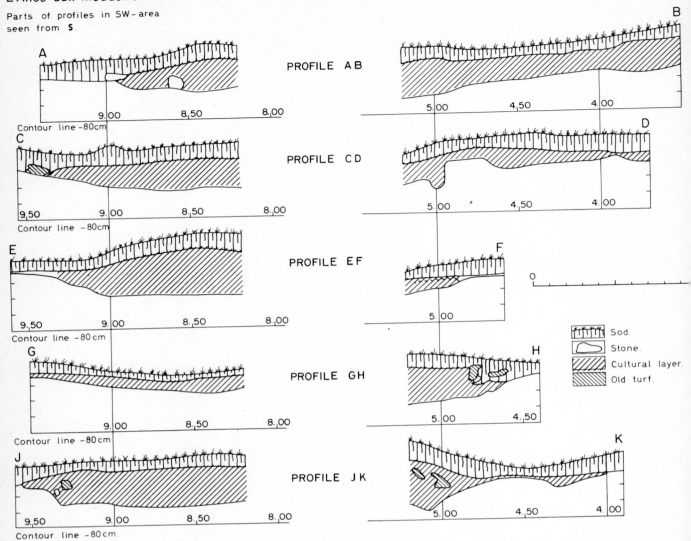

L'Anse aux Meadows

Parts of profiles in SW–area
seen from S.

PROFILE A B

Contour line –80cm

PROFILE C D

Contour line –80cm

PROFILE E F

Contour line –80 cm

PROFILE G H

Contour line –80cm

PROFILE J K

Contour line –80 cm.

Sod.
Stone.
Cultural layer.
Old turf.

Pl. 6

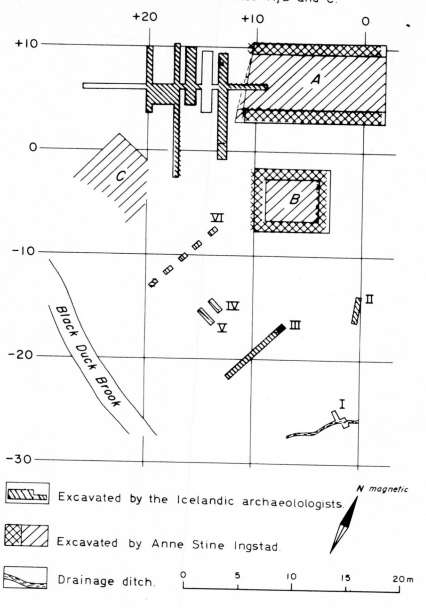

L'Anse aux Meadows

Plan of SE- and SW-area and
parts of house-sites A, B and C.

A

B

C

Black Duck Brook

VI

IV

V

III

II

I

◫◫◫ Excavated by the Icelandic archaeolologists.

▨ Excavated by Anne Stine Ingstad.

Drainage ditch.

N magnetic

0   5   10   15   20m

Pl. 7

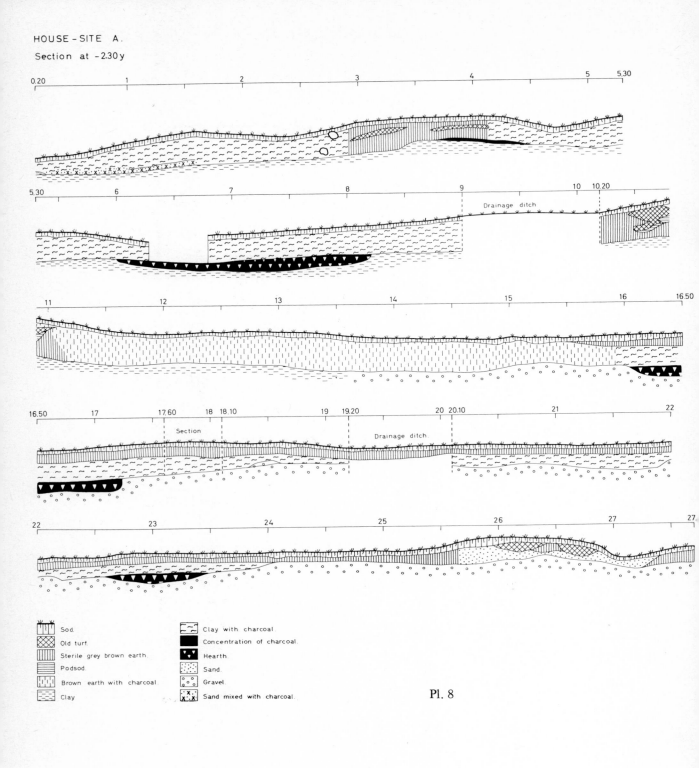

HOUSE - SITE A.
Section at -2.30 y

Drainage ditch

Drainage ditch

Section

Drainage ditch

Sod.
Old turf.
Sterile grey brown earth.
Podsod.
Brown earth with charcoal.
Clay.

Clay with charcoal.
Concentration of charcoal.
Hearth.
Sand.
Gravel.
Sand mixed with charcoal.

Pl. 8

HOUSE-SITE A.
Section at 21.10 x

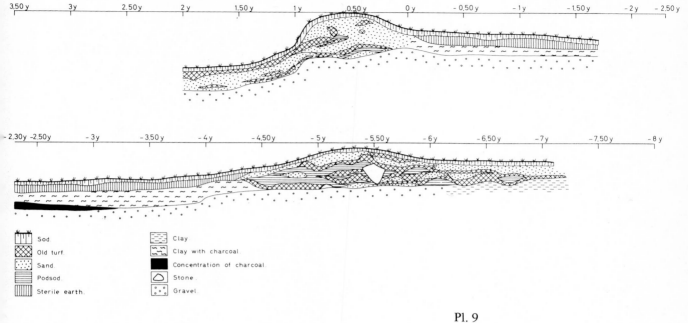

3.50 y   3 y   2.50 y   2 y   1.50 y   1 y   0.50 y   0 y   -0.50 y   -1 y   -1.50 y   -2 y   -2.50 y

-2.30 y -2.50 y   -3 y   -3.50 y   -4 y   -4.50 y   -5 y   -5.50 y   -6 y   -6.50 y   -7 y   -7.50 y   -8 y

Sod.
Old turf.
Sand.
Podsod.
Sterile earth.

Clay.
Clay with charcoal.
Concentration of charcoal.
Stone.
Gravel.

Pl. 9

HOUSE-SITE A
Section at 17.30 x

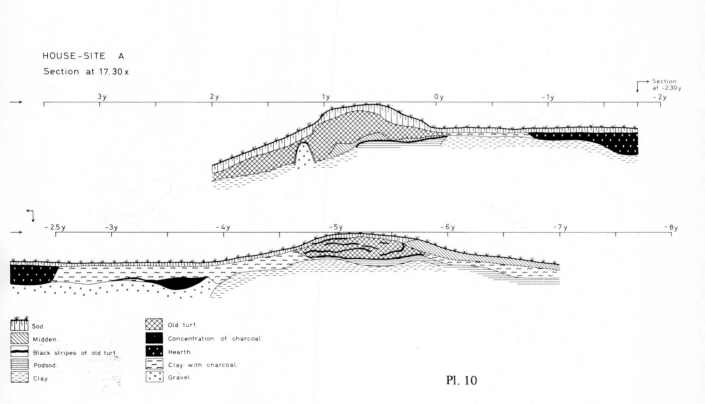

Section at -2.30 y

3 y   2 y   1 y   0 y   -1 y   -2 y

-2.5 y   -3 y   -4 y   -5 y   -6 y   -7 y   -8 y

Sod
Midden.
Black stripes of old turf.
Podsod.
Clay.

Old turf.
Concentration of charcoal.
Hearth.
Clay with charcoal.
Gravel.

Pl. 10

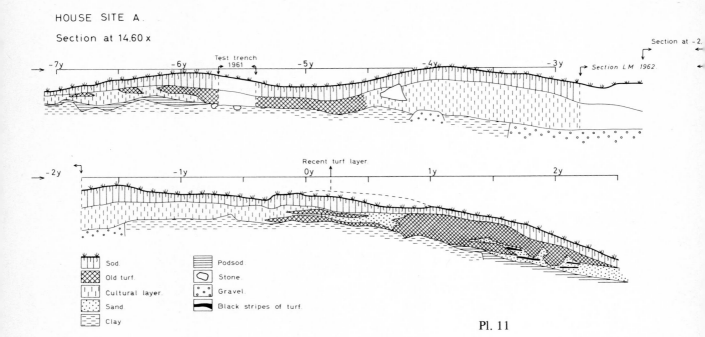

HOUSE SITE A.

Section at 14.60 x

Section at -2,

-7y   -6y   Test trench   -5y   -4y   -3y   Section LM 1962
              1961

-2y   -1y   Recent turf layer   0y   1y   2y

Sod.   Podsod.
Old turf.   Stone.
Cultural layer.   Gravel.
Sand   Black stripes of turf.
Clay

Pl. 11

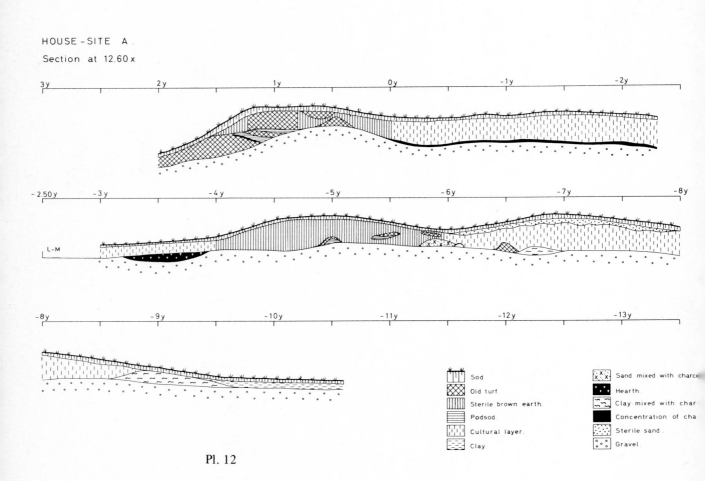

HOUSE - SITE A.

Section at 12.60 x

3y   2y   1y   0y   -1y   -2y

-2.50y   -3y   -4y   -5y   -6y   -7y   -8y

L-M

-8y   -9y   -10y   -11y   -12y   -13y

Sod   Sand mixed with charc
Old turf   Hearth
Sterile brown earth.   Clay mixed with char
Podsod   Concentration of cha
Cultural layer.   Sterile sand.
Clay   Gravel.

Pl. 12

HOUSE-SITE B.

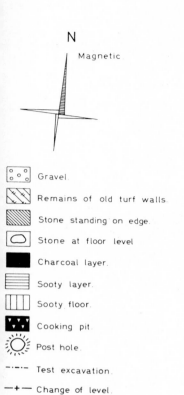

N

Magnetic

◦◦◦	Gravel.
⬚	Remains of old turf walls.
▨	Stone standing on edge.
⬭	Stone at floor level.
■	Charcoal layer.
▤	Sooty layer.
⦀	Sooty floor.
▼▼▼	Cooking pit.
⊙	Post hole.
–·–·–	Test excavation.
–+–	Change of level.

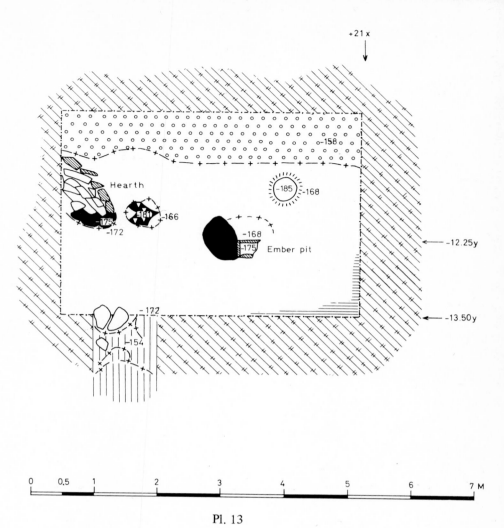

+21 x

o-158

Hearth

-185 -168

-161 -166

-175
-172

-168
-175 Ember pit

-12.25 y

-13.50 y

-172

-154

0	0.5	1		2		3		4		5		6		7 M

Pl. 13

HOUSE-SITE B

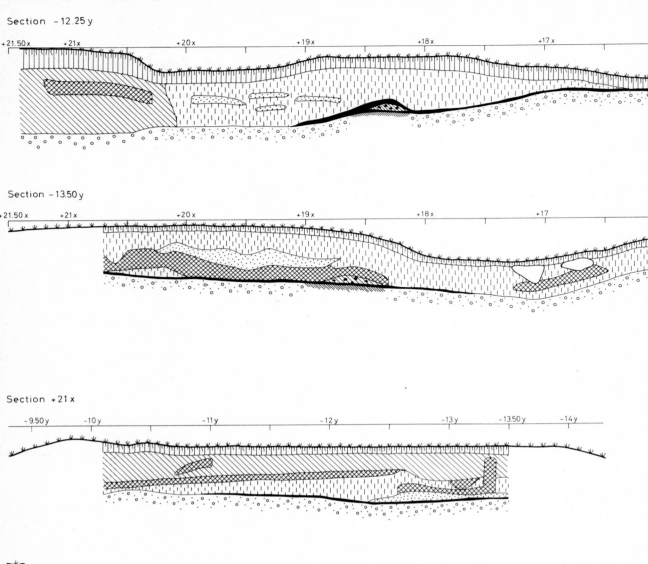

Section -12.25 y

Section -13.50 y

Section +21 x

	Sod.		Pod sod.
	Cultural layer.		Clay stamped hard.
	Sterile sand and humus.		Clay with charcoal.
	Old black turf.		Soot and charcoal.
	Red burnt clay.		

Pl. 14

HOUSE-SITE C.
Section A-B

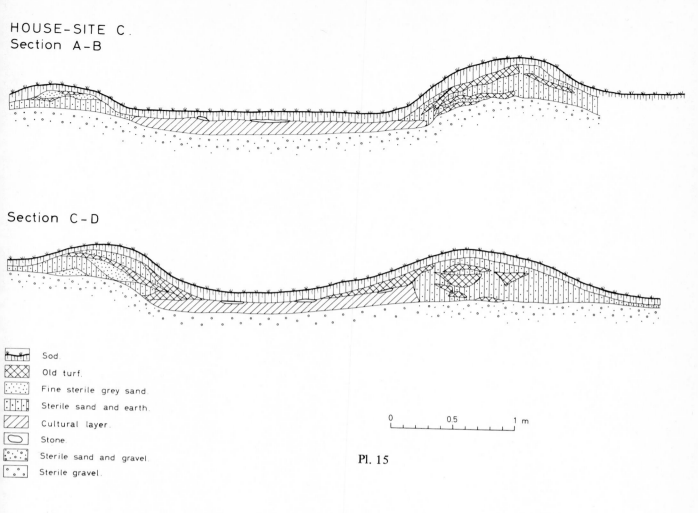

Section C-D

	Sod.
	Old turf.
	Fine sterile grey sand.
	Sterile sand and earth.
	Cultural layer.
	Stone.
	Sterile sand and gravel.
	Sterile gravel.

0   0.5   1 m

Pl. 15

HOUSE-SITES D AND E.

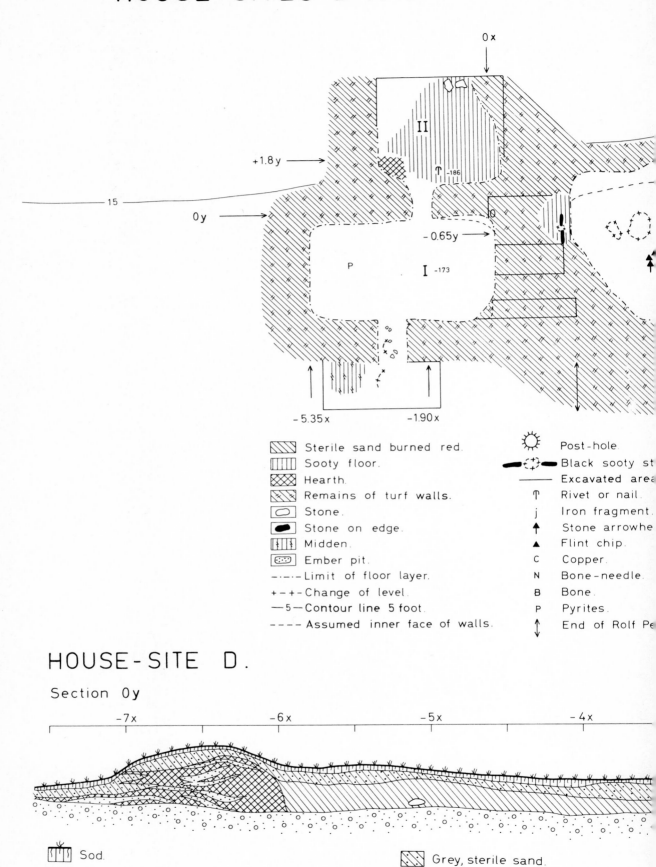

	Sterile sand burned red.		Post-hole.
	Sooty floor.		Black sooty st
	Hearth.		Excavated are
	Remains of turf walls.	↑	Rivet or nail.
	Stone.	j	Iron fragment.
	Stone on edge.	▲	Stone arrowhe
	Midden.	▲	Flint chip.
	Ember pit.	C	Copper.
—·—·—	Limit of floor layer.	N	Bone-needle.
+—+—	Change of level.	B	Bone.
—5—	Contour line 5 foot.	P	Pyrites.
— — —	Assumed inner face of walls.	↕	End of Rolf Pe

HOUSE-SITE D.

Section 0y

	Sod.		Grey, sterile sand.
	Cultural layer.		Sterile sand and gravel.
	Old black turf.		Pod sod.
	Sand mixed with black stripes and charcoal.		

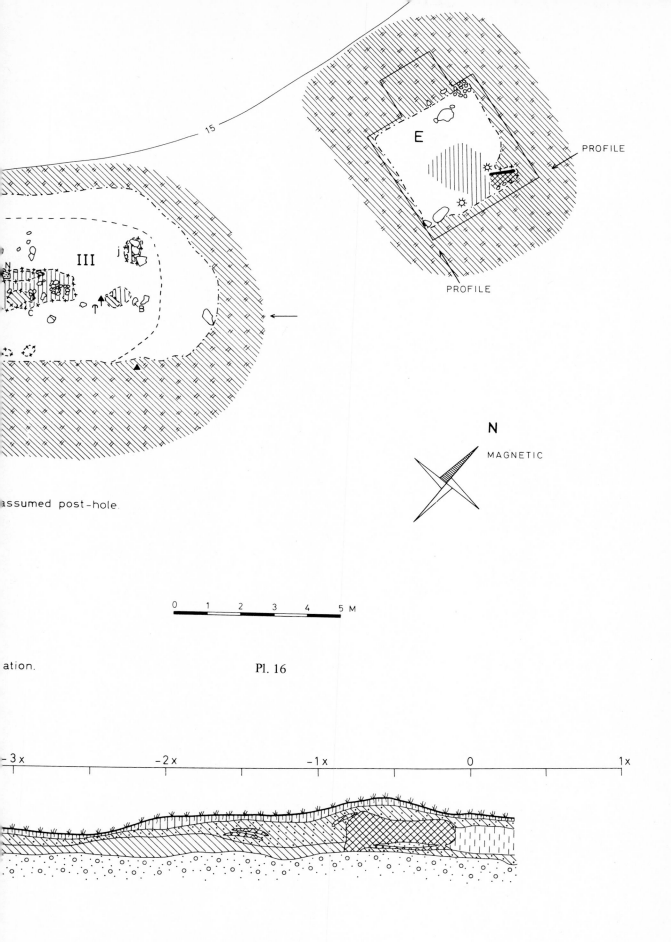

15

III

j

B

C

N

E

PROFILE

PROFILE

N
MAGNETIC

assumed post-hole.

| 0 | 1 | 2 | 3 | 4 | 5 M |

ation.

Pl. 16

-3x   -2x   -1x   0   1x

Pl. 17

HOUSE-SITE D.

Section – 5.35 x

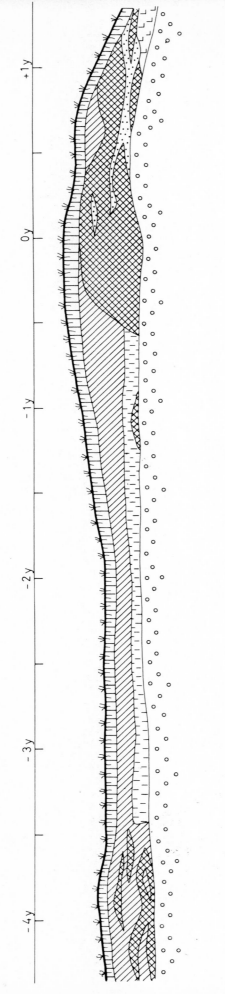

Section +1.8 y

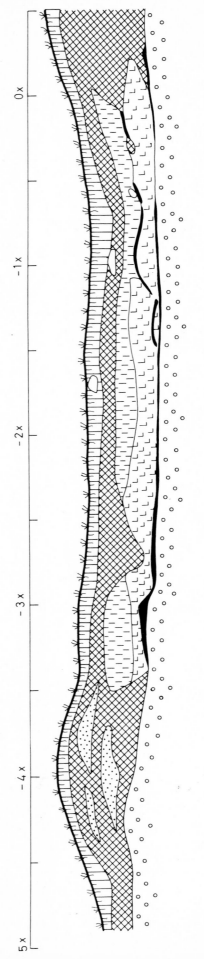

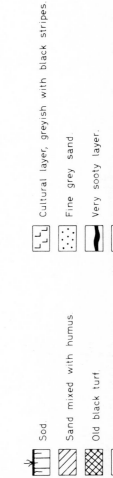

Sod	L L L Cultural layer, greyish with black stripes.
Sand mixed with humus.	Fine grey sand
Old black turf	Very sooty layer.
Cultural layer	o o Gravel

Pl. 18

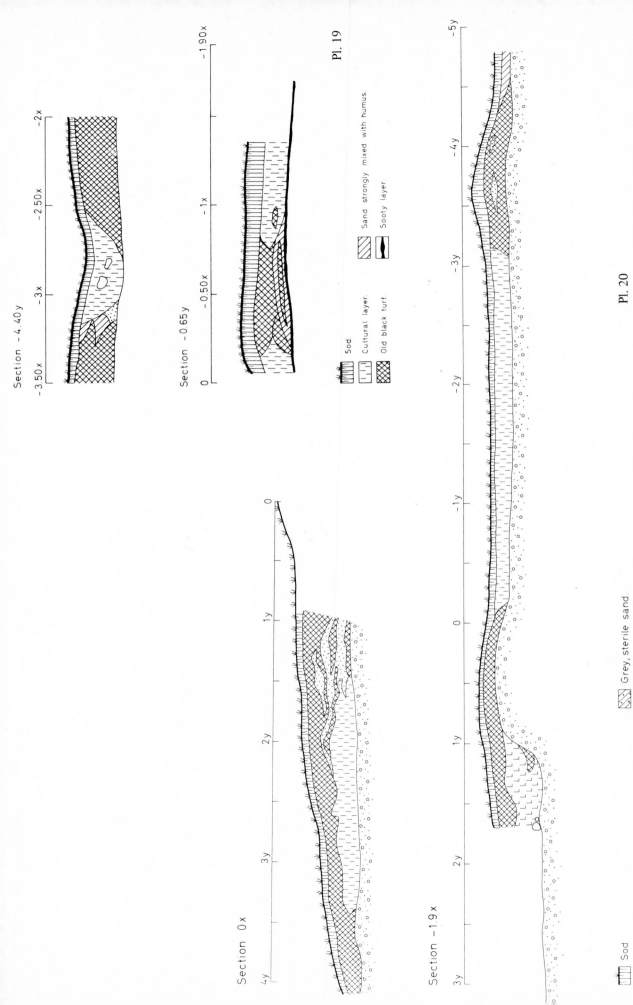

Section – 4.40y

-2x
-2.50x
-3x
-3.50x

Section – 0.65y

-1.90x
-1x
-0.50x
0

Pl. 19

Sod
Cultural layer.
Old black turf.

Sand strongly mixed with humus
Sooty layer.

Section 0x

0
1y
2y
3y
4y

Section –1.9x

-5y
-4y
-3y
-2y
-1y
0
1y
2y
3y

Pl. 20

Sod
Cultural layer.
Old black turf.
Sand mixed with black stripes and charcoal

Grey, sterile sand.
Sterile sand and gravel.
Pod sod
Grey sand with black stripes and charcoal.

HOUSE-SITE D III.

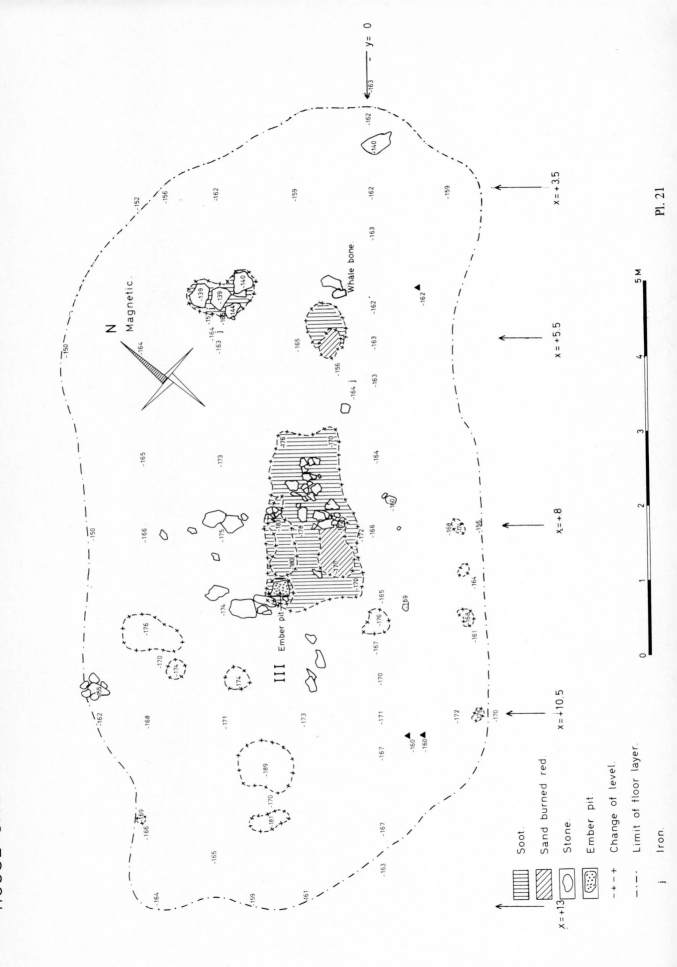

Whale bone

Magnetic.

N

III Ember pit.

Soot.
Sand burned red.
Stone.
Ember pit.
+–+ Change of level.
–·–· Limit of floor layer.
j Iron.

y= 0

x=+3.5

x=+5.5

x=+8

x=+10.5

x=+13

0 1 2 3 4 5 M

Pl. 21

HOUSE - SITE D III.

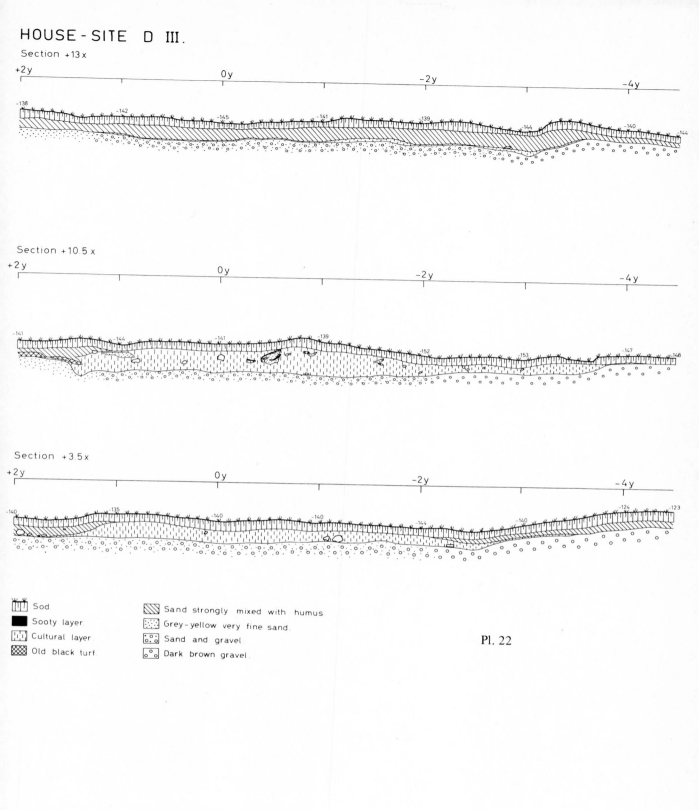

Section +13 x

Section +10.5 x

Section +3.5 x

	Sod.		Sand strongly mixed with humus.
	Sooty layer.		Grey-yellow very fine sand.
	Cultural layer.		Sand and gravel.
	Old black turf.		Dark brown gravel.

Pl. 22

HOUSE-SITE D III.

Section 0y

+13 x   +10 x   +8 x

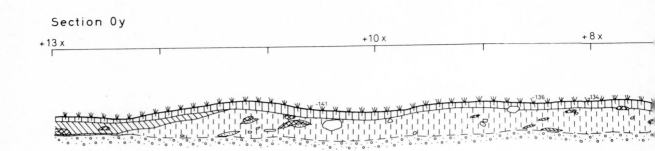

Section +8x

+4 y   +2 y   0 y

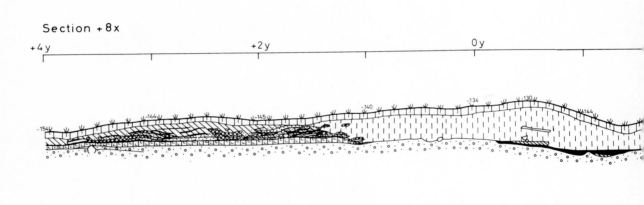

Section +5.5x

+4 y   +2 y   0 y

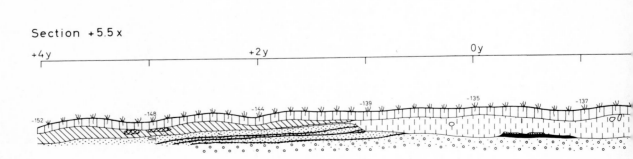

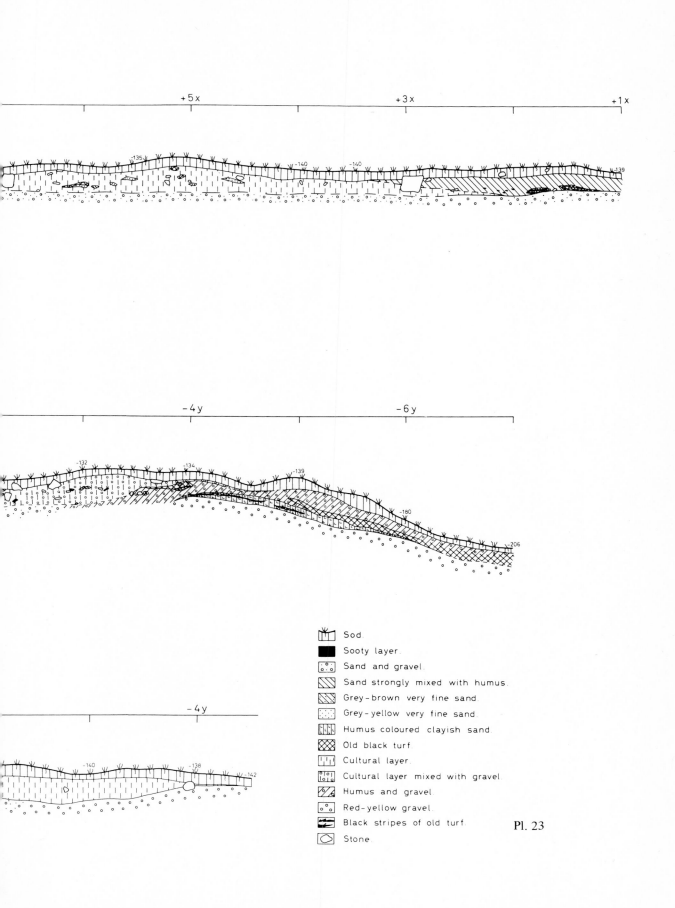

Sod.

Sooty layer.

Sand and gravel.

Sand strongly mixed with humus.

Grey–brown very fine sand.

Grey–yellow very fine sand.

Humus coloured clayish sand.

Old black turf.

Cultural layer.

Cultural layer mixed with gravel.

Humus and gravel.

Red–yellow gravel.

Black stripes of old turf.

Stone.

Pl. 23

HOUSE-SITE E.

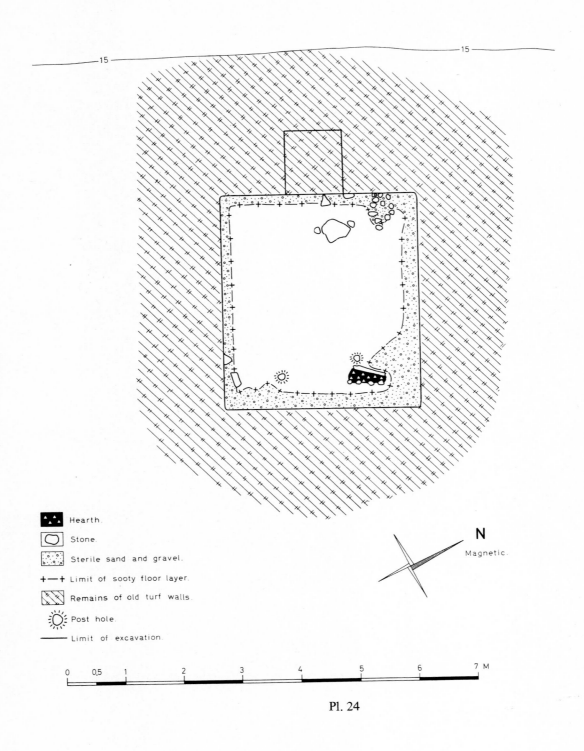

Hearth.

Stone.

Sterile sand and gravel.

+—+ Limit of sooty floor layer.

Remains of old turf walls.

Post hole.

—— Limit of excavation.

N

Magnetic.

0   0,5   1   2   3   4   5   6   7 M

Pl. 24

HOUSE-SITE E.

Section along the eastern wall showing depression in the turf layers.

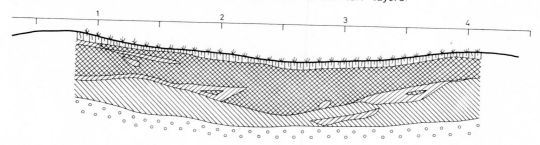

ction along the southern wall.

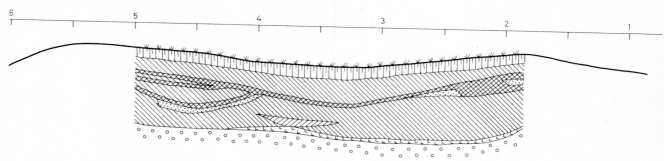

Section along the northern wall.

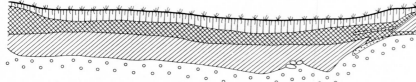

	Sod.
	Grey sterile sand.
	Old black turf.
	Sterile brown earth.
	Pod sod.
	Cultural layer with charcoal.
	Gravel.

Pl. 25

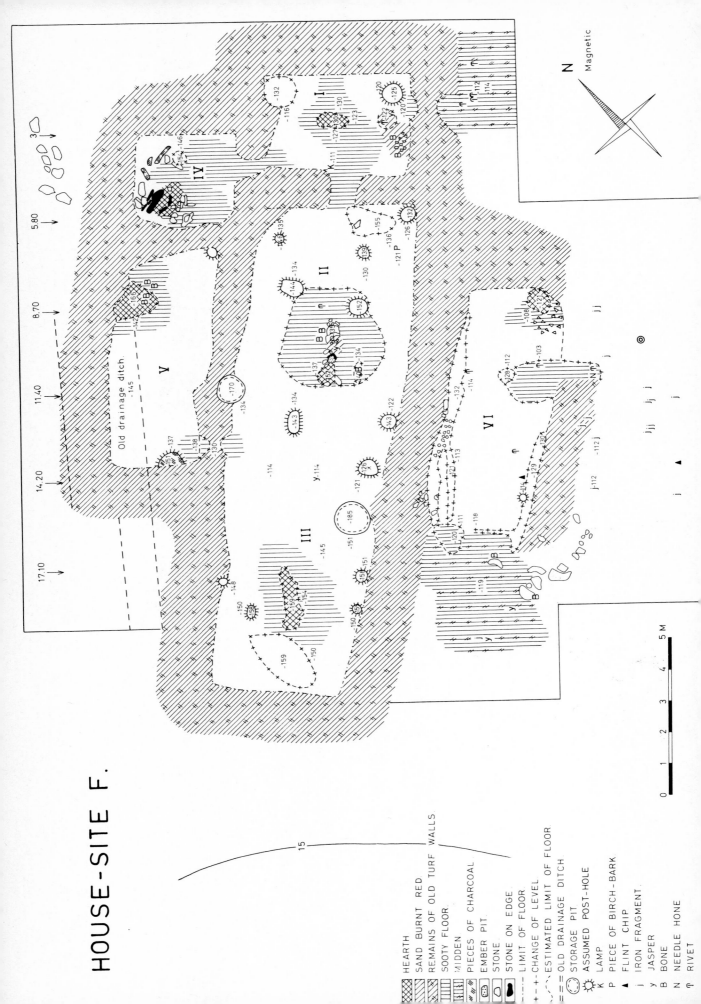

HOUSE-SITE F.

HEARTH
SAND BURNT RED
REMAINS OF OLD TURF WALLS.
SOOTY FLOOR
MIDDEN
PIECES OF CHARCOAL
EMBER PIT.
STONE
STONE ON EDGE.
LIMIT OF FLOOR
CHANGE OF LEVEL
ESTIMATED LIMIT OF FLOOR
OLD DRAINAGE DITCH
STORAGE PIT
ASSUMED POST-HOLE
K LAMP
P PIECE OF BIRCH-BARK
FLINT CHIP
j IRON FRAGMENT.
j JASPER
y NEEDLE HONE
B BONE
N NEEDLE HONE
RIVET

N
Magnetic

Old drainage ditch

0 1 2 3 4 5 M

HOUSE-SITE F. Section at 3 m.

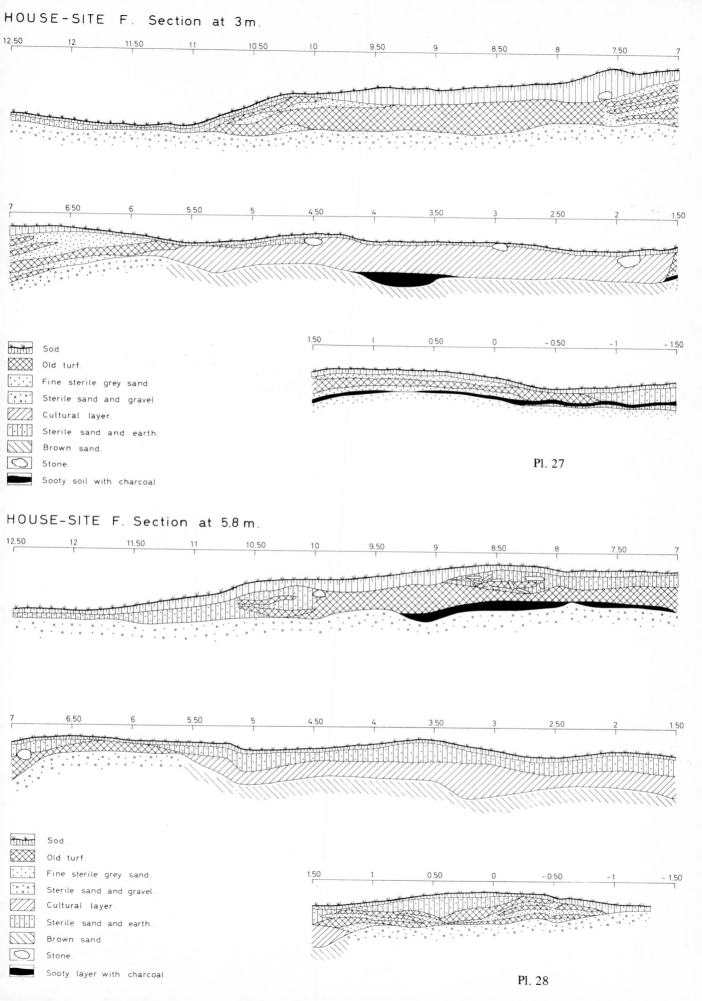

Sod

Old turf.

Fine sterile grey sand.

Sterile sand and gravel.

Cultural layer.

Sterile sand and earth.

Brown sand.

Stone.

Sooty soil with charcoal.

Pl. 27

HOUSE-SITE F. Section at 5.8 m.

Sod.

Old turf.

Fine sterile grey sand.

Sterile sand and gravel.

Cultural layer.

Sterile sand and earth.

Brown sand.

Stone.

Sooty layer with charcoal.

Pl. 28

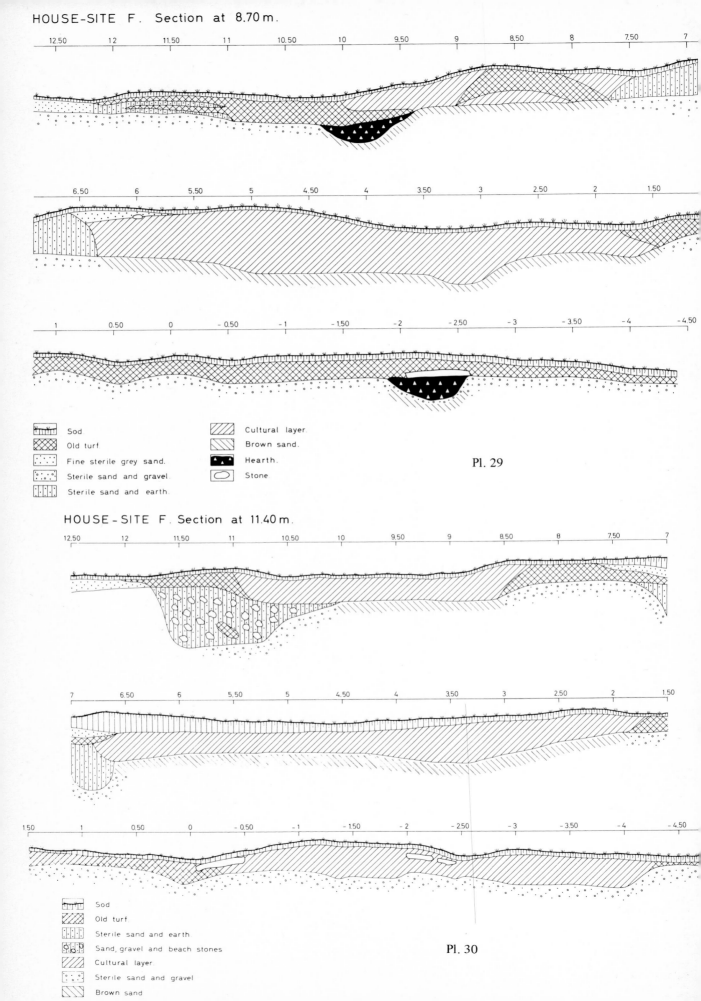

HOUSE-SITE F. Section at 8.70 m.

HOUSE-SITE F. Section at 11.40 m.

	Sod
	Old turf
	Fine sterile grey sand.
	Sterile sand and gravel.
	Sterile sand and earth.

	Cultural layer.
	Brown sand.
	Hearth.
	Stone

Pl. 29

	Sod
	Old turf.
	Sterile sand and earth.
	Sand, gravel and beach stones
	Cultural layer.
	Sterile sand and gravel
	Brown sand

Pl. 30

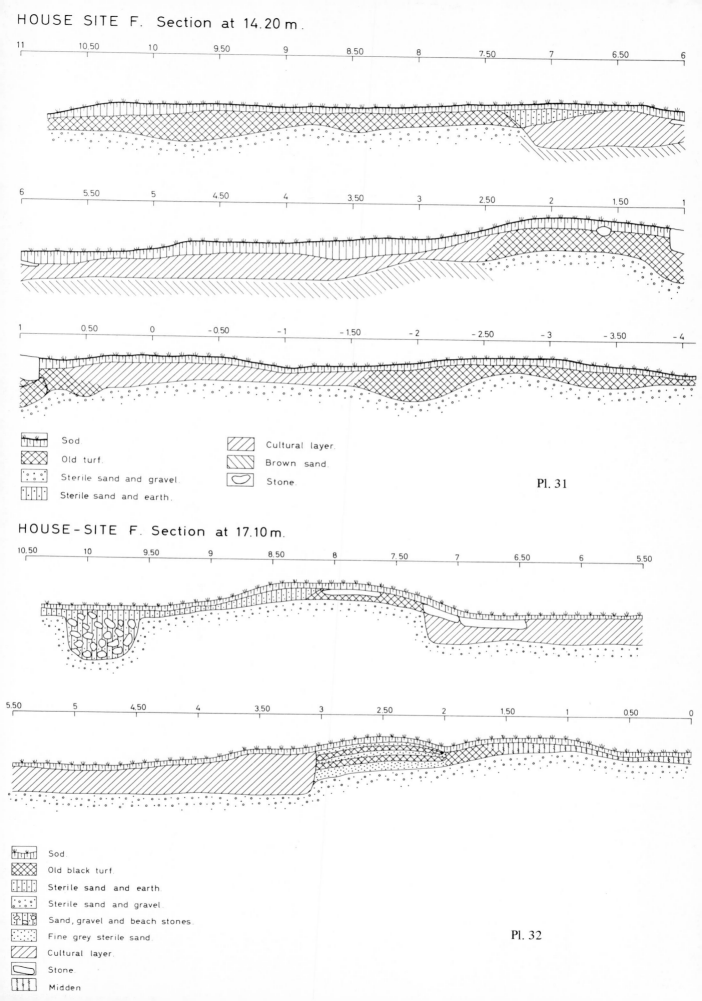

HOUSE SITE F. Section at 14.20 m.

| Sod |
| Old turf. |
| Sterile sand and gravel. |
| Sterile sand and earth. |
| Cultural layer. |
| Brown sand. |
| Stone. |

Pl. 31

HOUSE-SITE F. Section at 17.10 m.

| Sod. |
| Old black turf. |
| Sterile sand and earth. |
| Sterile sand and gravel. |
| Sand, gravel and beach stones. |
| Fine grey sterile sand. |
| Cultural layer. |
| Stone. |
| Midden. |

Pl. 32

HOUSE-SITE F.

Entrance to room I. 1.50 m NW of bases

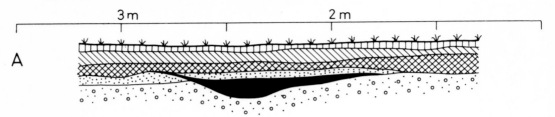

Entrance to room I. 0.50 m NW of bases

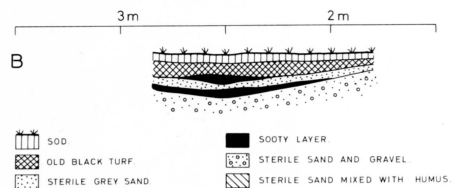

SOD.		SOOTY LAYER.
OLD BLACK TURF.		STERILE SAND AND GRAVEL.
STERILE GREY SAND.		STERILE SAND MIXED WITH HUMUS.

Pl. 33

Midden outside house-site G.

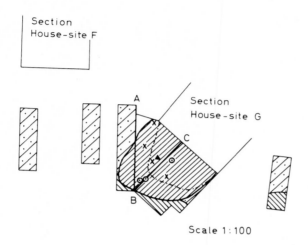

Section
House-site F

A

Section
House-site G

C

B

Scale 1:100

PROFILE A-B
Scale 1:20

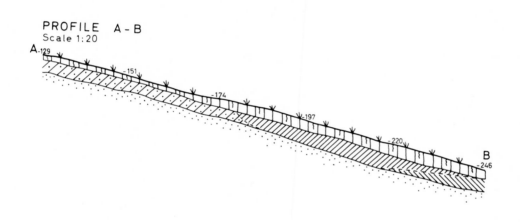

A -129
-151
-174
-197
-220
B
-246

PROFILE B-C
Scale 1:20

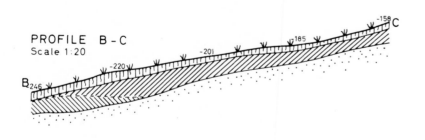

-158 C
185
-201
-220
B 246

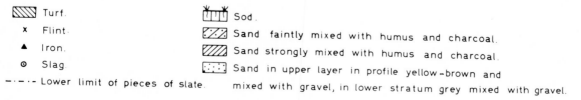

	Turf.		Sod.
x	Flint.		Sand faintly mixed with humus and charcoal.
▲	Iron.		Sand strongly mixed with humus and charcoal.
⊙	Slag.		Sand in upper layer in profile yellow-brown and
—·—·—	Lower limit of pieces of slate.		mixed with gravel, in lower stratum grey mixed with gravel.

Pl. 34

House-site G, upper level, 0.30 below surface of sod.

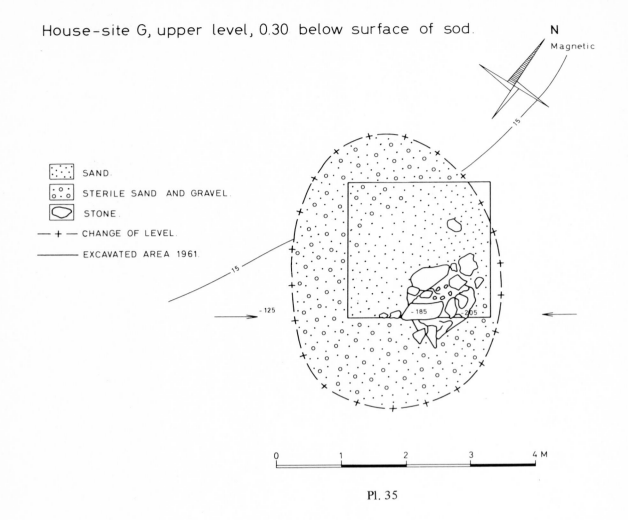

N
Magnetic

SAND.

STERILE SAND AND GRAVEL.

STONE.

— + — CHANGE OF LEVEL.

————— EXCAVATED AREA 1961.

15

15

− 125

− 185

− 205

0   1   2   3   4 M

Pl. 35

HOUSE-SITE G. Plan and section.

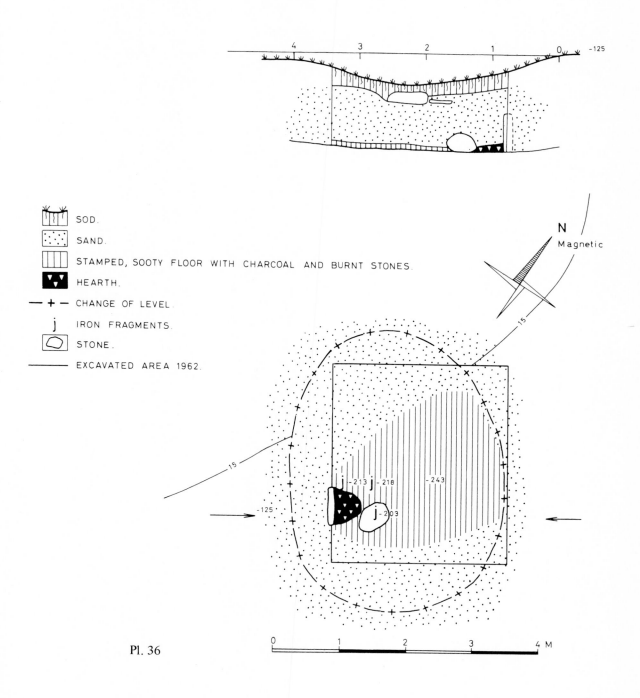

SOD.

SAND.

STAMPED, SOOTY FLOOR WITH CHARCOAL AND BURNT STONES.

HEARTH.

CHANGE OF LEVEL.

j IRON FRAGMENTS.

STONE.

EXCAVATED AREA 1962.

Pl. 36

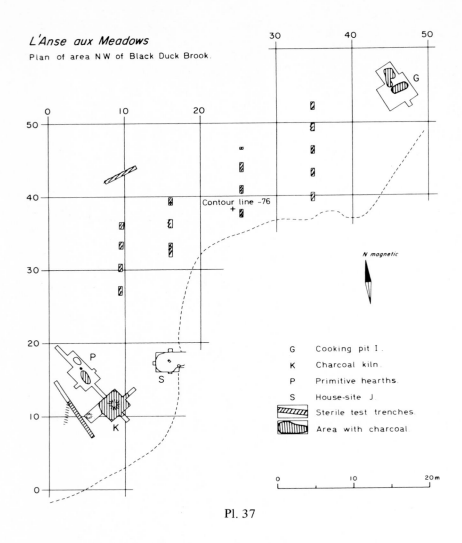

L'Anse aux Meadows

Plan of area N W of Black Duck Brook.

Contour line -76

N magnetic

G   Cooking pit I.
K   Charcoal kiln.
P   Primitive hearths.
S   House-site J
    Sterile test trenches.
    Area with charcoal.

0   10   20 m

Pl. 37

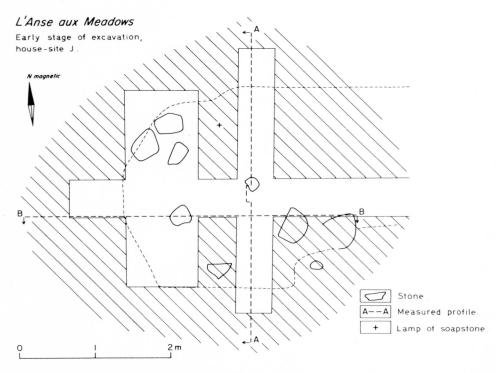

L'Anse aux Meadows

Early stage of excavation, house-site J.

N magnetic

    Stone
A——A   Measured profile.
+   Lamp of soapstone.

0   1   2 m

Pl. 38

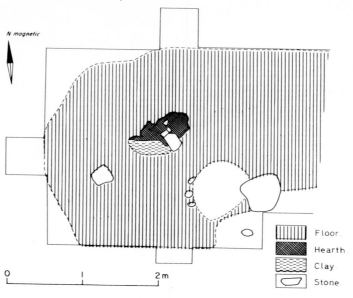

L'Anse aux Meadows

House-site J, excavated, floor.

N magnetic

	Floor.
	Hearth.
	Clay.
	Stone.

0   1   2 m

Pl. 39

L'Anse aux Meadows

House-site J. Profile A and B.

A

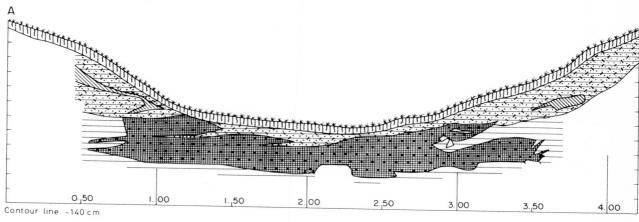

0.50   1.00   1.50   2.00   2.50   3.00   3.50   4.00

Contour line −140 cm.

	Sod.
	Stone.
	Old turf.
	Clay.
	Sand with humus and charcoal.
	Charcoal mixed with sand and slag.
	Sand and gravel.

0   1m

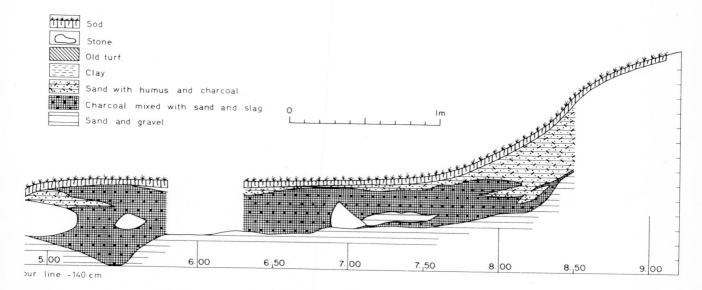

5.00   6.00   6.50   7.00   7.50   8.00   8.50   9.00

our line −140 cm.

Pl. 40

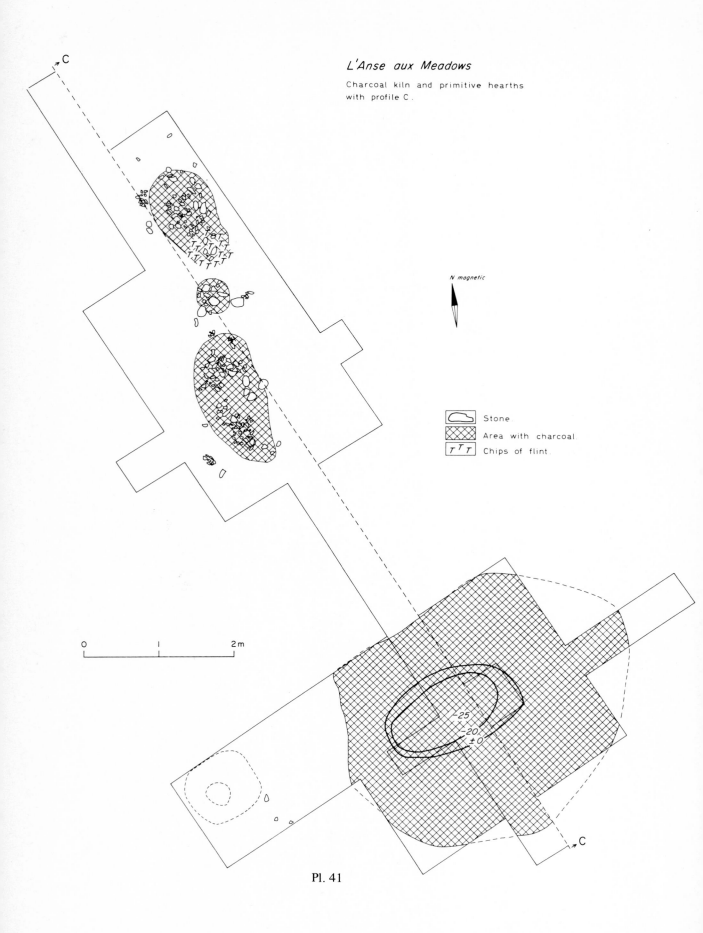

L'Anse aux Meadows

Charcoal kiln and primitive hearths
with profile C.

N magnetic

Stone.

Area with charcoal.

Chips of flint.

0   1   2 m

Pl. 41

L'Anse aux Meadows

Profile C through primitive
hearths and charcoal kiln,
seen from west

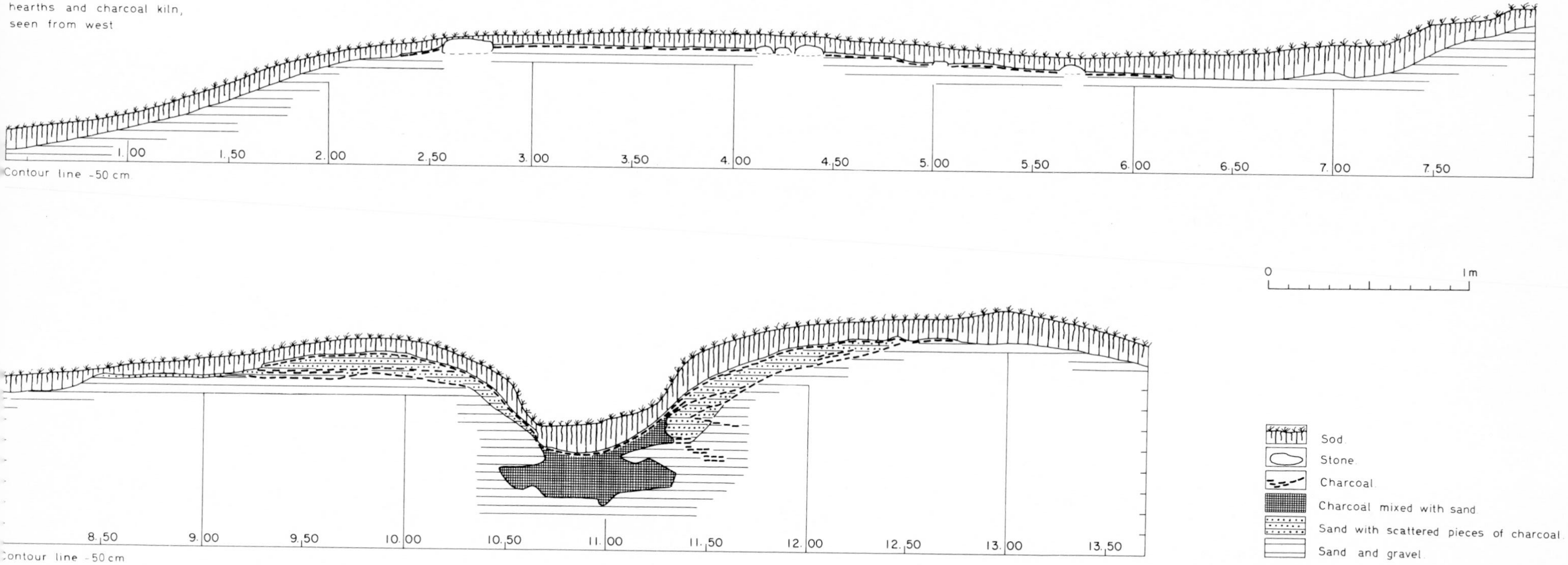

Sod

Stone

Charcoal

Charcoal mixed with sand

Sand with scattered pieces of charcoal.

Sand and gravel

0   1m

1,00 1,50 2,00 2,50 3,00 3,50 4,00 4,50 5,00 5,50 6,00 6,50 7,00 7,50

Contour line -50 cm

8,50 9,00 9,50 10,00 10,50 11,00 11,50 12,00 12,50 13,00 13,50

Contour line -50 cm

Pl. 42

L'Anse aux Meadows

Cooking pit I south of the bridge
and profiles D and E.

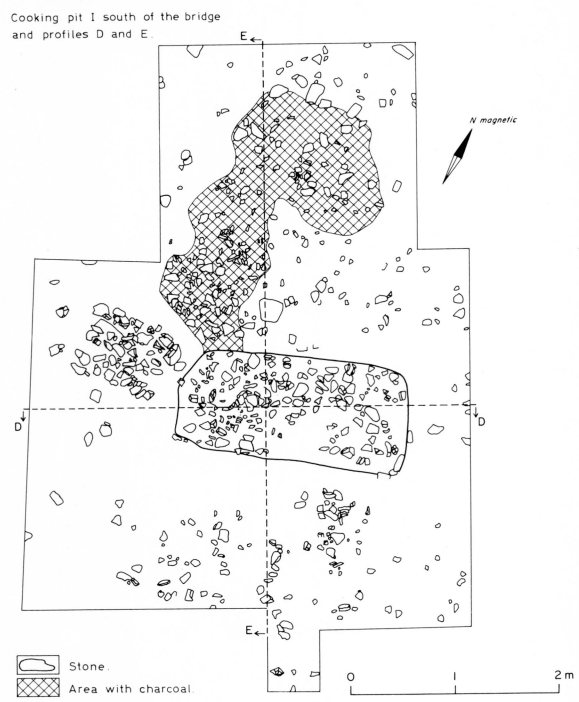

E

D   D

E

N magnetic

⬭ Stone.

▨ Area with charcoal.

0   1   2 m

Pl. 43

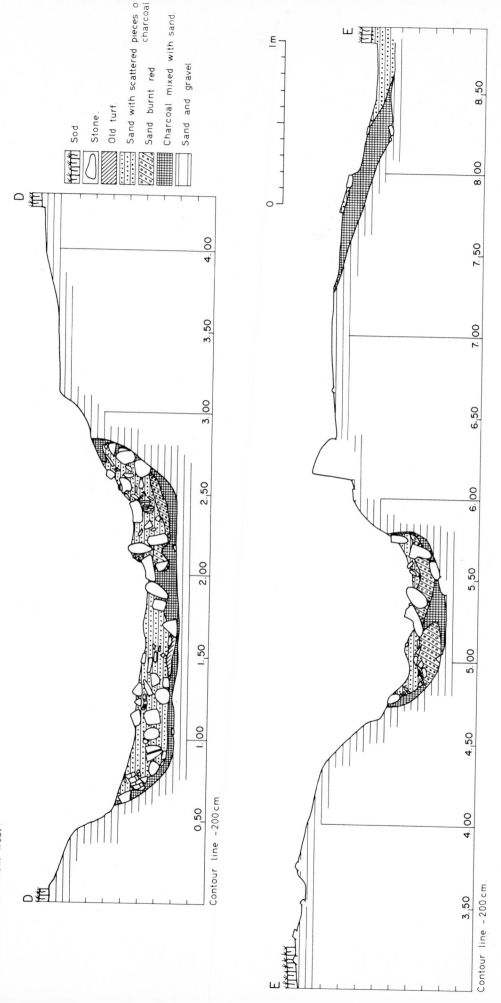

L'Anse aux Meadows

Cooking pit I. Profile D seen from north
and profile E seen from west.

Sod.
Stone.
Old turf.
Sand with scattered pieces o
charcoal
Sand burnt red
Charcoal mixed with sand.
Sand and gravel.

D

0,50   1,00   1,50   2,00   2,50   3,00   3,50   4,00

D

Contour line – 200 cm.

0   1m

E

3,50   4,00   4,50   5,00   5,50   6,00   6,50   7,00   7,50   8,00   8,50

E

Contour line – 200 cm.

Pl. 44

COOKING-PIT II

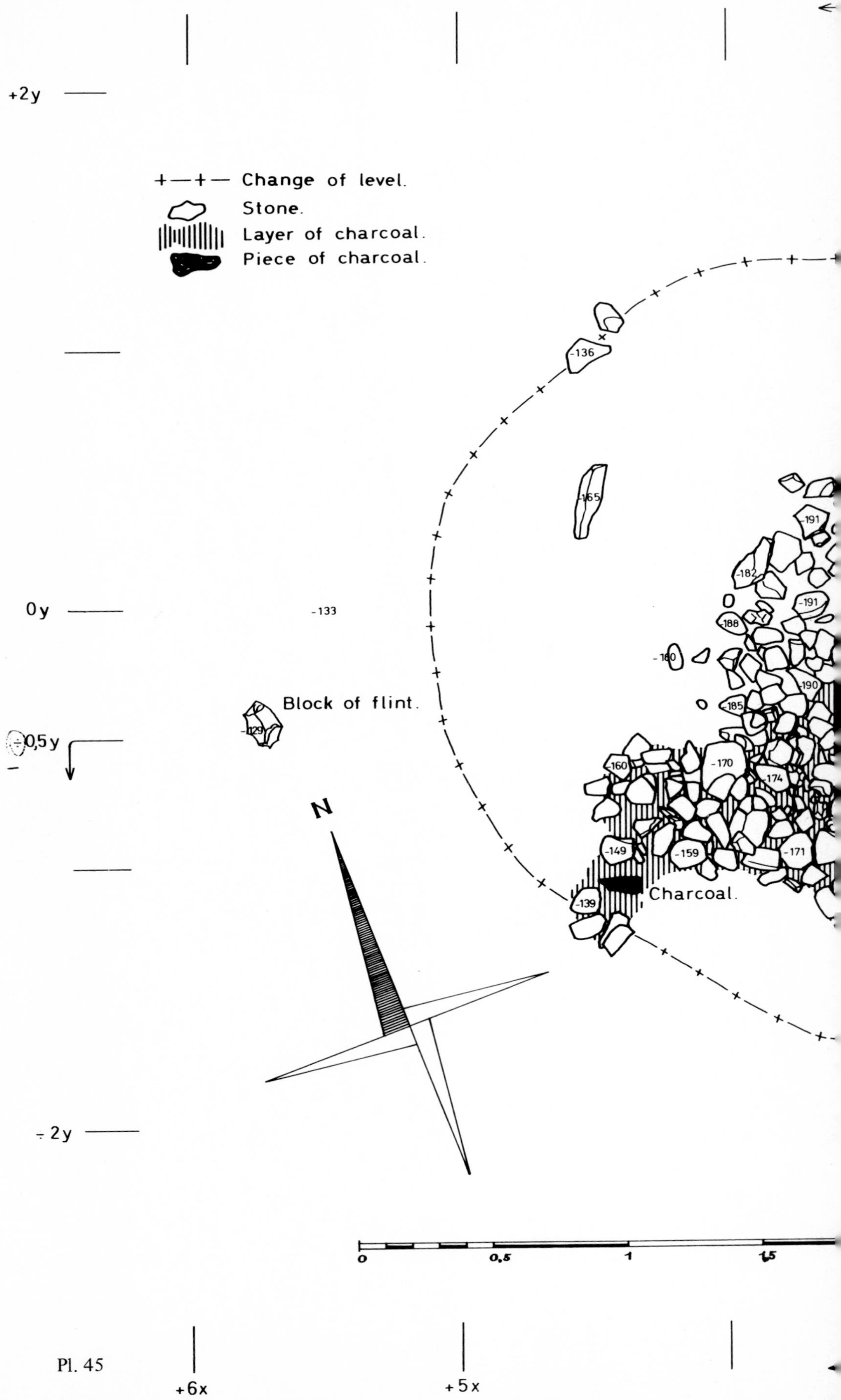

+2y
0y
÷0,5y
÷2y
Change of level.
Stone.
Layer of charcoal.
Piece of charcoal.
Block of flint.
Charcoal.
N
-136
-165
-191
-182
-191
-188
-180
-190
-185
-170
-160
174
-149
-159
-171
-139
-133
-129
0
0,5
1
1,5
+6x
+5x

Pl. 45

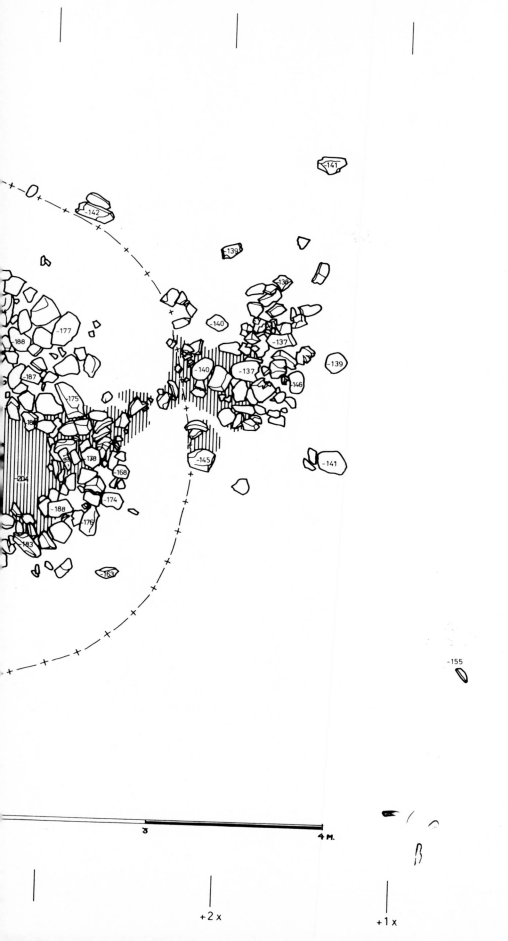

-141

-142

-139

-138

-177

-188

-140

-137

-187

-140   -137

-139

-175

-146

-188

-138

-168

-141

-204

-145

-174

-188

-176

-183

-163

-155

3   4 M.

β

+2 x   +1 x

COOKING-PIT II

Section 3.5x

−4y   −2y

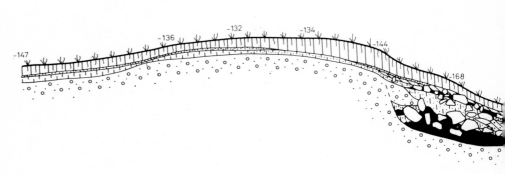

Section −0.5y

0x   +2x   +4x

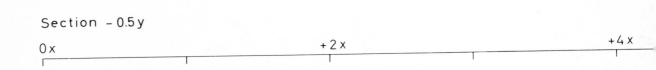

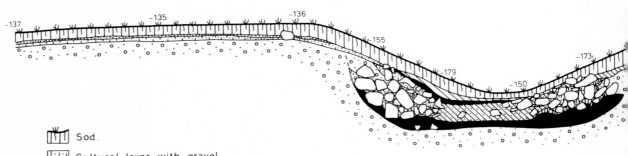

Sod.	
Cultural layer with gravel.	
Sooty layer.	
Sand and gravel.	
Sand strongly mixed with humus.	
Grey-brown very fine sand.	
Grey-yellow very fine sand.	
Cultural layer.	

Pl. 46

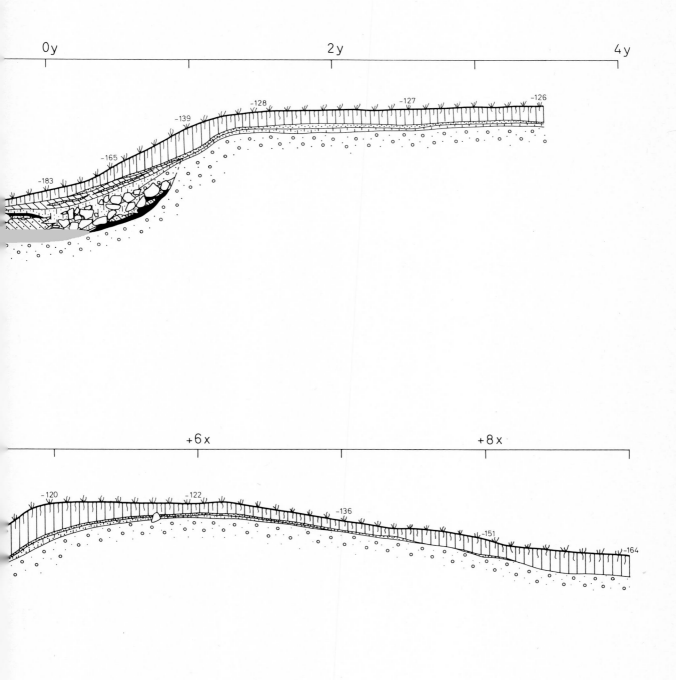

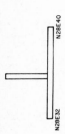

N28E40

N28E32

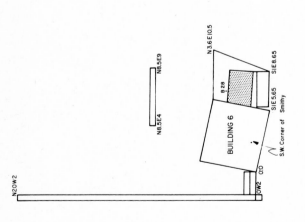

N8.5E9

N8.5E4

N20W2

N3.6E10.5

S1E8.65

B28

S1E5.65

BUILDING 6

S.W. Corner of
Smithy

0/0

0W2

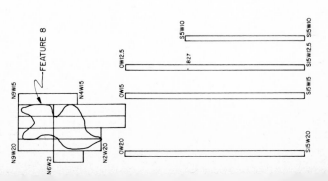

FEATURE 8

N9W15

N4W15

N9W20

N6W21

N2W20

0W20

0W15

0W12.5

B27

S5W10

S15W10   S15W10

S15W12.5

S15W15

S15W20

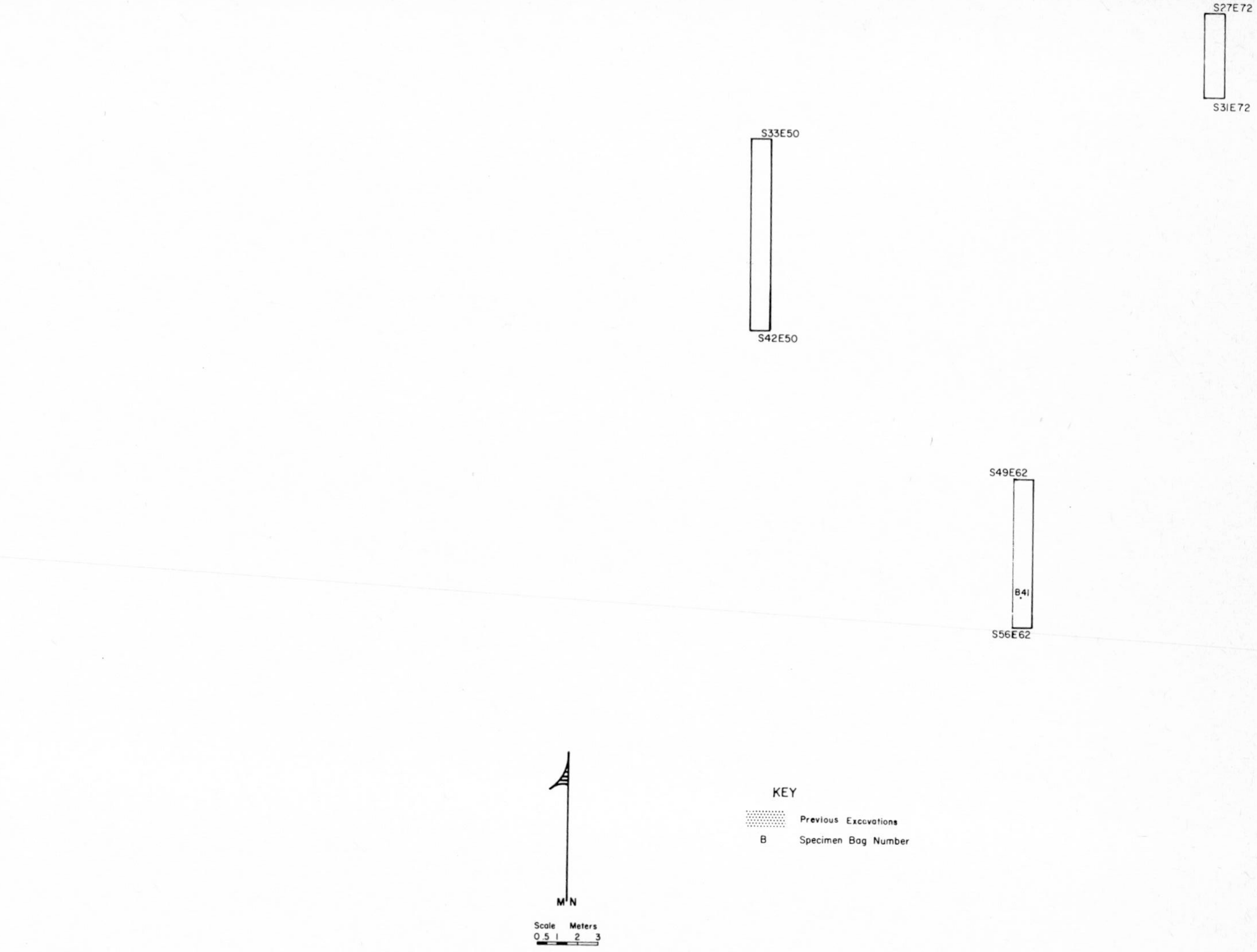

S27E72

S3IE72

S49E62

B4I

S56E62

S33E50

S42E50

KEY

Previous Excavations

B   Specimen Bag Number

MN

Scale   Meters
0 .5 1   2   3

GRID AND PLAN MAP
LANCE AUX MEADOWS, NEWFOUNDLAND

S77E30

S77E15

FIG I

Pl. 48

Section 0y.

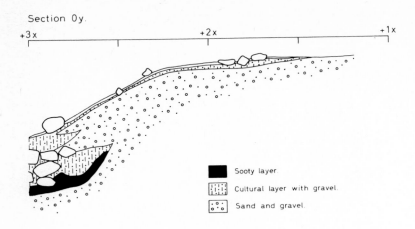

+3x   +2x   +1x

■ Sooty layer.

▦ Cultural layer with gravel.

▨ Sand and gravel.

Pl. 47

LANCE AUX MEADOWS
Feature I

N 59–57.5 E98 PROFILE

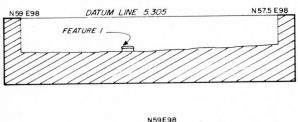

N 59 E98   DATUM LINE 5.305   N 57.5 E98

FEATURE I

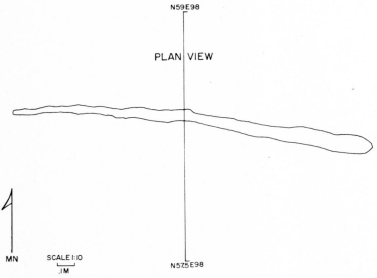

N59E98

PLAN VIEW

MN   SCALE I:IO
             .IM

N57.5E98

FIG. 4

Pl. 50

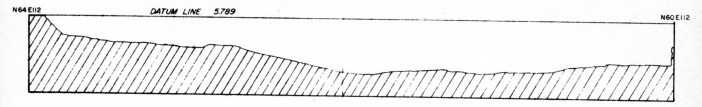

LANCE AUX MEADOWS
Feature 2

N 60-64 E112 PROFILE

N64 E112   DATUM LINE 5.789   N60 E112

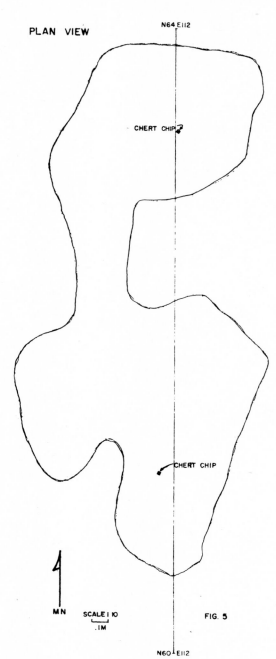

PLAN VIEW

N64 E112

CHERT CHIP

CHERT CHIP

MN   SCALE 1:10
              .1M

N60 E112

FIG. 5

Pl. 51

LANCE AUX MEADOWS

PLAN VIEW

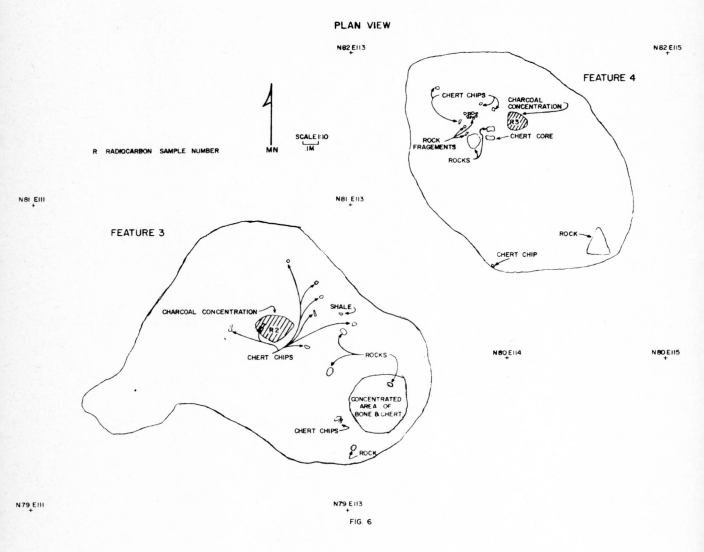

FIG. 6

Pl. 52

LANCE AUX MEADOWS
Feature 5

CROSS SECTION

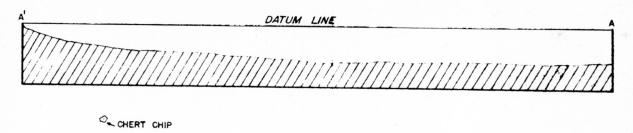

A' *DATUM LINE* A

◇← CHERT CHIP

◔← ROCK

PLAN VIEW

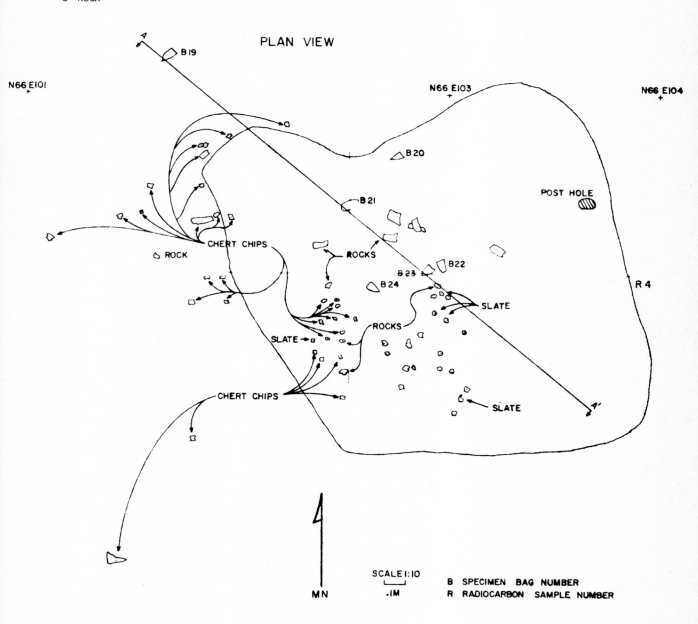

B 19

N66 E101

N66 E103

N66 E104

B 20

POST HOLE

B 21

CHERT CHIPS

ROCKS

ROCK

B 23 B 22

B 24

SLATE

R 4

ROCKS

SLATE

CHERT CHIPS

SLATE

MN

SCALE 1:10
.1M

B SPECIMEN BAG NUMBER
R RADIOCARBON SAMPLE NUMBER

N63 E101

N63 E103

N65 E104

Pl. 53   FIG. 7

LANCE AUX MEADOWS
Feature 6

PLAN VIEW

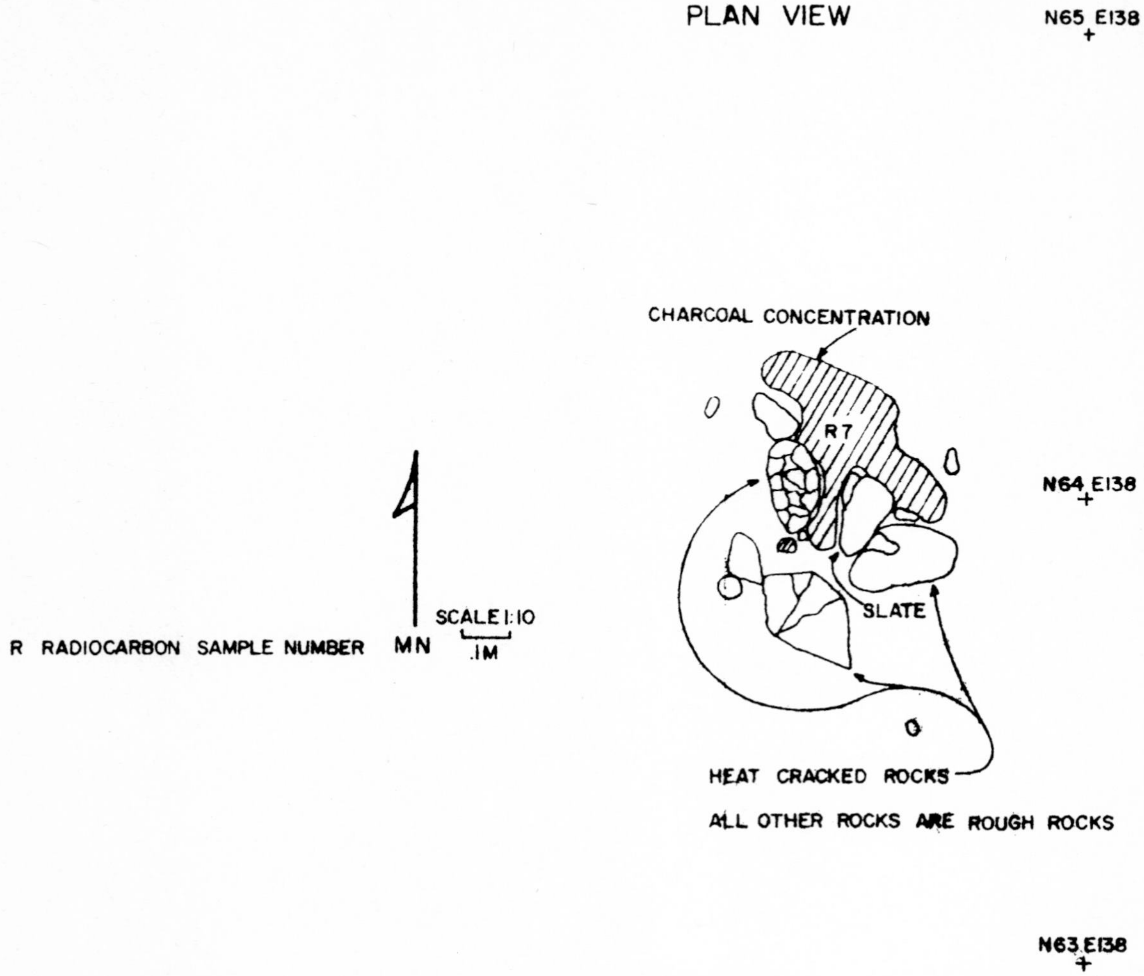

N65 E138
+

CHARCOAL CONCENTRATION

R 7

N64 E138
+

SLATE

R RADIOCARBON SAMPLE NUMBER   MN   SCALE 1:10
.1M

HEAT CRACKED ROCKS

ALL OTHER ROCKS ARE ROUGH ROCKS

N63 E138
+

Pl. 54   FIG. B

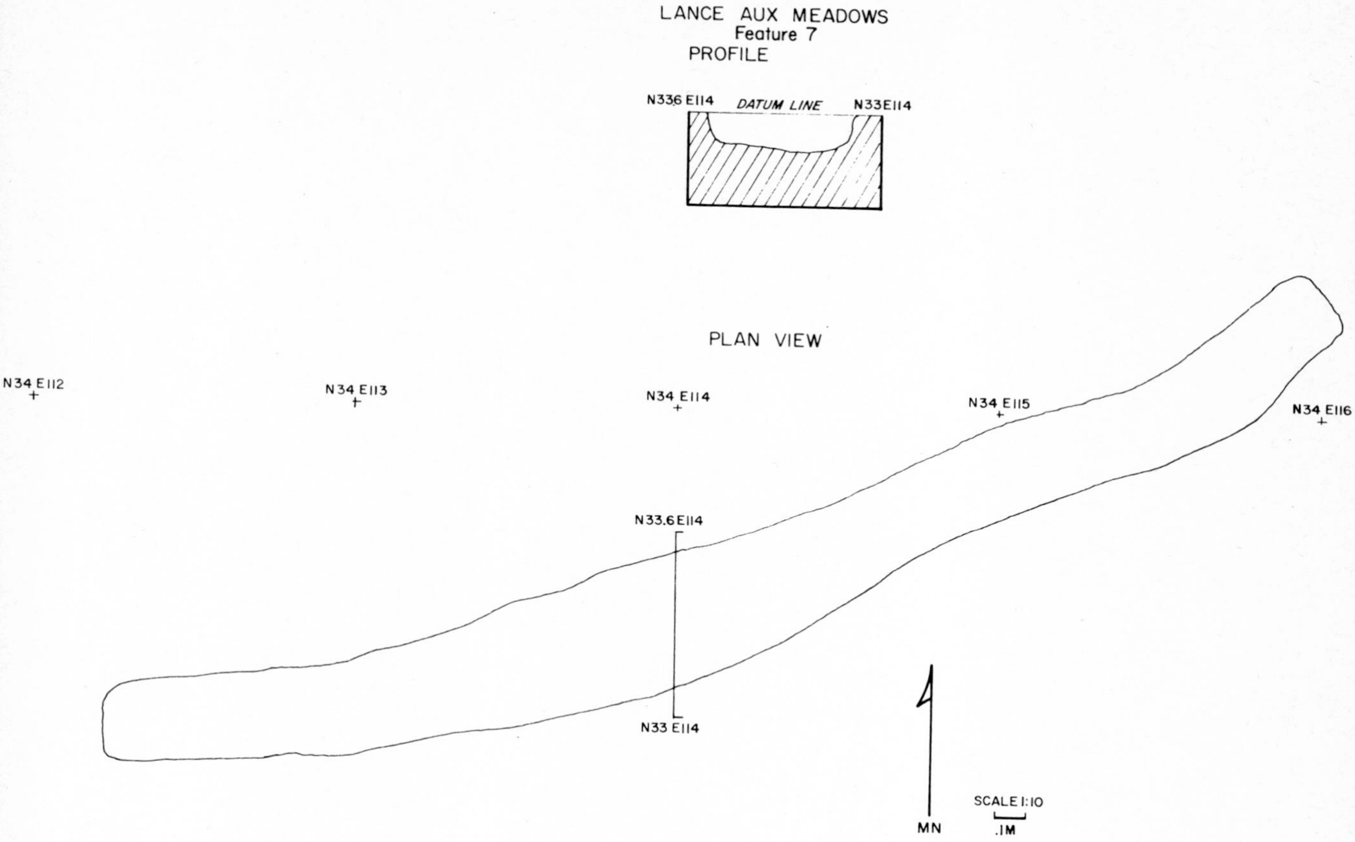

LANCE AUX MEADOWS
Feature 7
PROFILE

N336 E114   *DATUM LINE*   N33 E114

PLAN VIEW

N34 E112
+

N34 E113
+

N34 E114
+

N34 E115
+

N34 E116
+

N33.6 E114

N33 E114

MN

SCALE 1:10
.1M

FIG. 9

Pl. 55

LANCE AUX MEADOWS
Feature 8

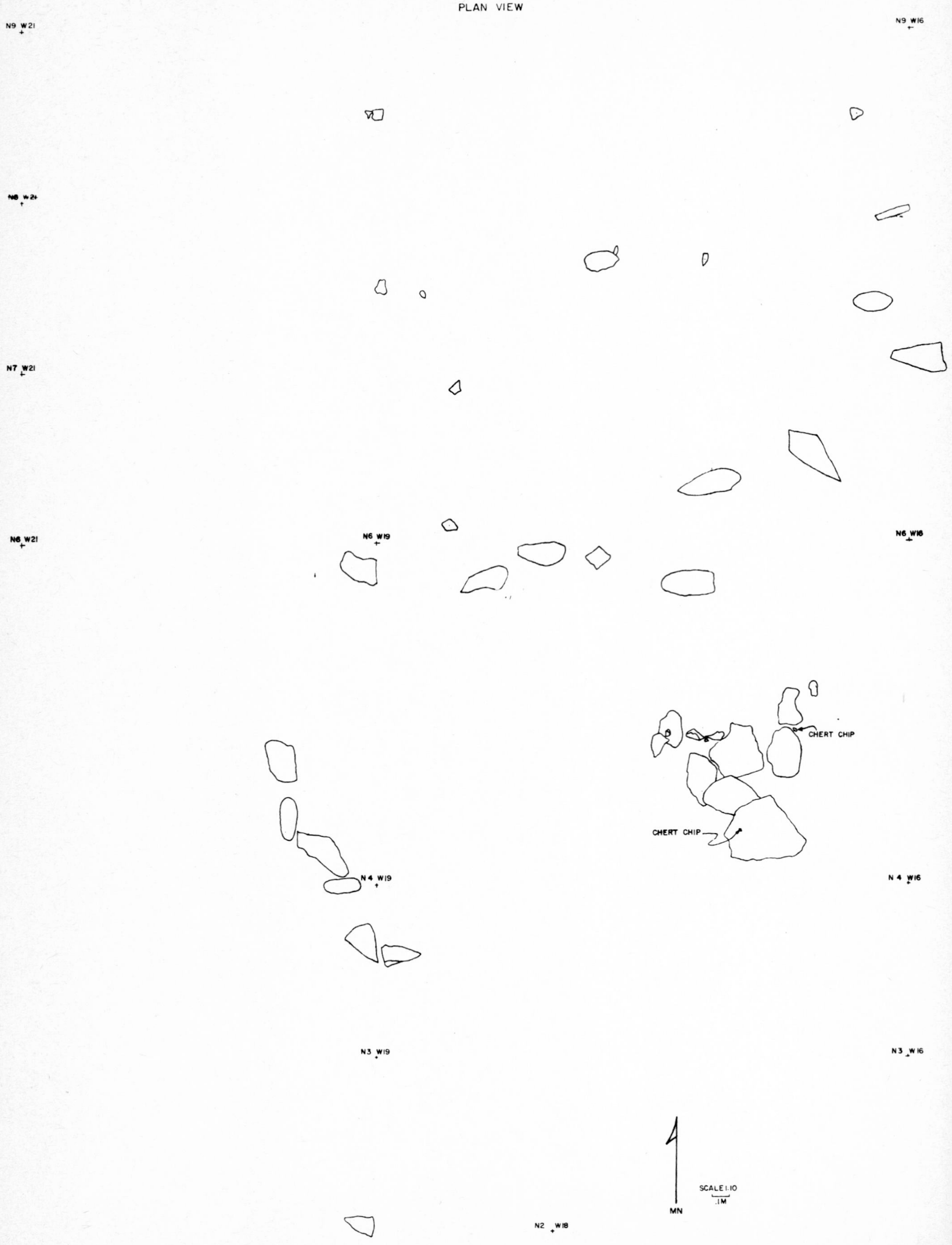

PLAN VIEW

N9 W21

N9 WI6

N8 W2I

N7 W2I

N6 W21   N6 WI9   N6 WI6

                                                          CHERT CHIP

                    CHERT CHIP

          N4 WI9   N 4 WI6

          N3 WI9   N3 WI6

                                                SCALE I:IO
                                                .I M
                              N2 WI8   MN

FIG. IO   Pl. 56

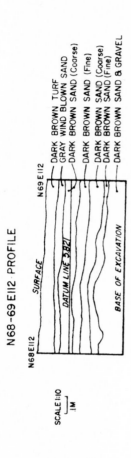

LANCE AUX MEADOWS
Profiles

N68-69 E112 PROFILE

N68E112   N69 E112

SURFACE

DATUM LINE 5.821

— DARK BROWN TURF
— GRAY WIND BLOWN SAND
— DARK BROWN SAND (Coarse)

— DARK BROWN SAND (Fine)

— DARK BROWN SAND (Coarse)
— DARK BROWN SAND (Fine)

— DARK BROWN SAND & GRAVEL

BASE OF EXCAVATION

SCALE 1:10
.1 M

N68 E133-138 PROFILE

N68 E133   N68 E138

SURFACE

DATUM LINE   5.866

— DARK BROWN TURF
— DARK ORGANIC LAYER MIXED WITH SAND
— GRAY SAND (Sterile)

BASE OF EXCAVATION

SCALE 1:20
.5M

N78E112-113 PROFILE

N78E112   N78E113

SURFACE

DATUM LINE   5.951

— DARK BROWN TURF
— GRAY WIND BLOWN SAND

— DARK BROWN SAND

BASE OF EXCAVATION

FIG. 3   Pl. 57

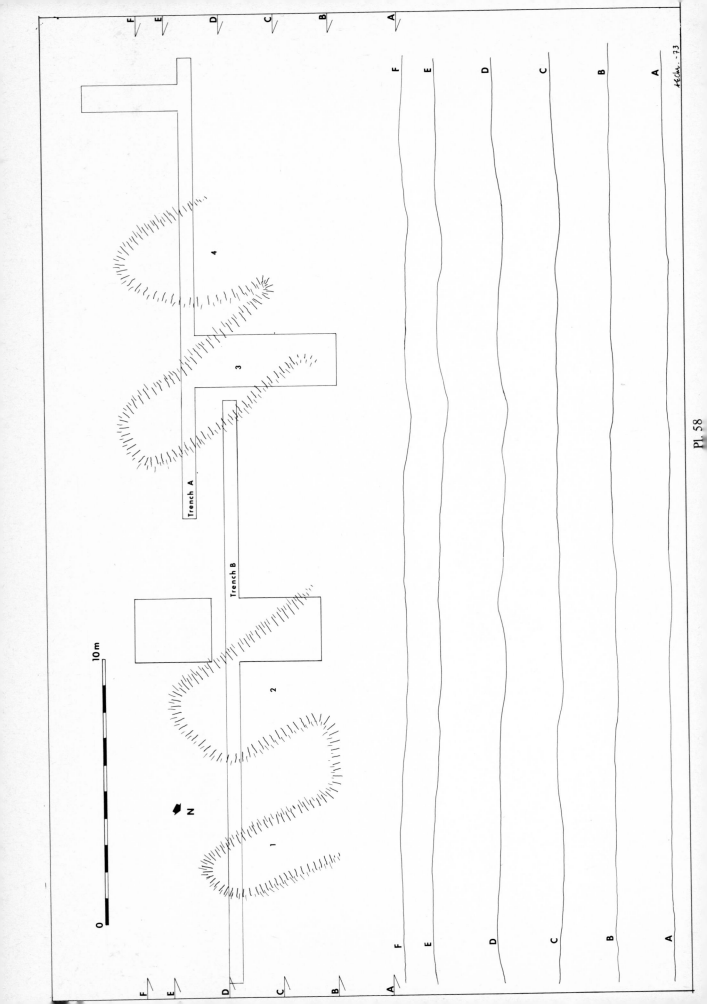

Trench A

Trench B

N

10 m

0

Pl. 58

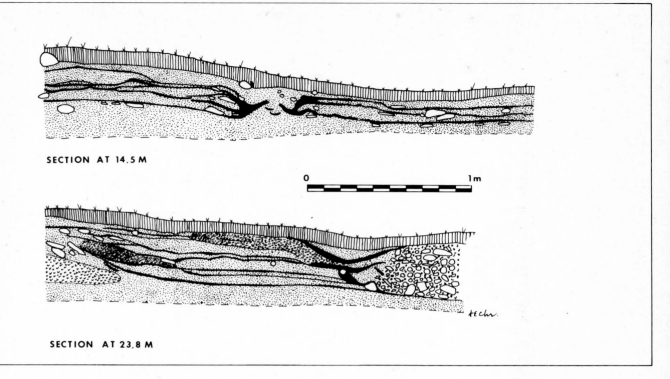

SECTION AT 14,5 M

0   1m

SECTION AT 23,8 M

Pl. 62

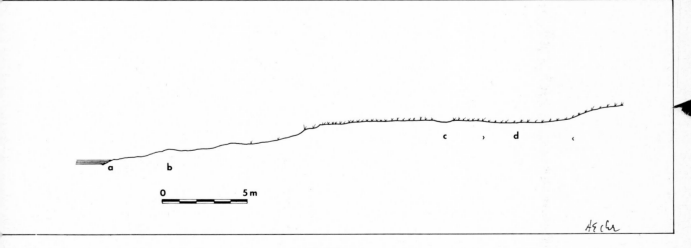

a   b

0   5m

Pl. 63